Rick Steves'

PARIS

2004

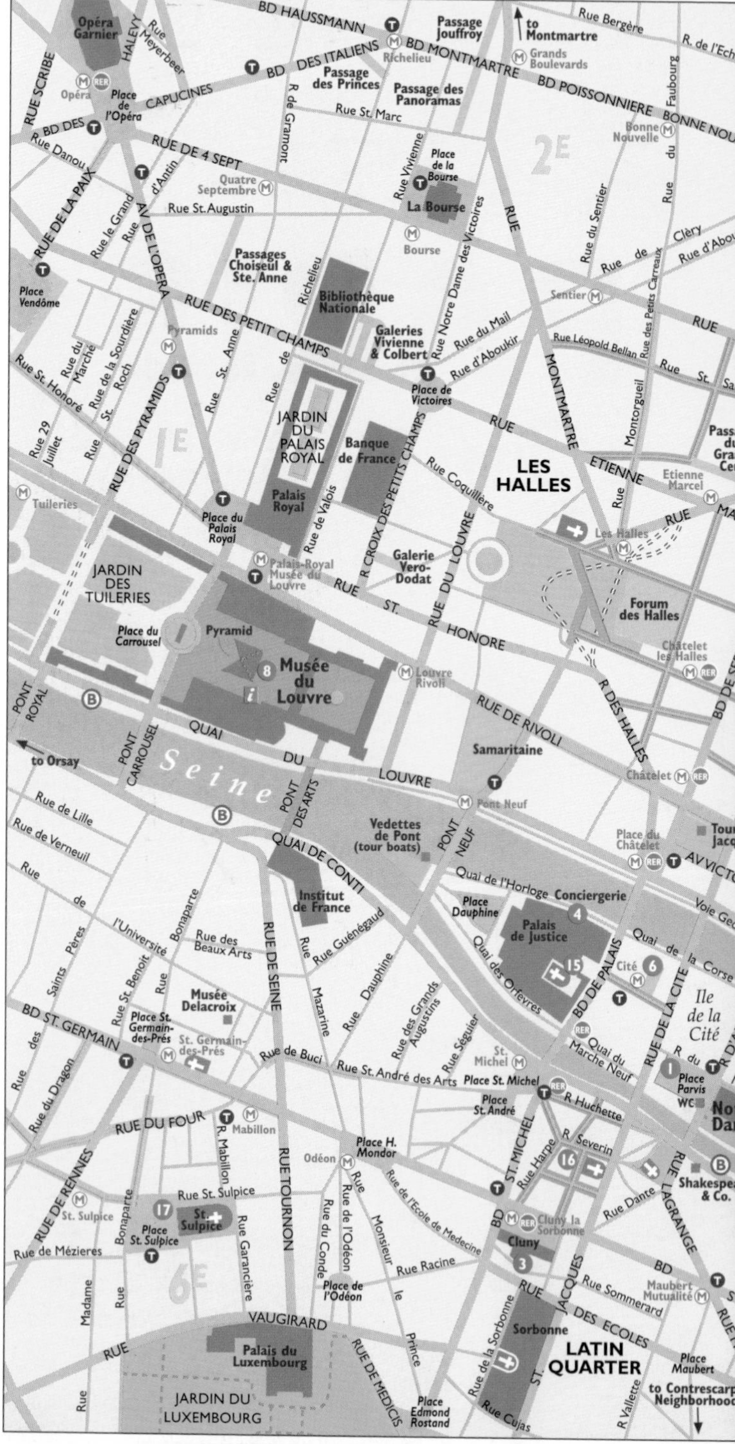
Opéra Garnier
BD HAUSSMANN
Passage Jouffroy
to Montmartre
Rue Bergère
Richelieu
BD MONTMARTRE
Grands Boulevards
BD DES ITALIENS
Passage des Princes
Passage des Panoramas
BD POISSONNIERE
BONNE NOUV
Place de l'Opéra
CAPUCINES
RUE SCRIBE
BD DES
Rue St. Marc
Bonne Nouvelle
RUE DE 4 SEPT
Place de la Bourse
2E
Quatre Septembre
Rue St. Augustin
La Bourse
Bourse
Rue du Sentier
Rue de Clèry
RUE DE LA PAIX
AV DE L'OPERA
Passages Choiseul & Ste. Anne
Bibliothèque Nationale
Place Vendôme
Sentier
RUE DES PETIT CHAMPS
Galeries Vivienne & Colbert
Rue du Mail
Rue d'Aboukir
Rue Léopold Bellan
Pyramids
RUE DES PYRAMIDS
Place de Victoires
Rue St. Honoré
Rue 29 Juillet
1E
JARDIN DU PALAIS ROYAL
Banque de France
R. CROIX DES PETITS CHAMPS
RUE MONTMARTRE
RUE ETIENNE MARCEL
Rue Montorgueil
LES HALLES
Etienne Marcel
Rue Coquillère
Tuileries
Place du Palais Royal
Palais Royal
Rue de Valois
Les Halles
Galerie Vero-Dodat
Palais-Royal Musée du Louvre
JARDIN DES TUILERIES
RUE ST. HONORE
RUE DU LOUVRE
Forum des Halles
Place du Carrousel
Pyramid
Musée du Louvre
Louvre Rivoli
Châtelet les Halles
PONT ROYAL
PONT CARROUSEL
RUE DE RIVOLI
R DES HALLES
to Orsay
QUAI DU LOUVRE
Seine
Samaritaine
Châtelet
Pont Neuf
PONT DES ARTS
PONT NEUF
Rue de Lille
Rue de Verneuil
QUAI DE CONTI
Vedettes de Pont (tour boats)
Place du Châtelet
AV VICTO
Quai de l'Horloge
Conciergerie
Institut de France
Place Dauphine
Palais de Justice
Rue de l'Université
Rue des Saints Pères
Bonaparte
Rue des Beaux Arts
RUE DE SEINE
Rue Guénégaud
Rue Mazarine
Rue Dauphine
Quai des Orfèvres
BD DE PALAIS
Cité
Quai de la Corse
Ile de la Cité
Musée Delacroix
Rue St. Benoit
Place St. Germain-des-Prés
St. Germain-des-Prés
BD ST. GERMAIN
Rue des Grands Augustins
Rue Séguier
Quai du Marché Neuf
RUE DE LA CITE
Rue de Buci
Rue St. André des Arts
St. Michel
Place St. Michel
Place St. André
R Huchette
Place Parvis
WC
Rue du Dragon
RUE DU FOUR
Mabillon
R. Mabillon
Place H. Mondor
Odéon
RUE TOURNON
R. Severin
Rue Harpe
BD ST. MICHEL
Rue Dante
RUE LAGRANGE
Shakespeare & Co.
RUE DE RENNES
St. Sulpice
Rue St. Sulpice
St. Sulpice
Place St. Sulpice
Rue de Mézieres
Rue Garancière
Rue de l'Odéon
Rue du Conde
Rue Monsieur le Prince
Rue de l'Ecole de Medecine
Cluny la Sorbonne
Cluny
Rue Racine
Maubert Mutualité
Rue Sommerard
RUE DES ECOLES
6E
Place de l'Odéon
RUE VAUGIRARD
Palais du Luxembourg
RUE DE MEDICIS
Sorbonne
Rue de la Sorbonne
RUE ST. JACQUES
LATIN QUARTER
Place Maubert
JARDIN DU LUXEMBOURG
Place Edmond Rostand
Rue Cujas
R Vallette
to Contrescarpe Neighborhood
Rue Madame

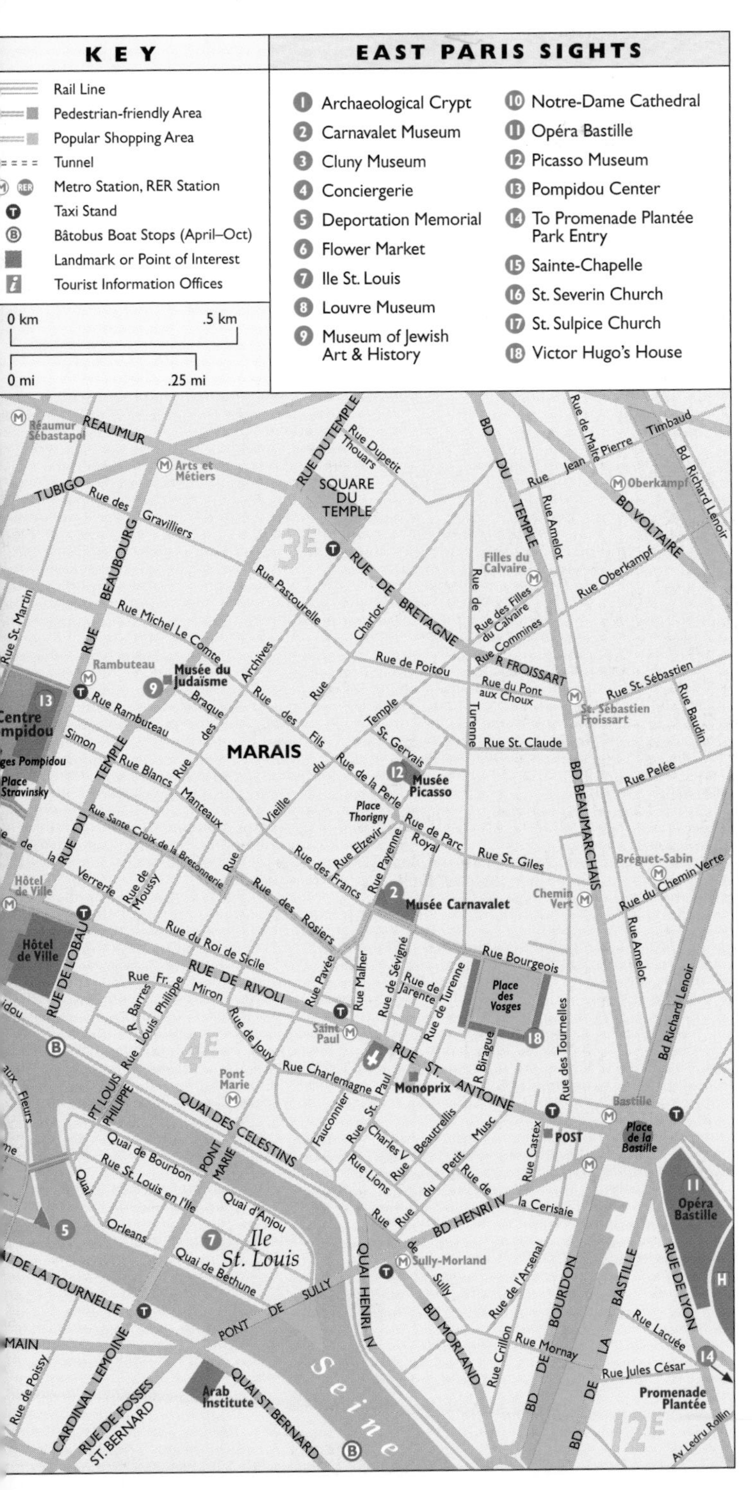
KEY
Rail Line
Pedestrian-friendly Area
Popular Shopping Area
Tunnel
Metro Station, RER Station
Taxi Stand
Bâtobus Boat Stops (April–Oct)
Landmark or Point of Interest
Tourist Information Offices
0 km
.5 km
0 mi
.25 mi
EAST PARIS SIGHTS
1 Archaeological Crypt
2 Carnavalet Museum
3 Cluny Museum
4 Conciergerie
5 Deportation Memorial
6 Flower Market
7 Ile St. Louis
8 Louvre Museum
9 Museum of Jewish Art & History
10 Notre-Dame Cathedral
11 Opéra Bastille
12 Picasso Museum
13 Pompidou Center
14 To Promenade Plantée Park Entry
15 Sainte-Chapelle
16 St. Severin Church
17 St. Sulpice Church
18 Victor Hugo's House
Réaumur Sébastapol
REAUMUR
Arts et Métiers
TUBIGO
Rue des Gravilliers
RUE DU TEMPLE
Rue Dupetit Thouars
SQUARE DU TEMPLE
3E
RUE DE BRETAGNE
BD DU TEMPLE
Rue Jean Pierre Timbaud
Rue de Malte
Oberkampf
BD VOLTAIRE
Bd Richard Lenoir
Rue Amelot
Filles du Calvaire
Rue Oberkampf
Rue des Filles du Calvaire
Rue de Commines
R FROISSART
Rue Pastourelle
Charlot
Rue de Poitou
Rue du Pont aux Choux
RUE BEAUBOURG
Rue St. Martin
Rue Michel Le Comte
Archives
Rambuteau
Musée du Judaïsme
Rue Rambuteau
Braque
Rue des Fils
Rue Temple
St. Gervais
Rue de Turenne
Rue St. Claude
Rue St. Sébastien
St. Sébastien Froissart
Rue Baudin
Centre Pompidou
Simon
MARAIS
Rue de la Perle
Musée Picasso
BD BEAUMARCHAIS
Rue Pelée
Place Stravinsky
Rue Blancs Manteaux
Vieille du
Place Thorigny
Rue de Parc Royal
Rue St. Giles
Rue Sainte Croix de la Bretonnerie
Rue Elzevir
Rue Payenne
Rue des Francs
Bréguet-Sabin
Rue du Chemin Verte
Hôtel de Ville
Verrerie
Rue de Moussy
Rue des Rosiers
Musée Carnavalet
Chemin Vert
Rue Amelot
Rue du Roi de Sicile
RUE DE LOBAU
Rue Bourgeois
Place des Vosges
RUE DE RIVOLI
Rue Fr. Miron
Rue Pavée
Rue Malher
Rue de Sévigné
Rue de Jarente
R. Barres
Rue Louis Philippe
Saint Paul
Rue des Tournelles
4E
Rue de Jouy
RUE ST. ANTOINE
R Birague
Pont Marie
Rue Charlemagne
Rue St. Paul
Monoprix
PT LOUIS PHILIPPE
QUAI DES CELESTINS
Fauconnier
Rue Charles V
Rue Beautreillis
Rue du Petit Musc
Rue Castex
POST
Bastille
Place de la Bastille
Quai de Bourbon
PONT MARIE
Rue St. Louis en l'Ile
Rue Lions
Rue de la Cerisaie
Opéra Bastille
Quai d'Anjou
BD HENRI IV
Orleans
Ile St. Louis
Quai de Bethune
Sully-Morland
Rue de Sully
Rue de l'Arsenal
BD BOURDON
BASTILLE
RUE DE LYON
DE LA TOURNELLE
PONT DE SULLY
QUAI HENRI IV
BD MORLAND
Rue Lacuée
Rue Crillon
Rue Mornay
Rue Jules César
Promenade Plantée
MAIN
Rue de Poissy
CARDINAL LEMOINE
RUE DE FOSSES ST. BERNARD
Arab Institute
QUAI ST. BERNARD
Seine
BD DE LA BASTILLE
12E
Av Ledru Rollin

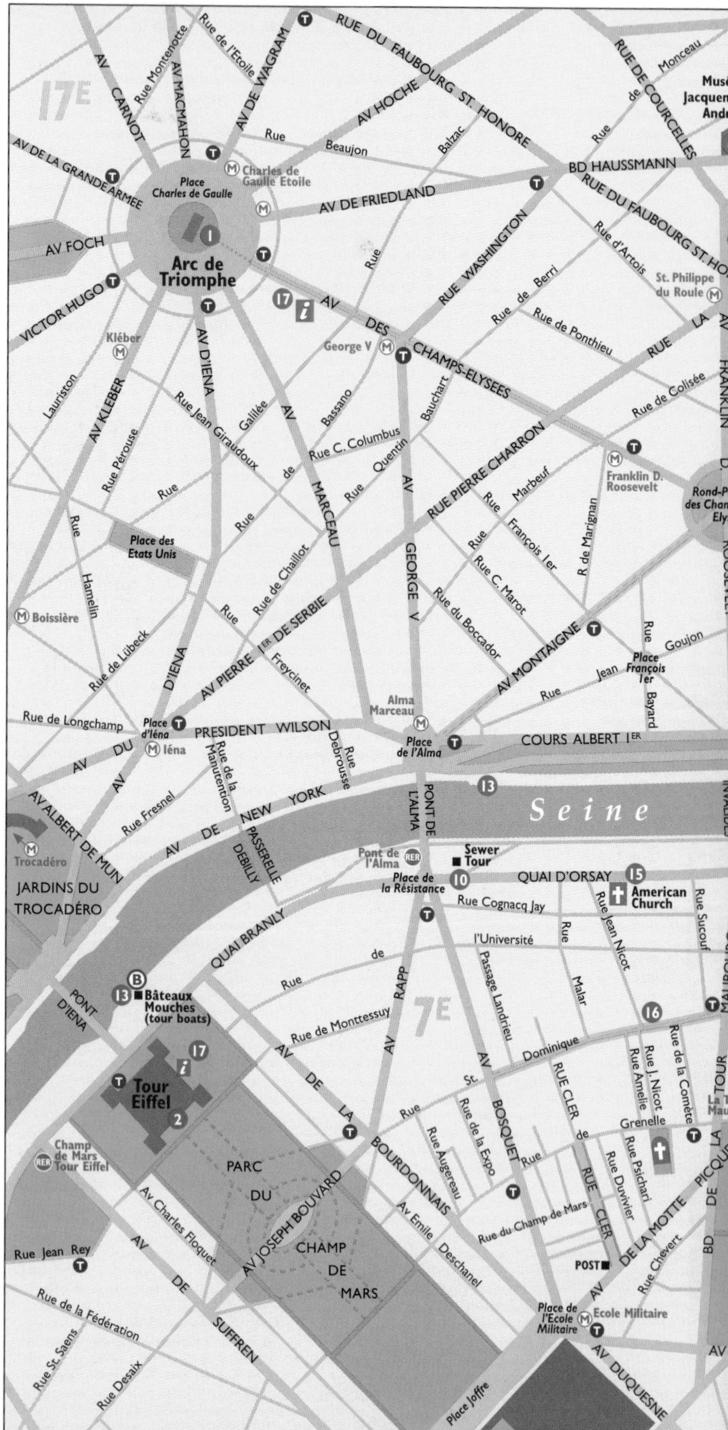
17E
Arc de Triomphe
Place Charles de Gaulle
Charles de Gaulle Etoile
AV DE WAGRAM
RUE DU FAUBOURG ST. HONORE
AV HOCHE
AV CARNOT
AV MACMAHON
Rue Montenotte
Rue de l'Etoile
Rue Beaujon
Balzac
BD HAUSSMANN
RUE DE COURCELLES
Rue de Monceau
Musée Jacquemart André
AV DE LA GRANDE ARMEE
AV DE FRIEDLAND
AV FOCH
VICTOR HUGO
AV D'IENA
AV DES CHAMPS-ELYSEES
RUE WASHINGTON
Rue d'Artois
Rue de Berri
Rue de Ponthieu
St. Philippe du Roule
RUE LA BOETIE
George V
Kléber
Lauriston
AV KLEBER
Rue Jean Giraudoux
Galilée
Bassano
Rue C. Columbus
Bauchart
Rue de Colisée
AV FRANKLIN D. ROOSEVELT
Franklin D. Roosevelt
Rond-Point des Champs Elysées
Rue Pérouse
Rue de Quentin
AV MARCEAU
AV GEORGE V
RUE PIERRE CHARRON
Rue Marbeuf
Rue François 1er
R de Marignan
Place des Etats Unis
Rue Hamelin
Rue de Chaillot
Rue C. Marot
Rue du Boccador
Boissière
Rue de Lübeck
AV PIERRE 1ER DE SERBIE
Rue Freycinet
AV MONTAIGNE
Rue Goujon
Rue Jean Goujon
Place François 1er
Rue Bayard
Alma Marceau
Rue de Longchamp
Place d'Iéna
AV PRESIDENT WILSON
Iéna
Rue de la Manutention
Rue Debrousse
Place de l'Alma
COURS ALBERT 1ER
13
PONT DE L'ALMA
Seine
AV DU
AV ALBERT DE MUN
Rue Fresnel
AV DE NEW YORK
PASSERELLE DEBILLY
Trocadéro
JARDINS DU TROCADÉRO
Pont de l'Alma
Sewer Tour
Place de la Résistance
10
QUAI D'ORSAY
15
American Church
Rue Cognacq Jay
Rue Jean Nicot
Rue Sucouf
QUAI BRANLY
Rue de l'Université
Passage Landrieu
Rue Malar
INVALIDES
AV RAPP
Bâteaux Mouches (tour boats)
PONT D'IENA
7E
16
BD DE LA TOUR MAUBOURG
Rue de Monttessuy
Tour Eiffel
17
2
AV DE LA BOURDONNAIS
AV BOSQUET
Rue St. Dominique
RUE CLER
Rue J. Nicot
Rue Amelie
Rue de la Comète
La Tour Maubourg
Rue de la Expo
Rue Augereau
Rue de Grenelle
Rue Psichari
Rue Duvivier
Champ de Mars Tour Eiffel
PARC DU CHAMP DE MARS
AV JOSEPH BOUVARD
Av Charles Floquet
Av Emile Deschanel
Rue du Champ de Mars
AV DE LA MOTTE PICQUET
POST
Rue Chevert
Rue Jean Rey
AV DE SUFFREN
Rue de la Fédération
Place de l'Ecole Militaire
Ecole Militaire
AV DUQUESNE
Rue St. Saens
Rue Desaix
Place Joffre

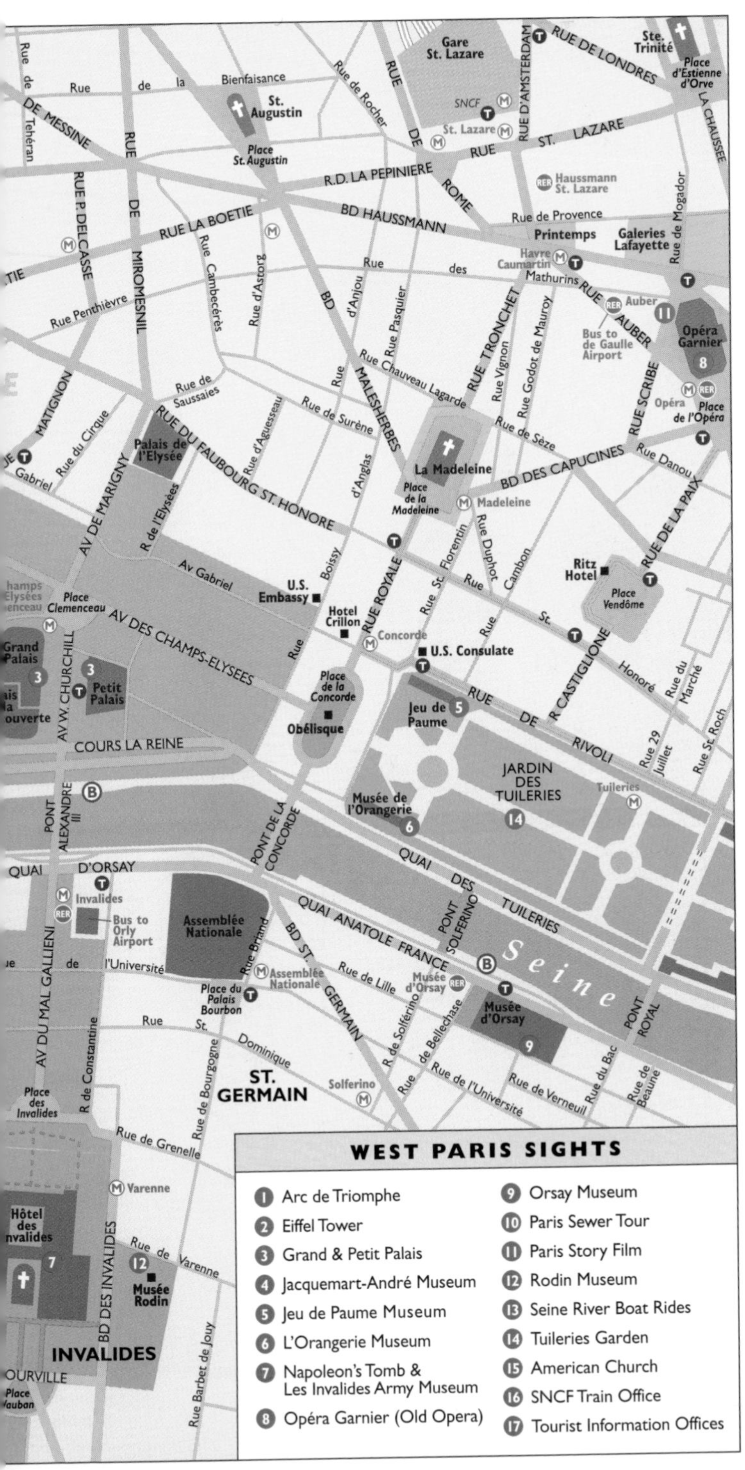

WEST PARIS SIGHTS
1 Arc de Triomphe
2 Eiffel Tower
3 Grand & Petit Palais
4 Jacquemart-André Museum
5 Jeu de Paume Museum
6 L'Orangerie Museum
7 Napoleon's Tomb & Les Invalides Army Museum
8 Opéra Garnier (Old Opera)
9 Orsay Museum
10 Paris Sewer Tour
11 Paris Story Film
12 Rodin Museum
13 Seine River Boat Rides
14 Tuileries Garden
15 American Church
16 SNCF Train Office
17 Tourist Information Offices
Gare St. Lazare
Ste. Trinité
Place d'Estienne d'Orve
St. Augustin
Place St. Augustin
SNCF
St. Lazare
Haussmann St. Lazare
Printemps
Galeries Lafayette
Havre Caumartin
Auber
Bus to de Gaulle Airport
Opéra Garnier
Opéra
Place de l'Opéra
La Madeleine
Place de la Madeleine
Madeleine
Ritz Hotel
Place Vendôme
Palais de l'Elysée
U.S. Embassy
Hotel Crillon
Concorde
U.S. Consulate
Place Clemenceau
Grand Palais
Petit Palais
Place de la Concorde
Obélisque
Jeu de Paume
JARDIN DES TUILERIES
Tuileries
Musée de l'Orangerie
Invalides
Bus to Orly Airport
Assemblée Nationale
Place du Palais Bourbon
Musée d'Orsay
Seine
ST. GERMAIN
Solferino
Place des Invalides
Varenne
Hôtel des Invalides
Musée Rodin
INVALIDES
RUE DE LONDRES
RUE D'AMSTERDAM
RUE ST. LAZARE
RUE DE ROME
R.D. LA PEPINIERE
BD HAUSSMANN
RUE LA BOETIE
BD MALESHERBES
RUE TRONCHET
RUE AUBER
RUE SCRIBE
BD DES CAPUCINES
RUE DE LA PAIX
RUE DU FAUBOURG ST. HONORE
RUE ROYALE
AV DES CHAMPS-ELYSEES
AV DE MARIGNY
AV W. CHURCHILL
COURS LA REINE
RUE DE RIVOLI
R CASTIGLIONE
PONT ALEXANDRE III
PONT DE LA CONCORDE
QUAI D'ORSAY
QUAI DES TUILERIES
QUAI ANATOLE FRANCE
PONT SOLFERINO
PONT ROYAL
BD ST. GERMAIN
AV DU MAL GALLIENI
BD DES INVALIDES
Rue de l'Université
Rue St. Dominique
Rue de Grenelle
Rue de Varenne
Rue de Lille
Rue de Verneuil
Rue du Bac
Rue de Bourgogne
Rue Barbet de Jouy

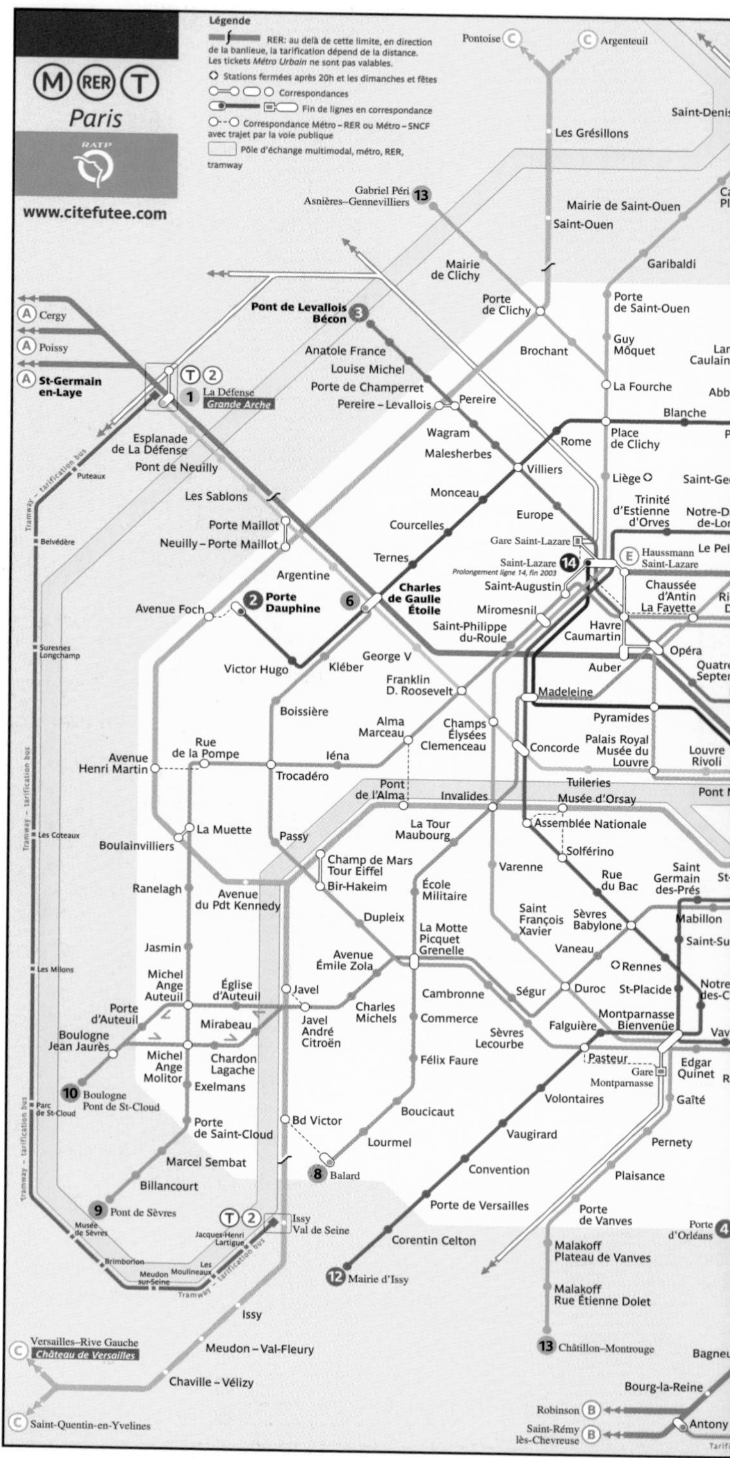

Légende
RER: au delà de cette limite, en direction de la banlieue, la tarification dépend de la distance. Les tickets Métro Urbain ne sont pas valables.
Stations fermées après 20h et les dimanches et fêtes
Correspondances
Fin de lignes en correspondance
Correspondance Métro – RER ou Métro – SNCF avec trajet par la voie publique
Pôle d'échange multimodal, métro, RER, tramway
M RER T
Paris
RATP
www.citefutee.com
Pontoise
Argenteuil
Saint-Denis
Les Grésillons
Gabriel Péri Asnières–Gennevilliers
Mairie de Saint-Ouen
Saint-Ouen
Garibaldi
Mairie de Clichy
Porte de Clichy
Porte de Saint-Ouen
Guy Môquet
Brochant
La Fourche
Blanche
Place de Clichy
Rome
Liège
Trinité d'Estienne d'Orves
Europe
Villiers
Cergy
Poissy
St-Germain en-Laye
Pont de Levallois Bécon
Anatole France
Louise Michel
Porte de Champerret
Pereire – Levallois
Pereire
Wagram
Malesherbes
Monceau
Courcelles
Ternes
La Défense Grande Arche
Esplanade de La Défense
Pont de Neuilly
Les Sablons
Porte Maillot
Neuilly – Porte Maillot
Argentine
Puteaux
Belvédère
Tramway – tarification bus
Gare Saint-Lazare
Saint-Lazare
Prolongement ligne 14, fin 2003
Haussmann Saint-Lazare
Chaussée d'Antin La Fayette
Saint-Augustin
Miromesnil
Saint-Philippe du-Roule
Havre Caumartin
Opéra
Auber
Madeleine
Pyramides
Palais Royal Musée du Louvre
Concorde
Tuileries
Avenue Foch
Porte Dauphine
Charles de Gaulle Étoile
Victor Hugo
Kléber
George V
Franklin D. Roosevelt
Boissière
Alma Marceau
Champs Élysées Clemenceau
Iéna
Trocadéro
Rue de la Pompe
Avenue Henri Martin
Suresnes Longchamp
Pont de l'Alma
Invalides
Musée d'Orsay
Assemblée Nationale
Solférino
Rue du Bac
La Muette
Boulainvilliers
Passy
La Tour Maubourg
Champ de Mars Tour Eiffel
Bir-Hakeim
Varenne
Saint Germain des-Prés
Les Coteaux
Ranelagh
Avenue du Pdt Kennedy
École Militaire
Dupleix
La Motte Picquet Grenelle
Saint François Xavier
Sèvres Babylone
Mabillon
Jasmin
Avenue Émile Zola
Vaneau
Rennes
Michel Ange Auteuil
Église d'Auteuil
Javel
Javel André Citroën
Charles Michels
Cambronne
Ségur
Duroc
St-Placide
Les Milons
Porte d'Auteuil
Mirabeau
Commerce
Sèvres Lecourbe
Falguière
Montparnasse Bienvenüe
Boulogne Jean Jaurès
Michel Ange Molitor
Chardon Lagache
Exelmans
Félix Faure
Pasteur
Gare Montparnasse
Edgar Quinet
Gaîté
Boulogne Pont de St-Cloud
Parc de St-Cloud
Porte de Saint-Cloud
Bd Victor
Boucicaut
Lourmel
Volontaires
Vaugirard
Pernety
Marcel Sembat
Balard
Convention
Plaisance
Billancourt
Pont de Sèvres
Porte de Versailles
Porte de Vanves
Porte d'Orléans
Issy Val de Seine
Corentin Celton
Musée de Sèvres
Jacques-Henri Lartigue
Brimborion
Meudon sur-Seine
Les Moulineaux
Malakoff Plateau de Vanves
Mairie d'Issy
Malakoff Rue Étienne Dolet
Issy
Châtillon–Montrouge
Versailles–Rive Gauche Château de Versailles
Meudon – Val-Fleury
Chaville – Vélizy
Bourg-la-Reine
Robinson
Antony
Saint-Rémy lès-Chevreuse
Saint-Quentin-en-Yvelines

ry-la-Ville – Coye

13 Saint-Denis – Université

Marché de St-Denis
Basilique de St-Denis
Cimetière de St-Denis
Hôpital Delafontaine
Cosmonautes
La Courneuve 6 Routes
Hôtel de Ville de La Courneuve
Tramway - tarification bus

Saint-Denis
Basilique de St-Denis
Saint-Denis Porte de Paris
Stade de France Saint-Denis
La Plaine Stade de France
La Courneuve Aubervilliers
Le Bourget

CDG Aéroport Charles de Gaulle B
Mitry – Claye B

Stade Géo André
Danton
La Courneuve – 8 Mai 1945
Maurice Lachâtre
Drancy – Avenir
Hôpital Avicenne
Gaston Roulaud
Escadrille Normandie – Niémen
La Ferme
Libération
Hôtel de Ville de Bobigny
Tramway - tarification bus
T 1

La Courneuve 8 Mai 1945 7
Fort d'Aubervilliers
Aubervilliers – Pantin Quatre Chemins
Pantin
5 Bobigny Pablo Picasso

12 Porte de la Chapelle
Marx Dormoy
Simplon
Marcadet Poissonniers
Château Rouge
Barbès Rochechouart
La Chapelle
Porte de la Villette
Corentin Cariou
Crimée
Riquet
Stalingrad
Bobigny – Pantin Raymond Queneau
Église de Pantin
Chelles–Gournay E
Villiers-sur-Marne Le Plessis-Trévise E
Prolongement à Tournan fin 2003

Ourcq
Porte de Pantin
Hoche
Laumière
Jaurès
Danube
Bolivar
Botzaris
7bis Pré St-Gervais
11 Mairie des Lilas
Gare du Nord
Magenta
7bis Louis Blanc
Château Landon
Gare de l'Est
Poissonnière
Colonel Fabien
Buttes Chaumont
Pyrénées
Jourdain
Place des Fêtes
Télégraphe
3bis Porte des Lilas
Belleville
Château d'Eau
Jacques Bonsergent
Strasbourg Saint-Denis
Goncourt
Couronnes
Saint-Fargeau
Ménilmontant
Pelleport
Bonne Nouvelle
Temple
République
Oberkampf
Arts et Métiers
Parmentier
Réaumur Sébastopol
Père Lachaise
Porte de Bagnolet
3 Gallieni
3bis Gambetta
Filles du Calvaire
Rue Saint-Maur
Châtelet Les Halles
Rambuteau
St-Sébastien Froissart
Saint-Ambroise
Philippe Auguste
9 Mairie de Montreuil
Hôtel de Ville
Richard Lenoir
Voltaire
Croix de Chavaux
Chemin Vert
Bréguet Sabin
Alexandre Dumas
Robespierre
St-Paul
Charonne
Porte de Montreuil
11
Bastille
Avron
Maraîchers
Saint-Michel Notre Dame
Pont Marie
Rue des Boulets
2
Buzenval
Marne-la-Vallée Parcs Disneyland A
Ledru-Rollin
Sully Morland
Faidherbe Chaligny
6 Nation
Vincennes
Cluny La Sorbonne
Saint-Mandé Tourelle
Maubert Mutualité
Porte de Vincennes
Boissy-Saint-Léger A
Cardinal Lemoine
Gare de Lyon
Reuilly – Diderot
Luxembourg
Quai de la Rapée
Montgallet
Picpus
Bérault
1 Château de Vincennes
Jussieu
Bel-Air
Gare d'Austerlitz
Daumesnil
Place Monge
Michel Bizot
10
Censier Daubenton
Dugommier
Port-Royal
Saint Marcel
Porte Dorée
Denfert Rochereau
Les Gobelins
Bercy
Campo Formio
Quai de la Gare
Porte de Charenton
Saint-Jacques
Cour St-Émilion
Corvisart
Place d'Italie
Chevaleret
Liberté
Glacière
5
Nationale
Bibliothèque François Mitterrand 14
Charenton – Écoles
Tolbiac
École Vétérinaire de Maisons-Alfort
Cité Universitaire
Maison Blanche
Porte d'Italie
Porte de Choisy
Porte d'Ivry
Ivry sur-Seine
Maisons-Alfort – Stade
Gentilly
Le Kremlin Bicêtre
Pierre Curie
Maisons-Alfort Alfortville
Maisons-Alfort Les Juilliottes
Mairie d'Ivry 7
Vitry sur-Seine
Créteil – L'Échat
Villejuif Léo Lagrange
Laplace
Villejuif Paul Vaillant-Couturier
Créteil – Université
Le Vert de Maisons
Arcueil – Cachan
7 Villejuif–Louis Aragon
8 Créteil–Préfecture
Les Ardoines
Massy–Palaiseau Versailles–Chantiers C
Orly Sud
Orly
Dourdan Saint-Martin-d'Étampes C
Malesherbes D
D Melun

AU CADET DE GASCOGNE
AU SINGE QUI LIT
Play Off

Rick Steves'

PARIS 2004

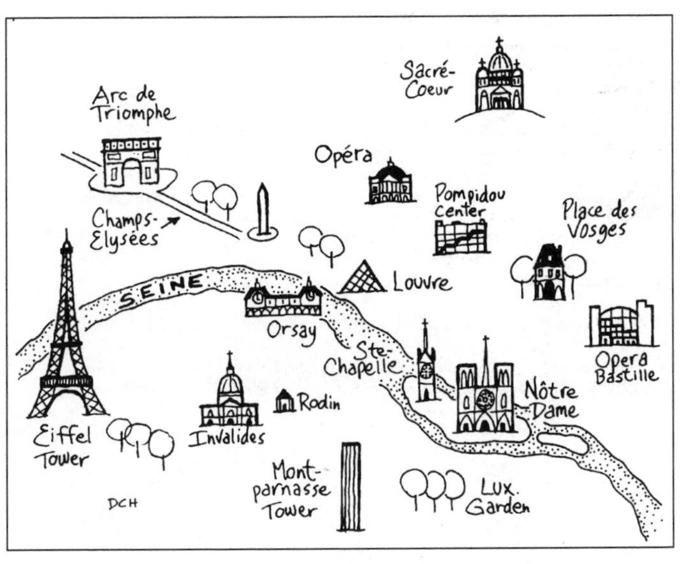

by Rick Steves, Steve Smith,
& Gene Openshaw

For a complete list of Rick Steves' Guidebooks, see page 8.

Avalon Travel Publishing, 1400 65th Street, Suite 250, Emeryville, CA 94608
Avalon Travel Pubishing is a division of Avalon Publishing Group, Inc.

Printed in the USA by Worzalla. Third printing February 2004.

Portions of this book were originally published in *Rick Steves' Mona Winks*, © 2001, 1998, 1996, 1993, 1988 by Rick Steves and Gene Openshaw; *Rick Steves' France, Belgium & the Netherlands* © 2002, 2001, 2000, 1999, 1998 by Rick Steves and Steve Smith; and in *Rick Steves' France* © 2003 by Rick Steves and Steve Smith.

ISBN 1-56691-522-8 • ISSN 1522-3299

For the latest on Rick's lectures, guidebooks, tours, and public television series, contact Europe Through the Back Door, Box 2009, Edmonds, WA 98020, tel. 425/771-8303, fax 425/771-0833, www.ricksteves.com, or e-mail: rick@ricksteves.com.

Europe Through the Back Door Managing Editor: Risa Laib
Europe Through the Back Door Editors: Jill Hodges, Cameron Hewitt
Avalon Travel Publishing Series Manager: Laura Mazer
Research Assistance: Karen Lewis Smith (cuisine), Kristen Kusnic (Chartres)
Copy Editor: Matthew Reed Baker
Production & Typesetting: Kathleen Sparkes, White Hart Design
Cover Design: Kari Gim, Laura Mazer
Interior Design: Jane Musser, Laura Mazer, Amber Pirker
Maps & Graphics: David C. Hoerlein, Rhonda Pelikan, Zoey Platt, Mike Morgenfeld
Photography: pp. 79, 87, 200: David C. Hoerlein; p. 350: Dominic Bonucelli; all others by Rick Steves
Front cover photo of Eiffel Tower: © Veronica Garbutts
Front matter color photos: p. i, Paris, France © Alex Bartel/PHOTOPHILE; p. viii, Place du Tertre, Paris, France © FOLIO, Inc.
Avalon Travel Publishing Graphics Coordinators: Justin Marler, Melissa Sherowski

CONTENTS

Paris

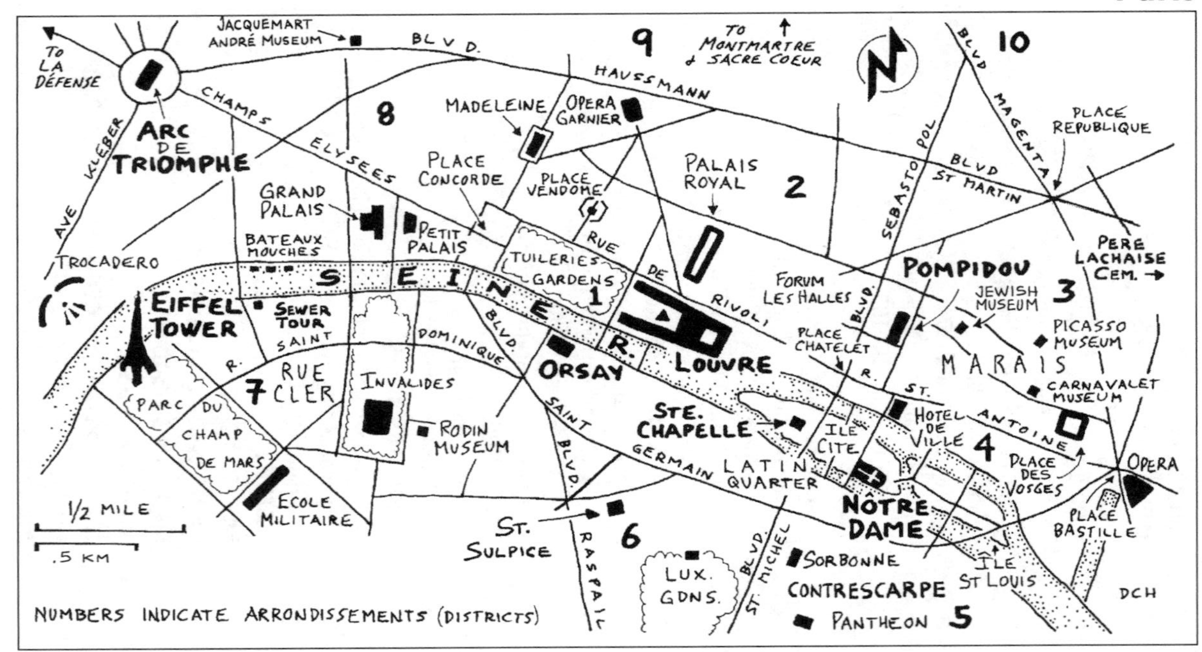

TO LA DÉFENSE
JACQUEMART ANDRÉ MUSEUM
BLVD. HAUSSMANN
9
TO MONTMARTRE & SACRE COEUR
10
BLVD MAGENTA
PLACE REPUBLIQUE
8
MADELEINE
OPERA GARNIER
ARC DE TRIOMPHE
CHAMPS ELYSEES
AVE KLEBER
PLACE CONCORDE
PLACE VENDOME
PALAIS ROYAL
2
SEBASTOPOL
BLVD ST MARTIN
GRAND PALAIS
PETIT PALAIS
BATEAUX MOUCHES
TROCADERO
RUE DE RIVOLI
TUILERIES GARDENS
1
PERE LACHAISE CEM.
FORUM LES HALLES
POMPIDOU
JEWISH MUSEUM
3
SEINE R.
EIFFEL TOWER
SEWER TOUR
R. SAINT DOMINIQUE
BLVD.
ORSAY
LOUVRE
PLACE CHATELET
PICASSO MUSEUM
MARAIS
R. ST. ANTOINE
CARNAVALET MUSEUM
RUE CLER
7
INVALIDES
PARC DU CHAMP DE MARS
RODIN MUSEUM
BLVD. SAINT GERMAIN
STE. CHAPELLE
ILE CITE
HOTEL DE VILLE
4
PLACE DES VOSGES
OPERA
LATIN QUARTER
ECOLE MILITAIRE
NÔTRE DAME
PLACE BASTILLE
1/2 MILE
.5 KM
ST. SULPICE
BLVD RASPAIL
6
LUX. GDNS.
BLVD. ST. MICHEL
SORBONNE
CONTRESCARPE
ILE ST LOUIS
PANTHEON
5
DCH
NUMBERS INDICATE ARRONDISSEMENTS (DISTRICTS)

INTRODUCTION

Paris—the City of Light—has been a beacon of culture for centuries. As a world capital of art, fashion, food, literature, and ideas, it stands as a symbol of all the fine things that human civilization can offer. Come prepared to celebrate, rather than judge, the cultural differences, and you'll capture the romance and joie de vivre that Paris exudes.

Paris offers sweeping boulevards, chatty crêpe stands, chic boutiques, and world-class art galleries. Sip decaf with deconstructionists in a sidewalk café, then step into an Impressionist painting in a tree-lined park. Climb Notre-Dame and rub shoulders with the gargoyles. Cruise the Seine, zip up the Eiffel Tower, and saunter down the avenue des Champs-Elysées. Master the Louvre and Orsay museums. Save some after-dark energy for one of the world's most romantic cities.

This Information Is Accurate and Up-to-Date

This book is updated every year. Most publishers of guidebooks that cover a city from top to bottom can afford an update only every two or three years. Since this book is selective, covering only the sights that make the top week or two in Paris, we can update it in person each summer (we even do a winter checkup). Still, things change. But if you're traveling with the current edition of this book, we guarantee you're using the most up-to-date information available in print. For the latest, visit www.ricksteves.com/update. Also at our Web site, check our Graffiti Wall (select "Rick Steves' guidebooks," then "Paris") for a huge, valuable list of reports and experiences—good and bad—from fellow travelers.

This book will help you have an inexpensive, hassle-free trip. Use this year's edition. Saving a few bucks by traveling with old information is not smart. If you're packing an old book, you'll learn the seriousness of your mistake…in Paris. Your trip costs at least $10 per waking hour. Your time is valuable. This guidebook saves lots of time.

Welcome to Our Paris City Guide

This book is organized in the following way:

Paris Orientation includes tourist information, public transportation basics, and easy-to-read maps. The "Planning Your Time" section offers a suggested schedule with thoughts on how best to use your limited time.

Sights provides a succinct overview of Paris' most important sights. They're arranged by neighborhood and include ratings: ▲▲▲—Don't miss; ▲▲—Try hard to see; ▲—Worthwhile if you can make it; no rating—Worth knowing about.

The **Walks** cover six of Paris' most enjoyable neighborhoods: Historic Paris (Notre-Dame and Sainte-Chapelle), Champs-Elysées, the Marais, rue Cler (near the Eiffel Tower), Montmartre, and the Left Bank.

The **Self-Guided Museum Tours** take you through Paris' most interesting museums: the Louvre, Orsay, Rodin, Marmottan, Cluny, Carnavalet, Picasso, Pompidou Center, and Napoleon's Tomb & Les Invalides. The Bus #69 Sightseeing Tour gives you an inexpensive overview of Paris.

Day Trips covers nearby sights, including the great châteaux of Versailles (includes self-guided tour), Vaux-le-Vicomte, Fontainebleau, and Chantilly; Chartres' majestic cathedral (includes self-guided tour); the Impressionist retreats of Claude Monet's Giverny and Vincent van Gogh's Auvers-sur-Oise; and, *finalement,* Disneyland Paris. For longer stays, we list accommodations for most day trip sights.

Sleeping is a guide to our favorite hotels, from budget deals to cushy splurges in three cozy neighborhoods, with orientation tips geared to make you feel at home.

Eating offers good-value restaurants ranging from inexpensive eateries to romantic bistros, arranged by neighborhood, with a special section on "Grand Cafés."

Paris with Children includes our top 10 recommendations to help keep your kids (and you) happy in Paris.

Shopping helps you shop painlessly and enjoyably, without letting it overwhelm your vacation or ruin your budget. Read up on Paris' great department stores, neighborhood boutiques, flea markets, and outdoor food markets.

Nightlife is a guide to entertainment and evening fun, with music, bus tours, and river cruises, plus information on how to easily translate *Pariscope,* the weekly entertainment guide.

Transportation Connections lays the groundwork for your smooth arrival and departure, covering connections by train and plane, with detailed information on Paris' two airports and six train stations.

The **French History** chapter takes you from Celtic times up to the present.

The **appendix** includes a pronunciation guide, a climate chart, telephone tips, French survival phrases, and a handy almanac of resources.

Throughout the book, when you see a ✪ in a listing, it means that the

TIPS FOR TACKLING OUR SELF-GUIDED TOURS

Sightseeing can be hard work. Our self-guided tours are designed to help make your visits to Paris' finest museums meaningful, fun, fast, and painless. To make the most of our tours, read the tour the night before your visit.

When you arrive at the sight, use the overview map to get the lay of the land and the basic tour route. Expect a few changes—paintings can be on tour, on loan, out sick, or shifted at the whim of the curator. Even museum walls are often moved. To adapt, pick up any available free floor plan as you enter. If you can't find a particular painting, just ask any museum worker. Point to the photograph in this book and ask, *"Où est?"* (oo ay; meaning, "Where is?").

We cover the highlights at sights. You might want to supplement with an audioguide (dry-but-informative recorded descriptions in English, about €5) or a guided tour (usually €6 or more). If guided tours in English are available, they're most likely to occur during peak season, though key museums offer them year-round. The quality of a tour depends on the guide's knowledge, fluency, and enthusiasm.

Museums have rules; if you're aware of them in advance, they're no big deal. Keep in mind that many sights have "last entry" times 30 to 60 minutes before closing. Guards usher people out before the official closing time. Cameras are normally allowed in museums, but no flashes or tripods (without special permission). A handheld camera with ASA-400 film and an F-2 aperture will take a fine picture (or buy slides at the museum bookstore). Video cameras are usually allowed. For security reasons, you're often required to check even small bags. Most museums have a free checkroom at the entrance. They're safe. If you have something you can't bear to part with, be prepared to stash it in a pocket or purse.

At the museum bookshop, thumb through the biggest guidebook (or scan its index) to be sure you haven't overlooked something that is of particular interest to you. If there's an on-site cafeteria, it's usually a good place to rest and have a snack or light meal. Museum WCs are free and generally clean.

sight is covered in more depth in one of our walks or self-guided tours—a page number will tell you where to look to find more information.

Browse through this book and choose your favorite sights. Then have a *fantastique* trip! You'll become your own guide with our self-guided walks and museum tours. You won't waste time on mediocre sights because, unlike other guidebooks, this one covers only the best.

Since lousy, expensive hotels are a major financial pitfall, we've worked hard to assemble good accommodations values. Traveling like a temporary local, you'll get the absolute most out of every mile, minute, and euro. And, as you explore the city we know and love, we're happy you'll be meeting some of our favorite Parisians.

Trip Costs

Five components make up your trip costs: airfare, surface transportation, room and board, sightseeing/entertainment, and shopping/miscellany.

Airfare: Don't try to sort through the mess. Find and use a good travel agent. A basic round-trip U.S.–Paris flight costs $700–1,100 (even cheaper in winter), depending on where you fly from and when.

Surface Transportation: For a typical one-week visit, allow about $50 for Métro tickets and a couple of day trips. Add an additional $70 if you opt for taxi rides to and from the airport (or you could save money taking a shuttle, airport bus, or the RER).

Room and Board: You can thrive in Paris on $80 a day per person for room and board. An $80-a-day budget allows $5 for breakfast, $10 for lunch, $20 for dinner, and $45 for lodging (based on 2 people splitting the cost of a $90 double room). That's doable. Students and tightwads do it on $40 ($20 per bed, $15–20 for meals and snacks). But budget sleeping and eating require using the skills and information covered in this book (and in much greater depth in *Rick Steves' Europe Through the Back Door*).

Sightseeing and Entertainment: Get the Paris Museum and Monument Pass, which covers most sights in Paris (for more information, see Sights chapter, page 27). You'll pay about $20 for a one-day pass, $40 for a three-day pass, and $60 for a five-day pass. (While you can buy the pass through some U.S. travel agents, it's easy and cheaper to buy in Paris). Without a museum pass, figure an average of $8.00 per major sight (e.g., Rodin Museum-$6, Louvre-$10), $4 for minor ones (climbing church towers), and $25 for bus tours and splurge experiences (concerts in the Sainte-Chapelle). An overall average of $15 a day works for most. Don't skimp here. After all, this category directly powers most of the experiences all the other expenses are designed to make possible.

Shopping and Miscellany: Figure $3 per ice-cream cone, coffee, or soft drink. Shopping can vary in cost from nearly nothing to a small fortune. Good budget travelers find that this category has little to do with assembling a trip full of lifelong and wonderful memories.

Exchange Rate

We've priced things throughout this book in the euro currency.

1 euro (€) = about $1.10

To convert prices in euros to dollars, add 10 percent: €45 = about $50.

Just like the dollar, one euro is broken down into 100 cents. Coins range from 1 cent to 2 euros, and bills from €5 to €500.

Prices, Times, and Discounts

The prices in this book, as well as the hours and telephone numbers, are accurate as of mid-2003. Europe is always changing, and we know you'll understand that this, like any other guidebook, starts to yellow even before it's printed.

In Europe—and in this book—you'll use the 24-hour clock. After 12 noon, keep going—13:00, 14:00, and so on. For anything over 12, subtract 12 and add p.m. (14:00 is 2:00 p.m.).

While discounts for sights and transportation are listed for only the most important sights in this book, students with International Student Identification Cards, teachers with proper identification, and youths under 18 often get discounts—but only if they ask.

When to Go

Late spring and fall have the best weather and the biggest crowds. Summers are generally hot and dry; if you wilt in the heat, look for a room with air-conditioning. It's fairly easy to find rooms in summer, and though many French businesses close in August, you'll hardly notice. Paris makes a great winter getaway. Airfares are cheap, the cafés are cozy, and the city feels lively but not touristy. The only problem—weather—is fixed by dressing correctly. Expect cold and rain, but no snow.

Red Tape and Business Hours

You need a passport, but no visa or shots, to travel in France.

Business Hours: Most shops are open Monday through Saturday (10:00–19:00) and closed Sunday, though many small markets, *boulangeries* (bakeries), and street markets are open Sunday mornings until noon. On Mondays, some businesses are closed until 14:00, and possibly all day. Saturdays are like weekdays (but most banks are closed).

Shopping: Shoppers interested in customs regulations and VAT refunds (the tax refunded on large purchases made by non-EU residents) can refer to page 343.

Watt's up? If you're bringing electrical gear, you'll need a two-prong adapter plug (sold cheap at travel stores like ours, www.ricksteves.com) and a converter. Travel appliances often have convenient, built-in converters; look for a voltage switch marked 120 (U.S.) and 240 (Europe).

Banking

Bring your ATM, credit, or debit card, along with a couple hundred dollars in cash as a backup. Traveler's checks are a waste of your time and money.

The best and easiest way to get cash in euros is to use the

omnipresent French bank machines (always open, lower fees, and quick processing). You'll need a PIN code—numbers only, no letters—to use with your Visa or MasterCard. Before you go, verify with your bank that your card will work and alert them that you'll be making withdrawals in Europe; otherwise, the bank may not approve transactions if it perceives unusual spending patterns. Bring two cards in case one gets damaged. "Cash machines" in French are signed *point d'argent* or *distributeur des billets;* the French just say "*distributeur*" (dee-stree-bew-tur).

Just like at home, credit or debit cards work easily at larger hotels, restaurants, and shops. Smaller businesses prefer payment in local currency. Smart travelers function with hard cash and plastic cards.

The Language Barrier and that French Attitude

You've no doubt heard that Parisians are "mean and cold and refuse to speak English." This is an out-of-date preconception left over from the days of Charles de Gaulle. Parisians are as friendly as any other people and no more disagreeable than New Yorkers. Like many big cities, Paris is a massive melting pot of international cultures; your evening hotel receptionist is just as likely to speak French with an accent as not. And, without any doubt, Parisians speak more English than Americans speak French. Be reasonable in your expectations: Waiters are paid to be efficient, not chatty. And Parisian postal clerks are every bit as speedy, cheery, and multilingual as ours are back home.

The biggest mistake most Americans make when traveling in France is trying to do too much with limited time. Hurried, impatient travelers who miss the subtle pleasures of people-watching from a sun-dappled café often misinterpret French attitudes. By slowing your pace and making an effort to understand French culture, you're much more likely to have a richer experience.

With five weeks' paid time off, your hosts can't comprehend why anyone would rush through a vacation. Parisians take great pride in their customs, clinging to their belief in cultural superiority despite the fact that they're no longer a world superpower. Let's face it: It's tough to keep on smiling when you've been crushed by a Big Mac, Mickey Moused by Disney, and drowned in instant coffee. Your hosts are cold only if you decide to see them that way. Polite and formal, the French respect the fine points of culture and tradition. In France, strolling down the street with a big grin on your face and saying hello to strangers is a sign of senility, not friendliness (seriously). Parisians think that Americans, while friendly, are hesitant to pursue more serious friendships. Recognize sincerity and look for kindness. Give them the benefit of the doubt.

Communication difficulties are exaggerated. To hurdle the language barrier, bring a small English/French dictionary, a phrase book (look for ours), a menu reader, and a good supply of patience. In transactions, a small notepad and pen minimize misunderstandings about prices; have vendors write the price down. If you learn only five phrases, learn and use these: *bonjour* (good day), *pardon* (pardon me), *s'il vous plaît* (please), *merci* (thank you), and *au revoir* (goodbye). The French place great importance on politeness. Begin every encounter with "*Bonjour, madame/monsieur*" and end every encounter with "*Au revoir, madame/monsieur.*"

The French are language perfectionists—they take their language (and other languages) seriously. Often they speak more English than they let on. This isn't a tourist-baiting tactic, but timidity on their part to speak another language less than fluently. Start any conversation with, "*Bonjour, madame/monsieur. Parlez-vous anglais?*" and hope they speak more English than you speak French.

Travel Smart

Your trip to Paris is like a complex play—easier to follow and really appreciate on a second viewing. While no one does the same trip twice to gain that advantage, reading this book in its entirety before your trip accomplishes much the same thing.

Reread this book as you travel, and visit local tourist information offices (abbreviated as "TI" in this book). Buy a phone card or mobile phone and use it for reservations and confirmations. Be positive and don't let one rude Parisian ruin your day. Ask questions. Most locals are eager to point you in their idea of the right direction. Wear your money belt. Those who expect to travel smart, do.

Plan ahead for banking, laundry, post-office chores, and picnics. Mix intense and relaxed periods. Every trip (and every traveler) needs at least a few slack days. Pace yourself. Assume you will return.

As you read through this book, plan your itinerary. Note the days when sights are closed. Sundays have pros and cons, as they do for traveling in the United States (special events and weekly markets, limited hours, shops and banks closed, limited public transportation, no rush hours). Saturdays are virtually weekdays. Popular places are even more popular on weekends and inundated on three-day weekends.

Major Holidays: In 2004, be ready for unusually big crowds during these holiday periods—Easter week (April 10–17), Labor Day weekend (April 30-May 2), VE Day (May 7–9), Ascension weekend (May 20–23), Pentecost weekend (May 28-31), Bastille Day (July 14), Assumption (Aug 15), All Saints' Day weekend (Oct 29–Nov 1), Armistice Day (Nov 11-14), and the winter holidays (Dec 20-Jan 5). Many sights close on the actual holiday (confirm closures at local tourist information offices).

French Tourist Offices in the United States

France's national tourist offices in the United States are a wealth of information. Before your trip, request any specific information you may want (such as city maps and schedules of upcoming festivals).

French Government Tourist Office: For questions and brochures (on regions, barging, and the wine roads), call 410/286-8310. Ask for the France Guide. Materials delivered in 4 to 6 weeks are free; there's a $4 shipping fee for information delivered in 5 to 10 days. Their Web site is www.franceguide.com, their e-mail is info@franceguide.com, and their offices are in...

New York: 444 Madison Ave., 16th floor, New York, NY 10022, fax 212/838-7855.

California: 9454 Wilshire Blvd. #310, Beverly Hills, CA 90212, fax 310/276-2835.

Rick Steves' Books, Videos, and DVDs

Rick Steves' Europe Through the Back Door 2004 gives you budget travel tips on minimizing jet lag, packing light, planning your itinerary, traveling by car or train, finding budget beds, changing money, avoiding rip-offs, hurdling the language barrier, using mobile phones, staying healthy, using your bidet, and lots more. The book also includes chapters on 38 of Rick's favorite "Back Doors."

Rick Steves' **Country Guides** are a series of nine, annually-updated guidebooks covering France (co-written with Steve Smith); Great Britain; Ireland (co-written with Pat O'Connor); Italy; Spain and Portugal; Scandinavia; Germany, Austria, and Switzerland; the Best of Europe; and—new for 2004—the Best of Eastern Europe.

Rick's **City and Regional Guides** include our new Provence & the French Riviera guidebook, along with this book, Rome, Venice, Florence, London, and Amsterdam. By the sleek Eurostar train, London is just three hours from Paris, and by the slick Thalys train, Amsterdam is only four hours away. Consider combining two or all three of these cities (and books) for a great visit.

Rick Steves' Easy Access Europe, new for 2004, is written for travelers who are mobility-impaired. This book offers our latest tips and information on sights, hotels, restaurants, and transportation in London, Paris, Bruges, Amsterdam, and the Rhine River—tailored for slow walkers and wheelchair users.

Rick Steves' Europe 101: History and Art for the Traveler (with Gene Openshaw) gives you the story of Europe's people, history, and art. Written for smart people who were sleeping in their history and art classes before they knew they were going to Europe, *101* helps Europe's sights come alive.

Rick Steves' Mona Winks (with Gene Openshaw) gives you fun, easy-to-follow, self-guided tours of Europe's top 25 museums and cultural sites. All of the *Mona Winks* chapters on Paris are included in this Paris guidebook. But if you'd like similar coverage for the great museums in London, Amsterdam, Venice, Florence, Rome, and Madrid, *Mona*'s for you.

Rick Steves' French Phrase Book is a fun, practical tool for independent budget travelers. This handy book has everything you'll need, including a menu decoder, conversation starters for connecting with locals, and an easy-to-follow telephone template for making hotel reservations.

Rick's new PBS-TV series, *Rick Steves' Europe,* keeps churning out shows. Out of 82 episodes (including the new series and *Travels in Europe with Rick Steves*), two shows cover Paris and seven half-hour shows cover other parts of France. These air nationally on public television stations and the Travel Channel. They are also available in information-packed home videos and DVDs (order online at www.ricksteves.com, or call 425/771-8303 for our free newsletter/catalog).

Rick Steves' Postcards from Europe, Rick's autobiographical book, packs 25 years of travel anecdotes and insights into the ultimate 3,000-mile European adventure. Through his guidebooks, Rick shares his favorite European discoveries with you. *Postcards* introduces you to his favorite European friends.

All of Rick's books are published by Avalon Travel Publishing (www.travelmatters.com).

Other Guidebooks

For most travelers, this book is all you need. But if you'd like more information, you may want to buy an additional guidebook. The Michelin Green Guide, which is somewhat scholarly, and the more readable *Paris Access* guide are both well-researched. Of the multitude of other guidebooks on France and Paris, many are high on facts and low on opinion, guts, or personality. If you'll be traveling elsewhere in France, *Rick Steves' France 2004* would come in handy.

Recommended Reading and Movies

To get the feel of Paris past and present, consider reading some of these books or seeing these films:

Non-Fiction: To better understand the French, check out *French or Foe* or *Savoir-Flair*! (both by Polly Platt) and *Fragile Glory* (by Richard Bernstein). *The Course of French History* (by Pierre Goubert) provides a good, succinct summary of French history. Other possibilities include: *A Moveable Feast* (Ernest Hemingway), *I'll Always Have Paris* (Art Buchwald), *A Corner in The Marais* (Alex Karmel), *Is Paris Burning?* (Larry Collins), *A Traveller's History of Paris* (Robert Cole), *Travelers' Tales: Paris* (James O'Reilly), *Paris: The Collected Traveler* (Barrie Kerper), *Culture Shock: France* (Sally Taylor), the *Marling Menu-Master for France*, and *The Paris Mapguide* (Michael Middleditch).

Fiction: *City of Darkness, City of Light* (Marge Piercy), *Le Divorce* and *Le Mariage* (both by Diane Johnson), *Inspector Maigret* series (George Simenon), *Sandman* (J. Robert Janes), *Murder in the Marais* (Cara Black),

Murder in Montparnasse (Howard Engel), *Les Misérables* and *The Hunchback of Notre-Dame* (both by Victor Hugo), *A Tale of Two Cities* (Charles Dickens), and the *Madeline* children's series (Ludwig Bemelmans).

Flicks: *Jules et Jim, The 400 Blows, Diva, Belle de Jour, The Accompanist, The Last Métro, Peppermint Soda, The Red Balloon, Ridicule, Les Misérables, Camille Claudel, Cyrano de Bergerac, Danton, Is Paris Burning?, Moulin Rouge, Madeline, French Kiss, The Moderns, Jefferson in Paris, American Dreamer, An American in Paris, Can-Can, Funny Face, Charade, Paris Blues, How To Steal A Million, Love In the Afternoon, The Last Time I Saw Paris, Gigi, The Phantom of the Opera, Victor/Victoria, Children of Paradise,* and the Three Colors trilogy: *Blue/White/Red.*

Maps

The black-and-white maps in this book, drawn by Dave Hoerlein, are concise and simple. Dave, who is well-traveled in Paris, designed these maps to help you quickly orient and painlessly get where you want to go. Once in Paris, simply check the color city map (and handy Métro map) at the front of this book, and you're ready to travel.

For a longer trip, consider the Rick Steves' France Planning Map, which shows France on one side and Paris on the other. Order online at www.ricksteves.com, or call 425/771-8303 for our free newsletter/catalog.

Tours of Paris and France by Rick Steves and Steve Smith

Travel agents will tell you about all the mainstream tours of Paris and France, but they won't tell you about ours. At Europe Through the Back Door, we organize and lead one-week tours of Paris and longer tours covering the highlights of France. The Paris tours, limited to 22 people, run year-round. For a longer tour, choose from "Paris and the Heart of France" (12 days in Paris, Normandy, Brittany, the Loire, and Burgundy), "Provence and the Riviera" (13 days), and "The Best of France" (18 days from Paris to Nice including Normandy, the Loire, Dordogne, Languedoc, Provence, and the Riviera). These depart each year April–October, are limited to 24–26 people per group, and have big, roomy buses and great guides. For details, call us at 425/771-8303 or check www.ricksteves.com.

Transportation

Transportation concerns within Paris are limited to the subway, buses, and taxis, all covered extensively in the Orientation chapter. Connections to day trip destinations are covered in those chapters. You don't want to drive in Paris. If you have a car, stow it (for parking information, see page 355).

For all the specifics on transportation throughout France by train or car, see *Rick Steves' France 2004.*

Telephones, Mail, and E-Mail

You'll want a locally purchased phone card *(une carte téléphonique)* for making hotel/restaurant reservations, verifying hours at sights, and phoning home. There are two basic types: a *télécarte* (tay-lay-kart) that can be used only in a public phone booth, and a *carte a code* (cart ah code) with a dial-up code that can be used with any phone. Either card can be purchased at any post office and from most newsstands and tobacco shops *(tabacs),* which you'll find everywhere in Paris, including at train stations and airports.

The *télécarte* represents the efficient card-operated system that has replaced coin-operated public phones throughout Europe. Insert the card in the phone and dial away. There are two denominations: *une petite* costs about €7; *une grande* about €15. To use the *télécarte,* simply take the phone off the hook, insert the card, and wait for a dial tone; the price of the call (local or international) is automatically deducted.

There are a variety of prepaid cards that work like those sold in the United States, allowing you to dial from the comfort of your hotel room, from a public phone booth (toll-free number), or from anywhere, and charge the call to the card at low rates. The *Carte Kertel* (kart kare-tel) and *Carte 365* are the most common (€7 and €15 cards available). There's even an international card *(Le Ticket de Téléphone International)* that offers cheaper rates for international calls.

These cards all work the same way and are simple to use. Scratch to get your PIN code. After dialing the toll-free access number, the message tells you to enter your PIN code followed by #. Once you hear the next message, dial your number, again followed by # (you don't have to listen to the sales pitch for more minutes). While a *carte a code* has cheaper per-minute rates than a *télécarte,* it's slower to use (more numbers to dial), so local calls are quicker with a *télécarte* from a phone booth.

U.S. Calling Card Services: Since direct-dialing rates have dropped, calling cards (offered by AT&T, MCI, and Sprint) are no longer the good value they used to be. In fact, they are a rip-off. You're likely to pay a $4 connection fee and $3 for the first minute; if you get an answering machine, it'll cost you $7 to say, "Sorry I missed you." Now it's much cheaper to make your international calls with a phone card purchased in Europe.

Dialing Direct: France has a direct-dial 10-digit telephone system. There are no area codes. To call to or from anywhere in France, including Paris, you dial the 10 numbers directly. All Paris numbers start with 01.

To call France from another country, start with the international access code (00 if you're calling from a European country; 011 from the United States and Canada), dial France's country code (33), and then drop the initial 0 of the 10-digit local number and dial the remaining nine digits. For example, the phone number of a good hotel in Paris is 01 47 05 49 15. To call it from home, dial 011 33 1 47 05 49 15.

To dial out of France, start your call with its international code (00), then dial the country code of the country you're calling, then the number you're calling. For example, to call our office in the United States, dial 00 (France's international access code), 1 (U.S. country code), then 425/771-8303 (our area code plus local number).

For a list of international access codes and country codes, see the appendix. European time is six/nine hours ahead of the East/West Coast of the United States.

Mobile Phones: Many travelers now buy cheap mobile phones in Europe to make both local and international calls. (Typical American mobile phones don't work in Europe, and those that do, have horrendous per-minute costs.) For about $75 you can get a phone with $20 worth of calls that will work in the country where you purchased it. (You can buy more time at newsstands or mobile phone shops.) For about $100 you can get a phone that will work in most countries once you pick up the necessary chip per country (about $25). If you're interested, stop by any European shop that sells mobile phones; you'll see prominent store window displays. Depending on your trip and budget, ask for a phone that works only in that country or one that can be used throughout Europe. If you're on a budget, skip mobile phones and use PIN cards instead.

Mail: The hours of French post offices (called PTT for "Post, Telegraph, and Telephone," signed as La Poste) vary, though most are open weekdays 8:00–19:00 and Saturday morning 8:00–12:00. Stamps and phone cards are also sold at *tabac* (tobacco) shops. It costs about €0.70 to mail a postcard to the United States.

To arrange for mail delivery, reserve a few hotels along your route in advance and give their addresses to friends. Or you can use the American Express Company's mail services (free for AmEx cardholders and a minimal fee for anyone else). Allow 10 days for a letter to arrive. Phoning is so easy that we've dispensed with mail stops altogether.

E-mail: E-mail has caught on among hoteliers; very few lack an e-mail address. As for Internet access, ask at your hotel for the nearest Internet (an-ter-net) café; some hoteliers even have Internet terminals in their lobbies.

Tipping

Tipping in France isn't as automatic and generous as it is in the United States, but for special service, tips are appreciated, if not expected. As in the United States, the proper amount depends on your resources, tipping philosophy, and the circumstance, but some general guidelines apply.

Restaurants: At cafés and restaurants, the service charge is included in the bill, though it's customary to tip five percent extra for good service (for details, see page 316). If you order a meal at a counter, don't tip.

Taxis: To tip the cabbie, round up. For a typical ride, round up to the next euro on the fare (to pay a €13 fare, give €14); for a long ride, round to the nearest €10 (for a €75 fare, give €80). If the cabbie hauls your bags and zips you to the airport to help you catch your flight, you might want to toss in a little more. But if you feel like you're being driven in circles or otherwise ripped off, skip the tip.

Special services: Tour guides at public sites and tour bus drivers often hold out their hands for tips after the tour; since we've already paid for the tour, we don't tip extra—but some tourists do give a euro or two, particularly for a job well done. We don't tip at hotels, but if you do, give the porter a euro for carrying bags and leave a couple of euros in your room at the end of your stay for the maid if the room was kept clean. In general, if someone in the service industry does a super job for you, a tip of a couple euros is appropriate...but not required.

When in doubt, ask: If you're not sure whether (or how much) to tip for a service, ask your hotelier or the tourist information office; they'll fill you in on how it's done on their turf.

Stranger in a Strange Land

We travel all the way to Europe to enjoy differences—to become temporary locals. You'll experience frustrations. Certain truths that we find "God-given" or "self-evident," like friendly waiters, ice in drinks, bottomless cups of coffee, hot showers, and bigger being better, are suddenly not so true. One of the benefits of travel is the eye-opening realization that there are logical, civil, and even better alternatives.

Tourism suffered throughout France in 2003. The poor economy kept many Europeans and Asians away, and the war in Iraq kept more Americans at bay. This was a severe blow to the average worker in the service industry (most with low-wage jobs). Whether you agree or disagree with French political leaders on this issue, remember that the people running your hotel and restaurants have no animosity toward you as an American. While most French differed with George Bush and Donald Rumsfeld, they don't hold American travelers accountable for the actions of their politicians. Unfortunately, some Americans took the French dispute over American policy in Iraq personally (renaming French fries to Freedom fries, and French toast to Freedom toast). Our French friends at first found this amusing, then alarming as self-righteous Americans boycotted more French products and businesses.

As you travel in France today, you'll find business owners happy to see you. Some might apologize for their leaders and others might be critical of Bush, but none will understand why many Americans took this issue so personally. American travelers have a greater responsibility than ever to represent our country in people-to-people diplomacy and to learn why most of the world disagreed with our invasion of Iraq.

Paris is an understandably proud city. To enjoy its people, you need to celebrate the differences. A willingness to go local ensures that you'll enjoy a full dose of Parisian hospitality.

Back Door Manners

While updating our guidebooks, we hear over and over again that our readers are considerate and fun to have as guests. Thank you for traveling as temporary locals who are sensitive to the culture. It's fun to follow you in our travels.

Send Us a Postcard, Drop Us a Line

If you enjoy a successful trip with the help of this book and would like to share your discoveries, please fill out the survey at the end of this book and send it to Europe Through the Back Door, Box 2009, Edmonds, WA 98020. We personally read and value all feedback. Thanks in advance—it helps a lot.

For our latest travel information, tap into our Web site: www.ricksteves.com. To check for any updates to this book, visit www.ricksteves.com/update. Rick's e-mail address is rick@ricksteves.com. Anyone is welcome to request a free issue of our Back Door quarterly newsletter (call 425/771-8303 or order it online at www.ricksteves.com).

Judging from all the positive feedback and happy postcards we receive from travelers who have used this book, it's safe to assume you'll enjoy a great, affordable vacation—with the finesse of an independent, experienced traveler.

From this point, "we" (your co-authors) will shed our respective egos and become "I."

Thanks, and *bon voyage*!

BACK DOOR TRAVEL PHILOSOPHY

From *Rick Steves' Europe Through the Back Door*

Travel is intensified living—maximum thrills per minute and one of the last great sources of legal adventure. Travel is freedom. It's recess, and we need it.

Experiencing the real Europe requires catching it by surprise, going casual…"Through the Back Door."

Affording travel is a matter of priorities. (Make do with the old car.) You can travel—simply, safely, and comfortably—anywhere in Europe for $80 a day plus transportation costs. In many ways, spending more money only builds a thicker wall between you and what you came to see. Europe is a cultural carnival and, time after time, you'll find that its best acts are free and the best seats are the cheap ones.

A tight budget forces you to travel close to the ground, meeting and communicating with the people, not relying on service with a purchased smile. Never sacrifice sleep, nutrition, safety, or cleanliness in the name of budget. Simply enjoy the local-style alternatives to expensive hotels and restaurants.

Extroverts have more fun. If your trip is low on magic moments, kick yourself and make things happen. If you don't enjoy a place, maybe you don't know enough about it. Seek the truth. Recognize tourist traps. Give a culture the benefit of your open mind. See things as different but not better or worse. Any culture has much to share.

Of course, travel, like the world, is a series of hills and valleys. Be fanatically positive and militantly optimistic. If something's not to your liking, change your liking. Travel is addictive. It can make you a happier American, as well as a citizen of the world. Our Earth is home to six billion equally important people. It's humbling to travel and find that people don't envy Americans. They like us, but, with all due respect, they wouldn't trade passports.

Globetrotting destroys ethnocentricity. It helps you understand and appreciate different cultures. Travel changes people. It broadens perspectives and teaches new ways to measure quality of life. Many travelers toss aside their hometown blinders. Their prized souvenirs are the strands of different cultures they decide to knit into their own character. The world is a cultural yarn shop. And Back Door travelers are weaving the ultimate tapestry.

Come on, join in!

ORIENTATION

Many people fall in love with Paris. Some see the essentials and flee, overwhelmed by the big city. With the proper approach, you'll fall head over heels for Europe's capital city.

This orientation to the City of Light will illuminate your trip. The day plans—for visits of one to seven days—will help you prioritize the many sights. You'll tap into Paris' information sources for current events. Most important, you'll learn to navigate Paris by Métro, bus, taxi, or foot. For most travelers, the key to the city is a Métro ticket.

Paris: A Verbal Map

Paris is split in half by the Seine River, divided into 20 *arrondissements* (proud and independent governmental jurisdictions), circled by a ring-road freeway (the *périphérique*) and speckled with Métro stations. You'll find Paris easier to navigate if you know which side of the river you're on, which *arrondissement* you're in, and which subway (Métro) stop you're closest to. If you're north of the river (the top half of any city map), you're on the Right Bank (*rive droite*). If you're south of it, you're on the Left Bank (*rive gauche*). The bull's-eye of your Paris map is Notre-Dame, which sits on an island in the middle of the Seine. Most of your sightseeing will take place within five blocks of the river.

Arrondissements are numbered, starting at the Louvre and moving in a clockwise spiral out to the ring road. The last two digits in a Parisian zip

Paris Arrondissements

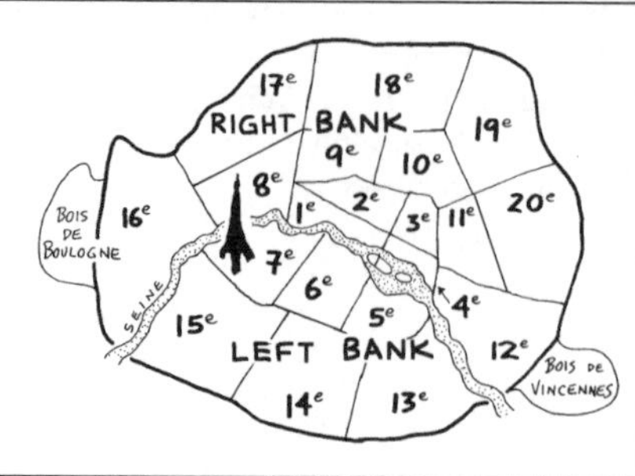

code are the *arrondissement* number. The abbreviation for the Métro stop is "Mo." In Parisian jargon, Napoleon's tomb is on *la rive gauche* (the Left Bank) in the *7ème* (7th *arrondissement*), zip code 75007, Mo: Invalides. Paris Métro stops are used as a standard aid in giving directions, even for those not using the Métro. As you're tracking down addresses, these words and pronunciations will help: *place* (plahs, square), *rue* (roo, road), and *pont* (pohn, bridge).

Arrival in Paris

For a comprehensive rundown on Paris' six train stations and two airports, see the Transportation Connections chapter on page 355.

PLANNING YOUR TIME

Paris in One, Two, or Three Busy Days

Sights are listed in descending order of importance. If you have only one day, just do Day 1 (below); for two days, add Day 2. If you want to fit in Versailles on a three-day visit, try the afternoon of the second day (easier) or third day.

Day 1

Morning: Follow Historic Paris Walk, featuring Ile de la Cité, Notre-Dame, Latin Quarter, and Sainte-Chapelle (consider lunch at nearby Samaritaine view café).

Afternoon: Tour the Louvre.

Evening: Cruise the Seine River or take the "Paris Illumination" nighttime bus tour.

Day 2

Morning: Follow Champs-Elysées Walk from Arc de Triomphe down the grand avenue des Champs-Elysées to Tuileries Garden (consider lunch at a café in the Tuileries Garden).

Midday: Cross the pedestrian bridge from the Tuileries Garden, then tour the Orsay Museum.

Afternoon: Tour the Rodin Museum or Napoleon's Tomb, or visit Versailles (take RER direct from Orsay).

Evening: Enjoy the Trocadéro scene and a twilight ride up the Eiffel Tower.

Day 3

Morning: Follow Marais Walk.

Afternoon: Stay in the Marais and tour your choice of the Carnavalet Museum, Pompidou Center, or Jewish Art and History Museum. (Or visit Versailles.)

Evening: Take Montmartre Walk, featuring the Sacré-Cœur basilica.

DAILY REMINDER

Monday: These sights are closed today—Orsay, Rodin, Marmottan, Montmartre, Carnavalet, Catacombs, Giverny, and Versailles; the Louvre is more crowded because of this, but the Denon wing (with *Mona Lisa,* Venus de Milo, and more highlights) stays open until 21:45. Napoleon's Tomb is closed the first Monday of the month. Some small stores don't open until 14:00. Street markets such as rue Cler and rue Mouffetard are dead today. Some banks are closed. It's discount night at most cinemas.

Tuesday: Many museums are closed today, including the Louvre, Picasso, Cluny, and Pompidou Center, as well as the châteaux of Chantilly (except July–Aug) and Fontainebleau. The Eiffel Tower, Orsay, and Versailles are particularly busy today.

Wednesday: All sights are open (Louvre until 21:45). The weekly *Pariscope* magazine comes out today. Most schools are closed, so many kids' sights are busy. Some cinemas offer discounts.

Thursday: All sights are open except the Sewer Tour. The Orsay is open until 21:45. Department stores are open late.

Friday: All sights are open except the Sewer Tour. Afternoon trains and roads leaving Paris are crowded; TGV reservation fees are higher.

Saturday: All sights are open (except the Jewish Art and History Museum). The fountains run at Versailles (July–Sept) and Vaux-le-Vicomte hosts candlelight visits (May–Oct); otherwise avoid weekend crowds at area châteaux. Department stores are busy. The Jewish Quarter is quiet.

Sunday: Some museums are two-thirds price all day and/or free the first Sunday of the month, thus more crowded (e.g., Louvre, Orsay, Rodin, Cluny, Pompidou, and Picasso). The fountains run at Versailles (early April–early Oct). Most of Paris' stores are closed on Sunday, but shoppers will find relief in the Marais neighborhood's lively Jewish Quarter and in Bercy Village, where many stores are open. Look for organ concerts at St. Sulpice and possibly other churches. The American Church hosts a free evening concert at 17:00 (Jan–June and Sept–Nov only). Most recommended restaurants in the rue Cler neighborhood are closed for dinner.

Paris in Five to Seven Days without Going In-Seine

Day 1

Morning: Follow Historic Paris Walk, featuring Ile de la Cité, Notre-Dame, Latin Quarter, Cluny Museum, and Sainte-Chapelle.

Afternoon: Enjoy the Luxembourg Garden and relax in a nearby café (see "Les Grands Cafés de Paris," page 332) or tour the nearby Pompidou Center.

Evening: Cruise the Seine River or take the "Paris Illumination" nighttime bus tour.

Day 2

Morning: Tour the Louvre (arrive 20 min before opening). Lunch at Café le Nemours.

Afternoon: Follow Champs-Elysées Walk from Arc de Triomphe down the grand avenue de Champs-Elysées to Tuileries Garden. (Reversing the morning and afternoon also works well because the Champs-Elysées Walk leaves you near the Louvre, though most have more energy for museums in the morning.)

Evening: Take Montmartre Walk, featuring the Sacré-Cœur basilica.

Day 3

Morning: Tour the Orsay Museum (arrive 15 min before opening).

Midday: Tour the Rodin Museum (picnic or café lunch in gardens).

Afternoon: Visit Napoleon's Tomb, then take the Rue Cler Walk and relax at the Café du Marché.

Evening: Enjoy dinner on the Ile St. Louis.

Day 4

Morning: Catch the RER and arrive early (9:00) at Versailles. Tour the palace's interior.

Midday: Have lunch on Versailles' market square.

Afternoon: Take the shortcut from the market square to Versailles' gardens, and visit Le Hameau and Trianon palaces. Return to Paris with some time for shopping.

Evening: Attend a concert at Sainte-Chapelle.

Day 5

Morning: Follow Marais Walk and tour the Carnavalet Museum. Lunch at Nectarine on place des Vosges or have a falafel on rue des Rosiers.

Afternoon: Tour the Pompidou Center and/or the Jewish Art and History Museum.

Evening: Enjoy the Trocadéro scene and a twilight ride up the Eiffel Tower.

Days 6 and 7

Choose from:
Shopping and cafés
Montmartre and Sacré-Cœur (by day)
Picasso, Cluny, Marmottan, or Jacquemart-André Museums, or Opéra Garnier
Day trip to Chartres
Day trip to Vaux-le-Vicomte and Fontainebleau
Day trip to Disneyland Paris
Evening: Night bus or boat tour (whichever you have yet to do)

Tourist Information

Avoid the Paris tourist offices (abbreviated as "TI" in this book) because of their long lines, short information, and charge for maps. This book, the *Pariscope* magazine (described below), and one of the freebie maps available at any hotel (or in the front of this book) are all you need. Paris' TIs share a single phone number: 08 36 68 31 12 (from the states, dial 011 33 8 36 68 31 12). The main TI is at 127 avenue des **Champs- Elysées** (daily 9:00–20:00), but the other TIs are less crowded: at **Gare de Lyon** (daily 8:00–20:00), at the **Eiffel Tower** (May–Sept daily 11:00–18:40, closed Oct–April), and at the **Louvre** (Wed–Mon 10:00–19:00, closed Tue). Both **airports** have handy TIs (called ADP) with long hours and short lines (see the Transportation Connections chapter).

Paris' TIs have an official Web site (www.paris-touristoffice.com) offering practical information on hotels, special events, museums, children's activities, fashion, nightlife, and more. Two other Web sites that are entertaining and at times useful are www.bonjourparis.com (which claims to offer a virtual trip to Paris, featuring interactive French lessons, tips on wine and food, and news on the latest Parisian trends) and the similar www.paris-anglo.com (with informative stories on visiting Paris, plus a directory of over 2,500 English-speaking businesses).

For a complete schedule of museum hours and English-language museum tours, pick up the free *Musées, Monuments Historiques, et Expositions* booklet from any museum.

Pariscope: The *Pariscope* weekly magazine (or one of its clones, €0.40 at any newsstand) lists museum hours, art exhibits, concerts, festivals, plays, movies, and nightclubs. Smart tour guides and sightseers rely on this for the latest listings (see "Tour of *Pariscope*" on page 350).

Maps: While Paris is littered with free maps, they don't show all the streets. You may want the huge Michelin #10 map of Paris. For an extended stay, I prefer the pocket-size, street-indexed *Paris Pratique* (about €6) with an easy-to-use Métro map.

Bookstores: There are many English-language bookstores in Paris where you can pick up guidebooks, for nearly double their American prices. Most carry this book. Others include Shakespeare and Company (daily 12:00–24:00, some used travel books, 37 rue de la Bûcherie, across the river from Notre-Dame, Mo: St. Michel, tel. 01 43 26 96 50), W. H. Smith (248 rue de Rivoli, Mo: Concorde, tel. 01 44 77 88 99), and Brentanos (37 avenue de L'Opéra, Mo: Opéra, tel. 01 42 61 52 50). My favorite is the friendly Red Wheelbarrow Bookstore in the Marais neighborhood, run by charming Penelope and Abigail (13 rue Charles V, Mo: St. Paul, tel. 01 42 77 42 17).

American Church: The American Church is a nerve center for the American émigré community. It distributes a free, handy, and insightful monthly English-language newspaper called the *Paris Voice*, which has useful reviews of concerts, plays, and current events; find it at about 200 locations in Paris (http://parisvoice.com). Also available is an advertisement paper called *France—U.S.A. Contacts*, which is full of useful information for those seeking work or long-term housing. The church faces the river between the Eiffel Tower and Orsay Museum (reception open Mon–Sat 9:30–22:30, Sun 9:00–19:30, 65 quai d'Orsay, Mo: Invalides, tel. 01 40 62 05 00).

Helpful Hints

Theft Alert: Pickpockets seem more numerous and determined than ever. Métro and RER lines that serve popular sights are infested with thieves. Wear a money belt, put your wallet in your front pocket, loop your day bag over your shoulders (consider wearing it in front), and keep a tight grip on a purse or shopping bag. Muggings are rare but do occur. If you're out late, avoid the dark riverfront quays and anywhere the lighting is dim and pedestrian activity minimal.

Paris Museum Pass: This worthwhile pass, covering most sights in Paris, is available at major Métro stations, TIs, and museums. For detailed information, see page 27.

Museum Strategy: Arriving 20 minutes before major museums open is line-time well spent. Remember, most museums require you to check daypacks and coats, and important museums have metal detectors that will slow your entry. If you're still ahead of the pack when you enter, consider hustling to the most popular works first.

Street Safety: Be careful on foot! Parisian drivers are notorious for ignoring pedestrians. Look both ways (many streets are one-way) and be careful of seemingly quiet bus/taxi lanes. Don't assume you have the right of way, even in a crosswalk. When crossing a street, keep your pace constant and don't stop suddenly. By law, drivers must miss pedestrians by one meter (1.5 meters in the countryside). Drivers carefully calculate your speed and won't hit you, provided you don't alter your route or pace. Watch out for a lesser hazard: *merde.* Parisian dogs decorate the city's sidewalks with 16 tons of droppings per day. People get injured by slipping in it.

Toilets: Carry small change for pay toilets, or walk into any sidewalk café like you own the place and find the toilet in the back. The restrooms in museums are free and the best you'll find, and if you have a museum pass, you can drop into almost any museum for the toilets. Modern, sanitary, street-booth toilets provide both relief and a memory (coins required, don't leave small children inside unattended). Keep toilet paper or tissues with you, as some toilets are poorly supplied.

Getting around Paris

By Métro: In Paris, you're never more than a 10-minute walk from a Métro station. Europe's best subway (open daily from 5:30 until 00:30) allows you to hop from sight to sight quickly and cheaply. Learn to use it.

Pickpockets and Panhandlers: Thieves spend their days in the Métro. Be on guard. For example, if your pocket is picked as you pass through a turnstile, you end up stuck on the wrong side while the thief strolls away. Stand away from Métro doors to avoid being a target for a just-before-the-door-close theft and run. Any jostling or commotion, especially when boarding or leaving trains, is likely the sign of a thief or a team of thieves in action. Make any fare inspector show proof of identity (ask locals for help if you're not certain).

Paris has a huge homeless population and higher than 11 percent unemployment; expect a warm Métro welcome by panhandlers, musicians, and those selling magazines produced by the homeless community.

Tickets and Passes: One ticket (€1.40) takes you anywhere in the system with unlimited transfers. Tickets are also good on the RER suburban trains (see below) and on city buses, although one ticket cannot be used as a transfer between subway and bus. Save 40 percent by buying a ***carnet*** (car-nay) of 10 tickets for €10 (a single ticket is €1.40, kids 4–10 pay €5 for a *carnet*). Buy tickets at any Métro station from a human or a machine (some machines also accept credit cards).

If you're staying in Paris for a week or more, consider the **Carte Orange** (kart oh-RAHNZH) for about €15, which gives you free run of the bus and Métro system for one week, starting Monday and ending Sunday; ask for the Carte Orange *coupon vert* and supply a passport-size photo. The month-long version costs about €50; request a Carte Orange *coupon orange* (good from the first day of the month to the last). These passes cover only central Paris; you can pay more for passes covering regional destinations (like Versailles). All passes can be purchased at any Métro station, most of which have photo booths where you can get the photo required for the pass. Despite what some Métro agents say, Carte Orange passes are definitely not limited to residents; if you're refused, simply go to another station to buy your pass. The overpriced **Paris Visite** passes were designed for tourists and offer minor reductions at minor sights (1 day-€9, 2 days-€14, 3 days-€19, 5 days-€28), but you'll get a better value with a cheaper *carnet* of 10 tickets or a Carte Orange.

How the Métro works: To get to your destination, determine the closest "Mo" stop and which line or lines will get you there. The lines have numbers, but they're best known by their direction or end-of-the-line stop. (For example, the La Défense/Château de Vincennes line runs between La Défense in the west and Vincennes in the east.) Once in the Métro station, you'll see blue-and-white signs directing you to the train going in your direction (e.g., "*direction:* La Défense"). Insert your ticket in the automatic turnstile (brown stripe down), pass through, reclaim your ticket, and *keep it until you exit the system*. Fare inspectors regularly check for cheaters and accept absolutely no excuses.

Transfers are free and can be made wherever lines cross. When you transfer, look for the orange *correspondance* (connections) signs when you exit your first train, then follow the proper direction sign.

While the Métro whisks you quickly from one point to another, be prepared to walk significant distances within stations to reach your platform (most noticeable when you transfer). Escalators are usually available for vertical movement, but they're not always in working order. To limit excessive walking, avoid transferring at these sprawling stations: Montparnasse-Bienvenüe, Chatelet-Les Halles, Charles de Gaulle-Etoile, Gare du Nord, and Bastille.

Before taking the *sortie* (exit) to leave the Métro, check the helpful *plan du quartier* (map of the neighborhood) to get your bearings, locate your destination, and decide which *sortie* you want. At stops with several *sorties,* you can save lots of walking by choosing the best exit.

After you exit the system, toss or tear your used ticket so you don't confuse it with your unused ticket—they look virtually identical.

By RER: The RER (Réseau Express Régionale; air-ay-air) is the suburban train system serving destinations such as Versailles, Disneyland Paris, and the airports. These routes are indicated by thick lines on your subway map and identified by letters A, B, C, and so on.

Within the city center, the RER works like the Métro but can be speedier (if it serves your destination directly) because it makes only a few stops within the city. Métro tickets are good on the RER when traveling in the city center. (You can transfer between the Métro and RER systems with the same ticket.) But to travel outside the city (to Versailles or the airport, for example), you'll need to buy a separate, more expensive ticket at the station window before boarding. Unlike in the Métro, you need to insert your ticket in a turnstile to exit the RER system. Also unlike the Métro, not every train stops at every station along the way; check the sign over the platform to see if your destination is listed as a stop (*toutes les gares* means it makes all stops along the way) or confirm with a local before you board.

By City Bus: The trickier bus system is worth figuring out. Métro tickets are good on both bus and Métro, though you can't use the same ticket to transfer between the two systems. One ticket gets you anywhere in central Paris, but if you leave the city center (shown as zone 1 on the diagram on board the bus), you must validate a second ticket. While the Métro shuts down about 00:30, some buses continue much later.

Enter through the front doors. Punch your Métro ticket in the machine behind the driver, or pay the higher cash fare. Get off the bus using the rear door. Even if you're not certain you've figured it out, do some joyriding (outside of rush hour). Lines #24, #63, and #69 are Paris' most scenic routes and make a great introduction to the city. Bus #69 is particularly handy, running east-west between the Eiffel Tower and the Père Lachaise Cemetery by way of rue Cler (recommended hotels), the quai d'Orsay, the Louvre, and the Marais (recommended hotels). J See Bus #69 Sightseeing Tour, page 239.

Schedules are posted at bus stops. Handy bus-system maps *(plan des autobus)* are available in any Métro station and are provided in your *Paris Pratique* map book if you invest €6. Big system maps, posted at each bus and Métro stop, display the routes. Individual route diagrams show the exact routes of the lines serving that stop. Major stops are displayed on the side of each bus. The handiest bus routes are listed for each recommended hotel neighborhood (see the Sleeping chapter, page 290).

By Taxi: Parisian taxis are reasonable—especially for couples and families. The meters are tamper-proof. Fares and supplements (described in English on the back windows) are straightforward. There's a €5 minimum. A 10-minute ride costs about €8 (versus €1 to get anywhere in town using a *carnet* ticket on the Métro). You can try waving down a taxi, but it's easier to ask for the nearest taxi stand (*Où est une station de taxi?*; oo ay oon stah-see-ohn duh taxi). Taxi stands are indicated by a circled T on many city maps, including Michelin's #10 Paris. A typical taxi takes three people (maybe 4 if you're polite and pay €2.60 extra); groups of up to five can use a *grand taxi,* which must be booked in advance—ask your hotel to call. If a taxi is summoned by phone, the meter starts as soon as the call is received, adding €3-4 to the bill. Higher rates are charged at night from 19:00 to 7:00, all day Sunday, and to either airport. There's a €1 charge for each piece of baggage and for train station pick-ups. To tip, round up to the next euro (minimum €0.50). Taxis are tough to find on Friday and Saturday nights, especially after the Métro closes (around 00:30). If you need to catch a train or flight early in the morning, book a taxi the day before.

Organized Tours of Paris

Bus Tours—Paris Vision offers handy bus tours of Paris, day and night (advertised in hotel lobbies); their "Paris Illumination" night tour is much more interesting and is explained on page 352.

Far better daytime bus tours are the hop-on, hop-off, double-decker buses that connect Paris' main sights while providing running commentary. These are ideal in good weather when you can sit on top. See also Batobus under "Boat Tours," below.

Two companies provide hop-on, hop-off bus service: **L'Open**

Tours and **Les Cars Rouges;** pick up their brochures showing routes and stops from any TI or on their buses. Both companies stop near the Eiffel Tower, on avenue Joseph Bouvard.

L'Open Tours, which uses yellow buses, provides more extensive coverage and offers three different routes, which roll by most of the important sights in Paris. Their Paris Grand Tour offers the best introduction. Tickets are good for any route. Buy your tickets from the driver (1-day ticket-€25, 2-day ticket-€27, kids 4–11 pay €13 for 1 or 2 days, 20 percent less if you have a *Carte Orange* Métro pass, allow 2 hours per tour). Two or three buses depart hourly from about 10:00 to 18:00; expect to wait 10–20 minutes at each stop (stops can be tricky to find). You can hop off at any stop, then catch a later bus. You'll see these bright-yellow, topless double-decker buses all over town; pick one up at the first important sight you visit, or start your tour at the Eiffel Tower stop (tel. 01 42 66 56 56).

Les Cars Rouges' bright red buses offer largely the same service with fewer stops on a single Grand Tour Route, for less money (2-day tickets, €23-adult, €12-kids 4–12, tel. 01 53 95 39 53).

Boat Tours—Several companies offer one-hour boat cruises on the Seine (by far best at night). The huge, mass-production **Bateaux-Mouches** boats, which depart every 20–30 minutes from the pont de l'Alma's right bank and right in front of the Eiffel Tower, are convenient to rue Cler hotels (€7, €4 for ages 4–12, daily 10:00–22:30, useless taped explanations in 6 languages and tour groups by the dozens, tel. 01 40 76 99 99). The smaller and more intimate **Vedettes du Pont-Neuf** depart only once an hour from the center of Pont-Neuf (twice an hour after dark), but they come with a live guide giving explanations in French and English and are convenient to Marais and Contrescarpe hotels (€9, €4.50 for ages 4–12, tel. 01 46 33 98 38).

From April through October, the **Batobus** hop-on, hop-off boats on the Seine connect eight popular stops every 15–25 minutes: Eiffel Tower, Champs-Elysées, Orsay/place de la Concorde, Louvre, Notre-Dame, St. Germain-des-Prés, Hôtel de Ville, and Jardin des Plantes. Pick up a schedule at any stop (or TI) and use the boats as a scenic alternative to the Métro. Tickets are available for one day (€2.50 per trip; €10 for 1 day, €5.50 under 12; €12.50 for 2 days, €6.50 under 12). Boats run from 10:00 to 19:00, or until 21:00 June through September.

Canauxrama offers a 2.5-hour cruise on a peaceful canal without the Seine in sight, starting from place de la Bastille and ending at Bassin de la Villette, near Métro stop Stalingrad (€14, €9 for kids, €11 for seniors and students, departs at 9:45 and 14:30 across from Opéra Bastille, just below boulevard de la Bastille, opposite #50, where the canal meets place de la Bastille, tel. 01 42 39 15 00).

Walking Tours—The company **Paris Walking Tours** offers a variety of excellent two-hour walks, led by British or American guides, nearly daily for €10 (tel. 01 48 09 21 40 for recorded schedule in English, fax 01 42 43 75 51, see www.paris-walks.com for their complete schedule). Tours focus on the Marais, Montmartre, Ile de la Cité and Ile St. Louis, and Hemingway's Paris. Ask about their family-friendly tours. Call ahead a day or two to learn their schedule and starting point. No reservations are required. These are thoughtfully prepared, relaxing, and humorous. Don't hesitate to stand close to the guide to hear.

Private Guide Service—For many, Paris merits hiring a Parisian as your personal guide. Two excellent licensed local guides who freelance for individuals and families are Arnaud Servignat, who runs Global Travel Partners (€215/4 hrs, €335/day, also does car tours of the country side around Paris, fax 01 42 57 00 38, arnaud.servignat@noos.fr or franceparisguide@noos.fr), and Marianne Siegler (€150/4 hrs, €250/day, reserve in advance if possible, tel. 01 42 52 32 51).

Bike Tours—Mike's Bullfrog Bike Tours attract a younger crowd for boisterous three- to four-hour rolls through Paris (€20, May–Nov daily at 11:00, also at 15:30 June–July, no CC, in English, no bikes or reservations needed, meet at south pillar of Eiffel Tower, mobile 06 09 98 08 60, www.mikesbiketours.com).

Excursion Tours—Many companies offer minivan and big bus tours to regional sights, including all of the day trips described in this book. **Paris Walking Tours** (mentioned above) are the best, with informative though infrequent tours of the Impressionist artist retreats of Giverny and Auvers-sur-Oise (€47–56, includes admissions, tel. 01 48 09 21 40 for recording in English, www.paris-walks.com).

Paris Vision and Euroscope both offer mass-produced, full-size bus and minivan tours to several popular regional destinations, including the Loire Valley, Champagne region, D-Day beaches, and Mont St. Michel. Their minivan tours are more expensive but more personal, given in English, and offer pick-up at your hotel (€130–200/person). Their full-size bus tours are multilingual and cost about half the price of a minivan tour—worth it for some simply for the ease of transportation to the sights (full-size buses depart from 214 rue de Rivoli, Mo: Tuileries, tel. 01 42 60 30 01, fax 01 42 86 95 36, www.parisvision.com). Euroscope leaves from 11 boulevard Haussmann (Mo: Opera or Chausée d'Antin, tel. 01 53 34 11 94, www.euroscope.com).

SIGHTS

The sights listed in this chapter are arranged by neighborhood for handy sightseeing. When you see a ✪ in a listing, it means the sight is covered in much more depth in one of my walks or self-guided tours.

Paris Museum Pass: In Paris, there are two classes of sightseers—those with a Paris museum pass and those who stand in line. Serious sightseers save time and money by getting this pass.

Most of the sights listed in this chapter are covered by the Paris museum pass, except for the Eiffel Tower, Montparnasse Tower, Marmottan Museum, Opéra Garnier, Notre-Dame treasury, Jacquemart-André Museum, Jewish Art and History Museum, Grande Arche de La Défense, Jeu de Paume Exhibition Hall, Catacombs, *Paris Story* film, and the ladies of Pigalle. Outside Paris, the pass covers the châteaux of Versailles, Chantilly, and Fontainebleau.

The pass pays for itself in two admissions and gets you into most sights with no lining up to buy tickets (1 day-€18, 3 consecutive days-€36, 5 consecutive days-€54, no youth or senior discount). It's sold at museums, main Métro stations (including Ecole Militaire and Bastille), and TIs (even at airports). Try to avoid buying the pass at a major museum (such as the Louvre), where supply can be spotty and lines long.

The pass isn't activated until the first time you use it (you enter the date on the pass). Think and read ahead to make the most of your pass, since some museums are free (e.g., Carnavalet and Victor Hugo's house), many sights are discounted on Sundays, and your pass must be used on consecutive days.

The pass isn't worth buying for children, as most museums are free for those under 18. Note that kids can skip the lines with their pass-holder parents.

The free museum and monuments directory that comes with your pass lists the latest hours, phone numbers, and specifics on what kids

PARIS AT A GLANCE

▲▲▲**Louvre** Europe's oldest and greatest museum, starring Mona Lisa and Venus di Milo. **Hours:** Wed–Mon 9:00–18:00, closed Tue. Denon wing open Mon until 21:45; all wings open Wed until 21:45.

▲▲▲**Orsay Museum** Nineteenth-century art, including Europe's greatest Impressionist collection. **Hours:** June 20–Sept 20 Tue–Sun 9:00–18:00; Sept 21–June 19 Tue–Sat 10:00–18:00, Sun 9:00–18:00; Thu until 21:45 year-round, closed Mon.

▲▲▲**Eiffel Tower** Paris' soaring exclamation point. **Hours:** March–Sept daily 9:00–24:00, Oct–Feb 9:30–23:00.

▲▲▲**Arc de Triomphe** Triumphal arch with viewpoint, marking start of Champs-Elysées. **Hours:** Outside always open; inside April–Sept daily 10:00–23:00, Oct–March daily 10:00–22:30.

▲▲▲**Sainte-Chapelle** Gothic cathedral with peerless stained glass. **Hours:** Daily 9:30–18:00.

▲▲▲**Versailles** The ultimate royal palace, with Hall of Mirrors, vast gardens, a grand canal, and smaller palaces. **Hours:** May–Sept Tue–Sun 9:00–18:30, Oct–April Tue–Sun 9:00–17:30, closed Mon. Gardens open early (7:00) and smaller palaces open late (12:00).

▲▲**Notre-Dame Cathedral** Paris' most beloved church, with towers and gargoyles. **Hours:** Church daily 8:00–18:45; tower April–Sept daily 9:30–19:30, Oct–March daily 10:00–17:30.

▲▲**Sacré-Cœur** White basilica atop Montmartre with spectacular views. **Hours:** Daily until 23:00.

▲▲**Napoleon's Tomb** The emperor's imposing tomb, flanked by army museums. **Hours:** April–Sept daily 10:00–18:00, Oct–March daily 10:00–17:00, closed first Mon of month.

▲▲**Rodin Museum** Works by the greatest sculptor since Michelangelo. **Hours:** April–Sept Tue–Sun 9:30–17:45; Oct–March Tue–Sun 9:30–17:00, closed Mon.

pay. The cutoff age for free entry varies from 5 to 18. Most major art museums let young people under 18 in for free, but anyone over age 5 has to pay to tour the sewers—go figure.

Included sights you're likely to visit (and admission prices without the pass): Louvre (€8.50), Orsay Museum (€7), Sainte-Chapelle (€5.50), Arc de Triomphe (€7), Les Invalides/Napoleon's Tomb (€6), Conciergerie (€5.50), Panthéon (€5.50), Sewer Tour (€4), Cluny Museum (€7), Pompidou Center (€5.50), Notre-Dame towers (€5.50) and crypt (€3.50), Picasso Museum (€5.50), Rodin Museum (€5), and the Cité des

▲▲**Marmottan Museum** Untouristy art museum focusing on Monet. **Hours:** Tue–Sun 10:00–18:00, closed Mon.

▲▲**Pompidou Center** Modern art in colorful building with city views. **Hours:** Wed–Mon 11:00–21:00, closed Tue.

▲▲**Jacquemart-André Museum** Art-strewn mansion. **Hours:** Daily 10:00–18:00.

▲▲**Cluny Museum** Medieval art with unicorn tapestries. **Hours:** Wed–Mon 9:15–17:45, closed Tue.

▲▲**Carnavalet Museum** Paris' history wrapped up in a 16th-century mansion. **Hours:** Tue–Sun 10:00–18:00, closed Mon.

▲▲**Jewish Art and History Museum** Displays history of Judaism in Europe. **Hours:** Mon–Fri 11:00–18:00, Sun 10:00–18:00, closed Sat.

▲▲**Deportation Memorial** Memorial to Holocaust victims, near Notre-Dame. **Hours:** April–Sept daily 10:00–12:00 & 14:00–19:00; Oct–March daily 10:00–12:00 & 14:00–17:00.

▲▲**Champs-Elysées** Paris' grand boulevard. **Hours:** Always open.

▲**Old Opera (Opéra Garnier)** 19th-century opera house open for tours. **Hours:** Daily 10:00–17:00 except during performances.

▲**La Défense and La Grande Arche** Paris' modern arch on outskirts of city. **Hours:** Elevator daily 10:00–19:00.

▲**Picasso Museum** World's largest collection of Picasso's works. **Hours:** April-Sept Wed–Mon 9:30–18:00; Oct-March 9:30-17:30, closed Tue.

▲**Catacombs** Underground tunnels lined with bones. **Hours:** Tue–Sun 10:00–17:00, closed Mon.

▲**Paris Sewer Tour** The lowdown on Paris plumbing. **Hours:** May-Sept Sat–Wed 11:00–17:00, Oct-April 11:00-16:00, closed Thu–Fri.

Sciences et l'Industrie museum (€9). Outside Paris, the pass covers the Palace of Versailles (€7.50, plus its Trianon châteaux-€5), Château of Fontainebleau (€5.50), and Château of Chantilly (€7).

Tally up what you want to see—and remember, an advantage of the pass is that you skip to the front of some lines, which saves hours of waiting, especially in summer. (Nevertheless, everyone must pass through the slow-moving metal-detector lines at some sights, and a few places, such as Notre-Dame's tower, can't accommodate a bypass lane.) With the pass, you'll pop freely into sights that you're walking by (even for a few minutes) that otherwise might not be worth the expense (e.g., Notre-Dame crypt, Conciergerie, and the Panthéon).

Museum Tips: The Louvre and many other museums are closed on Tuesday. The Orsay, Rodin, Marmottan, and Carnavalet Museums and Versailles are closed Monday. Most museums offer reduced prices on Sunday. Most sights stop admitting people 30–60 minutes before they close, and many begin closing rooms 45 minutes before the actual closing time.

For the fewest crowds, visit very early, at lunch, or very late. Most museums have slightly shorter hours October through March. French holidays can really mess up your sightseeing plans on Jan 1, May 1, July 14, Nov 1, Nov 11, and Dec 25.

The best Impressionist art museums are the Orsay (see tour on page 138), Marmottan (page 209), and L'Orangerie (closed until late 2004).

Paris Museums near the Tuileries Garden

Paris' grandest park, the Tuileries Garden, was once the private property of kings and queens and now links the museums of the Louvre, L'Orangerie, Jeu de Paume, and the Orsay.

▲▲▲Louvre (Musée du Louvre)—This is Europe's oldest, biggest, greatest, and second-most-crowded museum (after the Vatican). It's packed with Greek and Roman masterpieces, medieval jewels, Michelangelo statues, and paintings by the greatest artists from the Renaissance to the Romantics (mid-1800s).

Cost: €8.50, €6 after 18:00 on Mon and Wed, free on first Sun of month and for those under 18, covered by museum pass.

Hours: Wed–Mon 9:00–18:00, closed Tue. All wings open Wed until 21:45. On Mon, only the Denon wing is open until 21:45. Galleries start closing 30 minutes early. Closed Jan 1, Easter, May 1, Nov 1, and Dec 25. Tel. 01 40 20 51 51, recorded info tel. 01 40 20 53 17, www.louvre.fr.

Location: At Palais Royal-Musée du Louvre Métro stop. (The old Louvre Métro stop, called Louvre-Rivoli, is farther from the entrance.) ✪ See Louvre Tour on page 114.

▲L'Orangerie (Musée de l'Orangerie)—This Impressionist museum, lovely as a water lily, is due to reopen sometime late in 2004 after renovation (for the latest, ask at a Paris TI or any Paris museum). When it opens, you can step out of the tree-lined, sun-dappled Impressionist painting that is the Tuileries Garden, and into L'Orangerie (loh-rahn-zheh-ree), a little *bijou* of select works by Utrillo, Cézanne, Renoir, Matisse, and Picasso. On the ground floor, you'll find a line of eight rooms dedicated to these artists. Downstairs is the finale: Monet's water lilies. The museum's collection is small enough to enjoy in a short visit, but complete enough to see the bridge from Impressionism to the Moderns. And it's all beautiful (located in Tuileries Garden near place

Museums near Tuileries Garden

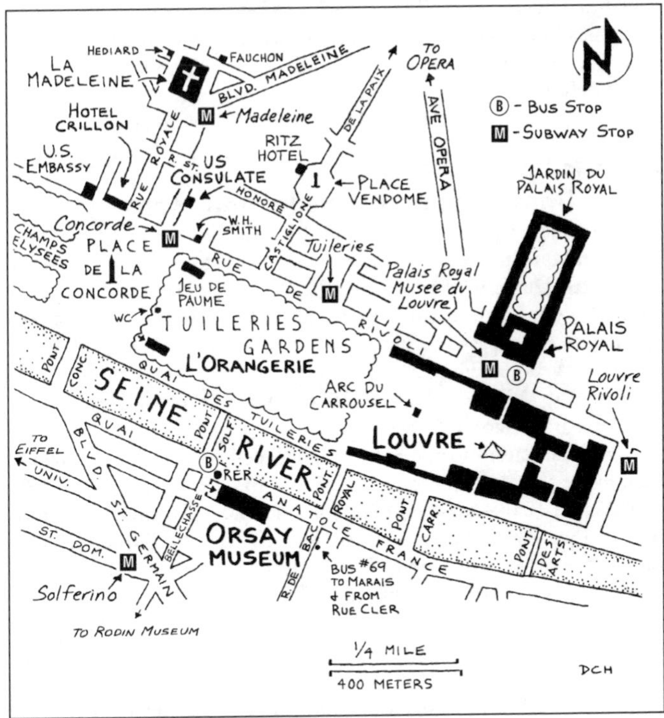

de la Concorde, Mo: Concorde). If you need a Monet fix, the Marmottan Museum (described under "Southwest Paris," below) is a good replacement until L'Orangerie reopens.

Jeu de Paume—This museum now hosts rotating exhibits of top contemporary artists (€6, not covered by museum pass, Tue 12:00–21:30, Wed–Fri 12:00–19:00, Sat–Sun 10:00–19:00, closed Mon, on place de la Concorde, just inside Tuileries Garden on rue de Rivoli side, Mo: Concorde).

▲▲▲Orsay Museum (Musée d'Orsay)—Paris' 19th-century art museum (actually, 1848–1914) includes Europe's greatest collection of Impressionist works.

Cost: €7; €5 after 16:15, on Sun, and for ages 18–25; free for youth under 18 and for anyone first Sun of month; covered by museum pass. English-language tours usually run at 11:30 daily except Sun, cost €6, take 90 min, and are also available on audioguide (€5).

Hours: June 20–Sept 20 Tue–Sun 9:00–18:00, Sept 21–June 19 Tue–Sat 10:00–18:00, Sun 9:00–18:00, Thu until 21:45 all year, always closed Mon. Last entrance is 45 min before closing, Impressionist Galleries start closing at 17:15. Tel. 01 40 49 48 14, www.musee-orsay.fr.

Location: Above the RER-C stop called Musée d'Orsay; the nearest Métro stop is Solferino, three blocks south of the Orsay. From the Louvre, it's a lovely 15-minute walk through the Tuileries and across the pedestrian bridge to the Orsay. ✪ See Orsay Museum Tour on page 138.

Historic Core of Paris: Notre-Dame, Sainte-Chapelle, and More

✪ All of these sights are covered in detail in the Historic Paris Walk (plus map) on page 46. Only the essentials are listed here.

▲▲Notre-Dame Cathedral—This 700-year-old cathedral is packed with history and tourists (free, daily 8:00–18:45; treasury-€2.50, not covered by museum pass, daily 9:30–17:30; ask about free English tours, normally Wed and Thu at 12:00 and Sat at 14:30; Mo: Cité, Hôtel de Ville, or St. Michel; clean €0.50 toilets in front of church near Charlemagne's statue). ✪ See page 48.

You can climb to the top of the facade between the towers and then to the top of the south **tower** (€5.50, April–Sept daily 9:30–19:30, Oct–March 10:00–18:00, last entry 45 min before closing, covered by museum pass, arrive early to avoid long lines). The **Paris Archaeological Crypt** is a worthwhile 15-minute stop with your museum pass (€3.50, Tue–Sun 10:00–18:00, closed Mon, enter 100 yards in front of church). You'll visit Roman ruins, trace the street plan of the medieval village, and see diagrams of how early Paris grew, all thoughtfully explained in English.

▲▲Deportation Memorial (Mémorial de la Déportation)—This memorial to the 200,000 French victims of the Nazi concentration camps draws you into their experience (free, April–Sept daily 10:00–12:00 & 14:00–19:00, Oct–March daily 10:00–12:00 & 14:00–17:00, east tip of the island Ile de la Cité, behind Notre-Dame and near Ile St. Louis, Mo: Cité). ✪ See page 54.

Ile St. Louis—The residential island behind Notre-Dame is known for its restaurants (see Eating chapter), great Berthillon ice cream (31 rue St. Louis-en-l'Ile), and shops (along rue St. Louis-en-l'Ile). ✪ See page 55.

Cité "Métropolitain" Stop and Flower Market—On place Louis Lépine, between Notre-Dame and Sainte-Chapelle, you'll find an early-19th-century subway entrance and a flower market (that chirps with a bird market on Sun).

▲▲▲Sainte-Chapelle—This triumph of Gothic church architecture is a cathedral of glass like no other (€5.50, €8 combo-ticket covers Conciergerie, both covered by museum pass, daily 9:30–18:00, Mo: Cité, tel. 01 44 07 12 38 for concert information). ✪ See page 60.

▲Conciergerie—Marie-Antoinette was imprisoned here, as were many others on the way to the guillotine (€5.50, €8 combo-ticket covers

Sainte-Chapelle, both covered by museum pass, April–Sept daily 9:30–18:30, Oct–March daily 10:00–17:00, good English descriptions). ✪ See page 65.

Southwest Paris: Eiffel Tower Neighborhood

▲▲▲Eiffel Tower (La Tour Eiffel)—It's crowded and expensive, but worth the trouble. To avoid most crowds, go early (by 8:45) or late in the day (after 18:00, after 20:00 in summer, last entry 1 hour before closing); weekends are worst. A TI/ticket booth is between the Pilier Nord (north pillar) and Pilier Est (east pillar). The stairs (yes, you can walk up partway) are next to the Jules Verne restaurant entrance (allow $300 per person for the restaurant, reserve 3 months in advance). A sign in the cheek-to-jowl elevator tells you to beware of pickpockets.

The tower is a 1,000-foot-tall ornament. In hot weather, it's six inches taller. It covers 2.5 acres and requires 50 tons of paint. Its 7,000 tons of metal are spread out so well at the base that it's no heavier per square inch than a linebacker on tiptoes. Visitors to Paris may find *Mona Lisa* to be less than expected, but the Eiffel Tower rarely disappoints, even in an era of skyscrapers.

Built a hundred years after the French Revolution (and in the midst of an Industrial one), the tower served no function but to impress. Bridge-builder Gustave Eiffel won the contest for the 1889 Centennial World's Fair by beating out such rival proposals as a giant guillotine. To a generation hooked on technology, the tower was the marvel of the age, a symbol of progress and of man's ingenuity. To others it was a cloned-sheep monstrosity. The writer Guy de Maupassant routinely ate lunch in the tower just so he wouldn't have to look at it.

Delicate and graceful when seen from afar, it's massive—even a bit scary—from close up. You don't appreciate the size until you walk toward it; like a mountain, it seems so close but takes forever to reach.

There are three observation platforms, at 200, 400, and 900 feet; the higher you go, the more you pay. Each requires a separate elevator (and line), so plan on at least 90 minutes if you want to go to the top and back. For most, the view from the second level is plenty. As you ascend through the metal beams, imagine being a worker, perched high above nothing, riveting this giant erector set together. On top, all of Paris lies before you, with a panorama guide. On a good day, you can see for 40 miles.

The **first level** has exhibits, a post office (daily 10:00–19:00, cancellation stamp will read Eiffel Tower), a snack bar, WCs, and souvenirs. Read the informative signs (in English) describing the major monuments, see the entertaining free movie on the history of the tower, and don't miss a century of fireworks—including the entire millennium blast—on video. Then consider a drink or a sandwich overlooking all of Paris at the snack café (outdoor tables in summer) or at the city's best view bar/restaurant, **Altitude 95** (€21–31 lunches, €55 dinners, dinner

Southwest Paris: Eiffel Tower Neighborhood

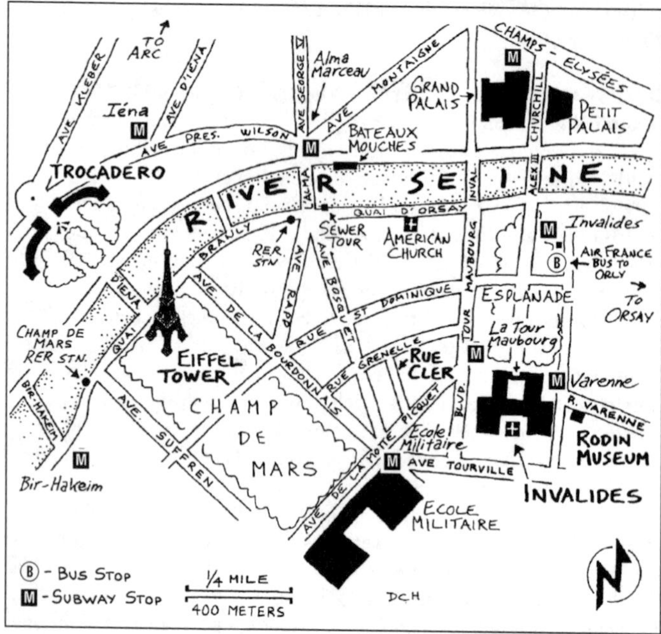

seatings at 19:00 and 21:00, reserve well ahead for a view table; before you ascend to dine, drop by the booth between the north/*nord* and east/*est* pillars to buy your Eiffel Tower ticket and pick up a pass that enables you to skip the line; tel. 01 45 55 20 04, fax 01 47 05 94 40).

The **second level** has the best views (walk up stairway to get above netting), a cafeteria, WCs, and an Internet gimmick to have your photo at the Eiffel Tower sent into cyberspace (at La Galerie des Visiteurs).

Cost and Hours: It costs €4 to go to the first level, €7.50 to the second, and €11 to go all the way (not covered by museum pass). On a budget? You can climb the stairs to the second level for only €3.50 (March–Sept daily 9:00–24:00, Oct–Feb daily 9:30–23:00, last entry 1 hour before closing, shorter lines at night, can catch Bateaux-Mouches boat for Seine cruise at base of tower, Mo: Trocadéro, RER: Champ de Mars-Tour Eiffel, tel. 01 44 11 23 23, www.tour-eiffel.fr). While you'll save no money, consider taking the lift up and the stairs down (from second level) for good exercise and views.

The best place to view the tower is from **Trocadéro Square** to the north; it's a 10-min walk across the river, and a happening scene at night, especially fun for kids. Consider arriving at the Trocadéro Métro stop for the view, then walking toward the tower. Another great viewpoint is the long, grassy field, le Parc du Champ de Mars, to the south (after about 20:00, the *gendarmes* look the other way as Parisians stretch out or picnic on the grass). However impressive it may be by day, the tower is an awesome thing to see at twilight, when it becomes engorged with light and virile Paris lies back and lets night be on top.

▲Paris Sewer Tour (Les Egouts de Paris)—This quick, fascinating, and slightly smelly visit (a perfumed hanky helps) takes you along a few hundred yards of underground water tunnels in the world's first underground sewer system. Discover what happens after you flush. Pick up the helpful English self-guided tour, then drop down into Jean Valjean's world of tunnels, rats, and manhole covers (Victor Hugo was friends with the sewer inspector when he wrote *Les Misérables*). You'll pass well-organized displays with helpful English information detailing the evolution of this amazing network of over 1,500 miles of tunnels that carry 317 million gallons of water daily through the world's longest sewer system. It's surprising to see how much work goes into something we take for granted.

Sewage didn't always disappear so readily. In the Middle Ages, wastewater was tossed from windows to a center street gutter, then washed into the river. In castles it ended up in the moat. In the 1500s, French Renaissance King Francois I moved from château to château (he had several) when the moat stench became too much—those who had to stay behind were not paid enough. Don't miss the slideshow, fine WCs just beyond the gift shop, and occasional tours in English (€4, covered by museum pass, May-Sept Sat-Wed 11:00-17:00, closes at 16:00 Oct-April, always closed Thu-Fri, where pont de l'Alma greets the Left Bank, Mo: Alma-Marceau, RER: Pont de l'Alma, tel. 01 53 68 27 81).

▲▲Napoleon's Tomb and Les Invalides Army Museum (Tombeau de Napoleon et le Musée de l'Armée)—The emperor lies majestically dead inside several coffins under a grand dome—a goose-bumping pilgrimage for historians. Napoleon is surrounded by Europe's greatest military museum, the Hôtel des Invalides, which provides interesting coverage of Napoleon, World War I, and World War II. The dome glitters with 26 pounds of gold (€6, students-€5, under 18 free, covered by museum pass, April–Sept daily 10:00–18:00, Oct–March daily 10:00–17:00, closed first Mon of month; Mo: La Tour Maubourg or Varenne, tel. 01 44 42 37 72, www.invalides.org). ✪ See Napoleon's Tomb & Les Invalides Tour on page 216.

▲▲Rodin Museum (Musée Rodin)—This user-friendly museum is filled with passionate works by the greatest sculptor since Michelangelo. See *The Kiss, The Thinker, The Gates of Hell,* and many more (€5, €3 on Sun and for students, free for youth under 18 and for anyone first Sun of month, covered by museum pass; €1 for gardens only, which may be Paris' best deal, as many works are well displayed in the beautiful gardens; April–Sept Tue–Sun 9:30–17:45, closed Mon, gardens close 18:45,

Oct–March Tue–Sun 9:30–17:00, closed Mon, gardens close 16:45; near Napoleon's Tomb, 77 rue de Varenne, Mo: Varenne, tel. 01 44 18 61 10, www.musee-rodin.fr). ✪ See Rodin Museum Tour on page 200.

▲▲Marmottan Museum (Musée Marmottan Monet)—In this private, intimate, untouristy museum, you'll find more than 100 paintings by Claude Monet (€6.50, not covered by museum pass, Tue–Sun 10:00–18:00, closed Mon, 2 rue Louis Boilly, Mo: La Muette, follow brown museum signs 6 blocks down chaussée de la Muette through park to museum, tel. 01 44 96 50 33, www.marmottan.com). ✪ See Marmottan Museum Tour on page 209.

Take a post-museum stroll down one of Paris' most pleasant (and upscale) shopping streets, the rue de Passy (2 blocks up chaussée de la Muette in opposite direction from La Muette Métro stop).

Southeast Paris: Left Bank

✪ For more information, see the Left Bank Walk on page 105, and the Historic Paris Walk (which dips into the Latin Quarter) on page 46.

▲Latin Quarter (Quartier Latin)—This Left Bank neighborhood, just opposite Notre-Dame, was the center of Roman Paris. But the Latin Quarter's touristy fame relates to its intriguing, artsy, bohemian character. This was perhaps Europe's leading university district in the Middle Ages, when Latin was the language of higher education. The neighborhood's main boulevards (St. Michel and St. Germain) are lined with cafés—once the haunts of great poets and philosophers, now the hangout of tired tourists. While still youthful and artsy, the area has become a tourist ghetto filled with cheap North African eateries.

▲▲Cluny Museum (Musée National du Moyen Age)—This treasure trove of medieval art fills the old Roman baths, offering close-up looks at stained glass, Notre-Dame carvings, fine goldsmithing and jewelry, and rooms of tapestries (€7, €5.50 on Sun, free first Sun of month, covered by museum pass, Wed–Mon 9:15–17:45, closed Tue, near corner of boulevards St. Michel and St. Germain, Mo: Cluny-La Sorbonne, St. Michel, or Odéon, tel. 01 53 73 78 16, www.musee-moyenage.fr). ✪ See Cluny Museum Tour on page 233.

St. Germain-des-Prés—A church was first built on this site in A.D. 452. The church you see today was constructed in 1163 and is all that's left of a once sprawling and powerful monastery. The colorful interior reminds us that Gothic churches originally were painted in bright colors. The area around the church hops at night with venerable cafés, fire-eaters, mimes, and scads of artists (Free, daily 8:00≠20:00, Mo: St. Germain-des-Prés).

▲St. Sulpice Organ Concert—For pipe-organ enthusiasts, this is a delight. The Grand-Orgue at St. Sulpice has a rich history, with a succession of 12 world-class organists (including Charles-Marie Widor and Marcel Dupré) going back 300 years. Widor started the tradition of opening the loft to visitors after the 10:30 service on Sundays. Daniel

Southeast Paris: Left Bank

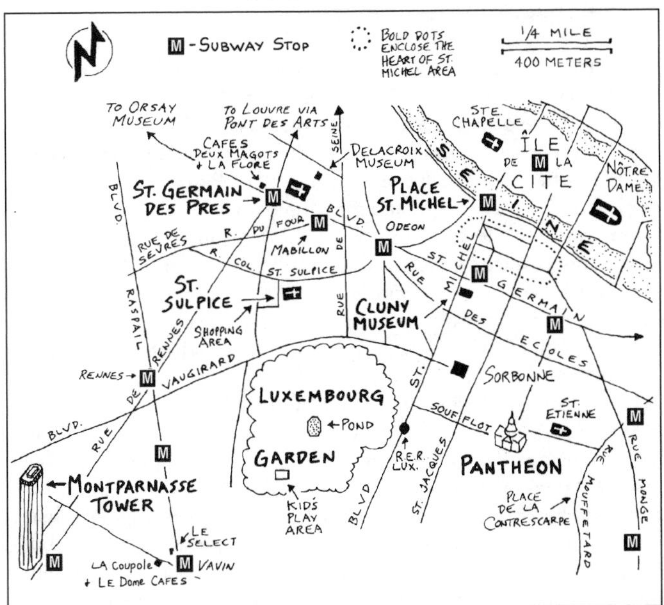

Roth continues to welcome guests in three languages while playing five keyboards at once. The 10:30 Sunday Mass is followed by a high-powered 25-minute recital at 11:40. Then, just after noon, the small, unmarked door is opened (left of entry as you face the rear). Visitors scamper like 16th notes up spiral stairs, past the 18th-century Stairmasters that were used to fill the bellows, into a world of 7,000 pipes, where they can watch the master play during the next Mass. You'll generally have 30 minutes to kill (there's a plush lounge) before the organ plays; visitors can leave at any time. If late or rushed, show up around 12:30 and wait at the little door. As someone leaves, you can slip in (daily 7:30–19:30, Mo: St. Sulpice or Mabillon). The Luxembourg Garden and St. Germain market (on rue Clément between St. Sulpice and Métro stop Mabillon) are both nearby and open daily.

▲▲Luxembourg Garden (Jardin du Luxembourg)—This lovely 60-acre garden is an Impressionist painting brought to life (see Left Bank Walk on page 105, and Paris with Children on page 336, open until dusk, Mo: Odéon, RER: Luxembourg). Enjoy the radiant flowerbeds, go jogging, or take in a chess game or puppet show. Notice any pigeons? The story goes that a poor Ernest Hemingway used to hand-hunt (read: strangle) them here. Paris Walking Tours offers a good tour of the park (see "Organized Tours of Paris," page 24).

Nearby are several grand cafes (see page 332) and the ho-hum Pantheon mausoleum (see page 45).

If you enjoy the Luxembourg Garden and want to see more, visit the more elegant Parc Monceau (Mo: Monceau) and the colorful Jardin des Plantes (Mo: Jussieu or Gare d'Austerlitz, RER: Gare d'Austerlitz).

Montparnasse Tower (La Tour Montparnasse)—The 59-story superscraper is cheaper and easier to get to the top of than the Eiffel Tower, and it has the added bonus of offering one of Paris' best views—since the Eiffel Tower is in sight and the Montparnasse Tower isn't. Buy the photo guide to the city, then go to the rooftop and orient yourself (€8.20, not covered by museum pass, daily in summer 9:30–23:30, off-season 10:00–22:00, disappointing after dark, entrance on rue de l'Arrivée, Mo: Montparnasse-Bienvenüe). The tower is an efficient stop when combined with a day trip to Chartres, which begins at the Montparnasse train station.

▲Catacombs—These underground tunnels contain the anonymous bones of six million permanent Parisians. In 1785, the Revolutionary Government of Paris decided to relieve congestion and improve sanitary conditions by emptying the city cemeteries (which traditionally surrounded churches) into an official ossuary. The perfect locale was the many miles of underground tunnels from limestone quarries, which were, at that time, just outside the city. For decades, priests led ceremonial processions of black-veiled, bone-laden carts into the quarries, where the bones were stacked into piles five feet high and as much as 80 feet deep behind neat walls of skull-studded tibiae. Each transfer was completed with the placement of a plaque indicating the church and district from which that stack of bones came and the date they arrived.

From the entry of the catacombs, a spiral staircase leads 60 feet down. Then you begin a one-mile subterranean walk. After several blocks of empty passageways, you ignore a sign announcing: "Halt, this is the empire of the dead." Along the way, plaques encourage visitors to reflect upon their destiny: "Happy is he who is forever faced with the hour of his death and prepares himself for the end every day." You emerge far from where you entered, with white limestone-covered toes, telling anyone in the know you've been underground gawking at bones. Note to wannabe Hamlets: An attendant checks your bag at the exit for stolen souvenirs. A flashlight is handy. Being under 6'2" is helpful (€5, not covered by museum pass, Tue–Sun 10:00–17:00, closed Mon, 1 place Denfert-Rochereau, Mo: Denfert-Rochereau, tel. 01 43 22 47 63).

Northwest Paris: Champs-Elysées, Arc de Triomphe, and Beyond

▲▲Champs-Elysées—The famous boulevard is Paris' backbone, and has the greatest concentration of traffic. From the Arc de Triomphe down the avenue des Champs-Elysées, all of France seems to converge on place de la Concorde, the city's largest square. While the boulevard has become a bit Americanized, a walk here is a must. ✪ See the Champs-Elysées Walk on page 69.

To reach the top of the Champs-Elysées, take the Métro to the Arc de Triomphe (Mo: Charles de Gaulle-Etoile) then saunter down the grand boulevard (Métro stops every few blocks: Charles de Gaulle-Etoile, George V, Franklin D. Roosevelt).

▲▲▲Arc de Triomphe—Napoleon had the magnificent Arc de Triomphe commissioned to commemorate his victory at the battle of Austerlitz. Climb to the top for a mesmerizing view of the traffic that swirls around the arch (€7, covered by museum pass, April–Sept daily 10:00–23:00, Oct–March daily 10:00–22:30, Mo: Charles de Gaulle-Etoile, use underpass to reach arch, tel. 01 55 37 73 77). ✪ See page 69.

▲Old Opera (Opéra Garnier)—This grand palace of the belle époque was built for Napoleon III and finished in 1875. (After completing this project, the architect—Garnier—went south to do the casino in Monte Carlo.) From the grand avenue de l'Opéra, once lined with Paris' most fashionable haunts, the newly restored facade seems to say "all power to the wealthy." While huge, the actual theater seats only 2,000. The real show was before and after, when the elite of Paris—out to see and be seen—strutted their elegant stuff in the extravagant lobbies. Think of the grand marble stairway as a theater itself. As you wander the halls and gawk at the decor, imagine the place filled with the beautiful people of the day. The massive foundations straddle an underground lake (creating the mysterious world of the *Phantom of the Opera*). Tourists can peek from two boxes into the actual red-velvet theater, where they see Marc Chagall's colorful ceiling (1964) playfully dancing around the eight-ton chandelier. Note the box seats next to the stage—the most expensive in the house, with an obstructed view of the stage but just right if you're there only to be seen. The elitism of this place prompted President François Mitterand to have a people's opera house built in the 1980s (symbolically on place de la Bastille, where the French Revolution started in 1789). This left the Opéra Garnier home only to ballet and occasional concerts (usually no performances from mid-July to mid-Sept). While the library/museum is of interest to opera buffs, anyone will enjoy the second-floor grand foyer and Salon du Glacier, iced with decor typical of 1900 (€6, not covered by museum pass, daily 10:00–17:00 except when in use for performance, €10 English tours summers only, normally at 12:00 and 14:00, 90 min, includes entry, call to confirm; enter through the front off place de l'Opéra, Mo: Opéra, tel. 01 40 01 22 53, www.opera-de-paris.fr). American Express and the *Paris Story* film are on the left side of the Opéra, and the venerable Galeries Lafayette department store is just behind.

***Paris Story* Film**—This entertaining film offers a good and painless overview of the city's turbulent and brilliant past, covering 2,000 years in

Northwest Paris: Champs-Elysées, Arc de Triomphe, and Beyond

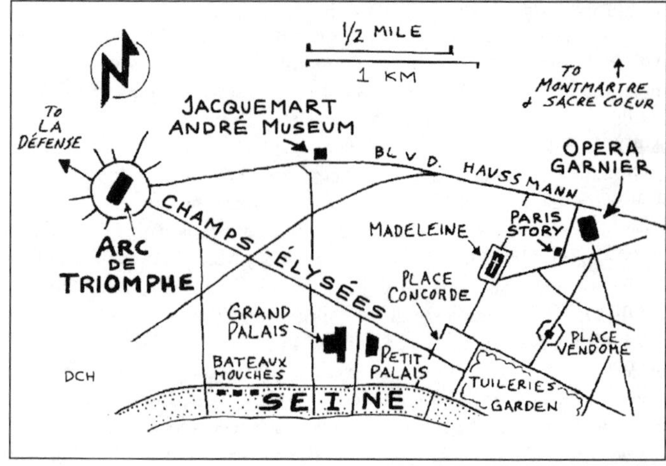

45 fast-moving minutes. The theater's wide-screen projection and cushy chairs provide an ideal break from bad weather and sore feet and make this a fun activity to do with kids (€8, ages 6 to 18-€5, family of 4-€21, not covered by museum pass, get a 20 percent discount with this book, shows on the hour daily 9:00–19:00, next to Opéra at 11 rue Scribe, Mo: Opéra, tel. 01 42 66 62 06).

▲▲Jacquemart-André Museum (Musée Jacquemart-André)—This thoroughly enjoyable museum showcases the lavish home of a wealthy, art-loving, 19th-century Parisian couple. After wandering the grand boulevards, you now get inside for an intimate look at the lifestyles of the Parisian rich and fabulous. Edouard André and his wife Nélie Jacquemart—who had no children—spent their lives and fortunes designing, building, and then decorating a sumptuous mansion. What makes this visit so rewarding is the fine audioguide tour (in English, free with admission). The place is strewn with paintings by Rembrandt, Botticelli, Uccello, Mantegna, Bellini, Boucher, and Fragonard—enough to make a painting gallery famous. Plan on spending an hour with the audioguide (€8, not covered by museum pass, daily 10:00–18:00, elegant café, 158 boulevard Haussmann, Mo: Miromesnil, tel. 01 42 89 04 91).

Petit Palais (and its Musée des Beaux-Arts)—The free museum, built for the Universal Exposition of 1900, is due to reopen after renovation in 2005. When it does, you'll find a broad collection of painting and sculpture from the 1600s to the 1900s. It feels like a museum of second-choice art, as the more famous museums in Paris have better collections from the same periods. Still, you'll find a few diamonds in the rough from Monet, Renoir, Boudin, and others; some interesting Art Nouveau pieces; and a smattering of works from Dutch, Italian, and Flemish Renaissance artists (across from Grand Palais, avenue Winston Churchill, just west of place de la Concorde, tel. 01 40 05 56 78).

▲View from Hôtel Concorde-Lafayette—For a remarkable (and free unless you buy a drink) Parisian panorama, take the Métro to the Porte Maillot stop, then find the unappealing concrete tower that houses this luxury hotel. Take the elevator in the rear of the lobby to floor 34 and enter a world of €8 beers, €6 espresso, and jaw-dropping views. If it's clear or the sun's about to set, spring for a drink (the ride was free).

▲La Défense and La Grande Arche—Beam yourself out to this *Star Wars*-like complex of glass towers and men in suits to contemplate the future of Paris and to experience the ultimate contrast of old and new. A business and shopping center, La Défense was first conceived nearly 60 years ago to create a USA-styled forest of skyscrapers to accommodate the business needs of the modern world. Today La Défense is home to 150,000 employees and 55,000 residents.

La Grande Arche is the centerpiece of this ambitious complex. Inaugurated in 1989 on the 200th anniversary of the French Revolution, it was dedicated to human rights and brotherhood. The place is big—38 floors holding offices for 30,000 people on more than 200 acres. They say that Notre-Dame Cathedral could fit under its arch.

You'll enjoy city views from the Arche elevator (€8, under 18-€6, family deals, not covered by museum pass, daily 10:00–19:00, includes a film on its construction and art exhibits, RER or Mo: La Défense, follow signs to Grande Arche, tel. 01 49 07 27 57).

The complex at La Défense is an interesting study in 1960s land-use planning, directing lots of business and development away from downtown and allowing central Paris to retain its more elegant feel. This makes sense to most Parisians, regardless of whatever else they feel about this controversial complex.

For a good visit, take the Métro to the La Défense stop, explore the Grande Arche, then stroll among the glass buildings to the Esplanade de la Défense Métro station, and return home from there. After enjoying the elegance of downtown Paris' historic, glorious monuments, it's clear that man can build bigger, but not more beautiful.

Northeast Paris: Marais Neighborhood and More

✪ To connect the sights with a fun, fact-filled stroll leading from place de la Bastille to the Pompidou Center, take the Marais Walk on page 79.

▲▲Pompidou Center (Centre Pompidou)—Europe's greatest collection of far-out modern art is housed in the Musée National d'Art Moderne, on the fourth and fifth floors of this colorful, exoskeletal building. Once ahead of its time, this 20th-century (remember that century?) art has been waiting for the world to catch up with it. After so many Madonnas-and-Children, a piano smashed to bits and glued to the wall is refreshing. Ride the escalator for a great city view from the top, and don't miss the free exhibits on the ground floor (€5.50, free on first Sun of the month, covered by museum pass, audioguide-€4, Wed–Mon 11:00–21:00, closed Tue and May 1; to use escalator you need museum ticket or museum pass, good mezzanine-level café is cheaper than cafés outside, Mo: Rambuteau, tel. 01 44 78 12 33, www.centrepompidou.fr).

The Pompidou Center and its square are lively, with lots of people, street theater, and activity inside and out—a perpetual street fair. Kids of any age enjoy the fun, colorful fountain (called *Homage to Stravinsky*) next to the Pompidou Center. ✪ See Pompidou Center Tour on page 163.

▲▲Jewish Art and History Museum (Musée d'Art et Histoire du Judaïsme)—This fascinating museum is located in a beautifully restored Marais mansion and tells the story of Judaism throughout Europe, from the Roman destruction of Jerusalem to the theft of famous artworks during World War II. Helpful, free audioguides and many English explanations make this an enjoyable history lesson (red numbers on small signs indicate the number you should press on your audioguide). Move along at your own speed. The museum illustrates the cultural unity maintained by this continually dispersed population. You'll learn about the history of Jewish traditions from bar mitzvahs to menorahs, and see the exquisite traditional costumes and objects around which daily life revolved. Don't miss the explanation of "the Dreyfus affair," a major event in early 1900s French politics. You'll also see photographs of and paintings by famous Jewish artists, including Chagall, Modigliani, and Soutine. A small but moving section is devoted to the deportation of Jews from Paris (€6.50, ages 18 to 26-€4, under 18 free, not covered by museum pass, Mon–Fri 11:00–18:00, Sun 10:00–18:00, closed Sat, 71 rue du Temple, Mo: Rambuteau or Hôtel de Ville a few blocks farther away, tel. 01 53 01 86 60, www.mahj.org).

▲Picasso Museum (Musée Picasso)—Tucked into a corner of the Marais and worth ▲▲▲ if you're a Picasso fan, this museum contains the world's largest collection of Picasso's paintings, sculptures, sketches, and ceramics, and includes his small collection of Impressionist art. The art is well-displayed in a fine old mansion with a peaceful garden café. The room-by-room English introductions help make sense of Picasso's work—from the Toulouse-Lautrec-like portraits at the beginning of his career, to his gray-brown Cubist period, to his Salvador Dalí–like finish. The well-done €3 English guidebook helps Picassophiles appreciate the context of his art and learn more about his interesting life. Most will be happy reading the posted English explanations while moving at a steady pace through the museum—the ground and first floors satisfied my curiosity (€5.50, free first Sun of month, covered by museum pass,

Northeast Paris: Marais Neighborhood and More

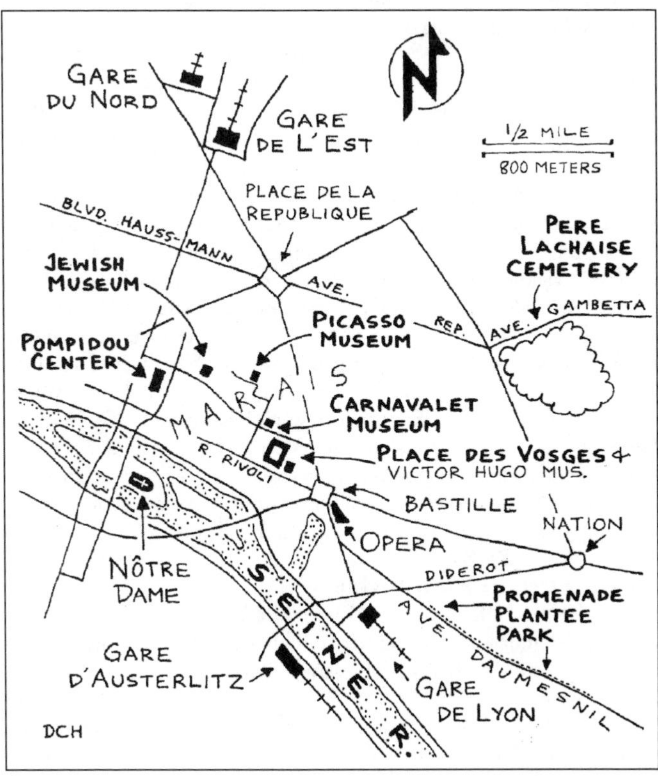

Apr-Sept Wed–Mon 9:30–18:00, Oct–March 9:30-17:30, closed Tue, 5 rue de Thorigny, Mo: St. Paul or Chemin Vert, tel. 01 42 71 25 21, www.musee-picasso.fr). ✪ See Picasso Museum Tour on page 191.

▲▲Carnavalet Museum (Musée Carnavalet)—The tumultuous history of Paris is portrayed well in this converted Marais mansion. Explanations are in French only, but many displays are fairly self-explanatory. You'll see paintings of Parisian scenes, French Revolution paraphernalia, old Parisian store signs, a small guillotine, a model of 16th-century Ile de la Cité (notice the bridge houses), and rooms full of 17th-century Parisian furniture (free, Tue–Sun 10:00–18:00, closed Mon, 23 rue de Sévigné, Mo: St. Paul, tel. 01 44 59 58 58, www.paris.fr/musees/musee_carnavalet). ✪ See Carnavalet Museum Tour on page 176.

Victor Hugo's House—France's literary giant lived in this house on place des Vosges from 1832 to 1848. Inside are posters advertising theater productions of his works, paintings of some of his most famous character creations, and a few furnished rooms (free, Tue–Sun 10:00–17:40, closed Mon, 6 place des Vosges, tel. 01 42 72 10 16).

▲Promenade Plantée Park—This two-mile-long, narrow garden walk on a viaduct was once used for train tracks and is now a joy. It runs from place de la Bastille (Mo: Bastille) along avenue Daumesnil to Saint-Mandé (Mo: Michel Bizot). Part of the park is elevated. At times, you'll walk along the street until you pick up the next segment. To reach the park from place de la Bastille, walk down rue de Lyon on the right side of the Opéra, then take avenue Daumesnil across the intersection with avenue Ledru Rollin; walk up the stairs and through the gate (free, opens Mon–Fri at 8:00, Sat–Sun at 9:00, closes at sunset). The shops below the viaduct's arches make for entertaining window-shopping.

▲Père Lachaise Cemetery (Cimetière du Père Lachaise)—Littered with the tombstones of many of the city's most illustrious dead, this is your best one-stop look at the fascinating, romantic world of "permanent Parisians." More like a small city, the place is confusing, but maps will direct you to the graves of Frédéric Chopin, Molière, Edith Piaf, Oscar Wilde, Gertrude Stein, Jim Morrison, and Héloïse and Abélard. In section 92, a series of statues memorializing World War II makes the French war experience a bit more real (helpful €1.50 maps at flower store near entry, closes at dusk, across street from Métro stop, Mo: Père Lachaise or bus #69).

North Paris: Montmartre

✪ Connect the sights with the Montmartre Walk on page 94.

▲▲Sacré-Cœur and Montmartre—This Byzantine-looking church, while only 130 years old, is impressive (church free: daily 7:00-23:00; €5 to climb dome: June–Sept daily 9:00–19:00, Oct–May daily 10:00–18:00). One block from the church, the place du Tertre was the haunt of Henri de Toulouse-Lautrec and the original bohemians. Today, it's mobbed with tourists and unoriginal bohemians, but it's still fun (go early in the morning to beat the crowds). Take the Métro to the Anvers stop (one more Métro ticket buys your way up the funicular and avoids the stairs) or the closer but less scenic Abbesses stop. A taxi to the top of the hill saves time and avoids sweat.

Pigalle—Paris' red-light district, the infamous "Pig Alley," is at the foot of butte Montmartre. *Oo la la.* It's more shocking than dangerous. Walk from place Pigalle to place Blanche, teasing desperate barkers and fast-talking temptresses. In bars, a €150 bottle of cheap champagne comes with a friend. Stick to the bigger streets, hang on to your wallet, and exercise good judgment. Cancan can cost a fortune, as can con artists in topless bars. After dark, countless tour buses line the streets, reminding us that tour guides make big bucks by bringing their groups to touristy nightclubs like the famous Moulin Rouge (Mo: Pigalle or Abbesses).

Near Paris: Versailles

▲▲▲Versailles—Every king's dream, Versailles was the residence of the French kings and the cultural heartbeat of Europe for about 100 years—until the Revolution of 1789 ended the notion that God deputized some people to rule for Him on earth. Louis XIV spent half a year's income of Europe's richest country turning his dad's hunting lodge into a palace fit for a divine monarch. Louis XV and Louis XVI spent much of the 18th century gilding Louis XIV's lily. In 1837, about 50 years after the royal family was evicted, King Louis-Philippe opened the palace as a museum. Europe's next-best palaces are Versailles wannabes.

Cost and Hours: €7.50 (main palace and both Trianon palaces covered by museum pass), €5.50 after 15:30, under 18 free. There are extra charges for tours, the gardens, and the Grand and Petit Trianon châteaux. On summer weekends, the fountains perform in the garden. The palace is open May–Sept Tue–Sun 9:00–18:30, Oct–April Tue–Sun 9:00–17:30, closed Mon (last entry 30 min before closing), www.chateauversailles.fr. ✪ See Versailles Tour on page 244.

Disappointments de Paris

Here are a few negatives to help you manage your limited time:

La Madeleine is a big, neoclassical church with a postcard facade and a postbox interior.

Paris' **Panthéon** (nothing like Rome's) is another neoclassical edifice, filled with the mortal remains of great Frenchmen who mean little to the average American tourist.

The **Bastille** is Paris' most famous non-sight. The square is there, but confused tourists look everywhere and can't find the famous prison of Revolution fame. The building's gone, and the square is good only as a jumping-off point for the Marais Walk (see page 79) or Promenade Plantée Park (see page 44).

Finally, much of the **Latin Quarter** is a frail shadow of its once-bohemian self. The blocks nearest the river are more Tunisian, Greek, and Woolworth's than old-time Paris. The neighborhood merits a wander, but you're better off focusing on the area around boulevard St. Germain and rue de Buci, and on the streets around the Maubert-Mutualité Métro stop.

HISTORIC PARIS **WALK**

From Notre-Dame to Sainte-Chapelle

Paris has been the capital of Europe for centuries. We'll start where it did, on Ile de la Cité, with a foray onto the Left Bank, on a walk that laces together 80 generations of history: from Celtic fishing village to Roman city, bustling medieval capital, birthplace of the Revolution, bohemian haunt of the 1920s café scene, and the working world of modern Paris. Allow four hours to do justice to this three-mile walk.

ORIENTATION

Many sights that charge admission are covered by the Paris museum pass, which for many is a great time and money saver (see page 29). The Archeological Crypt is a convenient place to buy a museum pass.

Notre-Dame: Free, church open daily 8:00–18:45; treasury-€2.50 (not covered by museum pass), daily 9:30–17:30; Sunday Mass at 8:00, 8:45, 10:00 (Gregorian), 11:30 (international), 12:30, and 18:30. Organ recitals at 16:30 on some days, usually Sat; ask. Leaflet with church schedule at booth inside entrance. Free English tours, normally Wed and Thu at 12:00 and Sat at 14:30. The tower climb takes 400 steps and €5.50—worth it for the gargoyle's-eye view of the city (April–Sept daily 9:30–19:30, Oct–March daily 10:00–18:00, last entry 45 min before closing, covered by museum pass but no bypass line for passholders; to avoid crowds in peak season, arrive before 10:00 or after 18:00).

Paris Archeological Crypt: €3.50, covered by museum pass, Tue–Sun 10:00–18:00, closed Mon, entry 100 yards in front of the cathedral.

Deportation Memorial: Free, April–Sept daily 10:00–12:00 & 14:00–19:00, Oct–March daily 10:00–12:00 & 14:00–17:00.

Sainte-Chapelle and Conciergerie: €5.50 each, €8 combo-ticket, both covered by museum pass, daily 9:30–18:00, Mo: Cité, tel. 01 44 07 12 38.

Historic Paris Walk

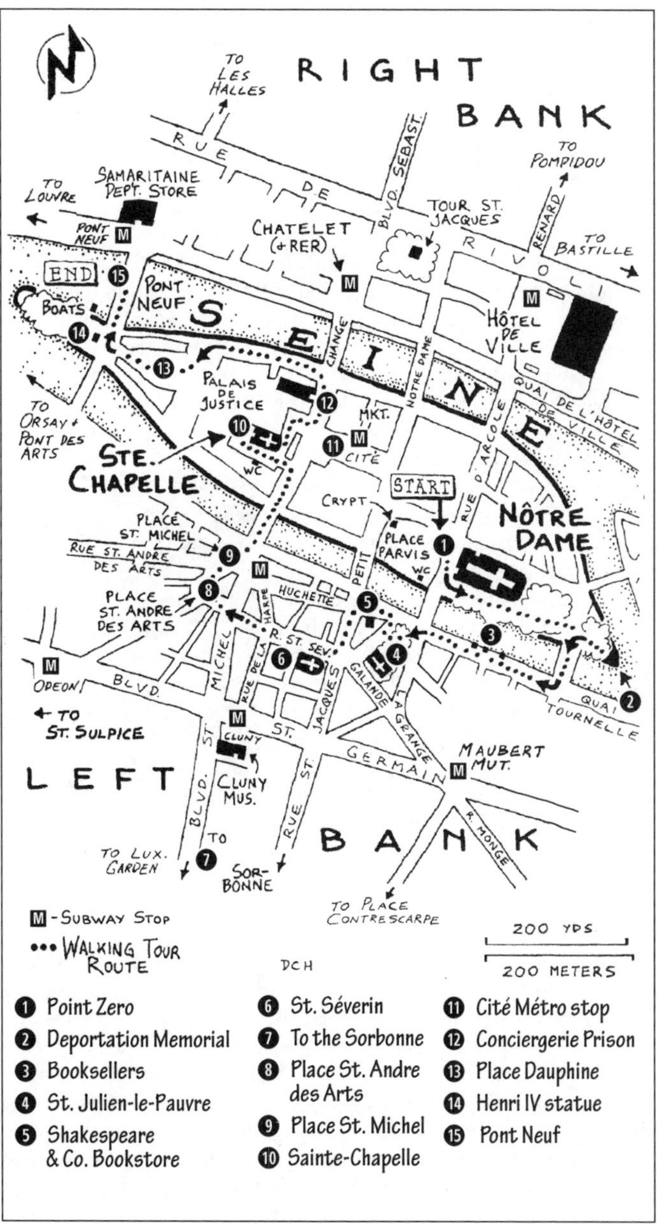

NOTRE-DAME

- *Start at Notre-Dame Cathedral on the island in the River Seine, the physical and historic bull's-eye of your Paris map (closest Métro stops are Cité, Hôtel de Ville, and St. Michel, each requiring a short walk). On the square in front of the cathedral, stand far enough back to take in the whole facade. Look at the circular window in the center.*

For centuries, the main figure in the Christian "pantheon" has been Mary, the mother of Jesus. Catholics petition her in times of trouble to gain comfort and to ask her to convince God to be compassionate with them. The church is dedicated to "Our Lady" (Notre-Dame), and there she is, cradling God, right in the heart of the facade, surrounded by the halo of the rose window. Though the church is massive and imposing, it has always stood for the grace and compassion of Mary, the "mother of God."

Imagine the faith of the people who built this. They broke ground in 1163 with the hope that someday their great-great-great-great-great-great grandchildren might attend the dedication Mass two centuries later in 1345. Look up the 200-foot-tall bell towers and imagine a tiny medieval community mustering the money and energy to build this. Master masons supervised, but the people did much of the grunt work themselves for free—hauling the huge stones from distant quarries, digging a 30-foot-deep trench to lay the foundations, and treading like rats on a wheel designed to lift the stones up, one by one. This kind of backbreaking, arduous manual labor created the real hunchbacks of Notre-Dame.

- *"Walk this way" toward the cathedral, and view it from the bronze plaque on the ground (30 yards from the central doorway) marked...*

Point Zero

You're standing at the center of France, the point from which all distances are measured. It was also the center of Paris 2,300 years ago, when the Parisii tribe fished here where the east-west river crossed a north-south road. The Romans conquered the Parisii and built their Temple of Jupiter where Notre-Dame is today (52 B.C.). When Rome fell, the Germanic Franks sealed their victory by replacing the temple with the Christian church of St. Etienne in the sixth century. See the outlines of the former church in the pavement (in smaller gray stones), showing where walls and columns were, angling out from Notre-Dame to Point Zero.

The grand equestrian statue (to your right, as you face the church) is

PARIS THROUGH HISTORY

250 B.C.	Small fishing village of the Parisii, a Celtic tribe.
52 B.C.	Julius Caesar conquers the Parisii capital of Lutetia (near Paris), and the Romans replace it with a new capital on the Left Bank.
A.D. 497	Rome falls to the Germanic Franks. King Clovis (482-511) converts to Christianity and makes Paris his capital.
885-6	Paris gets wasted in siege by Viking Norsemen = Normans.
1163	Notre-Dame cornerstone laid.
c. 1250	Paris is a bustling commercial city with a University and new construction such as Sainte-Chapelle and Notre-Dame.
c. 1600	King Henry IV beautifies Paris with buildings, roads, bridges, and squares.
c. 1700	Louis XIV makes Versailles his capital while Parisians grumble.
1789	Paris is the heart of France's Revolution, which condemns thousands to the guillotine.
1804	Napoleon Bonaparte crowns himself emperor in a ceremony at Notre-Dame.
1830 and 1848	Parisians take to the streets again in revolutions, fighting the return of royalty.
c. 1860	Napoleon's nephew, Napoleon III, builds Paris' wide boulevards.
1889	The centennial of the Revolution is celebrated with the Eiffel Tower. Paris enjoys wealth and middle-class prosperity in the belle époque (beautiful age).
1920s	After the draining Great War, Paris is a cheap place to live, attracting expatriates like Ernest Hemingway.
1940-44	Occupied Paris spends the war years under gray skies and gray Nazi uniforms.
2004	You arrive in Paris to make history.

of Charlemagne ("Charles the Great," 742-814), King of the Franks, whose reign marked the birth of modern France. He briefly united Europe and was crowned the first "Holy Roman Emperor" in 800, but after his death the kingdom was divided into what would become modern France and Germany. (Maybe even greater than Charles are the nearby pay toilets—the cleanest you'll find in downtown Paris.)

Before renovation 150 years ago, this square was much smaller, a characteristic medieval shambles facing a rundown church, surrounded by winding streets and higgledy-piggledy buildings. (Yellow bricks in the pavement show the medieval street plan and even identify some of the buildings.) The church's huge bell towers rose above this tangle of smaller buildings, inspiring Victor Hugo's story of a deformed bell-ringer who could look down on all of Paris.

Looking two-thirds of the way up Notre-Dame's left tower, those with binoculars or good eyes can find Paris' most photographed gargoyle. Propped on his elbows on the balcony rail, he looks down on all the tourists in line.

- *Much of Paris' history is right under your feet. Some may consider visiting it in the...*

Archeological Crypt

Two thousand years of dirt and debris have raised the city's altitude. In the Crypt museum (entrance 100 yards in front of Notre-Dame's entrance), you can see cellars and foundations from many layers of Paris: a Roman building with central heating; a wall that didn't keep the Franks out; the main medieval road that once led grandly up the square to Notre-Dame; even (wow) a 19th-century sewer.

- *Now turn your attention to the church facade. Look at the left doorway and, to the left of the door, find the statue with his head in his hands.*

Notre-Dame Facade

St. Denis

When Christianity began making converts in Roman Paris, the bishop of Paris (St. Denis) was beheaded. But those early Christians were hard to keep down. St. Denis got up, tucked his head under his arm, headed north, paused at a fountain to wash it off, and continued until he found just the right place to meet his maker. The Parisians were convinced by this miracle, Christianity gained ground, and a church soon replaced the pagan temple.

- *Above the central doorway, you'll find scenes from the Last Judgment.*

Central Portal

It's the end of the world, and Christ sits on the throne of judgment (just under the arches, holding both hands up). Below him, an angel and a demon weigh souls in the balance; the demon

Notre-Dame Facade

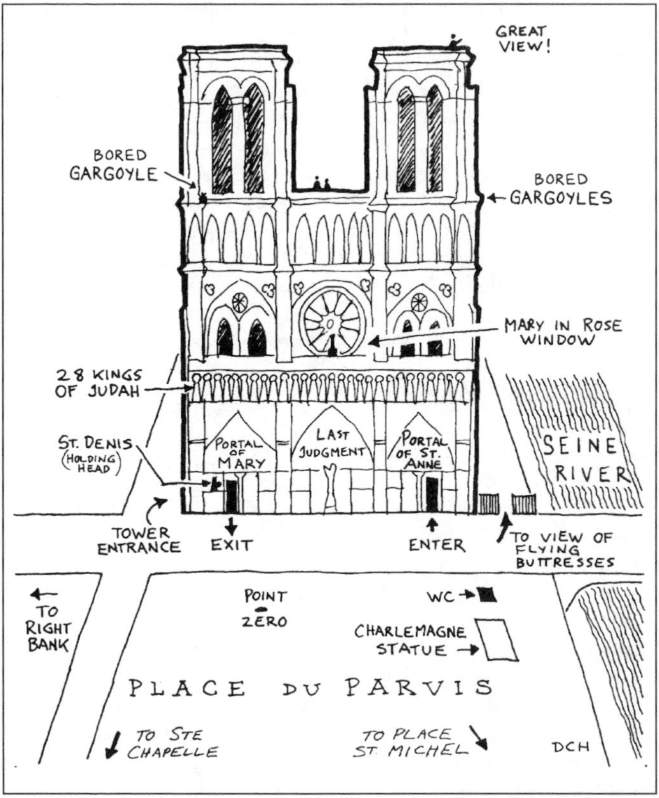

GREAT VIEW!
BORED GARGOYLE
BORED GARGOYLES
MARY IN ROSE WINDOW
28 KINGS OF JUDAH
ST. DENIS (HOLDING HEAD)
PORTAL OF MARY
LAST JUDGMENT
PORTAL OF ST. ANNE
SEINE RIVER
TOWER ENTRANCE
EXIT
ENTER
TO VIEW OF FLYING BUTTRESSES
TO RIGHT BANK
POINT ZERO
WC
CHARLEMAGNE STATUE
PLACE DU PARVIS
TO STE CHAPELLE
TO PLACE ST. MICHEL
DCH

cheats by pressing down. The good people stand to the left, gazing up to heaven. The naughty ones to the right are chained up and led off to a six-hour tour of the Louvre on a hot day. Notice the crazy, sculpted demons to the right, at the base of the arch. Find the flaming cauldron with the sinner diving into it headfirst. The lower panel shows Judgment Day, as angels with trumpets remind worshipers that all social classes will be judged—clergy, nobility, army, and peasants. Below that, Jesus stands between the 12 apostles—each barefoot and with their ID symbol (such as Peter with his keys).

• *Above the arches is a row of 28 statues, known as...*

The Kings of Judah

In the days of the French Revolution (1789–1799), these Biblical kings were mistaken for the hated French kings, and Notre-Dame represented the oppressive Catholic hierarchy. The citizens stormed the church, crying, "Off with their heads!" Plop, they lopped off the crowned heads of these kings with glee, creating a row of St. Denises that wasn't repaired for decades.

But the story doesn't end there. A schoolteacher who lived nearby collected the heads and buried them in his backyard for safekeeping. There they slept until 1977, when they were accidentally unearthed. Today, you can stare into the eyes of the original kings in the Cluny Museum, a few blocks away (see page 233).

- *Enter the church and find a spot where you can view the long, high central aisle. (Be careful: Pickpockets attend church here religiously.)*

Notre-Dame Interior

Nave

Remove your metaphorical hat and become a simple bareheaded peasant, entering the dim medieval light of the church. Take a minute to let your pupils dilate, then take in the subtle, mysterious light show God beams through the stained-glass windows. Follow the slender columns up 10 stories to the praying-hands arches of the ceiling and contemplate the heavens. Let's say it's dedication day for this great stone wonder. The priest intones the words of the Mass that echo through the hall: "*Terribilis est locus iste*"—"This place is *terribilis*," meaning awe-inspiring or even terrifying. It's a huge, dark, earthly cavern lit with an unearthly light.

This is Gothic. Taller and filled with light, this was a major improvement over the earlier Romanesque style. Gothic architects needed only a few structural columns, topped by pointed arches that crisscross the columns to support the weight of the roof. This let them build higher than ever, freeing up the walls for windows.

Notre-Dame is designed in the shape of a cross, with the altar placed where the crossbeam intersects. The church can hold up to 10,000 faithful.

- *Walk up to the main altar.*

Altar

This marks the spot where Mass is said and the bread and wine of Communion are blessed and distributed. In olden days, there were no chairs. This was the holy spot for Romans, Christians ... and even atheists. When the Revolutionaries stormed the church, they gutted it and turned it into a "Temple of Reason." A woman dressed up like the Statue of Liberty held court at the altar as a symbol of the divinity of Man. France today, while nominally Catholic, remains aloof from Vatican dogmatism. Instead of traditional wooden confessional booths, notice the open, glass-walled room (right aisle) where modern sinners seek counseling as much as forgiveness.

Right Transept

A statue of Joan of Arc (*Jeanne d'Arc*, 1412-1431), dressed in armor and praying, honors the French teenager who rallied the French soldiers to try to drive English invaders from Paris, before being burned at the stake for claiming to hear heavenly voices. Almost immediately, Parisians rallied to condemn Joan's execution, and finally, in 1909, here in Notre-Dame, the former "witch" was beatified.

Join the statue in gazing up to the blue and purple rose-shaped window—with teeny green Mary and baby Jesus in the center—the only one of the three still with its original medieval glass.

A large painting shows portly Thomas Aquinas (1225-1274) teaching while his students drink from the fountain of knowledge. This Italian monk did undergrad and master's work at the multicultural University of Paris, then taught there for several years while writing his theological works. His "scholasticism" used Aristotle's logic to examine the Christian universe, aiming to fuse faith and reason.

Just past the altar are the walls of the choir, where more intimate services can be held in this spacious building. Surrounding the choir are chapels, each dedicated to a particular saint. The faithful can pause at their favorite, light a candle as an offering, and meditate in the cool light of the stained glass. (The nearby treasury, containing lavish robes and golden reliquaries, lacks English explanations and probably isn't worth the €2.50 entry fee.)

Behind the altar, you'll see a fine 17th-century *pietà* flanked by two kneeling kings: Louis XIII and Louis XIV.

- *Amble around the ambulatory, spill back outside, and make a U-turn left. Walk to the back end of the church along the riverside.*

Notre-Dame Side View

Along the side of the church, you'll notice the flying buttresses. These 50-foot stone "beams" that stick out of the church were the key to the complex architecture of Gothic. The pointed arches we saw inside caused the weight of the roof to push outward rather than downward. The "flying" buttresses support the roof by pushing back inward. Gothic architects were masters at playing architectural forces against each other to build loftier and loftier churches, with walls opened up to stained glass windows.

Picture Quasimodo limping around along the railed balcony at the base of the roof among the gargoyles. These grotesque beasts sticking out from pillars and buttresses represent souls caught between heaven and earth. They also function as rain spouts (from the same French root as "gargle") when there are no evil spirits to battle.

The neo-Gothic 300-foot spire is a product of the 1860 reconstruction of the dilapidated old church. Victor Hugo's book *The Hunchback of Notre-Dame* (1831) inspired a young architecture student named Eugène-Emmanuel Viollet-le-Duc to dedicate his career to a major renovation in Gothic style. Find Viollet-le-Duc himself at the base of the spire among the green apostles and evangelists (visible from the back end of the church). The apostles look outward, blessing the city, while the architect (at top) looks up the spire, marveling at his fine work.

- *Behind Notre-Dame, cross the street, and enter the iron gate into the park at the tip of the island.*

Deportation Memorial *(Mémorial de la Déportation)*

This memorial to the 200,000 French victims of the Nazi concentration camps (1940-1945) draws you into their experience. France was quickly overrun by Nazi Germany, and Paris spent the war years under Nazi occupation. Jews and dissidents were rounded up and deported—many never returned.

As you descend the steps, the city around you disappears. Surrounded by walls, you have become a prisoner. Your only freedom is your view of the sky and the tiny glimpse of the river below. Enter the dark, single-file chamber up ahead. Inside, the circular plaque in the floor reads, "They went into the earth and they did not return."

The hallway stretching in front of you is lined with 200,000 lighted crystals, one for each French citizen who died. Flickering at the far end is the eternal flame of hope. The tomb of the unknown deportee lies at your feet. Above, the inscription reads, "Dedicated to the living memory of the 200,000 French deportees sleeping in the night and the fog, exterminated in the Nazi concentration camps." The side rooms are filled with triangles—reminiscent of the identification patches inmates were forced to wear—each

Ile St. Louis

bearing the name of a concentration camp. Above the exit as you leave is the message you'll find at all Nazi sites: "Forgive, but never forget."

Ile St. Louis

Back on street level, look across the river to the Ile St. Louis. If the Ile de la Cité is a tug laden with the history of Paris, it's towing this classy little residential dinghy laden only with high-rent apartments, boutiques, characteristic restaurants, and famous sorbet shops.

This island wasn't developed until much later (17th century) than the Ile de la Cité. What was a swampy mess is now harmonious Parisian architecture and one of Paris' most exclusive neighborhoods. Its uppity residents complain that the local ice cream shop—Berthillon—draws crowds until late into the night. (See page 329 for plenty of Ile St. Louis restaurant ideas.)

- *From the tip of Ile de la Cité, cross the bridge to the Left Bank and turn right. Walk along the river, toward the front end of Notre-Dame. Stairs detour down to the riverbank if you need a place to picnic. This side view of the church from across the river is one of Europe's great sights.*

LEFT BANK (RIVE GAUCHE)

The Left Bank of the Seine—"left" if you were floating downstream—still has many of the twisting lanes and narrow buildings of medieval times. The Right Bank is more modern and business-oriented, with wide boulevards and stressed Parisians in suits. Here along the riverbank, the "big business" is secondhand books, displayed in the green metal stalls on the parapet. These literary entrepreneurs pride themselves on their easygoing business style. With flexible hours and virtually no overhead, they run their businesses as they have since medieval times.

- *When you reach the bridge (pont au Double) that crosses over in front of Notre-Dame, veer to the left across the street to a small park (square Viviani) where you'll find the small rough-stone church of St. Julien-le-Pauvre. You'll pass Paris' oldest inhabitant—an acacia tree nicknamed Robinier after the guy who planted it in 1602—that may once have shaded the Sun King.*

Medieval Paris (1000–1400)

Picture Paris in 1250, when the church of St. Julien-le-Pauvre was still new. Notre-Dame was nearly done (so they thought), Sainte-Chapelle had just opened, the University was expanding human knowledge, and Paris was fast becoming a prosperous industrial and commercial center. The area around the church gives you some of the medieval feel. A half-timbered house stands to the right of the entrance. Many buildings in medieval times were built like this, with a wooden frame filled in with a plaster of mud, straw, and dung. Back then, the humble "half-timbered" structure would have been hidden by a veneer of upscale stucco.

Looking along nearby rue Galande, you'll see a few old houses leaning every which way. In medieval days, people were piled on top of each other, building at all angles, as they scrambled for this prime real estate near the main commercial artery of the day—the Seine. The smell of fish competed with the smell of neighbors in this knot of humanity.

Narrow dirt (or mud) streets sloped from here down into the mucky Seine, until modern quays and embankments cleaned that up.

- *Return to the river and turn left on rue de la Bûcherie. At #37, drop into the...*

Shakespeare and Company Bookstore

In addition to hosting butchers and fishmongers, the Left Bank has been home to scholars, philosophers, and poets since medieval times. This funky

bookstore—a reincarnation of the original shop from the 1920s—has picked up the literary torch. Sylvia Beach, an American with a passion for free thinking, opened Shakespeare and Company for the post-WWI Lost Generation who came to Paris to find themselves. American writers flocked here for the cheap rents, fleeing the uptight, Prohibition-era United States. Beach's bookstore was famous as a meeting place of Paris' literary expatriate elite. Ernest Hemingway borrowed books from here regularly. James Joyce struggled to find a publisher for his now-classic novel *Ulysses*—until Sylvia Beach published it. George Bernard Shaw, Gertrude Stein, and Ezra Pound also got their English fix here.

Today, the bookstore carries on that literary tradition. Struggling writers are given free accommodations upstairs in tiny rooms with views of Notre-Dame. Downstairs, travelers enjoy a great selection of used English books. Pick up the *Paris Voice* newspaper and say hi to owner George and his daughter ... Sylvia.

Notice the green water fountain (1900) in front of the bookstore, one of the many in Paris donated by the English philanthropist Sir Richard Wallace. The books below the carytids once held metal mugs for drinking the water.

- *Continue to the rue du Petit-Pont (which becomes rue St. Jacques). This busy north-south boulevard was the Romans' busiest boulevard 2,000 years ago, with chariots racing in and out of the city. (Roman-iacs can see remains from the third-century baths, along with a fine medieval collection, at the nearby Cluny Museum, 4 blocks away; see tour on page 233.)*

  Walking away from the river for one block, turn right at the Gothic church of St. Séverin and walk into the Latin Quarter.

St. Séverin

Don't ask me why, but it took a century longer to build this church than Notre-Dame. This is flamboyant, or "flame-like," Gothic, and you can see the short, prickly spires meant to make this building flicker in the eyes of the faithful. The church gives us a close-up look at gargoyles. This weird, winged species of flying mammal, now extinct, used to swoop down on unwary peasants, occasionally carrying off small children in their beaks. Today, they're most impressive in thunderstorms, when they vomit rain.

- *At #22 rue St. Séverin, you'll find the skinniest house in Paris, two windows wide. Rue St. Séverin leads right through…*

The Latin Quarter

While it may look more like the Greek Quarter today (cheap gyro sandwiches abound), this area is the Latin Quarter, named for the language you'd have heard on these streets if you walked them in the Middle Ages. The University of Paris (founded 1215), one of the leading educational institutions of medieval Europe, was (and still is) nearby.

A thousand years ago, the "crude" or vernacular local languages were sophisticated enough to communicate basic human needs, but if you wanted to get philosophical, the language of choice was Latin. The educated elite of medieval Europe was a class that transcended nations and borders. From Sicily to Sweden, they spoke and corresponded in Latin. Now the most Latin thing about this area is the beat you may hear coming from some of the subterranean jazz clubs.

Along rue St. Séverin, you can still see the shadow of the medieval sewer system. The street slopes into a central channel of bricks. In the days before plumbing and toilets, when people still went to the river or neighborhood wells for their water, flushing meant throwing it out the window. At certain times of day, maids on the fourth floor would holler, "*Garde de l'eau!*" ("Look out for the water!") and heave it into the streets, where it would eventually wash down into the Seine.

As you wander, remember that before Napoleon III commissioned Baron Haussmann to modernize the city with grand boulevards (19th century), Paris was just like this—a medieval tangle. The ethnic feel of this area is nothing new—it's been a melting pot and university district for almost 800 years.

Boulevard St. Michel

Busy boulevard St. Michel (or "boul' Miche") is famous as the main artery for Paris' café and artsy scene, culminating a block away (to the left), where it intersects boulevard St. Germain. Although nowadays you're more likely to find pantyhose at 30 percent off, there are still many cafés, boutiques, and bohemian haunts nearby.

The Sorbonne—the University of Paris' humanities department—is also close, if you want to make a detour. (Turn left on boulevard St. Michel and walk two blocks south. Gaze at the dome from the place de la Sorbonne courtyard or, when school is in session, poke your head into some of the buildings. The entrance at 17 rue de la Sorbonne can sell you an overpriced guidebook.) Originally founded as a theological school, the Sorbonne began attracting more students and famous professors—such as St. Thomas Aquinas and Peter Abélard—as its prestige grew. By the time the school expanded to include other subjects, it had a reputation for bold, new ideas. Nonconformity is a tradition here, and Paris remains a world center for new intellectual trends.

• *Cross boulevard St. Michel. Just ahead is…*

Place St. André-des-Arts

This tree-filled square is lined with cafés. In Paris, most serious thinking goes on in cafés. (For more information, see "Les Grands Cafés de Paris" on page 332.) For centuries, these have been social watering holes, where you can get a warm place to sit and stimulating conversation for the price of a cup of coffee. Every great French writer—from Voltaire and Jean-Jacques Rousseau to Jean-Paul Sartre and Jacques Derrida—had a favorite haunt.

Paris honors its writers. If you visit the Panthéon—a few blocks up boulevard St. Michel and to the left—you will find French writers (Voltaire, Victor Hugo, Emile Zola, and Rousseau), inventors (Louis Braille), and scientists (including Marie and Pierre Curie) buried in a setting usually reserved for warriors and politicians.

• *Adjoining this square is the triangular place St. Michel, with a Métro stop and a statue of St. Michael killing a devil. Note: If you were to continue west along rue St. André-des-Arts, you'd find more Left Bank action (see Left Bank Walk on page 105).*

Place St. Michel

You're standing at the traditional core of the Left Bank's artsy, liberal, hippie, bohemian district of poets, philosophers, and winos. Nearby, you'll find international eateries, far-out bookshops, street singers, pale girls in black berets, jazz clubs, and—these days—tourists. Small cinemas show avant-garde films, almost always in the *version originale* (v.o.). For colorful wandering and café-sitting, afternoons and evenings are best. In the morning, it feels sleepy. The Latin Quarter stays up late and sleeps in.

In less commercial times, place St. Michel was a gathering point for the city's malcontents and misfits. In 1830, 1848, and again in 1871, the citizens took the streets from the government troops, set up barricades *Les Miz*–style, and fought against royalist oppression. In World War II, the locals rose up against their Nazi oppressors (read the plaques under the dragons at the foot of the St. Michel fountain).

And in the spring of 1968, a time of social upheaval all over the world, young students battled riot batons and tear gas, took over the square, and declared it an independent state.

Factory workers followed their call to arms and went on strike, toppling the de Gaulle government and forcing change. Eventually, the students were pacified, the university was reformed, and the Latin Quarter's original cobblestones were replaced with pavement, so future scholars could never again use the streets as weapons.

- *From place St. Michel, look across the river and find the spire of the Sainte-Chapelle church, with its weathervane angel nearby. Cross the river on pont St. Michel and continue north along the boulevard du Palais. On your left, you'll see the doorway to the Sainte-Chapelle. You'll need to pass through a metal detector to get into the Sainte-Chapelle complex. Once past security, restrooms are ahead on the left. The line into the church may be long. (Museum passholders can go directly in.)*

  Enter the humble ground floor (pick up an English info flier and check the concert schedule if you're interested).

SAINTE-CHAPELLE

Sainte-Chapelle, the triumph of Gothic church architecture, is a cathedral of glass like no other. It was built in 1248 for King Louis IX (the only French king who is now a saint) to house the supposed Crown of Thorns. Its architectural harmony is due to the fact that it was completed under the direction of one architect and in only five years—unheard of in Gothic times. Recall that Notre-Dame took over 200 years.

The exterior is ugly. But those fat buttresses are all the support needed to hold up the roof, opening up the walls for stained glass. Inside the layout clearly shows an *ancien régime* approach to worship. The low-ceilinged basement was for staff and more common folks—worshiping under a sky filled with painted fleurs-de-lis, a symbol of the king. Royal Christians worshiped upstairs. The paint job, a 19th-century restoration, helps you imagine how grand this small, painted, jeweled chapel was. (Imagine Notre-Dame painted like this . . . .)

It takes 13 tourists to build a Gothic church: six columns, six buttresses, and one steeple.

- *Climb the spiral staircase to the Haute Chapelle. Leave the rough stone of the earth and step into the light.*

Sainte-Chapelle

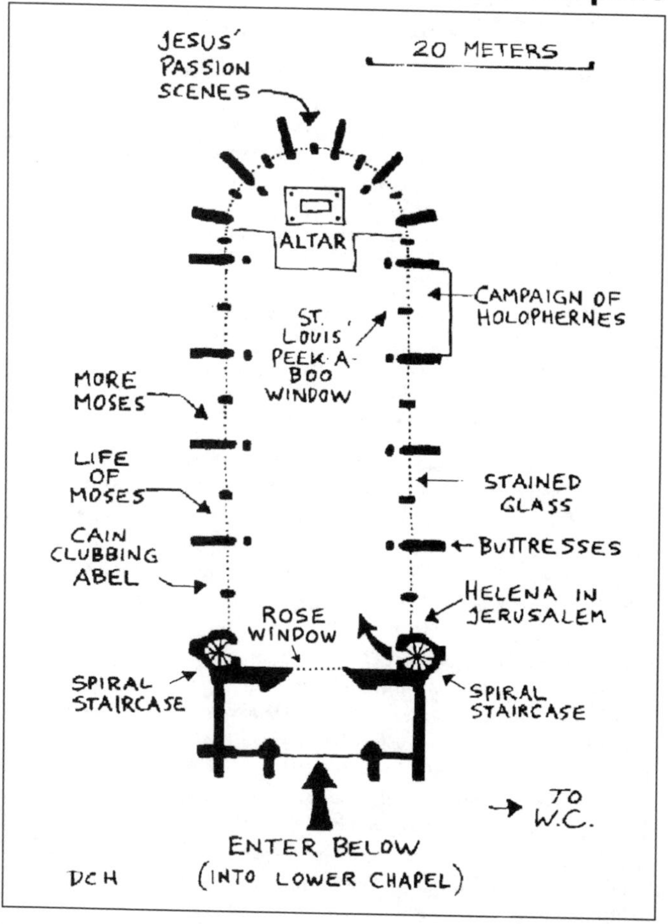

JESUS' PASSION SCENES
20 METERS
ALTAR
CAMPAIGN OF HOLOPHERNES
ST. LOUIS' PEEK-A-BOO WINDOW
MORE MOSES
LIFE OF MOSES
STAINED GLASS
CAIN CLUBBING ABEL
BUTTRESSES
HELENA IN JERUSALEM
ROSE WINDOW
SPIRAL STAIRCASE
SPIRAL STAIRCASE
TO W.C.
ENTER BELOW (INTO LOWER CHAPEL)
DCH

The Stained Glass

Fiat lux. "Let there be light." From the first page of the Bible, it's clear—light is divine. Light shines through stained glass like God's grace shining down to earth, and Gothic architects used their new technology to turn dark stone buildings into lanterns of light. For me, the glory of Gothic shines brighter here than in any other church.

STAINED GLASS SUPREME

Craftsmen made glass—which is, essentially, melted sand—using this recipe:

- Melt one part sand with two parts wood ash.
- Mix in rusty metals to get different colors—iron makes red, cobalt makes blue, copper green, manganese purple, cadmium yellow.
- Blow glass into a cylinder shape, cut lengthwise, and lay flat.
- Cut into pieces with an iron tool, or by heating and cooling a select spot to make it crack.
- Fit pieces together to form a figure, using strips of lead to hold in place.
- Place masterpiece so high on a wall that no one can read it.

There are 15 separate panels of stained glass, with more than 1,100 different scenes, mostly from the Bible. These cover the entire Christian history of the world, from the Creation in Genesis (first window on the left, as you face the altar), to the coming of Christ (over the altar), to the end of the world (the round "rose"-shaped window at the rear of the church). Each individual scene is interesting, and the whole effect is overwhelming.

- *Working clockwise from the entrance, here are some scenes worth a look. (Note: The sun lights up different windows at different times of day. Overcast days give the most even light. On bright, sunny days, some sections are glorious while others look like a sheet of lead.)*

Genesis—Cain clubbing Abel (first window on the left—always dark because of a building butted up against it): On the bottom level in the third circle from left, we see God create the round earth and hold it up. On the next level up, we catch glimpses of naked Adam and Eve. On the third level (far right circle), Cain, in red, clubs his brother Abel, creating murder.

Life of Moses (second window, the bottom row of diamond panels): The first panel shows baby Moses in a basket, placed by his sister in the squiggly brown river. Next, he's found by the pharaoh's daughter. Then, he grows up. And finally, he's a man, a prince of Egypt on his royal throne.

More Moses (third window, in middle and upper sections): You'll see various scenes of Moses, the guy with the bright yellow horns—the result of a medieval mistranslation of the Hebrew word for "rays of light," or halo.

Jesus' Passion Scenes (over the altar): These scenes from Jesus' arrest and crucifixion were the backdrop for the Crown of Thorns, which originally was displayed on the altar. Stand far enough back to look through the canopy to find Jesus in yellow shorts carrying his cross. A little below that, see Jesus being whipped (left) and—the key scene in this relic chapel—Jesus in purple being fitted with the painful Crown of Thorns (right). Finally (as high as you can see), Jesus on the cross is speared by a soldier.

Campaign of Holofernes: On the bottom row are four scenes of colorful knights. The second circle from the left is a battle scene (the campaign of Holofernes), showing three soldiers with swords slaughtering three men. The background is blue. The men have different-colored clothes—red, blue, green, mauve, and white. Notice some of the details. You can see the folds in the robes, the hair, and facial features. Look at the victim in the center—his head splotched with blood. Details like the folds in the robes (see the victim in white, lower left) came either by scratching on the glass or by baking on paint. It was a painstaking process of finding just the right colors, fitting them together to make a scene … and then multiplying by 1,100.

Helena in Jerusalem (first window on the right wall): This window tells the story of how Christ's Crown of Thorns found its way from Jerusalem to Constantinople to this chapel. Start in the lower left corner, where the Roman emperor Constantine (in blue, on his throne) waves goodbye to his Christian mom, Helena. She arrives at the gate of Jerusalem (next panel to the right). Her men (in the two-part medallion above Jerusalem) dig through ruins and find Christ's (tiny) cross and other relics. She returns to Constantinople with a stash of holy relics, including the Crown of Thorns. Nine hundred years later, French Crusader knights (the next double medallion above) invade the Holy Land and visit Constantinople. Finally, King Louis IX, dressed in blue (in the panel up one and to the right of the last one) returns to France with the sacred relic.

Rose Window (above entrance): It's Judgment Day, with a tiny Christ in the center of the chaos and miracles. This window is 200 years newer then the rest, from the Flamboyant period. Facing west and the sunset, it's best late in the day.

If you can't read much into the individual windows, you're not alone. (For some tutoring, a little book with color photos is on sale downstairs with the postcards.)

Altar

The altar was raised up high (notice the staircase for the priest) to better display the relic around which this chapel was built—the Crown of

Thorns. This was the crown put on Jesus when the Romans were torturing and humiliating him before his execution. King Louis IX, convinced he'd found the real McCoy, paid three times as much money for the thorns as was spent on this entire chapel. Today, the supposed Crown of Thorns is kept in the Notre-Dame Treasury (and shown only on Fridays during Lent).

Notice the little private viewing window in the right wall, near the altar. Louis was both saintly and shy. He liked to be able to go to church without dealing with the rigors of public royal life. Here he could worship still dressed in his jammies.

Lay your camera on the ground and shoot the ceiling. Those pure and simple ribs growing out of the slender columns are the essence of Gothic structure.

- *Exit Sainte-Chapelle. Back outside, as you walk around the church exterior, look down to see the foundation and notice how much Paris has risen in the 750 years since the Sainte-Chapelle was built.*

Palais de Justice

You're in a huge complex of buildings that has housed the local government since ancient Roman times. It was the site of the original Gothic palace of the early kings of France. The only surviving medieval parts are Sainte-Chapelle and the Conciergerie prison.

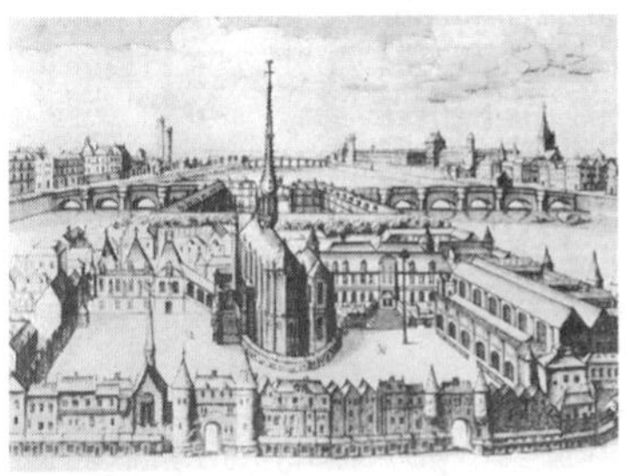

Paris' Palais de Justice in 1650, with Sainte-Chapelle, the Conciergerie, and Pont Neuf (then 30 years old) in the background.

Most of the site is now covered by the giant Palais de Justice, built in 1776, home of France's supreme court. The motto *Liberté, Egalité, Fraternité* over the doors is a reminder that this was also the headquarters of the Revolutionary government. Here, they doled out justice, condemning many to imprisonment in the Conciergerie downstairs or to the guillotine.

- *Now pass through the big iron gate to the noisy boulevard du Palais. Cross the street to the wide pedestrian-only rue de Lutèce.*

Sainte-Chapelle Area

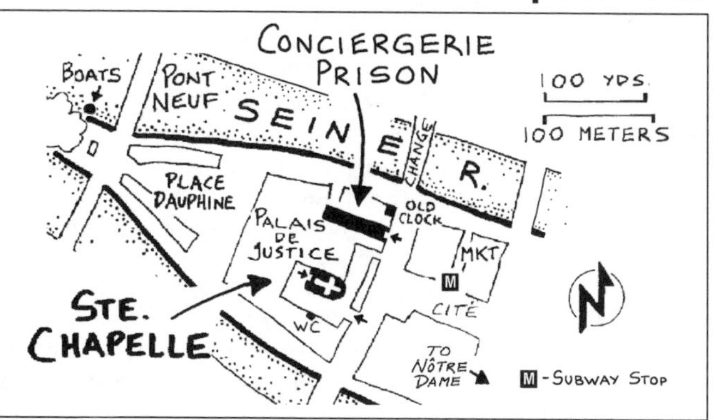

Cité "Metropolitain" Stop

Of the 141 original early-20th-century subway entrances, this is one of only a few survivors—now preserved as a national art treasure. (New York's Museum of Modern Art even exhibits one.) It marks Paris at its peak in 1900—on the cutting edge of modernism but with an eye to beauty. The curvy, plantlike ironwork is a textbook example of Art Nouveau, the style that rebelled against the erector-set squareness of the Industrial Age. In Paris, only the stations at Abbesses and Porte Dauphine survive with their canopies.

The flower and plant market on place Louis Lépine is a pleasant detour. On Sundays, this square is all aflutter with a busy bird market. And across the way is the Prefecture de Police, where Inspector Clouseau of *Pink Panther* fame used to work, and where the local resistance fighters took the first building from the Nazis in August of 1944, leading to the Allied liberation of Paris a week later.

- *Pause here to admire the view. Sainte-Chapelle is a pearl in an ugly architectural oyster. To the right of the Palais de Justice is the Conciergerie, with its entrance on boulevard du Palais. Though pretty barren inside, the Conciergerie echoes with history and is free with the museum pass.*

Conciergerie

Positioned next to the courthouse, the Conciergerie was the gloomy prison famous as the last stop for 2,780 victims of the guillotine, including France's last queen, Marie-Antoinette. Before then, kings had used the building to torture and execute failed assassins. (One of its towers along the river was called "the babbler," named for the painful sounds that leaked from it.) When the Revolution (1789) toppled the king, the building kept its same function, but without torture. The progressive Revolutionaries proudly unveiled a modern and more humane way to execute people—the guillotine.

Inside, pick up a free map and breeze through. See the spacious, low-ceilinged Hall of Men-at-Arms (Room 2) with four large fireplaces, used as a staff cafeteria in medieval times. This big room gives a feel for the grandeur of the Great Hall (upstairs, not open to visitors) where the Revolutionary tribunals grilled scared prisoners on their political correctness. The raised area at the far end of the room (Room 4, today's bookstore) was notorious as the walkway of the executioner, who was known affectionately as "Monsieur de Paris." The Prisoners' Gallery (Room 5) is a hall where the condemned milled about, waiting for the open-air cart (tumbrel) to pull up outside to carry them to the guillotine on place de la Concorde.

Upstairs in the Audio-Visual Room (top of the stairs), a video recreates prison life. Lining the walls are lists of the 2,780 citizens condemned to death by the guillotine. In alphabetical order, find: Georges Danton (prominent revolutionary who was later condemned for being insufficiently liberal, a nasty crime), Charlotte Corday (a noblewoman who snuck into the bathroom of the revolutionary writer, Jean-Paul Marat, and stabbed him while he bathed), Anne-Elizabeth Capet (whose crime was being "sister of the tyrant"), Louis XVI ("called Capet: last king of France"), Marie-Antoinette, and—oh the irony—Maximilien de Robespierre, the head of the Revolution, the man who sent so many to the guillotine, and who was eventually toppled, humiliated, imprisoned here, and beheaded.

Also upstairs, you'll walk by some reconstructed cells showing how the poor slept on straw while the wealthy got a cot.

Back downstairs, you wind up in the re-creation of Marie-Antoinette's Cell (Room 12), on the actual site of her original cell, though the building's layout has seen some changes. This was where the Queen spent her last days—separated from her 10-year-old son, and now widowed, because the King had already been executed. Mannequins and period furniture set the scene. The guard stands modestly behind a screen while the queen psyches herself up with a crucifix. In the glass display case, see her actual crucifix, napkin, and small water pitcher. On October 16, 1793, the queen walked the corridor, stepped onto the cart, and was slowly carried to place de la Concorde, where she had a date with "Monsieur de Paris."

- *Back outside, turn left on boulevard du Palais and head toward the river (north). On the corner is the city's oldest public clock. The mechanism of the present clock is from 1334, and even though the case is Baroque, it keeps on ticking.*

  Turn left onto quai de l'Horloge and walk west along the river, past the round medieval tower called "the babbler." The bridge up ahead is the pont Neuf, where we'll end this walk. At the first corner, veer left into a sleepy triangular square called place Dauphine.

Place Dauphine

It's amazing to find such coziness in the heart of Paris. This city of two million is still a city of neighborhoods, a collection of villages. The French Supreme Court building looms behind like a giant marble gavel. Enjoy the village-Paris feeling in the park. You may see lawyers on their lunch break playing *boules.*

- *Continue through place Dauphine. As you pop out the other end, you're face to face with a...*

Statue of Henry IV

Henry IV (1553-1610) is not as famous as his grandson, Louis XIV, but Henry helped make Paris what it is today—a European capital of elegant buildings and quiet squares. He built the place Dauphine (behind you), the pont Neuf (to the right), residences (to the left, down rue Dauphine), the Louvre's long Grand Gallery, and the tree-filled square Vert-Galant (directly behind the statue, on the tip of the island). The square is one of Paris' make-out spots; its name comes from Henry's own nickname, the Green Knight, as Henry was a notorious ladies' man.

BOULES

Each player starts with three iron balls, with the object of getting them close to the target, a small wooden ball called a *cochonnet.* The first player tosses the *cochonnet* about 30 feet, then throws the first of his iron balls near the target. The next player takes a turn. As soon as a player's ball is closest, it's the other guy's turn. Once all balls have been thrown, the score is tallied—the player with the closest ball gets one point for each ball closer to the target than his opponent's. The loser gets zero. Games are generally to 15 points.

A regulation *boules* field is 10-by-43 feet, but the game is played everywhere—just scratch a throwing circle in the sand, toss the *cochonnet,* and you're off. Strategists can try to knock the opponent's balls out of position, knock the *cochonnet* itself out of position, or guard their best ball with the other two.

The park is a great place to relax, dangling your legs over the concrete prow of this boat-shaped island.

- *From the statue, turn right onto the old bridge. Walk to the little nook halfway across.*

Pont Neuf

The pont Neuf, or "new bridge," is Paris' oldest standing bridge (built 1578-1607). Its 12 arches span the widest part of the river. Unlike other bridges, this one never had houses or buildings growing on it. The turrets were originally for vendors and street entertainers. In the days of Henry IV, who promised his peasants "a chicken in every pot every Sunday," this would have been a lively scene. From the bridge, look downstream (west) to see the next bridge, the pedestrian-only pont des Arts. Ahead on the Right Bank is the long Louvre Museum. Beyond that on the Left Bank is the Orsay. And what's that tall black tower in the distance?

The Seine

Our walk ends where Paris began—on the Seine River. From Dijon to the English Channel, the Seine meanders 500 miles, cutting through the center of Paris. The river is shallow and slow within the city, but still dangerous enough to require steep stone embankments (built 1910) to prevent occasional floods. You'll see tourist boats (Bateaux-Mouches) and commercial barges that carry 20 percent of Paris' transported goods. And on the banks, sportsmen today cast into the waters once fished by Paris' original Celtic inhabitants.

- *We're done. The closest Métro stop is Pont Neuf, across the bridge on the Right Bank.*

CHAMPS-ELYSEES **WALK**

Don't leave Paris without strolling the avenue des Champs-Elysées. This is Paris at its most Parisian: monumental sidewalks, stylish shops, grand cafés, and glimmering showrooms. This walk covers about three miles—from the Arc de Triomphe to the Tuileries Gardens—and takes three hours if done completely. It's a great stroll day or night. Métro stops are located about every three blocks on the Champs-Elysées (shahnz ay-lee-ZAY).

ORIENTATION

Arc de Triomphe: €7, covered by museum pass, elevator to museum (not to the top) only for the disabled, April–Sept daily 10:00–23:00, Oct–March daily 10:00–22:30, skip the ticket line if you have a museum pass, Mo: Charles de Gaulle-Etoile, tel. 01 43 80 31 31.

Sephora (perfumes): Daily 10:00–24:00, tel. 01 53 93 22 50.

Hôtel Crillon: High tea daily 15:30-19:00, tel. 01 44 71 15 00.

THE TOUR BEGINS

Start at the Arc de Triomphe (take the Métro to Charles de Gaulle-Etoile, then follow *sortie* Champs-Elysées/Avenue Friedland signs to "access Arc de Triomphe" signs). At the top of the Champs-Elysées, face the arch. The TI and underground WCs are on the other (south) side of Champs-Elysées, and an underground walkway leading to the arch is in front of you. Get to that arch (worthwhile even if you don't climb it; there's no charge to wander around the base).

The Arc de Triomphe (Exterior)

Construction on the 165-foot-high arch was begun in 1809 to honor Napoleon's soldiers, who, in spite of being vastly outnumbered by the

Champs-Elysées Walk

Austrians, scored a remarkable victory at the battle of Austerlitz. Patterned after the ceremonial arches of ancient Roman conquerors, it celebrates Napoleon as emperor of a "New Rome." On the arch's massive left pillar, a relief sculpture shows a toga-clad Napoleon posing confidently, while an awe-struck Paris—crowned by her city walls—kneels at his imperial feet. Napoleon died prior to the Arc's completion, but it was finished in time for his 1840 funeral procession to pass underneath, carrying his remains (19 years dead) from exile in St. Helena to Paris.

On the right pillar is the Arc's most famous relief, *La Marseillaise* (*Le Départ des Volontaires de 1792*, by François Rude). Lady Liberty—looking like an ugly reincarnation of Joan of Arc—screams, "Freedom is this way!" and points the direction with a sword. The soldiers below her are tired, naked, and stumbling, but she rallies them to carry on the fight against oppression.

Today, the Arc de Triomphe is dedicated to the glory of all French armies. If you stand directly beneath (on the faded eagle), you're surrounded by the lists of French victories since the Revolution—19th century on the arch, 20th century in the pavement. On the columns you'll see lists of generals (with a line under the names of those who died in battle). Nearby, stand on the bronze plaque at the foot of the Tomb of the Unknown Soldier (from World War I). Every day at 18:30 since just after World War I, the flame has been rekindled and new flowers set in place.

Like its Roman ancestors, this arch has served as a parade gateway for triumphal armies (French or foe) and important ceremonies. From 1940 to 1944, a large swastika flew from here as Nazis goose-stepped down the Champs-Elysées. In August 1944, Charles de Gaulle led allied troops under this arch as they celebrated liberation. Today, national parades start and end here with one minute of silence.

Interior and View from the Top

Ascend the Arc de Triomphe via the 284 steps (April–Sept daily 10:00–23:00, Oct–March daily 10:00–22:30). A wall mural by the ticket booth gives a sneak preview for the lazy (or those wondering if it's worth the climb).

Two-thirds of the way up, catch your breath in the small museum of the arch's history. Working clockwise around the room, see photographs of the post-World War I victory parade under the arch (*Le Defile de la Victoire*), led by Allied commander-in-chief, Marshal Ferdinand Foch. Under the words *De 1870 a 1914*, look for the picture of an enormous coffin placed under the arch to see how France mourned the death of the famous writer Victor Hugo. Read (in French) about the arch's relief sculptures (*Le Décor de l'Arc*) and stand next to screaming Lady Liberty's huge head. See various designs of the arch (*L'Achèvement de l'Arc de Triomphe*). And ponder what other grand structure might have been placed on this spot if Napoleon hadn't come up with an arch—how about a giant elephant? (*Le Carrefour de l'Etoile*).

From the top, you have an eye-opening view of *toute Paris*. **Looking east:** Gaze down the Champs-Elysées to the Tuileries Garden and the Louvre. Scan the cityscape of downtown Paris. Notice the symmetry. The beauty of Paris—basically a flat basin with a river running through it—is man-made, with a harmonious relationship between the width of its grand boulevards and the uniformity in the height and design of the buildings. Panning slowly to the right, see the twin towers of Notre-Dame, the "state-capitol-dome" of the Panthéon, a block of small skyscrapers on a hill (the Quartier d'Italie), the golden dome of the Invalides, and the lonely-looking Montparnasse Tower, standing like the box the Eiffel Tower came in. It served as a wake-up call in the early 1970s to preserve the building height restrictions and strengthen urban design standards.

Looking west: In the distance, the huge, white Grande Arche de la Défense, standing amid skyscrapers, is the final piece of a grand city axis—from the Louvre, up the Champs-Elysées to the Arc de Triomphe, continuing on as the avenue de la Grande Armée, ending in a forest of skyscrapers at La Défense, three miles away. Former French President François Mitterrand had the Grande Arche built as a centerpiece of this mini-Manhattan. Notice the contrast between the skyscrapers of La Défense and the uniform heights of the buildings closer to the Arc de Triomphe. Below you, the wide boulevard lined with grass and trees a little to your left is avenue Foch (named after the WWI hero) and is the best address to have in Paris (the Shah of Iran and Aristotle Onassis had homes here). The huge park at the end of avenue Foch is the Bois de Boulogne.

Gaze down at what appears to be a chaotic traffic mess. The 12 boulevards that radiate from the Arc de Triomphe (forming an *étoile*, or star) were part of Baron Haussmann's master plan for Paris: the creation of a series of major boulevards, intersecting at diagonals with monuments (such as the Arc de Triomphe) as centerpieces of those intersections. His plan did not anticipate the automobile—obvious when you watch the traffic scene below. But see how smoothly it really functions. Cars entering the circle have the right of way (the only roundabout in France with this rule); those in the circle must yield. Still, there are plenty of accidents, often caused by tourists oblivious to the rules. Tired of disputes, insurance companies split the fault and damages of any Arc de Triomphe accident 50–50. The trick is to make a parabola—get to the center ASAP and then begin working your way out two avenues before you want to exit.

• *We'll start our stroll down the Champs-Elysées at the Charles de Gaulle-Etoile Métro stop, on the north (sunnier) side of the street. Look straight down the Champs-Elysées to the Tuileries Garden at the far end.*

The Champs-Elysées

You're at the top of one of the world's grandest, most elegant, and celebrated streets, home to big business, celebrity cafés, glitzy nightclubs, high-fashion shopping, and international people-watching.

In 1667, Louis XIV opened the first section of the street as a short extension of the Tuileries Garden. This date is a considered the birth of Paris as a grand city. The Champs-Elysées soon became *the* place to cruise in your carriage. (It still is today—traffic can be jammed up even at midnight.) One hundred years later, the café scene arrived.

From the 1920s until the 1960s, this boulevard was pure elegance. Locals actually dressed up to come here. It was mainly residences, rich hotels, and cafés. Then, in 1963, the government pumped up the neighborhood's commercial metabolism by bringing in the RER (commuter underground). Suburbanites had easy access, and bam—there went the neighborhood.

• *Start your descent, pausing at the first tiny street you cross, rue de Tilsitt. This street is part of a shadow ring road—an option for drivers who'd like to avoid the chaos of the arch, complete with stoplights.*

A half-block down rue de Tilsitt is the Dresdner Bank building. It's one of the few survivors of a dozen uniformly U-shaped buildings of Haussman's original 1853 grand design. Peek into the foyer for a glimpse of 19th-century Champs-Elysées classiness.

Back on the main drag, look across to the other side of the Champs-Elysées at the big, gray concrete-and-glass "Publicis" building. Ugh. In the 1960s, venerable old buildings (similar to the Dresdner Bank building) were leveled to make way for new commercial operations, like Publicis. Then in 1985, a law prohibited the demolition of the old building fronts that gave the boulevard a uniform grace. Today, many modern businesses hide behind preserved facades.

The coming of McDonald's was a shock to the boulevard. At first, it was allowed only white arches painted on the window. Today, it spills out legally onto the sidewalk—provided it offers café-quality chairs and flower boxes—and dining *chez MacDo* has become typically Parisian. A €3 Big Mac here buys an hour of people-watching. (There's a public WC nearby.)

The *nouveau* Champs-Elysées, revitalized in 1994, has new benches and lamps, broader sidewalks, and an army of green-suited workers armed with high-tech pooper-scoopers. Blink away the modern elements, and it's not hard to imagine the boulevard pre-1963, with only the finest structures lining both sides all the way to the palace gardens.

Glitz

At the fancy car dealerships—Peugeot at #136 (showing off its futuristic concept cars next to the classic models) or Mercedes at #118 (like an English-language car show)—you can pick up your new sedan and a leather jacket and purse to match. In the 19th century, this was an area for horse stables; today, it's the district of garages, limo companies, and car dealerships.

Next to Mercedes is the famous Lido, Paris' largest cabaret (and a multiplex cinema). Check out the perky photos, R-rated videos, and shocking prices. Paris still offers the kind of burlesque-type spectacles combining music, comedy, and scantily-clad women performed here since the 19th century. Movie-going on the Champs-Elysées is also popular, at theaters that show the very latest releases. Check to see if there are films you recognize, then look for the showings *(séances)*. A "v.o." *(version originale)* next to the time indicates the film will be in its original language.

• *Now cross the boulevard. Spend one traffic light cycle at the island midstream enjoying the view. Look up at the Arc de Triomphe with its rooftop bristling with tourists. Notice the architecture—old and elegant, new, and new-behind-old facades.*

Café Culture

Fouquet's café-restaurant (#99), under the red awning, is a popular spot among French celebrities, serving the most expensive shot of espresso I've found in downtown Paris (€4.50). Opened in 1899 as a coachman's bistro, Fouquet's gained fame as the hangout of France's WWI biplane fighter pilots—those who weren't shot down by Germany's infamous "Red Baron." It also served as James Joyce's dining room. Since the early 1900s, Fouquet's has been a favorite of French actors and actresses. The golden plaques by the entrance honor winners of France's Oscar-like film awards, the Césars—see plaques to Gérard Depardieu, Catherine Deneuve, Roman Polanski, Juliette Binoche, and many famous Americans (but not Jerry Lewis). While the impressive interior is intimidating, the outdoor setting is great. Fouquet's was recently saved from foreign purchase and eventual destruction when the government declared it a historic monument.

Ladurée (a block downhill at #75, with green and purple awning) is a classic 19th-century tea salon/restaurant/*pâtisserie.* Its interior is right out of the 1860s. Wander around...even peeking into the cozy rooms upstairs. A coffee here is *très élégant.* The bakery makes traditional macaroons, cute little cakes, and gift-wrapped finger sandwiches.

• *Cross back to the lively (north) side of the street.*

At #92 (a bit uphill), a wall plaque marks the place Thomas Jefferson lived (with his 14-year-old slave, Sally Hemings) while minister to France (1785–1789). He'd replaced the popular Benjamin

Franklin, but quickly made his own mark, extolling the virtues of America's Revolution to a country approaching its own. A plaque just below marks the spot where a soldier (Robert Birlinger) died fighting the Germans during the liberation of Paris in August 1944.

The nearby Club Med (#88), with its travel ads to sunny destinations, is a reminder of the French commitment to the vacation. Since 1936 the French, by law, have enjoyed one month of paid vacation. In the swinging '60s, Club Med made hedonism accessible to the middle-class French masses.

French Shopping

Stroll into the Arcades des Champs-Elysées mall at #76. With its fancy lamps, mosaic floors, glass skylight, and classical columns, it captures faint echoes of the *années folles*—the "crazy years," as the roaring '20s were called in France. Architecture buffs can observe how flowery Art Nouveau became simpler, more geometrical Art Deco. Down the street, the Galerie du Claridge (at #74) is a fine example of an old facade—with an ironwork awning, balconies, *putti*, and sculpted fantasy faces—fronting a new building.

At #72, glide down Sephora's ramp into a vast hall of cosmetics and perfumes (daily 10:00–24:00). Grab a disposable white strip, spritz it with a sample, and sniff. The store is thoughtfully laid out: The entry hall is lined with the new products—all open and ready (with sniff strips) to sample. In the main showroom, women's perfumes line the left wall and men's line the (shorter) right wall—organized alphabetically by company from Armani to Versace. Stop first at the central "wheel of scents." The woman here helps shoppers explore their needs. She dishes out up to 400 samples until you find the scent of your dreams and then assembles a list of products to match. The wheel of scents is organized like a wheel of color (clockwise from fresh to strong). Follow the labeled progression: fresh, sea, flower, fruit, herb, wood, spicy, amber, and leather. Lemon is freshest. *Civette*—eau de cow pie—is strongest. (I'm not kidding...give it a whiff. Now you can mark your territory.) The best-seller: chocolate. Worst seller? Guess. Grab a basket and follow your nose. The mesmerizing music, chosen just for Sephora, actually made me crave cosmetics. Halfway down on your left in red, flashing numbers show the current prices of perfumes *(cours des parfums)* in cities throughout the world—allowing jet-setters to comparison shop.

The English pharmacy is open until midnight at the corner of rue la Boétie, and map-lovers can detour one block down this street to shop at Espace IGN (Institut Géographique National), France's version of the National Geographic Society (Mon–Fri 9:30–19:00, Sat 11:00–12:30 & 14:00–18:30, closed Sun, tel. 03 80 30 33 67).

International Shopping

A block farther down, the Virgin Megastore (#54) sells a world of music. The Disney, Gap, and Quicksilver stores are reminders of global economics—the French seem to love these places as much as Americans do. Hippo Citroën (#40) combines two French businesses—displaying the distinctive car inside a French chain restaurant. Renault, opposite Sephora, also has a cool concept-car exhibit, worth crossing the boulevard for.

Rond-Point and Beyond

At the Rond-Point des Champs-Elysées M. Dassault, the shopping ends and the park begins. This round, leafy traffic circle is always colorful, lined with flowers or seasonal decorations (thousands of pumpkins at Halloween, hundreds of decorated trees at Christmas).

A long block past the Rond Point, at Avenue de Marigny, look to the other side of the Champs-Elysées to find a new statue of Charles de Gaulle—ramrod straight and striding out as he did the day Paris was liberated in 1944. Charles stands in front of the glass- and steel-domed Grand and Petit Palais exhibition halls, built for the 1900 World's Fair. Today, these examples of the "can do" spirit of the early 20th century are museums. Impressive temporary exhibits fill the huge Grand Palais (on right, €8, not covered by museum pass; get details on current exhibitions from TIs or in *Pariscope*). The Petit Palais (left side), which is closed for renovation until 2005, houses a permanent collection of 19th-century paintings by Eugène Delacroix, Paul Cézanne, Claude Monet, Camille Pissarro, and other masters.

Beyond the two palaces, the pont Alexander III leads over the Seine to the golden dome of Les Invalides. This exquisite bridge, spiked with golden statues and ironwork lamps, was built to celebrate a turn-of-the-20th-century treaty between France and Russia. Like the Grand and Petit Palais, it's a fine example of belle-époque exuberance.

Les Invalides was built by Louis XIV as a veteran's hospital for his battle-weary troops (see Napoleon's Tomb Tour on page 216). The esplanade leading up to Les Invalides—possibly the largest patch of accessible grass in Paris—gives soccer balls and Frisbees a rare-in-Paris welcome.

From here, it's a straight shot down the last stretch of the Champs-Elysées. The plane trees (a kind of sycamore with peeling bark that does well in big-city pollution) are reminiscent of the big push Napoleon III made, planting 600,000 trees to green up the city.

- *View the 21-acre place de la Concorde from the obelisk in the center.*

Place de la Concorde

During the Revolution, this was the place de la Révolution. Many of the 2,780 beheaded during the Revolution lost their bodies here during the Reign of Terror. The guillotine sat here. A bronze plaque in the ground in front of the obelisk memorializes the place where Louis XVI, Marie-Antoinette, Georges Danton, Charlotte Corday, and Maximilien de Robespierre, among many others, were made "a foot shorter on top." Three people worked the guillotine: One managed the blade, one held the blood bucket, and one caught the head, raising it high to the roaring crowd.

The 3,300-year-old, 72-foot, 220-ton, red granite, hieroglyph-inscribed obelisk of Luxor now forms the centerpiece of place de la Concorde. It was carted here from Egypt in the 1830s, a gift to the French king. The gold pictures on the pedestal tell the story of its incredible two-year journey: Pulled down from the entrance to Ramses II's Temple of Amon in Luxor; encased in wood; loaded onto a boat built to navigate both shallow rivers and open seas; floated down the Nile, across the Mediterranean, along the Atlantic coast, and up the Seine; and unloaded here, where it was re-erected in 1836. Its glittering gold-leaf cap is a recent addition (1998), replacing the original stolen 2,500 years ago.

The obelisk also forms a center point along a line locals call the "royal perspective." You can hang a lot of history along this straight line (Louvre–obelisk–Arc de Triomphe–Grande Arche de la Défense). The Louvre symbolizes the old regime (divine-right rule by kings and queens). The obelisk and place de la Concorde symbolize the people's revolution (cutting off the king's head). The Arc de Triomphe calls to mind the triumph of nationalism (victorious armies carrying national flags under the arch). And the huge modern arch in the distance, surrounded by the headquarters of multinational corporations, heralds a future in which business entities are more powerful than nations.

Across the river (south) stands the building where the French National Assembly meets (similar to our Congress). On the north side of place de la Concorde is Hôtel Crillon, Paris' most exclusive hotel. It's the left one of two twin buildings that guard the entrance to rue Royale (which leads to the Greek-style church of the Madeleine). This hotel is so fancy that one of its belle-époque rooms is displayed in New York's Metropolitan museum. Eleven years before the king lost his head on this square, Louis XVI met with Benjamin Franklin in this hotel to sign a treaty recognizing the United States as an independent country.

(Today's low-profile, heavily-fortified American Embassy is located next door.) For a memorable splurge, consider high tea at the Crillon (see "Les Grands Cafés de Paris," page 332).

And from the base of the Champs-Elysées, the beautiful Tuileries Garden leads through the iron gates to the Louvre (with a public WC just inside on the right). Pull up a chair next to the pond or find one of the cafés in the gardens.

Nearby

Your guided walk is over. From here you can go: to the closest Métro stop (Concorde), north to a fancy shopping area (near place de la Madeleine; see page 344), into the park toward the Louvre, or across the river toward the Orsay (read on).

If you walk to the river, you'll cross a freeway underpass similar to the one at the pont de l'Alma, three bridges downstream, where Princess Diana lost her life in a 1997 car accident. The pont de la Concorde, built of stones from the Bastille prison (which was demolished by the Revolution in 1789), symbolizes that, with good government, *concorde* (harmony) can come from chaos. Stand mid-bridge and gaze upriver (east). If you use a clock as a compass, the Impressionist art museum L'Orangerie (due to reopen late in 2004) hides behind the trees at 10:00, and the tall building with the skinny chimneys at 11:00 is the architectural caboose of the sprawling Louvre palace. The thin spire of Sainte-Chapelle is dead center at 12:00, with the twin towers of Notre-Dame to its right. The Orsay Museum is closer on the right and connected with the Tuileries Garden by a sleek pedestrian bridge (the next bridge upriver).

MARAIS **WALK**

This walk takes you through one of Paris' most characteristic quarters, the Marais, and finishes in the artsy Beaubourg district. When in Paris, you naturally want to see the big sights, but to experience the city you also need to visit a vital neighborhood.

The Marais, containing more pre-Revolutionary lanes and buildings than anywhere else in town, is more atmospheric than touristy. It's medieval Paris and the haunt of the old nobility. After the aristocrats left, the Marais became a dumpy bohemian quarter so sordid it was nearly slated for destruction. But today, this thriving, trendy, real community is a joy to explore. It looks the way much of the city did until the mid-1800s, when Napoleon III had Baron Haussmann blast out the narrow streets to construct broad boulevards (wide enough for the guns and ranks of the army, too wide for revolutionary barricades), thus creating modern Paris. A big Haussmann-type boulevard was planned to slice efficiently through the Marais, but World War I got in the way.

The Marais walk is about two miles long. Allow two hours, and add another hour for each of these museums you might visit en route: Victor Hugo House, Carnavalet, Picasso, Jewish Art and History, and the Pompidou Center. The Jewish Quarter is quiet on Saturday.

Paris Walks offers guided tours of this area (see page 24).

ORIENTATION

Victor Hugo House: Free, Tue–Sun 10:00–17:40, closed Mon, 6 place des Vosges.

Carnavalet Museum: Free, Tue–Sun 10:00–18:00, closed Mon, 23 rue de Sévigné.

Picasso Museum: €5.50, covered by museum pass, April–Sept Wed–Mon 9:30–18:00, Oct-March Wed-Mon 9:30-17:30, closed Tue, 5 rue de Thorigny.

Marais Walk

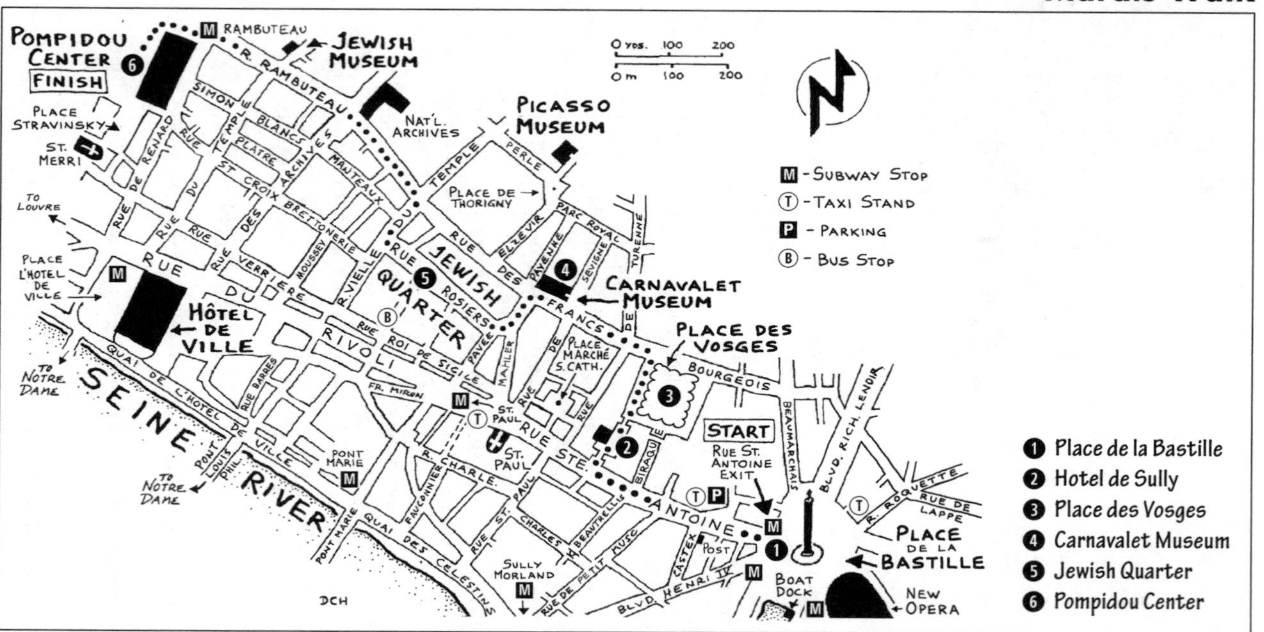
Pompidou Center
Finish
Place Stravinsky
St. Merri
Rambuteau
Jewish Museum
Nat'l. Archives
Picasso Museum
Place de Thorigny
Carnavalet Museum
Place des Vosges
Jewish Quarter
Place Marché S. Cath.
Start
Rue St. Antoine Exit
Place de la Bastille
New Opera
Boat Dock
St. Paul
Sully Morland
Pont Marie
Hôtel de Ville
Place l'Hotel de Ville
To Louvre
To Notre Dame
Seine River
Quai de l'Hotel de Ville
Quai des Celestins
Rue de Rivoli
Beaumarchais
Blvd. Rich. Lenoir
Blvd. Henri IV
0 yds. 100 200
0 m 100 200
M - Subway Stop
T - Taxi Stand
P - Parking
B - Bus Stop
1 Place de la Bastille
2 Hotel de Sully
3 Place des Vosges
4 Carnavalet Museum
5 Jewish Quarter
6 Pompidou Center
DCH

Jewish Art and History Museum: €6.50, ages 18 to 25-€4, under 18 free, not covered by museum pass, Mon–Fri 11:00–18:00, Sun 10:00–18:00, closed Sat, 71 rue du Temple.

Pompidou Center: €5.50, covered by museum pass, Wed–Mon 11:00–21:00, closed Tue.

THE TOUR

• *Start at the west end of place de la Bastille. From the Bastille Métro, exit following signs to rue St. Antoine (not the signs to rue du Faubourg St. Antoine). Ascend onto a noisy square dominated by the bronze Colonne de Juillet (July Column). The bronze god on the top is, like you, headed west.*

1. Place de la Bastille

There are more revolutionary images in the Métro station murals than on the square. While place de la Bastille is famous for its part in the French Revolution of 1789, little from that time remains. The actual Bastille, a royal fortress-turned-prison that once symbolized old-regime tyranny and now symbolizes the Parisian emancipation, is long gone. Only a brick outline of the fortress' round turrets survives (under the traffic where rue St. Antoine hits the square), though the story of the Bastille is indelibly etched into the city's psyche.

For centuries, the Bastille was used to defend the city (mostly from its own people). On July 14, 1789, the people of Paris stormed the prison, releasing its seven prisoners and hoping to find arms. They demolished the stone fortress and decorated their pikes with the heads of a few bigwigs. By shedding blood, the leaders of the gang made sure it would be tough to turn back the tides of revolution. Ever since, the French have celebrated July 14 as their independence day—Bastille Day.

The monument on the square—with its gilded statue of liberty—is a symbol of France's long struggle to establish democracy, commemorating the revolutions of 1830 and 1848. In 1830, the conservative King Charles X—who forgot all about the Revolution of the previous generation—needed to be tossed out. In 1848, a time of social unrest throughout Europe, the streets of Paris were barricaded by the working class, as dramatized in *Les Misérables*. Today, winged Mercury carries the torch of freedom into the future.

The southeast corner of the square is dominated (some say overwhelmed) by the flashy, curved, glassy-gray facade of the controversial **Opéra Bastille**. In a symbolic attempt to bring high culture to the masses, former French President

BASTILLE DAY IN FRANCE

Bastille Day—July 14, the symbolic kickoff date of the French Revolution—became the French national holiday in 1880. Traditionally, Parisians party at place de la Bastille starting at 20:00 on July 13, but the best parties are on the numerous smaller squares where firefighter units sponsor dances. At 10:00 on the morning of the 14th, a grand military parade fills the Champs-Elysées. Then, near midnight on the 14th, there's a fireworks display at the Eiffel Tower. *Vive la France!*

François Mitterrand chose this square for the opera house that would become Paris' main opera venue, edging out Paris' earlier "palace of the rich," the Garnier-designed opera house (see page 39). Designed by the Uruguayan architect Carlos Ott, this grand Parisian project was opened with fanfare by Mitterrand on the 200th Bastille Day, July 14, 1989. While tickets are heavily subsidized to encourage the unwashed masses to attend, how much high culture they have actually enjoyed here is a subject of debate. (For opera ticket information, see page 352.)

You'll now turn your back on this Haussmann-style grandeur and walk down what was—before the Revolution—one of the grandest streets in Paris, rue St. Antoine. In 1350, there was a gate to the city here, Porte St. Antoine, defended by a drawbridge and fortress—a *bastille*.

- *Passing the Banque de France on your right (opposite a fine map of the area on the curb), head west down rue St. Antoine about four blocks into the Marais. At #62 rue St. Antoine, enter the courtyard of Hôtel de Sully (open until 19:00, fine bookstore inside). If the Hôtel is closed, you'll need to backtrack one block to rue de Birague to reach the next stop, place des Vosges.*

2. Hôtel de Sully

During the reign of Henry IV, this area—originally a swamp *(marais)*—became the hometown of the French aristocracy. In the 17th century, big shots built their private mansions *(hôtels)* like this one close to Henry's ritzy place des Vosges. *Hôtels* that survived the Revolution now house museums, libraries, and national institutions.

The first (of two) courtyards is carriage-friendly and elegant, separating the mansion from the noisy and very public street. Walking through the passageway to the back courtyard, notice the skillfully carved and painted ceilings in the bookshop and stairway. The peaceful back courtyard, as was common, has an *orangerie* or greenhouse for homegrown fruits and veggies through the winter—it's behind the

French doors at the far end, now warming office workers. The bit of Gothic window tracery (on the right) is fun for a framed photo of your travel partner as a Madonna.

- *Continue through the small door at the far right corner of the second courtyard and pop out into one of Paris' finest squares.*

3. Place des Vosges

Walk to the center, where Louis XIII on horseback gestures, "Look at this wonderful square my dad built." He's surrounded by locals enjoying their community park. Children frolic in the sandbox, lovers warm benches, and pigeons guard their fountains while trees shade this retreat from the glare of the big city. (Or is it raining?)

Study the architecture: nine pavilions (houses) per side. The two highest—at the front and back—were for the king and queen (but were never used). Warm red brickwork—some real, some fake—is topped with sloped slate roofs, chimneys, and another quaint relic of a bygone era, TV antennas. Beneath the arcades are cafés, art galleries, and restaurants—it's a romantic place for dinner (see p. 313).

Henry IV (r. 1589-1610) built this centerpiece of the Marais in 1605 and called it "place Royal." As hoped, it turned the Marais into Paris' most exclusive neighborhood. Just like Versailles 80 years later, this was a magnet for the rich and powerful of France. With the Revolution, the aristocratic splendor of this quarter passed.

To encourage the country to pay its taxes, Napoleon promised to honor the district that paid first by renaming this square in its honor. The Vosges region (near Germany) paid first, and place Royal became place des Vosges.

In the 19th century, the Marais became a working-class quarter, filled with gritty shops, artisans, immigrants, and Jews. **Victor Hugo** lived at #6 when he wrote *Les Misérables.* You can visit his house (free, Tue–Sun 10:00–17:40, closed Mon, marked by the French flag in the corner closest to the Bastille; see page 43).

- *Exit the square at the northwest corner. (Walk behind Louis XIII's horse, cross the street, and turn left in the arcade.) Follow rue des Francs Bourgeois west two blocks to the…*

4. Carnavalet Museum

Housed inside a Marais mansion, this museum focuses on the history of Paris (closed Mon, 23 rue de Sévigné). Since this is the best possible look at the elegance of the neighborhood back when place des Vosges was place Royal—and the museum is free—it's worthwhile to interrupt this walk and splice in the Carnavalet Tour (page 176).

• *From the Carnavalet, continue west down rue des Francs Bourgeois. Turn left at the post office onto rue Pavée. A funky bookstore at #17 bis rue Pavée has more inside than meets the eye.*

Picasso fans will want to detour to the Picasso Museum (page 191), located two blocks north of here (closed Tue, 5 rue de Thorigny).

From rue Pavée, turn right onto rue des Rosiers (named for the roses that once lined the city wall), which runs straight for three blocks through Paris' Jewish Quarter, lively every day except Saturday.

5. Jewish Quarter

Once considered the largest in Western Europe, Paris' Jewish Quarter grew in three waves. First, with Jews escaping 19th-century Eastern European pogroms (surprise attacks on villages). Next, with Jews fleeing Nazi Germany (before 75 percent of the Jewish population was taken to concentration camps). And, most recently, with Algerian exiles, both Jewish and Muslim—living together peacefully here in Paris.

Today, while rue des Rosiers is lined with colorful Jewish shops and kosher eateries, the district is being squeezed by the trendy boutiques of modern Paris. Notice the old bath, or *hamam*, at #4—while the sign above it says "Hamam," it's now a furniture showroom. At #4-bis, the Ecole de Travail (trade school) has granite blocks on the sidewalk—an attempt to keep out any terrorists' cars. The plaque on the wall remembers the headmaster, staff, and students arrested and killed in Auschwitz in 1943 and 1944.

Jo Goldenberg's delicatessen/restaurant (first corner on left, #7 rue des Rosiers) serves typical—but not kosher—Eastern European Jewish cuisine. A plaque on the wall reminds locals of the 1982 terrorist bombing here that left six people dead. The nearby rue des Ecouffes (named for a bird of prey) is a derogatory reminder of the moneychangers' shops that once lined this lane.

This is a fine place for a lunch break. You'll be tempted by kosher pizza and plenty of €4-falafel-to-go joints (*emporter* = to go). The best falafels are at L'As ("The Ace") du Falafel, with a bustling New York deli atmosphere (at #34, sit-down or to go). The Sacha Finkelsztajn Yiddish bakery (at #27) is also good. Vegetarians appreciate the excellent cuisine at the popular Piccolo Teatro (closed Mon, near rue des Rosiers, 6 rue des Ecouffes, tel. 01 42 72 17 79).

• *Rue des Rosiers dead-ends into rue Vieille-du-Temple (where the Jewish Quarter's main drag meets Paris' gay district—generally to the left and along nearby rue Ste. Croix de la Bretonnerie). Turn right.*

Frank Bourgeois is waiting for you at the corner postcard/print shop.

Turn left on rue des Francs Bourgeois, which leads past the national archives (peek inside the courtyard) and turns into rue Rambuteau.

At #3 rue Rambuteau, check out the neighborhood's real estate prices in the window of the Immobilier. 300,000 euros for a one-bedroom flat?!

Continue on rue Rambuteau to rue du Temple. A half-block to the right is the Jewish Art and History Museum (closed Sat, 71 rue du Temple, see page 42). A block to the left is The Studio, a café wonderfully located in the 17th-century courtyard of a dance school. You can sip a café crème—or have a Tex-Mex meal—surrounded by ballet, tap-dance, and tango (daily, tasty salads, €12 plats du jour, 41 rue de Temple, tel. 01 42 74 10 38).

Continuing west on rue Rambuteau, the pipes and glass of the Pompidou Center mark your exit from the Marais and reintroduce you to the 21st century. Circle around the right side of that huge building to join the fray at the front entrance.

6. Pompidou Center

Survey this popular spot from the top of the sloping square. Tubular escalators lead up to a great view and the modern art museum (closed Tue, to use escalator must pay €5.50 for museum or show museum pass). ✪ See Pompidou Center Tour on page 163.

The Pompidou Center subscribes with gusto to the 20th-century architectural axiom, "form follows function." To get a more spacious and functional interior, the guts of this exoskeletal building are draped on the outside and color-coded: vibrant red for people lifts, cool blue for air ducts, eco-green for plumbing, don't-touch-it yellow for electrical stuff, and white for

bones. (Compare the Pompidou Center to another exoskeletal building, Notre-Dame.) Enjoy the adjacent *Homage to Stravinsky* fountains. Jean Tinguely and Niki de Saint-Phalle designed these as a tribute to the composer: Every fountain represents one of his hard-to-hum scores. For low-stress meals, try Le Mélodine, a self-service cafeteria at the Rambuteau Métro stop, or the fun Dame Tartine, which overlooks the *Homage to Stravinsky* fountains and serves a young clientele good, inexpensive meals.

- *With your back to the Pompidou Center's entrance, walk west along the cobbled pedestrian mall, crossing the busy boulevard de Sébastopol to the*

ivy-covered pavilions of Les Halles. Paris' down-and-dirty central produce market of 800 years was replaced by a glitzy but soulless shopping center in the late 1970s. The mall's most endearing layer is its grassy rooftop park. (The Gothic St. Eustache church overlooking this contemporary scene has a famous 8,000-pipe organ.)

For a more soulful shopping experience (similar to rue Cler), find your way behind St. Eustache church and cross rue Montmartre onto the delightfully traffic-free rue Montorgueil.

RUE CLER **WALK**

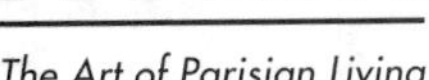

The Art of Parisian Living

Paris is changing quickly, but a stroll down this street puts you into a thriving, traditional Parisian neighborhood and provides a helpful orientation to the local culture.

Shopping for groceries is an integral part of daily life here. Parisians shop almost daily for three good reasons: Refrigerators are small (tiny kitchens), produce must be fresh, and it's an important social event. Shopping is a chance to hear about the butcher's vacation plans, see photos of the florist's new grandchild, relax over *un café,* and kiss the cheeks of friends (the French standard is twice for regular acquaintances, three times for friends you haven't seen in a while).

Rue Cler—traffic-free since 1984—offers plenty of space for tiny stores and their patrons to spill into the street. It's an ideal environment for this ritual to survive and for you to explore. The street is lined with all the necessary shops—wine, cheese, chocolate, bread—as well as a bank and a post office. And the shops of this community are run by people who've found their niche: boys who grew up on quiche, girls who know a good wine. If you see anyone in uniform, they're likely from the Ecole Militaire (military school, Napoleon's alma mater, two blocks away).

If you wish to learn the fine art of living Parisian-style, rue Cler provides an excellent classroom. And if you want to assemble the ultimate French picnic, there's no better place. The Rue Cler Walk is the only tour in this guidebook you should start while hungry.

Visit rue Cler when its market is open and lively (Tue–Sat 8:30–13:00 or 17:00–19:00, Sun 8:30–12:00, dead on Mon). Remember that these shops are busy serving regular customers. Be polite (say *Bonjour, Madame/Monsieur* as you enter and *Au revoir, Madame/Monsieur* when you leave) and be careful not to get in the way. Start your walk where the pedestrian section of rue Cler does, at rue de Grenelle (Mo: Ecole Militaire or bus #69 stop).

Rue Cler Walk

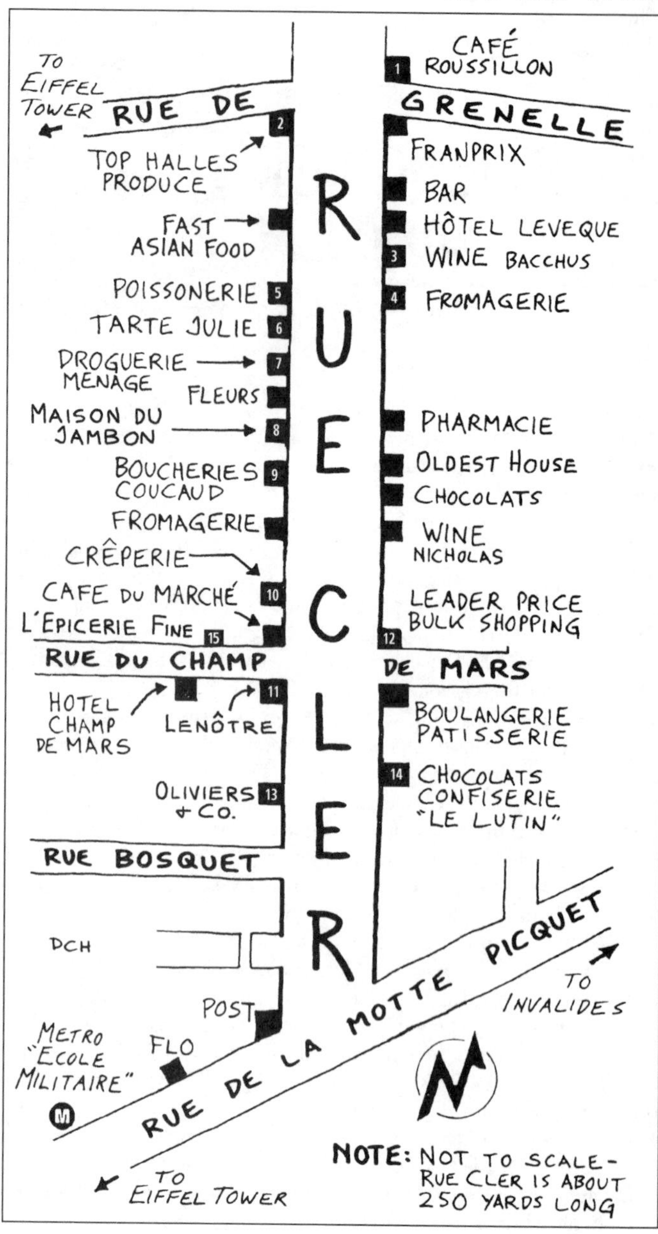

1. Café Roussillon

This place, a neighborhood fixture, recently dumped its old-fashioned, characteristic look for the latest café style—warm, natural wood tones, easy lighting, and music. The *tickets restaurant* and *chèque déjeuner* decals on the door advertise that this café accepts lunch "checks." In France, an employee lunch subsidy program is an expected perk. Employers issue a voucher check (worth about €5) for each day an employee works in a month. Sack lunches are rare, since a good lunch is sacred.

Inside, drinks at the always-active bar *(comptoir)* are about half the price of drinks at the tables. The blackboard lists wines sold by the little (7-centiliter) glass.

• *Kitty-corner from the café, find...*

2. Top Halles Fruits and Vegetables

Each morning, fresh produce is trucked in from farmers' fields to Paris' huge Rungis market—Europe's largest, near Orly Airport—and then dispatched to merchants with FedEx speed and precision. Locals generally shop with a trolley rather than use bags needlessly. Notice how the French resist excessive packaging and buy what's in season.

Parisians shop with their noses. Try it. Smell the cheap foreign strawberries. Then smell the torpedo-shaped French ones *(garriguettes)*. Find the herbs in the back. Is today's delivery in? Look at the price of those melons. What's the country of origin? It must be posted. If they're out of season, they come from Guadeloupe. Many people buy only local products.

The Franprix across the street is a small Safeway-type store. Opposite the Grand Hôtel Lévêque is Asie Traiteur. Fast Asian food to go is popular in Paris. These shops—about as common as bakeries now—are making an impact on Parisian eating habits.

• *Just past the Grand Hôtel Lévêque is...*

3. Wine Bacchus

Shoppers often visit the neighborhood wine shop last, once they've assembled their meal and are able to pick the appropriate wine. The wine is classified by region. Most "Parisians" have an affinity to their home region that affects their choice of wine. Notice the great prices. Wines of the month—in the center—sell for about €5. You can get a fine bottle for €10. The clerk is a counselor who works with your needs and budget. Notice the beer. Since this is a quality shop, there's nothing French—only Belgian specialty beers.

• *Next door, smell the...*

4. Fromagerie

A long, narrow, canopied cheese table brings the *fromagerie* into the street. Wedges, cylinders, balls, and miniature hockey pucks are all powdered white, gray, and burnt marshmallow—it's a festival of mold. Much of the street cart is devoted only to the goat cheeses. *Ooh la la* means you're impressed. If you like cheese, show greater excitement with more *las*. *Ooh la la la la*. My local friend once held the stinkiest glob close to her nose, took an orgasmic breath, and exhaled, "Yes, it smells like zee feet of angels." Try it.

Step inside and browse through some of the 400 types of French cheese. A cheese shop—known as "BOF" for *beurre, œuf,* and *fromage*—is where people go for butter, eggs, and cheese. In the back room are *les meules,* the big, 170-pound wheels of cheese (250 gallons of milk go into each wheel). The "hard" cheeses are cut from these. Don't eat the skin of these big ones … they roll them on the floor. But the skin on most smaller cheeses—the Brie, the Camembert—is part of the taste. "It completes the package," says my local friend.

At dinner tonight, you can take the cheese course just before or instead of dessert. On a good cheese plate, you have a hard cheese (like Emmentaler—a.k.a. "Swiss cheese"), a flowery cheese (maybe Brie or Camembert), a blue cheese, and a goat cheese—ideally from different regions. Because it's strongest, the goat cheese is usually eaten last.

- *Across the street, find the fish shop, known as the …*

5. Poissonnerie

Fresh fish is brought into Paris daily from ports on the English Channel, 110 miles away. In fact, fish here is likely fresher than in many towns closer to the sea because Paris is a commerce hub (from here, it's shipped to outlying towns). Anything wiggling? This place, like all such shops, has been recently upgraded to meet the new Europe-wide hygiene standards.

- *Next door is a particularly tempting storefront on rue Cler.*

6. No More Horse Meat

Now the place sells Greek food, but the restaurant's classy old storefront is a work of art that survives from the previous occupant. The inset stones and glass advertise horse meat: *Boucherie Chevaline.* The decorated front, from the 1930s and signed by the artist, would fit in a museum. But it belongs right here. And everyone knows you'll find Greek food here, not horse meat.

• *Next door is...*

7. Droguerie Ménage and More

At this French knickknack store, which sells everything but drugs, you can buy corkscrews, brooms, knives, and so on.

Wander on past the flower shop and pharmacy. (In France, the pharmacist makes the first diagnosis and prescription—if it's out of his league, he'll recommend a doctor.) Next to the pharmacy, notice the oldest and shortest building. It's from the early 1800s, when this street was part of a village near Paris and lined with buildings like this. Of course, over the years Paris engulfed these surrounding villages—and the street is a mishmash of architectural styles.

• *Across the street from this oldest house is...*

8. La Maison du Jambon

A *charcuterie* sells mouthwatering deli food to go. Because kitchens are so small, these gourmet delis are handy, allowing hosts to concentrate on the main course and buy beautifully prepared side dishes to complete a fine dinner. Notice the system: Order, take your ticket to the cashier to pay, and return with the receipt to pick up your food.

• *Next door is...*

9. Boucheries Coucaud

Sort through pigeons, quail, and rabbit. Look for things you may want to avoid in restaurants: *rognons* (kidneys), *foie* (liver), and *cœur de boeuf* (heart of beef). Hoist a duck and check the feet; they should be rough and calloused—an indication that they weren't stuck in an industrial kennel but ran wild on a farm. While Americans prefer beef, pork, and chicken, the French eat just as much rabbit *(lapin)*, quail *(caille)*, lamb *(agneau)*, and duck *(canard)*. The head of a calf is a delight for its many tasty bits. Horse, which came from Eastern Europe and was of questionable quality, has gone out of fashion only in the last decade. The meat is seasonal. In the winter, game swings from the ceiling.

• *Almost next door, you'll find the smallest business on rue Cler, the...*

10. Crêperie and More

Savory crêpes, called *galettes*, are made with buckwheat flour and come with ingredients we'd put in an omelette (cheese, ham, mushrooms, and so on). Request yours with "no salt" (*pas de sel*, pah duh sehl), as the ingredients are already salty enough. Dessert crêpes are made of wheat flour and come with everything you might enjoy on your ice-cream sundae.

The Café du Marché, on the corner, is *the* place to sit and enjoy the rue Cler action. For a reasonable meal, grab a chair and check the chalk menu listing the *plat du jour* (special of the day).

The shiny, sterile Leader Price grocery store (across the street) is a French Costco, selling bulk items. Because storage space is so limited in most Parisian apartments, bulk purchases are unlikely to become a big deal here. The latest trend for Parisians is to stock up on non-perishables by shopping online, pick up produce three times a week, and buy fresh bread daily.

- *From Café du Marché, cross rue de Champs du Mars to the store on the corner.*

11. Lenôtre

This specialty store is famous among locals as *the* deluxe place to buy a gift when invited to someone's home for dinner. When you're a French dinner guest, it's polite to bring some small gift: flowers, chocolates, wine, or an extra dessert. Parisians enjoy consuming very elegant treats from an over-the-top place like this. While expensive, a little delight from this place would send your host into orbit. Notice the proud little edible nametags.

- *Across rue Cler is a...*

12. Boulangerie

Since the French Revolution, the government has regulated the cost of a basic baguette. The *Prix du Pain* sign in the window tells you the going rate. Locals debate the merits of Paris' many *boulangeries.* It's said that a baker cannot be both good at bread and good at pastry. At cooking school, they major in one or the other, and locals say that when you do good bread, you have no time to do good pastry. Here, the baker does good bread. He has a man who does the tasty little pastries for him.

- *A bit farther along and across the street is...*

13. Oliviers & Co. Olive Oils

This shop, typical of an upscale neighborhood like this, sells fine gourmet goodies from the South of France and olive oil from around the Mediterranean. They are happy to give visitors a taste test—with tiny spoons—of three distinct oils.

- *Across the street, you'll find...*

14. Le Mére de Famille Gourmand Chocolats Confiseries

Corinne took over this shop from a woman who kept this neighborhood in fine chocolates for 30 years. The wholesalers want her to take the new products, but she keeps the old traditional candies, too. "The old ladies, they want the same sweets that made them so happy 80 years ago," Corinne says.

She dips and decorates her chocolates in the back, where the merchants used to live. As was the tradition in rue Cler shops, the merchants lived and produced in the back and sold in the front. This stop is best enjoyed from outside; formal Corinne can be brief with tourists.

- *For the perfect finale for this walk, backtrack a half-block to Cafe du Marché, turn left on rue de Champs du Mars, and within a few steps, find...*

15. L'Epicerie Fine

This fine foods boutique stands out from the rest because of its gentle owner, Pascal. His mission in life is to explain to travelers in fluent English what the French fuss over food is all about. Say *bonjour* to Pascal and let him tempt you with fine gourmet treats and generous tastes.

- *Rue Cler ends at the post office. The Ecole Militaire Métro stop is just around the corner. If you bought a picnic along this walk, you'll find benches and gardens nearby: from the post office, avenue de la Motte-Picquet leads to two fine parks—turn left for Les Invalides or right for the Eiffel Tower.*

MONTMARTRE **WALK**

Stroll along the hilltop of butte Montmartre amid traces of the people who've lived here—monks stomping grapes (1200s), farmers grinding grain in windmills (1600s), dust-coated gypsum miners (1700s), Parisian liberals (1800s), modernist painters (1900s), and all the struggling artists, poets, dreamers, and drunkards who came here for cheap rent, untaxed booze, rustic landscapes, and cabaret nightlife.

While many tourists make the almost obligatory trek to the top of Paris' butte Montmartre, eat an overpriced crêpe, and marvel at the view, most miss out on the neighborhood's charm and history—both uncovered in this stroll. Allow about two hours for this two-mile walk.

We'll start at the radiant Sacré-Cœur basilica, wander through the hilltop village, browse affordable art, ogle the Moulin Rouge nightclub, and catch echoes of those who once partied to a bohemian rhapsody during the belle époque.

ORIENTATION

Basilica of Sacré-Cœur: Free, daily 7:00-23:00; dome-€5, June–Sept daily 9:00–19:00, Oct–May daily 10:00–18:00.

Dalí Museum (L'Espace Dalí): €7, Sept-June daily 10:00–18:30, July–Aug daily 10:00-21:30.

Montmartre Museum: €4.50, not covered by museum pass, Tue–Sun 11:00–18:00, closed Mon.

When to Go: To avoid the crowds (worst on sunny weekends), arrive at Sacré-Cœur by 9:30. If crowds don't get you down, come for the sunset and stay for dinner (see Eating, page 313). This walk is best under clear skies when views are sensational.

Getting There: Start at Sacré-Cœur church, atop the hill. Closest Métro stops are Anvers, Abbesses, and Pigalle. There are several

Montmartre Walk

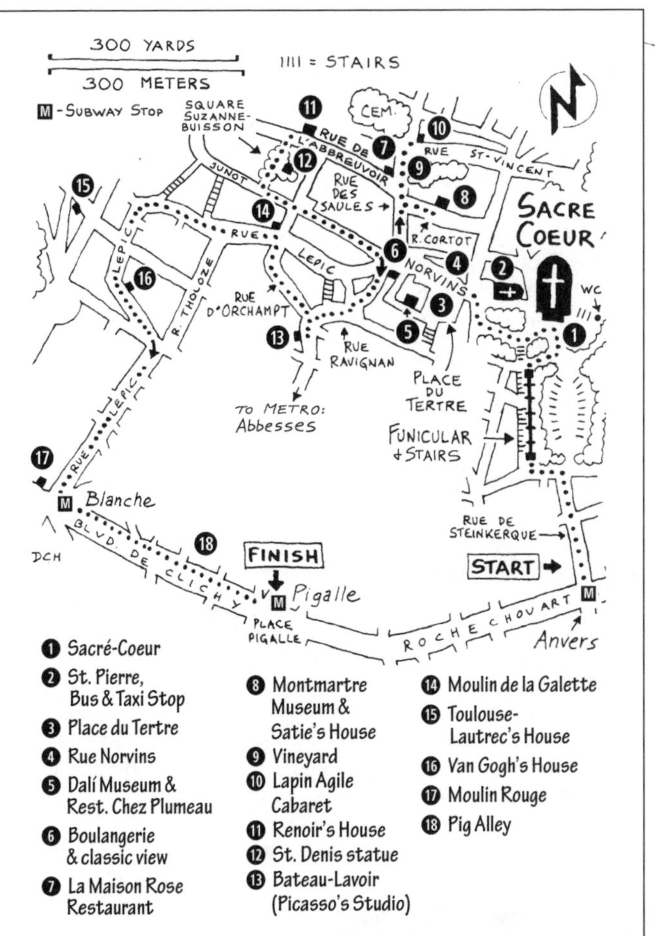

ways to avoid the climb up the hill. From near the Anvers stop, take the funicular (described below). The "Montmartrobus" (costs one Métro ticket, 4/hr) departs place Pigalle, dropping you right by place du Tertre. "Le Petit Train de Montmartre," a tourist tram with commentary, runs a circular route: place Pigalle to place du Tertre to Sacré-Cœur to place Blanche. Or catch a taxi (about €10 from the Seine River or Bastille to Sacré-Cœur).

Starring: Cityscape views, Sacré-Cœur, postcard scenes brought to life, and boring buildings where interesting people once lived.

THE TOUR BEGINS

To reach Sacré-Cœur by Métro, get off at Anvers. The peeling and neglected Elysées Montmartre theater across the street is the oldest cancan dance hall in Paris, and the famous Chat Noir (Black Cat) Cabaret was at #84. Today, the Elysées Montmartre is a rowdy dance club and concert hall, signaling this area's transition. Historically, people have moved to this neighborhood for cheap rent. While it still feels neglected, urban gentrification is underway as young professionals restore dilapidated apartments, hotels renovate for a more upscale clientele, and rents increase.

Walk two blocks up rue de Steinkerque (the street to the right of Elysées Montmartre), through a bizarre, low-rent urban bazaar, past cheap clothing and souvenir shops (pick up inexpensive postcards and €2 blue jeans) to the grassy park way below the white Sacré-Cœur church. The terraced hillside was once dotted with openings to gypsum mines, the source of the white "plaster of Paris" that plastered Paris' buildings for centuries.

- *Hike up to the church or ride the funicular (costs one Métro ticket, to the left, past the merry-go-round). The best view is just below the top flight of stairs.*

1. Sacré-Cœur Basilica and View

From Paris' highest point (420 feet), the City of Light fans out at your feet. Pan from left to right. The big triangular roof on your left is the Gare du Nord train station. The blue-and-red Pompidou Center is straight ahead, and the skyscrapers in the distance beyond define the southern limit of central Paris. Next is the domed Panthéon, atop Paris' other (and far smaller) butte. Then comes the modern Montparnasse Tower, and finally (if you're in position to see this far to the right), the golden dome of Les Invalides. Now face the church.

The Sacré-Cœur (Sacred Heart) **basilica,** with its onion domes and bleached-bone pallor, looks ancient but was built only a century ago by Parisians humiliated by German invaders. Otto von Bismarck's Prussian army laid siege to Paris for more than four months in 1870. Things got so bad for residents that urban hunting for dinner (to cook up dogs, cats, and finally rats) became accepted behavior. Convinced they were being punished for the country's liberal sins, France's Catholics raised money to build the church as a "praise the Lord anyway" gesture.

The five-domed, Roman-Byzantine basilica took 44 years to

build (1875-1919). It stands on a foundation of 83 pillars sunk 130 feet deep, necessary because the ground beneath was honeycombed with gypsum mines. The exterior is laced with gypsum, which whitens with age.

Interior: In the impressive mosaic high above the altar, Christ exposes his sacred heart, burning with love and compassion for humanity. He's adored by angels, popes, and gentlemen in business suits who pledge they will build a church (seen in the background). Right now, in this church, at least one person is praying for Christ to be understanding of the world's sins—part of a tradition that's been carried out here, day and night, 24/7, since Sacré-Cœur's completion.

• *Circle the church counterclockwise, starting at the first pillar to the left (as you face the altar), across from the statue of Mary.*

A small plaque shows where the 13 WWII bombs that hit Paris fell—all in a line, all near the church—killing no one. This fueled local devotion to the Sacred Heart and to this church.

Walking clockwise around the ambulatory, find a scale model of the church. Continuing behind the altar, notice the colorful mosaics of the Stations of the Cross. Between stations VII and VIII, rub St. Peter's bronze foot and look up to the heavens.

Continue your circuit around the church. Back near the entrance are stained glass windows dedicated to Joan of Arc (*Jeanne d'Arc*, 1412-1431) See the teenage girl as she hears the voices of two saints (*Jeanne entend ses voix*) and takes up the sword of the Archangel Michael. Next, she kneels to take communion, then kneels before the bishop (*Je suis envoie par Dieu...*) to tell him she's been sent by God to rally France's soldiers and save Orleans from English invaders. However, she's burned at the stake as a heretic (*Jeanne sur le bûcher*), dying with her eyes fixed on a crucifix and chanting, "Jesus, Jesus, Jesus..."

• *Exit the church. Once outside, a public WC is to your left, down 50 steps. To your right is the entrance to the church's...*

Dome and Crypt: For an unobstructed panoramic view of Paris, climb 260 feet up the tight and claustrophobic spiral stairs to the top of the **dome** (€5, June–Sept daily 9:00–19:00, Oct–May daily 10:00–18:00, especially worthwhile if you have kids with excess energy). The crypt is just a big empty basement.

• *Leaving the church, turn right and walk west along the ridge, following tree-lined rue Azaïs. At rue St. Eleuthère, turn right and walk uphill a block to the Church of St. Pierre-de-Montmartre (at top on right).*

The small square in front of the church is a convenient taxi stand and bus stop for the Monmartrobus to and from place Pigalle (costs one Métro ticket).

2. Church of St. Pierre-de-Montmartre

This church was the center of Montmartre's first claim to fame, a sprawling abbey of Benedictine monks and nuns. The church is one of

Paris' oldest (1147)—some say Dante prayed here—founded by King Louis VI and his wife, Adelaide. Find Adelaide's tombstone (*pierre tombale*) midway down on the left wall. Older still are the four gray columns inside that may have stood in a temple of Mercury or Mars in Roman times (two flank the entrance and two are behind the altar). The name "Montmartre" comes from the Roman "Mount of Mars," though later generations, thinking of their beheaded patron St. Denis, preferred a less pagan version, "Mount of Martyrs."

Along the right wall, rub St. Peter's toe (again), look up, and ask for *délivrance* from the tourist mobs outside. Now step back outside where a sign for the Café and Cabaret la Bohème reminds visitors that this was once the world capital of bohemian life in the late 19th and early 20th centuries. The artist-filled place du Tertre awaits.

3. Place du Tertre— Bohemian Montmartre

Lined with cafés, shaded by acacia trees, and filled with artists, hucksters, and tourists, the scene mixes charm and kitsch in ever-changing proportions. The place du Tertre has been the town square of the small village of Montmartre since medieval times.

In 1800, a wall separated Paris from this hilltop village. To enter Paris, you had to pass tollbooths that taxed anything for sale. Montmartre was a mining community where the wine flowed cheap (tax-free) and easy. Life here was a working-class festival of cafés, bistros, and dance halls. Painters came here for the ruddy charm, the light, and the low rents. In 1860, Montmartre was annexed into the growing city of Paris. The "bohemian" ambience survived, and it attracted sophisticated Parisians ready to get down and dirty in the belle époque of cancan. The Restaurant Mer Catherine is often called the first bistro, since this is where Russian soldiers first coined the word by saying, "I'm thirsty, bring my drink *bistro*!" (meaning "right away").

The square's artists, who at times outnumber the tourists, are the great-great-grandkids of the Renoirs, van Goghs, and Picassos who once roamed here—poor, carefree, seeking inspiration, and occasionally cursing a world too selfish to bankroll their dreams.

- *The tourist office (Syndicat d'Initiative, daily 10:00–19:00) across the square sells good maps and a so-so audioguide tour. Just south of the square is quiet, tiny place du Calvaire, with the recommended café Chez Plumeau. But for now, continue west along the main drag, called...*

MAURICE UTRILLO
(1883-1955)

Born to a free-spirited single mom and raised by his grandmother, Utrillo had his first detox treatment at age 18. Encouraged by his mother and doctors, he started painting as occupational therapy. That, plus guidance from his mother (and later, from his wife), allowed him to live productively into his seventies, becoming wealthy and famous, despite occasional relapses into drink and mental problems.

Utrillo grew up in Montmartre's streets. He fought, broke street lamps, and haunted the cafés and bars, buying drinks with masterpieces. A very free spirit, he's said to have exposed himself to strangers on the street, yelling, "I paint with this!"

His simple scenes of streets, squares, and cafés in a vaguely Impressionist style became popular with commoners and scholars alike. He honed his style during his "white period" (c. 1909-1914), painting a thick paste of predominantly white tints. In later years, after he moved out of Montmartre, he still painted the world he knew in his youth, using postcards and photographs as models.

Utrillo's mom, Suzanne Valadon, was a former trapeze performer and artist's model who posed for Toulouse-Lautrec, slept with Renoir, studied under Degas, and went on to become a notable painter in her own right. Her partner, a Spanish artist named André Utter, gave Maurice his family name (Utrillo = little Utter).

4. Rue Norvins

Montmartre's oldest and main street is still the primary commercial artery, serving the current trade—tourism.

- *If you're a devotee of Dalí, take a detour left on rue Poulbot, leading to the...*

5. Dalí Museum (L'Espace Dalí)

This beautifully lit black gallery offers a walk through statues, etchings, and paintings by the master of surrealism. Don't miss the printed interview on the exit stairs (€7, Sept-Jun daily 10:00–18:30, July–Aug daily 10:00-21:30, well-described in English, 11 rue Poulbot).

- *Return to rue Norvins and continue west a dozen steps to the intersection with rue des Saules, where you'll find a...*

6. Boulangerie and View

The venerable *boulangerie* (bakery) on the left, dating from 1900, is one of the last surviving bits of the old-time community, made famous in a painting by the artist Maurice Utrillo (see sidebar).

From the *boulangerie*, look back up rue Norvins, then backpedal a few steps to catch the classic view of the dome of Sacré-Cœur rising above the rooftops. The doorway of the nearby Auberge de la Bonne Franquet offers another famous dome view.

- *Let's leave the tourists. Follow rue des Saules downhill (north) onto the backside of Montmartre. A block downhill is...*

7. La Maison Rose Restaurant

The restaurant, made famous by an Utrillo painting, and once frequented by Utrillo, Pablo Picasso, and Gertrude Stein, is one of the few places that actually serves wine grown in the Montmartre vineyards across the street.

- *Turn right on rue Cortot and go half a block past vine-covered homes to the...*

8. Montmartre Museum and Satie's House

In what is now the museum (at 12 rue Cortot), Pierre-Auguste Renoir once lived while painting his best-known work, *Bal du Moulin de la Galette.* Every day, he'd lug the 4' x 6' canvas from here to the other side of the butte to paint (in *plein aire*) the famous windmill ballroom, which we'll see later.

A few years later, Utrillo lived and painted here with his mom, Suzanne Valadon. In 1893, she carried on a torrid six-month relationship with the lonely, eccentric man who lived next door at #6—composer Erik Satie ("Trois Gymnopedies"), who was eking out a living playing piano in Montmartre nightclubs. Also nearby, at 13 rue du Mont-Cenis (uphill and to the right), is the former Cabaret de Patachou (now a pleasant art gallery) where singer Edith Piaf (1915-1963) once trilled "La Vie en Rose."

The Montmartre Museum fills several floors in this creaky 17th-century manor house with paintings, posters, old photos, music, and memorabilia recreating the traditional cancan and cabaret Montmartre scene. Highlights are several original Toulouse-Lautrec posters for the Moulin Rouge, a few paintings by Valadon and Utrillo, the original Lapin Agile sign, and displays (mostly in French) on Montmartre's history, from gypsum mining to the Paris Commune to the Chat Noir Cabaret (€4.50, not covered by museum pass, Tue–Sun 11:00–18:00, closed Mon, some English descriptions).

- *Return to the rue des Saules and walk downhill past the Maison Rose restaurant one block to Paris' last remaining vineyard.*

9. Clos Montmartre Vineyard

What originally drew artists to Montmartre was country charm like this. Ever since the 12th century, the monks and nuns of the large abbey produced wine here. With vineyards, wheat fields, windmills, animals, and a village tempo of life, it was the perfect escape from grimy Paris. In 1576, puritanical laws taxed wine in Paris, bringing budget-minded drinkers to Montmartre. Today's vineyard is off-limits to tourists except during the annual grape-harvest fest (first Sat in Oct), when a thousand costumed locals bring back the boisterous old days and the vineyard's annual production of 300 liters is auctioned off to support local charities.

- *Continue downhill to the intersection with rue St. Vincent.*

10. Lapin Agile Cabaret

The faded poster above the door gives the place its name. A rabbit *(lapin)* makes an agile leap out of the pot while balancing the bottle of wine that he can now drink—rather than be cooked in. This was the village's hot spot. Picasso and other artists and writers (Renoir, Utrillo, Paul Verlaine, Aristide Bruant, Amedeo Modigliani, etc.) would gather for "performances" that ranged from serious poetry, dirty limericks, sing-alongs, and parodies of the famous to anarchist manifestos. Once, to play a practical joke on the avant-garde art community, patrons tied a paintbrush to the tail of the owner's donkey and entered the "abstract painting" that resulted in the Salon. Called *Sunset over the Adriatic,* it won critical acclaim and sold for a nice price.

- *Before heading back uphill to the boulangerie on rue Norvins, some may wish to make a detour (an extra 15 min) to a more residential part of Montmartre. If you're pooped, we'll meet you back up rue des Saules at the boulangerie.*

11. & 12. Detour to Renoir's House and St. Denis Statue

- *Walk up rue des Saules and turn right at La Maison Rose, heading west one block on rue de l'Abreuvoir. At the busty bust of the comic singer Dalida (1933–87, who popularized disco in France), continue straight (west) along the small walkway called allée des Brouillards. You'll pass another of Renoir's homes (at #6). Walk down the steps at the walkway's end, then stroll up through the small, fenced, multi-level park called square Suzanne Buisson.*

In the park, find the stone statue of headless St. Denis. The early Christian bishop was sentenced to death by the Romans for spreading Christianity. As they marched him up to the top of Montmartre to be executed, the Roman soldiers got tired, and just beheaded him near here. But Denis popped right up, picked up his head, and carried on another three miles north before he finally died. The statue of Denis cradles his head in his hands, looks over a regulation-size *boules* court... and gets ready to play ball.

- *At the top of the park, turn left onto avenue Junot, which turns into rue Norvins. (Don't you wish you could just walk right through these darn hills? You'll pass a statue that looks like it could do it.) The boulangerie is at the top of rue Norvins.*

  Once reunited at the boulangerie, we all go downhill (south)—not on car-filled rue Lepic—but down the pedestrian-only place J.B. Clement, hugging the buildings on our left. Turn right on rue Ravignan and follow it down to the "TIM Hôtel." Next door, at 13 place Emile Goudeau, is the...

13. Le Bateau-Lavoir, Picasso's Studio

A humble green facade marks the place where modern art was born. Here, in a lowly artists' abode (destroyed by fire in 1970, rebuilt a few years later), as many as 10 artists lived and worked. This former piano factory, converted to cheap housing, was nicknamed the "Laundry Boat" for its sprawling layout and crude facilities (sharing one water tap). It was "a weird, squalid place," wrote one resident, "filled with every kind of noise: arguing, singing, bedpans clattering, slamming doors, and suggestive moans coming from studio doors."

In 1904, a poor, unknown Spanish émigré named Pablo Picasso (1881-1973) moved in. He met dark-haired Fernande Olivier, his first real girlfriend, in the square outside. She soon moved in, lifting him out of his melancholy Blue Period into the rosy Rose Period. *La belle Fernande* posed nude for him, inspiring a freer treatment of the female form.

In 1907, Picasso started on a major canvas. For nine months, he produced hundreds of preparatory sketches, working long into the night. When he unveiled the work, even his friends were shocked. *Les Demoiselles d'Avignon* showed five nude women in a brothel (Fernande claimed they were all her), with primitive mask-like faces and fragmented bodies. Picasso had invented Cubism.

For the next two years, he and his neighbors Georges Braque and Juan Gris revolutionized the art world. Sharing paints, ideas, and girlfriends, they made Montmartre "The Cubist Acropolis," attracting free-thinking "Moderns" from all over the world to visit their studios—the artists Modigliani and Henri Rousseau, the poet Guillaume Apollinaire, and American expatriate writer, Gertrude Stein. By the time Picasso moved to better quarters (and dumped Fernande), he was famous. Still, Picasso would later say, "I know one day we'll return to Bateau-Lavoir. It was there that we were really happy—where they thought of us as painters, not strange animals."

- *Backtrack a half-block uphill and turn left on rue d'Orchampt. Squirt out the other end at the intersection with rue Lepic, where you're face-to-face with a wooden windmill.*

14. Moulin de la Galette

Only two windmills *(moulins)* remain on a hill that was once dotted with 30 of them. Originally, they pressed monks' grapes and farmers' grain, and crushed gypsum rocks into powdery plaster of Paris. When the gypsum mines closed (c. 1850) and the vineyards sprouted apartments, this windmill turned into the ceremonial centerpiece of a popular outdoor dance hall. Renoir's *Bal du Moulin de la Galette* (in the Orsay) shows it in its heyday—a sunny Sunday afternoon in the acacia-shaded gardens, with working-class people dancing, laughing, drinking, and eating the house crêpes, called *galettes*. Some call Renoir's version the quintessential Impressionist work and the painting that best captures—on a large canvas in bright colors—the joy of the Montmartre lifestyle.

- *Follow rue Lepic as it winds down the hill. The green-latticed building on the right side was also part of the Moulin de la Galette. Rounding the bend, look to the right down rue Tourlaque. The building one block down rue Tourlaque was...*

15. Henri de Toulouse-Lautrec's House

Find the building on the southwest corner with the tall, brick-framed art studio windows under the heavy mansard roof. Every night, Toulouse-Lautrec (1864-1901)—a nobleman turned painter, whose legs were deformed in a horse-riding accident during his teenage years—would dress up here and then journey down rue Lepic to the Moulin Rouge. One of Henri's occasional drinking buddies and fellow artist lived nearby.

- *Continue down rue Lepic and, at #54, find...*

16. Vincent van Gogh's House

Vincent van Gogh lived here with his brother, enjoying a grand city view from his top-floor window from 1886 to 1888. In those two short years, van Gogh transformed from a gloomy Dutch painter of brown and gray peasant scenes into an inspired visionary with wild ideas and Impressionist colors.

- *Follow the rue Lepic downhill as it makes a hard right at #36 and continue to place Blanche; check out the horse butcher at #30 as you descend. Notice the happy horses on the price stickers. This market street leg of the rue Lepic (lively only in the morning) has an energy like it did in the days when van Gogh lived here. Enjoy that notion for the delightful last stretch of rue Lepic before it hits the big street and a big change. On busy place Blanche is the...*

17. Moulin Rouge

Ooh la la. The new Eiffel Tower at the 1889 World's Fair was nothing compared to the sight of pretty cancan girls kicking their legs at the newly opened "Red Windmill." The nightclub seemed to sum up the belle époque—the age of elegance, opulence, sophistication, and worldliness. The big draw was amateur night of working-class girls in risqué dresses dancing "Le Quadrille" (dubbed cancan by a Brit). Wealthy Parisians slummed it by going there.

On most nights, you'd see a small man in a sleek black coat, checked pants, a green scarf, and a bowler hat peering through his pince-nez glasses at the dancers and making sketches of them—Henri de Toulouse-Lautrec. Perhaps he'd order an absinthe, the dense green liqueur (evil ancestor of today's *pastis*) that was the toxic muse for so many great (and so many forgotten) artists. Toulouse-Lautrec's sketches of dancer Jane Avril and comic La Goulue hang in the Orsay.

After its initial splash, the Moulin Rouge survived as a venue for all kinds of entertainment. In 1906, the novelist Colette kissed her female lover onstage, and the authorities closed the "Dream of Egypt" down. Yves Montand opened for Edith Piaf (1944) and the two fell in love offstage. It's hosted such diverse acts as Ginger Rogers, Dalida, and the Village People—together on one bill (1979). Mikhail Baryshnikov strode across its stage (1986). And the club celebrated its centennial (1989) with Ray Charles, Tony Curtis, Ella Fitzgerald and...Jerry Lewis.

Tonight they're showing...well, walk into the open-air entryway or step into the lobby to mull over the photos, show options, and prices.

- *The Blanche Métro stop is here in place Blanche, a good place to end. (Plaster of Paris from the gypsum found on this mount was loaded sloppily at place Blanche...the white square.) Others may want to sully themselves by walking east down...*

18. Pig Alley

The stretch of the boulevard de Clichy from place Blanche eastward (toward Sacré-Coeur) to place Pigalle is the den mother of all iniquities. Today, sex shops, peep shows, live sex shows, and hotdog stands line the busy boulevard de Clichy. Dildos abound.

It's raunchy now, but the area has always been the place where bistros had tax-free status, wine was cheap, and prostitutes roamed freely. In World War II, GIs nicknamed Pigalle "Pig Alley."

Bars lining the streets downhill from place Pigalle are lively with working girls eager to share a drink with anyone passing by. Escape home from the fine Art Nouveau Métro stop, Pigalle.

LEFT BANK **WALK**

The Left Bank is as much an attitude as it is an actual neighborhood. But this two-hour walk, which is a little over a mile—from the Seine to St. Germain-des-Prés to Luxembourg Garden—captures some of the artistic, intellectual, and counterculture spirit long associated with the south side of the river. We'll pass through an upscale area of art galleries, home-furnishing boutiques, antique dealers, bookstores, small restaurants, classic cafés, evening hotspots, and the former homes of writers, painters, and composers. Though trendy now, the area still has the offbeat funkiness that has always defined the Rive Gauche. (*Gauche*, or left-handed, implies social incorrectness, like giving a handshake with the wrong—left—hand.)

ORIENTATION

Delacroix Museum (Musée National Eugène Delacroix): €4, covered by museum pass, Thu-Mon 9:30-17:00, closed Tue-Wed, free first Sun of month. Tel. 01 44 41 86 50, www.musee-delacroix.fr.

St. Germain-des-Prés: Free, daily 8:00–20:00

St. Sulpice: Free, daily 7:30–19:30, Sunday morning organ concerts (see page 36).

Luxembourg Garden: Free, daily dawn until dusk.

THE TOUR BEGINS

- *Start on the pedestrian-only bridge across the Seine, the pont des Arts (next to Louvre, Mo: Pont Neuf or Louvre-Rivoli).*

Left Bank Walk

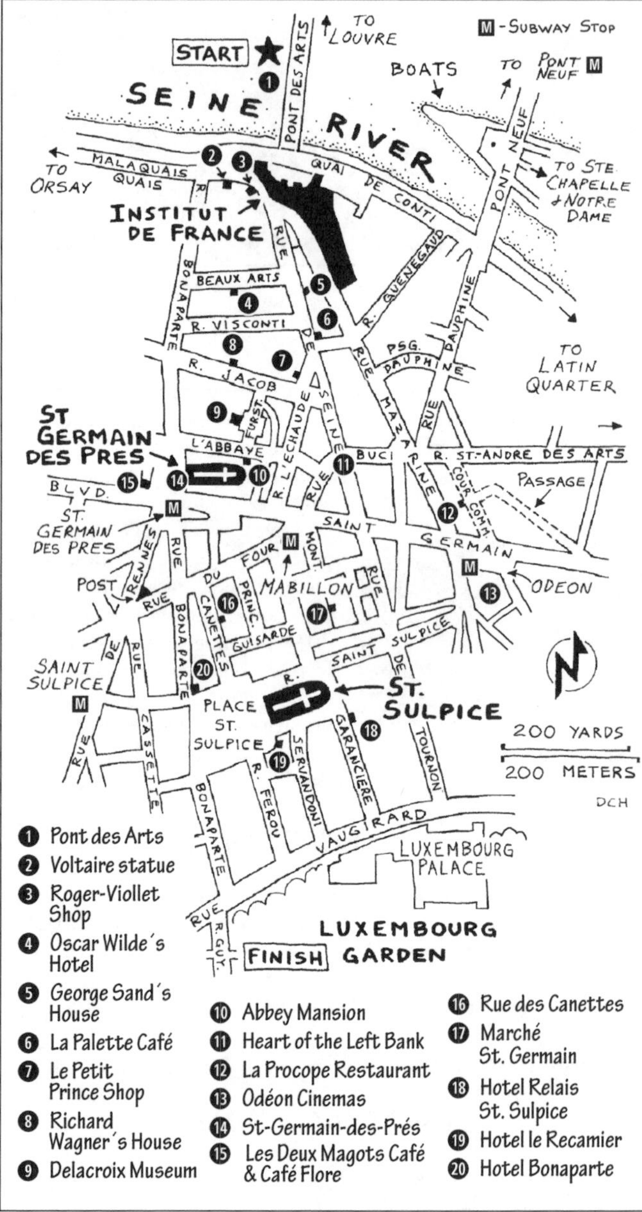

Pont des Arts

Before dozens of bridges crossed the Seine, the two riverbanks were like different cities—royalty on the right, commoners on the left.

Under the dome of the Institut de France (the building the pont des Arts leads to), 40 linguists meet periodically to decide whether it's acceptable to call computer software "*le software*" (as the French commonly do), or whether it should be the French word *logiciel* (which the linguists prefer). The Académie Française, dedicated to halting the erosion of French culture, is wary of new French words with strangely foreign sounds—like *le week-end*, *le marketing*, and *le fast-food*.

Besides the Académie Française, the Institut houses several other Académies, such as the Académie des Beaux-Arts, which is dedicated to subjects like music and painting, appropriate to the Left Bank.

- *Circle around the right side of the Institut de France building, to the head of rue de Seine. You're immediately met by a statue in a street-corner garden.*

Statue of Voltaire

"Jesus committed suicide." The mischievous philosopher Voltaire could scandalize a party with a wicked comment like that, said with an enigmatic smile and a twinkle in the eye (meaning if Christ is truly God, he could have prevented his crucifixion). Voltaire—a commoner more sophisticated than the royalty who lived across the river—introduces us to the Left Bank.

Born François-Marie Arouet (1694-1778), he took up Voltaire as his one-word pen name. Although Voltaire mingled with aristocrats, he was constantly in trouble for questioning the ruling class and fueling ideas that would soon spark a Revolution. He did 11 months in the Bastille prison, then spent 40 years in virtual exile from his beloved Paris. Returning as an old man, he got a hero's welcome so surprising it killed him.

The rue de Seine and adjoining streets are lined with art galleries and upscale shops selling lamps, sconces, vases, bowls, and statues for people who turn their living rooms into art.

- *From here, we'll head south down rue de Seine to boulevard St. Germain, making a few detours along the way. First stop is at 6 rue de Seine...*

Roger-Viollet

Look in the windows at black-and-white photos from Paris' history—a half-built Eiffel Tower, Hitler in Paris, etc. This humble shop is the funky origin of a worldwide press agency dealing in historic photographs. The family of photographer Henri Roger expanded his photographs into an archive of millions of photos, chronicling Paris's changes through the years.

- *At the first intersection, a half-block detour to the right leads to 13 rue des Beaux-Arts and the...*

L Hotel (Oscar Wilde's Hotel)

Oscar Wilde (1854-1900), the Irish playwright with the flamboyant clothes and outrageous wit, died in this hotel on November 30, 1900 (don't blame the current owners).

Just five years before, he'd been at his peak. He had several plays running simultaneously in London's West End, and he'd returned to London triumphant from a lecture tour through America. Then, news of his love affair with a Lord leaked out, causing a scandal, and he was sentenced to two years in prison for "gross indecency." Wilde's wife abandoned him, refusing to let him see their children again.

After his prison term, a poor and broken Wilde was exiled to Paris, where he succumbed to an ear infection and died here in a (then-) shabby hotel room. Among his last words in the rundown place were: "Either this wallpaper goes, or I do."

Wilde is buried in Père Lachaise Cemetery.

- *Return to rue de Seine and continue south. A plaque at 31 rue de Seine marks...*

George Sand's Home

George Sand (1804-76) divorced her abusive husband, left her children behind, and moved into this apartment, determined to become a writer. In the year she lived here (1831), she wrote articles for *Le Figaro* while turning her real-life experiences with men into a sensational novel *Indiana*. It made her a celebrity and allowed her to afford a better apartment.

George Sand is known for her novels, her cross-dressing (men's suits, slicked-down hair, and cigars), and for her complex love affair with a sensitive pianist from Poland, Frédéric Chopin.

- *At 43 rue de Seine is...*

La Palette Café

Though less famous than more historic cafés, this is a "real" one, where a *café crème*, beer, or glass of wine at an outdoor table costs less than €5. Inside, the tobacco-stained wood paneling, hole-in-the-ground toilet, and faded Art Nouveau decor exude Left Bank chic.

- *You could follow rue de Seine straight down to boulevard St. Germain. But we'll branch off, veering right down small rue de l'Echaudé. At 6 rue de l'Echaudé is...*

Le Petit Prince Shop

Books, dolls, cards, and T-shirts mass-market the quirky children's tale written by Antoine de Saint-Exupéry (1900-44). In *The Little Prince* (1943), a pilot crashes in the Sahara, where a mysterious little prince takes him to various planets, teaching him about life from a child's wise perspective.

"Saint-Ex" was himself a daring aviator who had survived wrecks in the Sahara. When the Nazis invaded, he fled to America, where he wrote and published *The Little Prince*. A year later, he enlisted and was shot down over the French Riviera by German planes.

- *A half-block detour to the right down rue Jacob (to #14) leads to...*

Richard Wagner's Home

Having survived a storm at sea on the way here, the young German composer (1813-1883) spent the gray winter of 1841-1842 in Paris in this building writing *The Flying Dutchman*, an opera about a ghost ship. It was the restless young man's lowest point of poverty. Six months later, a German company staged his first opera (*Rienzi*), plucking him from obscurity and leading to a production of *The Flying Dutchman* that launched his career.

Now the premises are occupied by a hip-looking bar.

- *Backtrack along rue Jacob, then turn right and continue south on rue Furstemberg to #6, the...*

Delacroix Museum

The painter Eugène Delacroix (1798-1863) lived here on this tiny, quiet square. Today his home is a museum with paintings and memorabilia, delightful for art-lovers and free for museum passholders.

You start in an **anteroom** with a chronology of his life. An ambassador's son, Delacroix moved to Paris and studied at the Beaux-Arts. By his early 20s, he had exhibited at the Salon. His *Liberty Leading the People* (1831, see Louvre, page 131) was an instant classic, a symbol of French democracy. Trips to North Africa added exotic, Muslim elements to his palette. He hobnobbed with aristocrats and with bohemians like George Sand and Frédéric Chopin (whom he painted). He painted large-scale murals for the Louvre, Hôtel de Ville, and Luxembourg Palace.

In 1857, his health failing, Delacroix moved here, seeking a quiet home/studio where he could concentrate on his final great works, for the Church of St. Sulpice (which we'll see later).

Next comes the **living room**, decorated with his mahogany writing desk and a haunting painting of Mary Magdalene. To the left is the **bedroom** (with fireplace) where he died in 1863, nursed by his long-time servant Jenny Le Guillou (see her portrait). Backtracking, you pass through the **library**, then go outside and down some stairs to his **studio** (*atelier*) in the pleasant backyard.

Delacroix built the studio to his own specifications, with high ceilings, big windows, and a skylight, ideal for an artist working prior to electric lights. See his easel and painting table, plus more paintings, including a small-scale study for *The Death of Sardanapalus,* which hangs in the Louvre. Some of Delacroix's most popular work was for book illustrations (lithographs for Goethe's *Faust*, Revolutionary history, and Shakespeare). Admire Delacroix's artistic range—from messy, colorful oils to meticulously-detailed lithographs.

Finally, in the peaceful **backyard**, soak up the meditative atmosphere that inspired Delacroix's religious paintings in St. Sulpice.

- *Rue Furstemberg runs directly into the Abbey Mansion. This mansion (1586) was the administrative center for the vast complex of monks gathered around the nearby church of St. Germain-des-Prés.*

  Facing the mansion, turn left on rue de l'Abbaye and work your way two blocks east to the intersection of rue de Seine and rue de Buci. This intersection is, arguably, the...

Heart of the Left Bank

Explore. The rue de Buci hosts *pâtisseries* and a produce market by day and bars by night. Mixing earthiness and elegance, here's your Left Bank. A right on rue de Buci leads to boulevard St. Germain. A left on rue de Buci leads to place St. Michel and the Latin Quarter.

- *Wherever you wander, we'll meet up a block south of here on boulevard St. Germain. But first, I'm making a several-block detour to find Voltaire's favorite café. Head east (left) on rue de Buci, which in a few blocks becomes rue St. André-des-Arts. At #61, turn right into the pedestrian-only passageway called Cour du Commerce St. André, where you'll find the back door to...*

Le Procope Restaurant

Le Procope (with its front door entrance at 13 rue de l'Ancienne Comédie, closed Sun) is just one of many eating options in this pleasant restaurant mall.

Founded in 1686, Le Procope is one of the world's oldest continuously operating restaurants and was one of Europe's first places to sample an exotic new stimulant—coffee—recently imported from the Muslim culture.

In the 1700s, Le Procope caffeinated the Revolution. Voltaire reportedly drank 30 cups a day, fueling his intellectual passion (his favorite table bears his carved initials). Benjamin Franklin recounted old war stories about America's Revolution. Robespierre, Danton, and Marat plotted coups over cups of double-short-two-percent-frappuccinos. And a young lieutenant named Napoleon Bonaparte ran up a tab he never paid.

Located midway between university students, royalty, and the counterculture Comédie Française, Le Procope attracted literary types who loved the free newspapers, writing paper, and quill pens.

Today, the coffeehouse is an upscale restaurant, with an affordable, if mediocre, *menu.*

- *The Cour du Commerce spills out onto boulevard St. Germain at an intersection (and Métro stop) called...*

Odéon

Paris' many lovers of film converge here for the latest releases at several multiplexes in the area. Looking south down rue de l'Odéon, you can see the classical columns of the front of the Théâtre de l'Odéon, the descendant of the original Comédie Française (which is now housed in Palais Royale).

- *Walk west along busy boulevard St. Germain for six blocks, passing fashionable, noisy cafés with outdoor terraces. You'll reach the large stone church and square of...*

St. Germain-des-Prés

Paris' oldest church, dating from the 11th century (the square belltower is original), stands on a site where a Christian church has stood since the fall of Rome. (The first church was destroyed by Vikings in the 885-86 siege.)

The inside is still painted in the medieval manner, as were Notre-Dame and others. The church is in Romanesque style, with round—not pointed—arches over the aisles of the nave.

The square outside is one of Paris' great gathering spots on warm evenings. Musicians, mimes, and fire-eaters entertain café patrons. The church is often lit up and open late. Jazz clubs cluster nearby. This is where the rich come to see and be seen, and the poor come for a night of free spectacle.

- *Note that Métro stop St. Germain-des-Prés is here, and the Mabillon stop is just a couple of blocks east. On place St. Germain-des-Prés, you'll find...*

Les Deux Magots Café and (next door) Café de Flore

Since opening in 1885, "The Two Chinamen Café" (wooden statues inside) has taken over Le Procope as the café of ideas. From Oscar Wilde's Aestheticism (1900) to Picasso's Cubism (1910s) to Hemingway's spare prose ('20s) to Sartre's Existentialism (with his girlfriend Simone de

Beauvoir and Albert Camus, 1930s and '40s) to rock singer Jim Morrison ('60s), worldwide movements have been born in the simple atmosphere of these two cafés.

- *From place St. Germain-des-Prés, cross boulevard St. Germain and head south on rue Bonaparte. Turn left on busy rue du Four, then right on...*

Rue des Canettes

Small, mid-priced restaurants, boutique shops, and comfortable brewpubs make this a pleasant area for evening life. Chez Georges (at #11) is the last outpost of funkiness (and how!) in an increasingly gentrified neighborhood.

- *A one-block detour left down rue Guisarde leads to more restaurants, shops, and pubs, and the Marché St. Germain shopping mall, a former farmer's market where fish and produce have been replaced by the Gap and other chain stores.*

  Continuing south on rue des Canettes leads to the church of...

St. Sulpice

The impressive neoclassical arcaded facade, with two round half-finished towers, is modeled on St. Paul's in London. It has a remarkable organ and offers Sunday morning concerts (see Sights, page 27).

Inside (first chapel on the right), find Delacroix's three murals (on the chapel's ceiling and walls) of fighting angels, completed in his final years. The most famous is the contemplative *Jacob Wrestling the Angel*, where the patriarch has fought the angel to a standstill, bringing him a well-earned blessing for his ordeal.

- *Continue south on rue Férou, which leads directly to the fenced-in Luxembourg Garden. Enter the garden by turning right on busy rue de Vaugirard, then left on rue Guynemer, where you'll find an entrance gate.*

Luxembourg Garden

Paris' most beautiful, interesting, and enjoyable garden/park/recreational area is a great place to watch Parisians at rest and play. These 60-acre private gardens, dotted with fountains and statues, are property of the French Senate, which meets here in the Luxembourg Palace.

The palace was begun in 1615 by Marie de Médicis. Recently widowed (by Henry IV) and homesick for Florence, she built the palace as a re-creation of her girlhood home, the Pitti Palace. When her son grew to be Louis XIII, he drove his mother from the palace, exiling her to Germany.

Luxembourg Garden has special rules governing its use (e.g., where cards can be played, where dogs can be walked, where joggers can run, and when and where music can be played). The brilliant flowerbeds are completely changed three times a year, and the boxed trees are brought out of the *orangerie* in May. Children enjoy the rentable toy sailboats, pony rides, and marionette shows (Les Guignols, or Punch and Judy; see page 336).

Challenge the card and chess players to a game (near the tennis courts) or find a free chair near the main pond and take a well-deserved break, here at the end of our Left Bank Walk.

Nearby

The grand neoclassical-domed Panthéon, now a mausoleum housing the tombs of great Frenchmen, is three blocks away (but probably only worth entering if you have a museum pass). The historic cafés of Montparnasse are a few blocks from the southwest-corner exit of the park (on rue Vavin, see "Les Grands Cafés de Paris," page 332).

- *Getting home: The Luxembourg Garden is ringed with Métro stops, all a 10-minute walk away. North of the garden, the two closest are St. Sulpice and Odéon (nearest RER: Luxembourg).*

LOUVRE **TOUR**

Paris walks you through world history in three world-class museums—the Louvre (ancient world to 1850), the Orsay (1850–1914, including Impressionism), and the Pompidou (20th century to today). Start your "art-yssey" at the Louvre. With more than 30,000 works of art, the Louvre is a full inventory of Western civilization. To cover it all in one visit is in-Seine. Let's focus on the Louvre's specialties—Greek sculpture, Italian painting, and French painting.

We'll see "Venuses" through history, from scrawny Stone Age fertility goddesses to the curvy *Venus de Milo*, from the wind-blown *Winged Victory of Samothrace* to placid medieval Madonnas, from *Mona Lisa* to the symbol of modern democracy. We'll see how each generation defines beauty differently and gain insight into long-ago civilizations by admiring the things they found beautiful.

In addition—for those with a little more time—we can visit some impressive chunks of stone from the "Cradle of Civilization," modern-day Iraq.

ORIENTATION

Cost: €8.50, €6 after 18:00 on Mon and Wed, free on first Sun of month and for those under 18, covered by museum pass. Tickets good all day; reentry allowed.

Hours: Wed–Mon 9:00–18:00, closed Tue. All wings open Wed until 21:45. On Mon, only the Denon wing is open until 21:45 (but it contains the biggies—*Mona Lisa* and *Venus de Milo*, etc.) and sometimes part of the Sully and Richelieu (Egyptian and Oriental antiquities) wings. Galleries start shutting down 30 minutes early. The last entry is 45 minutes before closing. Closed Jan 1, Easter, May 1, Nov 1, and Dec 25.

Crowds are worst on Sun, Mon, Wed, and mornings. Save money by visiting after 15:00.

The Louvre—A Bird's Eye View

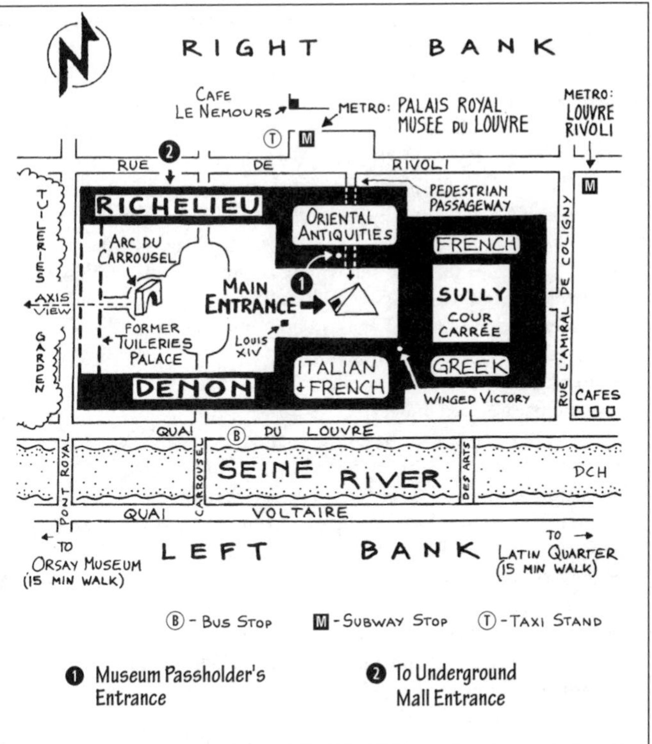

Getting There: The Métro stop Palais Royal-Musée du Louvre is closer to the entrance than the stop called Louvre-Rivoli. From the Palais Royal-Musée du Louvre stop, you can stay underground to enter the Louvre, or exit above ground if you want to enter the Louvre through the pyramid (more details below). There's a taxi stand on rue de Rivoli next to the Palais Royal-Musée du Louvre Métro station.

Getting In: There is no grander entry than through the main entrance at the pyramid in the central courtyard, but metal detectors (not ticket-buying lines) create a long line at times. There are several ways to avoid the line:

Museum passholders can use the group entrance in the pedestrian passageway between the pyramid and rue de Rivoli (under the arches, a few steps north of the pyramid, find the uniformed guard at the entrance, with the escalator down).

Otherwise, you can enter the Louvre from its (usually less-crowded) underground entrance, accessed through the "Carrousel du Louvre" shopping mall. Enter the mall at 99 rue de Rivoli (the door with the red awning, daily 8:30–23:00) or directly from the Métro stop Palais Royal-Musée du Louvre (stepping off the train, exit to the left, following signs to Carrousel du Louvre-Musée du Louvre).

Information: Pick up the free *Louvre Handbook* in English at the information desk under the pyramid as you enter. Tel. 01 40 20 51 51, recorded info tel. 01 40 20 53 17, www.louvre.fr.

Louvre Tours: The 90-minute English-language tours leave three times daily except Sun (normally at 11:00, 14:00, and 15:45, €3 plus your entry ticket, tour tel. 01 40 20 52 63). Digital audioguides (available for €5 at entries to the three wings, at top of escalators) give you a directory of about 130 masterpieces, allowing you to dial a rather dull commentary on included works as you stumble upon them. I prefer the free, self-guided tour described below.

Length of This Tour: Two hours.

Checkrooms: Located under the escalators. They will accept no cameras or any valuables in your bag. The coat check—which can have a torturously slow line (worst early in the morning and late afternoon)—does not take bags. The baggage check (which doesn't take coats that are not stuffed into bags) is separate from the coat check and generally has almost no line.

Cuisine Art: The underground shopping mall has a dizzying assortment of good-value, smoke-free eateries (up the escalator near the inverted pyramid). You'll also find a post office, handy TI, SNCF train office, glittering boutiques, and the Palais Royal-Musée du Louvre Métro entrance. Stairs at the far end take you right into the Tuileries Garden, a perfect antidote to the stuffy, crowded rooms of the Louvre. For a fine but more expensive light lunch than the Louvre's eateries, cross rue de Rivoli to the venerable Café le Nemours (adjacent to the Comédie Française; see page 313).

Photography: Photography without a flash is allowed.

Starring: *Venus de Milo*, *Winged Victory of Samothrace*, *Mona Lisa*, Raphael, Michelangelo, and the French painters.

Surviving the Louvre

Orient from underneath the glass pyramid. Pick up the free map at the information desk under the pyramid.

The Louvre, the largest museum in the Western world, fills three wings in this immense U-shaped palace. The Richelieu wing (north side of Louvre) houses Oriental antiquities (covered in the second part of this tour), plus

French, Dutch, and Northern art. The Sully wing (east side) has the extensive French painting and ancient Egypt collections.

For this part of the tour, we'll concentrate on the Louvre's Denon wing (south side), which houses many of the superstars: ancient Greek sculpture, Italian Renaissance painting, and French neoclassical and Romantic painting.

Expect changes. The sprawling Louvre is constantly in flux. If you can't find a particular work, ask a guard where it is. Point to the photo in your book and ask, "*Où est, s'il vous plaît?*" (it rhymes). And move quickly. Try to finish our once-over tour with enough energy left to browse.

DENON WING

THE TOUR BEGINS—GREEK STATUES (3,000 B.C.–A.D. 1)

- *From inside the big glass pyramid, you'll see signs to the three wings. Head for the Denon wing.*

  Escalate up one floor. After showing your ticket, take the first left you can, follow signs to Antiquités Grecques, and climb a set of stairs to the brick-ceilinged Salle 1: La Grèce préclassique (Salle = Room). Enter prehistory.

Pre-Classical Greece

These statues are noble but crude. The Greek Barbie dolls (3000 B.C.) are older than the pyramids, as old as writing itself. These pre-rational voodoo dolls whittle women down to their life-giving traits. Farther along, a woman *(Dame d'Auxerre)* pledges allegiance to stability. Another *(Core)* is essentially a column with breasts. A young, naked man *(Couros)* seems to have a gun to his back—his hands at his sides, facing front, with sketchy muscles and a mask-like face. "Don't move."

The early Greeks, who admired such statues, found stability more attractive than movement. Like their legendary hero, Odysseus, the Greek people had spent generations wandering, war-weary, and longing for the comforts of a secure home. The noble strength and sturdiness of these works looked beautiful.

Pre-Classical Greece

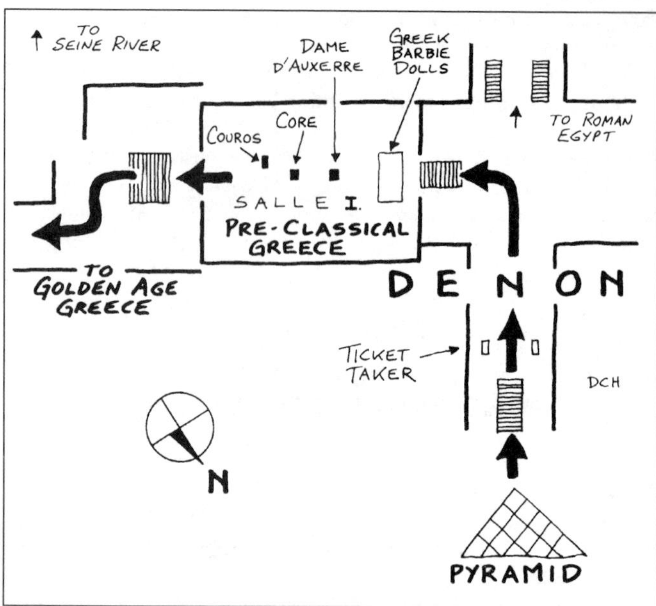

• *Exit Salle 1 at the far end and climb the stairs one flight. At the top, veer 10 o'clock left, where you'll soon see Venus de Milo, floating above a sea of worshiping tourists. It's been said that, among the warlike Greeks, this was the first statue to unilaterally disarm.*

Venus de Milo (Aphrodite, c. 100 B.C.)

The Venus de Milo (or goddess of love, from the Greek island of Melos) created a sensation when it was discovered in 1820. Europe was already in the grip of a classical fad, and this statue seemed to sum up all that ancient Greece stood for. The Greeks pictured their gods in human form (meaning humans are god-like), telling us they had an optimistic view of the human race. Venus' well-proportioned body embodies the balance and orderliness of the Greek universe.

Split Venus down the middle from nose to toes and see how the two halves balance each other. Venus rests on her right foot (called *contrapposto,* or "counterpoise"), then lifts her left leg, setting her whole body in motion. As the left leg rises, her right shoulder droops down. And as her knee points one way, her

Greek Statues

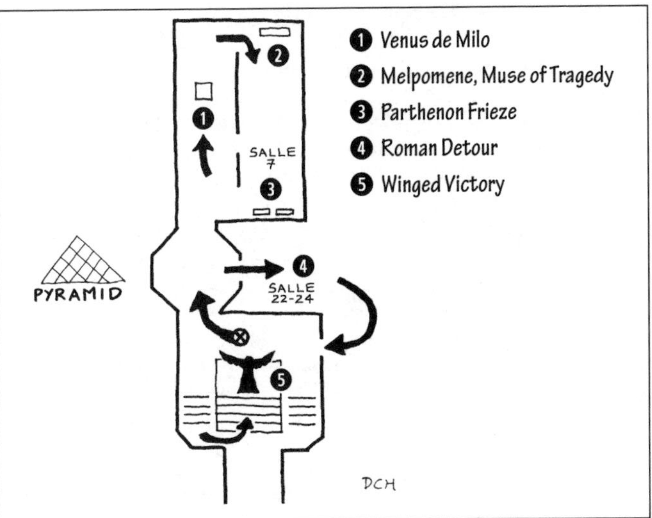

head turns the other. Venus is a harmonious balance of opposites, orbiting slowly around a vertical axis. The twisting pose gives a balanced S-curve to her body (especially noticeable from the back view) that the Greeks and succeeding generations found beautiful.

Other opposites balance as well, like the smooth skin of her upper half that sets off the rough-cut texture of her dress (size 14). She's actually made from two different pieces of stone plugged together at the hips (the seam is visible). The face is realistic and anatomically accurate, but it's also idealized, a goddess, too generic and too perfect. This isn't any particular woman, but Everywoman—all the idealized features that appealed to the Greeks.

Most "Greek" statues are actually later Roman copies. This is a rare Greek original. This "epitome of the Golden Age" was actually sculpted three centuries after the Golden Age, though in a retro-style.

What were her missing arms doing? Some say her right arm held her dress while her left arm was raised. Others say she was hugging a man statue or leaning on a column. I say she was picking her navel.

- *Orbit Venus. This statue is interesting and different from every angle. Remember the view from the back—we'll see it again later. Make your reentry to Earth behind Venus, with a U-turn to the right, doubling back down a room lined with Greek statues. Try to find even one that's not contrapposto. The large statue of Melpomene, holding the frowning mask of Tragedy, dominates the room. At the far end (in Salle 7, the Salle du Parthénon), you'll bump into two carved panels on the wall.*

GOLDEN AGE GREECE

The great Greek cultural explosion that changed the course of history unfolded over 50 years (around 450 B.C.) in Athens, a Greek town smaller than Muncie, Indiana. Having united the Greeks to repel a Persian invasion, Athens rebuilt, with the Parthenon as the centerpiece of the city. The Greeks dominated the ancient world through brain, not brawn, and the art shows their love of rationality, order, and balance. The ideal Greek was well-rounded—an athlete and a bookworm, a lover and a philosopher, a carpenter who plays the piano, a warrior and a poet. In art, the balance between timeless stability and fleeting movement made beauty.

In a sense, we're all Greek. Democracy, mathematics, theater, philosophy, literature, and science were practically invented in ancient Greece. Most of the art that we'll see in the Louvre either came from Greece or was inspired by it.

Parthenon Frieze *(Fragment de la Frise des Panathénées)*, c. 440 B.C.

These stone fragments once decorated the exterior of the greatest Athenian temple, the Parthenon, built at the peak of the Greek Golden Age. The right panel shows a centaur sexually harassing a woman. It tells the story of how these rude creatures crashed a party of humans. But the Greeks fought back and threw the brutes out, just as Athens (metaphorically) conquered its barbarian neighbors and became civilized.

The other relief shows the sacred procession of young girls who marched up the hill every four years with an embroidered veil for the 40-foot-high statue of Athena, the goddess of wisdom. Though headless, the maidens speak volumes about Greek craftsmanship. Carved in only a couple inches of stone, they're amazingly realistic—more so than anything we saw in the pre-Classical period. They glide along horizontally (their belts and shoulders all in a line), while the folds of their dresses drape down vertically. The man in the center is relaxed, realistic, and *contrapposto*. Notice the veins in his arm. The maidens' pleated dresses make them look as stable as fluted columns, but their arms and legs step out naturally—the human form is emerging from the stone.

- *Make a lo-o-o-ng (50-step) loop behind the Parthenon Frieze panels, turning left into Salle 22, the Antiquités Romaines, for a ...*

Roman Detour (Salles 22-24 and beyond)

Stroll among the Caesars and try to see the person behind the public persona. You might spot Augustus (*Auguste*), the first emperor, and his wily wife, Livia (*Livie*). Their son Tiberius (*Tibere*) was the Caesar that Jesus Christ "rendered unto." Curly-haired Domitia murdered her husband, Hadrian popularized the beard, Trajan ruled the Empire at its peak, Marcus Aurelius (*Marc Aurele*) presided stoically over Rome's slow fall. And you can't miss the many faces of the ubiquitous Emperor *Inconnu* ("unknown").

The pragmatic Romans (500 B.C.-A.D. 500) were great conquerors, but bad artists. One area in which the Romans excelled was realistic portrait busts, especially of their emperors, who were worshiped as gods on earth. Fortunately for us, the Romans also had a huge appetite for Greek statues and made countless copies. They took the Greek style and wrote it in capital letters, adding a veneer of sophistication to their homes, temples, baths, and government buildings.

The Roman rooms also contain sarcophagi and an impressive mosaic floor. Weary? Kick back and relax with the statues in the Etruscan Lounge (in Salle 18).

- *This Roman detour deposits you at the base of stairs leading up to the First Floor and the dramatic...*

Winged Victory of Samothrace (*Victoire de Samothrace*), c. 190 B.C.

This woman with wings, poised on the prow of a ship, once stood on a hilltop to commemorate a naval victory. Her clothes are windblown and sea-sprayed, clinging to her body close enough to win a wet T-shirt contest. (Notice the detail in the folds of her dress around the navel, curving down to her hips.) Originally, her right arm was stretched high, celebrating the victory like a Super Bowl champion, waving a "we're-number-one" finger.

This is the *Venus de Milo* gone Hellenistic, from the time after the culture of Athens was spread around the Mediterranean by Alexander the Great (c. 325 B.C.). As Victory strides forward, the wind blows her and her wings back. Her feet are firmly on the ground, but her wings (and missing arms) stretch upward. She is a pillar of vertical strength while the clothes curve and whip around her. These opposing forces create a feeling of great energy, making her the lightest two-ton piece of rock in captivity.

The earlier Golden Age Greeks might have considered this statue ugly. Her rippling excitement is a far cry from the dainty Parthenon maidens and the soft-focus beauty of Venus. And the statue's off-balance pose leaves you hanging, like an unfinished melody. But Hellenistic Greeks loved these cliff-hanging scenes of real-life humans struggling to make their mark.

In the glass case nearby is Victory's open right hand with an outstretched finger, discovered in 1950, a century after the statue itself was unearthed. When the French discovered this was in Turkey, they negotiated with the Turkish government for the rights to it. Considering all the other ancient treasures the French had looted from Turkey in the past, the Turks thought it only appropriate to give France the finger.

- *Enter the octagonal room to the left as you face the Winged Victory, with Icarus bungee-jumping from the ceiling. Bench yourself under a window and look out toward the pyramid.*

View from the Octagonal Room—The Louvre as a Palace

The Louvre, the former royal palace, was built in stages over eight centuries. On your right (the eastern Sully wing) was the original medieval fortress. Next, another palace, the Tuileries, was built 500 yards to the west—in the now-open area past the pyramid and past the triumphal arch. Succeeding kings tried to connect these two palaces, each one adding another section onto the long, skinny north and south wings. Finally, in 1852, after three centuries of building, the two palaces were connected, creating a rectangular Louvre. Nineteen years later, the Tuileries Palace burned down during a riot, leaving the U-shaped Louvre we see today.

The glass pyramid was designed by the American architect I. M. Pei (1989). Many Parisians hated the pyramid, like they used to hate another new and controversial structure 100 years ago—the Eiffel Tower.

In the octagonal room, a plaque at the base of the dome explains that France's Revolutionary National Assembly (the same people who brought you the guillotine) founded this museum in 1793. What could be more logical? You behead the king, inherit his palace and art collection, open the doors to the masses, and, *Voilà!* You have Europe's first public museum.

- *The Italian collection ("Peintures Italiennes") is on the other side of the Winged Victory. Cross in front of the Winged Victory to the other side and pause (in Salle 1) at the two Botticelli fresco paintings on the wall to the left. These pure maidens, like colorized versions of the Parthenon frieze, give us a taste of how ancient Greece would be "reborn" in the Renaissance. But first, continue into the large Salle 3.*

THE MEDIEVAL WORLD (1200-1500)

Cimabue—*The Madonna of the Angels* (1280)

During the Age of Faith (1200s), most every church in Europe had a painting like this one. Mary was a cult figure—bigger than even the 20th-century Madonna—adored and prayed to by the faithful for bringing baby Jesus into the world. After the collapse of the Roman Empire (c. A.D. 500), medieval Europe was a poorer and more violent place, with the Christian Church being the only constant in troubled times.

Altarpieces like this followed the same formula: Somber iconic faces, stiff poses, elegant folds in the robes, and generic angels. Violating 3-D space, the angels at the "back" of Mary's throne are the same size as those holding the front. These holy figures are laid flat on a gold background like cardboard cutouts, existing in a golden never-never-land, as though the faithful couldn't imagine them as flesh-and-blood humans inhabiting our dark and sinful earth.

Giotto—*St. Francis of Assisi Receiving the Stigmata* (c. 1290-1295)

Francis of Assisi (c. 1181–1226), a wandering Italian monk of renowned goodness, kneels on a rocky Italian hillside, pondering the pain of Christ's torture and execution. Suddenly he looks up, startled, to see Christ himself, with six wings, hovering above. Christ shoots lasers from his wounds to burn marks on the hands, feet, and side of the empathetic monk. Francis went on to breathe the spirit of the Renaissance into medieval Europe. His humble love of man and nature inspired artists like Giotto to portray real human beings with real emotions and living in a physical world of beauty.

Like a good filmmaker, Giotto (c. 1266–1337; JOT-toh) doesn't just *tell* us what happened, he *shows* us in present tense, freezing the scene at the most dramatic moment. Though the perspective is crude—Francis' hut is smaller than he is, and Christ is somehow shooting at Francis while facing us—Giotto gives a glimpse of the 3-D world of the coming

Renaissance. He paints a foreground (Francis), middle ground (his hut) and background (the hillside) to create the illusion of depth. Painting a 3-D world on a 2-D surface is tough, and after a millennium of Dark Ages, artists were rusty.

In the *predella* (the panel of paintings below the altarpiece), birds gather at Francis' feet to hear him talk about God. Giotto catches the late arrivals in mid-flight, an astonishing technical feat for an artist more than a century before the Renaissance. The simple gesture of Francis' companion speaks volumes about his amazement. Breaking the stiff, iconic mold for saints, Francis bends forward at the waist to talk to his fellow creatures, while the tree bends down symmetrically to catch a few words from the beloved hippie of Assisi.

- *The long Grand Gallery displays Italian Renaissance painting, some masterpieces, some not.*

The Grand Gallery

The Grand Gallery was built in the late 1500s to connect the old palace with the Tuileries Palace. From the doorway, look to the far end and consider this challenge: I hold the world's record for the Grand Gallery Heel-Toe-Fun-Walk-Tourist-Slalom, going end to end in one minute 58 seconds, two injured. Time yourself. Along the way, notice some of the...

Features of Italian Renaissance Painting

1. **Religious:** Lots of Madonnas, children, martyrs, and saints.
2. **Symmetrical:** The Madonnas are flanked by saints, two to the left, two to the right, and so on.
3. **Realistic:** Real-life human features are especially obvious in the occasional portrait.
4. **Three-Dimensional:** Every scene gets a spacious setting with a distant horizon.
5. **Classical:** You'll see some Greek gods and classical nudes, but even Christian saints pose like Greek statues, and Mary is a Venus whose face and gestures embody all that was good in the Christian world.

The Grand Gallery

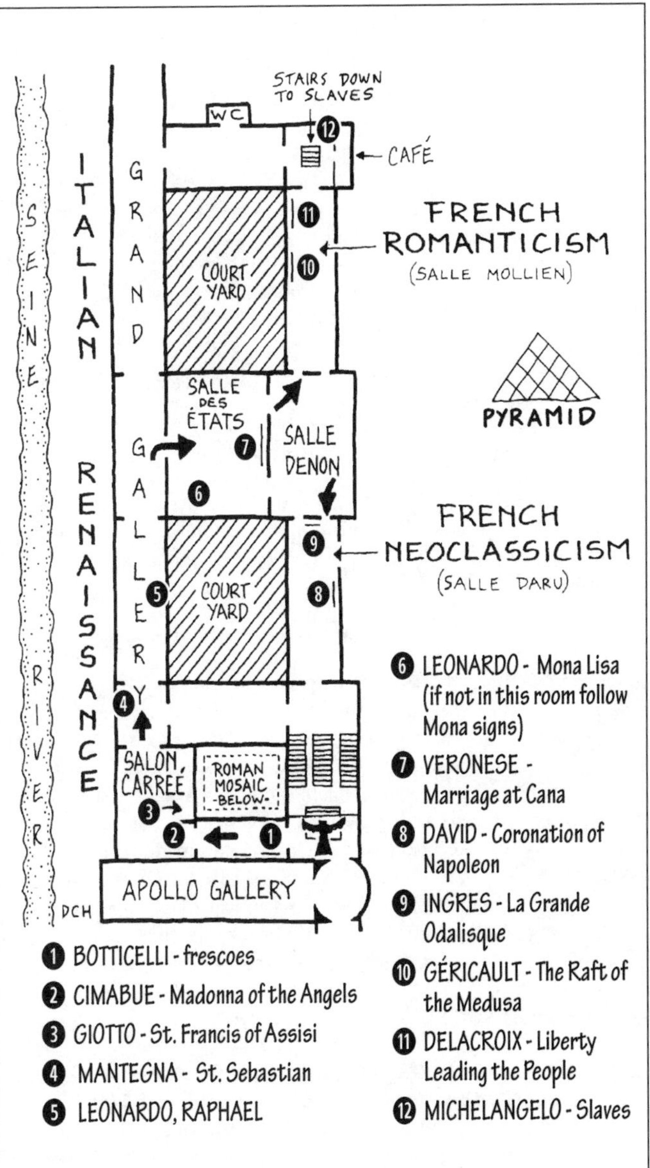

ITALIAN RENAISSANCE
(1400-1600)

A thousand years after Rome fell, plunging Europe into the Dark Ages, the Greek ideal of beauty was "reborn" in 15th-century Italy. The Renaissance—or "rebirth" of the culture of ancient Greece and Rome—was a cultural boom that changed people's thinking about every aspect of life. In politics, it meant democracy. In religion, it meant a move away from Church dominance and toward the assertion of man (humanism) and a more personal faith. Science and secular learning were revived after centuries of superstition and ignorance. In architecture, it was a return to the balanced columns and domes of Greece and Rome.

In painting, the Renaissance meant realism, and for the Italians, realism was spelled "3-D." Artists rediscovered the beauty of nature and the human body. With pictures of beautiful people in harmonious, 3-D surroundings, they expressed the optimism and confidence of this new age.

Andrea Mantegna—*St. Sebastian* (c. 1480)
This isn't the patron saint of acupuncture. St. Sebastian was a Christian martyr, although here he looks more like a classical Greek statue. Notice the *contrapposto* stance (all of his weight resting on one leg) and the Greek ruins scattered around him. His executioners look like ignorant medieval brutes bewildered by this enlightened Renaissance man. Italian artists were beginning to learn how to create human realism and earthly beauty on the canvas. Let the Renaissance begin.

- *Look for the following masterpieces by Leonardo and Raphael in the Grand Gallery.*

Leonardo da Vinci—*Virgin, Child, and St. Anne (La Vierge, l'Enfant Jésus, et Sainte-Anne)*, c. 1510
Three generations—grandmother, mother, and child—are arranged in a pyramid with Anne's face as the peak and the lamb as the lower-right corner. Within this balanced structure, Leonardo sets the figures in motion. Anne's legs are pointed to our left. (Is Anne *Mona?* Hmm.)

Her daughter Mary, sitting on her lap, reaches to the right. Jesus looks at her playfully while turning away. The lamb pulls away from him. But even with all the twisting and turning, this is still a placid scene. It's as orderly as the geometrically perfect universe created by the Renaissance god.

There's a psychological kidney punch in this happy painting. Jesus, the picture of childish joy, is innocently playing with a lamb—the symbol of his inevitable sacrificial death.

The Louvre has the greatest collection of Leonardos in the world—all five of them. Look for the neighboring *Virgin of the Rocks* and his androgynous *John the Baptist.* Leonardo was the consummate Renaissance man. Musician, sculptor, engineer, scientist, and sometimes painter, he combined knowledge from all areas to create beauty. If he were alive today, he'd create a Unified Field Theory in physics—and set it to music.

Raphael—*La Belle Jardinière* (1507)

Raphael (roff-eye-ELL) perfected the style Leonardo pioneered. This configuration of Madonna, Child, and John the Baptist is also a balanced pyramid with hazy grace and beauty. Mary is a mountain of maternal tenderness (the title translates as "The Beautiful Gardener"), as she eyes her son with a knowing look. Jesus looks up innocently, standing *contrapposto* like a chubby Greek statue.

With Raphael, the Greek ideal of beauty reborn in the Renaissance reached its peak. His work spawned so many imitators who cranked out sickly sweet, generic Madonnas that we often take him for granted. Don't. This is the real thing.

- *The* Mona Lisa (La Joconde) *is in the Salle des Etats, midway down the Grand Gallery. (If she's been moved elsewhere, you can't miss her. Just follow the signs and crowds.)*

Leonardo da Vinci—*Mona Lisa* (1503-1506)

Leonardo was already an old man when François I invited him to France. Determined to pack light, he took only a few paintings with him. One was a portrait of a Lisa del Giocondo, the wife of a wealthy Florentine merchant. When Leonardo arrived, François immediately fell in love with the painting, making it the centerpiece of the small collection of Italian masterpieces that would, in three centuries, become the

Louvre museum. He called it *La Gioconda.* We know it as a contraction of the Italian for "my lady Lisa"—*Mona Lisa.*

Mona may disappoint you. She's smaller than you'd expect, darker, engulfed in a huge room, and hidden behind a glaring pane of glass. So, you ask, "Why all the hubbub?" Let's take a closer look. Like any lover, you've got to take her for what she is, not what you'd like her to be.

The famous smile attracts you first. Leonardo used a hazy technique called *sfumato,* blurring the edges of *Mona*'s mysterious smile. Try as you might, you can never quite see the corners of her mouth. Is she happy? Sad? Tender? Or is it a cynical supermodel's smirk? Every viewer reads it differently, projecting his own mood onto *Mona*'s enigmatic face. *Mona* is a Rorschach inkblot…so how are you feeling?

Now look past the smile and the eyes that really do follow you (most eyes in portraits do) to some of the subtle Renaissance elements that make this work work. The body is surprisingly massive and statue-like, a perfectly balanced pyramid turned at an angle so that we can see its mass. Her arm is resting lightly on the chair's armrest almost on the level of the frame itself, like she's sitting in a window looking out at us. The folds of her sleeves and her gently folded hands are remarkably realistic and relaxed. The typical Leonardo landscape shows distance by getting hazier and hazier.

The overall mood is one of balance and serenity, but there's also an element of mystery. Her smile and long-distance beauty are subtle and elusive, tempting but always just out of reach, like strands of a street singer's melody drifting through the Métro tunnel. *Mona* doesn't knock your socks off, but she winks at the patient viewer.

- *The huge canvas at the far end of the Salle des Etats is…*

Paolo Veronese—*The Marriage at Cana* (1562-63)

Stand 10 steps away from this enormous canvas to where it just fills your field of vision, and suddenly…you're in a party! Help yourself to a glass of wine. This is the Renaissance love of beautiful things gone hog-wild. Venetian artists like Veronese painted the good life of rich, happy-go-lucky Venetian merchants.

In a spacious setting of Renaissance architecture, colorful lords and ladies decked out in their fanciest duds feast on a great spread of food and drink, while the musicians fuel the fires of good fun. Servants prepare and serve the food, jesters play, and animals roam. In the upper left, a dog and his master look on. A sturdy linebacker in yellow pours wine out of a jug

(right foreground). The man in white samples some wine and thinks, "Hmm, not bad," while nearby a ferocious cat battles a lion. The wedding couple at the far left is almost forgotten.

Believe it or not, this is a religious work showing the wedding celebration where Jesus turned water into wine. And there's Jesus in the dead center of 130 frolicking figures, wondering if maybe wine coolers might not have been a better choice. With true Renaissance optimism, Venetians pictured Christ as a party animal, someone who loved the created world as much as they did.

Now, let's hear it for the band! On bass—the bad cat with the funny hat—Titian the Venetian! And joining him on viola—Crazy Veronese!

- *Exit behind* The Marriage at Cana *into the Salle Denon. The dramatic Romantic room is to your left, and the grand neoclassical room is to your right. They feature the most exciting French canvases in the Louvre. In the neoclassical room, kneel before the largest canvas in the Louvre.*

FRENCH PAINTING—NEOCLASSICAL (1780–1850)

Jacques-Louis David—*The Coronation of Napoleon* (1806-1807)

Napoleon holds aloft an imperial crown. This common-born son of immigrants is about to be crowned emperor of a "New Rome." He has just made his wife, Josephine, the empress, and she kneels at his feet. Seated behind Napoleon is the pope, who journeyed from Rome to place the imperial crown on his head. But Napoleon felt that no one was worthy of the task. At the last moment, he shrugged the pope aside, grabbed the crown, held it up for all to see...and crowned himself. The pope looks p.o.'d.

After the French people decapitated their king during the Revolution (1793), their fledgling democracy floundered in chaos. France was united by a charismatic, brilliant, temperamental upstart general who kept his feet on the ground, his eyes on the horizon, and his hand in his coat—Napoleon Bonaparte. Napoleon quickly conquered most of Europe and insisted on

being made emperor (not merely king). The painter David (dah-veed) recorded the coronation for posterity.

The radiant woman in the gallery in the background center wasn't actually there. Napoleon's mother couldn't make it to see her boy become the most powerful man in Europe, but he had David paint her in anyway. (There's a key on the frame telling who's who in the picture.)

The traditional place of French coronations was the ultra-Gothic Notre-Dame cathedral. But Napoleon wanted a setting that would reflect the glories of Greece and the grandeur of Rome. So interior decorators erected stage sets of Greek columns and Roman arches to give the cathedral the architectural political correctness you see in this painting. (The *Pietà* statue on the right edge of the painting is still in Notre-Dame today.)

David was the new emperor's official painter and propagandist, in charge of color-coordinating the costumes and flags for public ceremonies and spectacles. (Find his self-portrait with curly gray hair in the *Coronation*, way up in the second balcony, peeking around the tassel directly above Napoleon's crown.) His "neoclassical" style influenced French fashion. Take a look at his *Madame Juliet Récamier* portrait on the opposite wall, showing a modern Parisian woman in ancient garb and Pompeii hairstyle reclining on a Roman couch. Nearby paintings, such as *The Death of Socrates* and *The Oath of the Horatii (Le Serment des Horaces)*, are fine examples of neoclassicism, with Greek subjects, patriotic sentiment, and a clean, simple style.

- *As you double back toward the Romantic room, stop at...*

Jean-Auguste-Dominique Ingres—*La Grande Odalisque* (1819)

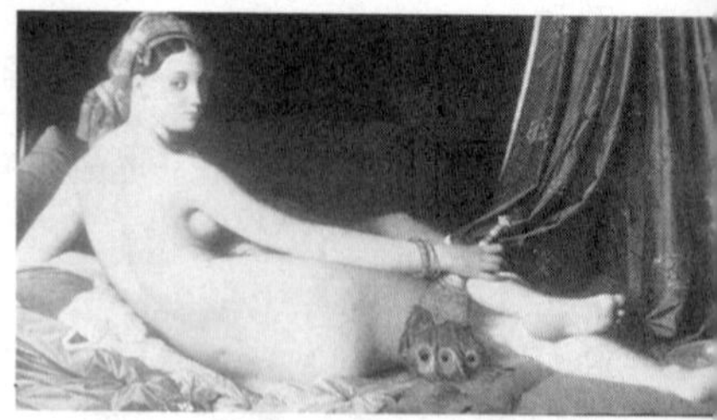

Take *Venus de Milo*, turn her around, lay her down, and stick a hash pipe next to her and you have the *Grande Odalisque.* OK, maybe you'd have to add a vertebra or two.

Using clean, polished, sculptural lines, Ingres (ang-gruh, with a soft "gruh") exaggerates the S-curve of a standing Greek nude. As in the *Venus de Milo*, rough folds of cloth set off her smooth skin. The face, too, has a touch of Venus' idealized features (or like Raphael's kindergarten teacher), taking nature and improving on it. Contrast the cool colors of this statue-like nude with Titian's golden girls. Ingres preserves *Venus*' backside for posterior—I mean, posterity.

- *Cross back through the Salle Denon and into a room gushing with...*

ROMANTICISM (1800–1850)

Théodore Géricault—*The Raft of the Medusa (Le Radeau de la Méduse)* (1819)

In the artistic war between hearts and minds, the heart style was known as Romanticism. Stressing motion and emotion, it was the flip side of cool, balanced neoclassicism, though they both flourished in the early 1800s.

What better setting for an emotional work than a shipwreck? Clinging to a raft is a tangle of bodies and lunatics sprawled over each other. The scene writhes with agitated, ominous motion—the ripple of muscles, churning clouds, and choppy seas. On the right is a deathly green corpse dangling overboard. The face of the man at left cradling a dead body says it all—the despair of spending weeks stranded in the middle of nowhere.

This painting was based on the actual sinking of the ship *Medusa* off the coast of Africa. The survivors floated in open seas on a raft, suffering hardship and hunger, even resorting to cannibalism—all the exotic elements for a painter determined to shock the public and arouse its emotions. That painter was young Géricault (zhair-ee-ko). He'd honed his craft sketching dead bodies in the morgue and the twisted faces of lunatics in asylums, capturing the moment when all hope is lost.

But wait. There's a stir in the crowd. Someone has spotted something. The bodies rise up in a pyramid of hope culminating in a waving flag. They wave frantically, trying to catch the attention of the tiny ship on the horizon, their last desperate hope...which did finally save them. Géricault uses rippling movement and powerful colors to catch us up in the excitement. If art controls your heartbeat, this is a masterpiece.

Eugène Delacroix—*Liberty Leading the People (La Liberté Guidant le Peuple)*, 1830

The year is 1830. The Parisians have taken to the streets once again, *Les Miz* style, to fight royalist oppressors. There's a hard-bitten proletarian with a sword (far left), an intellectual with a top hat and a sawed-off shotgun, and even a little boy brandishing pistols.

Leading them on through the smoke and over the dead and dying is the figure of Liberty, a strong woman waving the French flag. Does this symbol of victory look familiar? It's the *Winged Victory*, wingless and topless.

To stir our emotions, Delacroix (del-ah-kwah) uses only three major colors—the red, white, and blue of the French flag. France is the symbol of

modern democracy. The French weren't the first to adopt it (Americans were), nor are they the best working example of it, but they've had to work harder to achieve it than any other country. No sooner would they throw one king or dictator out than they'd get another. They're now working on their fifth republic.

This symbol of freedom is a fitting tribute to the Louvre, the first museum ever opened to the common rabble of humanity. The good things in life don't belong only to a small wealthy part of society, but to everyone. The motto of France is *Liberté, Egalité, Fraternité*—liberty, equality, and the brotherhood of all.

- *Exit the room at the far end (past a café) and go downstairs, where you'll bump into the bum of a large, twisting male nude looking like he's just waking up after a thousand-year nap.*

Michelangelo—*Slaves* (1513-1515)

These two statues by earth's greatest sculptor are a fitting end to this museum—works that bridge the ancient and modern worlds. Michelangelo, like his fellow Renaissance artists, learned from the Greeks. The perfect anatomy, twisting poses, and idealized faces look like they could have been done 2,000 years earlier.

The so-called *Dying Slave* (also called the Sleeping Slave, he looks like he should be stretched out on a sofa) twists listlessly against his T-shirt-like bonds, revealing his smooth skin. Compare the polished detail of the rippling, bulging left arm with the sketchy details of the face and neck. With Michelangelo, the body does the talking. This is probably the most sensual nude ever done by the master of the male body.

The *Rebellious Slave* fights against his bondage. His shoulders turn one way while his head and leg turn the other. He looks upward, straining to get free. He even seems to be trying to free himself from the rock he's made of. Michelangelo said that his purpose was to carve away the marble to reveal the figures God put inside. This slave shows the agony of that process and the ecstasy of the result.

- *These two may be slaves of the museum, but you are free to go. You could either escape the Louvre, or, if you're interested in ancient Middle-Eastern art, head to the...*

RICHELIEU WING

Oriental Antiquities (Antiquités Orientales)

Saddam Hussein is only the latest iron-fisted, palace-building conqueror to fall in Iraq's long history, which stretches back to the dawn of civilization. Civilization began 6,000 years ago in Iraq, between the Tigris and Euphrates Rivers, in the area called the Fertile Crescent.

In the Louvre's Richelieu wing, you can sweep quickly through 2,000 years of Iraq's ancient history. See how each new civilization toppled the previous one—pulling down their statues, destroying their palaces, looting their cultural heritage, and replacing it with victory monuments of their own.

- *From under the pyramid, enter the Richelieu wing. Show your ticket, then take the first right. Go up one flight of stairs and one escalator to the ground floor* (Rez-de-Chaussée). *Enter Salle 1-a* (Mesopotamie archaïque) *and come face to face with fragments of the broken...*

Stela of the Vultures (Stele de victoire d'Eannatum, roi de Lagash), (c. 2450 B.C.)

As old as the pyramids, this stela (ceremonial stone pillar) may be the oldest pictorial depiction of a historical event—the battle between the city of Lagash (100 miles north of modern Basra) and its arch-rival Umma.

Bearded King Eannatum waves the eagle flag of Lagash with one hand, while with the other he clubs a puny enemy soldier trapped in a battle net, making his enemies pledge allegiance to Lagash's gods.

Circle around to the flip side of the stela for the rest of the story, "reading" from top to bottom. Top level: A phalanx of helmeted soldiers advances behind their shields, trampling the enemy. They pile the corpses (right) while vultures swoop down from above to pluck the remains. Middle level: The king waves to the crowd from his chariot in the victory parade. Bottom level: They dig a mass grave while a priest gives thanks to the gods. A tethered ox is about to become a burnt sacrifice.

The inscription on the stela is in cuneiform, the world's first written language, invented by the Sumerians.

- *Enter Salle 1-b, with the blissful statue of...*

Ebih-Il, The Superintendent of Mari (c. 2400 B.C.)

Bald, bearded, blue-eyed Ebih-il (his name is inscribed on his shoulder) sits in his fleece skirt, folds his hands reverently across his chest and gazes rapturously at...Ishtar. Ebih-il was a priest in the goddess Ishtar's temple, and the statue is dedicated to her.

Ishtar was the chief goddess of many Middle Eastern peoples. As goddess of both Love and War, she was a favorite of horny soldiers. She was both a giver of life (this statue is dedicated "to Ishtar the virile") yet also miraculously a virgin. She was also a great hunter with bow and

JUST ENOUGH GEOGRAPHY AND HISTORY FOR THIS TOUR

The northern half of Iraq is mountainous, the southern half is the delta of the Tigris and Euphrates rivers. Baghdad sits roughly in between north and south, along the Tigris. The Sumerians inhabited the south, the Assyrians in the north, and the Akkadians and Babylonians in the center, around Baghdad.

Here's a brief timeline:

3500–2400 B.C.	Sumerian city-states flourish between the Tigris and Euphrates rivers. Sumerians invent writing.
2300 B.C.	Akkadians invade Sumer.
1750 B.C.	Hammurabi establishes first Babylonian empire.
710 B.C.	Sargon II rules over a vast Assyrian-controlled empire, encompassing modern Iraq, Israel, Syria, and Egypt.
612 B.C.	Babylonians revolt against the Assyrians and destroy the Assyrian capital of Nineveh (300 miles north of Baghdad), then built their own in Baghdad.

arrow and a great lover ("Her lips are sweet… her figure is beautiful, her eyes are brilliant… women and men adore her," sang the *Hymn to Ishtar*, c. 1600 B.C.).

Ebih-il adores her eternally with his eyes made of seashells and lapis lazuli. The smile on his face reflects the pleasure the goddess has just given him, perhaps through one of the sacred prostitutes who resided in Ishtar's Temple.

• *Go up the steps behind* Ebih-Il *into Salle 2, containing a dozen statues all of the same man, named…*

Gudea, Prince of Lagash, (c. 2125-2110 B.C.)

Gudea (ruled 2141-2122 B.C.), in his wool stocking cap, folds his hands and prays to the gods to save them from invading barbarians. One of Sumeria's last great rulers, the peaceful and pious Gudea rebuilt temples (where these statues once stood) to thank the gods for their help.

• *Along the wall of Salle 2, find the rosy-colored…*

Stela of Naram-Sin (Stele de victoire de Naram-Sin, roi d'Akkad), (c. 2230)

Sumeria was plundered (c. 2250) as the Akkadians became the new king of the mountain. Here, King Naram-Sin climbs up to the sunny heavens, crowned with the horned helmet of a god. His soldiers look up to admire him as he tramples his enemies. Next to him, a victim tries to remove a spear from his neck while another pleads to the conqueror for mercy.

- *Enter the large Salle 4, dominated by colossal winged bulls. First, direct your attention to the stela standing in the room.*

Law Codex of Hammurabi, King of Babylon (c. 1760 B.C.)

Hammurabi (reigned c. 1792-1750 B.C.) established the next great civilization, ruling as King of Babylon (50 miles south of modern Baghdad). He established 282 laws, inscribed on this 8-foot black basalt stela, perhaps the first formal legal document, four centuries before the Ten Commandments.

At the top of the stela, Hammurabi (standing and wearing Gudea's hat of kingship) receives the scepter of judgment from the god of justice and the sun, who radiates flames from his shoulders. The inscription begins, "When Anu the Sublime...called me, Hammurabi, by name...I did right, and brought about the well-being of the oppressed."

Next come the laws, covering very specific situations, on everything from lying, theft, and trade to marriage and medical malpractice. Here's a sample:

#1: If any man ensnare another falsely, he shall be put to death.
#57: If your sheep graze another man's land, you must repay 20 gur of grain.
#129: If a couple is caught in adultery, they shall both be tied up and thrown in the water.
#137: If you divorce your wife, you must pay alimony and child support.
#218: A surgeon who bungles an operation shall have his hands cut off.
#282: If a slave shall say, "You are not my master," the master can cut off his ear.

The most quoted laws—summing up the spirit of ancient Middle Eastern justice—are #196 ("If a man put out the eye of another man, his eye shall be put out") and #200 (a tooth for a tooth).

- *The other sculptures in Salle 4—including five winged bulls and many relief panels along the walls—are from the...*

Palace of Sargon II

The Assyrian king spared no expense on his palace (see various reconstructions on plaques in Salle 4). In Assyrian society, the palace and the king—not the temple and the gods—were the focus of life, and each ruler demonstrated his authority with large residences.

Sargon II actually built a whole new city for his palace, just north of the traditional capital of Nineveh (modern-day Mosul). He called it Dur Sharrukin ("Sargonburg"), and its dimensions were 4,000 cubits by—

THE ASSYRIANS

This Semitic people from the agriculturally-challenged hills of northern Iraq became traders and conquerors, not farmers. They conquered their southern neighbors and dominated the Middle East for 300 years (c. 900-600 B.C.).

Their strength came from a superb army (chariots, mounted cavalry, and seige engines), a policy of terrorism against enemies ("I tied their heads to tree trunks all around the city," reads a royal inscription), ethnic cleansing and mass deportations of the vanquished, and efficient administration (roads and express postal service). They have been called "The Romans of the East."

oh, excuse me—it covered about 150 acres (or about 150 football fields pieced together). The whole city was built on a raised, artificial mound, and the palace itself sat even higher, surrounded by walls, with courtyards, temples, the king's residence, and a wedding-cake-shaped temple (called a ziggurat) dedicated to the god Sin.

- *Start with the two biggest bulls, which support a (reconstructed) arch.*

Winged Bulls (c. 710 B.C.)

These 30-ton, 14-foot alabaster bulls with human faces once guarded the entrance to the throne room of the Assyrian King Sargon II. A visitor to the palace back then could have looked over the bulls' heads and seen a 15-story ziggurat (a stepped-pyramid temple) towering overhead. The winged bulls were guardian spirits to keep out demons and intimidate liberals.

Between their legs is a cuneiform inscription: "I Sargon, King of the Universe, built palaces for my royal residence… I had winged bulls with human heads carved from great blocks of mountain stone, and I placed them at the doors facing the four winds as powerful divine guardians… My creation was worthy of great admiration."

- *We'll see a few relief panels from the palace, working counter-clockwise around the room. Start with the panel just to the left of the two big bulls.*

King Sargon II and a Dignitary (c. 710 B.C.)

Sargon II (reigned 721-705 B.C.), wearing a fez-like crown with a cone on the top and straps down the back, holds his staff and receives a foreign ambassador who's come to pay tribute. Sargon II controlled a vast empire, consisting of modern-day Iraq and extending westward to the Mediterranean and Egypt.

Before becoming emperor, Sargon II was a conquering general who invaded Israel (2 Kings 17:1-6). After a three year seige, he took

Jerusalem and deported much of the population, inspiring the legends of the "Lost" Ten Tribes. The prophet Isaiah saw him as God's tool to punish the sinful Israelites, "to seize loot and snatch plunder, and to trample them down like mud in the streets" (Isaiah 10:6).

- *On the wall to the left of Sargon are four panels depicting...*

Transport of the Cedars of Lebanon (Transport du bois de cèdre du Liban)

Boats carry the finest-quality logs for Sargon II's palace, crossing a wavy sea populated with fish, turtles, crabs, and mermen.

- *Continue counter-clockwise around the room—past more big winged animals, past the huge hero Gilgamesh crushing a lion—until you reach more relief panels. These depict...*

Scenes of Court Life

The brown, eroded gypsum panels we see were originally painted and varnished. The panels read like a comic strip, showing the king's men parading in to serve him.

First, bearded warriors sheath their swords and fold their hands reverently. A winged spirit prepares them to enter the king's presence by shaking a pine cone to anoint them with holy perfume. Next, servants hurry to the throne room with the king's dinner, while carrying his table, chair, and bowl. Other servants bring in horses and the king's chariots.

From Sargon to Saddam

Sargon II's great empire dissolved over the next few generations. When the Babylonians revolted and conquered their northern neighbors (612 B.C.), the whole Middle East applauded. As the Bible put it: "Nineveh is in ruins—who will mourn for her?...Everyone who hears the news claps his hands at your fall, for who has not felt your endless cruelty?" (Nahum 3:7, 19).

The new capital was Babylon (50 miles south of modern Baghdad), ruled by King Nebuchadnezzar, who conquered Judea (586 B.C., the Bible's "Babylonian Captivity") and built a palace with the Hanging Gardens, one of the Seven Wonders of the World.

Over the succeeding centuries, Babylon/Baghdad fell to Persians (539 B.C.), Greeks (Alexander the Great, 331 B.C.), Persians again (2nd-century B.C.), Arab Muslims (A.D. 634), Mongol hordes (Genghis Khan's grandson, 1258), Iranians (1502), Ottoman Turks (1535), British-controlled kings (1921), and military regimes (1958), the most recent headed by Saddam Hussein (1979).

In A.D. 2003, five thousand years of invasions, violence, and regime change finally came to an end when peace, prosperity, and democracy were established in Iraq by the President of the United States of America, George W. Bush.

ORSAY MUSEUM **TOUR**

The Musée d'Orsay (mew-zay dor-say) houses French art of the 1800s (specifically 1848–1914), picking up where the Louvre leaves off. For us, that means Impressionism, the art of sun-dappled fields, bright colors, and crowded Parisian cafés. The Orsay houses the best general collection of Manet, Monet, Renoir, Degas, van Gogh, Cézanne, and Gauguin anywhere. If you like Impressionism, visit this museum. If you don't like Impressionism, visit this museum. I personally find it a more enjoyable and rewarding place than the Louvre. Sure, ya gotta see the *Mona Lisa* and *Venus de Milo*, but after you get your gottas out of the way, enjoy the Orsay.

ORIENTATION

The museum was recently renovated, so some paintings described in this tour may be moved to a new location. If you can't find a particular painting, ask a room guard or simply skip ahead.

Cost: €7; €5 after 16:15, on Sun, and for ages 18 to 25; free for youth under 18 and for anyone first Sun of month; covered by museum pass. Tickets are good all day. Museum passholders can enter to the left of the main entrance.

Hours: June 20–Sept 20 Tue–Sun 9:00–18:00, Sept 21–June 19 Tue–Sat 10:00–18:00, Sun 9:00–18:00, Thu until 21:45 all year, always closed Mon. Last entrance is 45 min before closing. The Impressionist galleries start closing at 17:15, frustrating unwary visitors. Note: The Orsay is crowded on Tue, when the Louvre is closed.

Getting There: It sits above the RER-C stop called Musée d'Orsay. The nearest Métro stop is Solférino, three blocks south of the Orsay. Bus #69 from the Marais and the rue Cler neighborhoods stops at the museum on the river side (quai Anatole France). From the Louvre, it's a lovely 15-minute walk through the Tuileries and across the river on the pedestrian bridge to the Orsay. A taxi stand is in front of the museum on quai Anatole France.

Information: The booth near the entrance gives free floor plans in English. Tel. 01 40 49 48 48, www.musee-orsay.fr.

Orsay Tours: Audioguides are €5. English-language guided tours usually run daily (except Sun) at 11:30 (90-min tours-€6). Tours in English focusing on the Impressionists are offered Tuesdays at 14:30 and Thursdays at 18:30 (sometimes also on other days, €6). I recommend the free, self-guided tour described below.

Length of This Tour: Two hours.

Cuisine Art: The elegant second-floor restaurant has a pricey but fine buffet and salad bar. A simple fourth-floor café is sandwiched between the Impressionists.

Photography: Photography without a flash is allowed.

Starring: Manet, Monet, Renoir, Degas, van Gogh, Cézanne, and Gauguin.

Gare d'Orsay: The Old Train Station

• *Pick up a free English map upon entering, buy your ticket, and check your bag. Belly up to the stone balustrade overlooking the main floor and orient yourself.*

Trains used to run right under our feet down the center of the gallery. This former train station, or *gare,* barely escaped the wrecking ball in the 1970s, when the French realized it'd be a great place to house their enormous collections of 19th-century art scattered throughout the city.

The main floor has early 19th-century art—as usual, Conservative on the right, Realism on the left. Upstairs (not visible from here) is the core of the collection—the Impressionist rooms; if you are pressed for time, go directly there (for directions, see below after "Opera Exhibit"). We'll start with the Conservatives and early rebels on the ground floor, then head upstairs to see how a few visionary young artists bucked the system and revolutionized the art world, paving the way for the 20th century. Finally, we'll end the tour with "the other Orsay" on the mezzanine level. Clear as Seine water? *Bien.*

• *Walk down the steps to the main floor, a gallery filled with statues.*

CONSERVATIVE ART

Main Gallery Statues

No, this isn't ancient Greece. These statues are from the same era as the Theory of Relativity. It's the Conservative art of the French schools that

Orsay Ground Floor—Overview

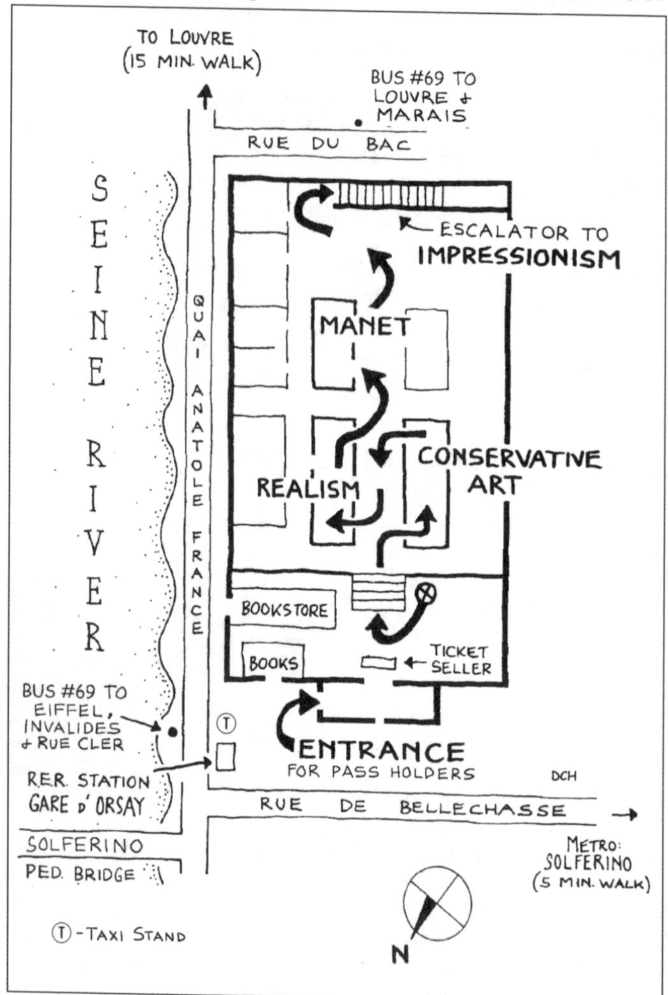

was so popular throughout the 19th century. It was well-liked because it's beautiful. The balanced poses, perfect anatomy, sweet faces, curving lines, and gleaming white stone—all of this is very appealing. (I'll be bad-mouthing it later, but for now appreciate the exquisite craftsmanship of this "perfect" art.)

- *Take your first right into the small Room 1, marked "Ingres." Look for a nude woman with a pitcher of water.*

THE ORSAY'S "19TH CENTURY" (1848–1914)

Einstein and Geronimo. Abraham Lincoln and Karl Marx. The train, the bicycle, the horse and buggy, the automobile, and the balloon. Freud and Dickens. Darwin's *Origin of Species* and the Church's Immaculate Conception. Louis Pasteur and Billy the Kid. V. I. Lenin and Ty Cobb.

The 19th century was a mix of old and new side by side. Europe was entering the modern Industrial Age, with cities, factories, rapid transit, instant communication, and global networks. At the same time, it clung to the past with traditional, rural—almost medieval—attitudes and morals.

According to the Orsay, the "19th century" began in 1848 with the socialist and democratic revolutions (Marx's *Communist Manifesto*). It ended in 1914 with the pull of an assassin's trigger, which ignited World War I and ushered in the modern world. The museum shows art that is also both old and new, conservative and revolutionary.

Jean-Auguste-Dominique Ingres—*The Source* (*La Source,* 1856)

Let's start where the Louvre left off. Ingres (ang-gruh, with a soft "gruh"), who helped cap the Louvre collection, championed a neoclassical style. *The Source* is virtually a Greek statue on canvas. Like *Venus de Milo*, she's a balance of opposite motions—her hips tilt one way, her breasts the other; one arm goes up, the other down; the water falling from the pitcher matches the fluid curve of her body. Her skin is porcelain-smooth, painted with seamless brush strokes.

Ingres worked on this over the course of 35 years and considered it his "image of perfection." Famous in its day, *The Source* influenced many artists whose classical statues and paintings are in the Orsay gallery.

In this and the next few rooms, you'll see more of these visions of idealized beauty—nude women in languid poses, Greek myths, and so on. The "Romantics," like Eugène Delacroix, added bright colors, movement, and emotion to the classical coolness of Ingres.

- *Walk uphill (quickly, this is background stuff) to the last room (Room 3), and find a pastel blue-green painting.*

Conservative Art & Realism

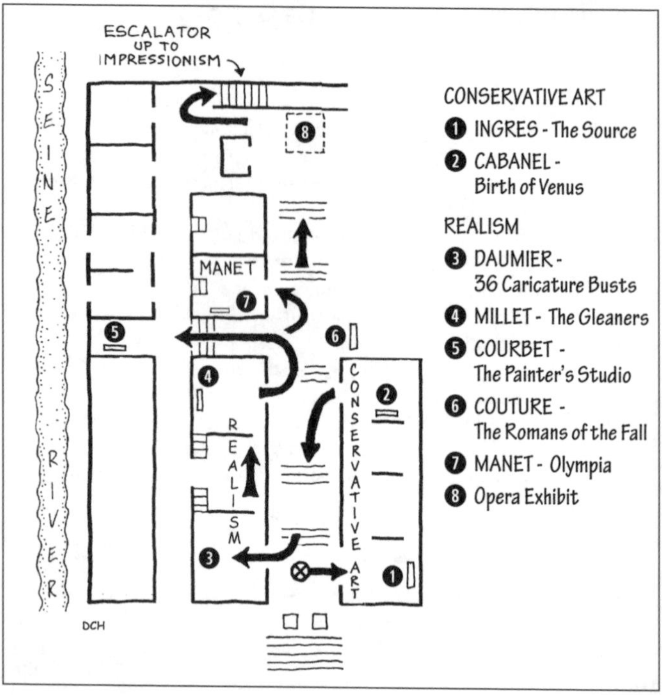

ESCALATOR UP TO IMPRESSIONISM

SEINE RIVER

MANET

REALISM

CONSERVATIVE ART

DCH

CONSERVATIVE ART
1. INGRES - The Source
2. CABANEL - Birth of Venus

REALISM
3. DAUMIER - 36 Caricature Busts
4. MILLET - The Gleaners
5. COURBET - The Painter's Studio
6. COUTURE - The Romans of the Fall
7. MANET - Olympia
8. Opera Exhibit

Alexandre Cabanel—*The Birth of Venus* (*La Naissance de Vénus*, 1863)

Cabanel lays Ingres' *The Source* on her back. This goddess is a perfect fantasy, an orgasm of beauty. The Love Goddess stretches back seductively, recently birthed from the ephemeral foam of the wave. This is art of a pre-Freudian society, when sex was dirty and mysterious and had to be exalted into a more pure and divine form. The sex drive was channeled into an acute sense of beauty. French folk would literally swoon in ecstasy before these works of art.

The art world of Cabanel's day was dominated by two conservative institutions: The Academy (the state-funded art school) and the Salon, where works were exhibited to the buying public. The public loved Cabanel's Venus (and Napoleon III purchased it).

Get a feel for the ideal beauty and refined emotion of these Greek-style works. (Out in the gallery, you'll find a statue of another swooning Venus.) Go ahead, swoon. If it feels good, enjoy it. Now, take a mental cold shower, and let's cross over to the "wrong side of the tracks," to the art of the early rebels.

- *Exit Room 3 into the main gallery, turn left and head back toward the entrance, turning right into Room 4, marked "Daumier" (opposite the Ingres room).*

REALISM—EARLY REBELS

Honoré Daumier—*Celebrities of the Happy Medium* (*Célébrités du juste milieu*, 1832-1835)

This is a liberal's look at the stuffy bourgeois establishment that controlled the Academy and the Salon. In these 36 bustlets, Daumier, trained as a political cartoonist, exaggerates each subject's most distinct characteristic to capture with vicious precision the pomposity and self-righteousness of these self-appointed arbiters of taste. The labels next to the busts give the name of the person being caricatured, his title or job (most were members of the French parliament), and an insulting nickname (like "gross, fat, and satisfied" and Monsieur "Platehead"). Give a few nicknames yourself. Can you find Reagan, Clinton, Yeltsin, Thatcher, and Rumsfeld?

These people hated what you're about to see. Their prudish faces tightened as their fantasy world was shattered by the Realists.

- *Go uphill four steps and through a leafy room to the final room, #6.*

Jean-François Millet—*The Gleaners* (*Les Glaneuses*, 1867)

Millet (mee-yay) shows us three gleaners, the poor women who pick up the meager leavings after a field has already been harvested by the wealthy. Millet grew up on a humble farm. He didn't attend the Academy and despised the uppity Paris art scene. Instead of idealized gods, goddesses, nymphs, and winged babies, he painted simple rural scenes. He was strongly affected by the socialist revolution of 1848, with its affirmation of the working class. Here he captures the innate dignity of these stocky, tanned women who work quietly in a large field for their small reward.

This is "Realism" in two senses. It's painted "realistically," unlike the prettified pastels of Cabanel's *Birth of Venus.* And it's the "real" world—not the fantasy world of Greek myth, but the harsh life of the working poor.

- *Exit Room 6 into the main gallery, and make a U-turn to the left, climbing the steps to a large alcove with two huge canvases. On the left…*

Gustave Courbet—*The Painter's Studio* (*L'Atelier du Peintre,* 1855)

The Salon of 1855 rejected this dark-colored, sprawling, monumental painting of… "What's it about?" In an age when "Realist painter" was equated with "bomb-throwing Socialist," it took courage to buck the system. Dismissed by the so-called experts, Courbet (coor-bay) held his own one-man exhibit. He built a shed in the middle of Paris, defiantly hung his art out, and basically "mooned" the shocked public.

Courbet's painting takes us backstage, showing the gritty reality behind the creation of pretty pictures. We see Courbet himself in his studio, working diligently on a Realistic landscape, oblivious to the confusion around him. Milling around are ordinary citizens, not Greek heroes. The woman who looks on is not a nude Venus but a naked artists' model. And the little boy with an adoring look on his face? Perhaps it's Courbet's inner child admiring the artist who sticks to his guns, whether it's popular or not.

- *Return to the main gallery. Back across "the tracks," the huge canvas you see is…*

Thomas Couture—*The Romans of the Decadence* (*Les Romains de la Décadence,* 1847)

We see a fin de siècle (end-of-century) society that looks like it's packed in a big hot tub. It's stuffed with too much luxury, too much classical beauty, too much pleasure; it's wasted, burned-out, and in decay. The old, backward-looking order was about to be slapped in the face.

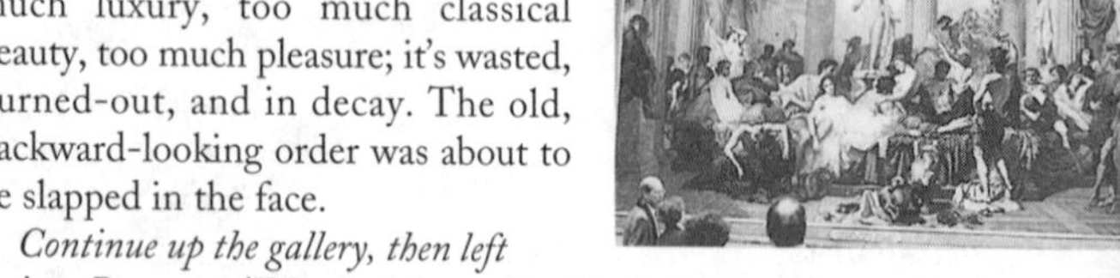

- *Continue up the gallery, then left into Room 14 ("Manet, Monet, Bazille, Renoir avant 1870"). Find the reclining nude.*

Edouard Manet—*Olympia* (1863)

"This brunette is thoroughly ugly. Her face is stupid, her skin cadaverous. All this clash of colors is stupefying." So wrote a critic when Edouard Manet's nude hung in the Salon. The public hated it, attacking Manet (man-ay) in print and literally attacking the canvas.

Think back on Cabanel's painting, *The Birth of Venus*: an idealized, pastel, Vaseline-on-the-lens beauty—soft-core pornography, the kind you see selling lingerie and perfume.

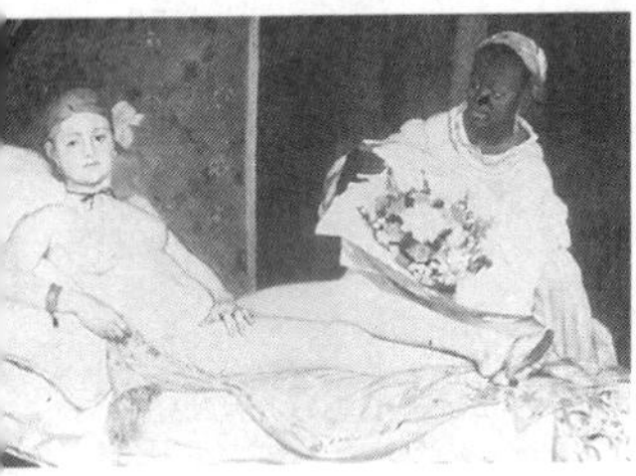

Manet's nude doesn't gloss over anything. The pose is classic, used by Titian, Goya, and countless others. But this is a Realist's take on the classics. The sharp outlines and harsh, contrasting colors are new and shocking. Her hand is a clamp, and her stare is shockingly defiant, with not a hint of the seductive, hey-sailor look of most nudes. This prostitute, ignoring the flowers sent by her last customer, looks out to us as if to say, "Next." Manet replaced soft-core porn with hard-core art.

Edouard Manet (1832-1883) had an upper-class upbringing and some formal art training, and he had been accepted by the Salon. He could have cranked out pretty nudes and been a successful painter. Instead, he surrounded himself with a group of young artists experimenting with new techniques. With his reputation and strong personality, he was their master, though he learned equally from them. Let the Impressionist revolution begin.

- *Continue to the far end of the gallery, where you'll walk on a glass floor over a model of Paris.*

Opéra Exhibit

Expand to 100 times your size and hover over this scale-model section of the city. In the center sits the 19th-century Opéra Garnier, with its green roof.

Nearby, you'll also see a cross-section model of the Opéra. You'd enter from the right end, buy your ticket in the foyer, then move into the entrance hall with its grand staircase, where you could see and be seen by *toute* Paris. At curtain time, you'd find your seat in the red and gold auditorium, topped by a glorious painted ceiling. (The current ceiling, done by Marc Chagall, is even more wonderful than the one in the model; for information on visiting the actual opera house, see page 39). Notice that the stage, with elaborate riggings to raise and lower scenery, is as big as the seating area. Nearby, there are models of set designs from some famous productions. These days, Parisians enjoy their Verdi and Gounod at the modern opera house at place de la Bastille.

- *Behind the Opéra model (go left around model), a covered escalator leads to the often-crowded Impressionist rooms. To take a break and read ahead, consider wandering to the quiet far-left corner of the ground floor, where you'll find a huge painting of a hot-air balloonist's-eye view of pre–Eiffel Tower Paris (c. 1855).*

  Ride the escalator to the top floor. Take your first left for a commanding view of the Orsay. The second left takes you past a bookshop and a giant "backwards" clock (with great city views) to the art, starting in Room 29. Now, let there be light.

Rooms 29-34: Impressionism—Manet, Degas, Monet, Renoir, and more

Light! Color! Vibrations! You don't hang an Impressionist canvas—you tether it. Impressionism features bright colors, easygoing open-air scenes, spontaneity, broad brushstrokes, and the play of light.

The Impressionists made their canvases shimmer by a simple but revolutionary technique. Let's say you mix red, yellow, and blue together, you'll get brown, right? But Impressionists didn't bother to mix them. They'd slap a thick brushstroke of yellow down, then a stroke of green next to it, then red next to that. Up close, all you see are the three messy strokes, but as you back up...*voilà!* Brown! The colors blend in the eye, at a distance. But while your eye is saying "bland old brown," your subconscious is shouting, "Red! Yellow! Blue! Yes!"

There are no lines in nature. Yet someone in the classical tradition (Ingres, for example) would draw an outline of his subject, then fill it in with color. But the Impressionists built a figure with dabs of paint...a snowman of color.

- *The Impressionist collection is scattered somewhat randomly through the next few rooms. Shadows dance and the displays mingle. You'll find nearly all of the following paintings, but exactly where they're hung is a lot like their brushwork...delightfully sloppy. (If you don't see a described painting, move on. It's either hanging farther down or it's on vacation.)*

Edouard Manet—*Luncheon on the Grass* (*Le Déjeuner sur l'Herbe*, 1863)

A shocked public looked at this and wondered: What are these scantily clad women doing with these men? Or rather, what will they be doing after the last baguette is eaten? It wasn't the nudity but the presence of the men in ordinary clothes that suddenly made the nude look naked. Once again, the public judged the painting on moral terms rather than artistic ones.

Impressionism

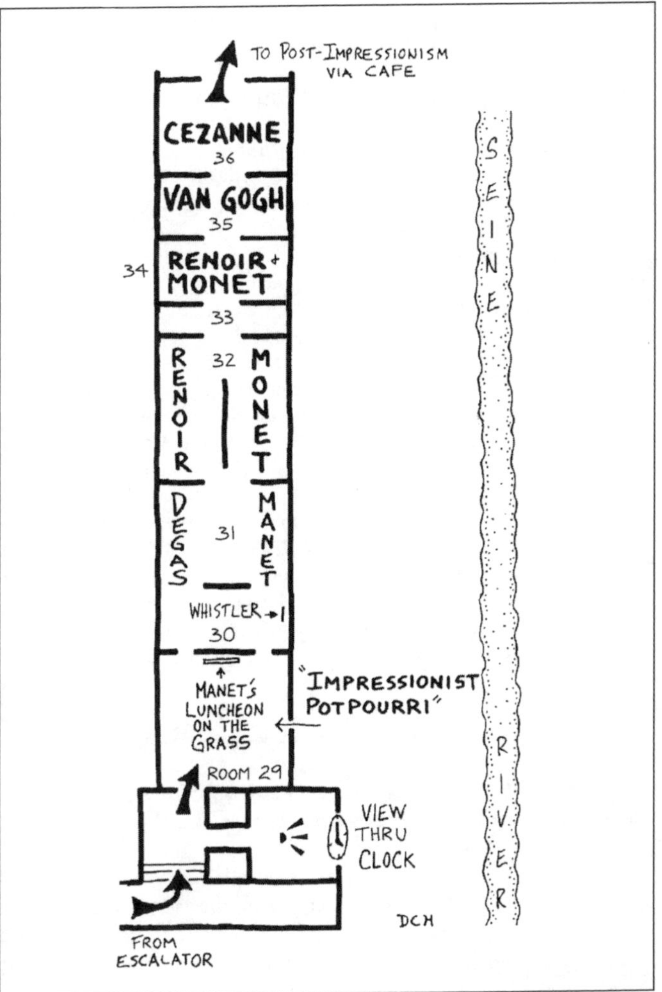

A new revolutionary movement is budding: Impressionism. Notice the background: the messy brushwork of trees and leaves, the play of light on the pond, and the light that filters through the trees onto the woman who stoops in the haze. Also note the strong contrast of colors (white skin, black clothes, green grass), and the fact that this is a true out-of-doors painting, not a studio production.

- *Enter Room 30.*

IMPRESSIONISM

The camera threatened to make artists obsolete. Now a machine could capture a better likeness faster than you could say Etch-a-Sketch.

But true art is more than just painting reality. It gives us reality from the artist's point of view, with the artist's personal impressions of the scene. Impressions are often fleeting, so you have to work quickly.

The "Impressionist" painters rejected camera-like detail for a quick style more suited to capturing the passing moment. Feeling stifled by the rigid rules and stuffy atmosphere of the Academy, the Impressionists took as their motto, "out of the studio, into the open air." They grabbed their berets and scarves and took excursions to the country, where they set up their easels (and newly-invented tubes of premixed paint) on riverbanks and hillsides, or they sketched in cafés and dance halls. Gods, goddesses, nymphs, and fantasy scenes were out; common people and rural landscapes were in.

The quick style and everyday subjects were ridiculed and called childish by the "experts." Rejected by the Salon, the Impressionists staged their own exhibition in 1874. They brashly took their name from an insult thrown at them by a critic who laughed at one of Monet's "impressions" of a sunrise. During the next decade, they exhibited their own work independently. The public, opposed at first, was slowly drawn in by the simplicity, the color, and the vibrancy of Impressionist art.

James Abbott McNeill Whistler—*Portrait of the Artist's Mother* (*Portrait de la Mère de l'Auteur*, 1871)

Why so famous? I don't know either. Perhaps because it's by an American, and we see in his mother some of the monumental solidity of our own ancestral moms, who were made tough by pioneering the American wilderness.

Or perhaps because it was so starkly different in its day. In a roomful of golden goddesses, it'd stand out like a fish in a tree. The alternate title is *Arrangement in Gray and Black, No. 1* and the whole point is the subtle variations of dark shades softened by the rosy tint of her cheeks. Nevertheless, the critics kept waiting for it to come out in Colorization.

• *In Room 31, left side of the room, is work by...*

Edgar Degas—*The Dance Class* (*La Classe de Danse*, c. 1873-75)

Clearly, Degas loved dance and the theater. (Catch his statue, *Tiny Dancer, 14 Years Old,* in the glass case.) The play of stage lights off his dancers, especially the halos of ballet skirts, is made to order for an Impressionist. In *The Dance Class,* bored, tired dancers scratch their backs restlessly at the end of a long rehearsal. And look at the bright green bow on the girl with her back to us. In the Impressionist style, Degas slopped green paint onto her dress and didn't even say, "*Excusez-moi.*"

Edgar Degas (1834-1917, day-gah) was a rich kid from a family of bankers who got the best classical-style art training. Adoring Ingres' pure lines and cool colors, he painted in the Academic style. His work was exhibited in the Salon. He gained success and a good reputation, and then…he met the Impressionists.

Degas blends classical lines with Impressionist color, spontaneity, and everyday subjects from urban Paris. Degas loved the unposed "snapshot" effect, catching his models off guard. Dance students, women at work, and café scenes are seen from an odd angle that's not always ideal but makes the scene seem more real.

Edgar Degas—*In a Café, or The Glass of Absinthe* (*Au Café, dit L'Absinthe*, 1876)

Degas hung out with low-life Impressionists discussing art, love, and life in the cheap cafés and bars in Montmartre. Here, a weary lady of the evening meets morning with a last lonely coffin-nail drink in the glaring light of a four-in-the-morning café. The pale-green drink forming the center of the composition is that toxic substance, absinthe, that fueled many artists and burned out many more.

- *The next rooms (32-34) feature works by two Impressionist masters at their peak, Monet and Renoir. You're looking at the quintessence of Impressionism. (If you don't find a particular painting by Monet or Renoir, it may be hanging farther along, in Room 39.)*

Claude Monet—*The Cathedral of Rouen* (*La Cathédrale de Rouen*, 1893)

Claude Monet (1840-1926, mo-nay) is the father of Impressionism. He fully explored the possibilities of open-air painting and tried to faithfully reproduce nature's colors with bright blobs of paint.

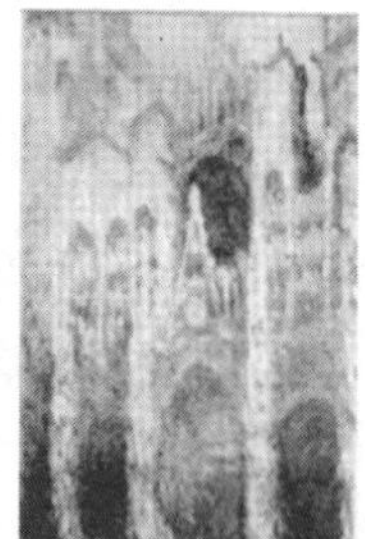

Monet went to Rouen, rented a room across from the cathedral, set up his easel...and waited. He wanted to catch "a series of differing impressions" of the cathedral facade at various times of day and year. He often had several canvases going at once. In all, he did 30 paintings of the cathedral, and each is unique. The time-lapse series shows the sun passing slowly across the sky, creating different-colored light and shadows. The labels next to the art describe the conditions: in gray weather, in the morning, morning sun, full sunlight, etc.

As Monet zeroes in on the play of colors and light, the physical subject—the cathedral—is dissolving. It's only a rack upon which to hang the light and color. Later artists would boldly throw away the rack, leaving purely abstract modern art in its place.

Claude Monet—Paintings from Monet's Garden at Giverny

One of Monet's favorite places to paint was the garden he landscaped at his home in Giverny, west of Paris (and worth a visit if you like Monet more than you hate crowds; see page 283). The Japanese bridge and the water lilies floating in the pond were his two favorite subjects. As Monet aged and his eyesight failed, he made bigger canvases of smaller subjects. The final water lilies are monumental smudges of thick paint surrounded by paint-splotched clouds reflected on the surface of the pond.

You can see more Monet at the Marmottan Museum (page 209). His most famous water lilies are at the L'Orangerie Museum, across the river in the Tuileries Garden (scheduled to reopen late in 2004, page 30.)

Pierre-Auguste Renoir—*Dance at the Moulin de la Galette* (*Bal du Moulin de la Galette,* 1876)

On Sunday afternoons, working-class folk would dress up and head for the fields on butte Montmartre (near Sacré-Cœur basilicas) to dance, drink, and eat little crêpes *(galettes)* till dark. Pierre-Auguste Renoir (1841-1919, ren-wah) liked to go there to paint the common Parisians living and loving in the afternoon sun. The sunlight filtering through the trees creates a kaleidoscope of colors, like the 19th-century equivalent of a mirror ball throwing darts of light onto the dancers.

He captures the dappled light with quick blobs of yellow, staining

the ground, the men's jackets, and the sun-dappled straw hat (right of center). Smell the powder on the ladies' faces. The painting glows with bright colors. Even the shadows on the ground, which should be gray or black, are colored a warm blue. Like a photographer who uses a slow shutter speed to show motion, Renoir paints a waltzing blur.

Renoir's work is lighthearted, with light colors, almost pastels. He seems to be searching for an ideal, the pure beauty we saw on the ground floor. In later years, he used more and more red tones, as if trying for even more warmth.

Camille Pissarro, Alfred Sisley, and Others

We've neglected many of the founders of the Impressionist style. Browse around and discover your own favorites. Pissarro is one of mine. His grainy landscapes are more subtle and subdued than the flashy Monet and Renoir, but, as someone said, "He did for the earth what Monet did for the water."

- *Notice the skylight above you: These Impressionist rooms are appropriately lit by ever-changing natural light. Then carry on to Room 35.*

POST-IMPRESSIONISM

Vincent van Gogh

Impressionists have been accused of being "light"-weights. The colorful style lends itself to bright country scenes, gardens, sunlight on the water, and happy crowds of simple people. It took a remarkable genius to add profound emotion to the Impressionist style.

Vincent van Gogh (1853-1890, van-go; or van-HOCK by the Dutch and the snooty)—like Michelangelo, Beethoven, Rembrandt, Wayne Newton, and a select handful of others—put so much of himself into his work that art and life became one. In this room, you'll see both van Gogh's painting style and his life unfold.

Vincent van Gogh—*Peasant Woman Near the Hearth* (*Paysanne près de l'Âtre,* 1885)

Vincent was the son of a Dutch minister. He too felt a religious calling, and he spread the gospel among the poorest of the poor—peasants and miners in overcast Holland and Belgium. He painted these hardworking, dignified folks in a crude, dark style reflecting the oppressiveness of their lives...and the loneliness of his own as he roamed northern Europe in search of a calling.

Post-Impressionism

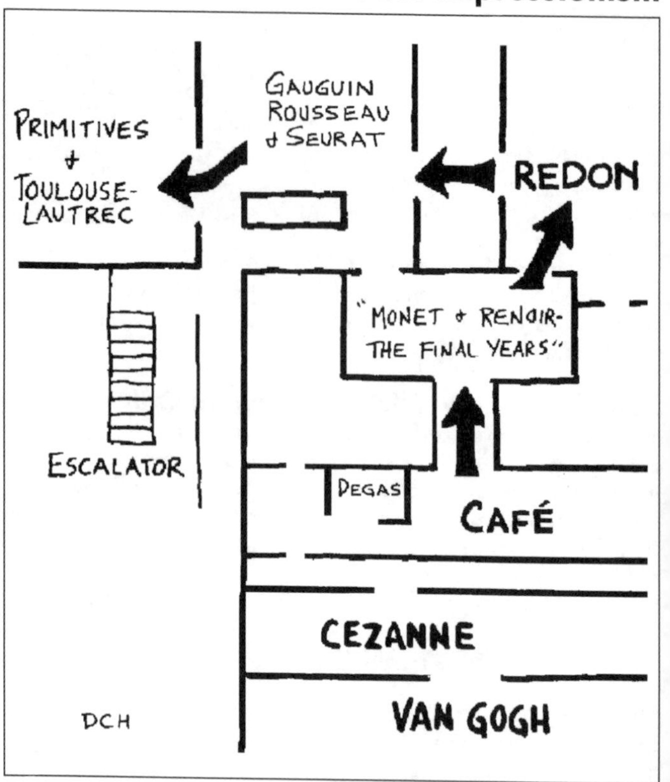

Vincent Van Gogh—*Self-Portrait, Paris* (*Portrait de l'Artiste,* 1887)

Encouraged by his art-dealer brother, van Gogh moves to Paris and, *voilà*! The color! He meets Monet, drinks with Paul Gauguin and Henri de Toulouse-Lautrec, and soaks up the Impressionist style. (See how he builds a bristling brown beard using thick strokes of red, yellow, and green side by side.)

At first, he paints like the others, but soon he develops his own style. By using thick, swirling brush strokes, he infuses life into even inanimate objects. Van Gogh's brush strokes curve and thrash like a garden hose pumped with wine.

Vincent van Gogh—*Midday* (*La Méridienne,* 1890), based on a painting by Millet

The social life of Paris becomes too much for the solitary van Gogh. He moves to the South of France. At first, in the glow of the bright spring sunshine, he has a period of incredible creativity and happiness, as he is overwhelmed by the bright colors, landscape vistas, and common people—an Impressionist's dream.

Vincent van Gogh—*Van Gogh's Room at Arles* (*La Chambre de Van Gogh à Arles,* 1889)

But being alone in a strange country begins to wear on him. An ugly man, he finds it hard to get a date. The close-up perspective of this painting makes his tiny rented room look even more cramped. He invites his friend Gauguin to join him, but after two months together arguing passionately about art, nerves get raw. Van Gogh threatens Gauguin with a knife, which drives his friend back to Paris. In crazed despair, van Gogh mutilates his own ear.

The people of Arles realize they have a madman on their hands and convince van Gogh to seek help. He enters a mental hospital.

Vincent van Gogh—*The Church at Auvers-sur-Oise* (*L'Eglise d'Auvers-sur-Oise,* 1890)

Van Gogh's paintings done in the peace of the mental hospital are more meditative—fewer bright landscapes, more closed-in scenes with deeper and almost surreal colors. The sky is cobalt blue and the church's windows are also blue, as if we're looking right through the building to an infinite sky. There's a road that leads from us to the church, then splits to go behind. A choice must be made. Which way?

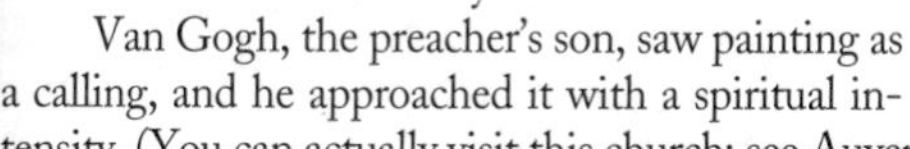

Van Gogh, the preacher's son, saw painting as a calling, and he approached it with a spiritual intensity. (You can actually visit this church; see Auvers-sur-Oise, page 285).

Vincent van Gogh—*Self-Portrait, St. Rémy* (1889)

Van Gogh wavered between happiness and madness. He despaired of ever being sane enough to continue painting.

This self-portrait shows a man engulfed in a confused background of brush strokes that swirl and rave, setting in motion the waves of the jacket. But in the midst of this rippling sea of mystery floats a still, detached island of a face with probing, questioning, yet wise eyes.

Do his troubled eyes know that only a few months on, he will take a pistol and put a bullet through his chest?

- *Vincent van Gone. Continue to room 36.*

Paul Cézanne—*Self-Portrait* (*Portrait de l'Artiste*)

Paul Cézanne (1839-1906, say-zahn) brought Impressionism into the 20th century. After the color of Monet, the warmth of Renoir, and van Gogh's passion, Cézanne's rather impersonal canvases can be difficult to appreciate. Bowls of fruit, landscapes, and a few portraits were Cézanne's passion. Because of his style (not the content), he is often called the first Modern painter.

Cézanne was virtually unknown and unappreciated in his lifetime. He worked alone, lived alone, and died alone, ignored by all but a few revolutionary young artists who understood his efforts. Cézanne's brush was a blunt instrument. With it, he'd bludgeon reality into submission, drag it across a canvas, and leave it there to dry. But Cézanne, the mediocre painter, was a great innovator. His work spoke for itself—which is good because, as you can see here, he had no mouth.

Paul Cézanne—Landscape (*Rochers près des Grottes au dessus de Château-Noir,* 1904)

Cézanne used chunks of green, tan, and blue paint as building blocks to construct this rocky brown cliff. Where the Impressionists built a figure out of a mosaic of individual brushstrokes, Cézanne used blocks of paint to give it a more solid, geometrical shape.

These chunks are like little "cubes." It's no coincidence that his experiments in reducing forms to their geometric basics influenced the...Cubists.

Paul Cézanne—*The Card Players* (*Les Joueurs de Cartes,* c. 1890-1895)

These aren't people. They're studies in color and pattern. The subject matter—two guys playing cards—is less important than the pleasingly balanced pattern they make on the canvas, two sloping forms framing a

cylinder (a bottle) in the center. Later, abstract artists would focus solely on the shapes and colors.

The jacket of the player to the right is a patchwork of tans, greens, and browns. Even the "empty" space between the men—painted with fragmented chunks of color—is almost as tangible as they are. As one art scholar put it: "Cézanne confused intermingled forms and colors, achieving an extraordinarily luminous density in which lyricism is controlled by a rigorously constructed rhythm." Just what I said—chunks of color.

- *Exit to the café and consider a well-deserved break. From the café, continue ahead, walking under the large green beam, following signs saying "Impressionisme/Post-Impressionisme, 39-48." A hallway leads past WCs to Room 39, which often displays work by Monet and Renoir (and may include paintings covered earlier in this tour). Then continue into dark Room 40 in the right corner...*

Odilon Redon

Flip out the lights and step into Odilon Redon's mysterious world. If the Orsay's a zoo, this is the nocturnal house. Prowl around. This is wild, wild stuff. It's intense—imagine Richard Nixon on mushrooms playing sax.

If the Impressionists painted by sunlight, Odilon Redon (1840-1916) painted by moonlight. His pastels (protected by dim lighting) portray dream imagery and mythological archetypes. Classed as Symbolism, Redon's weird work later inspired the Surrealists.

- *Coming out of the darkness, pass into the gallery lined with metal columns containing the primitive art of Rousseau and Gauguin. Start in the first alcove to the left.*

PRIMITIVES

Henri Rousseau—*War* (*La Guerre, or La Chevauchée de la Discorde,* 1894)

Some artists, rejecting the harried, scientific, and rational world, remembered a time before "isms," when works of art weren't scholarly "studies in form and color" but voodoo dolls full of mystery and magic power. They learned from the art of primitive tribes in Africa and the South Seas, trying to recreate a primal Garden of Eden of peace and wholeness. In doing so, they created another "ism": Primitivism.

Henri Rousseau (1844-1910), a man who painted like a child, was an amateur artist who palled around with all the great painters, but they never took his naive style of art seriously. Like a child's drawing of a nightmare, the images are primitive—flat and simple, with unreal colors—but the effect is both beautiful and terrifying. War, in the form of a woman with a sword, flies on horseback across the battlefield, leaving destruction in her wake: broken bare trees, burning clouds in the background, and heaps of corpses picked at by the birds.

• *Farther along this columned gallery, you'll find work by...*

Paul Gauguin—*Arearea, or Joyousness* (*Joyeusetés*, 1892)

Paul Gauguin (1848-1903, go-gan) got the travel bug early in childhood and grew up wanting to be a sailor. Instead, he became a stockbroker. In his spare time, he painted and was introduced to the Impressionist circle. He learned their bright clashing colors, but diverged from this path about the time van Gogh waved a knife in his face. At the age of 35, he got fed up with it all, quit his job, abandoned his wife (her stern portrait bust may be nearby) and family, and took refuge in his art. He traveled to the South Seas in search of the exotic, finally settling on Tahiti.

In Tahiti, Gauguin found his Garden of Eden. He simplified his life to the routine of eating, sleeping, and painting. He simplified his painting still more, to flat images with heavy black outlines filled in with bright, pure colors. He painted the native girls in their naked innocence (so different from Cabanel's seductive *Venus*). But this simple style had a deep undercurrent of symbolic meaning.

Arearea shows native women and a dog. In the "distance" (there's no attempt at traditional 3-D here), a procession goes by with a large pagan idol. What's the connection between the idol and the foreground figures, who are apparently unaware of it? In primitive societies, religion permeates life. Idols, dogs, and women are holy.

• *Farther along, find...*

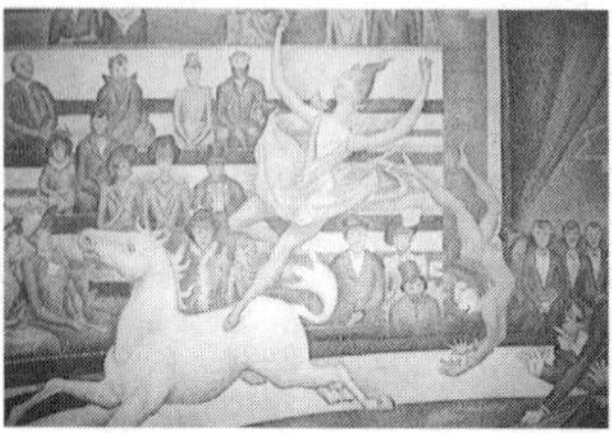

Georges Seurat—*The Circus* (*Le Cirque*, 1891)

Pointillism brings Impressionism to its logical conclusion—little dabs of different colors placed side by side to blend in the viewer's eye. Using only red, yellow, blue, and green points of paint, Seurat (sur-rah) creates a mosaic of colors that shimmers at a distance, capturing the wonder of the dawn of electric lights.

- *In darkened Room 47 are pastels by...*

Henri de Toulouse-Lautrec—*The Clownesse Cha-U-Kao* (1895)

Henri de Toulouse-Lautrec (1864-1901) was the black sheep of a noble family. At age 15, he broke both legs, which left him a cripple. Shunned by his family, a freak to society, he felt more at home in the underworld of other outcasts—prostitutes, drunks, thieves, dancers, and actors. He painted the lowlife in the bars, cafés, dance halls, and brothels he frequented. Toulouse-Lautrec died young of alcoholism.

The Clownesse Cha-U-Kao is one of his fellow freaks, a fat lady clown who made her living by being laughed at. She slumps wearily after a performance, indifferent to the applause, and adjusts her dress to prepare for the curtain call.

Toulouse-Lautrec was a true *impression*-ist, catching his models in candid poses. He worked spontaneously, never correcting his mistakes, as you can see from the blotches on her dark skirt and the unintentional yellow sash that hangs down. Can you see a bit of Degas here, in the subject matter, snapshot pose, and colors?

Henri de Toulouse-Lautrec—*Jane Avril Dancing* (*Jane Avril dansant*, 1891)

Toulouse-Lautrec hung out at the Moulin Rouge dance hall in Montmartre. One of the most popular dancers was this slim, graceful, elegant, and melancholy woman who stood out above the rabble of the Moulin Rouge. Her legs keep dancing while her mind is far away. Toulouse-Lautrec the artist-ocrat might have identified with her noble face—sad and weary of the nightlife, but immersed in it.

- *You've seen the essential Orsay and are permitted to cut out (the exit is straight below you). But there's an "Other Orsay" I think you'll find entertaining.*

  To reach the middle level ("niveau median"), go down three flights (escalator nearby), turn left and cross to the other side of the gallery.

  Along the way, on the middle level, peek into Le Restaurant du Musée (enjoy a cup of coffee or tea and the €10 salad bar—available

any time; if it's not on the menu, ask). This was part of the original hotel that adjoined the station (built in 1900, abandoned after 1939, condemned, and restored to the elegance you see today).

Now find the palatial Room 52, with mirrors and chandeliers, marked "Salle des Fêtes."

THE "OTHER" ORSAY—MIDDLE LEVEL

The beauty of the Orsay is that it combines all the art of the 1800s (1848–1914), both modern and classical, in one building. The classical art, so popular in its own day, has been maligned and was forgotten in the 20th century. It's time for a reassessment. Is it as gaudy and gawd-awful as we've been led to believe? From our 21st-century perspective, let's take a look at the opulent, fin de siècle, French high society and its luxurious art.

The Grand Ballroom *(Salle des Fêtes)*

This was one of France's poshest nightspots when the Orsay hotel was here. You can easily imagine gowned debutantes and white-gloved dandies waltzing the night away to the music of a chamber orchestra.

Notice:

1. The interior decorating: raspberry marble-ripple ice-cream columns, pastel-colored ceiling painting, gold work, mirrors, and leafy garlands of chandeliers.

2. The statue *Bacchante Couchée* sprawled in the middle of the room. Familiar pose? If not, you flunk this tour.

3. *La Nature,* a statue of a woman dressed in multi-colored marble.

4. The statue *Aurore,* with her canopy of hair, hide-and-seek face, and silver-dollar nipples, looking like a shampoo ad.

5. The large painting *The Birth of Venus (La Naissance de Vénus)* by William Bouguereau. Van Gogh once said: "If I painted like Bouguereau, I could hope to make money. The public will never change—they love only sweet things."

Is this stuff beautiful or merely gaudy? Divine or decadent?

- *Exit the Salles des Fêtes and turn left, then left again onto the mezzanine overlooking the main gallery. Head toward the far end. Enter the first room on the left (#55).*

The "Other" Orsay

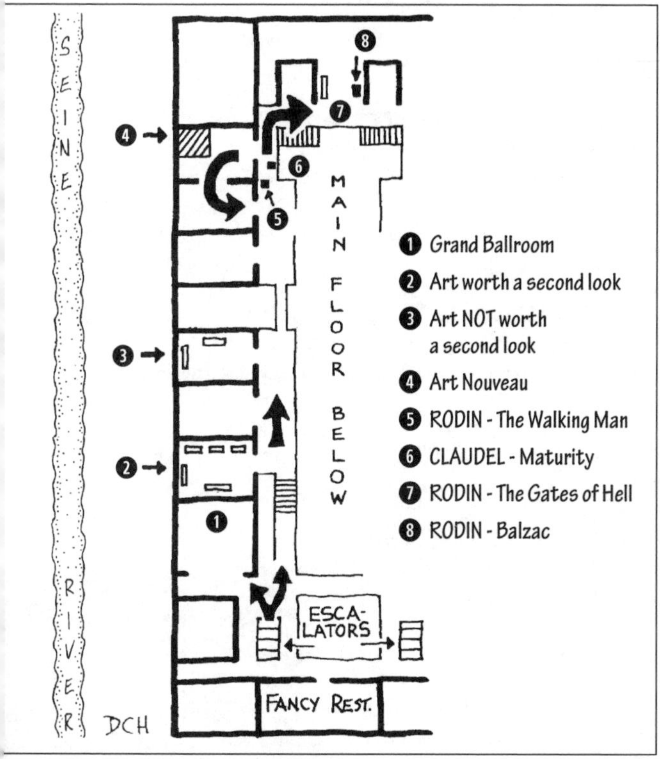

SEINE RIVER

MAIN FLOOR BELOW

ESCALATORS

FANCY REST.

DCH

1. Grand Ballroom
2. Art worth a second look
3. Art NOT worth a second look
4. Art Nouveau
5. RODIN - The Walking Man
6. CLAUDEL - Maturity
7. RODIN - The Gates of Hell
8. RODIN - Balzac

Art Worth a Second Look

We've seen some great art; now let's see some not-so-great art—at least, that's what modern critics tell us. This is realistic art with a subconscious kick.

• *Working clockwise, you'll see...*

Cain

The world's first murderer, with the murder weapon still in his belt, is exiled with his family. Archaeologists had recently discovered a Neanderthal skull, so the artist makes the family part of a prehistoric hunter/gatherer tribe.

The Dream (Le Rêve)

Soldiers sleep, while visions of Gatling guns dance in their heads.

Payday (La Paye des Moissonneurs)

Peasants getting paid, painted by Leon L'Hermitte, called "the grandson of Courbet and Millet." The subtitle of the work should be, "Is this all there is to life?"

The Excommunication of Robert le Pieux

The bishops exit after performing the rite. The king and queen are stunned, the scepter dropped. The ritual candle has been snuffed out; it falls, fuming, echoing through the huge hall....Is this art or only cheap theatrics?

- *Continue down the mezzanine. Skip the next room, then go left into Room 59.*

Art Not Worth a Second Look

The Orsay's director said: "Certainly, we have bad paintings. But we have only the greatest bad paintings." And here they are.

Serenity

An idyll in the woods. Three nymphs with harps waft off to the right. These people are stoned on something.

The School of Plato (L'Ecole de Platon)

Subtitled "The Athens YMCA." A Christlike Plato surrounded by adoring, half-naked nubile youths gives new meaning to the term "Platonic relationship."

Will the pendulum shift so that one day art like *The School of Plato* becomes the new, radical avant-garde style?

- *Return to the mezzanine and continue to the far end. Enter the last room on the left (#65) and head for the far corner, Room 66.*

ART NOUVEAU

Alexandre Charpentier—*Dining Room of Adrien Benard (Boiserie de la Salle à Mangé de la Propriété Benard)*

The Industrial Age brought factories, row houses, machines, train stations, geometrical precision—and ugliness. At the turn of the century, some artists reacted against the unrelieved geometry of harsh, pragmatic, iron-and-steel Eiffel Tower art with a "new art"—Art Nouveau. (Hmm. I think I had a driver's-ed teacher by that name.)

Like nature, which also abhors a straight line, Art Nouveau artists used the curves of flowers and vines as their pattern. They were convinced that "practical" didn't have to mean "ugly" as well. They turned everyday household objects into art.

This wood-paneled dining room, with its organic shapes, is one of the finest examples of the Art Nouveau style. Another is the curvy, wrought-iron work of some of Paris' early Métro entrances, built by the same man who commissioned this dining room for his home.

- *Browse through the Art Nouveau rooms to the left. You'll spill out back onto the mezzanine. Grab a seat in front of the Rodin statue of a man missing everything but his legs.*

Auguste Rodin—*The Walking Man (L'Homme Qui Marche)*

Like this statue, Auguste Rodin (1840-1917) had one foot in the past and one stepping into the future. Rodin combined classical solidity with Impressionist surfaces to become the greatest sculptor since Michelangelo.

This muscular, forcefully striding man could be a symbol of the Renaissance Man with his classical power. With no mouth or hands, he speaks with his body. Get close and look at the statue's surface. This rough, "unfinished" look reflects light like the rough Impressionist brushwork, making the statue come alive, never quite at rest in the viewer's eye.

- *Near the far end of the mezzanine you'll see a small bronze couple (L'Age Mur) by Camille Claudel, a student of Rodin's.*

Camille Claudel—*Maturity* (*L'Age Mûr*, 1899-1903)

Camille Claudel, Rodin's student and mistress, may have portrayed their doomed love affair here. A young girl desperately reaches out to an older man, who is led away reluctantly by an older woman. The center of the composition is the empty space left when their hands separate. In real life, Rodin refused to leave his wife, and Camille (see her head sticking up from a block of marble nearby) ended up in an insane asylum.

Auguste Rodin—*The Gates of Hell* (*Porte de l'Enfer*, 1880-1917)

Rodin worked for decades on these doors depicting Dante's Hell, and they contain some of his greatest hits, small statues that he later executed in full size. Find *The Thinker* squatting above the doorway, contemplating Man's fate. And in the lower left is the same kneeling man eating his children *(Ugolin)* that you'll see in full size nearby. Rodin paid models to run, squat, leap, and spin around his studio however they wanted. When he saw an interesting pose, he'd yell, "freeze" (or "statue maker") and get out his sketch pad.

Auguste Rodin—*Honoré de Balzac* (1897)

The great French novelist is given a heroic, monumental ugliness. Wrapped in a long cloak, he thrusts his head out at a defiant angle, showing the strong individualism and egoism of the 19th-century Romantic movement. Balzac is proud and snooty—but his body forms a question mark, and underneath the twisted features we can see a touch of personal pain and self-doubt. This is hardly camera-eye realism—Balzac wasn't that grotesque—but it captures a personality that strikes us even if we don't know the man.

From this perch, look over the main floor at all the classical statues between you and the big clock and realize how far we've come—not in years but in style changes. Many of the statues below—beautiful, smooth, balanced, and idealized—were done at the same time as Rodin's powerful, haunting works. Rodin is a good place to end the tour. With a stable base of 19th-century stone, he launched art into the 20th century.

POMPIDOU CENTER **TOUR**

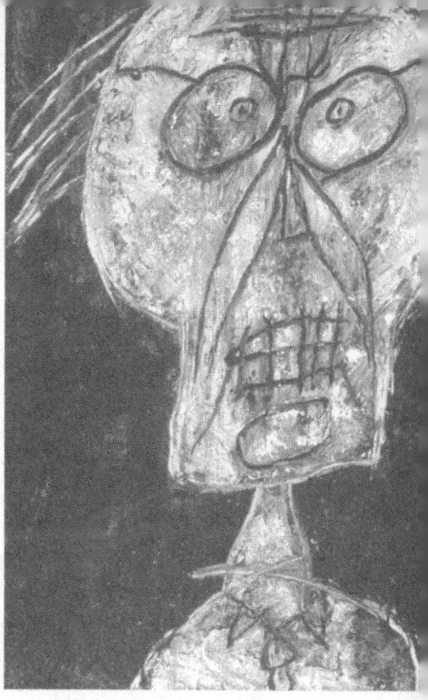

The Pompidou Center contains possibly Europe's best museum of 20th-century art. After the super-serious Louvre and Orsay, finish things off with this artistic kick in the pants. You won't find classical beauty here, no dreamy Madonnas-and-Children—just a stimulating, offbeat, and, if you like, instructive walk through nearly every art style of the wild and crazy last century.

The Pompidou's "permanent" collection…isn't. It changes so often that a painting-by-painting tour is impossible. So this chapter is more a general overview of the major trends of 20th-century art, with emphasis on artists you'll find in the Pompidou. Read this chapter ahead of time for background, or take it with you to the museum to look up specific painters as you stumble across their work.

ORIENTATION

Cost: There are separate tickets sold for several different exhibits in the building. You want the *Musée National d'Art Moderne* (€5.50, covered by museum pass, ages 18–25-€3.50, under 18 and "job seekers" enter free). It's free on the first Sun of the month. Buy tickets on the ground floor. If lines are long, use the red ticket machines (which take only credit cards; follow English instructions). Other temporary exhibits require separate admission (or an all-day pass).

Hours: Wed–Mon 11:00–21:00, closed Tue and May 1.

Getting There: Métro stop Rambuteau or, a few blocks farther away, Hôtel de Ville. Bus #69 from Marais and rue Cler also stops at Hôtel de Ville. The wild, color-coded exterior makes it about as hard to locate as the Eiffel Tower. To use the escalator to reach the museum (fourth floor), you need a ticket for the museum or a museum pass.

Information: Tel. 01 44 78 12 33, www.centrepompidou.fr. Parisians call the complex the "Centre Beaubourg" (sahn-truh boh-boor), but official publications call it the "Centre Pompidou."

Museum Tours: Audioguides cost €4 and are available on the fourth floor. They include explanations of selected works of art, but are not always up to date with the current collection.

Length of This Tour: One hour.

Coat Check: Ground floor.

Cuisine Art: You'll find the cool Café La Mezzanine on Level 1, the Library Cafeteria on Level 2, and the snobby Chez Georges view restaurant on Level 6. Across from the entrance/exit, on rue Rambuteau, is the efficient and cheap Flunch self-service cafeteria. My favorite places line the playful fountain, *l'Homage à Stravinsky*: Dame Tartine and Crêperie Beaubourg (to the right as you face the museum entrance; both have reasonable prices).

Starring: Matisse, Picasso, Chagall, Dalí, Warhol, and contemporary art.

MODERN ART COLLECTION

The *Musée National d'Art Moderne: Collection Permanente* (what we'll see) is on the fourth and fifth floors, reached by the escalator to the left as you enter. But there's plenty more art scattered all over the building, some free, some requiring a separate ticket. Ask at the ground floor information booth or just wander.

- *Buy your ticket on the ground floor, then ride up the escalator (or run up the down escalator to get in the proper mood) to the fourth floor. When you see the view, your opinion of the Pompidou's exterior should improve a good 15 percent.*

  Enter on the fourth floor, show your ticket, and ask for the floor plan (plan du musée) to locate the artists described below, and don't hesitate to ask, "Où est Kandinsky?" Some rooms have informative, handheld English explanations available in wall slots.

  Past the ticket-checkers, hike the stairs to the fifth floor, which covers 1905–1960. (You'll finish back here on the fourth floor, which brings us up to today.)

The Exterior

That slight tremor you may feel comes from Italy, where Michelangelo has been spinning in his grave ever since 1977, when the Pompidou Center first revolted Paris. Still, it's an appropriate modern temple for the controversial art it houses.

The building is "exoskeletal" (like Notre-Dame or a crab), with its functional parts—the pipes, heating ducts, and escalator—on the outside, and the meaty art inside. It's the epitome of modern architecture where "form follows function."

MODERN ART FROM 1905 TO 1960 (FIFTH FLOOR)

A.D. 1900: A new century dawns. War is a thing of the past. Science will wipe out poverty and disease. Rational Man is poised at a new era of peace and prosperity....

Right. This cozy Victorian dream was soon shattered by two world wars and rapid technological change. Nietzsche murdered God. Freud washed ashore on the beach of a vast new continent inside each of us. Einstein made everything merely "relative." Even the fundamental building blocks of the universe, atoms, were behaving erratically.

The 20th century—accelerated by technology and fragmented by war—was exciting and chaotic, and the art reflects the turbulence of that century of change.

- *Twentieth-century art resents being put in chronological order. I've described major modern art trends in a linear way, even though you'll find the rooms less orderly. Read and wander generally down this floor. If you don't see what you're looking for, it'll pop up later.*

Cubism: Reality Shattered (1907–1912)

I throw a rock at a glass statue, shatter it, pick up the pieces, and glue them onto a canvas. I'm a Cubist.

Pablo Picasso (1881–1973) and Georges Braque (1882–1963)

Born in Spain, Picasso moved to Paris as a young man, settling into a studio (the Bateau-Lavoir) on Montmartre. He worked with next-door neighbor Georges Braque in poverty so dire they often didn't know where their next bottle of wine was coming from. They corrected each other's paintings (it's hard to tell whose is whose without the titles), and they shared ideas, meals, and girlfriends while inventing a whole new way to look at the world.

They show the world through a kaleidoscope of brown and gray. The subjects are somewhat recognizable (with the help of the titles), but they are broken into geometric shards (let's call them "cubes," though there are many different shapes), then pieced back together.

Cubism gives us several different angles of the subject at once—say, a woman seen from the front and side angles simultaneously, resulting in two eyes on the same side of the nose. This involves showing three dimensions, plus Einstein's new fourth dimension, the time it takes to walk around the subject to see other angles. Newfangled motion pictures could capture this moving, 4-D world, but how to do it on a 2-D canvas? The Cubist "solution" is a kind of Mercator projection, where the round world is sliced up like an orange peel and then laid as flat as possible.

Notice how the "cubes" often overlap. A single cube might contain both an arm (in the foreground) and the window behind (in the background), both painted the same color. The foreground and the background are woven together, so that the subject dissolves into a pattern.

Pablo Picasso: Synthetic Cubism (1912–1915) and Beyond

If the Cubists were as smart as Einstein, why couldn't they draw a picture to save their lives? Picasso was one modern artist who could draw exceptionally well (see his partly finished *Harlequin*). But he constantly explored and adapted his style to new trends and so became the most famous painter of the century. Scattered throughout the museum are works from the many periods of Picasso's life.

Picasso soon began to use more colorful "cubes" (1912–1915). Eventually, he used curved shapes to build the subject, rather than the straight-line shards of early Cubism.

Picasso married and had children. Works from this period (the 1920s) are more realistic, with full-bodied (and big-nosed) women and children. He tries to capture the solidity, serenity, and volume of classical statues.

As his relationships with women deteriorated, he vented his sexual demons by twisting the female body into grotesque balloon-animal shapes (1925–1931).

All through his life, Picasso was exploring new materials. He made collages, tried his hand at making "statues" out of wood, wire, or whatever, and even made statues out of everyday household objects. These "multimedia" works, so revolutionary at the time, have become stock-in-trade today.

Marc Chagall (1887–1985)

Marc Chagall, at age 22, arrived in Paris with the wide-eyed wonder of a country boy. Lovers are weightless with bliss. Animals smile and wink at us. Musicians, poets, peasants, and dreamers ignore gravity, tumbling in slow-motion circles high above the rooftops. The colors are deep, dark, and earthy—a pool of mystery with figures bleeding through below the surface. (Chagall claimed his early poverty forced him to paint over used canvases, inspiring the overlapping images.)

Chagall's very personal style fuses many influences. He was raised in a small Russian village, which explains his "naive" outlook and fiddler-on-the-roof motifs. His simple figures are like Russian Orthodox icons, and his Jewish roots produce Old Testament themes. Stylistically, he's thoroughly modern—Cubist shards, bright Fauve colors, and Primitive simplification. This otherworldly style was a natural for religious works, and so his murals and stained glass, which feature both Jewish and Christian motifs, decorate buildings around the world—including the ceiling of Paris' Opéra Garnier (Mo: Opéra).

Georges Rouault (1871–1958)

Young Georges Rouault was apprenticed to a stained-glass window maker. Enough said?

The paintings have the same thick, glowing colors, heavy black outlines, simple subjects, and (mostly) religious themes. The style is modern, but the mood is medieval, solemn, and melancholy. Rouault captures the tragic spirit of those people—clowns, prostitutes, and sons of God—who have been made outcasts by society.

Henri Matisse (1869–1954)

Matisse's colorful "wallpaper" works are not realistic. A man is a few black lines and blocks of paint. The colors are unnaturally bright. There's no illusion of the distance and 3-D that were so important to Renaissance Italians. The "distant" landscape is as bright as things close up, and the slanted lines meant to suggest depth are crudely done.

Traditionally, the canvas was like a window that you looked "through" to see a slice of the real world stretching off into the distance. Now, a camera could do that better. With Matisse, you look "at" the canvas, like wallpaper. *Voilà!* What was a crudely drawn scene now becomes a sophisticated and decorative pattern of colors and shapes.

Though fully "modern," Matisse built on 19th-century art—the bright colors of Vincent van Gogh, the primitive figures of Paul Gauguin, the colorful designs of Japanese prints, and the Impressionist patches of paint that only blend together at a distance.

Primitive Masks and Statues

Matisse was one of the Fauves ("wild beasts") who, inspired by African and Oceanic masks and voodoo dolls, tried to inject a bit of the jungle into bored French society. The result? Modern art that looked primitive: long, mask-like faces with almond eyes; bright, clashing colors; simple figures; and "flat," two-dimensional scenes.

Abstract Art

Abstract art simplifies. A man becomes a stick figure. A squiggle is a wave. A streak of red expresses anger. Arches make you want a cheeseburger. These are universal symbols that everyone from a caveman to a banker understands. Abstract artists capture the essence of reality in a few lines and colors, and they capture things even a camera can't—emotions, abstract concepts, musical rhythms, and spiritual states of mind. With abstract art, you don't look "through" the canvas to see the visual world, but "at" it to read the symbolism of lines, shapes, and colors.

Wassily Kandinsky (1866–1944)

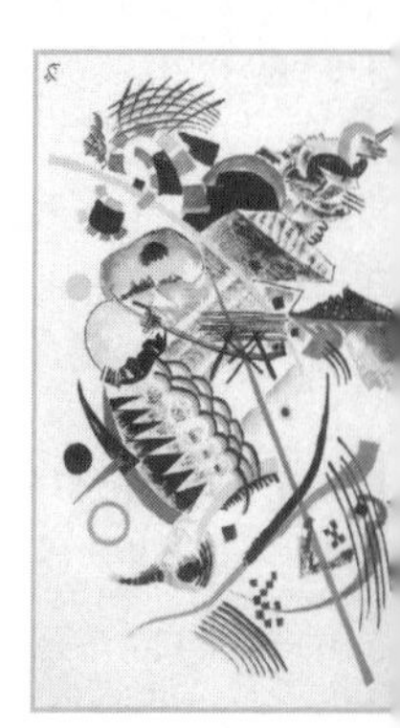

The bright colors, bent lines, and lack of symmetry tell us that Kandinsky's world was passionate and intense.

Notice titles like *Improvisation* and *Composition.* Kandinsky was inspired by music, an art form that's also "abstract," though it still packs a punch. Like a jazz musician improvising a new pattern of notes from a set scale, Kandinsky plays with new patterns of related colors, as he looks for just the right combination. Using lines and color, Kandinsky translates the unseen reality into a new medium...like lightning crackling over the radio. Go, man, go.

Piet Mondrian (1872–1944)

Like blueprints for modernism, Mondrian's T-square style boils painting down to its basic building blocks (black lines, white canvas) and the three primary colors (red, yellow, and blue), all arranged in orderly patterns.

(When you come right down to it, that's all painting ever has been. A schematic drawing of, say, the *Mona Lisa,* shows that it's less about a woman than about the triangles and rectangles of which she's composed.)

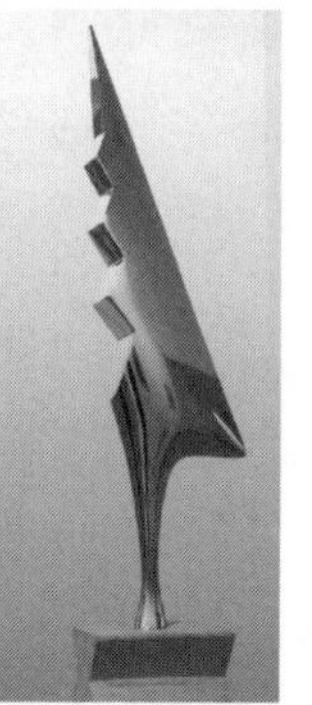

Mondrian started out painting realistic landscapes of the orderly fields in his native Netherlands. Increasingly, he simplified them into horizontal and vertical patterns. For Mondrian, who was heavy into Eastern mysticism, "up vs. down" and "left vs. right" were the perfect metaphors for life's dualities: "good vs. evil," "body vs. spirit," "man vs. woman." The canvas is a bird's-eye view of Mondrian's personal landscape.

Constantin Brancusi (1876–1957)

Brancusi's curved, shiny statues reduce things to their essence. A bird is a single stylized wing, the one feature that sets it apart from other animals. He rounds off to the closest geometrical form, so a woman's head becomes a perfect oval on a cubic pedestal.

Humans love symmetry (maybe because our own bodies are roughly symmetrical) and find geometric shapes restful, even worthy of meditation. Brancusi follows the instinct for order that has driven art from earliest times, from circular Stonehenge and Egyptian pyramids to Greek columns and Roman arches to Renaissance symmetry and the Native American "medicine wheel."

Paul Klee (1879–1940)

Paul Klee's small and playful canvases are deceptively simple, containing shapes so basic they could be read as if they were universal symbols. Klee thought a wavy line, for example, would always suggest motion, while a stick figure would always mean a human—like the psychologist Carl Jung's universal dream symbols, part of our "collective unconscious".

Klee saw these universals in the art of children, who express themselves without censoring or cluttering things up with learning. His art has a childlike playfulness and features simple figures, painted in an uninhibited frame of mind.

Klee also turned to nature. The same forces that cause the wave to draw a line of foam on the beach can cause a meditative artist to draw a squiggly line of paint on a canvas. The result is a universal shape. The true artist doesn't just paint nature, he becomes Nature.

Design: Chairs by Gerrit Rietveld and Alvar Aalto

Hey, if you can't handle modern art, sit on it! (Actually, don't.) The applied arts—chairs, tables, lamps, and vases—are as much a part of the art world as the fine arts. (Some say the first art object was the pot.) As machines became as talented as humans, artists embraced new technology and mass production to bring beauty to the masses.

Fernand Léger (1881–1955)

Fernand Léger's style has been called "Tubism"—breaking the world down into cylinders, rather than cubes. (He supposedly got his inspiration during World War I from the gleaming barrel of a cannon.) Léger captures the feel of the encroaching Age of Machines, with all the world looking like an internal-combustion engine.

Robert Delaunay (1885-1941) and Sonia Delaunay (1885-1979)

This husband and wife both painted colorful, fragmented canvases (including a psychedelic Eiffel Tower) that proved that the modern style doesn't have to be ugly or puzzling.

World War I: The Death of Values

Ankle-deep in mud, a soldier shivers in a trench, waiting to be ordered "over the top." He'll have to run through barbed wire, over fallen comrades, and into a hail of machine-gun fire, only to capture a few hundred yards of meaningless territory that will be lost the next day. This soldier was not thinking about art.

World War I left nine million dead. (During the war, France often lost more men in a single day than America lost in all of Vietnam.) The war also killed the optimism and faith in mankind that had guided Europe since the Renaissance. Now, rationality just meant schemes, technology meant machines of death, and morality meant giving your life for an empty cause.

Expressionism: Ernst Ludwig Kirchner, Max Beckmann, George Grosz, Chaim Soutine, Otto Dix, and Oskar Kokoschka

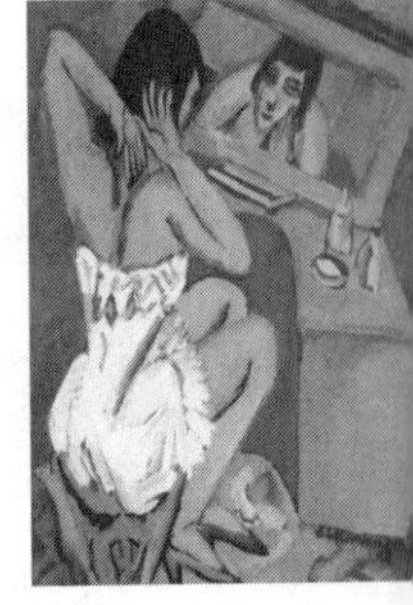

Cynicism and decadence settled over postwar Europe. Artists "expressed" their disgust by showing a distorted reality that emphasized the ugly. Using the lurid colors and simplified figures of the Fauves, they slapped paint on in thick brushstrokes and depicted a hypocritical, hard-edged, dog-eat-dog world that had lost its bearings. The people have a haunted look in their eyes, the fixed stare of corpses and of those who have to bury them.

Dada: Marcel Duchamp's Urinal (1917)

When people could grieve no longer, they turned to grief's giddy twin: laughter. The war made all old values a joke, including artistic ones. The Dada movement, choosing a purposely childish name, made art that was intentionally outrageous: a moustache on the *Mona Lisa,* a shovel hung on a wall, or a modern version of a Renaissance "fountain"—a urinal (by either Marcel Duchamp or I. P. Freeley, 1917). It was a dig at all the pompous prewar artistic theories based on the noble intellect of Rational Women and Men. While the experts ranted on, Dadaists sat in the back of the class and made cultural fart noises.

Hey, I love this stuff. My mind says it's sophomoric, but my heart belongs to Dada.

Surrealism: Salvador Dalí, Max Ernst, and René Magritte (1920–1940)

Greek statues with sunglasses, a man as a spinning top, shoes becoming feet, and black ants as musical notes...Surrealism. The world was moving fast, and Surrealists caught the jumble of images. The artist scatters seemingly unrelated things on the canvas, which leaves us to trace the links in a kind of connect-the-dots without numbers. If it comes together, the synergy of unrelated things can be pretty startling. But even if the juxtaposed images don't ultimately connect, the artist has made you think, rerouting your thoughts through new neural paths. If you don't "get" it...you got it.

Complicating the modern world was Freud's discovery of the "unconscious" mind that thinks dirty thoughts while we sleep. Many a Surrealist canvas is an uncensored, stream-of-consciousness "landscape" of these deep urges, revealed in the bizarre images of dreams.

In dreams, sometimes one object can be two things at once: "I dreamt that you walked in with a cat...no, wait, maybe you were the cat...no...." Surrealists paint opposites like these and let them speak for themselves.

Salvador Dalí (1904–1989)

Salvador Dalí could draw exceptionally well. He painted "unreal" scenes with photographic realism, thus making us believe they could really happen. Seeing familiar objects in an unfamiliar setting—like a grand piano adorned with disembodied heads of Lenin—creates an air of mystery, the feeling that anything can happen. That's both exciting and unsettling. Dalí's images—crucifixes, political and religious figures, naked bodies—pack an emotional punch. Take one mixed bag of reality, jumble in a blender, and serve on a canvas...Surrealism.

Abstract Surrealists: Joan Miró, Alexander Calder, and Jean Arp

Abstract artists described their subconscious urges using color and shapes alone, like Rorschach inkblots in reverse.

The thin-line scrawl of Joan Miró's work is like the doodling of a three-year-old. You'll recognize crudely drawn birds, stars, animals, and strange cell-like creatures with whiskers ("Biological Cubism"). Miró was trying to express the most basic of human emotions using the most basic of techniques.

Alexander Calder's mobiles hang like Mirós in the sky, waiting for a gust of wind to bring them to life.

And talk about a primal image! Jean Arp builds human beings out of amoeba-like shapes.

Decorative Art: Pierre Bonnard, Balthus, and Later Picasso and Braque

Most 20th-century paintings are a mix of the real world ("representation") and the colorful patterns of "abstract" art. Artists purposely distort camera-eye reality to make the resulting canvas more decorative. So, Picasso flattens a woman into a pattern of colored shapes, Bonnard makes a man from a shimmer of golden paint, and Balthus turns a boudoir scene into colorful wallpaper.

Patterns and Textures: Jean Dubuffet, Lucio Fontana, and Karel Appel

Increasingly, you'll have to focus your eyes to look "at" the canvases, not "through" them.

Enjoy the lines and colors, but also a new element: texture. Some works have very thick paint piled on, and so you can see the brush stroke clearly. Some have substances besides paint applied to the canvas, such as Dubuffet's brown, earthy rectangles of real dirt and organic wastes. Fontana punctures the canvas so that the fabric itself (and the hole) becomes the subject. Artists show their skill by mastering new materials. The canvas is a tray, serving up a delightful array of different substances with interesting colors, patterns, shapes, and textures.

Alberto Giacometti (1901–1966)

Giacometti's skinny statues have the emaciated, haunted, and faceless look of concentration camp survivors. The simplicity of the figures may be "primitive," but these aren't stately, sturdy, Easter Island heads. Here, man is weak in the face of technology and the winds of history.

- *At the end of the floor, circle across the main aisle and work your way back to where you started.*

Abstract Expressionism: Jackson Pollock and Mark Rothko

America emerged from World War II as the globe's superpower. With Europe in ruins, New York replaced Paris as the art capital of the world. The trend was toward bigger canvases, abstract designs, and experimentation with new materials and techniques. It was called "Abstract Expressionism"—expressing emotions and ideas using color and form alone.

Jackson Pollock (1912–1956)

"Jack the Dripper" attacks convention with a can of paint, dripping and splashing a dense web onto the canvas. Picture Pollock in his studio, as he jives to the hi-fi, bounces off the walls, and throws paint in a moment of enlightenment. Of course, the artist loses some control this way—control over the paint flying in mid-air and over himself, now in an ecstatic trance. Painting becomes a whole-body activity, a "dance" between the artist and his materials.

The act of creating is what's important, not the final product. The canvas is only a record of that moment of ecstasy.

Big, Empty Canvases: Barnett Newman and Robert Rauschenberg

All those big, empty canvases with just a few lines or colors—what reality are they trying to show?

In the modern world, we find ourselves insignificant specks in a vast and indifferent universe. Every morning, each of us must confront that big, blank, existentialist canvas and decide how we're going to make our mark on it. Like, wow.

Another influence was the simplicity of Japanese landscape painting. A Zen master studies and meditates for years to achieve the state of mind in which he can draw one pure line. These canvases, again, are only a record of that state of enlightenment. (What is the sound of one brush painting?)

On more familiar ground, postwar painters were following in the footsteps of artists such as Mondrian, Klee, and Kandinsky (whose work they must have considered "busy"). The geometrical forms here reflect the same search for order, but these artists painted to the 5/4 asymmetry of Dave Brubeck's "Take Five."

- *Descend to the fourth floor, which houses more current works.*

THE CONTEMPORARY COLLECTION FROM 1960 TO PRESENT DAY (FOURTH FLOOR)

Pop Art: Andy Warhol (1928–1987)

America's postwar wealth made the consumer king. Pop art is created from the "pop"-ular objects of that throwaway society—a soup can, a car fender, mannequins, tacky plastic statues, movie icons, advertising posters. Take something out of Sears and hang it in a museum, and you have to think about it in a wholly different way.

Is this art? Are all these mass-produced objects beautiful? Or crap? If they're not art, why do we work so hard to acquire them? Pop art, like Dada, questions our society's values.

Andy Warhol (who coined the expression "15 minutes of fame" and became a pop star) concentrated on another mass-produced phenomenon: celebrities. He took publicity photos of famous people and repeated them. The repetition—like the constant bombardment we get from repeated images on television—cheapens even the most beautiful things.

Contemporary Art

The modern world is history. Picasso and his ilk are now gathering dust and boring art students everywhere. Enter the "postmodern" world as seen through the eyes of current artists.

You'll see fewer traditional canvases or sculptures. Artists have traded paintbrushes for blowtorches and are exploring new materials and new media. (Miró said he was out to "murder" painting.) Mixed media work is the norm, combining painting, sculpture, photography, welding, film/slides/video, computer programming, new resins, plastics, industrial techniques, and lighting and sound systems.

Here are some of the trends as the 21st-century odometer turns:

Op Art: "Op"-tical illusions play tricks with your eyes (like the way a spiral starts to spin when you stare at it).

Found Art: Artists raid dumpsters, recycling junk into the building blocks for larger "assemblages."

Deconstruction: Modern artists critique (or "deconstruct") society by examining things so familiar that we take them for granted. A familiar object loaded with meaning (a crucifix), removed from its usual circumstances (a church), and placed in a new setting (in a jar of urine, to cite one notorious art project), can make you see it in a different way.

Video and Film: Clips of inane, ordinary events, repeated ad nauseam.

Words: Plaques of inane slogans or ad copy, repeated ad nauseam.

The Occasional Sculpture: This is usually an abstract, unrecognizable form that emphasizes the material from which it's made.

The Occasional Canvas: This comes as a familiar relief.

Natural Objects: A rock in an urban setting is inherently interesting.

New Realism: Hyper-realistic canvases try to recreate the "look" of a photo or video image.

Installations: An entire room is given to an artist to prepare. Like entering an art funhouse, you walk in without quite knowing what to expect (I'm always thinking, "Is this safe?"). Using the latest technology, the artist engages all your senses, by controlling the lights, sounds, and sometimes even smells.

Contraptions: Weird, useless, Rube Goldberg machines make fun of technology.

Interaction: Some exhibits require your participation, whether you push a button to get the contraption going, touch something, or just walk around the room. In some cases, the viewer "does" art rather than just stares at it. If art is really meant to change, it has to move you, literally.

Performance Art: A kind of mixed media of live performance.

Many artists—who in another day would have painted canvases—have turned to music, dance, theater, and performance art. This art form is often interactive, by dropping the illusion of a performance and encouraging audience participation. When you finish with the Pompidou Center, go outside for some of the street theater.

Playful Art: Children love the art being produced today. If it doesn't put a smile on your face, well, then you must be a jaded grump like me, who's seen the same repetitious s#%t passed off as "daring" since Warhol stole it from Duchamp. I mean, it's *so* 20th-century.

VIEW ART

Before leaving, escalate up to the sixth floor. Near the *très* snooty Chez Georges view restaurant (where just looking is not OK), take a walk along the tube that runs the length of the building for great Paris cityscapes.

CARNAVALET MUSEUM **TOUR**

Musée Carnavalet—Histoire de Paris

At the Carnavalet Museum, French history unfolds in a series of stills—like a Ken Burns documentary, except you have to walk. The Revolution is the highlight, but you get a good overview of everything, from Louis XIV–period rooms, to Napoleon, to the belle époque.

ORIENTATION

Cost: Free.

Hours: Tue–Sun 10:00–18:00, closed Mon. Avoid lunchtime (12:00-14:00), since many rooms close.

Getting There: It's in the heart of the Marais district at 23 rue de Sévigné (Mo: St. Paul), and on the Marais Walk (page 79).

Information: Get the free (necessary) map. Tel. 01 44 59 58 58, www.paris.fr/musees/musee_carnavalet.

Length of This Tour: 90 minutes.

Starring: François I, Louis XIV, Louis XV, Louis XVI, the Bastille, Robespierre, the guillotine, Napoleon, Napoleon III, the Paris Commune, and la belle époque.

OVERVIEW

The museum, which opened in 1880, is housed in two Marais mansions connected by a corridor. The first half of the museum (pre-Revolution) is difficult to follow—rooms numbered out of order, no English descriptions, and sections closed due to understaffing. See this part quickly, so that you can concentrate your energies on the Revolution and beyond. If you get lost or frustrated, we'll meet up again in Room 45 (on the first floor) where the Revolution begins.

MAIN BUILDING—1500-1789

• *Begin outside in the...*

Courtyard

You're surrounded by the in-your-face richness of the *ancien régime*—back when people generally accepted the notion that some were born to rule and most were born to be ruled. And the embodiment of that age stands atop the statue in the center: Louis XIV, the ultimate divine monarch.

Notice the date: July 14, 1689, exactly 100 years before the French Revolution ended all that. This statue is a rare surviving pre-Revolutionary bronze. In 1792, nearly all of them were melted down to make weapons, as Revolutionary France took on the rest of Europe in an all-out war. Notice the relief below—a great piece of counter-Reformation propaganda. France (the angel with the royal shield) and heaven (portrayed by the angel protecting the Communion Host) are literally stomping the snakes and reformers of Protestantism (Hus, Calvin, Wycliffe, and Luther).

• *Now find Room 7 on the ground floor. It's not obvious where it is—grab a free map and ask a guard (Où est salle sept?; oo ay sahl set). Once again, if you get lost or rooms are closed, we'll meet up again in Room 45, on the first floor.*

Rooms 7–10: 1500s—Renaissance and Reformation

In Room 7, a **model of Ile de la Cité** (made by a monk around 1900) shows the medieval city before France became a world power—crowded, narrow-laned, and steeple-dotted, with houses piled even on top of bridges. There's Notre-Dame on the east end, and Sainte-Chapelle, with its royal palace and gardens, on the west. The only straight road in town was the old Roman road that splits the island north-south (and is still used today).

King François I (1494–1547, reigned 1515-1547, Room 7) brought Paris into the modern world. Handsome, athletic François—a writer of poems, leader of knights, and lover of women—embodied the optimism of the Italian Renaissance. "*Le grand roi François*" (it rhymes) centralized the government around his charismatic self and made a rebuilt Louvre his home. He affirmed his absolute right to rule every time he ordered something done—"For such is our pleasure!"

Renaissance open-mindedness brought religious debate, even leading to open warfare between

Catholics and Protestants (called Huguenots in France). Depicted in Room 8, the Catholic **King Charles IX** (1550-1574, reigned 1560-1574) and his mother, **Catherine de Médicis** plotted to assassinate several prominent Protestants, but it quickly snowballed into the slaughter of thousands of Parisian Huguenots on St. Bartholomew's Day in 1572. Paintings (in Rooms 8 and 9) show events organized by the **Catholic League:** parades, Bible studies, and the occasional Protestant barbecue to keep the faithful in good spirits.

King Henry IV (1553-1610, reigned 1589-1610, Louis XIV's grandfather) was perhaps France's most popular king. His **bust** (Room 10) depicts him with a faint smile and smile lines around the eyes, capturing his reputation as a witty conversationalist and friend of commoners. Henry helped reconcile Catholics and Protestants and rebuilt Paris. Still, that didn't stop a Revolutionary mob from tearing his equestrian statue to pieces ***(Fragment du monument)***. See **engravings** of Henry's second wife, Marie de Médicis and of some of Henry's building projects (including place Dauphine and the place des Vosges). The grotesque **stone faces** are four of the 300 that adorn Henry's greatest creation, the pont Neuf.

- *Head upstairs to the first floor. Browse around the furnished rooms, getting a feel for the luxurious life of France's kings and nobles before the Revolution. In fact, several rooms are straight out of the mansions lining the nearby place des Vosges. Use the following material as background. See you in Room 45.*

FIRST FLOOR—THE LUXURY OF LOUIS XIV, XV, AND XVI

Louis XIV (1638-1715, reigned 1643-1715)

The flowery walls, Greek-myth ceiling paintings, and powdered-wig portraits give a tiny glimpse of the opulence of Louis XIV and his greatest monument, the palace at Versailles. You'll see luxurious wallpaper, tables, chairs, parquet floors, clocks, gaming tables, statues, paintings, and even a doghouse that costs more than a peasant hut. Versailles was the physical symbol of Louis' absolute power over the largest, most populous, and richest nation in Europe.

Louis XIV Style: Baroque. In rooms from this period, ceilings are decorated with curved ornamental frames (cartouches) that hold paintings of Greek myths, and furnishings are gilded. The heavy tables and chairs have thick, curved legs, animal feet, and bronze-corner protectors.

Louis XV (1710-1774, reigned 1715–1774)

Louis XV ascended the throne of Europe's most powerful nation when his great-grandfather, the Sun King, died after reigning for 72 years.

Only five years old at the time, he was for many years a figurehead, while the government was run by his mentors: a regent during his childhood, his teacher during his youth, one of his many mistresses (Madame de Pompadour) during his middle age, and bureaucrats by the end. Louis was intelligent and educated, and he personally embraced the budding democratic ideals of the Enlightenment, but he spent his time at Versailles, where he gamed and consorted with Europe's most cultured and beautiful people. Meanwhile, France's money was spent on costly wars with Austria and England (including the American "French and Indian War"). Louis, basking in the lap of luxury and the glow of the Enlightenment, looked to the horizon and uttered his prophetic phrase: "*Après moi—le déluge!*" ("After me—the flood!")

Louis XV Style: Rococo. The rooms are decorated in pastel colors, with lighter decoration and exotic landscapes. The chairs are made of highly polished, rare woods, with delicate curved legs and padded seats and backs. Note the Chinese decor and objects such as the Ming vase.

Louis XVI (1754-1793, reigned 1774–1792)

With a flood watch in effect, the next Louis stubbornly clung to the rules of the *ancien régime* (the traditional chessboard society with king on top, pawns on bottom, and bishops that walk diagonally).

While peasants groaned in the fields, picture the rich in their mansions: parties lit by chandeliers glimmering off mirrors, the sound of a string quartet, exotic foods from newly colonized lands, billiards in one room and high-stakes card games in another, a Molière comedy downstairs, dangerous talk by radicals like Voltaire and Jean-Jacques Rousseau, and dangerous liaisons among social butterflies—male and female—dressed in high heels, makeup, wigs, and perfume.

Louis XVI Style: Neoclassical. Influenced by recently-excavated Pompeii, the rooms are simpler—with classical motifs—and the furniture is straighter. The chairs' straight legs taper to a point.

- *From Room 45, follow signs to "Revolution, 19th and 20th centuries." A long corridor leads to the next building. Hike up the hardwood stairs to the second floor and La Révolution Française.*

SECOND FLOOR

The Revolution: 1789–1799

No period of history is as charged with the full range of human emotions and actions as the French Revolution: bloodshed, martyrdom, daring speeches, murdered priests, emancipated women, back-stabbing former friends—all done in the name of government "by, for, and of the people." Common people, with their everyday concerns, were driving the engine of history. Or perhaps they were only foam bubbles swept along in the shifting tides of vast socioeconomic trends.

Room 101: The Estates-General

It's 1789, France is bankrupt from wars and corruption, and the people want change. The large **allegorical painting *L'espoir du bonheur*** shows King Louis XVI in the boat of France, navigating stormy seas. Lady Truth is trying to light the way, but the winged demon of tyranny keeps nagging at the king. Above shines the fleur-de-lis, whose petals are labeled with the three social groups that held all power in France: clergy, king, and nobles. Now they are laced together by the new power...the people.

In May, the king called each sector of society together at Versailles to solve the financial crisis. But in a bold and unheard-of move, the Third Estate (the people), tired of being outvoted by the clergy and nobility, split and formed their own National Assembly (see ***The Oath of the Jeu-de-Paume*** on the opposite wall, a preparatory sketch by Jacques-Louis David for a huge canvas that was never painted). Amid the chaos of speeches, debate, and deal-making, they raised their hands, bravely pledging to stick together until a new constitution was written. Vacillating between democratic change and royalist repression, **Louis XVI** (see his pink-faced portrait to the left) ordered the Assembly to dissolve (they refused), sent 25,000 Swiss mercenary soldiers to Paris, and fired his most popular, liberal minister.

Room 102: The Bastille (July 14, 1789)

The Bastille (see the **model**) was a medieval fortress turned prison. With its eight towers and 100-foot-high walls, it dominated the Parisian skyline, a symbol of oppression. (See the series of **paintings** that illustrate some of the following events.)

On the hot, muggy morning of July 14, Paris' citizens waited on edge, listening to reports of attacks on the populace by the king's Swiss guards. A crowd formed and marched on the Invalides armory and seized 30,000 rifles...but no gunpowder. Word spread that it was stored across town at the Bastille. The mob grew bigger and angrier as it went.

By noon, they stood at the foot of the walls of the Bastille and demanded gunpowder. They captured the fort's governor, and two citizens managed to scale the wall and cut the chains. The drawbridge crashed down, and the mob poured through. Terrified guards opened fire, killing dozens and wounding hundreds. At the battle's peak, French soldiers in red and blue appeared on the horizon...but whose side were they on? A loud cheer went up as they pointed their cannons at the Bastille, and the fort surrendered. The mob trashed the Bastille, opened the dark dungeons, and brought seven prisoners into the light of day. They then stormed City Hall (Hôtel de Ville) and arrested the mayor, who was literally torn apart by the hysterical crowd. His head was stuck on a stick and carried through the city. The Revolution had begun.

Today, the events of July 14 are celebrated every Bastille Day, with equally colorful festivities. The Bastille itself was soon dismantled stone by stone—nothing remains but the open space of place de la Bastille—but the memory became a rallying cry throughout the Revolution: "*Vive le quatorze juillet!*" ("Long live July 14th!").

Room 103 *(La Fête de la Fédération)*: The Celebration (1789)

Imagine the jubilation! To finally be able to shout out things formerly whispered in fear.

The large painting of ***La Fête de la Fédération*** shows the joy and exuberance of the newly freed people, as they celebrate the first Bastille Day (July 14, 1790). Liberty! Equality! Fraternity! Members of every social class (even including, it appears, three women) hugged, kissed, and mingled on the Champs de Mars, where the Eiffel Tower stands today. An artificial mound was built for heroes of the Revolution to ascend while a choir sang. Women, dressed up to symbolize Truth, Freedom, Justice, and other capital-letter virtues, were worshiped in a new kind of secular religion. Public demonstrations like these must have infuriated the king, queen, bishops, and nobles, who were now quarantined in their palaces, fuming impotently.

The ***Declaration of the Rights of Man and the Citizen*** (see 2 different versions) made freedom the law. The preamble makes it clear that "*Le Peuple Français*" (the French people)—not the king—were the ultimate authority. "Men are born free and equal," it states, possessing "freedom of the individual, freedom of conscience, freedom of speech."

Room 104 *(De la Monarchie à la République)*: Louis XVI Quietly Responds (1789–1792)

Louis XVI (see the bust)—studious, shy, aloof, and easily dominated—was stunned by the ferocious summer of 1789. The Bastille's violence spread to the countryside, where uppity peasants tenderized their

masters with pitchforks. The Assembly was changing France with lightning speed: abolishing Church privileges, nationalizing nobles' land, and declaring the king irrelevant. Louis accepted his role as a rubber-stamp monarch, hoping the furor would pass and trying to appear idealistic and optimistic.

But looming on the horizon was...***Le docteur Joseph-Ignace Guillotin*** (see portrait, opposite window). The progressive Assembly abolished brutal medieval-style torture and executions. In their place, Dr. Guillotin proposed a kinder, gentler execution device that would make France a model of compassion. The guillotine—also known as "the national razor," or, simply, "The Machine"—could instantly make someone "a head shorter at the top." (In 1977, it claimed its last victim; now capital punishment is abolished.)

Room 105 *(La famille royale)*: Royalty Loses Its Head (1793)

Louis' wife, **Queen Marie-Antoinette** (several portraits), became the focus of the citizens' disgust. Reports flew that she spent extravagantly and plunged France into debt. More decisive than her husband, she steered him toward repressive measures to snuff out the Revolution. Worst of all, she was foreign-born, known simply as "The Austrian," and soon Austria was trying to preserve the monarchy by making war on the French. When Marie was informed that the Parisians had no bread to eat, a rumor spread that she had sneered, "Let them eat cake!" ("Cake" was the term for the burnt crusts peeled off the oven and generally fed only to the cattle.)

Enraged and hungry, 6,000 Parisian women (backed by armed men) marched through the rain to Versailles to demand lower bread prices. On the night of October 5, 1789, a small band infiltrated the palace, burst into the Queen's room, killed her bodyguards, and chased her down the hall. The royal family was kidnapped and taken to Paris, where—though still monarchs—they were under house arrest in the Tuileries Palace (which once stood where the Louvre today meets the Tuileries Garden).

Three years later, the royal family became actual prisoners (see the reconstructed and rather cushy **Prison du Temple** in Room 106) after trying to escape to Austria to begin a counter-revolution. One of their servants pretended to be a German baroness, while Louis dressed up as her servant (the irony must have been killing him). When a citizen recognized Louis from his portrait on a franc note, the family was captured, thrown into prison, and soon put on trial as traitors to France. The National Convention (the Assembly's successor) declared the monarchy abolished.

The royal family—Louis, Marie-Antoinette, and their eight-year-old son—was tearfully split up (see the painting **Les adieux de Louis XVI a sa famille**, in Room 105), and Marie-Antoinette was imprisoned in the Conciergerie.

On January 21, 1793 (see **execution painting**), King Louis XVI (excuse me, "Citizen Capet") was led to the place de la Concorde and laid face down on a slab, and then—shoop!—a thousand years of monarchy that had dated back before Charlemagne was decapitated. On October 16, 1793 (see **painting**), Marie-Antoinette also met her fate on place de la Concorde. Genteel to the end, she apologized to the executioner for stepping on his foot. The blade fell, the blood gushed, and her head was shown to the crowd on a stick—an exclamation point for the new rallying cry: *Vive la nation!*

Little Louis XVII died in prison at age 10. (Notice his cute **portrait** —***Le Dauphin***—in the corner next to his mother portrayed as a widow in prison.) Rumors spread that the boy-king had escaped, fueled by Elvis-type sightings and impersonators. But recent DNA evidence confirms that the *dauphin* (heir to the throne) did indeed die in prison in 1795.

Room 108 *(La Convention–La Terreur)*: The Reign of Terror (1793–1794)

Here are **portraits** of key players in the Revolutionary spectacle. Some were moderate reformers, some radical priest-killers. With Europe ganging up on the Revolution, they all lived in fear that any backward step could tip the delicate balance of power back to the *ancien régime.* Enemies of the Revolution were everywhere—even in their own ranks.

By the summer of 1793, the left-of-center Jacobin party took control of France's fledgling democracy. Pug-faced but silver-tongued **Georges Danton** (see portrait of a Newt Gingrich look-alike) drove the Revolution with his personal charisma and bold speeches: "To conquer the enemies of the fatherland, we need daring, more daring, daring now, always daring." He led the "Committee of Public Safety" to root out and execute those enemies, even moderates opposed to the Jacobins.

More radical still, **Jean-Paul Marat** (the "Friend of the People," portrait next to Danton) dressed and burped like a man of the street, but he wrote eloquently against all forms of authority. Wildly popular with the commoners, he was seen by others as a loose cannon. A beautiful 25-year-old noblewoman named **Charlotte Corday** decided it was her mission in life to save France by silencing him. On July 11, 1793, she entered his home under the pretext of giving him names of counter-revolutionaries. Marat, seated in a bathtub to nurse a skin condition, wrote the names down and said, "Good. I'll have them all guillotined." Corday stood up, whipped a knife out from under her dress, and stabbed him through the heart. Corday was guillotined, and Marat was hailed as a martyr to the cause.

Marat's death was further "proof" that counter-revolutionaries were everywhere. For the next year (summer of 1793 to summer of 1794, see **paintings of guillotine scenes**), the Jacobin government arrested, briefly tried, then guillotined everyone suspected of being "enemies of the Revolution": nobles, priests, the rich, and many true Revolutionaries who simply belonged to the wrong political party. More than 2,500 Parisians were beheaded, 18,000 were executed by other means, and tens of thousands died in similar violence throughout the country. The violence begun at the **Bastille** in July 1789 would climax in July 1794.

Master of the Reign of Terror was **Maximilien de Robespierre** (the portrait opposite Danton's), a 35-year-old lawyer who promoted the Revolution with a religious fervor. By July 1794, the guillotine was slicing 30 necks a day. In Paris' main squares, grim executions alternated with politically correct public spectacles that honored "Liberty," "Truth," and the heroes of France. As the death toll rose, so did public cynicism. Finally, Robespierre even sentenced to death his old friend Danton, who had spoken out against the bloodshed. As Danton knelt under the blade, he joked, "My turn." The people had had enough.

Room 109 *(Thermidor—Le Directoire)*: Terror Ends (July 1794)

Engravings show the chaos—riots, assassinations, food shortages, inflation—that fueled Robespierre's meteoric fall from power. Robespierre's own self-righteousness made him an easy target. On July 27, 1794, as Robespierre prepared to name the daily list of victims, his fellow committee members started yelling "Tyrant!" and shouted him down. Stunned by the sudden fall from grace, Robespierre unsuccessfully attempted suicide by shooting himself in the mouth.

The next day, he walked the walk he'd ordered thousands to take. Hands tied behind his back, he was carried through the streets on a two-wheeled cart, while citizens jeered and spat on him. At the guillotine, the broken-down demagogue had no last words, thanks to his wounded jaw. When the executioner yanked off the bandage, Robespierre let out a horrible cry, the blade fell, and the Reign of Terror came to an end.

From 1795 to 1799, France caught its breath, ruled by the Directory, a government so intentionally weak and decentralized (two houses of parliament, five executives, and no funding) that it could never create another Robespierre.

FRENCH NATIONAL ANTHEM: "LA MARSEILLAISE"

The genteel French have a gory past.

Allons enfants de la Patrie,	(Let's go, children of the fatherland,)
Le jour de gloire est arrivé.	(The day of glory has arrived.)
Contre nous de la tyrannie	(The blood-covered flag of tyranny)
L'étendard sanglant est levé.	(Is raised against us.)
L'étendard sanglant est levé.	(Is raised against us.)
Entendez-vous dans les campagnes	(Do you hear these ferocious soldiers)
Mugir ces féroces soldats?	(Howling in the countryside?)
Qui viennent jusque dans nos bras	(They're coming nearly into our grasp)
Egorger vos fils et vos compagnes.	(To slit the throats of your sons and your women.)
Aux armes, citoyens,	(Grab your weapons, citizens,)
Formez vos bataillons,	(Form your battalions,)
Marchons, marchons,	(March on, march on,)
Qu'un sang impur	(So that their impure blood)
Abreuve nos sillons.	(Will fill our trenches.)

Room 110 *(La Guerre)*: France vs. Europe

The blade that dropped on Louis XVI rattled royal teacups throughout Europe. Even as early as 1792, France had to defend its young democracy against Austria and Prussia. France's new army was composed of ordinary citizens from a universal draft and led by daring young citizen-officers, who sang a stirring, bloodthirsty new song, "La Marseillaise." Surprisingly, they quickly defeated the apathetic mercenaries they faced. France vowed to liberate all Europe from tyranny. Europe feared that, by "exporting Revolution," France would export democracy…plus senseless violence and chaos.

A young Corsican named **Napoleon Bonaparte** (see the bust) rose quickly through the ranks and proved himself by fighting royalists in Italy, Egypt, and on the streets of Paris. In 1799, the 29-year-old general returned to Paris as a conquering hero. Backed by an adoring public, he dissolved the Directory, established order, and gave himself the Roman-style title of "first consul."

Room 111 *(Vandalisme et Conservation)*: The Revolution vs. Religion

Three-fourths of France's churches were destroyed or vandalized during the Revolution, a backlash against the wealthy and politically repressive Catholic Church. In Notre-Dame, Christ was mothballed, and a woman dressed as "Dame Reason" was worshiped on the altar.

Room 113: Souvenirs of Revolution

After the Reign of Terror, *Liberté, Egalité, Fraternité* was just a slogan, remembered fondly on commemorative **plates and knickknacks**. The Revolution was history.

- *The visit continues down four flights of stairs—or down the elevator—on the ground floor.*

Room 115 *(Le Premier Empire)*: Napoleon Conquers Europe (1799–1815)

Here's **Napoleon I** (1769-1821, reigned as emperor 1804-15; see portrait, also breastplate, pistols, and death mask in glass case) at the peak of power, master of Western Europe. Dressed in his general's uniform, he's checking the maps to see who's left to conquer. Behind him is a throne with his imperial seal. This Corsican-born commoner, educated in Paris' military schools, became a young Revolutionary and a daring general, rising to prominence as a champion of democracy. Once in power, he preached revolution, but in fact became a dictator and crowned himself emperor (1804).

During the Empire, all things classical became popular. Wealthy socialites such as **Juliette Récamier** (see painting) donned robes and lounged on couches, while Paris was rebuilt with neoclassical monuments, such as the Arc de Triomphe, to make it the "New Rome."

In 1812, Napoleon foolishly invaded Russia, thus starting a downward spiral that ended in defeat by allied Europe at the Battle of Waterloo in Belgium (1815). Napoleon was exiled, and died (1821) on the island of St. Helena, off the coast of Africa.

Room 118 *(La Restauration)*: The Monarchy Restored (1815–1830)

After almost 25 years in exile, royalty returned. **Louis XVIII** (1755-1824, reigned 1815-1824) was the younger brother of headless Louis XVI; he returned to Paris with the backing of Europe's royalty and reclaimed the crown as a constitutional monarch (see the crowd scene of ***Entrée du Louis XVIII à Paris, le 3 mai 1814***).

The next king, retro-looking **Charles X** (1757-1836, reigned 1824-1830, youngest brother of Louis XVI), in glorious coronation robes, revived the fashion and oppression of the *ancien régime,* as he plotted to dissolve the people's Assembly. But the French people were not about to turn the clock back.

Room 119 *(Juillet 1830):* Revolution of 1830

Parisians again blocked off the narrow streets with barricades to fight the king's red-coated soldiers (see various **street battle paintings**). The people stormed the Louvre (biggest painting) and the king's palace, and slaughtered the mercenary Swiss Guards. After "Three Glorious Days" of fighting, order was restored by Louis-Philippe (see **model**), an unassuming nobleman who appeared on the balcony of the Hôtel de Ville and was cheered by royalists, the middle class, and peasants alike. They made him king.

Room 120 *(La Monarchie de Juillet):* Constitutional Monarchy (1830–1848)

King Louis-Philippe (1773-1850, reigned 1830-1848, see black bust)—a former lieutenant turned banker, with a few drops of royal blood—was a true constitutional monarch, harmlessly presiding over an era of middle-class progress fueled by the Industrial Revolution. Still, liberal reforms came too slowly. New factories brought division between wealthy employers and poor workers, and only 200,000 out of 30 million French citizens (1:150) could vote.

Room 121 *(La Deuxième République):* Revolution of 1848

In February 1848—a time of Europe-wide depression and socialist strikes—Parisians took to the streets again **(battle scenes).** They battled at the Bastille, Palais-Royal, Panthéon, and place de la Concorde, and they toppled the king. Even prosperous accountants and shoe salesmen caught the spirit of revolution. After five decades of dictators (including Napoleon), retread Bourbons (the Restoration), and self-proclaimed monarchs (Louis-Philippe), France was back in the hands of the people—the Second Republic.

Room 122 *(Le Romantisme):* Romanticism

Freedom of expression, the uniqueness of each person, the glories of the human spirit and the natural world—these values from the 1789 Revolution were extolled by artists of the 1800s known as Romantics. Working clockwise, you'll see **caricature busts** of many famous Frenchmen and visitors to the center of European culture, Paris: Victor Hugo (author of *Les Misérables* and *The Hunchback of Notre-Dame*), Frédéric Chopin (Polish pianist who charmed Parisian society), Giuseppe Verdi (composer of stirring operas—*Aida*, etc.), and Gioacchino Rossini (*Lone Ranger* theme). There are also **paintings** of Romantic painter Eugène Delacroix and of glamorous pianist Franz Liszt and his mistress Marie d'Agoult—the ultimate Romantic. She left her husband and children to follow the dynamic Liszt on a journey of self-discovery in Italy and Switzerland—"the years of pilgrimage."

- *Journey upstairs and to the left toward* "Paris: Du Second Empire à nos jours"—*From the Second Empire to Today.*

Room 128 *(Le Second Empire)*: Napoleon III and the Second Empire (1852–1870)

Louis-Napoleon Bonaparte (1808-1873, reigned as emperor 1852-1871; in the big painting, with red pants and sash, waxed moustache, and goatee) was the nephew of the famous Emperor Napoleon I. He used his well-known name to get elected president by a landslide in 1848, then combined democracy with monarchy to be voted "Emperor Napoleon III." He suppressed opposition but promoted liberal reforms and economic and colonial expansion.

Here he hands an order to **Baron Georges Haussmann** (mutton-chop sideburns) to modernize Paris. Haussmann cut the wide, straight boulevards of today to move goods, open up the crowded city...and prevent barricades for future revolutions. Parks, railroad stations, and the Opéra Garnier made Paris the model for world capitals. (Room 129 shows building projects.)

The **boat-like cradle** (Room 128) is a copy of the famous cradle of Napoleon II (1811–1832, known to history as the King of Rome), the only son of Napoleon I, who died at 21 of tuberculosis before ever ruling anything.

Napoleon III pursued popular wars (the **model** in Room 129 celebrates Crimean War vets, 1855) and unpopular ones (backing Austrian Emperor Maximilian in Mexico). In the summer of 1870, he personally led a jubilant French Army to crush upstart Prussia—"On to Berlin!" Uh-oh.

Room 130 *(Le siège de Paris)*: The Franco-Prussian War (1870–1871)

Within weeks, the overconfident French were surrounded, Napoleon III himself was captured, and he surrendered. Paris was stunned. (See the big **painting of crowd** hearing the news on the legislature steps.) The Germans quickly put a stranglehold on Paris, and a long, especially cold winter settled in.

Some would not give up. Without an emperor, they proclaimed yet another democratic republic (France's third in a century) and sent minister Léon Gambetta in a newfangled balloon **(painting)** over the Germans' heads to rally the countryside to come save Paris. The Parisians themselves held out bravely (**painting** of Tuileries as army camp), but German efficiency and modern technology simply overwhelmed the French.

Room 131 *(La Commune)*: The Paris Commune (Spring 1871)

The Republic finally agreed to a humiliating surrender. Paris' liberals—enraged at the capitulation after such a brave winter and fearing a return of monarchy—rejected the surrender and proclaimed their own government, the Paris Commune. **Portraits** honor the proud idealists, who barricaded themselves inside Paris' neighborhoods, refusing to bow to the German emperor.

Then, in one "bloody week" in May **(battle scenes)**, French troops backing the Republic stormed through Paris, leaving 15,000 dead, 5,000 jailed, and 8,000 deported. The Commune was snuffed out, but the memory was treasured by generations of liberals in popular **souvenirs:** a jar of bread from the hungry winter, a carrier pigeon's feather, a box reading "*Vive la Commune!*"

The church of Sacré-Cœur (see a **painting** way up high) was built after the war as a form of national penance for the sins of liberalism.

Rooms 132–142 *(La Belle Epoque)*: The Beautiful Age (1871–1914)

The Third Republic restored peace to a prosperous middle-class society. The **Eiffel Tower** (Room 132) marked the 1889 centennial of the Revolution, and the **Statue of Liberty** (Room 133) honored America's revolution.

Paris was a capital of world culture, a city of **Impressionist painters** (Room 135); of writers and actors, including the actress **Sarah Bernhardt** (Room 136), called the world's first international star ("a force of nature, a fiery soul, a marvelous intelligence, a magnificent creature of the highest order," raved one of the smitten); of **Georges Bizet** (Room 136), composer of *Carmen;* of balls, carriages, cafés, and parks (**paintings,** Rooms 137–140).

And it was the city of Art Nouveau. Two delightful turn-of-the-century Parisian shops—spliced into this old-regime mansion—illustrate the curvy, decorative Art Nouveau style: the *très chic* **Café de Paris** (Room 141) and the **Boutique Fouquet** (Room 142). Imagine browsing through jewelry in the spindly splendor of this world of peacocks peering through stained glass and nubile nymphs atop fountains.

Room 145: World War I (1914–1918)

Three costly wars with Germany—Franco-Prussian, World War I, and World War II—drained France. Although **Marshal Foch** (big painting above the elevator) is hailed as the man who coordinated the Allied armies to defeat Germany in World War I, France was hardly a winner.

More than 1.5 million Frenchmen died, a generation was lost, and the country would be a pushover when Hitler invaded in 1940. France's long history as a global superpower was over.

Room 147 *(La vie littéraire du XXe siècle)*: Remembrance of Things Past

The last room is filled with portraits of Paris' 20th-century literary greats. By producing such figures as the writer **Marcel Proust** (see his reconstructed bedroom) and the dreamy writer/filmmaker **Jean Cocteau,** France has remained a cultural superpower.

PICASSO MUSEUM **TOUR**

The 20th century's greatest artist was the master of many styles (Cubism, Surrealism, Expressionism, etc.) and of many media (painting, sculpture, prints, ceramics, and assemblages). Still, he could make anything he touched look unmistakably like "a Picasso."

The Picasso Museum walks you through the evolution of the artist's long life and many styles. The women he loved and the global events he lived through appear in his canvases, filtered through his own emotional response. You don't have to admire Picasso's lifestyle or like his modern painting style. But a visit here might make you appreciate the sheer vitality and creativity of this hard-working and very unique man.

ORIENTATION

Cost: €5.50, free first Sun of month, covered by museum pass.
Hours: Apr-Sept Wed–Mon 9:30–18:00, Oct–March Wed-Mon 9:30-17:30, closed Tue.
Information: Tel. 01 42 71 25 21. www.musee-picasso.fr.
Getting There: 5 rue de Thorigny, Mo: St. Paul or Chemin Vert.
Length of This Tour: One hour.

OVERVIEW

Start upstairs on the first floor. A thoughtfully laid-out series of rooms leads you chronologically through Picasso's life. I applaud the curators. This chapter follows the museum's logic and is intended as a supplement to their excellent English information. It's also shorter, for those who want to see the whole museum quickly, then browse. While the order of the rooms is fairly permanent, the museum rotates its large collection of paintings often, so don't be dismayed if you don't find a particular work.

Pablo Picasso (1881-1973)

Born in Spain, the son of an art teacher, the teenaged Picasso q advanced beyond his teachers. He mastered camera-eye realism b showed an empathy for the people he painted that was insightful b his years. (Unfortunately, the museum has very few early works. doubters of Picasso's genius warm to him somewhat after seeing his lent draftsmanship and facility with oils.) As a teenager in Barcelo fell in with a bohemian crowd that mixed wine, women, and art.

In 1900, Picasso set out to make his mark in Paris, the undis world capital of culture. He rejected the surname his father had give (Ruiz) and chose his mother's instead, making it his distinctive one brand: Picasso.

Room 1: Early years and Blue Period (1895-1903)

The brash Spaniard quickly became a poor, homesick foreigner, abs the styles of many painters (especially Henri de Toulouse-Lautrec) searching for his own artist's voice. He found companionship a fellow freaks and outcasts on butte Montmartre (see paintings of j circus performers, and garish cabarets). When his best friend com suicide (*Death of Casagemas*, 1901), Picasso plunged into a "Blue Pe painting emaciated beggars, hard-eyed pimps, and himself, bund against the cold, with eyes all cried out (*Autoportrait*, 1901).

Room 2: *Les Demoiselles d'Avignon* (1904-19

In 1904, Picasso moved into his Bateau-Lavoir home/stud Montmartre (see Montmartre Walk, page 94), got a steady girlfrien suddenly saw the world through rose-colored glasses (the Pink P 1904-05, though the museum has very few of these).

Only 25 years old, Picasso reinvented painting. Fascinated primitive power of African and Iberian tribal masks (seen in Room sketched human faces with simple outlines and almond eyes (*Autop* 1906). Intrigued by the body of his girlfriend Fernande Olivi sketched it from every angle, then experimented with showing several different views on the same canvas (see various nude studies).

A hundred paintings and nine months later, Picasso gave birth to a monstrous canvas of five nude, fragmented prostitutes with mask-like faces—*Les Demoiselles d'Avignon* (1907). The painting hangs in New York's Museum of Modern Art, but you'll see a similar-looking painting in Room 3

(*Three Figures Under a Tree*, 1907-1908). His friends were speechless, his enemies reviled it, and almost overnight, Picasso was famous.

Room 3: Masks and Cubist Experiments (1907-1909)

Picasso went to the Louvre for a special exhibit on Cézanne, then returned to the Bateau-Lavoir to expand on Cézanne's chunky style and geometric simplicity—oval-shaped heads, circular breasts, and diamond thighs (see landscapes). Picasso rejected traditional 3-D. Instead of painting, say, a distant hillside in dimmer tones than the trees in the bright foreground, Picasso did it all bright, making the foreground blend into the background, and turning a scene into an abstract design. Modern art was being born.

Room 4: Cubism (1910-1917)

With his next-door neighbor, Georges Braque, Picasso invented Cubism, a fragmented "cube"-shaped style. He'd fracture a musician (*Man with a Violin*, 1911) into a barely-recognizable jumble of facets, and of facets within facets. Even empty space is composed of these "cubes," all of them the same basic color, that weave together the background and foreground. Picasso sketches reality from every angle, then pastes it all together, a composite of different views. The monochrome color (mostly gray or brown) is less important than the experiments with putting the 3-D world on a 2-D canvas in a modern way. (For more on Cubism, see the Pompidou Chapter, page 163.)

In a few short years, Picasso had turned painting in the direction it would go for the next 50 years.

Room 4b: Synthetic Cubism

Analytic Cubism (1907-1913) broke the world down into small facets, to "analyze" the subject from every angle. Now it was time to "synthesize" it back together with the real world.

These "constructions" are still-life paintings (a 2-D illusion) augmented with glued-on real-life materials—wood, paper, rope, or chair caning (the real 3-D world). The contrast between real objects and painted objects makes it clear that while traditional painting is a mere illusion, art can be more substantial.

Personally, Picasso's life had fragmented into a series of relationships with women. He finally met (1917) and married a graceful Russian dancer with the Ballet Russes, Olga Kokhlova (*Portrait of Olga in an Armchair*, 1917, in Room 4).

Room 5: Picasso's Personal Collection

Picasso had an encyclopedic knowledge of art history and a caricaturist's ability to easily "quote" another artist's style, which he would adapt to his own uses. In this room, see Picasso's sources, from Pierre-Auguste Renoir's plump women to Cézanne's chunky surfaces to the simple outlines and bright colors of Henri Matisse, his friend and rival in the contest to be Century's Greatest Painter. He and Matisse, who met in Paris and later lived near each other in the south of France, would occasionally trade masterpieces, letting the other pick out their favorite.

Room 6: Classicism, Family Life at the Beach (1918-1924)

Now he was a financially secure husband and father (see the portrait of his 3-year-old son, *Paul en Harlequin*, 1924), and with the disastrous Great War over, Picasso took his family for summer vacations on the Riviera. There, he painted peaceful scenes of women and children at the beach.

A trip to Rome inspired him to emulate the bulky mass of ancient statues, transforming them into plump but graceful women, with Olga's round features. Picasso could create the illusion of a face or body bulging out from the canvas, like a cameo or classical bas-relief. Watching kids drawing in the sand with a stick, he tried drawing a figure without lifting the brush from the canvas.

Room 7: Surrealism and Women (1925-1929)

In 1927, middle-aged Picasso stopped a 17-year-old girl outside the Galeries Lafayette department store (by the Opéra Garnier) and said "Mademoiselle, you have an interesting face, can I paint it? I am Picasso." She said, "Who?"

The two had little in common, but the unsophisticated Marie-Thérèse Walter and the short balding artist developed a strange attraction for each other. Soon, Marie-Thérèse moved into the house next door to Picasso and his wife, and they began an awkward three-wheeled relationship. Worldly Olga was jealous, young Marie-Thérèse was insecure and clingy, and Picasso the workaholic artist faithfully chronicled the erotic/neurotic experience.

Using a Surrealist style, he lets the id speak. These women—a jumble of clashing colors and twisted limbs—open their toothy mouths and scream their frustration (*Large Nude on a Red*

Armchair, 1929). The artist and his model were becoming hopelessly entangled. Picasso needed a big ego to keep his big id out of trouble.

• *From Room 7, consider a detour up to the second floor, which hosts temporary exhibits on Picasso and selections from his 2,000 prints. Our tour continues downstairs in...*

Room 8: The Bathers and Room 9: Boisgeloup (1930-1935)

Picasso twists women into balloon-animal shapes lounging on the beach. With his increasing fame, even Picasso's sandcastles were worth hanging in a museum.

See the photo in a glass case (Room 8) of young athletic Marie-Thérèse with her classic profile—big chin and long nose with a straight bridge. Picasso would never tire of portraying her (see several versions of *Head of a Woman*, 1931, in Room 10). In 1935, Marie-Thérèse gave birth to their daughter, Maya.

Room 10: Spain—Bullfights, Minotaurs, *Guernica*

Picasso, an unrepentantly macho Spaniard, loved bullfights, seeing them as a metaphor for the timeless human interaction between the genders. Me bull, you horse, I gore you.

The minotaur (a bull-headed man) symbolized man's warring halves: half rational human (Freud's superego) and half raging beast (the id). Picasso could be both tender and violent with women, thus playing out both sides of this love/war duality.

Take the Spanish imagery in this room—of bulls, screaming horses, a woman with a candle—put it all on one monumental canvas (bigger even than the big collage in Room 11) and you get *Guernica* (1937, on display in Madrid), Picasso's most famous work, which summed up the pain of Spain's brutal Civil War (1936-1939).

• *Down on basement level...*

PICASSO'S RESIDENCES

The Spaniard lived almost all of his adult life in France, mostly in Paris and the south of France. Over the years, Picasso had 13 different studios in Paris, mainly in the Montmartre and Montparnasse neighborhoods. Picasso liked both France and Spain, but after 1936, he vowed never again to set foot in Fascist-controlled Spain, and he never did.

PICASSO'S WOMEN

Women were Picasso's main subject. As an artist, he used women both as models and as muses. Having sex with his model allowed him to paint not just the woman's physical features but also the emotional associations of their relationship. At least that's what he told his wife.

In today's psychobabble, Picasso was an egotistic and abusive male, a sex addict fueled by his own insecurities and inability to connect intimately with women.

In the lingo of Picasso's crowd—steeped in the psychoanalysis of Freud and Jung—relations with women allowed him to express primal urges, recover repressed memories, confront his relationship with his mother, discover hidden truths, connect with his anima (female side), and recreate the archetypal experiences lived since the beginning of time.

After about 1910, Picasso almost never painted (only sketched) from a posed model. His "portraits" of women were often composites of several different women from his large catalog of memories, filtered through emotional associations.

Here are some of Picasso's models/mistresses/muses:

María Picasso y López—his mom—wrote him a letter almost every day until her death. In childhood, Picasso was raised as a lone boy among the many women of his extended family.

Dark-haired **Fernande Olivier**, an artist's model who'd lived a wild life, was Picasso's first real love. They lived together (1904-1909) on Montmartre (with a dog and a 10-year-old street urchin they'd taken in) when Picasso was inventing Cubism, and her features are seen in *Les*

Room 12: Sculpture Garden

Picture Picasso with goggles and a blow-torch, creating 3-D Cubist statues out of scrap metal. He was the master of many media (as we'll see) and often turned 20th-century industrial junk into art. In the figure just down the ramp en route to Room 13, a ladle becomes a head, sticks are legs, and garden claws are hands. A true scavenger, Picasso took what he found, played with it, and transformed it into something interesting.

Room 13: The Muses

Picasso met the artsy, sophisticated photographer Dora Maar over coffee at Les Deux Magots in 1936. She photographed him in his studio working on *Guernica*, and they became involved. Picasso still kept ties with Marie-Thérèse while also working out a complicated divorce from Olga.

Compare portraits of his two mistress/muses. Blonde Marie-

Demoiselles d'Avignon. Fernande claimed that Picasso locked her in or hid her shoes so she couldn't go out while he was gone.

In May, 1913, Fernande left him for good, his father died, and **Eva Gouel** moved in. Picasso launched into Synthetic Cubism. Eva died two years later of tuberculosis.

Elegant **Olga Kokhlova** (1896-1955) gave Picasso a son (Pablo, Jr.) and 10 years of stability. They lived high class, hobnobbing with the international set surrounding the Ballet Russes.

Athletic **Marie-Thérèse Walter** (1910-1977) knew nothing of art and never mixed with Picasso's sophisticated crowd. But even as she put on weight, Picasso found her figure worthy to paint. They had a daughter together named Maya (b.1935).

Sparkly-eyed **Dora Maar** (1909-1998) was the anti-Marie-Thérèse—a woman who could converse with Picasso about his art.

Françoise Gilot (born 1921), a painter herself, is often depicted with a flower, perhaps symbolizing the new life (and two children) she gave to an aging Picasso. She stubbornly forced Picasso to sever ties with Dora Maar before she'd settle in. When Picasso dumped her for his next conquest (1954), she went on to write a scathing tell-all book. Their children, Claude and Paloma, grew up amid lawsuits over whether they could use their father's famous last name.

Jacqueline Roque (1927-1986) married the god of painting when he was 80 and she was 33. She oulived him but later took her own life.

So, I guess Picasso's ideal model would be a composite—a brainy but tubercular dancer with a curvaceous figure, as well as a youthful flower-child who could pose like a slut but remind him of his mother.

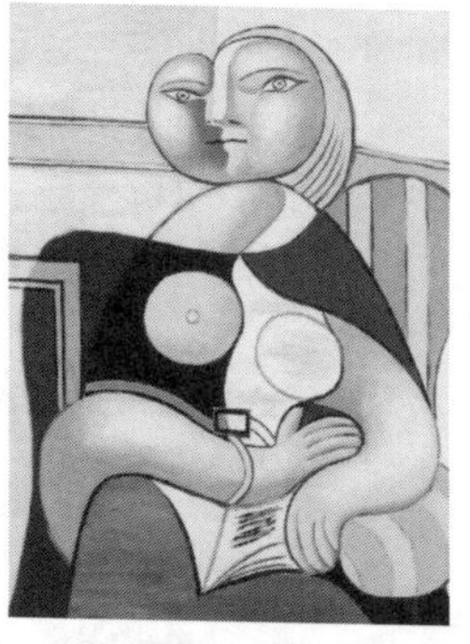

Thérèse, with her big straight nose and round chin, is full-figured and curvy (The Body). Dark-haired Dora Maar is slender, with long red nails and sparkling, intelligent eyes (The Mind).

Dora is often pictured crying. Go figure. She's attached to a physically abusive married man who refuses to leave his other mistress.

Room 14: Ceramics

The minute Picasso discovered ceramics (1947), the passion consumed him. Working in a small family-owned ceramics factory in the south of France, he shaped the wet clay, painted it, and fired up a dozen or more pieces a day—2,000 in a single year. He created plates with faces, bird-shaped vases, woman-shaped bottles, bull-shaped statues, and colorful tiles. Working in this timeless medium, he gives a modernist's take on classic motifs: red-and-black Greek vases, fauns, primitive goddesses, Roman amphorae, etc.

Room 15: Multimedia

A bicycle seat with handlebar horns becomes the *Head of a Bull* (1942). This is quintessential Picasso—a timeless motif (minotaurs) made of 20th-century materials and done with a twinkle in his eye.

Room 16: World War II (1940-1945)

In 1940, Nazi tanks rolled into Paris. Picasso decided to stay for the duration and live under gray skies and gray uniforms. Not only did he suffer from wartime shortages, condescending Nazis, and the grief of having comrades killed or deported, he had girl trouble. "The worst time of my life," he said. His beloved mother had died, and he endured the endless, bitter divorce from Olga, all the while juggling his two longtime feuding mistresses—as well as the occasional fling.

Still, he continued working, and his canvases from this period are only slightly more gray and gloomy.

Room 18: The South of France (1948-1954)

Sun! Color! Water! Spacious skies! Freedom!

At war's end, he left Paris and all that emotional baggage behind, finding fun in the sun in the South of France. Sixty-five-year-old Pablo Picasso was reborn, enjoying worldwide fame and the love of a beautiful 23-year-old painter named Françoise Gilot. She soon gave him a fresh start at fatherhood and gave birth to son Claude and daughter Paloma.

Picasso spent mornings swimming in the Mediterranean, days painting, evenings partying with friends, and late nights painting again, like a madman. Dressed in rolled-up white pants and a striped sailor's shirt, bursting with pent-up creativity, he often cranked out more than a painting a day. Ever-restless Picasso had finally found his Garden of Eden and rediscovered his *joie de vivre.*

These works set the tone for the rest of Picasso's life—sunny, lighthearted, childlike, experimenting in new media, and using motifs of the sea, of Greek mythology (fauns, centaurs), and animals (birds, goats, and pregnant baboons). His childlike doves became an international symbol of peace. These joyous themes announce Picasso's newfound freedom in a newly liberated France.

- *Head upstairs to...*

Room 19: The Studio/ Luncheon on the Grass (1955-1961)

With no living peers in the world of art, the great Picasso dialogued with dead Masters, reworking paintings by Edouard Manet and Diego de Velázquez. Oh yes, also in this period he meets mistress number...um, whatever—27-year-old Jacqueline Roque, whom he married.

Room 20: The Last Period (1961-1973)

He was fertile to the end, still painting with bright thick colors at age 91. Throughout his long life, Picasso was intrigued with portraying people—always people, ignoring the background—conveying their features with a single curved line and their moods with colors. These last works have the humor and playfulness of someone much younger. As it is said of Picasso, "When he was a child, he painted like a man. When he was old, he painted like a child."

RODIN MUSEUM **TOUR**

Auguste Rodin (1840–1917) was a modern Michelangelo, sculpting human figures on an epic scale, revealing through the body their deepest thoughts and feelings. Like many of Michelangelo's unfinished works, Rodin's statues rise from the raw stone around them, driven by the life force. With missing limbs and scarred skin, these are prefab classics, making ugliness noble. Rodin's people are always moving restlessly. Even the famous *Thinker* is moving. While he's plopped down solidly, his mind is a million miles away. The museum presents a full range of Rodin's work, housed in a historic mansion where he once lived and worked. The gardens are picnic-perfect (BYO), but there's also a pleasant, if pricey, café.

ORIENTATION

Cost: €5, €3 on Sun and for students, free for youth under 18 and for anyone on the first Sun of month; €1 for garden only; all covered by museum pass.

Hours: April–Sept Tue–Sun 9:30–17:45, garden closes at 18:45. Oct–March Tue–Sun 9:30–17:00, garden closes at 16:45. Closed Mon. Last entrance 30 minutes before closing.

Getting There: It's at 77 rue de Varenne, near Napoléon's Tomb (Mo: Varenne). Bus #69 stops at Grenelle-Bellechasse.

Information: Tel. 01 44 18 61 10, www.musee-rodin.fr.

Museum Tours: Audioguides covering the museum and gardens cost €4.

Length of This Tour: One hour.

THE TOUR BEGINS

- *As you enter the mansion, pick up a museum plan with room numbers (this tour is keyed to that plan), turn left, and walk through the shop to start a circular tour of the ground floor.*

Rodin Museum

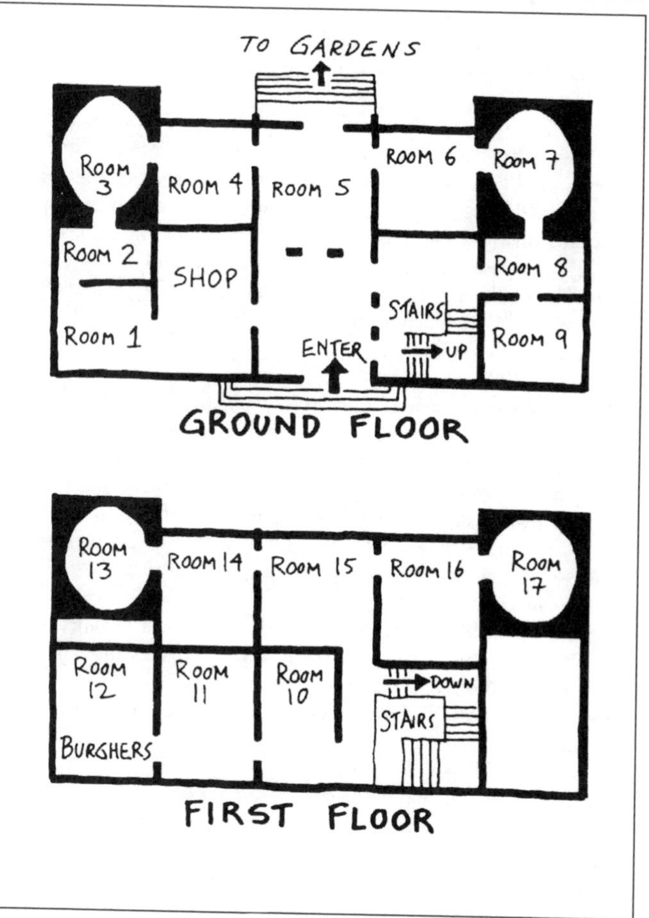

Room 1: Rodin's early works match the belle époque style of the time—noble busts of bourgeois citizens, pretty portraits of their daughters, and classical themes. Born of working-class roots, Rodin taught himself art by sketching statues at the Louvre and then sculpting copies.

The Man with the Broken Nose (*L'Homme au nez cassé*, 1865)—a deliberately ugly work—was 23-year-old Rodin's first break from the norm. He meticulously sculpted this deformed man (one of the few models the struggling sculptor could afford), but then the clay statue froze in his unheated studio, and the back of the head fell off. Rodin loved it! The Salon hated it. Rodin persevered. (Note: the Museum rotates the display of two different versions: the broken-headed one and another, repaired version Rodin made later that the Salon accepted.)

See the painting of Rodin's future wife, Rose Beuret *(Portrait de Madame Rodin)*, who suffered with him through obscurity and celebrity.

Room 2: To feed his new family, Rodin cranked out small-scale works with his boss' name on them—portraits, ornamental vases, nymphs, and knickknacks to decorate buildings. Still, the series of mother-and-childs (Rose and baby Auguste?) allowed him to experiment on a small scale with the intertwined twosomes he'd do later.

His job gave him enough money to visit Italy, where he was inspired by Michelangelo's boldness, monumental scale, restless figures, and "unfinished" look. Rapidly approaching middle age, Rodin was ready to rock.

Room 3: Rodin moved to Brussels, where his first major work, *The Bronze Age* (*L'âge d'airain*, 1877), brought controversy and the fame that surrounds it. This nude youth, perhaps inspired by Michelangelo's "Dying Slave" in the Louvre, awakens to a new world. It was so lifelike that Rodin was accused of not sculpting it himself but simply casting it directly from a live body. The boy's left hand looks like he should be leaning on a spear, but it's just that missing element that makes the pose more tenuous and interesting.

The art establishment still snubbed Rodin as an outsider, and no wonder. Look at his ultra-intense take on the winged symbol of France *(La Défense)*—this Marseillaise screams, "Off with their heads!" at the top of her lungs. Rodin was a slave to his muses, and some of them inspired monsters.

Room 4: Like the hand of a sculptor, *The Hand of God* (*La main de Dieu*, 1896) shapes Adam and Eve from the mud of the earth, to which they will return. Rodin himself worked in "mud," using his hands to model clay figures, which were then reproduced in marble or bronze, usually by his assistants. Spin this masterpiece on its turntable. Rodin wants you to see it from every angle. He first worked from the front view, then checked the back and side profiles, then filled in the in-between.

In *The Kiss* (1888-1889), a passionate woman twines around a solid man for their first, spontaneous kiss. In their bodies, we can almost read the thoughts, words, and movements that led up to this meeting of lips. *The Kiss* was the first Rodin work the public loved. Rodin despised it, thinking it simple and sentimental.

Other works in this room show embracing couples who seem to emerge from the stone just long enough to love. Rodin left many works "unfinished," reminding us that all creation is a difficult process of dragging a form out of chaos.

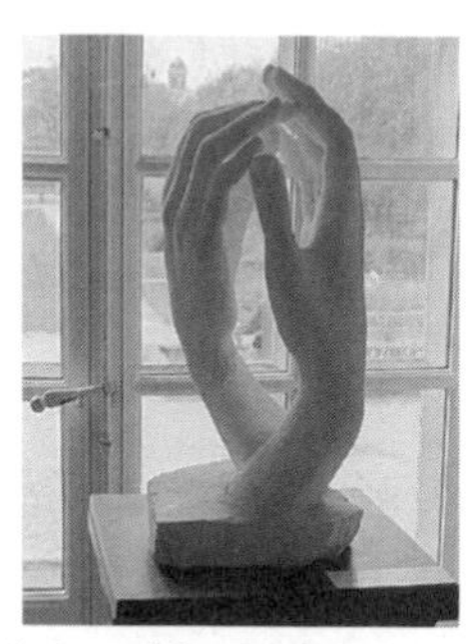

Room 5: The two hands that form the arch of *The Cathedral* (*La Cathédrale*, 1908) are actually two right hands (a man's and a woman's?).

In the room's center, a bronze man strides forward, as bold as the often-controversial Rodin. The armless and headless *Walking Man* (*L'Homme Qui Marche*, 1900-1907) plants his back foot forcefully, as though he's about to step, while his front foot already has stepped. Rodin, who himself had one foot in the past, one in the future, captures two poses at once.

Rodin worked with many materials—he chiseled marble, modeled clay, cast bronze, worked plaster, painted, and sketched. He often created different versions of the same subject in different media.

Room 6: This room displays works by Camille Claudel, mostly in the style of her master. The 44-year-old Rodin took 18-year-old Camille as his pupil, muse, colleague, and lover. We can follow the arc of their relationship:

Rodin was inspired by young Camille's beauty and spirit, and he often used her as a model. (See several versions of her head.)

As his student, "Mademoiselle C" learned from Rodin, doing portrait busts in his lumpy style. Her bronze bust of Rodin (by the door) shows the steely-eyed sculptor with strong front and side profiles, barely emerging from the materials he worked with.

Soon they were lovers. *The Waltz* (*La Valse*, 1892) captures the spinning exuberance the two must have felt as they embarked together on a new life. The couple twirls in a delicate balance.

But Rodin was devoted as well to his lifelong companion, Rose (see her face emerging from a block of marble). Claudel's *Maturity* (*L'Age Mûr*, 1895-1907) shows the breakup. A young woman on her knees begs the man not to leave her, as he's led away reluctantly by an older woman. The center of the composition is the hole left when their hands drift apart.

Rodin did leave Camille. Overwhelmed by grief and jealousy, she went crazy and had to be institutionalized until she died. *The Wave* (*La Vague*, 1900), carved in green onyx in a very un-Rodin style, shows tiny, helpless women huddled under a wave about to engulf them.

Rooms 7 and 8: What did Rodin think of women? Here are many different images from which you can draw conclusions.

Eve (1881) buries her head in shame, hiding her nakedne she can't hide the consequences of that first sin—she's pregnant.

Rodin became famous, wealthy, and respected, and society la wanted him to do their portraits. In Room 8, you'll also see his la tress *(La Duchesse de Choiseul),* who lived with him here in this m

Room 9: This dimly lit room is filled with Rodin's sketches (t rary exhibits occasionally occupy this space). The first flash of insp for a huge statue might be a single line sketched on notepaper. wanted nude models in his studio at all times—walking, dancir squatting—in case they struck some new and interesting pose. thought of sculpture as simply "drawing in all dimensions."

- *Upstairs, you'll find a glass display case that tries hard to explain..*

The Bronze Casting Process

Rodin made his bronze statues—not by hammering sheets of n but by using the classic "lost wax" technique. He'd start by shapi figure out of wet plaster. This figure becomes a model that's c with a form-fitting mold. Pour molten bronze into the narrow between the model and the mold around it, let it cool, remove the and—*voilà*!—you have a hollow, bronze statue ready to be polish varnished. With a mold, you could produce other copies, which there are many authorized bronze versions of Rodin's masterpieces all over the world.

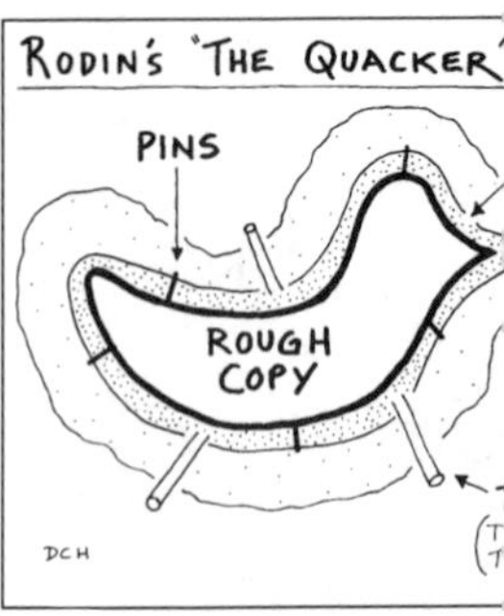

As the display case teaches, there are actually a number of additional steps, involving two models and two molds. Rodin used the original plaster model to make a first mold, which was used to make a heat-resistant clay copy of the original plaster model. He sanded down the clay copy, coated it with a wax skin, and then touched up the wax to a face details. He used this touched-up copy to make the more d final mold. He fitted the mold with ventilation tubes and startec ing in the molten bronze. The wax melted away—the "lost wax nique—and the bronze cooled and hardened in its place, thus fo the final bronze statue.

Rooms 10 and 11: *The Thinker* was to have been the c piece of a massive project that Rodin wrestled with for decades— way encrusted with characters from Dante's *Inferno.* These *Gates* were never completed (we'll later see the unfinished piece in the garden), but the studies for it (in this room) are some of Rodin's masterpieces.

These figures struggle to come into existence. Rodin was fascinated with the theory of evolution—not Darwin's version of the survival of the fittest, but the Frenchman Jean-Baptiste Lamarck's. His figures survive not by the good fortune of random mutation (Darwin), but by their own striving (Lamarck). They are driven by the life force, a restless energy that animates and shapes dead matter (Lamarck and Henri-Louis Bergson). Rodin must have felt that force even as a child, when he first squeezed soft clay and saw a worm emerge.

In Room 11, you'll see studies of the human body in all its aspects—open, closed, wrinkled, intertwined.

Room 12: A virtual unknown until his mid-30s, Rodin slowly began receiving major commissions for public monuments. *The Burghers of Calais* (*Bourgeois de Calais*, in the center of the room) depicts the actual event in 1347, when, in order to save their people, the city fathers surrendered the keys of the city—and their own lives—to the enemy. Rodin portrays them not in some glorious pose drenched in pomp and allegory, but as a simple example of men sacrificing their lives together. As they head to the gallows, with ropes already around their necks, each shows a distinct emotion, ranging from courage to despair. Compare the small plaster model in this room with the final, life-size bronze group outside the window in the garden (near the street).

• *Double back to the wing overlooking the gardens.*

Room 15: Rodin's feverish attempts to capture a portrait of the novelist Balzac ranged from a pot-bellied Bacchus to a headless nude cradling an erection. In a moment of inspiration, Rodin threw a plaster-soaked robe over the nude and watched it dry into what would become the proud, final, definitive version.

The museum's film clip shows Rodin—now old, bearded, and famous—making the marble chips fly. In fact, he rarely picked up a chisel and left that task to assistants.

Room 17: Legendary lovers kiss, embrace, and intertwine in yin-yang bliss.

Room 14: See Rodin's portrait busts of celebrities and some paintings by (yawn, are we through yet?) Vincent van Gogh, Claude Monet, and Pierre-Auguste Renoir. Rodin enjoyed discussions with Monet and other artists and incorporated their ideas in his work. Rodin is often considered an Impressionist because he captured spontaneous "impressions" of figures and created rough surfaces that catch reflected light.

Room 13: By the end of his life, Rodin was more famous than his works. Get a sense of Rodin's working process by comparing the small plaster "sketches" (in the glass case) with the final, large-scale marble versions that line the walls.

THE GARDENS

Rodin lived and worked in this mansion, renting rooms alongside Henri Matisse, the poet Rainer Maria Rilke (Rodin's secretary), and the dancer Isadora Duncan. He loved placing his creations in the overgrown gardens. These are his greatest works, Rodin at his most expansive. The epic human figures are enhanced, not dwarfed, by nature.

- *Leaving the house, there are five more stops: Two on the left and three on the right. Beyond these stops is a big, breezy garden ornamented with statues, a cafeteria, and a WC.*

***The Thinker* (*Le Penseur,* 1906)**

Leaning slightly forward, tense and compact, every muscle working toward producing that one great thought, Man contemplates his fate. No constipation jokes, please.

This is not an intellectual, but a linebacker who's realizing there's more to life than frat parties. It's the first man evolving beyond his animal nature to think the first thought. It's anyone who's ever worked hard to reinvent himself or to make something new or better. Said Rodin: "It is a statue of myself."

There are 29 other authorized copies of this statue, arguably the most famous in the world.

- *To the left of* The Thinker, *you'll find...*

***Balzac* (1898)**

The iconoclastic novelist turns his nose up at the notion he should be honored with a statue. This final version also stands in the Musée d'Orsay and on a street median in Montparnasse. When the statue was unveiled, the crowd booed, a fitting tribute to both the defiant novelist and the bold man who sculpted him.

- *Along the street near the ticket booth are...*

***The Burghers of Calais* (1889)**

The six city fathers trudge to their execution, and we can read in their

Rodin Museum Gardens

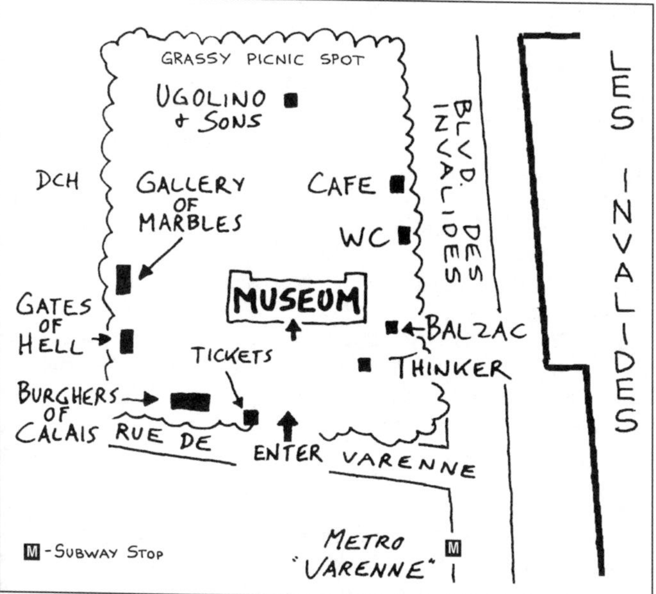

faces and poses what their last thoughts are. They mill about, dazed, as each one deals with the decision he's made to sacrifice himself for his city.

• *Circling counterclockwise...*

The man carrying the key to the city tightens his lips in determination. The bearded man is weighed down with grief. Another buries his head in his hands. One turns, seeking reassurance from his friend, who turns away and gestures helplessly. The final key-bearer (in back) raises his hand to his head.

Each is alone in his thoughts, but they're united by their mutual sacrifice, by the base they stand on, and by their weighty robes—gravity is already dragging them down to their graves.

Pity the poor souls, then thank King Edward III, who, at the last second, pardoned them.

• *Follow* The Thinker's *gaze to the opposite side of the house. Standing before a tall white backdrop is a big dark door*—The Gates of Hell.

The Gates of Hell (Porte de l'Enfer, 1880-1917)

These doors (never meant to actually open) were never finished for a museum that was never built. But the vision of Dante's trip into hell gave Rodin a chance to explore the dark side of human experience. "Abandon hope all ye who enter in," was hell's motto. The three Shades at the top of the door point down—that's where we're going. Beneath the Shades, pondering the whole scene from above, is Dante as the Thinker. Below him, the figures emerge from the darkness just long enough to tell their sad tale of depravity. There's Paolo and Francesca (in the center of the right door), who were driven into an illicit love affair that brought them here. Ugolino (left door, just below center) crouches in prison over his kids. This poor soul was so driven by hunger that he ate the corpses of his own children. On all fours like an animal, he is the dark side of natural selection. Finally, find what some say is Rodin himself (at the very bottom, inside the right doorjamb, where it just starts to jut out), crouching humbly.

You'll find some of these figures writ large in the garden. *The Thinker* is behind you, *The Shades* (c. 1889) are 30 yards to the right, and *Ugolino* (1901-1904) dines in the fountain at the far end.

It's appropriate that the *Gates*—Rodin's "cathedral"—remained unfinished. He was always a restless artist for whom the process of discovery was as important as the finished product.

• *To the right of* The Gates of Hell *is a glassed-in building, the...*

Gallery of Marbles

Unfinished, they show human features emerging from the rough stone. Imagine Rodin in his studio, working to give them life.

Victor Hugo (at the far end of the Gallery), the great champion of progress (and author of *Les Misérables*), leans back like Michelangelo's nude *Adam,* waiting for the spark of creation. He tenses his face and cups his ear, straining to hear the call from the blurry Muse above him. Once inspired, he can bring the idea to life (just as Rodin did) with the strength of his powerful arms. It's been said that all of Rodin's work shows the struggle of mind over matter, of brute creatures emerging from the mud and evolving into a species of thinkers.

MUSEE MARMOTTAN MONET **TOUR**

The Marmottan has the best collection of works by the master Impressionist, Claude Monet. In this mansion on the fringe of urban Paris, you can walk through Monet's life, from black-and-white sketches to colorful open-air paintings to the canvas that gave Impressionism its name. The museum's highlights are scenes of his garden at Giverny, including larger-than-life water lilies.

ORIENTATION

Cost: €6.50, €4 for students under 25 and anyone over 60, free for children under 8. The Marmottan is not covered by the museum pass.

Hours: Tue–Sun 10:00–18:00 (last entrance 17:30), closed Mon, May 1, and Dec 25.

Getting There: It's in northwest Paris at 2 rue Louis Boilly. Métro, RER, and buses all work: Take the Métro to La Muette, then walk six blocks in 10 minutes, following brown signs down chaussée de la Muette through the delightful, kid-filled park to the museum. Or take the RER-C from the rue Cler area (Invalides or Pont de l'Alma), get off at Boulainvilliers stop, follow *sortie* Singer, turn left on rue Singer, turn right up rue Boulainvilliers, and then turn left down chaussée de la Muette to the museum. Bus #63 is handy from the rue Cler area or from the Latin Quarter (buses #32, #22, and #52 also serve the museum).

Information: Tel. 01 44 96 50 33, www.marmottan.com.

Length of This Tour: One hour.

Photography: Not allowed. Cameras must be checked.

Starring: Claude Monet, including: *Impression: Sunrise* (shown above); portraits of Rouen Cathedral, Gare St. Lazare, and Houses of Parliament; scenes from Giverny; and water lilies.

OVERVIEW

The museum traces Monet's life chronologically, but in a way that's as rough and fragmented as a Monet canvas. The collection is reorganized periodically, so have patience and keep the big picture.

Basement: Entirely devoted to Monet, with works from throughout his life—mostly from his gardens at Giverny (including water lilies).

Ground floor: Bookstore, some Monet memorabilia, and an eclectic collection of non-Monet objects (including a beautifully displayed series of illuminated manuscript drawings).

First Floor (upstairs): Paintings by Impressionist colleagues (Pierre-Auguste Renoir, Camille Pissarro, Berthe Morisot, and more), period furnishings.

GROUND FLOOR

- *Turn left after entering and walk to the end of the hall to the timeline on the wall.*

Claude Monet (1840-1926)

Claude Monet was the leading light of the Impressionist movement that revolutionized painting in the 1870s. Fiercely independent and dedicated to his craft, Monet gave courage to Renoir and others in the face of harsh criticism.

A wall chart (in French) shows major events of Monet's life: 1840—birth; 1865—first acceptance of two of his paintings by *le jury*; 1870—marriage to Camille and draft dodge to London (*Londres*) to avoid the Franco-Prussian War; 1873—*Impression: Sunrise*, for the first Impressionist exhibition he organized with friends; the birth of several of his children; 1883—move to Giverny; and 1926—his death.

Memorabilia and Portraits of Monet and his Family

One of Monet's actual palettes is displayed nearby, alongside portraits of his children. Monet's first wife, Camille, died in 1879, leaving Monet to raise 12-year-old Jean and babe-in-arms Michel. (Michel would grow up to inherit the family home and many of the paintings that ended up here.) But Monet was also involved with Alice Hoschede, who had recently been abandoned by her husband. Alice moved in with her six kids and took care of the dying Camille, and the two families made a Brady Bunch merger. Baby Michel became bosom buddies with Alice's baby, Jean-Pierre, while teenage Jean Monet and stepsister Blanche fell in love and later married.

- *Drop downstairs and trace the stages of Monet's life. The basement is one big room divided into three "rooms." Start with Monet's black-and-white drawings in a glass case (usually in the center of the first room, but you may need to hunt for these; they've even been sighted upstairs on the top floor).*

BASEMENT LEVEL, FIRST ROOM FROM LE HAVRE TO LONDON (1857-1900)

Growing Up in Le Havre (1840-1860): Caricature Drawings (c. 1858)

Teenage Monet's first works—black-and-white, meticulously drawn, humorous sketches of small-town celebrities—are as different as can be from the colorful, messy oils that would make him famous. Still, they show his gift for quickly capturing an overall impression with a few simple strokes.

- *Now work clockwise around the first alcove, starting at the stairs.*

The son of a grocer, Monet defied his family, insisted he was an artist, and sketched the world around him—beaches, boats, and small-town life. A fellow artist, Eugène Boudin, encouraged him to don a scarf, set up his easel outdoors, and paint the scene exactly as he saw it. Today, we say: "Well, duh!" But "open-air" painting was unorthodox for artists trained to study their subjects thoroughly in the perfect lighting of a controlled studio setting.

At 19, Monet went to Paris but refused to enroll in the official art schools. The letters (in the glass case) from Monet asking for survival money from his friends show the price he paid for his early bohemian lifestyle.

The 1870s: Pure Impressionism

Monet teamed up with Renoir and Alfred Sisley, leading them on open-air painting safaris to the countryside. Inspired by the realism of Edouard Manet, they painted everyday things—landscapes, seascapes, street scenes, ladies with parasols, family picnics—in bright, basic colors.

In 1870, Monet married his girlfriend, Camille (the dark-haired woman in many of his paintings), and moved just outside Paris to the resort town of Argenteuil. Playing host to Renoir, Manet, and others, he perfected the Impressionist style—painting nature as a mosaic of short brushstrokes of different colors placed side by side, suggesting shimmering light.

First, he simplified. In *The Beach at Trouville* (*Sur la Plage à Trouville*, 1870-1871), a lady's dress is a few thick strokes of paint. With paintings

like *Stroll Near Argenteuil* (*Promenade près d'Argenteuil*, 1873), Monet gradually broke things down into smaller dots of different colors. If you back up from a Monet canvas, the colors blend into one (for example, red plus green plus yellow equals a brown boat). Still, they never fully resolve, creating the effect of colorful, shimmering light. Monet limited his palette to a few bright colors—cobalt blue, white, yellow, two shades of red, and emerald green abound. But no black—even shadows are a combination of bright colors.

Monet's constant quest was to faithfully reproduce nature in colored blobs of paint. His eye was a camera lens set at a very slow shutter speed to admit maximum light. Then he "developed" the impression made on his retina with an oil-based, pigmented solution. Even as the heartbroken Monet watched Camille die of tuberculosis in 1879, he was (he admitted later) intrigued by the changing colors in her dying face.

Impression: Sunrise (*Impression, Soleil levant*, 1873)

Here's the painting that started the revolution—a simple, serene view of boats bobbing under an orange sun. At the first public showing by Monet, Renoir, Degas, and others in Paris in 1874, critics howled at this work and ridiculed the title. "Wallpaper," one called it. The sloppy brushstrokes and ordinary subject looked like a study, not a finished work. The style was dubbed "Impressionist"—an accurate name.

The misty harbor scene obviously made an "impression" on Monet, who faithfully rendered the fleeting moment in quick strokes of paint. The waves are simple horizontal brushstrokes. The sun's reflection on the water is a few thick, bold strokes of orange tipped with white. They zigzag down the canvas, the way a reflection shifts on moving water.

Monet the Traveler

In search of new light and new scenes, Monet traveled throughout France and Europe. As you enjoy canvases painted in all kinds of weather, picture Monet at work—hiking to a remote spot; carrying an easel, several canvases, brushes (large-size), a palette, tubes of paint (an invention that made open-air painting practical), food and drink, a folding chair, and an umbrella; and wearing his trademark hat, with a cigarette on his lip. He weathered the elements, occasionally putting himself in danger by clambering on cliffs to get the shot.

The key was to work fast, before the weather changed and the light shifted, completely changing the colors. Monet worked "wet-in-wet," applying new paint before the first layer dried, mixing colors on the canvas, and piling them up into a thick paste.

The 1890s: Series

Monet often painted the same subject several times under different light (such as one of Paris' train stations, the *Gare St. Lazare,* 1870s). In the 1890s, he conceived of a series of paintings to be shown as a group, giving a time-lapse view of a single subject.

He rented several rooms offering different angles overlooking the *Rouen Cathedral* and worked on up to 14 different canvases at a time, shuffling the right one onto the easel as the sun moved across the sky. The cathedral is made of brown stone, but at sunset it becomes gold and pink with blue shadows, softened by thick smudges of paint. The true subject is not the cathedral, but the full spectrum of light that bounces off it.

These series—of the cathedral, of haystacks, poplars, and mornings on the Seine—were very popular. Monet, poverty-stricken until his mid-40s, was slowly becoming famous, first in America, then London, and finally in France.

- *Just before leaving the first room, you'll see...*

The 1900s: London

Turning a hotel room into a studio, Monet—working on nearly a hundred different canvases simultaneously—painted the changing light on the River Thames. The *London Houses of Parliament, reflected in the Thames* (*Londres, Le Parlement, Reflets sur la Tamise,* 1905) stretch and bend with the tide. *Charing Cross Bridge* is only a few smudgy lines enveloped in fog.

London's fog epitomized Monet's favorite subject—the atmosphere that distorts distant objects. That filtering haze gives even different-colored objects a similar tone, resulting in a more harmonious picture. When the light was just right and the atmosphere glowed, the moment of "instantaneity" had arrived, and Monet worked like a madman.

In truth, many of Monet's canvases were begun quickly in the open air, then painstakingly perfected later in the studio. He composed his scenes with great care—clear horizon lines give a strong horizontal axis, while diagonal lines (of trees or shorelines) create solid triangles. And he wasn't above airbrushing out details that might spoil the composition—such as Cleopatra's Needle near Charing Cross.

- *Continue into the next room.*

ROOMS TWO AND THREE PAINTINGS OF GIVERNY (1883–1926)

Rose Trellises and the Japanese Bridge (several versions)

In 1883, Monet's brood settled into a farmhouse in Giverny (50 miles west of Paris). Financially stable and domestically blissful, he turned Giverny into a garden paradise and painted nature without the long commute.

These canvases immerse you in Monet's garden at Giverny. Each canvas is fully saturated with color, the distant objects as bright as the close ones. Monet's mosaic of brushstrokes forms a colorful design that's beautiful even if you just look "at" the canvas like wallpaper. He wanted his paintings to be realistic and three-dimensional, but with a pleasant, two-dimensional pattern.

In the last half of his life, Monet's world shrank—from the broad vistas of the world traveler to the tranquility of his home, family, and garden. But his artistic vision expanded as he painted smaller details on bigger canvases and helped invent modern abstract art.

In 1890, Monet started work on his Japanese garden, inspired by tranquil scenes from the Japanese prints he collected. He diverted a river to form a pond, planted willows and bamboo on the shores, filled the pond with water lilies, then crossed it with this wooden footbridge. As years passed, the bridge became overgrown with wisteria (compare the early bridge canvas behind you and the later bridge canvases in front of you). He painted it at different times of day and year, exploring different color schemes.

Monet uses the bridge as the symmetrical center of simple, pleasing designs. The water is drawn with horizontal brushstrokes that get shorter as you move up the canvas ("farther away"), creating the illusion of distance. The horizontal water contrasts with the vertical willows, while the bridge "bridges" the sides of the square canvas and laces the scene together.

In 1912, Monet began to go blind. Cataracts distorted his perception of depth and color, and sent him into a tailspin of despair. The (angry?) red paintings date from this period.

Early Water Lilies (*Nymphéas*, several versions)

As his vision slowly failed, Monet concentrated on painting close-ups of the surface of the pond and its water lilies by using red, white, yellow, lavender, and various combos. Some lilies are just a few broad strokes on a bare canvas (a study), while others are piles of paint formed with overlapping colors.

But more than the lilies, the paintings focus on the changing reflections on the surface of the pond. Pan slowly around the room and watch the pond go from predawn to bright sunlight to twilight.

Early lily paintings (c. 1900) show the shoreline as a reference point. But increasingly, Monet cropped the scene ever closer, until there was no shoreline, no horizon, no sense of what's up or down. Lilies float among clouds. Stepping back from the canvas, you see the lilies just hang there on the museum wall, suspended in space. The surface of the pond and the surface of the canvas are one. Modern, abstract art—a colored design on a flat surface—is just around the corner.

• *Enter the final, round room and find the big tree trunk.*

Big Weeping Willow (*Saule Pleureur,* 1918-1919)

Get close—Monet did—and analyze the trunk. Rough "brown" bark is made of thick strokes (an inch wide and 4 inches long) of pink, purple, orange, and green. Impressionism lives. But to get these colors to resolve in your eye, you'd have to back up all the way to Giverny.

Later Water Lilies (*Nymphéas,* 1915–1926)

Like Beethoven going deaf, blind Monet wrote his final symphonies on a monumental scale. He planned a series of huge, six-foot-tall canvases of water lilies to hang in special rooms at L'Orangerie (scheduled to reopen in late 2004). He built a special studio with skylights and wheeled easels, and he worked on these paintings obsessively. A successful eye operation in 1923 gave him new energy. Here at the Marmottan are smaller-scale studies for that series.

Some lilies are patches of thick paint circled by a squiggly "caricature" of a lily pad. Monet simplifies in a way that Henri Matisse and Pablo Picasso would envy. But getting close, you see that the lily is made of many brushstrokes, and also that each brushstroke is itself a mixture of different colored paints.

Monet is thought of as a lightweight, but he deals with the fundamentals of life, especially in his later work, featuring green lilies floating among lavender clouds reflected in the blue water. Staring into Monet's pond, we see the intermingling of the four classical elements, earth (foliage), air (the sky), fire (sunlight), and water—the primordial soup where life begins.

When Monet died in 1926, he was famous. Starting with meticulous line drawings, he had evolved into an open-air realist, then Impressionist color-analyst, then serial painter, and finally master of reflections. As the subjects of his work became fuzzier, the colors and patterns predominated. Monet builds a bridge between Impressionism and modern abstract art.

FIRST FLOOR COLLECTION

Check out the fine collection of paintings by Monet's Impressionist colleagues: Renoir, Paul Gauguin, Pissarro, Morisot (find her portrait by Manet), and others before saying *au revoir* to this museum.

NAPOLEON'S TOMB & LES INVALIDES **TOUR**

If you've ever considered being absolute dictator of a united Europe, come here first. Hitler did, but still went out and made the same mistakes as his role model. (Hint: Don't invade Russia.)

Napoleon's tomb rests beneath the golden dome of Les Invalides church. Around the church, in a former veterans' hospital built by Louis XIV, are various military museums, where you can see Napoleon's horse stuffed and mounted, WWI machine guns, and much more. The best exhibit is the World War II wing in the Army Museum (page 224).

ORIENTATION

Cost: €6, students-€5, free for those under 18, covered by museum pass.

Hours: April–Sept daily 10:00–18:00, Oct–March daily 10:00–17:00. Closed the first Monday of every month, Jan 1, May 1, Nov 1, and Dec 25.

Getting There: The tomb is at the Hôtel des Invalides at 129 rue de Grenelle (near Rodin Museum, Mo: La Tour Maubourg, Varenne, or Invalides). Bus #69 from the Marais and rue Cler area is also handy. The museum is a 10-minute walk from rue Cler.

Information: English handouts at the ticket office (tel. 01 44 42 37 72, www.invalides.org).

Length of This Tour: Women—two hours, men—three hours, Republican men—all day.

Cuisine Art: A reasonable cafeteria is next to the ticket office, and the rear gardens are picnic-perfect.

- *Start at Napoleon's tomb, underneath the golden dome. It's at the back end (farthest from the Seine) of this vast complex of churches and museums.*

NAPOLEON'S TOMB

Enter the church, gaze up at the dome, then lean over the railing and bow to the emperor lying inside the red, porphyry-scrolled tomb. If the lid were opened, you'd find an oak coffin inside, which holds another ebony coffin, housing two lead ones, then mahogany, then tinplate...until finally you'd find Napoleon himself staring up, with his head closest to the door. When his body was exhumed from the original grave and transported here (1840), it was still perfectly preserved, even after 19 years in the ground.

Born of humble Italian heritage on the French-owned isle of Corsica, Napoleon Bonaparte (1769–1821) went to school at Paris' Ecole Militaire (Military School), then rose quickly through the ranks amid the chaos of the Revolution. The charismatic "Little Corporal" won fans by fighting for democracy at home and abroad. In 1799, he assumed power and, within five short years, conquered most of Europe. The great champion of the Revolution had become a dictator, declaring himself emperor of a new Rome.

Napoleon's red tomb on its green base stands 15 feet high in the center of a marble floor. It's exalted by the dome above, where dead Frenchmen cavort with saints and angels, forming a golden halo over Napoleon.

Napoleon is surrounded by family. After conquering Europe, he installed his big brother, Joseph, as king of Spain (turn around to see Joseph's black-and-white marble tomb in the alcove to the left of the door); his little brother, Jerome, became king of Westphalia (to right of door); and his baby boy, Napoleon II (downstairs), sat in diapers on the throne of Rome.

In other alcoves, you'll find more dead war heroes, including Marshal Ferdinand Foch, the Commander in Chief of the multinational Allied forces in World War I, his tomb lit with otherworldly blue light. These heroes, plus many painted saints, make this the French Valhalla in the Versailles of churches.

The Crypt

- *The stairs behind the altar (with the corkscrew columns) take you down to crypt level for a closer look at the tomb.*

Wandering clockwise, read the names of Napoleon's battles on the floor around the base of the tomb. Rivoli marks the battle where the rookie 26-year-old general took a ragtag band of "citizens" and thrashed the professional Austrian troops in Italy, returning to Paris a celebrity. In

Egypt (*Pyramides*), he fought Turks and tribesmen to a stands exotic expedition caught the public eye, and he returned home a

Napoleon's huge victory over Austria at Austerlitz on t anniversary of his coronation made him Europe's top dog. At the the million-man Great Army (*La Grande Armée*), he made a three blitz attack through Germany and Austria. As a general, he was relying on top-notch generals and on a mobile force of indep armies. His personal charisma on the battlefield was said to be 10,000 additional men.

Pause in the battles to gaze at the grand statue of Napol emperor in the alcove at the head of the tomb—royal scepter anc Earth in his hands. By 1804, all of Europe was at his feet. He elaborate ceremony in Notre-Dame, where he proclaimed hi Josephine, as empress, and himself—the 36-year-old son of immigrants—as emperor. The laurel wreath, the robes, and the eagles proclaim him the equal of the Caesars. The floor at the feet marks the grave of his son, Napoleon II (*Roi de Rome*, 1811-

Around the crypt are relief panels showing Napoleon's co tive side. Dressed in toga and laurel leaves, he dispenses justice, and pork-barrel projects to an awed populace.

- *In the first panel to the right of the statue...*

He establishes an Imperial University to educate naked boys th out "*tout l'empire.*" The roll of great scholars links modern Fran those of the past: Plutarch, Homer, Plato, and Aristotle. Three later, his various building projects (canals, roads, and so on) are cel with a list and his quotation, "Everywhere I passed, I left durable b

Hail Napoleon. Then, at his peak, came his fatal mistake.

- *Continue around the tomb to the Battle of Moscow (Moscowa)...*

Napoleon invaded Russia with 600,000 men and returned t with 60,000 frostbitten survivors. Two years later, the Russians m into Paris, and Napoleon's days were numbered. After a brief e the isle of Elba, he skipped parole, sailed to France, bared his and said, "Strike me down or follow me!" For 100 days, they fo him, finally into Belgium, where the British hammered the Fre the Battle of Waterloo (conspicuously absent on the floor's Exiled again by a war tribunal, he spent his last days in a crud on the small South Atlantic island of St. Helena.

- *To get to the Courtyard of Honor and the various military museur the church with Napoleon's tomb, make a U-turn right and march the cafeteria and ticket hall. Halfway down the long hallway, on t right through the glass, you'll see...*

Napoleon's Tombstone *(Pierre Tombal)*

This bare stone slab beside weeping willows once rested atop Nap grave on the island of St. Helena. The epitaph was never finishe the French and British wrangled over what to call the hero/tyrant. The stone read simply, "Here lies..."

- *Continuing on, you'll spill out into the large Courtyard of Honor, where Napoleon honored his troops and de Gaulle once kissed Churchill. The Army Museum flanks both sides of the courtyard.*

LES INVALIDES AND THE ARMY MUSEUM *(MUSÉE DE L'ARMEE)*

Your tomb ticket also admits you to a number of other military museums scattered around the complex (listed in the free English map/guide in ticket hall). Here are four I recommend and give information on:

▲▲Army Museum: East wing—French military history, with focus on Napoleon (entrance on east side of courtyard).

▲Army Museum: West wing—Weapons through the ages, with a good World War I section (entrance on west side of courtyard).

▲▲▲World War II wing—Interesting coverage of this critical war (entrance at southwest corner of courtyard, near Napoleon's tombstone).

Liberation Museum—Story of WWII French Resistance, but no English descriptions (near tombstone).

Pick your favorite war. With limited time, visit only the excellent World War II wing. Most displays consist of dummies in uniforms and endless glass cases full of muskets, without historical context.

- *Cross the courtyard, enter the east wing under the golden letters, and go up to the second floor (European) to reach the east wing exhibits (elevator available, WC downstairs).*

ARMY MUSEUM: EAST WING

This museum traces uniforms and weapons through French history, from Louis XIV to World War I, with emphasis on Napoleon. As you circle the second floor, you'll follow the history and art of French warfare from about 1700 to 1850: Pre-Revolution, Revolution, Napoleon, and Restoration. Red banners give an English overview in each room.

Salle Louis XIV: Louis XIV unified the army as he unified the country, creating the first modern nation-state with a military force. In this room and several more, you'll see how gunpowder was quickly turning swords, pikes, and lances to pistols, muskets, and bayonets. Uniforms become more uniform and everyone gets a standard-issue flintlock.

Les Invalides

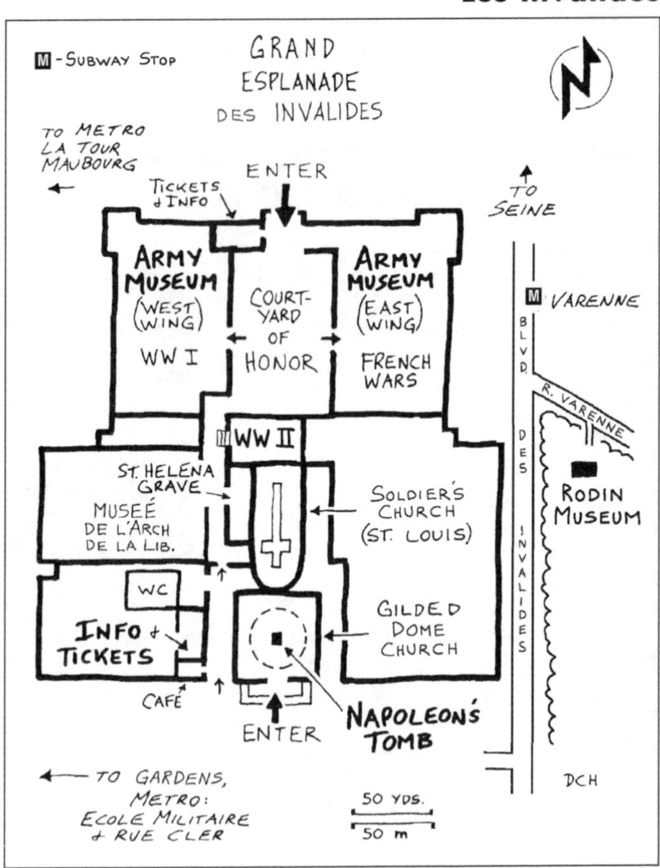

• *A few rooms later…*

Salle Guerres de la République: With the Revolution, the king's Royal Army became the people's National Guard, protecting their fledgling democracy from Europe's monarchies, while spreading revolutionary ideas by conquest. At the Battle of Lodi (1796, see the model with tiny toy soldiers), the French and Austrians faced off on opposites sides of a northern Italian river, trying to capture the crucial bridge and using cannons to clear the way for a cavalry charge. Young, relatively obscure Bonaparte personally sighted the French cannons on the enemy—normally the job of a lesser officer—which turned the tide of battle and earned himself a reputation and nickname, "The Little Corporal."

Salle Boulogne: See General Bonaparte's hat, sword, and medals. The tent (behind screen) shows his bivouac equipment: a bed with mosquito netting, a director's chair, and a table that you can imagine his generals hunched over as they made battle plans.

Back in the hall, a glass case displays a French-Breton dictionary *(Grammaire Françoise-Celtique)*, providing French soldiers the necessary lingo to survive in the "foreign" region of Brittany.

- *Turning the corner...*

Salle Austerlitz: Now at the peak of his power, Emperor Napoleon (in the famous portrait by Jean-Auguste-Dominique Ingres) stretches his right arm to supernatural lengths.

Salle Eylau: Behold Napoleon's beloved Arabian horse, Le Vizir, who weathered many a campaign and grew old with him in exile (stuffed in a glass case).

Salle Montmirail: A portrait catches a dejected Napoleon after his first abdication in 1814. A glass case is dedicated to Napoleon's son, the "Roi de Rome." His little soldier boots are there, and an engraving shows the child king in a royal carriage. When he grew up (miniature portrait in the center), he looked a lot like his dad—a fact that kept French Royalists wary until his death. Junior's mother (engraving to the left) was Marie-Louise, whom Napoleon married after divorcing barren Josephine.

- *Turn the corner into a long, blue corridor, the...*

Corridor de Tarascon: Napoleon's big white dog (in a glass case), his companion in exile on Elba, suffered the same fate as the horse. On the wall to the left of the dog hang proclamations of thanks and good-byes, announcing the surrender at Waterloo, that Napoleon sent to his soldiers and the French people. Directly behind the dog (other side of the wall), a shining breastplate shows the effectiveness of British artillery in the battle of Waterloo. A dozen steps further along at the blue drapes, you'll find Napoleon's death mask and a reconstruction of a room in his final home on St. Helena (inside the drapes). Picture a lonely man suffering from ulcers sitting here in his nightcap and slippers, playing chess, not war.

Exit the long blue corridor, and you'll see an American flag (in a glass case) along with the French tricolor flag, honoring the Marquis de Lafayette of France, the general who helped George Washington take Yorktown.

- *Turn right to exit.*

The Musée des Plans Reliefs (top floor of east wing) has 1
18th-century models (1:1,600 scale) of France's cities, usec
French to devise strategies to thwart enemy attacks (see Englis
the door). Survey a city and ponder which hillside you'd use to la
attack. Big models of Mont St. Michel and Antibes lie at eit
Other floors of this wing are filled with temporary exhibits.

ARMY MUSEUM: WEST WING

Across the courtyard is a twin museum in the west wing. The
floor covers military implements, from stone axes to Axis powe
the entrance, two long, interesting rooms of armor and n
weaponry have good English descriptions.

WORLD WAR I WING

Upstairs on the second floor, you'll find a small but fascinating
War I wing (14–18 Gallerie) that makes warfare feel less glorious

• *Working clockwise around this long room, you'll find:*

Scale Model of "Grosse Bertha": Boom! August 1914: Th
War began, pitting modern machinery like the cannon Big Ber
times bigger than this model)—lobbing 420-caliber, 300-pound
against men on horseback carrying bayonets (see mannequin
case opposite).

Map, 1914: Germany swept through Belgium to attack France.
had been sparked by the assassination of the Austrian archdu
Serbian terrorist. It quickly escalated into a World War, as E
nations took sides in the regional struggle (you'll see mannequins
many nations' uniforms). France and Britain (along with others)
off against Germany (and others). For the first year, the war follow
ditional course, with both sides trying to outflank the other.

Map, 1915—*L'année sterile:* France stalled the German
at the Battle of the Marne, and the two sides froze into a new
warfare. They dug trenches to protect their territory and fough
in the narrow space between, called No Man's Land.

Machine Guns: As soldiers with rifles and bayonets went "over
of the trenches and charged across No Man's Land, they were me
relentless hail of bullets from these modern weapons. Routinely, m
diers died in a single day of battle than America lost in 10 years of V
(The inventor of the machine gun thought his invention would e
assuming that no one would send a soldier into its flurry of bullets

Model of Trench: Soldiers lived in the elaborate system of trenches, where they suffered from disease, rats, and boredom. A crooked trench-rifle (opposite the model) was designed to shoot over the top.

• *At the far end of the room, find a...*

Model of the Battle of Verdun: On February 21, 1916, history's biggest and longest battle began. Day after day for nine months, French and German soldiers spilled over the top of trenches to fight on this small, 3.5-square-mile battlefield in eastern France. Press the buttons to see how little territory was won, lost, then recaptured—maybe a few hundred yards—at a cost of 700,000 casualties (337,000 dead, wounded, and missing on each side).

• *Down the other half of the room, you'll find grenades and helmets with bullet holes, along with...*

Maps of Other Fronts: The Western Front between France and Germany is the most famous battle line, but this first World War was fought in Russia, Poland, the Italian Alps, Serbia, and beyond.

Model Airplanes: This was the first war in which airplanes played a role. Goggled-and-scarved pilots in biplanes fought "dogfights" to gain air superiority, not so much to bomb as to conduct surveillance of enemy positions.

American Soldier and Poster: "I want YOU!" says Uncle Sam. In 1917, a formerly neutral America sent U.S. soldiers, dubbed "doughboys" to fight alongside the French and British. (Also in the room, see more mannequins representing many of the nations in this world war.)

Map, 1917: Even after two years of warfare, the combatants' positions look virtually the same as on the map of 1915.

Model Tank: World War I invented the technology of war that would be perfected in World War II. (Fortunately, one of the weapons deployed during the Great War—poison gas—has been used sparingly since.)

• *Finally, near the end of the room is a...*

Painting—The Victory Parade, July 14, 1919 *(Le Défile de la Victoire, le 14 Juillet 1919)*: At 11:00 a.m. on the 11th day of the 11th month, 1918, fighting ceased. Who won? Germany surrendered and France could hold a victory parade like this one down the avenue des Champs-Elysées, but there were no winners. Ten million men died in the "war to end all wars," and it proved to be only a prelude to its sequel, World War II.

(The next floor up displays models of artillery over the years.)

- *The entrance to the World War II wing is located in the southwest corner of the main courtyard; go upstairs, following signs to "General de Gaulle: Deuxième Guerre Mondiale, 39/45." The museum another as well: "France Libre, France Combattante."*

ARMY MUSEUM: WORLD WAR II WING

World War II was the most destructive of Earth's struggles. In this exhibit, the war unfolds in photos, displays, and newsreels, with special emphasis on the French contribution. You may never have realized that it was Charles de Gaulle who won the war for us.

The free museum map is helpful for locating the displays we'll see. Climb to the top floor and work back down, from Germany's quick domination (third floor) to the Allies turning the tide (second floor) to the final surrender (first floor).

There are fine English descriptions. Make time!

Third Floor: Axis Aggression

Room 1: Treaty of Versailles to 1939 *(Du Traité de Versailles à 1939):* In 1918, the "war to end all wars" ground to a halt, leaving 10 million dead, a defeated Germany, and a devastated (if victorious) France. For the next two decades, Adolf Hitler would feed off German resentment over the Treaty of Versailles, which had humiliated and ruined Germany.

Room 2: The Defeat of 1940 *(La Défaite de 1940):* On September 1, 1939, Hitler invaded Poland, starting World War II. France and Britain mobilized, but Germany did nothing for six months. Then, in the spring of 1940 came the Blitzkrieg ("lightning war"), and Germany's better-trained and better-equipped soldiers and tanks swept west through Belgium. France was immediately overwhelmed, and British troops barely escaped across the English Channel from Dunkirk. Within a month, Nazis were goose-stepping down the Champs-Elysées, and Hitler was on his way to Napoleon's tomb.

Room 3: The Appeal of June 18, 1940: Just like that, virtually all of Europe was dominated by fascists. During those darkest days, as France fell and Nazism spread across the Continent, one Frenchman—an obscure military man named Charles de Gaulle—refused to admit defeat. He escaped to London, made inspiring speeches over the radio, and slowly convinced a small audience of French expatriates that victory was still possible.

Room 4: Charles de Gaulle (1890–1970): This 20th-century John of Arc had an unshakable belief in his mission to save France. He was born into a literate, upper-class family, raised in military academies, and became a WWI hero and POW. After the war, he helped administer the occupied Rhineland. When World War II broke out, he was only a minor officer (the title of "Brigadier General" was hastily acquired during the invasion). He had limited political experience and was virtually unknown to the French public. But he rallied France, became the focus of French patriotism, and later guided the country in the postwar years.

Rooms 5 and 6: The Vichy Government *(La France après l'Armistice, L'Empire colonial: un enjeu)*: After the surrender, Germany ruled northern France (including Paris) but allowed the French to administer the south and the colonies (North Africa). This puppet government, centered in the city of Vichy, was right-wing and traditional, bowing to Hitler's demands as he looted France's raw materials and manpower for the war machine. (The movie *Casablanca,* set in Vichy-controlled Morocco, shows French officials following Nazi orders while French citizens defiantly sing "The Marseillaise.")

Room 7: The Battle of Britain—June 1940–June 1941 *(La Bataille d'Angleterre, Du Refus de la Défaite à l'Esprit de Résistance)*: Facing a "New Dark Age" in Europe, British Prime Minister Winston Churchill pledged, "We will fight on the beaches....We will fight in the hills. We will never surrender."

In June 1940, Germany mobilized to invade Britain across the Channel. From June to September, they paved the way, sending bombers—up to 1,500 planes a day—to destroy military and industrial sites. When Britain wouldn't budge, Hitler concentrated on London and civilian targets—this was "The Blitz" of the winter of 1940, which killed 30,000 and left London in ruins. But Britain hung on, armed with newfangled radar, speedy Spitfires, and an iron will.

They also had the Germans' secret "Enigma" code. The "Enigma machine" (in display case), with its set of revolving drums, allowed German commanders to scramble orders in a complex code that could safely be broadcast to their troops. The British (with crucial help from Poland) captured a machine, broke the code (a project called "Ultra"), then monitored German airwaves.

For the rest of the war, they had advance knowledge of many top-secret plans. (Occasionally, Britain even let Germany's plans succeed—sacrificing their own people—to avoid suspicion.)

By spring of 1941, Hitler had given up any hope of invading the Isle of Britain. Churchill said of his people: "This was their finest hour."

Room 10: Germany Invades the Soviet Union—June 1941 *(L'Allemagne Envahit l'Union Soviétique):* Perhaps hoping to one-up Napoleon, Hitler sent his state-of-the-art tanks speeding toward Moscow (betraying his former ally, Joseph Stalin). By winter, the advance had stalled at the gates of Moscow and was bogged down by bad weather and Soviet stubbornness. The Third Reich had reached its peak. From now on, Hitler would have to fight a two-front war. The French Renault tank (displayed) was downright puny compared to the big, fast, high-caliber German Panzers. This war was often a battle of factories, to see who could produce the latest technology fastest and in the greatest numbers. And what nation might that be...?

Room 12: The United States Enters the War *(Les Etats-Unis Entrent dans la Guerre):* "On December 7, 1941, a date which will live in infamy" (as F.D.R. put it), Japanese planes made a sneak attack on the U.S. base at Pearl Harbor, Hawaii, and destroyed the pride of the Pacific fleet in two hours.

The United States quickly declared war on Japan and her ally, Germany. In two short years, America had gone from isolationist observer to supplier of Britain's arms to full-blown war ally against fascism. The United States now faced a two-front war—in Europe against Hitler, and in Asia against Japan's imperialist conquest of China, Southeast Asia, and the South Pacific.

America's first victory came when Japan tried a sneak attack on the U.S. base at Midway Island (June 3, 1942). This time—thanks to the Allies who cracked the "Enigma" code—America had the aircraft carrier U.S.S. *Enterprise* (see model) and two of her buddies lying in wait. In five minutes, three of Japan's carriers (with valuable planes) were fatally wounded, their major attack force was sunk, and Japan and the United States were dead-even and settling in for a long war of attrition.

Though slow to start, America eventually had an army of 16 million strong, 80,000 planes, the latest technology, $250 million a day, unlimited raw materials, and a population fighting for freedom to a boogie-woogie beat.

• *Continue downstairs to the second floor.*

Second Floor: The Tide Turns

In 1942, the Continent was black with fascism and Japan was secure on a distant island. The Allies had to chip away on the fringes.

Room 13: Battle of the Atlantic *(La Bataille de l'Atlantique):* German U-boats (short for *Unterseeboot*, see model) and battleships such as the *Bismarck* patrolled Europe's perimeter, where they laid mines and kept America from aiding Britain. (Until long-range transport planes were invented near war's end, virtually all military transport was by ship.) The Allies traveled in convoys with air cover, used sonar and radar, and dropped depth charges, but for years they endured the loss of up to 60 ships per month.

Room 14: El-Alamein, Stalingrad, and Guadalcanal—The War Turns: Three crucial battles in autumn of 1942 put the first chink in the fascist armor. Off the east coast of Australia, 10,000 marines took an airstrip on Guadalcanal, while 30,000 Japanese held the rest of the tiny, isolated island. For the next six months, the two armies were marooned together, duking it out in thick jungles and malaria-infested swamps while their countries struggled to reinforce or rescue them. By February 1943, America had won and gained a crucial launch pad for bombing raids.

A world away, German tanks under General Erwin Rommel rolled across the vast deserts of North Africa. In October 1942, a well-equipped, well-planned offensive by British General Bernard Montgomery attacked at El-Alamein, Egypt. "Monty" drove "the Desert Fox" east into Tunisia for the first real Allied victory against the Nazi *Wehrmacht* war machine.

Then came Stalingrad. In August 1942, Germany attacked the Soviet city, an industrial center and gateway to the Caucasus oil fields. By October, the Germans had battled their way into the city center and were fighting house-to-house, but their supplies were running low, the Soviets wouldn't give up, and winter was coming. The snow fell, their tanks had no fuel, and relief efforts failed. Hitler ordered them to fight on through the bitter cold. On the worst days, 50,000 men died. (America lost a total of 58,000 in Vietnam.) Finally, on January 31, 1943, the Germans surrendered, against Hitler's orders. The six-month totals? Eight hundred thousand German and other Axis soldiers dead, 1.1 million Soviets dead. The Russian campaign put hard miles on the German war machine.

Also in 1942, the Allies began long-range bombing of German-held territory, including saturation bombing of civilians. It was global war and total war.

Room 15: The Allies Land in North Africa *(Le Débarquement en Afrique du Nord, La Campagne de Tunisie):* Winston Churchill and U.S. President Franklin D. Roosevelt (see photo with de Gaulle), two of the century's most dynamic and strong-willed statesmen,

decided to attack Hitler indirectly by invading Vichy-controlled Morocco and Algeria. On November 8, 1942, 100,000 Americans and British—under the joint command of an unknown, low-key problem-solver named General Dwight ("Ike") Eisenhower—landed on three separate beaches (including Casablanca). More than 120,000 Vichy French soldiers, ordered by their superiors to defend the fascist cause, confronted the Allies and...gave up.

The Allies moved east, but bad weather, their own inexperience, and the powerful Afrika Korps under Rommel stopped them in Tunisia. But with flamboyant General George S. ("Old Blood-and-Guts") Patton punching from the west and Monty pushing from the south, they captured the port town of Tunis on May 7, 1943. The Allies now had a base from which to retake Europe.

Room 17: The French Resistance *(L'Unification de la Résistance, La Lutte Clandestine)*: Inside occupied France, other ordinary heroes fought the Nazis—the "underground," or Resistance. Within loaves of bread, bakers hid radios to secretly contact London. Barmaids passed along tips from tipsy Nazis. Communists in black berets cut telephone lines. Farmers hid downed airmen in haystacks. Housewives spread news from the front with their gossip. Printers countered Nazi propaganda with pamphlets.

Jean Moulin (see photo in museum), de Gaulle's assistant, secretly parachuted into France and organized these scattered heroes into a unified effort. In May 1943, Moulin was elected chairman of the National Council of the Resistance. A month later, he was arrested by the Gestapo (Nazi secret police), imprisoned, tortured, and sent to Germany, where he died in transit. Still, Free France now had a (secret) government again, rallied around de Gaulle, and was ready to take over when liberation came.

Room 18: The Red Army *(L'Armée Rouge Reprend l'Initiative)*: Monty, Patton, and Ike were certainly heroes, but the war was won on the Eastern Front by Soviet grunts, who slowly bled Germany dry.

Room 21: The Allies Land in Italy *(Premiers Débarquements Alliés en Europe)*: On July 10, 1943, the assault on Hitler's European fortress began. More than 150,000 Americans and British sailed from Tunis and landed on the south shore of Sicily. (See maps showing the campaigns.) Speedy Patton and methodical Monty began a "horse race" to take the city of Messina (the United States won the friendly competition by a few hours). They met little resistance from 300,000 Italian soldiers and were actually cheered as liberators by the Sicilian people. Their real enemies were the 50,000 German troops sent by Hitler to bolster his ally, Benito Mussolini. By September, the island was captured. On the mainland, Mussolini was arrested by his own people, and Italy surrendered to the Allies. Hitler quickly poured troops into Italy (and reinstalled Mussolini) to hold off the Allied onslaught.

In early September, the Allies launched a two-pronged landing onto the beaches of southern Italy. Finally, after four long years of war, free men set foot on the European continent.

Room 22: The Italian Campaign *(La Campagne d'Italie)*: Lieutenant General Mark Clark, leading the slow, bloody push north to liberate Rome, must have been reminded of the French trenches he'd fought in during World War I. As in that bloody war, the fighting in Italy was a war of attrition, fought on the ground by foot soldiers and costing many lives for just a few miles.

In January 1944, the Germans dug in between Rome and Naples at Monte Cassino, a rocky hill topped by the monastery of St. Benedict. Thousands died as the Allies tried inching up the hillside. In frustration, the Allies air-bombed the historic monastery, killing hundreds of monks...but no Germans, who dug in deeper. Finally, after four months of vicious, sometimes hand-to-hand combat, the Allies (Americans, Brits, Free French, Poles, Italian partisans, Indians, etc.) stormed the monastery, and the German back was broken.

Meanwhile, 50,000 Allies had landed on Anzio (a beach near Rome) and held the narrow beachhead for months against massive German attacks. When reinforcements arrived, they broke out and joined the two-pronged assault on the capital. Without a single bomb threatening its historic treasures, Rome fell on June 4, 1944.

Room 23: D-Day—June 6, 1944, "Operation Overlord": Three million Allies and six million tons of materiel were massed in England in preparation for the biggest fleet-led invasion in history—across the Channel to France, then eastward to Berlin. The Germans, hunkered down in northern France, knew an invasion was imminent, but the Allies kept it top secret. On the night of June 5, 150,000 soldiers boarded ships and planes without knowing where they were headed until they were underway. Each one carried a note from General Eisenhower: "The tide has turned. The free men of the world are marching together to victory."

At 6:30 in the morning on June 6, 1944, Americans spilled out of troop transports into the cold waters off a beach in Normandy, code-named Omaha. The weather was bad, seas were rough, and the prep bombing had failed. The soldiers, many seeing their first action, were dazed and confused. Nazi machine guns pinned them against the sea. Slowly, they crawled up the beach on their stomachs. A thousand died. They held on until the next wave of transports arrived.

All day long, Allied confusion did battle with German indecision; the Nazis never really counterattacked, thinking D-Day was just a ruse instead of the main invasion. By day's end, the Allies had taken several beaches along the Normandy coast and began building artificial harbors, providing a tiny port-of-entry for the reconquest of Europe. The stage was set for a quick and easy end to the war. Right.

- *Go downstairs to the...*

First Floor: The War Ends... Very Slowly (June 1944–August 1945)

Room 24: Battle of Normandy *(La Bataille de Normandie)*: For a month, the Allies (mostly Americans) secured Normandy, by taking bigger ports (Cherbourg and Caen) and amassing troops and supplies for the assault on Germany. In July, they broke out and sped eastward across France, with Patton's tanks covering up to 40 miles a day. They had "Jerry" on the run.

Room 25: Landing in Provence, August 1944 *(Le Débarquement de Provence)*: On France's Mediterranean coast, American troops under General Alexander Patch landed near Cannes, took Marseilles, and headed north to meet up with Patton.

Room 26: "Les Maquis": French Resistance guerrilla fighters helped reconquer France from behind the lines. (Don't miss the folding motorcycle in its parachute case.) The liberation of Paris was started by a Resistance attack on a German garrison.

Room 27: Liberation of Paris: As the Allies marched on Paris, Hitler ordered his officers to torch the city—but they sanely disobeyed and prepared to surrender. On August 26, 1944, General Charles de Gaulle walked ramrod-straight down the Champs-Elysées, followed by Free French troops and U.S. GIs passing out chocolate and Camels. Two million Parisians went ape.

Room 28: On to Berlin—Offensive from the West *(Vers Berlin—Offensives de l'Ouest)*: The quick advance through France, Belgium, and Luxembourg bogged down at the German border in autumn of 1944. Patton outstripped supply lines, a parachute invasion of Holland (Battle of Arnhem) was disastrous, and bad weather grounded planes and slowed tanks.

On December 16, the Allies met a deadly surprise. An enormous, well-equipped, energetic German army appeared from nowhere, punched a "bulge" deep into Allied lines, and demanded surrender. General Anthony McAuliffe sent a one-word response—"Nuts!"—and the tide turned. The Battle of the Bulge was Germany's last great offensive.

The Germans retreated across the Rhine River, blowing up bridges behind them. The last bridge, at Remagen, was captured by the Allies just long enough to cross and establish themselves on German soil. Soon U.S. tanks were speeding down the autobahns and Patton could wire the good news back to Ike: "General, I have just pissed in the Rhine."

Soviet soldiers did the dirty work of taking fortified Berlin, by launching a final offensive in January 1945 and surrounding the city in April. German citizens fled west to surrender to the more-benevolent Americans and Brits. Hitler, defiant to the end, hunkered in his underground bunker.

On April 28, 1945, Mussolini and his girlfriend were killed and hung by their heels in Milan. Two days later, Adolf Hitler and his new bride, Eva Braun, avoided similar humiliation by committing suicide (pistol in mouth) and having their bodies burned beyond recognition. Germany formally surrendered on May 8, 1945.

In Corridor to the left of Room 28: Concentration Camps: Lest anyone mourn Hitler or doubt this war's purpose, gaze on photos from Germany's concentration camps. Some camps held political enemies and prisoners of war, including two million French. Others were expressly built to exterminate peoples considered "genetically inferior" to the "Aryan master race"—particularly Jews, Gypsies, homosexuals, and the mentally ill.

Room 29: War of the Pacific *(Pacifique—Les Grandes Offensives Americaines)*: Often treated as an afterthought, the final campaign against Japan was a massive American effort, costing many lives but saving millions from Japanese domination.

Japan was an island bunker surrounded by a vast ring of fortified Pacific islands. America's strategy was to take one island at a time, "island hopping" until close enough for B-29 Superfortress bombers to attack Japan itself. The war spread across thousands of miles. In a new form of warfare, ships carrying planes led the attack and prepared tiny islands for troops to land and build an airbase. While General Douglas MacArthur island-hopped south to retake the Philippines ("I have returned!"), others pushed north toward Japan.

In February 1945, marines landed on Iwo Jima, a city-size island-volcano close enough to Japan (800 miles) to launch air raids. Twenty thousand Japanese had dug in on the volcano's top and were picking off the advancing Americans. On February 23, several U.S. soldiers raised the Stars and Stripes on the mountain (that famous photo), which inspired their mates to victory at a cost of nearly 7,000 men.

Japan Surrenders *(Capitulation du Japon)*: On March 9, Tokyo was firebombed and 90,000 were killed. Japan was losing, but a land invasion would cost hundreds of thousands of lives. The Japanese had a reputation for choosing death over the shame of surrender—they even sent bomb-laden "kamikaze" planes on suicide missions.

America unleashed its secret weapon, an atomic bomb (originally suggested by German-turned-American Albert Einstein). On August 6, a B-29 dropped one (named "Little Boy") on the city of Hiroshima and instantly vaporized 100,000 people and four square miles. Three days later, a second bomb fell on Nagasaki. The next day Emperor Hirohito unofficially surrendered. The long war was over, and U.S. sailors returned home to kiss their girlfriends in public places.

War Totals *(Le Bilan de la Guerre)*: The death toll for World War II (Sept 1939–Aug 1945) totaled 80 million soldiers and civilians. The Soviet Union lost 26 million, China 13 million, France 580,000, and the United States 340,000.

World War II changed the world, with America emerging as the dominant political, military, and economic superpower. Europe was split in two. The western half recovered, with American aid. The eastern half remained under Soviet occupation. For 45 years, the United States and the Soviet Union would compete—without ever actually doing battle—in a "Cold War" of espionage, propaganda, and weapons production that stretched from Korea to Cuba, from Vietnam to the moon.

- *Before you leave Les Invalides, go down a long hall between the ticket office and bookshop, near the exit of the World War II wing, to find the...*

LIBERATION MUSEUM (MUSEE DE L'ORDRE DE LA LIBERATION)

This museum tells the story of the Resistance in World War II (free, no English descriptions). The French refer to World War II as "The War of '39–40," but this proud collection makes it clear that the French were busy during the Nazi occupation.

CLUNY MUSEUM **TOUR**

Musée National du Moyen Age

The "National Museum of the Middle Ages" doesn't sound quite so boring as I approach middle age myself. Aside from the solemn religious art, there is some lively stuff here.

Paris emerged on the world stage in the "Middle Ages," the time between ancient Rome and the Renaissance. Europe was awakening from a thousand-year slumber. Trade was booming, people actually owned chairs, and the Renaissance was moving in like a warm front from Italy.

ORIENTATION

Cost and Hours: €7, €5.50 on Sun, free on first Sun of the month, covered by museum pass, Wed–Mon 9:15–17:45, closed Tue.

Getting There: The entrance is a block above the intersection of boulevards St. Germain and St. Michel at 6 place Paul Painlevé (Mo: Cluny-La Sorbonne, St. Michel, or Odéon; bus #63 from rue Cler or #86 from the Marais).

Information: Pick up the free and handy museum map guide. Tel. 01 53 73 78 16, www.musee-moyenage.fr.

Length of This Tour: One hour.

Baggage Check: Required and free.

THE TOUR BEGINS

- *The museum hosts frequent special exhibits slightly affecting the permanent collection described below.*

Room 2 (first room after the bookshop): The first art you see is not some grim, gray crucifixion but six colorful wool-and-silk tapestries that celebrate the secular pleasures of life on a country estate. The humans

Cluny Ground Floo

Cluny-La Sorbonne

M - Subway Stop

BLVD. SAINT GERMAIN

BLVD. SAINT MICHEL

RUE DE CLUNY

RUE DU SOMMERARD

MUSEUM GARDENS

COURTYARD

STAIRS UP TO LADY & UNICORN TAPESTRIES

PLACE PAUL-PAINLEVÉ

DCH

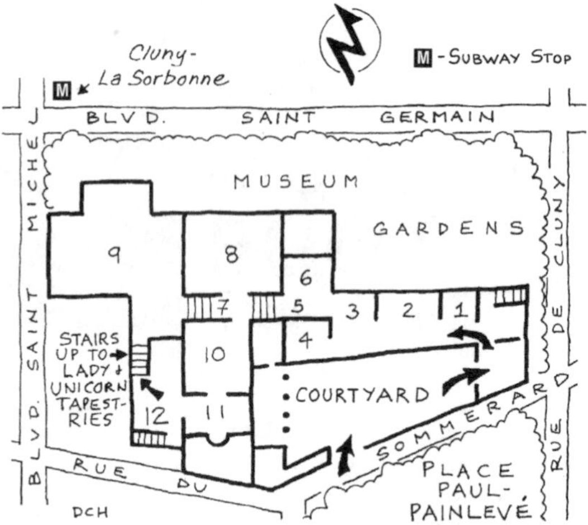

Room 2: Six tapestries

Room 3: Fabrics brought back by crusaders

Room 6: Stained glass

Room 8: Stone heads from Notre-Dame

Room 9: Roman bath (A.D. 200)

Room 10: Byzantine ivories and altarpieces

Room 12: *Vendange* harvest tapestry

Upstairs: *Lady and the Unicorn* tapestries

mingle harmoniously with the trees, flowers, and animals of the glorious physical world.

Reading clockwise: 1) A lady with a puppy spins wool while her husband relaxes with the morning paper. 2) A naked woman takes a chilly bath and enjoys fruits, jewels, and music—the good things of a material world becoming increasingly less sinful. 3) The family picks fruit from their plentiful orchards. 4) A lady embroiders a pillow. 5) Out in the garden, the sexes mingle unchaperoned by the Church. A lady takes a breath mint while a troubadour puts the moves on her servant. 6) A lord goes hunting with his falcon, dog, and servant.

Having survived their Y1K crisis, these people realize the world won't end, and they turn their attention to the beauty of their surroundings.

Room 3: Colorful woven fabrics were brought back to France by crusaders, who went off to conquer barbarian infidels but returned with tales of enlightened peoples on the fringes of Europe.

Room 6: Enter the Dark Ages, when life was harsh and violent, angels and demons made regular appearances, and the Church was your only refuge. This room offers a rare close-up look at stained glass, which gave the poor a glimpse of the glories of heaven. These panels (many from the cathedral of light, Sainte-Chapelle) give us a window into the magical, supernatural, miraculous—and often violent—medieval mind.

Read clockwise around the room at eye level (the bottom): 1) The angel Gabriel blasts his horn on Resurrection morning, which rousts the grateful dead from their coffins. Notice that Gabriel's royal purple robe is made up of several different pieces of glass—purples, whites, blues—held together with lead. 2) Naked Christ is baptized in the squiggly River Jordan. 3) A red-faced, horned, horny demon, accompanied by an equally lascivious wolf and henchman, carries off a frightened girl in red to do unspeakable acts. 4) Blond, pious Joseph is sold into slavery to camel merchants by his plotting brothers.

Next wall: 5) Samson is about to pull down the temple… 6) Then he has his eyes gouged out by Philistines. 7) Slaughter on the battlefield. Men with bloodstained hands and faces hack at each other with golden swords. 8) Aaron, disobeying God and Moses, worships a golden calf. 9) A king on a throne closes his eyes to all this wickedness.

Next wall (with some panels from the first Gothic church, St. Denis): 10) Two monks with prayer books gaze up, as one of their brothers disappears into heaven. The Latin inscription, *"hec est via,"* means "This is the way." 11) Seated Jesus, in a royal purple robe, is consoled by two angels. 12) Theophilus ("Lover of God") has struck a Faustian deal with the devil and is now feeling buyer's remorse. 13) Sleeping St. Martin is visited by a heavenly vision. 14) Angels in Rock-and-Roll Heaven.

Last wall: Four apostles—John (*Ioannes*), James, Peter (*Petrus*, with key), and Paul.

Room 8: These 21 stone heads (sculpted 1220–1230) of the Biblical kings of Judah once decorated the front of Notre-Dame. In 1793, an angry mob of Revolutionaries mistook the kings of Judah for the kings of France and abused and decapitated the statues. (Today's heads on the Notre-Dame statues are reconstructions.) Someone gathered up the heads and buried them in his backyard near the present-day Opéra

Garnier. There they slept for two centuries, unknown and noseless, until 1977, when some diggers accidentally unearthed them and brought them to an astounded world. Their stoic expressions accept what fate, time, and liberals have done to them.

The statue of Adam (nearby) is also from Notre-Dame. He's scrawny and flaccid by Renaissance standards. And it will be another 200 years before naked Adam can step out from behind that bush.

Room 9: This echoing cavern was a Roman frigidarium. Pretty cool. The museum is located on the site of a Roman bathhouse, which was in the center of town during the Roman years. After hot baths and exercise in adjoining rooms, ordinary Romans would take a cold dip in the sunken pool (in the alcove), then relax cheek to cheek with notables such as Emperor Julian the Apostate (see his statue), who lived right next door. As the empire decayed in the fourth century, Julian avoided the corrupt city of Rome and made Paris a northern power base.

The 40-foot-high ceiling is the largest Roman vault in France, and it took the French another 1,000 years to improve on that crisscross-arch technology. The sheer size of this room—constructed in A.D. 200 when Rome was at its peak—gives an idea of the epic scale in which the Romans built, and it inspired Europeans to greatness during the less civilized Middle Ages.

The four square column fragments (*Pilier des Nautes*) are the oldest man-made objects you'll see from Paris. These pillars once supported a 20-foot-high altar to the king of the gods in the Temple of Jupiter, where Notre-Dame now stands. The carving on one ("TIB. CAESARE") says it was built in the time of the Emperor Tiberius, A.D. 14–37, and was paid for by the Parisian boatmen's union (see them holding their shields). On another column find the horned Celtic god Cernunnos, The Stag Lord and god of the hunt. The eclectic Romans allowed this local "druid" god to support the shrine of Jupiter, in league with their own Vulcan, who hammers, and Castor and Pollux, who pet their horses.

Room 10: Rome lived on after the fall of the empire. The finely carved Byzantine ivories (first glass case) show how pagan gods, emperors, and griffins became Christian saints, gargoyles, and icons. Constantinople—the eastern half of the empire that survived the fall—preserved Roman tastes and imagery. In painting, Byzantine gold-background icons inspired medieval altarpieces, like some in this room.

Rome also lived on in the Roman-esque grandeur of Christian churches like St.

Germain-des-Prés (see the 12 column capitals). In the central capital, Christ sits in robes on a throne, ruling the world like a Roman emperor. These capitals were originally painted, much like the painted wooden statues across the room.

Don't leave this room before eyeing the tusk of a narwhal (on the wall), which must have convinced superstitious folk to believe in unicorns.

Room 12: The large tapestry shows grape-stomping peasants during the *vendange,* the annual autumn harvest and wine celebration. A peasant man treads grapes in a vat, while his wife collects the juice. A wealthy man gives orders. Above that, a peasant with a pimple turns a newfangled mechanical press. On the right, you'll see the joy of picking—pawns, knights, and queens all working side by side.

- *Go upstairs to...*

Room 13—"The Lady and the Unicorn" Tapestries: As Europeans emerged from the Dark Ages, they rediscovered the beauty of the world around them.

These six mysterious tapestries were designed by an unknown (but probably French) artist before 1500 and were woven in Belgium out of wool and silk. Loaded with symbols—some serious, some playful—they have been interpreted many ways, but, in short, the series deals with each of the five senses (handheld English explanations that you can pick up from slots hanging on the wall add more detail).

- *Moving clockwise around the room...*

Taste: A blond lady takes candy from a servant's dish to feed it to her parakeet. A unicorn and a lion look on. At the lady's feet, a monkey also tastes something, while the little white dog behind her wishes he had some. This was the Age of Discovery, when Columbus and Vasco da Gama spiced up Europe's bland gruel with new fruits, herbs, and spices.

The lion (symbol of knighthood?) and unicorn (symbol of "bourgeois nobility," purity, or fertility?) wave flags with the coat of arms of the family that bought the tapestries—three silver crescents in a band of blue.

Hearing: Wearing a stunning dress, the lady plays sweet music on an organ, which soothes the savage beasts around her. The pattern and folds of the tablecloth are lovely. Humans and their fellow creatures live in harmony in an enchanted blue garden filled with flowers, all set in a red background.

Sight: The unicorn cuddles up and looks at himself in the lady's mirror, pleased with what he sees. The lion turns away and snickers. As the Renaissance dawns, vanity is a less-than-deadly sin.

Admire the great artistic skill in some of the detail work, the necklace and the patterns in her dress. This tapestry had qual trol in all its stages: the drawing of the scene, its enlargement an fer to a cartoon, and the weaving. Still, the design itself is c Renaissance 3-D standards. The fox and rabbits, supposedly in tance, simply float overhead, as big as the animals at the lady's f

Smell: The lady picks flowers and weaves them into a smelling wreath. On a bench behind, the monkey apes her. The trees, and animals are exotic and varied. Each detail is exquisit but step back, and they blend together into pleasing patterns.

Touch: This is the most basic and dangerous of the senses. The lady "strokes the unicorn's horn," if you know what I mean, and the lion gets the double entendre. Unicorns, a species extinct since the Age of Reason, were so wild that only the purest virgins could entice and tame them. Medieval Europeans were exploring the wonders of love and the pleasures of sex. The Renaissance is coming.

Tapestry #6: The most talked-about tapestry gets its name from the words on our lady's tent: *À Mon Seul Désir* ("To My Sole Desire"). What *is* her only desire?

Is it jewelry, as she grabs a necklace from the jewel box? C putting the necklace away and renouncing material things, in follow her only desire?

Our lady has tried all things sensual and is now prepared t the one true impulse. Is it God? Or love? Her friends the unic lion open the tent doors. Flickering flames cover the tent. Perha stepping out from the tent. Or is she going in to meet the objec desire? Human sensuality is awakening, an old dark age is endi the Renaissance is emerging.

THE REST OF THE MUSEUM

While the Unicorn tapestry is the Cluny's prize, there's much mc enth-century Visigoth crowns (Room 16), the chapel (Room 20 medieval garden (outside and explained in the museum map gui

BUS #69 SIGHTSEEING **TOUR**

Why pay €25 for a tour company to give you an overview of Paris when there are city bus routes like #69 that cost €1.40? Hop on the bus and settle in for a ride through some of the city's most interesting neighborhoods. On this ride from the Eiffel Tower to Pére Lachaise Cemetery, you'll learn how great Paris' bus system is, and wonder why you've been tunneling by Métro under this gorgeous city. And if you're staying in the Marais or rue Cler neighborhoods, line #69 is a useful route for just getting around town.

ORIENTATION

Cost: €1.40

Getting There: Eastbound line #69 leaves from the Eiffel Tower on avenue Joseph Bouvard (the street that becomes rue St. Dominique as it crosses the Champs de Mars). The stop is at the eastern end of the avenue (just before the avenue de la Bourdonnais) across from the Eiffel Tower.

Bus Tips: This tour is best done in the direction it's written (east from the Eiffel Tower to Père Lachaise cemetery) since one-way streets change the route in the other direction. Métro tickets work on buses, but you can't use the same ticket to transfer between the systems or use them for more than one bus ride. You can also buy a ticket from the bus driver. Board through the front door and exit through the rear door. All tickets must be validated in the machine behind the driver. Grab a window seat—right side is best. Get on at one of the first stops to secure a good seat. Buses run every 10 to 20 minutes (6:30–21:30).

When to Go: Avoid rush hours (8:00-9:30 & 17:00-19:00).

Length of This Tour: One hour.

OVERVIEW

Handy line #69 crosses the city east-west, running between the Eiffel Tower and Père Lachaise, and passing these great monuments and neighborhoods: Eiffel Tower, Ecole Militaire, rue Cler, Les Invalides, Louvre Museum, Ile de la Cité, Ile St. Louis, Hôtel de Ville, Pompidou Center, Marais, Bastille, and Père Lachaise. You don't to have to do the whole enchilada; get on and off wherever you like. Many find the Bastille a good ending point (where you can hop out and begin our walking tour of the Marais, page 79). This ride also ties in well after a visit to the Eiffel Tower. Think of this as an overview. The sights you'll survey are written up in more depth elsewhere in the book. OK—let's roll.

Champs de Mars and Eiffel Tower

Your tour begins below this 1,000-foot, reddish-brown hood ornament. While you're waiting for the bus, you could read up on the Eiffel Tower (page 33). The park surrounding you is called the Champs de Mars park (for the god of war, Mars) and served as a parade ground for the military school (Ecole Militaire) that seals the park at the right end. Napoléon Bonaparte is the school's most famous graduate. In 1889 the Champs de Mars was covered with a massive temporary structure that housed exhibitions of all sorts to celebrate the same event for which the Eiffel Tower was built, the Centennial World's Fair. The apartments surrounding the park are among the most exclusive in Paris, and the grass that runs down the center of the park is off-limits—at least until the *gendarmes* are off-duty (about 20:30), when soccer balls, Frisbees, pets, and (it seems) the whole neighborhood descend on the grass.

- *Leaving the Champs de Mars, the bus slices through the 7th arrondissement along its primary shopping street.*

Rue St. Dominique

Clothing boutiques, food shops, and cafés line this well-coiffed street. One of your authors lived on this street for three years and learned that you can get anything you need on rue St. Dominique (but not at any hour), and that many locals never leave the area to shop elsewhere. Paris functions as a city of a thousand small neighborhoods. If you forget your money when it's time to pick up your clothes, your local dry cleaner knows you and trusts you'll pay him another time. If the plumber can only come by when you're at work, you can leave your keys with the nearest shop owner, who will make sure he gets them. Notice how well your driver navigates past delivery trucks and illegally parked cars.

This area has long been popular with Americans—the American Church (two blocks to the left), American Library, American University, and lots of my readers call this area home.

- *After crossing boulevard de la Tour Maubourg, you'll enter the open world of Esplanade des Invalides.*

Esplanade des Invalides

This sprawling esplanade links the river and Europe's first veteran's hospital, Les Invalides, built under Louis XIV (see Tour, page 216). Napoleon lies powerfully dead under the brilliant golden dome.

Afternoon *boules* (lawn bowling), near the Invalides building on the far right, is a thrilling spectator sport. I spend more time watching the player's expressions and mannerisms that the game itself (see Boules sidebar, page 67). In summer, American football games are played on the grassy esplanade with teams composed of Franco-American friends. They even have a league and drink beer after the games. The Rodin museum lies just beyond the upper lefthand side of the esplanade.

Now, look the other way, and see the pont d'Alexandre III (Alexander III Bridge) crossing the Seine. Spiked with golden statues and ironwork lamps, the bridge was built to celebrate a turn-of-the-20th-century treaty between France and Russia. Just across the bridge are the glass-and steel-domed Grand and Petit Palais exhibition halls, built for the 1900 World's Fair. Like the bridge, they are fine examples of belle époque architecture. Impressive temporary exhibits fill the huge Grand Palais, while the smaller Petit Palais (closed through 2004) houses a permanent collection of 19th-century paintings by Eugène Delacroix, Paul Cézanne, Claude Monet, Pablo Picasso, and other masters.

- *Leaving Les Invalides, you'll re-enter narrow streets lined with government buildings. Many of France's most important ministries occupy this staid side of Les Invalides (look for police guarding doorways and for people in suits speaking in hushed tones).*

Boulevard St. Germain and Rue du Bac

You'll emerge from the street flanked by government buildings onto the stylish and leafy boulevard St. Germain, where colorful furniture stores tempt this neighborhood's upper-crust residents. Several blocks farther down lies the boulevard St. Germain with the cafés frequented by existentialists Albert Camus and Jean-Paul Sartre. But we turn left onto rue du Bac and cross streets (to the right) filled with antiques and smart hotels. The Orsay museum is a few blocks to the left (if you need an art break, the best stop for this museum is just before the river—see tour on page 138).

- *Next, you'll cross the river and enter the Right Bank.*

Jardin des Tuileries and Louvre Museum

The Tuileries Garden lies straight ahead as you cross the Seine. This was the royal garden of the Louvre palace—come here after touring the

Louvre to clear your mind (see Louvre Tour, page 114). There are several cafés scattered among these pretty gardens and ponds with toy boats for rent. After turning right along the river, you'll see the immense Grand Gallery of the Louvre dominating the left side of the street, and café-boats on the right (there are about 2,000 barges docked on the Seine in Paris). At the end of the Grand Gallery on the right is the view-perfect pedestrian bridge, pont des Arts (the beginning of the Left Bank Walk, see page 105). That curved building with a dome on the other side is where the Académie Française has met since the 1600s to defend the French language from corrupting influences (like English) and to compose the official French dictionary.

- *Next on the right is the island where Paris was founded. Be ready for quick right-left-right head movements.*

Ile de la Cité

The river splits around this island where Paris began over 2,000 years ago. The medieval towers of the Conciergerie (named for the concierge who ran these offices when the king moved to the Louvre) guard the Ile de la Cité's law courts (Palais de Justice). Next to the courthouse was the prison famous as the last stop for those about to be guillotined. That needle that emerges from the center is Sainte-Chapelle's spire. Quickly back to the left is Paris' primary department-store shopping district, with standards such as Samaritaine. Now look back to your right for peek-a-boo views of the dome of the Panthéon in the distance, and closer, Notre-Dame soon after the Conciergerie. Back to the left, the grand Hôtel de Ville (Paris' city hall) stands proudly behind playful fountains. Each of the 20 *arrondissements* (governmental areas) in Paris has its own city hall and this one is the big daddy of them all. Look beyond city hall to see the clashing colors of the Pompidou Center. A quick look back right finds the bridge that connects Paris' two islands.

- *Our bus leaves the river after city hall, and angles left around a church and into the Marais, turning right on rue St. Antoine.*

Le Marais

This is jumbled, medieval Paris at its finest. It's been a swamp, aristocratic district, and bohemian hangout. Today classy stone mansions sit alongside trendy bars, antique shops, and fashion-conscious boutiques. The Picasso Museum, Carnavalet Museum, Victor Hugo's House, Jewish Art and History Museum, and the Pompidou Center all have Marais addresses. You'll get a snapshot look at the Marais' red-brick centerpiece square, place des Vosges, on your left a few blocks after turning on to rue St. Antoine.

- *The green pillar in the center of the huge place de la Bastille draws you toward it. If your trip ends here, get off before entering place de la Bastille. Options if you get off: Marais Walk (page 79), canal boat tour (page 25), Promenade Plantée Park (page 44), Opera House (page 39), and Marais eateries (page 325).*

Place de la Bastille

The namesake of this square, a fortress-turned-prison that symbolized royal tyranny, is long gone. But for centuries, the fortress that stood here was used to defend the city, mostly from its own people. On July 14, 1789, angry Parisians swarmed the Bastille, released its prisoners, and kicked off the French Revolution. Since then, the French celebrate their Independence Day on July 14 (a.k.a. Bastille Day) as enthusiastically as we commemorate July 4.

- *You'll cross over the canal St. Martin in the middle of place de la Bastille (look to the right). The canal runs from the Seine under the tree-lined boulevard Richard Lenoir (on the left) to northern Paris. You'll curve in front of the new Opéra Bastille. Leaving place de la Bastille, you'll angle left up rue de la Roquette all the way to Père Lachaise.*

Rue de la Roquette

This street begins at the Bastille in a young and hip, less-touristed neighborhood of galleries, seedy bars, and cheap eateries. The first street to the right is rue de Lappe (described on page 354). One of the wildest nightspots in Paris, rue de Lappe is filled with a dizzying array of wacky bistros, bars, and dance halls.

Continuing farther east, you can't help but notice the change in the diversity of the riders—apartments become cheaper the farther from the center you go in this direction.

- *The bus eventually turns left onto boulevard de Ménilmontant at Père Lachaise. Get off here and take a short stroll into the cemetery—see page 44 (Mo: Père Lachaise, one block up boulevard de Ménilmontant).*

Père Lachaise Cemetery

Navigating the labyrinthian rows is a challenge, but maps will help you find the graves of greats such as Frédéric Chopin, Oscar Wilde, Gertrude Stein, and Jim Morrison. The tour is over. What better place for your final stop?

VERSAILLES **TOUR**

If you've ever wondered why your American passport has French writin in it, you'll find the answer at Versailles (vehr-sigh). The powerful cour of Louis XIV at Versailles set the standard of culture for all of Europe right up to modern times. Versailles was every king's dream palace Today, if you're planning to visit just one palace in all of Europe, mak it Versailles. And if you have a car, or simply prefer a smaller town bas for Paris, see my hotel recommendations on page 311.

ORIENTATION

Cost: There are several different parts of the palace, each with a separat admission. The **State's Apartments** (our self-guided tour) is €7.50, cov ered by the museum pass; €5.50 after 15:30, under 18 free. The palace i also theoretically free for all teachers, professors, and architecture students Guided tours cost extra (see "Touring Versailles from A to D" sidebar).

The **gardens** cost €3 (not covered by museum pass) except o summer weekends, when the fountains blast and the price shoots up t €5.50 (see "Fountain Spectacles," below).

Entering the **Grand and Petit Trianon Palaces** costs €5 togethe €3 after 15:30 (both covered by museum pass).

If you don't have a Paris museum pass, consider getting the Versaille Pass, which covers your entrance, gives you priority access to everythin (no lines), and includes an audioguide (€21, sold at Versailles train sta tion, RER stations that serve Versailles, and at FNAC department stores)

Hours: The **palace** is open May–Sept Tue–Sun 9:00–18:30, Oct–Apri Tue–Sun 9:00–17:30, closed Mon (last entry 30 min before closing) The **Grand and Petit Trianon Palaces** are open daily April–Oc 12:00–18:00, Nov–March 12:00–17:00, closed Mon. The **garden** i open daily from 7:00 (8:00 in winter) to sunset (as late as 21:30 or a early as 17:30).

Versailles

WALKING TIMES

Train Station to Chateau = 10 min.

Chateau to Grand Trianon = 30 min.

Grand Trianon to Le Hameau = 20 min.

Le Hameau to Chateau = 30 min.

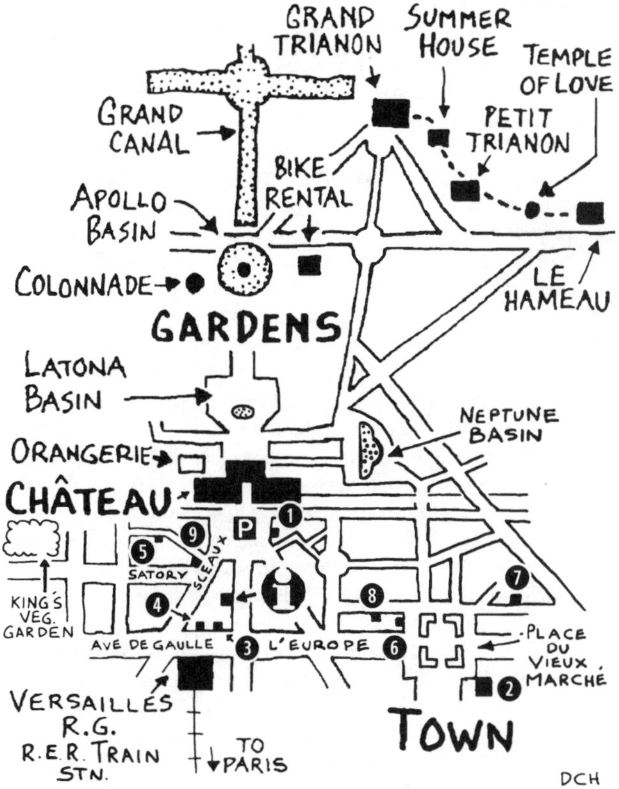

GRAND TRIANON
SUMMER HOUSE
TEMPLE OF LOVE
GRAND CANAL
PETIT TRIANON
BIKE RENTAL
APOLLO BASIN
COLONNADE
LE HAMEAU
GARDENS
LATONA BASIN
NEPTUNE BASIN
ORANGERIE
CHÂTEAU
KING'S VEG. GARDEN
SATORY
SCEAUX
AVE DE GAULLE
L'EUROPE
PLACE DU VIEUX MARCHÉ
VERSAILLES R.G. R.E.R. TRAIN STN.
TO PARIS
TOWN
DCH

1. Hôtel de France
2. Hôtel le Cheval Rouge
3. Hôtel Ibis Versailles
4. Hôtel du Palais
5. Hôtel d'Angleterre
6. Rest. La Boeuf á la Mode
7. Rest. Fenêtres sur Cour
8. Rest. A la Côte Bretonne
9. Rest. Le Limousin

When to Go: In summer, Versailles is especially crowded around 10:00 and 13:00, and all day Tue and Sun. Remember, the crowds gave Marie-Antoinette a pain in the neck, too, so relax and let them eat cake. For fewer crowds, go early or late: Either arrive by 9:00 (when the palace opens, touring the palace first, then the gardens) or after 15:30 (you'll get a reduced entry ticket but you'll probably miss the last guided tours of the day, which generally depart at 15:00). If you arrive midday, see the gardens first and the palace later, at 15:00. The gardens and palace are great late. On my last visit, at 18:00 I was the only tourist in the Hall of Mirrors...even on a Tuesday.

Getting There: Take the **RER-C train** (€5 round-trip, 30 min one-way) from any of these RER stops: Gare d'Austerlitz, St. Michel, Musée d'Orsay, Invalides, Pont de l'Alma, and Champ de Mars. Any train whose name starts with a V (e.g., "Vick") goes to Versailles; don't board other trains. Get off at the last stop (Versailles R.G. or "Rive Gauche"—not Versailles C.H., which is farther from the palace), and exit through the turnstiles by inserting your ticket.

To reach the château, turn right out of the station, then left at the first boulevard. It's a 10-minute walk to the palace.

Your Eurailpass covers this inexpensive trip, but it uses up a valuable "flexi" day. If you really want to use your railpass, consider seeing Versailles on your way into or out of Paris. To get free passage, show your railpass at an SCNF ticket window—for example, at the Invalides or Musée d'Orsay RER stop—and get a *contremarque de passage.* Keep this ticket to exit the system.

When returning to Paris from Versailles, look through the windows past the turnstiles for the departure board. Any train leaving Versailles serves all downtown Paris RER stops on the C line (they're marked on the schedule as stopping at *"toutes les gares jusqu'à Austerlitz,"* meaning "all stations up to Austerlitz").

Taxis for the 30-minute ride between Versailles and Paris cost about €25.

To reach Versailles from Paris by **car,** get on the *périphérique* freeway that circles Paris and take the toll-free autoroute A-13 toward Rouen. Follow signs into Versailles, then look for "*château*" signs and park in the huge pay lot in front of the palace. The drive takes about 30 minutes one-way.

Information: A helpful TI is just past the Sofitel Hôtel on your walk from the RER station to the palace (May–Sept daily 9:00–19:00, Oct–April daily 9:00–18:00, tel. 01 39 24 88 88, www.chateauversailles.fr). You'll also find information booths inside the château (at entrances A, B-2, and C) and, during peak season, kiosks scattered around the courtyard. The useful brochure "Versailles Orientation Guide" explains your sightseeing options.

Length of This Tour: Allow two hours for the palace and two for the gardens. Including two hours to cover your round-trip transit time, it's a six-hour day trip from Paris.

Baggage Check: Available at door A.

Cuisine Art: The cafeteria and WCs are next to the general entrance (door A). There's a sandwich kiosk and a decent restaurant at the canal in the garden.

You'll find restaurants on the street to the right of the parking lot (as you face the château), though the best eateries line the pleasant market square, place du Marché, in the town center (turn right out of the train station, cross avenue de Paris, and continue about 5 blocks to place du Marché); see page 264 for a list of recommended restaurants. For a shortcut to Versailles' gardens from place du Marché, walk 10 minutes west down rue de la Paroisse. The château is to your left after entering, and the main gardens, Trianon Palaces, and Hameau are straight ahead. The quickest way to the château's front door is along avenue de St. Cloud and rue Colbert.

A handy McDonald's is immediately across from the train station (WC without crowds), and many restaurants line rue de Satory, midway between the station and the palace.

Fountain Spectacles: Classical music fills the king's backyard, and the garden's fountains are in full squirt, July–Sept Sat and early April–early Oct Sun (schedule for both days: 11:00–12:00 & 15:30–17:00 & 17:20–17:30). On these "spray days," the gardens cost €5.50 (not covered by museum pass, ask for a map of fountains). Louis had his engineers literally reroute a river to fuel these fountains. Even by today's standards, they are impressive. Pick up the helpful brochure of the fountain show ("Les Grandes Eaux Musicales") at any information booth for a guide to the fountains. Also ask about the impressive *Les Fêtes de Nuit* nighttime spectacle (July–mid-Sept some Sat).

Starring: Louis XIV and the *ancien régime.*

THE TOUR BEGINS

• *Start outside the palace at the equestrian statue of Louis XIV.*

The Original Château and the Courtyard

The part of the palace directly behind the horse statue (the section with the clock) is the original château, once a small hunting lodge where little Louis XIV spent his happiest boyhood years. The Sun King's private bedroom (the three arched windows beneath the clock), naturally, faced the rising sun. The palace and grounds are laid out on an east-west axis.

Once king, Louis XIV expanded the lodge, by attaching wings to create the present U-shape. Later, the long north and south wings were built. The total cost of the project has been estimated at half of France's entire GNP for one year.

TOURING VERSAILLES FROM A TO D

Versailles' highlights are the State Apartments (including the magnificent Hall of Mirrors) and the gardens, dotted with the Trianon Palaces—both covered on our self-guided tour. Versailles aficionados should spend extra time and money to see the lavish King's Private Apartments, the Opera House, and more, which can be visited only with an audioguide or live guide.

The price of any tour is added to the €7.50 entry fee to Versailles (entry covered by Paris museum pass, but tours are not). If you don't have a pass, keep your ticket as proof you've paid for admission, in case you decide to take a guided tour after you've wandered through the palace by yourself.

• *Stand in the courtyard to orient yourself to Versailles' entrances.*

Entrance A: State Apartments, Self-Guided Tour—To tour the palace on your own (by following my tour, below, or a €4 audioguide), join the line at entrance A if you need to pay admission. Those with a museum pass are allowed in through entrance B-2 without a wait. Enter the palace and take a one-way walk through the State Apartments from the King's Wing, through the Hall of Mirrors, and out via the Queen's and Nobles' Wing.

Entrance B-2—Museum passholders can avoid the line to buy tickets at Entrance A by using this entrance to get into the State Apartments.

Entrance C: King's Private Apartments—Using a dry but informative audioguide, you tour Louis XIV's private bedroom, some other rooms, and the Hall of Mirrors.

Entrance D: Various Guided Tours—You can select a one-hour guided tour from a variety of themes, such as the daily life of a king or the lives of such lesser-known nobles as the well-coiffed Madame de Pompadour (€4, join first English tour available). Or consider the 90-minute tour (€6) of the King's Private Apartments (Louis XV, Louis XVI, and Marie-Antoinette) and the chapel. This tour, which is the only way visitors can see the sumptuous Opera House, can be long depending on the quality of your guide.

For a live tour, make reservations immediately upon arrival, as tours can sell out by 13:00 (first tours generally begin at 10:00, last tours depart usually at 15:00 but as late as 16:00).

Versailles' Entrances

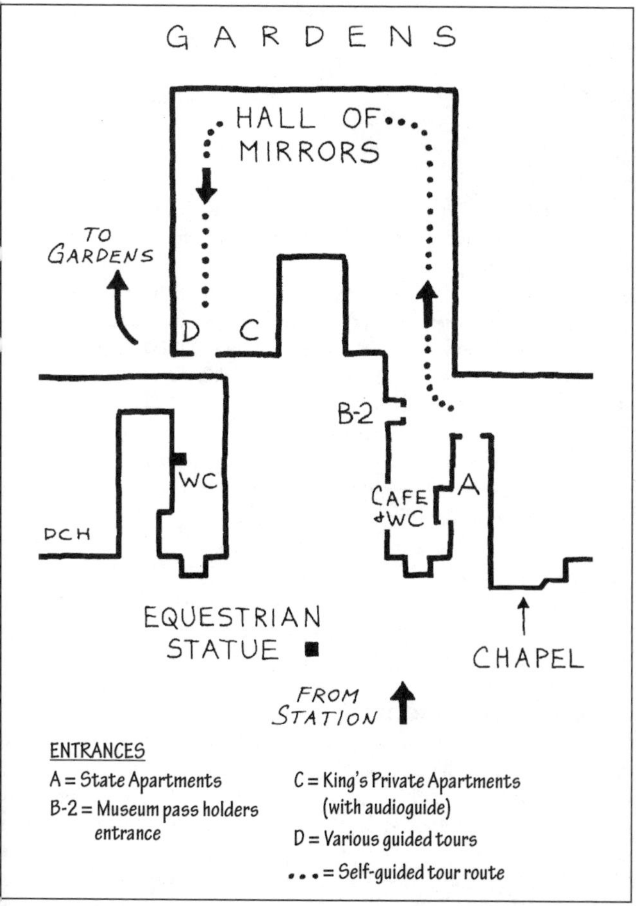

GARDENS

HALL OF MIRRORS

TO GARDENS

D C

B-2

WC

CAFE + WC

A

DCH

EQUESTRIAN STATUE

CHAPEL

FROM STATION

ENTRANCES

A = State Apartments

B-2 = Museum pass holders entrance

C = King's Private Apartments (with audioguide)

D = Various guided tours

• • • = Self-guided tour route

The Gardens—If you want to visit these first, go around the left side of the palace. The spacious gardens stretch for miles behind the palace, featuring landscaped plots, statues, bubbling fountains, a Grand Canal, and several smaller palaces, interesting both outside and in.

Think how busy this court yard must have been 300 year ago. There were as many a 5,000 nobles here at any on time, each with an entourage They'd buzz from games to par ties to amorous rendezvous i sedan-chair taxis. Servants ra about delivering secret message and roast legs of lamb. Horse drawn carriages arrived at the fancy gate with their finely dressed passen gers, having driven up the broad boulevard that ran direct from Paris (th horse stables still line the boulevard). Incredible as it seems, both th grounds and most of the palace were public territory where even the lowli est peasant could come to gawk (so long as they followed a dress code) Then as now, there were hordes of tourists, pickpockets, palace workers and men selling wind-up children's toys.

- *You'll see signs marking the various entrances (A, B, B-2, C, and D) int the U-shaped palace. For this tour of the State Apartments, which covers the ceremonial center of the palace, start at Entrance A (if you need to pa admission) or Entrance B-2 (if you have a museum pass).*

  You'll be directed, first, through the 21 rooms of the history museum, with paintings on the background of Versailles and its kings.

  Our tour starts upstairs, in the room that overlooks the lavish Royal Chapel with its pipe organ. (Note: As you jostle through the crowded corridors of the palace, pickpockets will be working the tourist crowds.)

The State Apartments

Royal Chapel: Every morning at 10:00, the organist and musician struck up the music, these big golden doors opened, and Louis XIV an his family walked through to attend Mass. While Louis XIV sat her on the upper level and looked down on the golden altar, the lowly noble below knelt with their backs to the altar and looked up—worshipin Louis worshiping God. Important religious ceremonies took place here including the marriage of young Louis XVI to Marie-Antoinette.

In the vast pagan "temple" that is Versailles, built to glorify on man, Louis XIV, this Royal Chapel is a paltry tip of the hat to tha "other" god—the Christian one. It's virtually the first, last, and onl hint of Christianity you'll see in the entire complex. Versailles cele brates Man, not God, by raising Louis XIV to almost godlike status the personification of all good human qualities. In a way, Versailles i the last great flowering of Renaissance humanism and revival of th classical world.

- *Take a map flier and enter the next room, a large room with a fireplace and a colorful painting on the ceiling.*

Hercules Drawing Room: Pleasure ruled. The main suppers, balls, and receptions were held in this room. Picture elegant partygoers in fine silks, wigs, rouge, lipstick, and fake moles (and that's just the men), as they dance to the strains of a string quartet.

On the wall opposite the fireplace is an appropriate painting showing Christ in the middle of a Venetian party. The work by Paolo Veronese, a gift from the Republic of Venice, was one of Louis XIV's favorites, so they decorated the room around it. (Stand by the fireplace for the full effect: The room's columns, arches, and frieze match the height and style of Veronese's painted architecture, which makes the painting an extension of the room.)

The ceiling painting of Hercules being crowned a god gives the room its name. Hercules (with his club) hurries up to heaven on a chariot, late for his wedding to the king of the gods' daughter. Louis XIV built the room for his own daughter's wedding reception in the style of the day—pure Baroque. As you wander, the palace feels bare, but remember that entire industries were created to furnish and decorate the place with carpets, mirrors, furniture, and tapestries.

- *From here on, it's a one-way tour—getting lost is not allowed. Follow the crowds into the small green room with a goddess in pink on the ceiling. The names of the rooms generally come from the paintings on the ceilings.*

The King's Wing

Cornucopia Room: If the party in the Hercules Room got too intense, you could always step in here for some refreshments. Silver trays were loaded up with liqueurs, exotic stimulants (coffee), juice, chocolates, and, on really special occasions, three-bean salad.

The ceiling painting shows the cornucopia of riches poured down on invited guests. Around the edges of the ceiling are painted versions of the king's actual dinnerware and treasures. The two black chests-of-drawers are from Louis' furniture collection (most of it was lost in the Revolution). They rest on heavy bases and are heavily ornamented—the so-called "Louis XIV style."

Louis himself might be here. He was a gracious host who enjoyed letting his hair down at night. If he took a liking to you, he might sneak you through those doors there (in the middle of the wall) and into his own private study, where he'd show off his collection of dishes, medals, jewels, or…the *Mona Lisa,* which hung on his wall.

The paintings on the walls are of Louis XIV's heirs. He reigned more than 70 years and outlived three of them, finally leaving the crown to his pink-cheeked, five-year-old great-grandson, Louis XV (on the right).

Venus Room: Love ruled at Versailles. In this room, couples would cavort beneath the Greek goddess of love (on the ceiling), who sends

KINGS AND QUEENS AND GUILLOTINES

- *You could read this on the train ride to Versailles. Relax, the palace is the last stop.*

Come the Revolution, when they line us up and make us stick out our hands, will you have enough calluses to keep them from shooting you? A grim thought, but Versailles raises questions like that. It's the symbol of the *ancien régime*, a time when society was divided into rulers and the ruled, when you were born to be rich or to be poor. To some it's the pinnacle of civilization, to others the sign of a civilization in decay. Either way, it remains one of Europe's most impressive sights.

Versailles was the residence of the king and seat of France's government for a hundred years. Louis XIV (reigned 1643–1715) moved out of the Louvre in Paris, the previous royal residence, and built an elaborate palace in the forests and swamps of Versailles, 10 miles west. The reasons for the move were partly personal—Louis XIV loved the outdoors and disliked the sniping environs of stuffy Paris—and partly political.

Louis XIV was creating the first modern, centralized state. At Versailles, he consolidated Paris' scattered ministries so that he could personally control policy. More important, he invited to Versailles all of France's nobles, so that he could control them. Living a life of almost enforced idleness, the "domesticated" aristocracy couldn't interfere with the way Louis ran things. With 18 million people united under one king (England had only 5.5 million), a booming economy, and a powerful military, France was Europe's number-one power.

Around 1700, Versailles was the cultural heartbeat of Europe, and French culture was at its zenith. Throughout Europe, when you said "the king," you were referring to the French king...Louis XIV. Every king wanted a palace like Versailles. Everyone learned French. French taste in clothes, hairstyles, table manners, theater, music, art, and kissing spread across the Continent. That cultural dominance has continued, to some extent, right up to this century.

down a canopy of golden garlands to ensnare mortals in delicious *amour*. Notice how a painted garland goes "out" the bottom of the central painting, becomes a golden garland held by a satyr, transforms into a gilded wood garland, and then turns back to a painting again. Baroque artists loved to mix their media to fool the eye. Another illusion is in the paintings at both ends of the room—the painted columns match the room's real ones and so extend this grand room into mythical courtyards.

Don't let the statue of a confident Louis XIV as a Roman emperor

Louis XIV

At the center of all this was Europe's greatest king. He was a true Renaissance man, a century after the Renaissance: athletic, good-looking, a musician, dancer, horseman, statesman, art-lover, lover. For all his grandeur, he was one of history's most polite and approachable kings, a good listener who could put even commoners at ease in his presence.

Louis XIV called himself the Sun King because he gave life and warmth to all that he touched. He was also thought of as Apollo, the Greek god of the sun. Versailles became the personal temple of this god on earth, decorated with statues and symbols of Apollo, the sun, and Louis XIV himself.

Louis XIV was a hands-on king who personally ran affairs of state. All decisions were made by him. Nobles, who in other countries were the center of power, became virtual slaves dependent on Louis XIV's generosity. For 70 years, he was the perfect embodiment of the absolute monarch. He summed it up best himself with his famous rhyme—"*L'état, c'est moi!*" (lay-tah say-mwah): "The state, that's me!"

Another Louis or Two to Remember

Three kings lived in Versailles during its century of glory. Louis XIV built it and established French dominance. Louis XV, his great-grandson (Louis XIV reigned for 72 years), carried on the tradition and policies, but without the Sun King's flair. During Louis XV's reign (1715-1774), France's power abroad was weakening, and there were rumblings of rebellion from within.

France's monarchy was crumbling, and the time was ripe for a strong leader to reestablish the old feudal order. They didn't get one. Instead, they got Louis XVI (reigned 1774–1792), a shy, meek bookworm, the kind of guy who lost sleep over Revolutionary graffiti…because it was misspelled. Louis XVI married a sweet girl from the Austrian royal family, Marie-Antoinette, and together they retreated into the idyllic gardens of Versailles while Revolutionary fires smoldered.

fool you. He started out as a poor little rich kid with a chip on his shoulder. His father died before Louis was old enough to rule, and, during the regency period, the French Parliament treated little Louis and his mother like trash. They were virtual prisoners, humiliated in their home (the Royal Palace of the Louvre in Paris)and getting by with bland meals, hand-me-down leotards, and pointed shoes. Once Louis XIV attained power and wealth, there was one topic you never discussed in his presence—poverty. Maybe Versailles was his way of saying, "Living well is the best revenge."

Diana Room: Here in the billiards room, Louis and his men played on a table that stood in the center of the room, while ladies sat surrounding them on Persian-carpet cushions and music wafted in from the next room. Louis was a good pool player, a sore loser, and a king—he rarely lost.

The famous bust of Louis by Giovanni Lorenzo Bernini (in the center) shows a handsome, dashing, 27-year-old playboy-king. His gaze is steady amid his windblown cloak and hair. Youn Louis loved life. He hunted animals by day (notice Diana the Huntres on the ceiling) and chased beautiful women at night.

Games were actually an important part of Louis' political strateg known as "the domestication of the nobility." By distracting the noble with the pleasures of courtly life, he was free to run the government hi way. Billiards, dancing, and concerts were popular, but the biggest dis traction was gambling, usually a card game similar to blackjack. Louis len money to the losers, making them even more indebted to him. The goo life was an addiction, and Louis kept the medicine cabinet well-stocked.

As you move into the next room, notice the fat walls that hid thi servants, who were to be at their master's constant call—but out of sigh when not needed.

Mars Room: Decorated with a military flair, this was the room fo Louis' Swiss bodyguards. On the ceiling, there's Mars, the Greek go of war, in a chariot pulled by wolves. The bronze cupids in the corne are escalating from love arrows to heavier artillery.

Out the window are sculpted gardens in the style of a tradition Italian villa—landscaped symmetrically, with trimmed hedges and cone shaped trees lining walkways that lead to fountains.

Mercury Room: Louis' life was a work of art, and Versailles was th display case. Everything he did was a public event designed to show hi subjects how it should be done. This room served as Louis' official (nc actual) bedroom, where the Sun King would ritually rise each mornin to warm his subjects.

From a canopied bed (like this 18th-century one), Louis woul get up, dress, and take a seat for morning prayer. Meanwhile, th nobles stand behind a balustrade, in awe of his piety, nobility, an clean socks. At breakfast, they murmur with delight as he deftly decap itates his boiled egg with a knife. And when Louis went to bed a night, the dukes and barons would fight over who got to hold th candle while he slipped into his royal jammies. Bedtime, wake-up, an meals were all public rituals.

The clock dates from Louis' time. When the cocks crowed at the top of the hour and the temple doors opened, guess who popped out?

Apollo Room: This was the grand throne room. Louis held court from a 10-foot-tall, silver-canopied throne on a raised platform placed in the center of the room. (Notice the metal rings in the ceiling that once supported the canopy.)

Everything in here reminds us that Louis XIV was not just any ruler, but the Sun King, who lit the whole world with his presence. On the ceiling, the sun god Apollo drives his chariot, dragging the sun across the heavens to warm the four corners of the world (counterclockwise from above the exit door): 1) Europe, with a sword; 2) Asia, with a lion; 3) Africa, with an elephant; and 4) good old America, an Indian maiden with a crocodile. Notice the ceiling's beautifully gilded frame and Goldfinger maidens.

The famous portrait by Hyacinthe Rigaud over the fireplace gives a more human look at Louis XIV. He's shown in a dancer's pose, displaying the legs that made him one of the all-time dancing fools of kingery. At night, they often held parties in this room, actually dancing around the throne.

Louis XIV (who was 63 when this was painted) had more than 300 wigs like this one, and he changed them many times a day. This fashion first started when his hairline began to recede, then sprouted all over Europe, and even to the American colonies in the time of George Washington.

Louis XIV may have been treated like a god, but he was not an overly arrogant man. His subjects adored him because he was a symbol of everything a man could be, the fullest expression of the Renaissance Man. Compare the portrait of Louis XIV with the one across the room of his last successor, Louis XVI—same arrogant pose, but without the inner confidence to keep his head on his shoulders.

The War Room: "Louis Quatorze was addicted to wars..." and France's success made other countries jealous and nervous. At the base of the ceiling, we see Germany (with the double eagle), Holland (with its ships), and Spain (with a red flag and roaring lion) ganging up on Louis XIV. But Lady France (center of ceiling), protected by the shield of Louis XIV, hurls thunderbolts down to defeat them. The stucco relief on the wall shows Louis XIV on horseback, triumphing over his fallen enemies.

Versailles was good propaganda. It showed the rest of the world how rich and powerful France was. One look at this eye-saturating view of the gardens sent visitors reeling. But Louis XIV's greatest triumph may be the next room, the one that everybody wrote home about.

The Hall of Mirrors: No one had ever seen anything like this hall when it was opened. Mirrors were still a great luxury at the time, and the number and size of these monsters were astounding. The hall is nearly 250 feet long. There are 17 arched mirrors, matched by 17 windows reflecting that breathtaking view of the gardens. Lining the hall are 24 gilded candelabras, eight busts of Roman emperors, and eight classical-style statues (7 of them ancient). The ceiling decoration chronicles Louis' military accomplishments, topped off by Louis himself in the central panel (with cupids playing cards at his divine feet), doing what he did best—triumphing. Originally, two huge carpets mirrored the action on the ceiling.

Imagine this place lit by the flames of thousands of candles, filled with ambassadors, nobles, and guests dressed in silks and powdered wigs. At the far end of the room sits the king, on the canopied throne moved temporarily from the Apollo Room. Servants glide by with silver trays of hors d'ouevres and an orchestra fuels the festivities. The mirrors reflect an age when beautiful people loved to look at themselves. It was no longer a sin to be proud of good looks or fine clothes, or to enjoy the good things in life: laughing, dancing, eating, drinking, flirting, and watching the sun set into the distant canal.

From the center of the hall, you can fully appreciate the epic scale of Versailles. The huge palace (by architect Louis Le Vau), the fantasy interior (by Charles Le Brun), and the endless gardens (by André Le Nôtre) made Versailles *le* best. In 1871, after the Prussians defeated the French, Otto von Bismarck declared the establishment of the German Empire in this room. And in 1919, here in the Hall of Mirrors, Germany and the Allies signed the Treaty of Versailles, ending World War I (and, some say, starting World War II).

- *Enter the small Peace Room.*

The Peace Room: By the end of Louis XIV's long life, he was tired of fighting. In this sequel to the War Room, peace is granted to Germany, Holland, and Spain as cupids play with the discarded cannons, armor, and swords.

The oval painting above the fireplace shows 19-year-old Louis XV bestowing an olive branch on Europe. Beside him is his wife, Marie from Poland, cradling their baby twin daughters.

The Peace Room marks the beginning of the queen's half of the palace. On Sundays, the queen held chamber-music concerts here for family and friends (notice the gilded music motifs).

- *Enter the first room of the Queen's Wing, with its canopied bed.*

The Queen's and Nobles' Wing

The Queen's Bedchamber: It was here that the queen rendezvoused with her husband. Two queens died here. This is where 19 princes were born. The chandelier is where two of them were conceived. Just kidding.

True, Louis XIV was not the most faithful husband. There was no attempt to hide the fact that the Sun King warmed more than one bed, for he was above the rules of mere mortals. Adultery became acceptable—even fashionable—in court circles. The secret-looking door on the left side of the bed was for Louis' late-night liaisons—it led straight to his rooms.

Some of Louis XIV's mistresses became more famous and powerful than his rather quiet queen, but he was faithful to the show of marriage and had genuine affection for his wife. Their private apartments were connected, and Louis XIV made a point of sleeping with the queen as often as possible, regardless of whose tiara he tickled earlier in the evening.

This room looks like it did in the days of the last queen, Marie-Antoinette, who substantially redecorated the entire wing. That's her bust over the fireplace, and the double eagle of her native Austria in the corners. The big chest to the left of the bed held her jewels.

The queen's canopied bed is a reconstruction. The bed, chair, and wall coverings switched with the seasons. This was the cheery summer pattern.

Drawing Room of the Nobles: The queen's circle of friends met here, seated on the stools. Discussions ranged from politics to gossip, food to literature, fashion to philosophy. The Versailles kings considered themselves enlightened monarchs who promoted the arts and new ideas. Folks like Voltaire—a political radical—and the playwright Molière participated in the Versailles court. Ironically, these discussions planted the seeds of liberal thought that would grow into the Revolution.

Queen's Antechamber: The royal family dined here publicly, while servants and nobles fluttered around them. admired their table manners, and laughed at the king's jokes like courtly Paul Shaffers. A typical dinner consisted of four different soups, two whole birds stuffed with truffles, mutton, ham slices, fruit, pastries, compotes, and preserves.

THE KING'S VEGETABLE GARDEN *(LE POTAGER DU ROI)*

When Louis XIV demanded fresh asparagus in the middle of winter, he got it, thanks to his vegetable garden. Located a few blocks from the château, the 22-acre garden—still productive—is open to visitors. Stroll through symmetrically laid-out plots planted with vegetables both ordinary and exotic, among thousands of fruit trees. The garden is surrounded by walls and sunk below street level to create its own microclimate. Overseeing the central fountain is a statue of the agronomist Jean de la Quintinie, who wowed Louis XIV's court with Versailles-sized produce. Even today, the garden sprouts 20 tons of vegetables and 50 tons of fruit a year, which you can buy in season (€4.50 on weekdays, €6.50 on weekends, April-Oct daily 10:00–18:00, 10 rue du Maréchal Joffre, see map on page 249).

The central portrait is of luxury-loving, "Let-them-eat-cake" Marie-Antoinette, who became a symbol of decadence to the peasants. The portrait at the far end is a public-relations attempt to soften her image, by showing her with three of her children.

Queen's Guard Room: On October 6, 1789, a mob of revolutionaries—appalled by their queen's taste in wallpaper—stormed the palace. They were fed up with the ruling class leading a life of luxury in the countryside while they were starving in the grimy streets of Paris.

The king and queen locked themselves in. Some of the revolutionaries gained access to this upper floor. They burst into this room where Marie-Antoinette was hiding, overcame her bodyguards, and dragged her and her husband off. (Some claim that, as they carried her away, she sang "Louis, Louis, oh-oh...we gotta go now.")

The enraged peasants then proceeded to ransack the place, as revenge for the years of poverty and oppression they'd suffered. Marie-Antoinette and Louis XVI were later taken to the place de la Concorde in Paris, where they knelt under the guillotine and were made a foot shorter at the top.

Did the king and queen deserve it? Were the revolutionaries destroying civilization or clearing the decks for a new and better one? Was Versailles a symbol of progress or decadence?

Coronation Room: No sooner did they throw out a king than they got an emperor. The Revolution established democracy, but it was shaky in a country that wasn't used to it. In the midst of the confusion, the upstart general Napoleon Bonaparte took control and soon held dictatorial powers. This room captures the glory of the Napoleon years, when he conquered most of Europe. In the huge canvas on the left-hand wall, we see him crowning himself emperor of a new, revived "Roman" Empire. (While also painted by the master, Jacques-Louis David, this is a lesser-quality version of the famous one hanging in the Louvre.)

Turn and face the windows to see the portrait (between the windows) of a dashing, young, charismatic Napoleon in 1796, when he was just a general in command of the Revolution's army in Italy. Compare this with the adjacent portrait from 10 years later—looking less like a revolutionary and more like a Louis. Above the young Napoleon is a portrait of Josephine, his wife and France's empress. In David's *Distribution of Eagles* (opposite the *Coronation*), the victorious general (in imperial garb) passes out emblems of victory to his loyal troops. In *The Battle of Aboukir* (opposite the window), Joachim Murat—Napoleon's general and brother-in-law—looks bored as he slashes through a tangle of dark-skinned warriors. His horse, though, has a look of "What are we doing in this mob? Let's get out of here!" Let's.

- *The exit staircase puts you outside on the left (south) side of the palace, where you enter the gardens.*

The Gardens—Controlling Nature

Louis was a divine-right ruler. One way he proved it was by controlling nature like a god. These lavish grounds, elaborately planned out, pruned, and decorated, showed everyone that Louis was in total command.

- *Buy your ticket (not covered by museum pass) and enter the gardens, then turn left toward the stone railing about 70 yards away. You'll pass through flowers and cookie-cutter patterns of shrubs and green cones. Stand at the railing overlooking the courtyard below and the Louis-made lake in the distance.*

The Orangerie: The warmth from the Sun King was so great that he could even grow orange trees in chilly France. Louis XIV had a thousand of these to amaze his visitors. In winter, they were kept in the greenhouses (beneath your feet) that surround the courtyard. On sunny days, they were wheeled out in their silver planters and scattered around the grounds.

- *From the stone railing, turn about-face*

and walk to the back side of the palace, with two large pools of water. Sit on the top stair and look away from the palace.

View down the Royal Drive: This, to me, is the most stunning spot in all of Versailles. In one direction, the palace. Stretching out in the other direction, the endless grounds. Versailles was laid out along an eight-mile axis that included the grounds, the palace, and the town of Versailles itself, one of the first instances of urban planning since Roman times and a model for future capitals such as Washington, D.C. and Brasilia.

Looking down the Royal Drive (also known as "The Green Carpet"), you see the round Apollo fountain far in the distance. Just beyond that is the Grand Canal. The groves on either side of the Royal Drive were planted with trees from all over, laid out in an elaborate grid and dotted with statues and fountains. Of the original 1,500 fountains, 300 remain.

Looking back at the palace, you can see the Hall of Mirrors—it's the middle story, with the arched windows.

- *Stroll down the steps to get a good look at the frogs and lizards that fill the round Latona Basin.*

The Latona Basin: Absolutely everything in the garden has a symbolic meaning. The theme of Versailles is Apollo, the god of the sun, associated with Louis XIV. This round fountain tells the story of the birth of Apollo and his sister, Diana. On top of the fountain are Apollo and Diana as little kids with their mother, Latona (they're facing toward the Apollo fountain). Latona, an unwed mother, was insulted by the local peasants. She called on the king of the gods, Zeus (the children's father), to avenge the insult. Zeus swooped down and turned all the peasants into the frogs and lizards that ring the fountain.

- *As you walk down past the basin toward the Royal Drive, you'll pass by "ancient" statues done by 17th-century French sculptors. The Colonnade is hidden in the woods on the left-hand side of the Royal Drive, about three-fourths of the way to the Apollo Basin.*

The Colonnade: Versailles had no prestigious ancient ruins, so the king built his own. This prefab Roman ruin is a 100-foot circle of 64 marble columns supporting arches. Beneath the arches are small birdbath fountains. Nobles would picnic in the shade to the tunes of a string quartet and pretend that they were the enlightened citizens of the ancient world.

The Apollo Basin: The fountains of Versailles were its most famous attraction, a marvel of both art and engineering. This one was the centerpiece, showing the sun god—Louis XIV—in his sunny chariot, as he starts his journey across the sky. The horses are half-submerged, giving

GETTING AROUND THE GARDENS

It's a 30-minute hike from the palace, down to the canal, past the two Trianon palaces to the Hamlet—our self-guided tour. The fast-looking, slow-moving tram for tired tourists leaves from behind the château (north side) and serves the Grand Canal and the Trianon palaces; you can hop on and off as you like (€5, 4/hr, 4 stops but not the Hamlet, commentary is nearly worthless). A horse carriage also departs from the north side of the palace. You can rent bikes near the Grand Canal (1 hr-€6).

the impression, when the fountains play, of the sun rising out of the mists of dawn. Most of the fountains were only turned on when the king walked by, but this one played constantly for the benefit of those watching from the palace.

All the fountains are gravity-powered. They work on the same principle as blocking a hose with your finger to make it squirt. Underground streams (pumped into Versailles by Seine River pressure) feed into smaller pipes at the fountains, which shoot the water high into the air.

Looking back at the palace from here, realize that the distance you just walked is only a fraction of this vast complex of buildings, gardens, and waterways. Be glad you don't have to mow the lawn.

The Grand Canal: Why visit Venice when you can just build your own? In an era before virtual reality, this was the next best thing to an actual trip. Couples in gondolas would pole along the waters accompanied by barges with orchestras playing "O Sole Mio." The canal is actually cross-shaped, this being the long arm, one mile from end to end. Of course, this too is a man-made body of water with no function other than to please. Originally, actual gondoliers, imported with their boats from Venice, lived in a little settlement next to the canal.

The Trianon Area—Retreat from Reality

Versailles began as an escape from the pressures of kingship. In a short time, the palace was as busy as Paris ever was. Louis XIV needed an escape from his escape and built a smaller palace out in the tulies. Later, his successors retreated still farther into the garden and built a fantasy world of simple pleasures from which to ignore the real world, which was crumbling all around them.

- *You can rent a bike or catch the pokey tourist train, but the walk is half the fun. It's about a 30-minute walk from here to the end of the tour, plus another 30 minutes to walk back to the palace.*

Grand Trianon: This was the king's private residence away from th main palace. Louis usually spent a couple of nights a week here, but th two later Louises spent more and more time retreating. While the mai palace of Versailles was a screen separating French reality from the roya utopia, the Trianon palaces were engulfed in the royals' fantasy worl and therefore favored.

The facade of this one-story building is a charming combinatio of pink, yellow, and white, a cheery contrast to the imposing Baroqu facade of the main palace. Ahead you can see the gardens through th columns. The king's apartments were to the left of the columns.

The flower gardens were changed daily for the king's pleasure—fo new color combinations and new "nasal cocktails."

Walk around the palace (to the right), if you'd like, for a view o the gardens and rear facade.

• *Facing the front, do an about-face. The Summer House is not down the driveway but about 180 yards away, along the smaller pathway at abou 10 o'clock.*

Summer House of the French Garden: This small white buildin with four rooms fanning out from the center was one more step away fro the modern world. Here, the queen spent summer evenings with famil and a few friends, listening to music or playing parlor games. All avenues of *la douceur de vivre*—"the sweetness of living"—were explored. To the left are the buildings of the Ménagerie, where cows, goats, chickens, and ducks were bred.

• *Continue frolicking along the path until you run into the…*

Petit Trianon: Louis XV developed an interest in botany. He wanted t spend more time near the French Gardens, but the Summer House jus wasn't big enough. He built the Petit Trianon (the "small" Trianon), a mas terpiece of neoclassical architecture. This gray, cubical building has four dis tinct facades, each a perfect and harmonious combination of Greek-styl columns, windows, and railings. Walk around it and find your favorite.

Louis XVI's wife, Marie-Antoinette, made this her home base Despite her bad public reputation (see Carnavalet Museum Tour, pag 176), Marie-Antoinette was a sweet girl from Vienna who never quite fi in with the fast, sophisticated crowd at Versailles. Here at the Peti Trianon, she could get away and recreate the simple home life sh remembered from her childhood. On the lawn outside, she installed a merry-go-round.

• *Five minutes more will bring you to the…*

Temple of Love: A circle of 12 marble Corinthian columns supporting a dome decorates a path where lovers would stroll. Underneath, there's a statue of Cupid making a bow (to shoot arrows of love) out of the club of Hercules. It's a delightful monument to a society whose rich could afford that ultimate luxury, romantic love. When the Revolution came, I bet they wished they'd kept the club.

• *And finally, you'll reach…*

The Hamlet (Le Hameau): Marie-Antoinette longed for the simple life of a peasant. Not the hard labor of real peasants—who sweated and starved around her—but the fairy-tale world of simple country pleasures. She built this complex of 12 buildings as her own private village.

This was an actual working farm with a dairy, a water mill, and domestic animals. The harvest was served at Marie-Antoinette's table. Marie-Antoinette didn't do much work herself, but she "supervised," dressed in a plain white muslin dress and a straw hat.

The Queen's House is the main building, actually two buildings connected by a wooden gallery. Like any typical peasant farmhouse, it had a billiard room, library, elegant dining hall, and two living rooms.

Nearby was the small theater. Here, Marie-Antoinette and her friends acted out plays, far from the rude intrusions of the real world…

• *The real world and the main palace are a 30-minute walk to the southeast. Along the way, stop at the Neptune Basin near the palace, an impressive miniature lake with fountains, and indulge your own favorite fantasy.*

SLEEPING

For a laid-back alternative to Paris within easy reach of the big city by RER train (5/hr, 30 min), Versailles, with easy, safe parking and reasonably priced hotels, can be a good overnight stop. Park in the château's main lot while looking for a hotel, or leave your car there overnight (free, 19:30–8:00). Get a map of Versailles at your hotel or at the TI.

SLEEP CODE

S = Single, D = Double/Twin, T = Triple, Q = Quad, b = bathroom, s = shower only, CC = Credit Cards accepted, no CC = Credit Cards not accepted. Everyone speaks English.

Hôtel de France***, in an 18th-century townhouse, offers four-star value, with air-conditioned, appropriately royal rooms, a pleasant courtyard, comfy public spaces, a bar, and a restaurant (Db-€145, Tb-€180,

Qb-€240, just off parking lot across from château, 5 rue Colbert, tel. 01 30 83 92 23, fax 01 30 83 92 24, www.hotelfrance-versailles.com).

Hôtel le Cheval Rouge**, built in 1676 as Louis XIV's stables, now houses tourists. It's a block behind the place du Marché in a quaint corner of town on a large, quiet courtyard with free parking and sufficiently comfortable rooms (Ds-€51, Db-€68–80, Tb-€90, Qb-€95, 18 rue André Chénier, tel. 01 39 50 03 03, fax 01 39 50 61 27, www.chevalrouge.fr.st).

Ibis Versailles** offers fair value and modern comfort, but no air conditioning (Db-€71, cheaper weekend rates can't be reserved ahead, across from RER station, 4 avenue du Général de Gaulle, tel. 01 39 53 03 30, fax 01 39 50 06 31).

Hôtel du Palais, facing the RER station, has clean, sharp rooms—the cheapest I list in this area. Ask for a quiet room off the street (Ds-€45, Db-€52, extra person-€11, piles of stairs, 6 place Lyautey, tel. 01 39 50 39 29, fax 01 39 50 80 41, hotelpalais@ifrance.com).

Hôtel d'Angleterre**, away from the frenzy, is a tranquil old place with smiling, Polish Madame Kutyla in control. Rooms are comfortable and spacious. Park nearby in the château lot (Db-€58–88, extra bed-€15, just below palace to the right as you exit, 2 rue de Fontenay, tel. 01 39 51 43 50, fax 01 39 51 45 63, hotel.angleterre@voila.fr).

EATING

In the pleasant town center, around place du Marché Notre-Dame, you'll find a variety of reasonable restaurants, cafés, and a few cobbled lanes (market days Sun, Tue, and Fri until 13:00; see map on page 245). The square is a 15-minute walk from the château (veer left when you leave château). From the place du Marché, consider shortcutting to Versailles' gardens by walking 10 minutes west down rue de la Paroisse. The château will be to your left after entering, the main gardens, Trianon palaces, and Hameau straight ahead. The quickest way to the château's front door is along avenue de St. Cloud and rue Colbert.

These places are on or near place du Marché Notre-Dame, and all are good for lunch or dinner. **La Bœuf à la Mode** is a bistro with traditional cuisine right on the square (€25 *menu*, daily, 4 rue au Pain, tel. 01 39 50 31 99). **Fenêtres sur Cour** is the romantic's choice, where you dine in a glass gazebo surrounded by antique shops, just below the square in the "antique village," on place de la Geôle (closed all day Mon and Tue–Wed eves, tel. 01 39 51 97 77). **À la Côte Bretonne** is the place to go for crêpes in a cozy setting (daily, a few steps off the square on traffic-free rue des Deux Ponts, at #12).

Rue Satory is a pedestrian-friendly street lined with restaurants, on the south side of the château near Hôtel d'Angleterre (10-min walk, angle right out of the château). **Le Limousin** is a warm, traditional restaurant on the corner nearest the château, with mostly meat dishes (allow €35 with wine, daily, lamb is a specialty, 4 rue de Satory, tel. 01 39 50 21 50).

CHARTRES CATHEDRAL **TOUR**

Many of the children who watched the old church burn to the ground on June 10, 1194, grew up to build Chartres cathedral and attend the dedication Mass in 1260. That's astonishing, considering that other Gothic cathedrals, such as Paris' Notre-Dame, took hundreds of years to build. Having been built so quickly, Chartres is arguably Europe's best example of pure Gothic, with a unity of architecture, statues, and stained glass that captures the spirit of the Age of Faith.

Chartres' pleasing, cobbled old center is overshadowed by its great cathedral. Discover the picnic-friendly park behind the cathedral and wander the quiet alleys and peaceful squares. For accommodations and eateries, see the end of this chapter.

ORIENTATION

Cost: Free to enter church; costs €4.60 and 300 steps to climb north tower (free for kids and on first Sun of month).

Hours: Daily 7:00–19:00. Tower hours: May–Aug Mon–Sat 9:00–18:00, Sun 13:00–18:30; Sept–Oct & March–April daily 9:30–11:30 & 14:00–17:00; Nov–Feb daily 10:00–11:30 & 14:00–16:00 (last entry 30 min before closing, entrance inside church after bookstore on left).

Getting There: Chartres is a one-hour train trip from Paris' Gare Montparnasse (about €11.60 one-way, 10/day, last train on Sat departs Chartres about 19:00; figure on a round-trip total of 3 hrs from Paris to cathedral doorstep and back). Upon arrival in Chartres, confirm your return schedule. Leaving the train station and heading uphill, you'll soon see the medieval church rise above the modern city of Chartres.

Bring: Binoculars, if you got 'em.

Information: The helpful TI has a map with a self-guided walking tour

Chartres

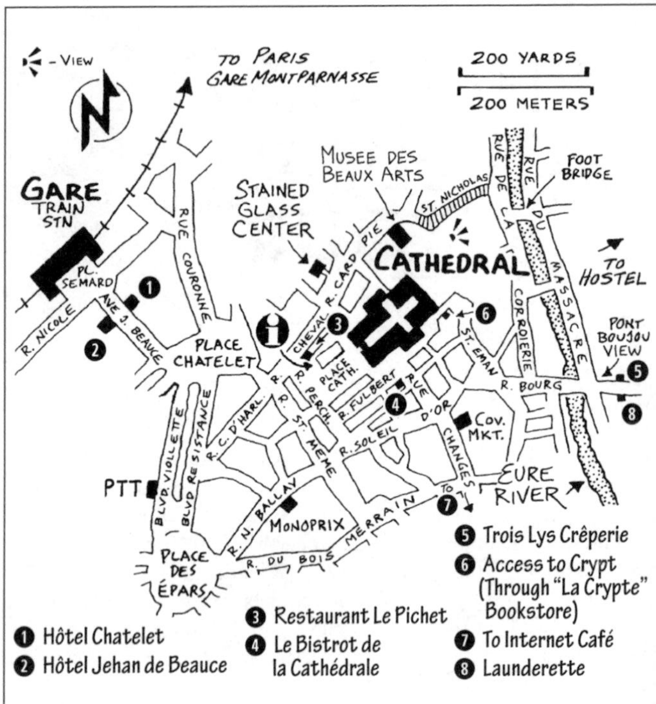

of Chartres and rents audioguides that accompany the tour (April-Sept Mon–Sat 9:00–19:00, Sun 9:30–17:30, Oct-March Mon-Sat 10:00-18:00, Sun 10:00-13:00 & 14:30-16:30, located 100 yards in front of church, tel. 02 37 18 26 26). The church has two bookstores, one inside near the entrance, the other outside near the south porch (church tel. 02 37 21 22 07).

Cathedral Tours by Malcolm Miller: This fascinating English scholar illuminates a new detail of the church with every tour. The one-hour tours, offered Mon–Sat at 12:00 and 14:45, cost €11 and are led by either Malcolm Miller or his capable assistant. These are worthwhile, even if you've taken this self-guided tour. Tours begin at the bookstore inside the church. Private tours can be arranged (tel. 02 37 28 15 58, fax 02 37 28 33 03). For a detailed look at Chartres' windows, sculpture, and history, pick up Malcolm Miller's two guidebooks (sold at cathedral).

Audioguides: You can rent audioguides from the cathedral bookstore. Circuits are available on the cathedral (€3.80, 45 min), the choir only

(€2.90, 25 min), or both (€5.65, 70 min). If you are staying the night in Chartres, consider renting an audioguide for a tour of the so-often-missed old town (€5.50, €8.50 for 2, about 2 hours, available at the TI). You'll need to leave your passport as a deposit.

The Crypt: The foundations can be visited only as part of a guided tour in French (with an English handout). You'll see remnants of the earlier churches, a modern copy of the old wooden Mary-and-baby statue, and hints of the old well and Roman wall (30-min tours start in La Crypte bookstore, located outside church near south porch).

Length of This Tour: One hour, but Chartres is an all-day excursion from Paris.

Cuisine Art: For restaurant (and hotel) recommendations, see the end of this chapter.

THE CHARTRES GENERATION—THE 1200s

• *Kill train time by reading this.*

From king to bishop and knight to pawn, French society was devoted to the Christian faith. It inspired knights to undertake the formidable Crusades, artists to re-create heaven in statues and stained glass, and architects to build skyscraping cathedrals filled with the mystic light of heaven. They aimed for a golden age, blending faith and reason, though misguided faith often outstripped reason, resulting in very un-Christian intolerance and violence.

Timeline

1194—The old cathedral burns down.

c. 1200—The University of Paris is founded, using human reason to analyze Christian faith. Borrowing from the pagan Greek philosopher Aristotle, scholars described the Christian universe as a series of concentric rings spinning around the Earth in geometrical perfection.

1202—The pope calls on all true Christians to rescue the Holy Land from Muslim "infidels" in the Fourth Crusade (1202–1204). This crusade ends disastrously in the sacking of Constantinople, a Christian city.

1206—Chartres' cornerstone is laid. The style is *opus francigenum* ("French-style work")—which is what the people in Gothic times called Gothic. Chartres is just one of several great cathedrals under construction in Europe.

1207—Francis of Assisi, a rebellious Italian youth, undergoes a conversion to a life of Christian poverty and love. His open spirit inspires many followers, including France's King Louis IX (a generation later).

1209—France's King Philip Augustus, based in Paris, invades southern France and massacres fellow Christians (the Cathars or Albigensians) as heretics.

1212—Thousands of boys and girls idealistically join the Children's Crusade to save the Holy Land. Most die in transit or are sold into slavery.

1220—The external structure of Chartres cathedral is nearly finished. Work begins on the statues and stained glass.

1226—Eleven-year-old Louis IX is crowned as *rex et sacerdos,* "King and Priest," beginning a 45-year golden age combining church and state. His mother, Blanche of Castile (granddaughter of Eleanor of Aquitaine), is his lifelong mentor.

1230—Most of Chartres' stained glass is completed.

1244—At age 30, Louis IX falls sick and sees a vision in a coma that changes his life. His personal trustworthiness helps unify the nation. He reforms the judicial system along Christian lines, helping the poor.

1245—The last Albigensian heretics are burned at Montségur, in a crusade ordered by Louis IX and his mother, Blanche.

1248—Louis IX personally leads the Seventh Crusade by walking barefoot from Paris to the port of departure. During the fighting, he is captured and ransomed. He later returns home a changed man. Humbled, he adopts the poverty of the Franciscan brotherhood. His devotion earns him the title of St. Louis.

1260—Chartres cathedral is dedicated. The church is the physical embodiment of the Age of Faith, with architecture as mathematically perfect as God's Creation, sculpture serving as sermons in stone, and stained glass lit by the light of God.

Mary's Church ("Notre-Dame" = "Our Lady" of Chartres)

The church is (at least) the fourth church on this spot dedicated to Mary, the mother of Jesus, who has been venerated here for some 1700 years. There's even speculation that the pagan Romans dedicated a temple to a mother-goddess. In earliest times, Mary was honored next to a natural spring of healing waters (not visible today). In the ninth century, the church acquired Mary's veil (which is sometimes displayed in the church) as the focus of devotion. A crude wooden statue of Mary also attracted pilgrims; the statue was destroyed in 1793, but copies remain.

The Book of Chartres

Historian Malcolm Miller calls Chartres a picture book of statues, stained glass, and symbolic architecture, telling the entire Christian story—from Creation to Christ's birth (the north side of the church), from Christ and his followers up to the present (south entrance), to the end of time when Christ returns as judge (west entrance).

The Christian universe is a complex web of heaven and earth, angels and demons, and prophets and martyrs. Much of the medieval symbolism is obscure today. Expect to be overwhelmed by the thousands of things to see, but appreciate the perfect unity of this Gothic masterpiece.

Chartres Cathedral

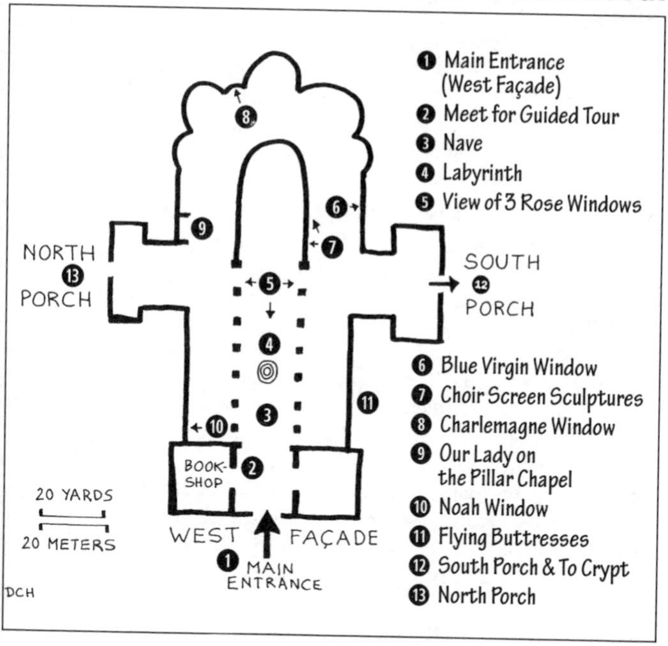

NORTH PORCH 13
SOUTH PORCH 12
BOOK-SHOP
20 YARDS
20 METERS
WEST FAÇADE
1 MAIN ENTRANCE
DCH

1. Main Entrance (West Façade)
2. Meet for Guided Tour
3. Nave
4. Labyrinth
5. View of 3 Rose Windows
6. Blue Virgin Window
7. Choir Screen Sculptures
8. Charlemagne Window
9. Our Lady on the Pillar Chapel
10. Noah Window
11. Flying Buttresses
12. South Porch & To Crypt
13. North Porch

THE TOUR BEGINS

1. The Main Entrance (West Facade), c. 1150: The two mismatched steeples, three doors, rose window, and various statues are the only survivors of the intense, lead-melting fire that incinerated the rest of the church in 1194. The church of today was rebuilt behind this facade in a single generation (1194–1260).

Towers: The right (south) tower, with a stone steeple, is original Romanesque. The left (north) tower lost its wooden steeple in the 1194 fire. In the 1500s, it was topped by a steeple bigger than the tapered lower half was meant to hold.

The West Doors: Christ, the center of Christian history, sits above the **central door,** surrounded by symbolic animals.

The anorexic statues between the doors are pillars of the faith that foretold the coming of Christ. With solemn gestures and faces, they patiently endure the wait.

History's pivotal event is shown above the

right door, where Mary (seated) produces baby Jesus from her loins. This Mary-and-baby sculpture is a 12th-century stone version of an older wooden statue (burned 1793). Centuries of pilgrims have visited Chartres to see Mary's statue, gaze at her veil, and ponder the mystery of how God in Heaven became Man on Earth, as He passed through immaculate Mary like sunlight through stained glass.

• *Enter the church and wait for your pupils to enlarge.*

2. Nave: The church has a long, tall central nave, flanked by raised side aisles for crowd flow, so pilgrims could circle the church without disturbing worshipers. The 12 pillars lining the nave support pointed crisscrossed arches on the ceiling, which lace together the heavy stone vaulting. The pillars are supported by flying buttresses on the outside of the church (which we'll see later). This skeleton structure was the miracle of Gothic, allowing tall buildings with ribbed walls and lots of stained-glass windows (like the big saints in the upper stories of the nave). The floor of the nave slopes in to the center, for easy drainage when hosing down dirty pilgrims who camped here.

3. The Labyrinth: The round maze inlaid in black stone on the floor of the nave is a spiritual journey. Pilgrims enter from the west rim by foot or on knees and wind inward, meditating. And 1,000 feet later, they hope to meet God in the middle. (Current world record for reaching enlightenment is 3:42.)

• *Walk up the nave to where the transept crosses. As you face the altar, north is to the left.*

4. The Rose Windows—North, South, and West: The three big, round "rose" (floral-shaped) windows over the entrances open like flowers to receive sunlight at different times of day. All three are predominantly blue and red, but each has different "petals," and each tells a different part of the Christian story in a kaleidoscope of fragmented images.

Having trouble making out the tiny, distant details? As we've all read, stained glass was a way to teach Bible stories to the illiterate medieval masses…who apparently owned state-of-the-art binoculars. Yes, the windows tell stories, but obviously, their main purpose was to light a dark church in a colorful and decorative way.

The **north rose window** charts history from the distant past up to the birth of Jesus. On the outer rim, murky, ancient (barely visible) prophets foretell Christ's coming. Then (circling inward), there's a ring

GOD = LIGHT

You can try to examine the details, but a better way to experience the mystery of Chartres is to just sit and stare at these enormous panels, as they float in the dark of empty space like holograms or space stations or the Queen of Heaven's crown jewels. Ponder the medieval concept that God is light.

To the Chartres generation, the church was a metaphor for how God brings his creation to life, like the way light animates stained glass. They were heavy into mysticism, feeling a oneness with all creation in a moment of enlightenment. The Gospel of John (as well as a writer known to historians as the Pseudo-Dionysius) was their favorite. Here are select verses from John 1:1–12 (loosely translated):

In the beginning was The Word.
Jesus was the light of the human race.
The light shines in the darkness, and the darkness
cannot resist it.
It was the real light coming into the world, the light that
enlightens everyone.
He was in the world, but the world did not recognize Him.
But to those who did,
He gave the power to become the children of God.

of red squares with kings who are Christ's direct ancestors. Still closer, a circle of white doves and winged angels zero in on the central event of history—Mary, the heart of the flower, with her newborn baby, Jesus.

This window was donated by King Louis IX (who built Paris' Sainte-Chapelle) and his mom, Blanche of Castile. See their coats of arms just below the rose—Louis IX's yellow fleur-de-lis on a blue background and Blanche's yellow castles on a red background.

In the **south rose window,** the Old Testament prophecies are fulfilled. Christ sits in the center (dressed in blue, with a red background), setting in motion the radiating rings of angels, beasts, and apocalyptic elders who labor to bring history to its close. The five lancet windows below show Old Testament prophets lifting New Testament writers on their shoulders (in first window on left, see white-robed Luke riding piggyback on dark-robed Jeremiah), demonstrating how the ancients prepared the way for Christ. A dark Christ rings in history's final Day of Judgment at the center of the **west rose window.** Around him, winged angels blow their trumpets and the dead rise, face judgment, and are sent to hell or raised to eternal bliss. The frilly edge of this glorious "rose" is flecked with tiny, clover-shaped dewdrops.

5. The Blue Virgin Window: Mary, dressed in blue on a rich red background, cradles purple Jesus, while the dove of the Holy Spirit descends on her. This is some of the oldest stained glass (1150), a survivor of the 1194 fire, which was reinserted into this new window frame around 1230. The Blue Virgin was one of the most popular stops for pilgrims—especially pregnant ones—of the cult of the Virgin-about-to-give-birth. Devotees prayed, carried stones to repair the church, or donated to the church coffers; Mary rewarded them with peace of mind, easy births, and occasional miracles.

Below Mary, see **Christ being tempted** by a red-faced, horned, smirking devil.

Hail, maiden, what's your sign? Pick up chicks at the **Zodiac Window** (second window to the left). The 12 signs are in the right half of the window; read from the bottom up—Pisces, Aries, Gemini (in the cloverleaf), Taurus, Cockroach, Leo, Virgo, etc.

6. The Choir Screen—Life of Mary: In the center of the church sits the stone **choir** (the enclosed area behind the altar where church officials sat), ringed with **41 statue groups** illustrating Mary's life (by various sculptors, 1520–1714). Although the Bible says little about the mother of Jesus, legend and lore fleshed out her life.

Scene #1 (south side) shows an angel telling her dad that Mary's on the way. In #4, Anne gives birth to Mary. In #6, Mary marries Joseph. In #10, she gives birth to Jesus in a manger. In #12, the Three Kings arrive. Scenes #15–27 show her famous son's life. In #28, Jesus is crucified. In #34, the resurrected Jesus appears to his mother. In #38, Mary dies; in #39, she's raised by angels into heaven; and in #41, she's crowned Queen of Heaven by the Father, Son, and the Holy Ghost.

The **plain windows** surrounding the choir date from the 1770s, when the dark mystery of medieval stained glass was replaced by the open light of the French Enlightenment. The plain windows and the choir are some of the only "new" features. Most of the 1200s church has remained, despite style changes, Revolutionary vandals, and war bombs.

• *Due to the damage that even ordinary light inflicts on fragile objects, Mary's veil may not be on display during your visit.*

7. Mary's Veil: Sitting in a glass case with a gold frame held by angels, this is the torn, 2,000-year-old **veil** supposedly worn by Mary when she gave birth to Jesus. Since the ninth century, this has been the main object of adoration for the cult of the Virgin, and stories abound of its magical powers.

In A.D. 911, with the city surrounded by Vikings, the bishop hoisted the veil like a battle flag and waved it at the invaders. It scared the bejesus out them with visions of extended labor, and the town was saved.

When the fire of 1194 incinerated the old church, the veil was feared lost. Lo and behold, several days later they found it miraculously unharmed in the crypt (beneath today's choir). The people were so stoked, they worked like madmen to erect this grand cathedral in which to display it.

8. Charlemagne Window: The window tells the story of how the veil ended up here. **Charlemagne** (bottom left semicircle), the great king of the Franks (A.D. 742–814) and first Holy Roman Emperor (800–814), sits on his throne between two advisers and plans a great adventure—a crusade to the Holy City of Jerusalem. Next (the semicircle just above), he attacks the Muslim infidels occupying Jerusalem. Charlemagne (heart-shaped shield) stabs a Saracen (round shield) in the neck and drives the Muslims out of the city.

On the way home, Charlemagne stops in the great Christian city of Constantinople (in the diamond directly to the right), where he's welcomed at the gate by the emperor. The emperor rewards him (semicircle directly to the right) with three chests of holy relics... including Mary's veil. Charlemagne returns home (the circle above the diamond) to his palace in Aix-la-Chapelle, kneels, and places the relics before the altar. Charlemagne's grandson, Charles the Bald, gave the veil to Chartres in 876.

The fashion-conscious will notice the clothes are from the 1220s, when the window was made.

9. Chapel of Our Lady on the Pillar: A 16th-century **statue of Mary and baby**—draped in cloth, crowned and sceptered—sits on a column in a wonderful carved-wood alcove. This is today's pilgrimage center, built to keep visitors from clogging up the altar area. Modern pilgrims honor the Virgin by leaving flowers, lighting candles, and kissing the column.

10. The Noah Window: Read Chartres' windows from left to right and bottom to top.

Bottom-left is a man making a wheel. He's one of the donors of this window. His colleagues to the right are from the axe- and barrel-maker guilds.

Then comes the story of **Noah** (read from the bottom up): God tells Noah he'll destroy the earth (#1, bottom diamond). Noah hefts an axe to build an ark, while his son hauls wood (diamond #2). He loads horses (cloverleaf, above left), purple elephants (cloverleaf, above right), and other animals. The psychedelic ark sets sail (diamond #3). Waves cover the earth and drown the wicked (two cloverleaves). The ark survives (diamond #4), and Noah releases a dove. Finally, up near the top (diamond #7), a rainbow arches overhead, God drapes himself over it, and Noah and his family give thanks.

• *Exit the church (through the main entrance or the door in the south transept) to view its south side.*

11. South Exterior—Flying Buttresses: Six flying buttresses on the south side (the arches that stick out from the upper walls) push against six pillars lining the nave inside, and they help to hold up the heavy stone ceiling and sloped, lead-over-wood roof. The ceiling and roof push down onto the pillars, of course, but also outward (north and south) because of the miracle of Gothic, the pointed arch. These flying buttresses push back, channeling the stress outward to the six vertical buttresses, then down to the ground. The result is a tall cathedral held up by slender pillars buttressed from the outside, allowing the walls to be opened up for stained glass.

The church is built from large blocks of limestone. Peasants trod in hamster-wheel contraptions to raise these blocks into place—a testament to their great faith.

12. South Porch: The three doorways of the south entrance show the world from Christ to the present, as Christianity triumphs over persecution.

Center Door—Christ and Apostles: Standing between the double doors, **Jesus** holds a book and raises his arm in blessing. He's a simple, itinerant, bareheaded, barefoot rabbi, but underneath his feet he tramples symbols of evil, the dragon and lion (which is which?). Christ's face is among the most noble of all Gothic sculpture.

Christ is surrounded by his **apostles,** who spread the good news to a hostile world. **Peter** (to the left as you face Jesus), with curly hair and beard, holds the key to the kingdom of heaven and the slender cross on which he was crucified upside down. **Paul** (to the right of Jesus) fingers the sword of his martyrdom and contemplates the inevitable loss of his head and the hair upon it. In fact, all of the apostles were killed or persecuted, and their faces are humble, with sad eyes. But their message prevailed, and under their feet they crush the squirming emperors who once persecuted them.

The final triumph comes above the door in the **Last Judgment.** Christ sits in judgment, raising his hands, while Mary and John beg him to take it easy on poor humankind. Beneath Christ, the souls are judged—the righteous on our left, and the wicked on the right, who are thrown into the fiery jaws of hell. Farther to the right (above the statues of Paul and the apostles), horny demons subject wicked women to an eternity of sexual harassment.

Left Door—Martyrs: Eight martyrs flank the left door. **St. ,awrence** (second from left) cradles the grill on which he was barbe-ued alive. His last brave words to the Romans actually were: "You can urn me over—I'm done on this side." **St. George** (far right) wears the :nightly uniform of the 1200s, when Chartres was built and King Louis X was crusading. Depicted beneath the martyrs are gruesome **methods of torture** (e.g., George stretched on the wheel), many of which were ised in the 1200s against heretics, Muslims, Jews, and Albigensians (the Cathar sect of southern France).

Right Door—Confessors: Among these eight pillars of the faith, ind **Jerome** (third from the right), holding the Bible he translated into everyday Latin; and **Gregory** (second from the right), the pope who organized church hierarchy and wrote Gregorian chants.

Reach the north side by circling around the back end of the church (great views) or by cutting through the church.

13. The North Porch: In the Book of Chartres, the north porch s chapter one, from the Creation up to the coming of Christ.

Center Door: Baby Mary (headless), in the arms of **her mother Anne** (the statue between the double doors), marks the culmination of he Old Testament world.

History begins in the tiny details in the concentric arches over the loorway. **God creates Adam** (at the peak of the outer arch) by cradling his head in his lap like a child.

Melchizedek (farthest to the left of Mary and Anne), with cap and cup, is the Biblical model of the *rex et sacerdos* (king-priest), the title bestowed on King Louis IX.

Abraham (second from left) holds his son by the throat and raises a knife to slit him for sacrifice. Just then, he hears something and turns his head up to see God's angel, who stops the bloodshed. The drama of this frozen moment anticipates Renaissance naturalism by 200 years.

John the Baptist (fourth to the right from Mary/Anne), the last Old Testament prophet who prepared the way for Jesus, holds a lamb, the symbol of Christ. John is skinny from his diet of locusts and honey. His body twists and flickers like a flame.

All these **prophets,** with their beards turning down the corners of their mouths, have the sad, wise look of having been around since the beginning of time and having seen it all—from Creation to Christ to Apocalypse. They are some of the last work done on the church, completing the church's stone-and-glass sermon.

Imagine all this painted and covered with gold leaf in preparation for the dedication ceremonies in 1260, when the Chartres generation could finally stand back and watch as their great-grandchildren, carrying candles, entered the cathedral.

SLEEP CODE

S = Single, D = Double/Twin, T = Triple, Q = Quad, b = bathroom, s = shower only, CC = Credit Cards accepted, no CC = Credit Cards not accepted. Everyone speaks English.

SLEEPING AND EATING

(€1 = about $1.10, country code: 33)

Chartres, a good getaway from Paris, can also be a first or last overnigh stop for those flying to/from Orly Airport.

Chartres has a **launderette** (across from recommended Troi Lys Crêperie, near pont Boujou, 15-min walk from cathedral) and th **Tout va Bien** Internet café (Mon–Sat 8:00–21:00, 2 rue de la Mairie 5-min walk from cathedral down rue des Changes).

These hotels face each other (200 yards straight out of train station, 300 yards below cathedral): **Hôtel Châtelet***** is comfortable, fron its welcoming lobby to its spotless, spacious, well-furnished rooms (Sb-€65–78, Db-€72–84, extra person-€10, streetside rooms are cheaper parking-€6, 6 avenue Jehan de Beauce, tel. 02 37 21 78 00, fax 02 37 3 23 01, www.hotelchatelet.com, hchatel@club-internet.fr). **Hôtel Jeha de Beauce**** is basic, clean, and quiet, with some tiny bathrooms (S-€33 D-€42, Ds-€45, Db-€56, Tb-€64, 19 avenue Jehan de Beauce, tel. 0 37 21 01 41, fax 02 37 21 59 10).

Eating: Le Pichet, run by friendly Marie-Sylvie and Xavier, is reasonable and homey with good daily specials (menus from €11, oper Thu-Tue for lunch, Thu-Sat for dinner, closed Wed, 19 rue du Cheva Blanc, near TI, tel. 02 37 21 08 35). **Le Bistrot de la Cathédrale** is fin for salads and basic bistro fare, but you'll pay for the view (menus fron €15, on south side of cathedral at 1 cloître Notre-Dame, tel. 02 37 36 5 60). **Trois Lys Crêperie** makes cheap crêpes just across the river on pon Boujou (3 rue de la Porte Guillaume, tel. 02 37 28 42 02).

MORE DAY **TRIPS**

Grand Châteaux near Paris • Impressionist Excursions: Giverny and Auvers-sur-Oise • Disneyland Paris

GRAND CHATEAUX NEAR PARIS

The region around Paris (Ile de France) is dotted with sumptuous palaces. Paris' booming upper class made it the heartland of European château-building in the 16th and 17th centuries. Most of these châteaux were lavish hunting lodges—getaways from the big city. The only things they defended were noble and royal egos. Try to avoid visiting on weekends, when they are most crowded.

Consider four very different châteaux:

▲▲▲**Versailles**—for its history, grandeur, and accessibility (closed Mon).

▲▲▲**Vaux-le-Vicomte**—for sheer beauty and intimacy (open daily, Nov-Feb closed early).

▲▲**Fontainebleau**—for its history, fine interior, and pleasant city (closed Tue).

▲**Chantilly**—for its beautiful setting and fine collection of paintings (closed Tue except in summer).

If you only have time for one château, choose between Vaux-le-Vicomte and Versailles (see tour on page 244). Except for Versailles, these châteaux are quiet on weekdays. Versailles, Fontainebleau, and Chantilly are covered by the Paris museum pass.

Vaux-le-Vicomte

While Versailles is most travelers' first choice for its sheer historic weight, Vaux-le-Vicomte (voh luh vee-komt) offers a more intimate interior and a better sense of 17th-century château life. Located in a huge forest, with magnificent gardens and no urban sprawl in sight, Vaux-le-Vicomte gave me just a twinge of palace envy.

Vaux-le-Vicomte was the architectural inspiration of Versailles and

Day Trips from Paris

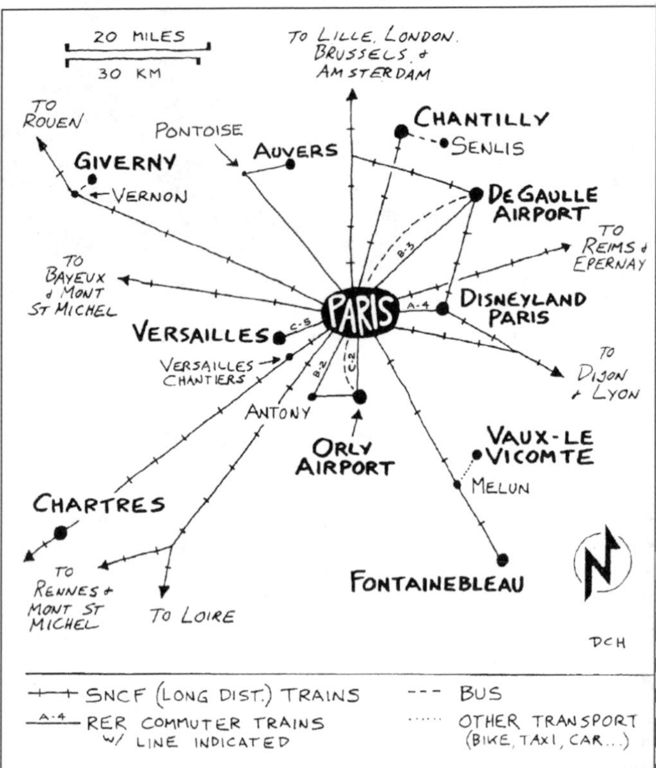

set the standard for European châteaux to come. The proud owner, Nicolas Fouquet (Louis XIV's finance minister), threw a château-warming party. Louis XIV was so jealous that he arrested his host, took his architect (Louis Le Vau), artist (Charles Le Brun), and landscaper (André Le Nôtre), and proceeded with the construction of the bigger and costlier (but not necessarily more splendid) palace of Versailles. Monsieur Fouquet's party and later arrest feature prominently in the third Musketeer book by Alexandre Dumas, and at least two versions of *The Man in the Iron Mask* were filmed here.

Vaux-le-Vicomte is more expensive than Versailles to get to (because of cab fare), but a joy to tour. Most rooms have English explanations. For more information, rent a €3 audioguide (with a pro-Fouquet perspective) or get a souvenir booklet at the gift shop. Outside the gift shop is a reasonably-priced café (limited menu, daily 11:30–18:00 and, during candlelit visits, until midnight).

Start your tour with the fine exhibit of carriages *(équipages)* in the old stables. Wax figures and an evocative soundtrack get you in the proper mood. Next, stroll like a wide-eyed peasant across the stone bridge (any fish down there?) and up the front steps into the château. Turn around to admire the symmetry and elegance of the stables; horses lived well here.

As you wander through Fouquet's dream home, you'll understand Louis XIV's jealousy. Versailles was a simple hunting lodge when this was built. The furniture in Vaux-le-Vicomte is not original—Louis XIV confiscated the real thing for Versailles. You'll see cozy bedrooms upstairs and grand living rooms downstairs (billiards room, library, card room, and dining room; feel free to fast-forward the 90-min audioguide tour). The kitchen and wine cellar are in the basement. Climb the cupola for a great view (€2).

Survey the garden from the back steps of the palace. Landscaper Le Nôtre's first claim to fame, this garden was the cutting edge of sculpted French gardens. He integrated ponds, shrubbery, and trees in a style that would be copied in palaces all over Europe. Take the 30-minute walk (one-way) to the Hercules viewpoint atop the grassy hill far in the distance. Rentable golf carts (Club Cars, 45 min-€14, €125 deposit) make the trip easier, and the funky Nautilles (pedal boats in the shape of water animals, 30 min-€10) are fun for kids. Picnics are not allowed.

Cost and Hours: €13 for gardens, château, and carriage museum, not covered by museum pass. Open March–early Nov daily 10:00–18:00, closed early Nov–early March, tel. 01 64 14 41 90, www.vaux-le-vicomte.com. The impressive fountains run 15:00–18:00 the second Sat and last Sat of each month (April–Oct).

Candlelit Visits: Two thousand candles and piped-in classical music illuminate the palace May–Sept Sat and holiday nights (open 20:00–24:00); call to ask about any upcoming holidays. These *visites aux chandelles* are worth the €16 entry, but remember, it doesn't get really dark until 22:00 in late May, June, and early July, and the last train to Paris leaves Melun at about 22:00.

Getting to Vaux-le-Vicomte: To reach Vaux-le-Vicomte by a train-and-taxi combination, take the RER-D train to Melun from Paris' Gare du Nord or Châtelet-Les Halles stations. Faster SNCF *banlieue* trains to Melun leave from Paris' Gare de Lyon (about €7.50 one-way, hrly, 35 min). From Melun's station, taxis make the 15-minute drive to Vaux-le-Vicomte (€17 Mon–Sat, €21 eves and Sun, taxi tel. 01 64 52 51 50, other numbers posted above taxi stand). Ask a staff person at the château to call a cab for your return or schedule a pick-up time with your driver. In either direction, seek others to split the fare with. If you have time to kill before your return train, or just want to make more of your excursion, consider exploring Melun's small medieval center, 10 easy minutes on foot from the station (walk down avenue Gallieni past the ugly concrete buildings, turn right on rue Thiers and cross the river).

Several tour companies offer bus excursions to Vaux-le-Vicomte; see under Organized Tours of Paris, page 24.

By car from Paris, take the A-6 autoroute toward Lyon, then follow signs to Melun. In Melun, follow signs to Meaux (N-36), then Vaux-le-Vicomte.

Adding Fontainebleau: Vaux-le-Vicomte and Fontainebleau can be combined into a full, though manageable, day trip by car, taxi, or train from Paris (except on Tue, when Fontainebleau is closed). Fontainebleau is 12 minutes by train from Melun (allow €35-40 by taxi).

Sleeping near Vaux-le-Vicomte: Modern and ugly, but handy and cheap, **Ibis Hôtel** is between Melun and the château, just off N-105 (Db-€60, less on weekends, tel. 01 60 68 42 45, fax 01 64 09 62 00). It'd be better to drive 15 minutes to Fontainebleau and sleep at one of the recommended hotels (below).

Château of Fontainebleau

Fontainebleau's history rivals that of more modern Versailles. Many French kings have called this glamorous hunting lodge home. Louis XIII was born here, Louis XV married here, and Napoleon was baptized here. The little emperor also welcomed the pope to this château during his coronation celebration, and it was here that he abdicated his rule when exiled to Elba in 1814. Many years later, General Patton set up headquarters at this château on his way to Berlin.

While Vaux-le-Vicomte and Versailles are French-designed, Fontainebleau was built a century earlier by an Italian. The palace you see today was largely financed by Renaissance King François I. Inspired by his travels through Renaissance Italy, he hired Italian artists to build his palace.

Visit the information room to quickly orient yourself, using its huge model of the château (first door on your right in the grand courtyard). The palace entry is 50 yards farther down. Your ticket provides access to the Chinese rooms and the main rooms of the château. Napoleon buffs can enjoy the interesting little museum of Napoleonic history or a visit to his apartments. Both can be visited only with a guided tour in French (some English possible, €3 each, hours vary, call ahead or ask on arrival). The €3 audioguides give

good room-by-room descriptions (allow one hour)and basic English explanations are posted throughout.

In the main château, start downstairs with the small but impressive Chinese collection of Napoleon III's empress, then climb to the main rooms of the palace. Highlights include the stunning Renaissance hall of François I, the opulent dance hall with piped-in music *(salle de bal),* Napoleon's throne room, and Diana's Gallery (library). The gardens, designed a century later by the landscaper André Le Nôtre, are worth a stroll. Rent a rowboat for the *étang des carpes* (carp pond), or walk its path for a good view of the château complex.

Cost and Hours: €5.50, covered by museum pass, free first Sun of the month. Open April-Sept Wed–Mon 9:30–18:00, closed Tue; Oct-March 9:30–17:00; last entry 45 minutes before closing.

Getting to Fontainebleau: Catch a train at the Grande Ligne tracks from Paris' Gare de Lyon in the direction of Montereau (about €9 one-way, 40 min) to the Fontainebleau-Avon station. Cross under the tracks and catch the bus to the château (Cars Verts, about €1.50, every 10 min). Get return train times before leaving the station, as there can be big gaps. Your train might make an unscheduled stop in the middle of the forest to drop off hikers. Taxis to the château cost about €7; to nearby Vaux-le-Vicomte costs €35-40 (taxi tel. 01 64 22 00 06).

Town of Fontainebleau: Turn right out of the château courtyard and keep right to reach the town center, where cafés and restaurants abound. The helpful **TI** is two blocks across from the château behind Hôtel Londres at 4 rue Royale and has hiking maps and bikes for rent (Mon–Sat 10:00–18:30, Sun 10:00–12:30 & 15:00-17:00, tel. 01 60 74 99 99). Return bus stops to the station are across the street from the Hotel Londres, opposite the chateau entrance and at la Poste in the city center.

Sleeping and Eating in Fontainebleau: The **Hôtel Londres***** is run by gentle Philippe and Mama, who have left no stone unturned in their zeal to make everything perfect. The rooms are big, immaculate and *très* country-French, many have point-blank views of the château (smaller Db-€106, larger Db with château view-€130–140, 1 place du Général de Gaulle, tel. 01 64 22 20 21, fax 01 60 72 39 16, www.hoteldelondres.com). Turn right out of the château entrance and keep right for about five blocks to reach **Hôtel Legris et Parc*****, a quiet getaway with a garden, pool, and a country-classy restaurant (menus from €28). Rooms are faded, but fine (standard Db-€70, bigger Db-€90, Tb/Qb suites-€135, 36 rue Paul Seramy, tel. 01 64 22 24 24, fax 01 64 22 22 05, legris.et.parc@wanadoo.fr).

To eat well, try one of these central places: **Croquembouche** (*menus* from €20, closed Wed and Sun, 43 rue de France, tel. 01 64 22 01 57) or dine by candlelight under medieval arches at the **Caveau des Ducs** (good €20-30 menus, daily, 24 rue de Ferrare, tel. 01 64 22 05 05).

Château of Chantilly

Chantilly (shahn-tee-yee), 35 minutes north of Paris, floats serenely on a reflecting pond amid grand gardens. Unfortunately, the château interior is disappointing. Its best rooms can be seen only on a boring French-language guided tour, and the fine works of art in the picture galleries are poorly displayed. Still, Chantilly can be a rewarding experience for art-lovers needing a break from the big city. Allow most of a day for Chantilly.

This extravagant hunting palace was destroyed during the Revolution. Today's château was largely rebuilt during the 19th century. It's divided into two parts: the painting gallery, with art by Raphael, Titian, Nicolas Poussin, Eugène Delacroix, and others; and the private apartments, which require a French-language tour. The highlight of the otherwise dull apartments is the first stop: the prince's library, lined with more than 13,000 books and beautiful copies of pages from *Les Très Riches Heures du Duc du Berry,* a much-admired 15th-century illuminated manuscript.

The gardens immediately behind the château are formal and austere. With your back to the château, follow the signs to the right to *le Hameau.* This little hamlet, with an enchanting garden café, was the prototype for the more famous *hameau* at Versailles. Just beyond is a small kiosk offering boat trips along the canals.

Cost and Hours: €7, €4 for gardens only, covered by museum pass, March–Oct Wed–Mon 10:00–18:00, closed Tue; July–Aug also open Tue 10:00–18:00; Nov–Feb Wed–Fri and Mon 10:30–12:45 & 14:00–17:00, Sat–Sun 10:00–18:00, closed Tue, tel. 03 44 62 62 62, www.chateaudechantilly.com.

Live Horse Stables (*Les Ecuries Vivant*): The Prince de Condé believed he'd be reincarnated as a horse, so he built this opulent horse château for his next go-round. You'd have to have similar beliefs to pay the €8 entry for this horse museum (although it's impressive and thorough). The museum features 40 live horses in their stables, and demonstrations at 15:30 weekdays, weekends at 11:15, 15:15 and 17:15, (April–Oct Wed–Mon 14:00–17:00, weekends 10:00-17:30; July–Aug also open Tue 14:00–17:30; Nov–March Mon and Wed–Fri 14:00–18:00, Sat–Sun 10:30–17:30, closed Tue, tel. 03 44 57 13 13).

Getting to Chantilly: Leave from Paris' Gare du Nord for Chantilly-Gouvieux. While the RER serves Chantilly, service is faster on the main lines at Grandes Lignes level. Ask any information desk for the next departure (about €7 one-way, nearly hrly, 35 min). Upon arrival in Chantilly, confirm return times (fewer trips on weekends). The TI is across from the station (Mon–Sat 9:00–12:30 & 14:00–18:00, tel. 03 44 67 37 37). To get to the château, get lucky and catch the once an hour bus (marked "le Duc"), or walk 30 minutes (follow signs, stay on path, turn right before gas station, cross grass field, "château" in distance is stables, real château is beyond that); or take a taxi (allow €6, tel. 06 05 45 37 55).

IMPRESSIONIST EXCURSIONS: GIVERNY AND AUVERS-SUR-OISE

Giverny

Claude Monet's gardens at Giverny are like his paintings—brightly-colored patches that are messy but symmetrical. Flowers were his brushstrokes, a bit untamed and slap-dash, but part of a carefully composed mosaic. Monet spent his last (and most creative) years at Giverny (zhee-vayr-nee), the Camp David of Impressionism (1883–1926).

In 1883, middle-aged Claude Monet, his wife Alice, and their eight children from two families settled into a farmhouse here, 50 miles west of Paris. Monet, now a famous artist and happiest at home, would spend 40 years in Giverny, traveling less with each passing year. He built a pastoral paradise complete with a Japanese garden and a pond full of floating lilies.

In the last half of his life (beginning in 1912), Monet—the greatest visionary, literally, of his generation—began to go blind with cataracts. He used larger canvases and painted fewer details. The true subject is not really the famous water lilies, but the changing reflections on the surface of the pond—of the blue sky, white clouds, and green trees that line the shore.

All kinds of people flock to Giverny. Gardeners admire the earth-moving landscaping and layout, botanists find interesting new plants, and art lovers can see paintings they've long admired come to life. Fans enjoy wandering around the house where Monet spent half his life and seeing the boat he puttered around in, as well as the hen-house where his family got the morning omelets. It's a busy place, so come early or late.

There are two gardens, separated by train tracks and split by a busy road, plus the house, which displays Monet's prized collection of Japanese prints.

Buy your ticket and go directly to the garden by the house. Monet cleared this land of pine trees, and laid out symmetrical beds, split down the middle by a "grand alley" covered with iron trellises of climbing roses. He did his own landscaping: flowerbeds of lilies, iris, and clematis, and arbors of climbing roses. The arched trellises form a natural tunnel that leads your eye down the path (an effect exploited in his Rose Trellis paintings that you can see in Paris at the Marmottan Museum). Hollyhocks, daisies, and poppies are thrown together in Monet's careless manner. But each flowerbed has an overall color scheme that con to the look of the whole garden.

Take the underpass that leads to the Japanese bridge, under w willows, over the pond filled with water lilies, and past countless that leave artists aching for an easel. Monet landscaped like he pai he built an Impressionist mosaic of blocks of color. Once he'd plan gardens, he painted them, from every angle, at every time of day kinds of weather. Assisted by his favorite daughter, Blanche painter, who married Monet's son Jean from an earlier marria worked on several canvases at once, moving with the sun from one next. In a series of canvases, you can watch the sunlight sweep o gardens from early dawn to twilight.

Back on the other side, continue your visit with a wander t his mildly interesting home. The jammed gift shop at the exit is th skylit skylighted studio where Monet painted his water-lily maste

Hours and Cost: €5.50, €4 for gardens only, April–Oct T 10:00–18:00, closed Mon and Nov–March, tel. 02 32 51 94 65.

Avoiding Crowds: While lines may be long and tour grou trample the flowers, true fans still find magic in the gardens. Mi crowds by arriving before 10:00 (get in line) or after 16:00.

Getting to Giverny: Take the Rouen-bound train from Gare St. Lazare station to Vernon (about €22 round-trip, lor in service, know schedule before you go). From the Vernon tra tion to Monet's garden (2.5 miles one-way), you have three options: bus, taxi, and bike. The Vernon-Giverny **bus** is sched meet most trains (4/day, make sure the driver knows you plan to by bus and on which trip, otherwise he may not make the last C pickup). If you miss the last bus, find others to share a **taxi** (abc for up to 3, €12 for 4, tel. 06 07 34 36 68, tel. 06 76 08 50 78, 02 32 21 31 31). The ticket office at Monet's home in Giverny schedules and can call a taxi if you don't see one waiting by t stop. The return bus stop is on the main road from Vernon, just Monet's home. You can also rent a **bike** at the bar opposite th station, and follow a paved bike path *(piste cyclable)* that runs al abandoned railroad right-of-way (the bike path begins across th from Vernon in Veronnet). Pleasant little Vernon is good for kil hour if you missed your train.

Big tour companies do a Giverny day trip from Paris for €65; ask at your hotel.

Nearby Sight: The American Art Museum (Musée Américain, turn left when leaving Monet's place and walk 100 y devoted to American artists who followed Claude to Giverny. and his garden had a great influence on American artists of his da bright, modern gallery—with a good but small Mary Cassatt secti well-explained in English (same price and hours as Monet's

IMPRESSIONISM

Impressionism was a revolutionary movement in European art—the rage in the 1880s. Artists abandoned photo-realism in favor of a wispy style that captured light, glimmers, feelings, and impressions. Impressionists—capturing nature as a mosaic of short brushstrokes of different colors placed side by side, suggesting shimmering light—were committed to conveying the subtleties of nature. And there is no better nature for an Impressionist ready to paint than Monet's delightful mix of weeping willows, luminous clouds, delicate bridges, reflecting ponds...and lush water lilies.

though its most appealing feature might be its garden café (€9 salads, picnics possible at the far end).

Sleeping and Eating in Giverny: The adorable **Hôtel La Musardière**** is two blocks to the right out of Monet's home (Db-€52–70, Tb-€67–80, 132 rue Claude Monet, 27620 Giverny, tel. 02 32 21 03 18, fax 02 32 21 60 00, iraymonde@aol.com). You'll find a café and sandwich stand near the entrance to Monet's home, but the garden café at the American Art Museum is better—peaceful and surrounded by gardens Monet would appreciate.

Auvers-sur-Oise

There's no better place to get a feel for life during the Impressionist era than on the banks of the lazy Oise River, about a 45-minute drive (or one-hour train ride) northwest of Paris.

Auvers-sur-Oise (oh-vay soor wahz) is famous as the village where Vincent van Gogh committed suicide after relocating from southern France to be near his sympathetic doctor (Paul Gachet). But many other artists enjoyed this peaceful rural retreat, including Charles-François Daubigny, Jean-Baptiste-Camille Corot, Camille Pissarro, and Paul Cézanne.

Today, this modest little town opens doors to visitors with a handful of sights, walking trails leading to scenes painted by the artists (some with copies of the paintings posted), and a tranquil break from the big city. Come for the afternoon (some sights are closed in the morning) and avoid weekends if you can. Auvers has cafés, restaurants and bakeries with sandwiches. Most sights are closed Mondays and Tuesdays and from November to Easter.

Start at the eager-to-help **TI,** which has good information on all village sights, bus and RER train schedules, and a helpful €0.50 map of Auvers showing the walking routes, with famous art scenes posted

(April–Oct daily 9:30–12:30 & 14:00–18:00, Nov–March 9:30–12:30 & 14:00–17:00, tel. 01 30 36 10 06).

The skippable **Musée Daubigny**, one floor up from the TI, houses a small collection of works from artists who came to work with Monsieur Daubigny, an ardent defender of the Impressionists (€3, Wed–Sun 14:00–18:00, closed Mon–Tue).

The best way to spend a few hours in Auvers is to wander the streets between the TI and the château and find locations where paintings were set, and to visit the dazzling château (see below).

The most worthwhile sight in Auvers is **Château d'Auvers** (follow "Château" signs along the small road that runs above the TI, 15 min on foot). The entire château has been brilliantly transformed into a re-creation of life during the Impressionist years. Elaborate multimedia displays use headphones, video screens, and lasers to guide you along the Impressionist route that led from Montmartre to the sea, giving you a keen appreciation of life's daily struggles and pleasures during this time (€10, good family rates, open April–Sept Tue–Sun 10:30–18:00, closed Mon; Oct–March Tue–Sun 10:30–16:30, closed Mon; tel. 01 34 48 48 45).

You can walk through the same crow-infested wheat fields Vincent did. From the château, return to Auvers along the same road, but veer left when you reach rue Daubigny, then turn right on rue du Montier, and turn right again up a dirt trail. As you stroll through the wheat fields (can be muddy), ponder how amazed the artist would be at his popularity today. You can go as far as the cemetery and visit the tombs of Vincent and his brother Theo (15 min on trail), or take the dirt trail shortcut a few hundred yards before the cemetery, down to the **Church at Auvers** (see painting at Orsay Museum). From here, it's a short walk down to the train station and bus stop to Pontoise.

Some van Gogh fans make a pilgrimage to **Auberge Ravoux**, where Vincent died after shooting himself. Informative English-information plaques in the free courtyard explain Vincent's tragic life and wood steps lead to his small room (€5, daily 10:00–18:00, closed Nov–early March, includes 12-min slideshow and maybe a visit with English commentary, otherwise tour on your own). Food connoisseurs skip the visit and have a tasty lunch in the auberge's perfectly preserved restaurant (€27 menu).

Sleeping and Eating in Auvers: Auvers is a handy first or last stop for drivers using Charles de Gaulle airport. I can't imagine a better way to begin or end a trip than at **Chambre d'Hôtes la Ramure**, where charming Sylvie opens the doors of her lovely stone home to travelers. The three rooms have fireplaces, oak floors, high ceilings, and real furniture (Db-€60–70, 2 connecting rooms for families-€100, includes breakfast, no CC, 100 yards on road that leads from rear of Auvers' church, look for Chambre d'Hôtes sign, tel. 01 30 36 79 32, mobile 06 81 31 30 86, http://www.perso.club-internet.fr/laramure, laramure@club-internet.fr).

Or sleep luxuriously at the small, friendly, and polished **Hostellerie du Nord*****, with modern, spacious rooms and a seriously good restaurant requiring reservations (Db-€93–124, suites-€185, menus-€48-59, a block from train station at 6 rue du Général de Gaulle, tel. 01 30 36 70 74, fax 01 30 36 72 75, www.hostelleriedunord.fr). The place to eat in Auvers is **Auberge Ravoux,** unchanged, except for its prices, since 1876, when painters would meet here over a good meal (€27 menu, closed Sun eve and all day Mon, below TI on place de la Mairie, tel. 01 30 36 60 60).

Getting to Auvers: Frequent trains to Auvers (via Pontoise) leave from Gare du Nord and Gare St. Lazare, but by far the easiest trip is via RER-C to Pontoise (catch in Paris at St. Michel, Orsay, Invalides, or Pont de l'Alma stops, 2-3/hr, 40 min, €5). Pontoise is the end of the line. To get to Auvers, a 10-minute ride away, take the train (if it's leaving soon) or hop on bus #95 (runs more frequently than train, catch it to the right out of the station; look for the posted schedule—you're at "Chemin de la Gare" in Pontoise and you want the "Marie" stop in Auvers). Taxis wait outside the Pontoise station to the left (€10 to Auvers, tel. 01 30 75 95 95, for a bit more money the same taxi can pick you up in Auvers for the return). If you arrive in Auvers by train, you can reach the TI by turning left on the main road leaving Auvers' station (look for signs, TI has bus schedules to Pontoise). For a taxi in Auvers, call 06 71 60 50 06 or 06 08 24 54 88.

By **car,** Auvers is about 45 minutes northwest of Paris, off autoroute A-15 (exit #7, then follow direction: Beauvais).

DISNEYLAND PARIS

Europe's Disneyland is a remake of California's, with most of the same rides and smiles. The main difference is that Mickey Mouse speaks French (and you can buy wine with your lunch). My kids went ducky. It's easy to get to, and worth a day, if Paris is handier than Florida or California. Saturday, Sunday, Wednesday, public holidays, and any day in July and August are the most crowded. After dinner, crowds are gone. Food is fun and not outrageously priced. (Still, many smuggle in a picnic.) The free FASTPASS system is a worthwhile timesaver (get FASTPASS card at entry, good for 5 most popular rides, at ride insert card in machine to get a window of time to enter—often within about 45 min). You'll also save time by buying your tickets ahead (at airport TIs, over 100 Métro stations, or along the Champs-Elysées at the TI, Disney Store, or Virgin Megastore). Disney brochures are in every Paris hotel. For Disneyland information and reservations, call 01 60 30 60 30 (www.disneylandparis.com).

Walt Disney Studios: This zone, which opened in 2002 next to the original 10-year-old amusement park, has a Hollywood focus geared for an older crowd, with animation, special effects, and movie magic "rides." The Aerosmith Rock 'n' Roller Coaster is nothing special. The highlight is the Stunt Show Spectacular, filling a huge back-lot stadium five times a day for 45 minutes of car chases and thriller filming tips. An actual movie sequence is filmed with stunt drivers, audience bit players, and brash MTV-style hosts.

Cost: Disneyland Paris and Walt Disney Studios charge the same and you pay separately for each. Only the three-day passes (called "Hopper" tickets) include entry to both parks. From April through October, adults pay approximately €40 for one day (2 days-€72, 3-day "Hopper" ticket-€110) and kids ages 3–11 pay €30 for one day (2 days-€62, 3-day "Hopper" ticket-€82). Regular prices are discounted about 25 percent off-season. Kids under 3 are always free. Ask about summer evening deals (lower entry prices from 17:00 to 23:00), but these discounts may be discontinued. The only budget deal (and, I think, the only way the Walt Disney Studios are worth visiting) is to pay for a full-price Walt Disney Studios ticket, which gets you into the Disneyland Park for free during the last three hours of that day.

Hours: Both parks are open April–June daily 9:00–20:00, July–Aug daily 9:00–23:00, and Sept–March Mon–Fri 10:00–20:00, Sat–Sun 9:00–20:00.

Sleeping at Disneyland: Most are better off sleeping in reality (Paris), though with direct buses and freeways to both airports, Disneyland makes a convenient first- or last-night stop. Seven different Disney-owned hotels offer accommodations at or near the park in all price ranges. Prices are impossible to pin down as they vary by season and by the "package deal" you choose (deals that include park entry are usually a better value). The cheapest is **Davy Crockett,** but you'll need a car. **Hôtel Santa Fe**** offers the best midrange value, with shuttle service to the park every 12 minutes. The most expensive is **Disneyland Hotel****,** right at the park entry, about twice the price of the Santa Fe. To reserve any Disneyland hotel, call 01 60 30 60 30, fax 01 60 30 60 65, or check www.disneylandparis.com. The prices you'll be quoted include entry to the park.

Transportation Connections—Disneyland Paris

By train: TGV trains connect Disneyland directly with **Charles de Gaulle airport** (10 min), the **Loire Valley** (1.5 hrs, Tours-St. Pierre des Corps station, 15 min from Amboise), **Avignon** (3 hrs, TGV station), **Lyon** (2 hrs, Part Dieu station), and **Nice** (6 hrs, main station).

By RER: The slick one-hour RER trip is the best way to Disneyland from downtown Paris. Take RER line A-4 to Marne-la-Vallée-Chessy (from Charles de Gaulle-Etoile, Auber, Châtelet-Les Halles, or Gare de Lyon stations, about €7.75 each way, hrly, drops you one hour later right in the park). The last train back to Paris leaves shortly after midnight. Be sure to get a ticket that is good on both the

RER and Métro; when returning, remember to use your same RER ticket for your Métro connection in Paris.

By bus: Both airports have direct shuttle buses to Disneyland Paris (€13, daily 8:30–19:45, every 45 min).

By car: Disneyland is about 40 minutes east of Paris on the A-4 autoroute (direction Nancy/Metz, exit #14). Parking is €8 per day at the park.

SLEEPING

I've focused on three safe, handy, and colorful neighborhoods: the village-like rue Cler (near the Eiffel Tower), artsy and trendy Marais (near place de la Bastille), and lively, park-packed Luxembourg (on the Left Bank).

For each neighborhood, I list good hotels, helpful hints, and restaurants (see Eating chapter, page 313). Before choosing a hotel, read the descriptions of the three neighborhoods closely. Each offers different pros and cons, and your neighborhood is as important as your hotel for the success of your trip. Less expensive and less central accommodations are also listed in various chapters: Versailles, Chartres, Day Trips (Fontainebleau, Giverny, Auvers-sur-Oise, and Disneyland Paris), and Shopping (place de Bercy).

Reserve ahead for Paris—the sooner the better. Conventions clog Paris in September (worst), October, May, and June (very tough). Holidays are busy. In 2004, expect crowds during Easter week (April 10–17), Labor Day weekend (April 30-May 2), VE Day (May 7–9), Ascension weekend (May 20–23), Pentecost weekend (May 28–31), Bastille Day (July 14), Assumption (Aug 15), All Saints' Day weekend (Oct 29–Nov 1), Armistice Day (Nov 11–14), and the winter holidays (Dec 20–Jan 5). In August, when Paris is quiet, some hotels offer lower rates. But August is also a time when paying extra for a place with air-conditioning can be money well spent. For tips on reserving hotels, see "Making Reservations," below.

A comfortable hotel in Paris costs less than a comparable hotel in London, Amsterdam, Rome, or in most major U.S. cities. It's a good hotel city. Still, reserve as far as possible in advance for the best values. I like places that are clean, small, central, traditional, friendly, and a good value. Most places I list have at least four of these six virtues.

In this book, the price for a double room will normally range from €40 (very simple, toilet and shower down the hall) to €250 (grand lobbies, maximum plumbing, and more), with most clustering around €90–120.

If you have any trouble finding a room using my listings, try www.parishotel.com and www.viamichelin.com. You can select from various neighborhood areas (e.g., Eiffel Tower area), give the dates of your visit and preferred price range, and presto—they'll list options with rates. You'll find the hotels listed in this book to be better located and more objectively reviewed, but as a last resort, the Web site services are handy.

Hotels

The French have a simple hotel rating system depending on amenities (zero through four stars, indicated in this book by * through ****). One star is simple, two has most of the comforts, and three is generally a two-star with a fancier lobby and more elaborately designed rooms. Four stars offer more luxury than you have time to appreciate. Two- and three-star hotels are required to have an English-speaking staff. Nearly all hotels we recommend have someone who speaks English. One- and two-star hotels are the best budget values, though some three-star hotels (and even a few four-star hotels) can justify the extra cost. Generally, the number of stars does not reflect room size. Lately, the star system is less reliable. Unclassified hotels (no stars) can be bargains or depressing dumps. Look before you leap and lay before you pay (upon departure).

Hotels in France must charge a daily room tax *(taxe du séjour)* that is normally added to the bill (about €1 per person per day). While some hotels include it in the price list, most add it to your bill.

Old, characteristic, budget Parisian hotels have always been cramped. Retrofitted with toilets, private showers, and elevators (as most are today), they are even more cramped. Recommended hotels have an elevator unless otherwise noted.

Most hotels have a few singles, triples, and quads. While groups sleep cheap, traveling alone can be expensive. Singles (except for the rare closet-type rooms that fit only 1 twin bed) are simply doubles used by one person—so they cost about the same as a double. Because rooms with double beds and showers are cheaper than rooms with twin beds and baths, room prices vary within each hotel. A triple and a double are often the same room, with a small double bed and a sliver single, so a third person sleeps very cheaply. Quad rooms usually have two double beds. Hotels cannot legally allow more people in a room than what's shown on their price list.

Receptionists often don't mention the cheaper rooms (they assume you want a private bathroom). Study the price list on the Web site or posted at the desk. These are the types of rooms and beds:

Une chambre sans douche or *sans WC*: Room without a private shower or toilet (uncommon these days)

Une chambre avec cabinet de toilette: Room with a toilet but no shower (some hotels charge for down-the-hall showers)

Une chambre avec salle de bain: Room with private bathtub and toilet.

Une chambre avec salle douche: Room with private shower and toilet
Chambres communiquantes: Connecting rooms (ideal for families)
Un grand lit: Double bed (55 inches wide)
Deux petits lits: Twin beds (30–36 inches wide)
Deux lits séparés: Two beds separated
Un lit de cent-soixante: Queen-size bed (literally 160 centimeters, or 63 inches wide)

You can save as much as €20–25 by finding the rare room without a private shower or toilet. A room with a bathtub costs €5–10 more than a room with a shower and is generally larger. Hotels often have more rooms with tubs than showers and are inclined to give you a room with a tub (which the French prefer).

A double bed is €5–10 cheaper than twins, though rooms with twin beds tend to be larger and French double beds are smaller than American double beds. Hotels rarely offer queen-size beds (a bed that's 63 inches wide—most doubles are 55). To see if a hotel has queen-size beds, ask, "*Avez-vous un lit de cent-soixante?,*" (ah-vay-voo uh lee duh sahn-swah-sahnt). Some hotels push two twins together under king-size sheets and blankets.

If you prefer a double bed (instead of twins) and a shower (instead of a tub), you need to ask for it—and you'll save up to €30 at more expensive hotels. If you'll take either twins or a double, ask generically for *une chambre pour deux* (room for two) to avoid being needlessly turned away.

You'll almost always have the option of breakfast at your hotel, which is pleasant and convenient, but it's more than the price of breakfast at the corner café, with less ambience (though you get more coffee at your hotel). Some hotels offer only the classic continental breakfast for about €6–8, but others offer buffet breakfasts for about €8–15 (cereal, yogurt, fruit, cheese, croissants, juice, and hard-boiled eggs)—which I usually spring for. While hotels hope you'll buy their breakfast, it's optional unless otherwise noted.

Rooms are safe. Still, keep cameras and money out of sight. Towels aren't routinely replaced every day; drip-dry and conserve. If that French Lincoln-log pillow isn't your idea of comfort, American-style pillows (and extra blankets) are sometimes in the closet or available on request. To get a pillow, ask for "*Un oreiller, s'il vous plaît*" (un oh-ray-yay, see voo play). If you're planning to visit Paris in the summer, the extra expense of an air-conditioned room can be money well spent. When using the air-conditioner, remember that 20 degrees Celsius = 68 degrees Fahrenheit (also see thermometer diagram in appendix).

Get advice from your hotel for safe parking (consider long-term parking at either airport—Orly is closer—and a taxi in). Garages are plentiful (€14–23/day, with special rates through some hotels). Meters are free in August.

SLEEP CODE

To give maximum information in a minimum of space, I use the following code to describe the accommodations. Prices listed are per room, not per person. Unless otherwise noted, breakfast is included (but usually optional). English is generally spoken.

- **S** = Single room (or price for one person in a double).
- **D** = Double or Twin room. "Double beds" are often two twins sheeted together and are usually big enough for nonromantic couples.
- **T** = Triple (generally a double bed with a single).
- **Q** = Quad (usually two double beds).
- **b** = Private bathroom with toilet and shower or tub.
- **s** = Private shower or tub only (the toilet is down the hall).
- **no CC** = Doesn't accept credit cards; pay in local cash.
- **SE** = Speaks English. This code is used only when it seems predictable that you'll encounter English-speaking staff.
- **NSE** = Does not speak English. Used only when it's unlikely you'll encounter English-speaking staff.

According to this code, a couple staying at a "Db-€140, SE" hotel would pay a total of €140 (about $155) for a double room with a private bathroom. The hotel accepts credit cards or Italian cash (euros); you can assume a hotel takes credit cards unless you see "no CC" in the listing. The staff speaks English.

To help you sort easily through these listings, I've divided the rooms into three categories based on the price for a standard double room with bath:

- $$$ **Higher Priced:** Most rooms more than €180.
- $$ **Moderately Priced:** Most rooms between €130–180.
- $ **Lower Priced:** Most rooms under €130.

Your hotelier can direct you to the nearest Internet café (*café internet*, kah-fay an-ter-net) and self-service launderette (*laverie automatique*, lah-vay-ree oh-to-mah-teek).

Hostels

Parisian hostels charge about €25 per bed. Some require a hostel membership. Get a hostel card before you go if you need one. Travelers of any age are welcome if they don't mind dorm-style accommodations and meeting other travelers. Travelers without a hostel card can generally spend the night for a small, extra "one-night membership" fee at those places requiring membership. Cheap meals are sometimes available, and kitchen facilities are usually provided for do-it-yourselfers.

Apartments

It's easy, though not necessarily cheaper, to rent a furnished apa in Paris. Consider this option if you're either traveling with a fa staying two weeks or longer. For listings, see the end of this cha

Country Code and Exchange Rate

To phone France, you'll need to know its country code: 33. France from the United States or Canada, dial 011 - 33 - local n (without the initial 0). If calling France from another European c dial 00 - 33 - local number (without the initial 0).

The exchange rate: €1 = about $1.10

Making Reservations

Reserve ahead for Paris, the sooner the better. To reserve from h mail, fax, or call the hotel. E-mail is preferred (see the reservatio online at www.ricksteves.com/reservation). Phone and fax costs a sonable. To fax, use the form in the appendix. Most hotels lis accustomed to English-only speakers.

If you're not sure how long you'll stay, guess long (it's very add days at the last minute), but then cancel once you know t length of your stay—some hotels require seven days notice.

A two-night stay in August would be "2 nights, 16/8 18/8/04"—Europeans write the date day/month/year, and Eu hotel jargon uses your day of departure.

If you e-mail or fax a reservation request and receive a re with rates and stating that rooms are available, this is not a con tion. You must confirm that the rates are fine and that inde want the room. One night's deposit is generally required. A cre will usually be accepted as a deposit, though you may need to signed traveler's check or a bank draft in the local currency. Do your credit-card number as a deposit unless you're absolutely su want to stay at the hotel on the dates you requested and are cle they have a room available. If you don't show up, you'll be bi one night, and even if you cancel, you may not receive your deposit back.

Reconfirm your reservation a few days in advance for safety. to honor (or cancel) your reservation.

RUE CLER ORIENTATION

Rue Cler is a safe, tidy, village-like pedestrian street. It's so Fren when I step out of my hotel in the morning, I feel like I must hav a poodle in a previous life. How such coziness lodged itself betw high-powered government district and the wealthy Eiffel Tow Invalides areas, I'll never know. This is a neighborhood of wid lined boulevards, stately apartment buildings, and lots of Ame

The American Church, American Library, American University, and many of my readers call this area home.

Become a local at a rue Cler café for breakfast or join the afternoon crowd for *une bière pression* (a draft beer). On rue Cler, you can eat and browse your way through a street full of tart shops, delis, cheese shops, and colorful outdoor produce stalls. Afternoon *boules* (lawn bowling) on the Esplanade des Invalides is a relaxing spectator sport (look for the dirt area to the upper right as you face Les Invalides; see Boules sidebar on page 67). The manicured gardens behind the golden dome of Les Invalides are free, peaceful, and filled with flowers (close at about 19:00). Take an evening stroll above the river through the parkway between pont de l'Alma and pont des Invalides.

For an after-dinner cruise on the Seine, it's a 15-minute walk to the river and the Bateaux-Mouches (see page 353). For a post-dinner cruise on foot, saunter into Champ de Mars park to admire the glowing Eiffel Tower (see also Nightlife, page 350, and Paris with Children, page 336).

Cross the Champ de Mars park to mix it up with bargain-hunters at the twice-weekly open-air market, **Marché Boulevard de Grenelle,** under the Métro a few blocks southwest of Champ de Mars park (Wed and Sun until 12:30, between Mo: Dupleix and Mo: La Motte Picquet-Grenelle). The Epicerie de la Tour **grocery** is open until midnight (197 rue de Grenelle). Rue St. Dominique is the area's boutique-browsing street. **Cyber World Café** is at 20 rue de l'Exposition (open daily, tel. 01 53 59 96 54).

Your neighborhood **TI** is at the Eiffel Tower (May–Sept daily 11:00–18:40, closed Oct–April, all-Paris TI tel. 08 36 68 31 12). There's a **post office** at the end of rue Cler on avenue de la Motte Picquet, and a handy **SNCF train office** at 78 rue St. Dominique (Mon–Fri 9:00–19:00, Sat 10:00–12:30 & 14:00–18:00, closed Sun).

The **American Church and Franco-American Center** is the community center for Americans living in Paris and should be one of your first stops if you're planning to stay awhile (reception open Mon–Sat 9:00–22:00, Sun 9:00–19:30, 65 quai d'Orsay, tel. 01 40 62 05 00). Pick up copies of the *Paris Voice* for a monthly review of Paris entertainment, and *France-U.S.A. Contacts* for information on housing and employment through the community of 30,000 Americans living in Paris. The interdenominational services at 11:00 on Sunday, the coffee hour after church, and the free Sunday concerts (Sept–May 18:00, not every week) are a great way to make some friends and get a taste of émigré life in Paris.

Key **Métro** stops are Ecole Militaire, La Tour Maubourg, and Invalides. The **RER-C** line runs from the Pont de l'Alma and Invalides stations, serving Versailles to the west; Auvers-sur-Oise to the north; and the Orsay Museum, Latin Quarter (St. Michel stop), and Austerlitz train station to the east.

Smart travelers take advantage of these helpful **bus routes** (see Rue

Rue Cler Hotels

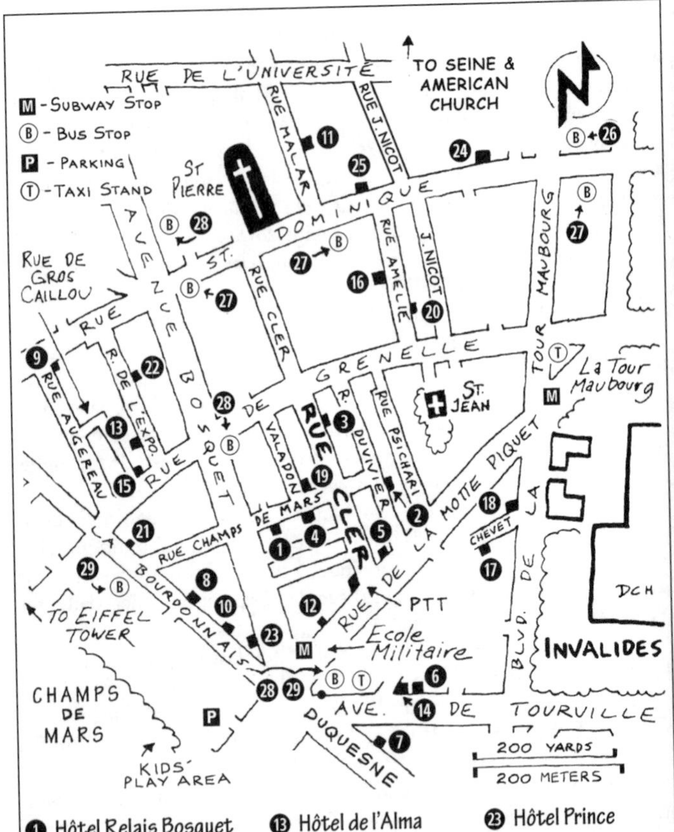

1. Hôtel Relais Bosquet
2. Hôtel Beaugency
3. Hôtel Leveque
4. Hôtel du Champ de Mars
5. Hôtel la Motte Piquet
6. Hôtel le Tourville
7. Hôtel Splendid
8. Hôtel de la Bourdonnais
9. Hôtel Londres Eiffel
10. Eber-Mars Hôtel
11. Hôtel de la Tulipe
12. Hôtel Royal Phare
13. Hôtel de l'Alma
14. Hôtel de Turenne
15. Hôtel de la Paix
16. Hôtel les Jardins Eiffel & Hôtel Amélie
17. Hôtel Muguet
18. Hôtel de l'Empereur
19. Hôtel du Cadran
20. Best Western Park Hotel
21. Hôtel Kensington
22. Hôtel de la Tour Eiffel
23. Hôtel Prince
24. Hôtel le Pavillon
25. SNCF Office
26. Bus #28 to St. Lazare Station
27. Bus #69 to Orsay, Louvre & Marais
28. Bus #92 to Arc de Triomphe
29. Bus #87 to Lux. Garden

Cler Hotels map for stop locations): Line #69 runs along rue St. Dominique and serves Les Invalides, Orsay, Louvre, Marais, and Père Lachaise cemetery (see Bus #69 Sightseeing Tour, page 239). Line #63 runs along the river (the quai d'Orsay), serving the Latin Quarter along boulevard St. Germain to the east, and Trocadéro and the Marmottan Museum to the west. Line #92 runs along avenue Bosquet north to the Champs-Elysées and Arc de Triomphe and south to the Montparnasse Tower. Line #87 runs on avenue de la Bourdonnais and serves St. Sulpice, Luxembourg Garden, and the Sèvres-Babylone shopping area. Line #28 runs on boulevard La Tour Maubourg and serves Gare St. Lazare.

In the Rue Cler Neighborhood
(7th arrondissement, Mo: Ecole Militaire or La Tour Maubourg)

Rue Cler is the glue that holds this handsome neighborhood together. From here you can walk to the Eiffel Tower, Napoleon's Tomb, the Seine River, and the Orsay and Rodin Museums. Hotels here are relatively spacious and a great value, considering the elegance of the neighborhood and the high prices of the more cramped hotels of the trendy Marais.

Many of my readers stay in this neighborhood. If you want to disappear into Paris, choose a hotel away from the rue Cler, or in the other neighborhoods I list. And if nightlife matters, sleep elsewhere. The first five hotels listed below are within Camembert-smelling distance of rue Cler; the others are within a 5- to 10-minute stroll.

The Heart of Rue Cler

$$$ Hôtel Relais Bosquet*** is modern, spacious, and a bit upscale, with snazzy, air-conditioned rooms, electric darkness blinds, and big beds. Gerard and his staff are politely formal and friendly (Sb-€125–150, standard Db-€145, spacious Db-€165, extra bed-€30, parking-€14, 19 rue du Champ de Mars, tel. 01 47 05 25 45, fax 01 45 55 08 24, www.relaisbosquet.com).

$$$ Hôtel la Motte Picquet***, at the end of rue Cler, is like staying in an antique dollhouse. Most of its 18 adorable, spendy rooms face a busy street, but the twins are on the quieter rue Cler (Sb-€105–121, Db-€129-165, 30 avenue de la Motte Picquet, tel. 01 47 05 09 57, fax 01 47 05 74 36, www.paris-hotel-mottepicquet.com).

$$ Hôtel Beaugency***, on a quieter street a short block off rue Cler, has 30 small, cookie-cutter rooms. Rooms have automated air-conditioning that shuts off once you go to bed (Sb-€105, Db-€115-125, Tb-€145, first breakfast free with this book, 21 rue Duvivier, tel. 01 47 05 01 63, fax 01 45 51 04 96, www.hotel-beaugency.com).

Warning: The next two hotels listed here—while good values—are busy with my readers (reserve long in advance).

$ Grand Hôtel Lévêque** is ideally located, with a helpful staff

(Christophe and female Pascale SE), a singing maid, and a Starshi *Enterprise* elevator. It's a classic old hotel with well-designed rooms tha have all the comforts, including air-conditioning and ceiling fans. It feel a bit frayed at the edges but remains a solid value (S-€56, Db-€86-106 Tb-€122 for 2 adults and 1 child only, breakfast-€7, first breakfast fre for readers of this book, 29 rue Cler, tel. 01 47 05 49 15, fax 01 45 50 4 36, www.hotel-leveque.com, info@hotelleveque.com).

$ Hôtel du Champ de Mars**, with charming pastel rooms an helpful English-speaking owners Françoise and Stephane, is a homie rue Cler option. This plush little hotel has a Provence-style, small-tow feel from top to bottom. Rooms are small, but comfortable and an excel lent value. Single rooms can work as tiny doubles (Sb-€68, Db-€72–78 Tb-€94, 30 yards off rue Cler at 7 rue du Champ de Mars, tel. 01 4 51 52 30, fax 01 45 51 64 36, www.hotel-du-champ-de-mars.com stg@club-internet.fr).

Near Rue Cler

The following listings are a 5- to 10-minute walk from rue Cler, nea Métro stop Ecole Militaire or RER stop Pont de l'Alma.

$$$ Hôtel le Tourville**** is the most classy and expensive of m rue Cler listings. This four-star place is surprisingly intimate and friendl from its designer lobby and vaulted breakfast area to its pretty but sma pastel rooms (small standard Db-€145, superior Db-€215, Db with privat terrace-€240, junior suite for 3–4 people-€310, air-con, 16 avenue d Tourville, tel. 01 47 05 62 62, fax 01 47 05 43 90, hotel@tourville.com).

$$$ Hôtel Splendid*** is Art Deco modern, professional, an worth your while if you land one of its three suites with great Eiffe Tower views. Fifth-floor rooms have small terraces (Db-€126–150, D suite-€200-225, 29 avenue de Tourville, tel. 01 45 51 24 77, fax 01 4 18 94 60, www.hotels-exclusive.com/hotels/splendid).

$$$ Hôtel de la Bourdonnais*** is a *très* Parisian place, mixin slightly faded Old World elegance with professional service, comfort able public spaces, and mostly spacious, traditionally decorated room (avoid the few *petite* rooms, Sb-€120, Db-€150, Tb-€160, Qb-€180, 5 person suite-€210, air-con, 111 avenue de la Bourdonnais, tel. 01 47 0 45 42, fax 01 45 55 75 54, www.hotellabourdonnais.fr).

$$ Hôtel Londres Eiffel*** is my closest listing to the Eiffel Towe and Champ de Mars park. It offers immaculate, warmly decorate rooms, cozy public spaces, Internet access, and air-conditioning. Th helpful staff takes good care of their guests. It's less convenient to th Métro (10-min walk); handy bus #69 and the RER stop Pont de l'Alm are better options (Sb-€95-99, Db-€110-140, Tb-€150-165, extr bed-€17, 1 rue Augerau, tel. 01 45 51 63 02, fax 01 47 05 28 96, www .londres-eiffel.com, info@londres-eiffel.com).

$$ Eber-Mars Hôtel**, with helpful owner Jean-Marc, is a goo midrange value with larger-than-average rooms and a beam-me-up-Jacques, coffin-sized elevator (small Db-€75, large Db-€90-110, Tb-€135, extra bed-€25, pricey €10 breakfast, 117 avenue de la Bourdonnais, tel. 01 47 05 42 30, fax 01 47 05 45 91, www.hotelseber.com).

$$ Hôtel de la Tulipe*** is a unique place three blocks from rue Cler toward the river, with friendly Bernhard behind the desk. The smallish but artistically decorated rooms—each one different—come with little, stylish bathrooms and surround a seductive wood-beamed lounge and a peaceful, leafy courtyard (Db-€110-140, Tb-€170, 2-room suite-€220-250, no elevator, 33 rue Malar, tel. 01 45 51 67 21, fax 01 47 53 96 37, www.hoteldelatulipe.com).

$ Hôtel Royal Phare** is a simple yet solid value facing the busy Ecole Militaire Métro stop. Rooms are unimaginative but pink-pastel-comfortable; those on the courtyard are far quieter (Sb-€62, Db-€72-77, Tb-€92, 40 avenue de la Motte Picquet, tel. 01 47 05 57 30, fax 01 45 51 64 41, www.hotel-royalphare-paris.com).

$ Hôtel de l'Alma*** is well-located on "restaurant row," with cheery rooms, small bathrooms, a nice little courtyard, and very reasonable rates only with this book (Sb-€80, Db-€90, includes breakfast, 32 rue de l'Exposition, tel. 01 47 05 45 70, fax 01 45 51 84 47, www.alma-paris-hotel.com, Carine SE).

$ Hôtel de Turenne,** with sufficiently comfortable, air-conditioned rooms and so-so bed quality, is a good value particularly when it's hot. It also has five truly single rooms and several connecting rooms (Sb-€61, Db-€71–83, Tb-€98, extra bed-€10, 20 avenue de Tourville, tel. 01 47 05 99 92, fax 01 45 56 06 04, hotel.turenne.paris7@wanadoo.fr).

$ Hôtel de la Paix **, a smart hotel located away from the fray on a quiet little street, offers 23 plush, well-designed rooms and is a good value (Sb-€61, Db-€91-100, Tb-€110-120, fine buffet breakfast, 19 rue du Gros-Caillou, tel. 01 45 51 86 17, fax 01 45 55 93 28, hotel.de.la.paix@wanadoo.fr).

Near Métro: La Tour Maubourg

The next three listings are within two blocks of the intersection of avenue de la Motte Picquet and boulevard de la Tour Maubourg.

$$$ Hôtel les Jardins Eiffel*,** on a quiet street, feels like a modern motel, but earns its three stars with professional service, its own parking garage, a spacious lobby, and 80 comfortable, air-conditioned rooms—some with private balconies (ask for a room *avec petit balcon*). Even better: Readers of this book get free buffet breakfasts (Db-€130–€160, extra bed-€21 or free for a child, parking-€20/day, 8 rue Amélie, tel. 01 47 05 46 21, fax 01 45 55 28 08, www.hoteljardinseiffel.com, Marie SE).

$$ Hôtel Muguet,** a peaceful, stylish and immaculate hotel, gives you three-star comfort for a two-star price. This delightful hotel offers 48 tasteful, air-conditioned rooms, a greenhouse lounge, and a small garden courtyard. The hands-on owner, Catherine, gives her guests a res secure home in Paris (Sb-€87, Db-€97–105, Tb-€135, 11 rue C tel. 01 47 05 05 93, fax 01 45 50 25 37, www.hotelmuguet.com).

$ Hôtel de l'Empereur** lacks intimacy but is roomy and fair value. Its 38 pleasant, woody rooms come with sturdy furnit all the comforts except air-conditioning. Streetside rooms hav but some noise; fifth-floor rooms have small balconies and Nap views (Sb-€70–80, Db-€80-100, Tb-€120, Qb-€140, 2 rue Chev 01 45 55 88 02, fax 01 45 51 88 54, www.hotelempereur.com, Al

The Other Side Of Champs de Mars Park

To stay in a peaceful neighborhood with many qualities of the r area (in the 7th *arrondissement*), cross Champs de Mars park an the 15th *arrondissement*. While it's a 10- to 15-minute walk to r you get more space for your money and fewer fellow Americans.

$$ Hôtel Ares*** is a handsome hotel situated on a quiet block toward the river from avenue de le Motte Picquet. The hot classy lobby with elbow room, and comfortable rooms you can stre in (Sb-€105, Db-€122, Tb-€155, Qb-€180, between avenue de and avenue de Grenelle—not to be confused with rue de Grene crosses rue Cler—at 7 rue du Général Larminat, Mo: La Motte P Grenelle, tel. 01 47 34 74 04, fax 01 47 34 48 56, aresotel@easyne

Lesser Values in the Rue Cler Area

Given this fine area, these are acceptable last choices.

$$$ Hôtel du Cadran*,** while perfectly located, has a shin but no charm and tight, narrow, pricey rooms (Db-€152–170, du Champ de Mars, air-con, tel. 01 40 62 67 00, fax 01 40 62 www.hotelducadran.com).

$$$ Best Western Park Hotel*,** is a dead-quiet, concre ness hotel with all the comforts, a friendly staff, pleasant if u tional rooms, and a nifty and spacious rooftop terrace (Db-€1 17 bis rue Amélie, tel. 01 45 55 10 01, fax 01 47 05 28, 68, r tion@eiffelpark.com).

$$ Hôtel Prince,** just across avenue Bosquet from th Militaire Métro stop, has good-enough rooms, many overlookin street (Sb-€73, Db-€87-113, 66 avenue Bosquet, tel. 01 47 05 fax 01 47 53 06 62, www.hotel-paris-prince.com).

$ Hôtel Amélie** is another midrange possibility (Db-€95-10 Amélie, tel. 01 45 51 74 75, fax 01 45 56 93 55, hotelamelie@wana

$ Hôtel Kensington** is impersonal with miniscule rooms, fair value (Sb-€53, Db-€67–82, 79 avenue de la Bourdonnais, te 05 74 00, fax 01 47 05 25 81, www.hotel-kensington.com).

$ Hôtel de la Tour Eiffel** is a modest little place wit priced rooms, but cheap furnishings and foam mattresses (Sb-€6

€80, Tb-€100, 17 rue de l'Exposition, tel. 01 47 05 14 75, fax 01 47 53 99 46, Muriel SE).

$ Hôtel le Pavillon** is quiet, with basic rooms, no elevator, and cramped halls in a charming location (Sb-€72, Db-€80, Tb, Qb, or Quint/b-€105, 54 rue St. Dominique, tel. 01 45 51 42 87, fax 01 45 51 32 79, patrickpavillon@aol.com).

MARAIS ORIENTATION

Those interested in a more Soho/Greenwich Village locale should make the Marais their Parisian home. Only 15 years ago, it was a forgotten Parisian backwater, but now the Marais is one of Paris' most popular residential, tourist, and shopping areas. This is jumbled, medieval Paris at its finest, where classy stone mansions sit alongside trendy bars, antique shops, and fashion-conscious boutiques. The streets are a fascinating parade of artists, students, tourists, immigrants, and babies in strollers munching baguettes. The Marais is also known as a hub of the Parisian gay and lesbian scene. This area is *sans* doubt livelier (and louder) than the rue Cler area.

In the Marais, you have these sights close at hand: Picasso Museum, Carnavalet Museum, Victor Hugo's House, Jewish Art and History Museum, and the Pompidou Center. You're also a manageable walk from Paris' two islands (Ile St. Louis and Ile de la Cité), home to Notre-Dame and the Sainte-Chapelle. The Opéra Bastille, Promenade Plantée park, place des Vosges (Paris' oldest square), Jewish Quarter (rue des Rosiers), and nightlife-packed rue de Lappe are also walkable. (For sight descriptions, see "Northeast Paris," page 41; for the Opéra, see page 39.)

The Marais has two good open-air markets: the sprawling Marché de la Bastille on place de la Bastille (Thu and Sun until 12:30) and the more intimate Marché de la place d'Aligre (daily 9:00–12:00, a few blocks behind Opéra on place d'Aligre). Two little grocery shops are open until 23:00 on rue St. Antoine (near intersection with rue Castex).

The nearest **TIs** are in the Louvre (Wed–Mon 10:00–19:00, closed Tue) and Gare de Lyon (daily 8:00–20:00, all-Paris TI tel. 08 36 68 31 12). Most banks and other services are on the main drag, rue de Rivoli, which becomes rue St. Antoine. For your Parisian Sears, find the **BHV** next to the Hôtel de Ville. Marais **post offices** are on rue Castex and on the corner of rue Pavée and rue des Francs Bourgeois. A rare Internet café, @aron, is at 3 rue des Ecouffes (tel. 01 42 71 05 07).

Métro service to the Marais neighborhood is excellent, with direct service to the Louvre, Champs-Elysées, Arc de Triomphe, La Défense (all on line 1), rue Cler area (line 8 from Bastille stop) and four major train stations: Gare de Lyon, Gare du Nord, Gare de l'Est, and Gare d'Austerlitz. Key Métro stops in the Marais are, from east to west: Bastille, St. Paul, and Hôtel de Ville (Sully-Morland, Pont Marie, and Rambuteau stops are also handy). There are also several helpful **bus routes:** Line #69 on rue St. Antoine takes you to the Louvre, Orsay, and Rodin museums, plus Napoleon's Tomb, and ends at the Eiffel Tower. Line #86 runs down boulevard Henri IV, crossing Ile St. Louis and serving the Latin Quarter along boulevard St. Germain. Line #96 runs on rues Turenne and François Miron and serves the Louvre and boulevard St. Germain (near Luxembourg Garden), ending at the Gare Montparnasse. Line #65 gets you to the Gare d'Austerlitz, Gare de l'Est, and Gare du Nord train stations from place de la Bastille.

You'll find **taxi stands** on place de la Bastille, on the north side of rue St. Antoine (where it meets rue Castex), and on the south side of rue St. Antoine (in front of St. Paul church).

In the Marais Neighborhood (4th arrondissement)

The Marais runs from the Pompidou Center to the Bastille (a 15-min walk), with most hotels located a few blocks north of the main east–west drag, the rue de Rivoli/rue St. Antoine. It's about 15 minutes on foot from any hotel in this area to Notre-Dame, Ile St. Louis, and the Latin Quarter. Strolling home (day or night) from Notre-Dame along the Ile St. Louis is marvelous.

$$$ Hôtel de la Place des Vosges** is so well-located—in a medieval building on a quiet street just off place des Vosges—that the staff can take or leave your business (Sb-€90, Db-€140, 16 rooms, one flight of stairs then elevator, 12 rue de Birague, Mo: St. Paul, tel. 01 42 72 60 46, fax 01 42 72 02 64, hotel.place.des.vosges@gofornet.com).

$$ Hôtel Castex***, newly-renovated and on a quiet street near the place de la Bastille, feels Spanish from the formal entry to the red-tiled floors and dark wood accents. A clever system of connecting rooms allows families total privacy between two rooms. Rooms are slender but sharp and air-conditioned, and the new elevator is big (Sb-€115, Db-€140, Tb-€220, good buffet breakfast-€8, just off place de la Bastille and rue St. Antoine, 5 rue Castex, Mo: Bastille, tel. 01 42 72 31 52, fax 01 42 72 57 91, www.castexhotel.com, info@castexhotel.com).

$$ Hôtel Bastille Spéria***, a short block off the place de la Bastille, offers business-type service. The 42 plain but cheery rooms have air-conditioning, thin walls, and curiously cheap and sweaty foam mattresses. It's English-language-friendly, from the *International Herald Tribunes* in the lobby to the history of the Bastille posted in the elevator (Sb-€100, Db-€110–135, child's bed-€20, excellent but pricey buffet breakfast-€12.50, 1 rue de la Bastille, Mo: Bastille, tel. 01 42 72 04 01, fax 01 42 72 56 38, www.hotel-bastille-speria.com, info@hotel-bastille-speria.com).

$$ Hôtel des Chevaliers***, a little boutique hotel one block northwest of place des Vosges, offers small, pleasant rooms with modern comforts. Eight of its 24 rooms are off the street and quiet—worth requesting

1. Hôtel Castex
2. Hôtel Bastille Speria
3. Hôtel de la Place des Vosges
4. Hôtel des Chevaliers
5. Hôtel St. Louis Marais
6. Grand Hôtel Jeanne d'Arc
7. Hôtel Lyon-Mulhouse
8. Hôtel Sévigné
9. Hôtel Pointe Rivoli
10. Hôtel de 7ème Art
11. To Hôtel de la République
12. MIJE Hostels
13. Hôtel Axial & Hotel Sansonnet
14. Hôtel de la Bretonnerie
15. Hôtel Caron de Beaumarchais
16. Hôtel de Vieux Marais
17. Hôtel Beaubourg
18. Hôtel de Nice
19. Grand Hôtel du Loiret
20. BHV Department Store
21. Red Wheelbarrow Bookstore
22. SNCF Office
23. Bus #69 to Louvre, Orsay & Eiffel Tower
24. Bus #s 86 & 87 to Latin Quarter

M - Subway Stop
T - Taxi Stand
P - Parking
B - Bus Stop

Pompidou Center
Place Stravinsky
St. Merri
To Louvre
Place l'Hotel de Ville
To Notre Dame
Hotel de Ville
Seine River
Jewish Museum
Nat'l. Archives
Picasso Museum
Place de Thorigny
Jewish Quarter
Carnavalet Museum
Place des Vosges
Rue St. Antoine Exit
Place de la Bastille
New Opera
Boat Dock
Pont Marie
Sully Morland
St. Paul
Rambuteau
0 yds. 100 200
0 m 100 200
DCH

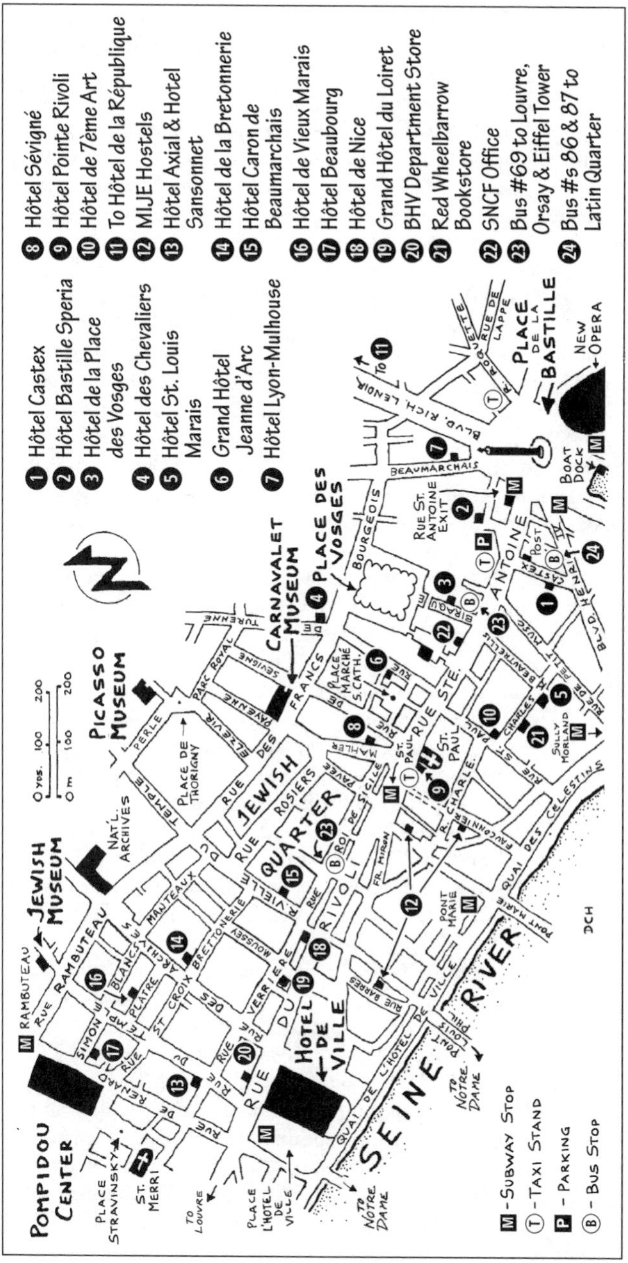

(Db-€120–135, prices depend on season, 30 rue de Turenne, Mo: St. Pau tel. 01 42 72 73 47, fax 01 42 72 54 10, info@hoteldeschevaliers.com Christele and Laurence SE).

$$ Hôtel St. Louis Marais** is a tiny, welcoming place, lost on quiet residential street between the river and rue St. Antoine, with a inviting lobby, 16 cozy rooms, and an owner who cares (Sb-€91, sma Db-€107, standard Db-€125, no elevator but only three floors, ask abou their new annex rooms, all at street level, 1 rue Charles V, Mo: Sull Morland, tel. 01 48 87 87 04, fax 01 48 87 33 26, www.saintlouis marais.com).

$$ Hôtel de 7ème Art,** two blocks south of rue St. Antoin toward the river, is a relaxed, Hollywood-nostalgia place, run by hip friendly, young people, with a full-service café-bar and Charlie Chapli murals. Its 23 rooms lack imagination, but are comfortable and a fa value. The large rooms are American-spacious (small Db-€77, standar Db-€88–100, large Db-€115–135, extra bed-€20, 20 rue St. Paul, Mo St. Paul, tel. 01 44 54 85 00, fax 01 42 77 69 10, hotel7art@wanadoo.fr

$ Grand Hôtel Jeanne d'Arc,** a well-tended hotel with thought fully appointed rooms, is ideally located for (and very popular with) con noisseurs of the Marais. Rooms on the street can be noisy until the ba close. Sixth-floor rooms have a view, and corner rooms are wonderful bright in the City of Light. Reserve this place way ahead (Sb-€55-70 Db-€80, larger twin Db-€95, Tb-€113, good Qb-€130, 3 rue de Jarent Mo: St. Paul, tel. 01 48 87 62 11, fax 01 48 87 37 31, informatio @hoteljeannedarc.com, Gail SE).

$ Hôtel Lyon-Mulhouse,** with half of its 40 pleasant rooms on busy street off place de la Bastille, is a good value. Its bigger, quiete rooms at the back are worth the extra euros (Sb-€55, Db-€66, twin Db €85, Tb-€90–95, Qb-€115, 8 boulevard Beaumarchais, Mo: Bastille, te 01 47 00 91 50, fax 01 47 00 06 31, hotelyonmulhouse@wanadoo.fr).

$ Hôtel Sévigné,** is a sharp little air-conditioned place wit lavender halls, tidy, comfortable rooms at fair prices, and a dour owne (Sb-€64, Db-€74-86, Tb-€10, 2 rue Malher, Mo: St. Paul, tel. 01 4 72 76 17, fax 01 42 78 68 26, www.le-sevigne.com).

$ Hotel Pointe Rivoli*, across from the St. Paul Métro stop, is jumbled, treehouse of rooms in the thick of the Marais, with Pari steepest stairs (no elevator) and modest rooms at reasonable rates (Sb €60, Db-€70, Tb-€100, 125 rue St. Antoine, Mo: St. Paul, tel. 01 42 7 14 23, fax 01 42 72 51 11, pointerivoli@libertysurf.fr).

$$ Hôtel de la République,** owned by the people who run th Castex (see above), is in a less appealing, out-of-the-way location, com pared to other listed Marais hotels, it often has rooms when others don (Sb-€53, Db-€61, near place de la République, 31 rue Albert Thoma 75010 Paris, Mo: République, tel. 01 42 39 19 03, fax 01 42 39 22 6 www.republiquehotel.com).

$ MIJE Youth Hostels: The Maison Internationale de la Jeunesse et des Etudiants (MIJE) runs three classy old residences clustered a few blocks south of rue St. Antoine. Each offers simple, clean, single-sex, one- to four-bed rooms for travelers under the age of 30 (exceptions are made for families). None has an elevator or double beds, each has an Internet station, and all rooms have showers. You can stay seven days maximum and prices given are per person and favor single travelers (two people can find a double in a very simple hotel for similar rates). You can pay more to have your own room, or pay less and room with as many as three others (Sb-€48, Db-€38, Tb-€32, Qb-€26, no CC, includes breakfast but not towels, which you can get from a machine; required membership card-€2.50 extra/person; rooms locked 12:00–15:00 and at 1:00). The hostels are: **MIJE Fourcy** (€10 dinners available to anyone with a membership card, 6 rue de Fourcy, just south of rue de Rivoli), **MIJE Fauconnier** (11 rue du Fauconnier), and the best, **MIJE Maubisson** (12 rue des Barres). They all share the same contact information (tel. 01 42 74 23 45, fax 01 40 27 81 64, www.mije.com) and Métro stop (St. Paul). Reservations are accepted, though you must arrive by noon.

Near the Pompidou Center

These hotels are farther west and closer to the Pompidou Center than to place de la Bastille.

$$$ Hôtel Axial Beaubourg*,** a block from Hôtel de Ville toward the Pompidou Center, has a minimalist lobby and 28 pricey but plush rooms, many with wood beams. If you cancel with less than seven days' notice, you'll lose your one-night deposit (standard Db-€145, big Db-€185, air-con, 11 rue du Temple, Mo: Hôtel de Ville, tel. 01 42 72 72 22, fax 02 42 72 03 53, www.axialbeaubourg.com).

$$$ Hôtel Caron de Beaumarchais*** feels like a folk-museum, with its 20 sweet little rooms and a lobby cluttered with bits from an elegant 18th-century Marais house. Short antique collectors love this place (small back-side Db-€145, larger Db on the front–€160, air-con, 12 rue Vielle du Temple, Mo: Hôtel de Ville, tel. 01 42 72 34 12, fax 01 42 72 34 63, www.carondebeaumarchais.com).

$$$ Hôtel de la Bretonnerie*,** three blocks from the Hôtel de Ville, is a fine Marais splurge. It has an on-the-ball staff, a big, welcoming lobby, elegant decor, and tastefully-appointed rooms with an antique, open-beam warmth (perfectly good standard "classic" Db-€114, bigger "charming" Db-€148, Db suite-€190, Tb suite-€215, Qb suite-€245, between rue Vielle du Temple and rue des Archives at 22 rue Ste. Croix de la Bretonnerie, Mo: Hôtel de Ville, tel. 01 48 87 77 63, fax 01 42 77 26 78, www.bretonnerie.com, Francoise SE).

$$ Hôtel de Vieux Marais** is tucked away on a quiet street two blocks east of the Pompidou Center with bright, spacious, and well-designed rooms. The we-try-harder owner, Marie-Hélène, loves her work and gives this place its charm. Greet Leeloo, the hotel hound (Db-€110-140, extra bed-€23, air-con, just off rue des Archives at 8 rue du Plâtre, Mo: Rambuteau or Hôtel de Ville, tel. 01 42 78 47 22, fax 01 42 78 34 32, www.vieuxmarais.com).

$$ Hôtel Beaubourg*** is a good three-star value on a quiet street in the shadow of the Pompidou Center. Its 28 rooms are wood-beam comfy, and the inviting lounge is warm and pleasant (Db-€115, some with balconies-€135, twins are considerably larger than doubles, includes breakfast, 11 rue Simon Le Franc, Mo: Rambuteau, tel. 01 42 74 34 24, fax 01 42 78 68 11, htlbeaubourg@hotellerie.net).

$$ Hôtel de Nice,** on the Marais' busy main drag, is a turquoise-and-rose, "Marie-Antoinette does tie-dye" place. Its narrow halls are littered with paintings, and its 23 rooms are filled with thoughtful touches and include tight bathrooms. Twin rooms, which cost the same as doubles, are larger and on the street side—but have effective double-paned windows (Sb-€68, Db-€105, Tb-€125, Qb-€135, extra bed-€20, 42 bis rue de Rivoli, Mo: Hôtel de Ville, tel. 01 42 78 55 29, fax 01 42 78 36 07).

$ Hotel Sansonnet,** a block from Hôtel de Ville toward the Pompidou Center, is a spotless, homey and unassuming oasis with no elevator but with 26 comfortable, well-maintained, and top-value rooms (Sb-€48-68, Db-€60–80, 48 rue de la Verrerie, Mo: Hôtel de Ville, tel. 01 48 87 96 14, fax 01 48 87 30 46, www.hotel-sansonnet.com, info@hotel-sansonnet.com).

$ Grand Hôtel du Loiret** is a bare-bones and basic place where you get what you pay for (S-€37, Sb-€47–62, D-€42, Db-€56–72, Tb-€72–84, 8 rue des Mauvais Garçons, Mo: Hôtel de Ville, tel. 01 48 87 77 00, fax 01 48 04 96 56, hotelduloiret@hotmail.com).

Near the Marais on Ile St. Louis

The peaceful, residential character of this river-wrapped island, its brilliant location, and homemade ice cream have drawn Americans for decades, allowing hotels to charge top euro for their rooms. There are no budget values here, but the island's coziness and proximity to the Marais, Notre-Dame, and the Latin Quarter compensate for higher rates. The hotels listed below are shown on the map on page 55. All are on the island's main drag, the rue St. Louis-en-l'Ile, where I list several restaurants (see page 329). Use Mo: Pont Marie or Sully Morland.

$$$ Hôtel du Jeu de Paume**,** located in a 17th-century tennis center, is the most expensive hotel I list in Paris. When you enter its magnificent lobby, you'll understand why. Greet Scoop, the hotel dog, then ride the glass elevator for a half-timbered-treehouse experience, and marvel at the cozy lounges. The 30 quite comfortable rooms are carefully designed and *très* tasteful, though small for the price (you're paying for the location and public spaces). Most face a small garden and all are pin-drop peaceful (Sb-€160, standard Db-€220, larger Db-€230–260, deluxe Db-€285, Db suite-€460, 54 rue St. Louis-en-l'Ile, tel. 01 43 26 14 18, fax 01 40 46 02 76, www.jeudepaumehotel.com).

The following two hotels are owned by the same person. For both, if you must cancel, do so a week in advance or pay fees:

$$$ Hôtel de Lutèce*** is the better, cozier value on the island, with a sit-a-while wood-paneled lobby, a fireplace, and warmly designed air-conditioned rooms. Twin rooms are larger and the same price as double rooms (Sb-€127, Db-€152, Tb-€170, 65 rue St. Louis-en-l'Ile, tel. 01 43 26 23 52, fax 01 43 29 60 25, www.hotel-ile-saintlouis.com).

$$$ Hôtel des Deux Iles*** is brighter and more colorful with marginally smaller rooms and the same rates (59 rue St. Louis-en-l'Ile, tel. 01 43 26 13 35, fax 01 43 29 60 25).

LUXEMBOURG-CONTRESCARPE ORIENTATION

I've patched together three small neighborhoods (St. Sulpice, Panthéon, and rue Mouffetard) to construct this diverse hotel area. St. Sulpice has a picturesque, pleasing square and Paris' best window-shopping. The Panthéon is stately and reserved, and the rue Mouffetard is light-hearted and youthful.

Sleeping in the Luxembourg-Contrescarpe area puts the Latin Quarter, Luxembourg Garden, boulevard St. Germain, Cluny Museum, Latin Quarter, and the Jardin des Plantes within easy walking distance. Here you get the best of many worlds—two lively areas (Latin Quarter and rue Mouffetard), two fine parks, and the classy trappings that surround the monumental Panthéon and St. Sulpice church. To walk from one end of this area to the other (from St. Sulpice church to the bottom of rue Mouffetard) takes about 25 minutes.

Having the Luxembourg Garden at your back door allows strolls through meticulously cared-for flowers, a great kids' play area (see Paris with Children, page 336), and a purifying escape from city traffic. Place St. Sulpice offers an elegant, pedestrian-friendly square and some of Paris' best boutiques (see Shopping, page 340). The rue Mouffetard is the bohemian soul of this area, running south from its heart, place de la Contrescarpe, to rue de Bazeilles. Two thousand years ago, it was the principal Roman road south to Italy. Today, this small, meandering street has a split personality. The lower part thrives in the daytime as a pedestrian market street. The upper part sleeps during the day but comes alive after dark, teeming with bars, restaurants, and nightlife.

The flowery Jardin des Plantes park, just east of rue Mouffetard, is ideal for afternoon walks, picnics, naps, and kids (see Paris with Children, page 336). The doorway at 49 rue Monge leads to a hidden **Roman arena** (Arènes de Lutèce). Today, *boules* players occupy the stage while couples cuddle on the seats. Admire the Panthéon from the outside (it's not worth paying to enter), and peek inside the exquisitely beautiful St. Etienne-du-Mont church.

Place Monge hosts a good **outdoor market** on Wednesday, Friday, and Sunday mornings until 13:00. The **street market** at the bottom of rue Mouffetard is colorful (Tue–Sat 8:00–12:00 & 15:30–19:00, Sun 8:00–12:00, 5 blocks south of place de la Contrescarpe). Lively cafés at place de la Contrescarpe hop with action until late.

The nearest **TI** is at the Louvre museum. The **post offices** (PTT) are between rue Mouffetard and rue Monge at 10 rue de l'Epée-de-Bois, and at the corner of rue des Ecoles and rue du Cardinal Lemoine. Edmicro Internet Access is two blocks north of place Contrescarpe (Tue–Fri, 11:00–20:00, Sat and Mon 14:00–20:00, closed Sun, 29 rue Descartes). **Bus** #47 runs along rue Monge north to Notre-Dame, the Pompidou Center, Gare de l'Est, and Gare du Nord.

Near St. Sulpice Church (6th arrondissement)

These three are all within a block of St. Sulpice, and two blocks from the famous boulevard St. Germain. Métro stops St. Sulpice and Mabillon are equally close. To locate hotels, see map on page 106.

$$$ Hôtel Relais St. Sulpice***, on the small street just behind St. Sulpice church, feels like a cozy bar with a melt-in-your-chair lounge and beautifully-designed rooms, most of which surround a leafy atrium courtyard. The dazzling breakfast room sits below the glass atrium near the sauna (Db-€165-205, good buffet breakfast-€12, air-con, 3 rue Garancière, tel. 01 46 33 99 00, fax 01 46 33 00 10, relaisstsulpice@wanadoo.fr).

$$$ Hôtel Bonaparte** sits between boutiques a few steps from place St. Sulpice on the smart rue Bonaparte. While the rooms don't live up to the handsome entry, they are homey, comfortable, and generally spacious with big bathrooms, molded ceilings, and clashing bedspreads (Sb-€90-135, Db-€118-150, Tb-€155, air-con, 61 rue Bonaparte, tel. 01 43 26 97 37, fax 01 46 33 57 67).

$$ Hôtel le Récamier**, which feels like grandma's house, is an overlooked prize tucked in the corner of place St. Sulpice. Flowery wallpaper, dark halls, and spotless, just-what-you-need rooms (with no TV!)—some with views of the square—make this an ideal Paris refuge. How such a low-key place escaped the trendy style of other hotels in this chic area, I'll never know (S-€90, Sb-€110, Db-€115-130, Tb-€155, Qb-€200, includes breakfast, 3 bis place St. Sulpice, tel. 01 43 26 04 89, fax 01 46 33 27 73).

Near the Panthéon (5th arrondissement)

The following two wannabe-four-star hotels face the Panthéon's right transept and are owned by the same family (ask about their promotional rates, which can be offered anytime, even during some summer weeks). The rates are sky-high and the rooms aren't big, but the quality is tops. I prefer the first hotel.

Luxembourg-Contrescarpe Hotels & Restaurants

Use Métro stops Cardinal Lemoine or Maubert-Mutualité, c RER stop Luxembourg for these hotels.

$$$ **Hôtel du Panthéon***** welcomes you with a cushy lobby and 3 country-French-cute rooms with air-conditioning and every possible com fort. Fifth-floor rooms have sliver balconies, but sixth-floor rooms hav the best views (Sb-€188, Db-€218, Tb-€235, 19 place du Panthéon, te 01 43 54 32 95, fax 01 43 26 64 65, www.hoteldupantheon.com).

$$$ **Hôtel des Grands Hommes***** was built to look good—and does. The lobby is to be admired but not enjoyed, and the 31 room reflect an interior designer's dream. They're generally tight but adorabl with great attention to detail and little expense spared. Fifth- and sixth floor rooms have balconies (sixth-floor balconies, with grand views, ar big enough to use). For more luxury, splurge for a suite (Sb-€188, stan dard Db-€218, Db suite-€390, air-con, 17 place du Panthéon, tel. 0 46 34 19 60, fax 01 43 26 67 32, www.hoteldesgrandshommes.com).

$$ **Hôtel des Grandes Ecoles***** is simply idyllic. A short alley lead to three buildings protecting a flower-filled garden courtyard, preserving sense of tranquility that is rare in a city this size. Its 51 rooms are reasonabl spacious and comfortable, with large beds. This romantic place is deservedl popular, so call well in advance, though reservations are not accepted mor than 4 months ahead (Db-€105–115, a few bigger rooms-€130, extra bed €20, parking-€30, 75 rue du Cardinal Lemoine, Mo: Cardinal Lemoine tel. 01 43 26 79 23, fax 01 43 25 28 15, www.hotel-grandes-ecoles.com mellow Marie speaks some English, Maman does not).

$$ **Hôtel Elysa-Luxembourg***** sits on a busy street and is m closest listing to Luxembourg Garden. It has plush, air-conditione rooms, but little personality (Db-€125-140, 6 rue Gay Lussac, tel. 0 43 25 31 74, fax 01 46 34 56 27, www.elysa-luxembourg.fr).

$ **Hôtel Central***, wedged between two cafés, has a smoky, ding reception, a steep, slippery stairway, so-so beds, and basic-but-cheery-if somewhat-mildewed rooms. To an optimist, this hotel defines unpre tentiousness; to a pessimist, it's a dive with a charming location Regardless, it's cheap (all rooms with showers, though toilets are dow the hall, Ss-€29–37, Ds-€39–45, no CC, no elevator, 6 rue Descartes Mo: Cardinal Lemoine, tel. 01 46 33 57 93, sweet Pilar NSE).

$ **Hôtel de Senlis**** is a fair deal hiding quietly two blocks fron Luxembourg Garden, with modest rooms, carpeted walls, and meta closets. Most rooms have beamed ceilings, and all rooms could use decorator with taste (Sb-€67, Db-€72–87, Tb-€95, Qb-€110, 7 ru Malebranche, Mo: Cluny-La Sorbonne, tel. 01 43 29 93 10, fax 01 4 29 00 24, www.hoteldesenlis.fr).

$ **Hôtel Medicis** is as cheap, stripped-down, and basic as it gets, wit a soiled linoleum charm, a happy owner, and a great location (S-€16, D €31, 214 rue St. Jacques, tel. 01 43 54 14 66, hotelmedecis@aol.com Denis speaks English).

$ **Hôtel du Brésil****, one block from Luxembourg Garden, has ttle character and some smoky rooms, but reasonable rates, making it n acceptable last resort (Sb-€64, Db-€68–85, 10 rue le Goff, tel. 01 43 4 76 11, fax 01 46 33 45 78, hoteldubresil@wanadoo.fr).

t the Bottom of Rue Mouffetard

)f my recommended accommodations in this area, these are farthest om the Seine and other tourists, in an appealing workaday area. They equire a longer walk or Métro ride to sights but may have rooms when thers don't. Use Métro stops Censier-Daubenton or Les Gobelins.

$$ **Comfort Hôtel Cardinal***** is a well-designed hotel with less haracter but agreeable decor and modern comforts like air-conditioning. oom prices vary enormously depending on demand, so the low-end rices listed could be available anytime—it's worth a call to check their ates (Sb-€68-100, standard Db-€88-138, large Db-€135-185, 20 rue ascal, tel. 01 47 07 41 92, fax 01 47 07 43 80, hotelcardinal@aol.com).

$ Don't let **Port-Royal-Hôtel***'s lone star fool you—this 46-room lace is polished bottom to top and has been well-run by the same proud amily for 66 years. You could eat off the floors of its spotless, comfy ooms. Ask for a room off the street (S-€39–50, D-€66, big hall showers-2.50, Db-€76, deluxe Db-€89, no CC, requires cash deposit, climb stairs om rue Pascal to busy boulevard de Port Royal, 8 boulevard de Port oyal, tel. 01 43 31 70 06, fax 01 43 31 33 67, www.portroyalhotel.fr.st).

$ **Hôtel de l'Espérance**** is a solid two-star value. It's quiet, pink, uffy, and comfortable, with thoughtfully appointed rooms complete vith canopy beds and a flamboyant owner (Sb-€70, Db-€73–86, small b-€101, 15 rue Pascal, Mo: Censier-Daubenton, tel. 01 47 07 10 99, ax 01 43 37 56 19, hotel.esperance@wanadoo.fr).

$ **Hôtel de France**** is set on a busy street, with adequately comortable rooms, fair prices, and charming owner, Madame Margo. The est and quietest rooms are *sur le cour* (on the courtyard), though streetide rooms are OK (Sb-€66, Db-€76–80, requires one-night nonefundable deposit, 108 rue Monge, tel. 01 47 07 19 04, fax 01 43 36 2 34, hotel.de.fce@wanadoo.fr).

$ **Y&H Hostel** is easygoing and English-speaking, with Internet ccess, kitchen facilities, and basic but acceptable hostel conditions (beds n four-bed rooms-€23, beds in double rooms-€26, sheets-€2.50, no C, rooms closed 11:00–16:00 but reception stays open, 2:00 curfew, eservations require deposit, 80 rue Mouffetard, Mo: Cardinal Lemoine, el. 01 47 07 47 07, fax 01 47 07 22 24, smile@youngandhappy.fr).

FOR LONGER STAYS

taying a week or longer? Consider the advantages that come with renting a furnished apartment. Complete with a small, equipped kitchen and living room, this option is great for families. Among the many English speaking organizations ready to help, the following have proven mos reliable. Their Web sites are generally excellent and essential to under standing your options.

Paris Appartements Services rents studios and one-bedroom apartments in the Opéra, Louvre, and Marais neighborhoods (2 ru d'Argout, 75002 Paris, tel. 01 40 28 01 28, fax 01 40 28 92 01 www.paris-appartements-services.fr).

Apalachee Bay is British-owned and offers an extensive range o carefully selected, furnished apartments (21 rue de Madrid, 75008 Paris tel. 01 42 94 13 13, fax 01 42 94 83 01, www.bridgestreet.com).

Locaflat offers accommodations ranging from studios to five-room apartments (63 avenue de la Motte Picquet, 75015 Paris, tel. 01 43 0 78 79, fax 01 40 56 99 69, www.locaflat.com).

Lodgis has studios from €400 per week and €900 euros per month (16 rue de la Folie Méricourt, 75011 Paris, tel. 01 48 07 11 06 www.lodgis.com).

EATING

The Parisian eating scene is kept at a rolling boil. Entire books (and lives) are dedicated to the subject. Paris is France's wine and cuisine melting pot. While it lacks a style of its own (only French onion soup is truly Parisian), it draws from the best of France. Paris could hold a gourmet's Olympics and import nothing.

Parisians eat long and well. Relaxed lunches, three-hour dinners, and endless hours of sitting in outdoor cafés are the norm. They have a legislated 35-hour workweek and a self-imposed 36-hour eat-week. Local cafés, cuisine, and wines become a highlight of any Parisian adventure—sightseeing for your palate. Even if the rest of you is sleeping in a cheap hotel, let your taste buds travel first-class in Paris. (They can go coach in London.)

You can eat well without going broke, but choose carefully—you're just as likely to blow a small fortune on a mediocre meal as you are to dine wonderfully for €20. By following the suggestions offered below, you'll have a better dining experience.

Breakfast

Petit déjeuner (puh-tee day-zhu-nay) is typically *café au lait,* hot chocolate, or tea; a roll with butter and marmalade; and a croissant, though more hotels are starting to provide breakfast buffets with fruit, cereal, yogurt, and cheese (usually for a few extra euros and well worth it). While breakfasts are available at your hotel (about €6–15), they're cheaper at corner cafés (but no coffee refills; see also "Café Culture," below). It's fine to buy a croissant or roll at a bakery and eat it with your cup of coffee at a café. Better still, some bakeries offer worthwhile breakfast deals with juice, croissant, and coffee or tea for about €3 (the chain of bakeries called La Brioche Dorée is one example). If the urge for an egg in the morning gets the best of you, drop into a café and order *une omelette* or *œufs sur le plat* (fried eggs). You could also buy or bring from home plastic bowls and spoons, buy a box of cereal and a small box of milk, and eat in your room before heading out for coffee.

Picnics

Great for lunch or dinner, Parisian picnics can be first-class affairs and adventures in high cuisine. Be daring. Try the smelly cheeses, ugly pâtés, sissy quiches, and minuscule (usually drinkable) yogurts. Local shopkeepers are accustomed to selling small quantities of produce. Try the tasty salads to go and ask for *une fourchette en plastique* (a plastic fork).

Gather supplies early for a picnic lunch; you'll probably visit several small stores to assemble a complete meal, and many close at noon. Look for a *boulangerie* (bakery), a *crémerie* or *fromagerie* (cheeses), a *charcuterie* (deli items, meats, and pâtés), an *épicerie* or *magasin d'alimentation* (small grocery store with veggies, drinks, and so on), and a *pâtisserie* (delicious pastries). For fine picnic shopping, check out our street market recommendations in the Shopping chapter. While wine is taboo in public places in the United States, it's *pas de problème* in France.

S*upermarchés* offer less color and cost, more efficiency, and adequate quality. Department stores often have supermarkets in the basement along with top-floor cafeterias offering not really cheap but low-risk, low-stress, what-you-see-is-what-you-get meals. For a quick meal to go, look for food stands and bakeries selling take-out sandwiches and drinks. For an affordable sit-down meal, try a *crêperie* or café.

In stores, unrefrigerated soft drinks and beer are one-half the price of cold drinks. Milk and boxed fruit juice are the most inexpensive drinks. Avoid buying drinks to go at streetside stands; you'll find them far cheaper in a shop. Try to keep a water bottle with you. Water quenches your thirst better and cheaper than anything you'll find in a store or café. I drink tap water in Paris and use that to refill my bottle.

For good lunch picnic sites, consider these suggestions. The Palais Royal (across the place du Palais Royal from the Louvre) is a good spot for a peaceful, royal picnic, as is the little triangular Henry IV Park on the west tip of Ile de la Cité. The pedestrian pont des Arts bridge, across from the Louvre, has unmatched views and plentiful benches. For great people-watching, try the Pompidou Center (by the *Homage to Stravinsky* fountains), the elegant place des Vosges (closes at dusk), the gardens at the Rodin Museum, and Luxembourg Garden.

Café Culture

French cafés (or *brasseries*) provide reasonable light meals and a refuge from museum and church overload. Feel free to order only a bowl of soup or a salad for lunch or dinner at a café.

Cafés generally open by 7:00, but closing hours vary. Unlike restaurants, which open only for lunch and dinner, meals are served throughout the day at cafés, so if you want a late lunch or an early dinner—find a café.

It's easier for the novice to sit and feel comfortable when you know the system. Check the price list first. Prices, which must be posted prominently, vary wildly between cafés. And cafés charge different prices for the same drink depending upon where you want to be seated. Prices are posted: *comptoir* (counter/bar) or the more expensive *salle* (seated). At large cafés, outside tables are most expensive and prices rise after 20:00.

Your waiter probably won't overwhelm you with friendliness. Notice how hard they work. They almost never stop. Cozying up to clients (French or foreign) is probably the last thing on their minds.

The **standard menu items** (generally served day and night) are the *croque-monsieur* (grilled ham-and-cheese sandwich) and *croque-madame* (*croque monsieur* with a fried egg on top). The *salade composée* (com-po-zay) is a hearty chef's salad. Sandwiches are least expensive but plain unless you buy them at the *boulangerie* (bakery). To get more than a piece of ham (*jambon*; zhahm-bohn) or chicken (*poulet*; poo-lay) on a baguette, order *jambon-* or *poulet-crudité* (crew-dee-tay), which means garnished with lettuce, tomatoes, cucumbers, and so on. Omelets come lonely on a plate with a basket of bread. The **daily special**—*plat du jour* (plah dew zhoor)—is your fast, hearty hot plate for €10–14. At most cafés (though never at a restaurant), feel free to order only appetizers—which many find lighter, more fun, and more interesting than entrées. Regardless of what you order, bread is free; to get more, just hold up your breadbasket and ask, "*Encore, s'il vous plaît.*"

House **wine** at the bar is cheap (about €3 per glass, cheapest by the pitcher—*pichet,* pee-shay), and the local beer is cheaper on tap (*une pression*, oon pres-yohn) than in the bottle (*bouteille*, boo-teh-ee). France's best **beer** is Alsatian; try Kronenbourg or the heavier Pelfort. *Une panaché* (pan-a-shay) is a refreshing French shandy (7-Up and beer). For a fun, bright, nonalcoholic drink of 7-Up with mint syrup, order *un diablo menthe* (dee-ah-bloh mahnt). Kids love the local lemonade (*citron pressé;* see-trohn preh-say) and the flavored syrups mixed with bottled water (*sirops à l'eau*; see-roh ah loh). The ice cubes melted after the last Yankee tour group left.

If you order **coffee or tea,** here's the lingo:

Coffee

- *un express* (uh nex-press) = shot of espresso
- *une noisette* (oon nwah-zette) = espresso with a shot of milk
- *café au lait* (kah-fay oh lay) = coffee with lots of milk. Also called *un grand crème* (large size; uh grahn krehm) or *un petit crème* (average size; uh puh-tee krehm)
- *un grand café noir* (uh grahn kah-fay nwahr) = cup of black coffee, closest to American style
- *un décaffiné* (uh day-kah-fee-nay) = decaf; can modify any of the above drinks

Tea

- *un thé nature* (uh tay nah-tour) = plain tea
- *un thé au lait* (uh tay oh lay) = tea with milk
- *un thé citron* (uh tay see-trohn) = tea with lemon
- *un infusion* (uhn an-few-see-yohn) = herbal tea

By law, the waiter must give you a glass of tap water with your coffee if you request it; ask for *un verre d'eau, s'il vous plaît* (uh vayr doh, see voo play).

Tipping

Virtually all cafés and restaurants include a service charge in the bill (usually 15 percent), but it's polite to round up for a drink or meal well-served. This bonus tip is usually about 5 percent of the bill (e.g., if your bill is €19, leave €20). In the rare instance that service is not included (the menu states *service non compris*), tip 15 percent. When you hand your payment plus a tip to your waiter, you can say, "*C'est bon*" (say bohn), meaning, "It's good." If you order your food at a counter, don't tip.

Restaurants

Choose restaurants filled with locals, not places with big neon signs boasting, We Speak English. Consider your hotelier's opinion. If a restaurant doesn't post its menu *(la carte)* outside, move along.

If you want the menu, ask for *la carte* (and order à la carte like the locals do); if you ask for the *menu* (muh-noo), you'll get a fixed-price meal. *Menus*, which offer three or four courses, are generally a good value: You get your choice of soup, appetizer, or salad; your choice of three or four main courses with vegetables; plus a cheese course and/or a choice of desserts. Service is included, but wine and other drinks are generally extra. Restaurants that offer a *menu* for lunch often charge about €6 more for the same *menu* at dinner.

If you'd rather dine à la carte, ask the waiter for help deciphering the French. Go with his or her recommendations and anything *de la maison* (of the house), as long as it's not an organ meat (*tripes, rognons, andouillette*—yuck). Galloping gourmets should bring a menu translator; the *Marling Menu Master* is excellent. The *Rick Steves' French Phrase Book,* with a Menu Decoder, works well for most travelers. The wines are often listed in a separate *carte des vins.*

In France, an *entrée* is the first course and *le plat* is the main course. *Le plat* or *le plat du jour* (plate of the day) is the main course with vegetables (usually €10–14). If all you want is a salad, find a café instead. By American standards, the French undercook meats: rare or *saignant* (seh-nyahn) is close to raw; medium or *à point* (ah pwahn) is rare; and well-done or *bien cuit* (bee-yehn kwee), is medium.

Parisians are willing to pay for bottled water with their meal (*eau minérale;* oh mee-nay-rahl) because they prefer the taste over tap water f you prefer a free pitcher of tap water, ask for *une carafe d'eau* (oon kah-ahf doh). Otherwise, you may unwittingly buy bottled water. To get inexpensive wine at a restaurant, order table wine in a pitcher (*un pichet;* pee-shay), rather than a bottle (though finer restaurants usually offer only bottles of wine). If all you want is a glass of wine, ask for *un verre de vin* (uh vehr duh van). A half carafe of wine is *un demi-pichet* (uh duh-mee pee-shay), a quarter carafe (ideal for one) is *un quart* (uh car).

To get a waiter's attention, simply say, "*S'il vous plaît*" (see voo play)—please.

PARISIAN CUISINE

There is no Parisian cuisine to speak of. The principal advantage of dining in Paris is that you can sample fine cuisine from throughout France. Many restaurants specialize in a particular region's cuisine (in this book, I list restaurants specializing in food from Provence, Burgundy, Alsace, Normandy, Dordogne, Languedoc, and the Basque region). So be a galloping gourmet and try a few of these regional restaurants (see the note on "French Specialties by Region," page 318). For general, classic, anywhere-in-France dishes, consider these suggestions:

First Course *(Entrée)*

Soupe à l'oignon: Hot, salty, and filling, French onion soup is a beef broth served with cheesy bread croutons floating on top.

Salade au chèvre chaud: A mixed green salad topped with warmed goat cheese and toasted bread croutons.

Salade niçoise: While famous as a specialty from Nice, this classic salad is served throughout France. There are many versions, though most include a base of green salad topped with green beans, boiled potatoes (sometimes rice), tomatoes, anchovies, lots of tuna, and hard-boiled eggs.

Crudités: A mix of raw and lightly-cooked, fresh vegetables usually including grated carrots, celery root, tomatoes, and beets, often with a hefty dose of vinaigrette dressing. If you want the dressing on the side, say, "*La sauce à côté, s'il vous plaît*" (lah sohss ah co-tay see voo play).

Escargots: Snails cooked in parsley-garlic butter. You don't even have to like the snail itself. Just dipping your bread in garlic butter is more than satisfying. Prepared a variety of ways, the classic is *à la bourguignonne* (served in their shells).

Huîtres: Oysters served raw any month and delivered fresh from nearby Brittany. This food is particularly popular at Christmas and New Year's, when every café seems to have overflowing baskets lining the storefront.

Pâtés* and *Terrines: Slowly cooked ground meat (usually pork, though chicken and rabbit are also common) that is highly seasoned and served in slices with mustard and *cornichons* (little pickles). Pâtés are smoother than the similarly prepared, but more chunky *terrines.*

FRENCH SPECIALTIES BY REGION

Alsace: The German influence is obvious: sausages, potatoes, onions, and sauerkraut. Look for *choucroute garni* (sauerkraut and sausage—although it seems a shame to eat it in a fancy restaurant), the more traditionally Alsatian *baeckeoffe* (potato, meat, and onion stew), *rösti* (an oven-baked potato-and-cheese dish), fresh trout, and foie gras.
Burgundy: Considered by many to be France's best, Burgundian cuisine is peasant cooking elevated to an art. This wine region excels in *coq au vin* (chicken with wine sauce), *bœuf Bourguignon* (beef stew cooked with wine, bacon, onions, and mushrooms), *œufs en meurette* (eggs poached in red wine), *escargots* (snails), and *jambon persillé* (ham with garlic and parsley).
Basque: Mixing influences from the mountains, sea, Spain, and France, it's dominated by seafood, tomatoes, and red peppers. Look for anything *basquaise* (cooked with tomatoes, eggplant, red peppers, and garlic), such as *thon* (tuna) or *poulet* (chicken). Try *piperade,* a dish combining peppers, tomatoes, garlic, and eggs (ham optional), and *ttoro,* a seafood stew that is the Basque answer to bouillabaisse.
Languedoc and Périgord: The cuisine of these regions is referred to in Paris as Southwest cuisine *(cuisine du sudouest)*. It's hearty peasant cooking using full-bodied red wines and lots of duck. Try the hearty *cassoulet*

Foie gras: Rich and buttery in consistency, it's made from the swollen livers of force-fed geese (or ducks, in *foie de canard*). Spread it on bread with your knife, and do not add mustard to this pâté dish.

Main Course *(Plat Principal)*

Coq au vin: This Burgundian dish is chicken marinated ever so slowly in red wine, then cooked until it melts in your mouth. It's served (often family-style) with vegetables.
Bœuf bourguignon: Another Burgundian specialty, this classy beef stew is cooked slowly in red wine, then served with onions, potatoes, and mushrooms.
Steak: Referred to as *pavé, bavette,* or *entrecôte,* French steak is usually thinner than American steak and is always served with sauces (*au poivre* is a pepper sauce, *une sauce roquefort* is a cheese sauce).
Steak tartare: This wonderfully French dish is for adventurous type only. It's very lean, raw hamburger served with spices (usually Tabasco onions, salt, and pepper on the side) and topped with a raw egg.
Gigot d'agneau: Leg of lamb served in many styles, often with white

(white bean, duck, and sausage stew), *canard* (duck), *pâté de foie gras* (goose liver pâté), *pommes sarladaise* (potatoes fried in duck fat), *truffes* (truffles, earthy mushrooms), and anything with *noix* (walnuts).

Normandy and Brittany: Normandy specializes in cream sauces, organ meats (sweetbreads, tripe, and kidneys—the "gizzard salads" are great), and seafood *(fruits de mer)*. Dairy products are big here. Munch some *moules* (mussels) and *escalope normande* (veal in cream sauce). Brittany is famous for its oysters and crêpes. Both regions use lots of *cidre* (hard apple cider) in their cuisine.

Provence: The almost extravagant use of garlic, olive oil, herbs, and tomatoes makes Provence cuisine France's liveliest. To sample it, order anything *à la provençale*. Among the area's spicy specialties are *ratatouille* (a thick mixture of vegetables in an herb-flavored tomato sauce), *brandade* (a salt cod, garlic, and cream mousse), *aioli* (a garlicky mayonnaise often served atop fresh vegetables), *tapenade* (a paste of puréed olives, capers, anchovies, herbs, and sometimes tuna), *soupe au pistou* (vegetable soup with basil, garlic, and cheese), and *soupe à l'ail* (garlic soup).

Riviera: The Côte d'Azur gives Provence's cuisine a Mediterranean flair. Local specialties are *bouillabaisse* (the spicy seafood stew/soup that seems worth the cost only for those with a seafood fetish), *bourride* (a creamy fish soup thickened with *aioli* garlic sauce), and *salade niçoise* (nee-swaz; a tasty tomato, potato, olive, anchovy, and tuna salad).

beans. The best lamb is *pré salé*, which means the lamb has been raised in salt-marsh lands (like at Mont St. Michel).

Confit de canard: This Southwest favorite is duck that has been preserved in its own fat, then cooked in its fat, and often served with potatoes cooked in the same fat. Not for dieters.

Saumon: You'll see salmon dishes served in various styles. The salmon usually comes from the North Sea and is always served with sauce, most commonly a sorrel sauce.

Cheese Course *(Le Fromage)*

In France, the cheese course is served just before (or instead of) dessert. It not only helps with digestion, it gives you a great opportunity to sample the tasty regional cheeses. There are more than 400 different French cheeses to try. Most restaurants will offer a cheese platter from which you select a few different cheeses (three is average). Those most commonly served in Paris are *brie de Meaux* (mild and creamy, from just outside Paris), Camembert (semi-creamy and pungent, from Normandy), *chèvre* (goat cheeses with a sharp taste, usually from the Loire), and Roquefort (strong and blue-veined, from south-central France).

If you'd like a little of each type of cheese from the cheese plate, say, *"Un peu de chaque, s'il vous plaît"* (uh puh duh shahk, see voo play). If you serve yourself from the cheese plate, observe French etiquette and keep the shape of the cheese. To avoid being gauche, politely shave off a slice from the side or cut small wedges.

Dessert *(Le Dessert)*

Crème brulée: A rich, creamy, dense, and caramelized custard.
Tarte tatin: This is apple pie like grandma never made, with caramelized apples cooked upside down, but served upright.
Mousse au chocolat: Chocolate mousse.
Ile flottante: This lighter dessert consists of islands of meringue floating on a pond of custard sauce.
Profiteroles: Cream puffs filled with vanilla ice cream, smothered in warm chocolate sauce.
Tartes: Narrow strips of fresh fruit, baked in a crust and served in thin slices (without ice cream).
Sorbets: Known to us as sherbets, these light, flavorful, and fruity ices are sometimes laced with brandy.

Coffee *(Café)*

If you order espresso, it will always come after dessert. To have coffee with dessert, ask for *"café avec le dessert"* (kah-fay ah-vehk luh day-sayr).

EATING IN PARIS

My recommendations are centered around the same three great neighborhoods listed in the Sleeping chapter; you can come home exhausted after a busy day of sightseeing and find a good selection of restaurants right around the corner. And evening is a fine time to explore any of these delightful neighborhoods, even if you're sleeping elsewhere.

To save piles of euros, review the budget eating tips above and restaurant recommendations below, and consider dinner picnics (great take-out dishes available at *charcuteries*).

Restaurants open for dinner around 19:00, and small local favorites get crowded after 21:00. When lunch is served, it generally begins at 11:30 and goes until 14:00, with last orders taken at about 13:30. Beware: Many restaurants close Sunday and Monday. Most of the restaurants listed below accept credit cards.

The Rue Cler Neighborhood

The rue Cler neighborhood caters to its residents. Its eateries, while not destination places, have an intimate charm. My favorites are small mom-

PRICE CODE

To help you choose among these listings, I've divided the restaurants into three categories, based on the price for a typical meal without wine.

$$$ Higher Priced—Most meals €34 or more.
$$ Moderately Priced—Most meals between €20–34.
$ Lower Priced—Most meals under €20.

nd-pop places that love to serve traditional French food at good prices to local clientele. You'll generally find great dinner *menus* for €20–30 and *lats du jour* for around €12-15. Eat early with tourists or late with locals.

$$$ **Le Bourdonnais,** boasting one Michelin star, is the neighborood's intimate gourmet splurge. You'll find friendly but formal service n a plush and very subdued 10-table room. Micheline Coat, your hostss, will treat you well (€43 lunch *menu*, €66 dinner *menu*, daily, 113 venue de la Bourdonnais, tel. 01 47 05 47 96).

$$$ **Café de l'Esplanade,** the latest buzz, is your opportunity to e surrounded by chic, yet older and sophisticated Parisians enjoying op-notch traditional cuisine as foreplay. There's not a tourist in sight. t's a sprawling place—half its tables with well-stuffed chairs fill a plush, iving-room–like interior, and the other half are lined up outside under ts elegant awning facing the street and car park. Dress competitively, s this is *the* place to be seen in the 7th *arrondissement* (€20 *plats du jour*, lan on €45 plus wine for dinner, open daily, reserve—especially if you vant a curbside table, smoke-free room in the back, bordering Les nvalides at 52 rue Fabert, tel. 01 47 05 38 80).

$$ **Léo le Lion,** a warm, charming souvenir of old Paris, is popular vith locals. Expect to spend €25 per person for fine à la carte choices closed Sun, 23 rue Duvivier, tel. 01 45 51 41 77).

$$ Save **Le Florimond** for a special occasion. Locals come for clasic French cuisine like grandma used to make, served with care in an ntimate, warm setting—and so should you. Since it's a neighborhood avorite, it's best to reserve ahead. Friendly English-speaking Laurent vill take good care of you (€30 *menu*, closed Sun, good and reasonable vine selection, 19 avenue de la Motte Picquet, tel. 01 45 55 40 38).

$$ At **L'Affriolé,** you'll compete with young professionals for a table. This small and trendy place is well-deserving of its rave reviews. Item elections change daily and the wine list is extensive, with some good barains (€32 *menu*, closed Sun, 17 rue Malar, tel. 01 44 18 31 33).

$$ **Au Petit Tonneau** is a purely Parisian experience. Fun-loving wner-chef Madame Boyer prepares everything herself, wearing her tall

Rue Cler Restaurants

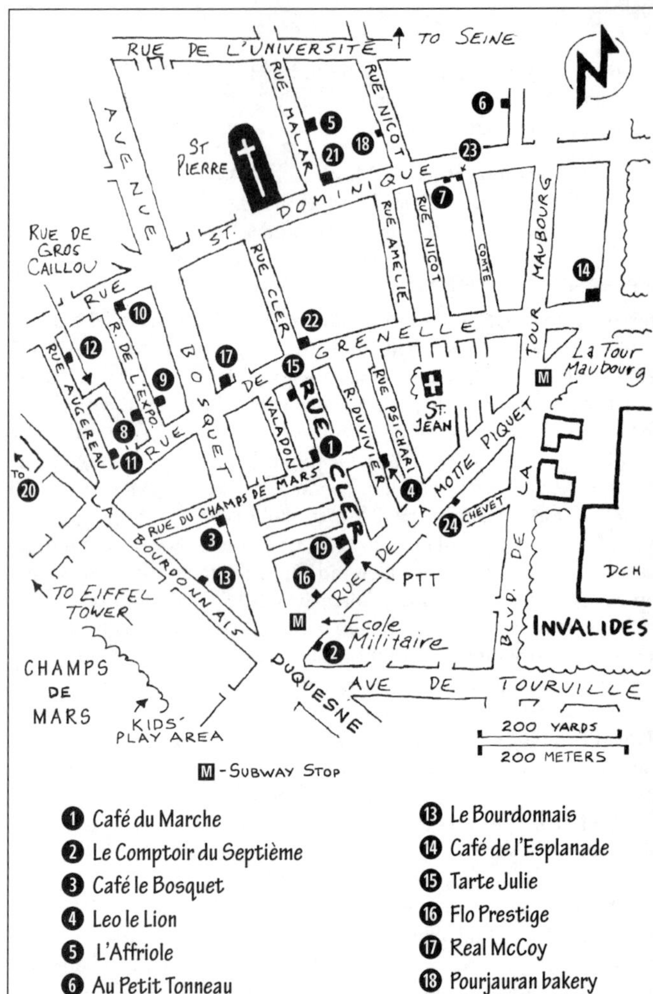

1. Café du Marche
2. Le Comptoir du Septième
3. Café le Bosquet
4. Leo le Lion
5. L'Affriole
6. Au Petit Tonneau
7. Brasserie Thoumieux
8. P'tit Troquet & Casa Sergio
9. Restaurant la Serre
10. La Fontaine de Mars
11. La Varangue
12. Chez Agnes
13. Le Bourdonnais
14. Café de l'Esplanade
15. Tarte Julie
16. Flo Prestige
17. Real McCoy
18. Pourjauran bakery
19. Petite Brasserie PTT
20. To Le Sancerre
21. Le Toulouse
22. Café la Roussillon
23. O'Brien's Pub
24. Le Florimond

chef's hat like a crown as she rules from her family-style kitchen. The small dining room is plain and a bit smoky (allow €35/person with wine, open daily, 20 rue Surcouf, tel. 01 47 05 09 01).

$$ **Thoumieux,** the neighborhood's classy, traditional Parisian brasserie, is a local institution and deservedly popular. It's big and dressy, with formal but good-natured waiters. They serve a €14 lunch *menu,* a €31 dinner *menu* (3 courses with wine), and really good *crème brulée* (daily, 79 rue St. Dominique, tel. 01 47 05 49 75).

$$ **Le P'tit Troquet** is a petite place taking you back to Paris in the 1920s, gracefully and earnestly run by Dominique. The delicious three-course €27 *menu* comes with fun, traditional choices (closed Sun, 28 rue de l'Exposition, tel. 01 47 05 80 39).

$$ **La Casa di Sergio** is *the* place for gourmet Italian cuisine served family-style. Only Sergio could make me enthusiastic about Italian food in Paris. Sergio, a people-loving Sicilian, says he's waited his entire life to open a restaurant like this. Eating here involves a little trust...just sit down and let Sergio spoil you (€26–34 *menus,* closed Sun, 20 rue de l'Exposition, tel. 01 45 51 37 71).

$$ **La Fontaine de Mars** is a longtime favorite for locals, charmingly situated on a classic tiny Parisian street and jumbled square. It's a happening scene, with tables jammed together for the serious business of good eating. Reserve in advance or risk eating upstairs without the fun street-level ambience (allow €40/person with wine, nightly, where rue de l'Exposition and rue St. Dominique meet, at 129 rue St. Dominique, tel. 01 47 05 46 44).

$$ **Chez Agnès** is the smallest restaurant listed in this book. Eccentric and flowery, it's truly a family-style place where engaging Agnès (with dog Gypsy at her side) does it all—working wonders in her minuscule kitchen, and serving, too, without a word of English. Don't come for a quick dinner; she expects to get to know you (€23 *menu,* closed Mon, 1 rue Augereau, tel. 01 45 51 06 04).

$ **Café du Marché,** with the best seats, coffee, and prices on rue Cler, serves hearty €9 salads and good €10 *plats du jour* for lunch or dinner to a trendy, smoky, mainly French crowd. This easygoing café is ideal if you want a light dinner (good dinner salads) or a more substantial but simple meal. Arrive before 19:30; it's packed at 21:00. A chalkboard lists the plates of the day—each a meal (Mon–Sat 11:00–23:00, closes at 17:00 on Sun, at the corner of rue Cler and rue du Champ de Mars, at 38 rue Cler, tel. 01 47 05 51 27, well-run by Frank, Jack, and Bruno). You'll find similar dishes and prices with better (but smoky) indoor seating **Le Comptoir du Septième,** two blocks away on a busy street at the Ecole Militaire Métro stop (daily, 39 avenue de la Motte Picquet, tel. 01 45 55 90 20).

$ **Petite Brasserie PTT** is popular with postal workers, offering traditional café fare at reasonable prices next to the PTT on rue Cler (closed Mon, opposite 53 rue Cler).

$ Café le Bosquet is a vintage Parisian brasserie with dressy waiters and classic indoor or sidewalk tables on a busy street. Come here for a bowl of French onion soup, a salad, or a three-course set *menu* for €16 (closed Sun, many choices from a fun menu, the house red wine is plenty good, corner of rue du Champs de Mars and avenue Bosquet, at 46 avenue Bosquet, tel. 01 45 51 38 13).

$ La Varangue is an entertaining one-man show featuring English-speaking Phillipe, who ran a French catering shop in Pennsylvania for three years, then returned to Paris to open his own place. He lives upstairs, and clearly has found his niche serving a Franco-American clientele who are all on a first-name basis. The food is cheap and good (try his snails and chocolate cake—but not together), the tables are few, and he opens early, at 17:30. Norman Rockwell would dig his tiny dining room (€10 *plats du jour* and a €14.50 *menu,* closed Sun, always a veggie option, 27 rue Augereau, tel. 01 47 05 51 22).

$ Le Toulouse is a friendly, easygoing boutique/restaurant serving southwest French cuisine featuring duck, *cassoulet*, and hearty salads at very fair prices (closed Sun, 86 rue St Dominique, tel. 01 45 56 04 31).

$ Restaurant la Serre is also worth considering and reasonable (*plats du jour* €11–15, closed Sun-Mon, good onion soup and duck specialties, 29 rue de l'Exposition, tel. 01 45 55 20 96, Margot).

$ Le Sancerre wine bar-café is wood-beam warm and ideal for a light lunch or dinner, or just a glass of wine after a long day of sightseeing. The owner's cheeks are the same color as his wine (open Mon-Fri until 21:30, closed Sat night and Sun, great omelets, 22 avenue Rapp, tel. 01 45 51 75 91).

Picnicking

The rue Cler is a moveable feast that gives "fast food" a good name. The entire street is clogged with connoisseurs of good eating. Only the health-food store goes unnoticed. A festival of food, the street is lined with people whose lives seem to be devoted to their specialty: polished produce, rotisserie chicken, crêpes, or cheese. For a self-guided tour of all the temptations, see the Rue Cler Walk on page 87.

For a magical picnic dinner at the Eiffel Tower, assemble it in no fewer than five shops on rue Cler and lounge on the best grass in Paris (the police don't mind after dusk), with the dogs, Frisbees, a floodlit tower, and a cool breeze in the parc du Champ de Mars.

The **crêpe stand** next to Café du Marché does a wonderful top-end dinner crêpe for €4. **Asian delis** (generically called *Traiteur Asie*) provide tasty, low-stress, low-price, take-out treats (€6 dinner plates; two delis have tables on the rue Cler—one across from Grand Hôtel Lévêque, and the other near the rue du Champ de Mars). **La Maison du Jambon** overflows with delicious dishes ready to go (on rue Cler midway between rues Grenelle and Champs de Mar). The elegant **Flo Prestige** *harcuterie* is open daily until 23:00 and offers mouthwatering meals to o (at the Ecole Militaire Métro stop). **Real McCoy** is a little shop selling American food and sandwiches (closed Sun, 194 rue de Grenelle). There are small, **late-night groceries** at 186 and 197 rue de Grenelle open nightly until midnight).

Breakfast

Café la Roussillon (daily, at corner of rue de Grenelle and rue Cler) erves American breakfasts and a dynamite Sunday brunch at fair prices. The **Pourjauran** bakery, offering great baguettes, hasn't changed in 70 ears (at 20 rue Jean Nicot). The **bakery** at 112 rue St. Dominique is vorth the detour, with classic decor and tables where you can enjoy your *afé au lait* and croissant.

Nightlife

This sleepy neighborhood is not the place for night owls, but there are a ew notable exceptions. **Café du Marché** and its brother, **Le Comptoir du Septième** (both listed above), hop with a Franco-American crowd ntil about midnight, as does the flashier **Café la Roussillon** (nightly, at orner of rue de Grenelle and rue Cler). **O'Brien's Pub** is a relaxed, Parisian rendition of an Irish pub (77 avenue St. Dominique).

The Marais Neighborhood

The trendy Marais is filled with locals enjoying good food in colorful and tmospheric eateries. The scene is competitive and changes all the time. Here is an assortment of places—all handy to recommended hotels—that offer good food at reasonable prices, plus a memorable experience. For naximum ambience, go to the place des Vosges or place du Marché Ste. Catherine (several places listed below in each of these squares).

$$$ **Ma Bourgogne** is a good match for the classy place des Vosges with a certain snob appeal. You'll sit under arcades in a whirlpool of Frenchness as bow-tied and black-aproned waiters serve traditional Burgundian specialties: steak, *coq au vin,* lots of French fries, escargot, and great red wine. Service at this institution comes with food but no smiles (allow €38/person with wine, open daily, dinner reservations smart, no CC, at northwest corner at #19, tel. 01 42 78 44 64).

$$$ **L'Excuse**, one of the neighborhood's top restaurants, is a good splurge for a romantic, dressy evening in a hushed atmosphere, with lounge-lizard music and elegant Mediterranean nouveau cuisine. The plates are petite but creative and presented with panache (€37 *menu*, closed Sun, reserve ahead, request downstairs—ideally by the window, 14 rue Charles V, tel. 01 42 77 98 97).

$$ ***Restaurants on place du Marché Ste. Catherine:*** This tiny square just off rue St. Antoine is an international food festival cloaked in extremely Parisian, leafy-square ambience. On a balmy evening, this is

clearly a neighborhood favorite, with five popular restaurants offering €20–30 meals. Survey the square and you'll find two French-style bistros (**Le Marché** and **Au Bistrot de la Place,** both open daily), a fun Italian place, a popular Japanese/Korean restaurant, and a Russian eatery with an easy but adventurous menu. You'll eat under the trees surrounded by a futuristic-in-1800 planned residential quarter.

$$ **L'Impasse,** a cozy, neighborhood bistro on a quiet alley, serves an enthusiastically French, €26 three-course *menu* (great escargots, scallops, and steak). Françoise, a former dancer and artist, runs the place *con brio* and, judging by the clientele, she's a fixture in the neighborhood. It's a spacious place where everything is made fresh (closed Sun, 4 impasse de Guéménée, tel. 01 42 72 08 45). Françoise promises anyone with this book a free glass of *byrrh*—it's pronounced "beer," but it's a French port-like drink. The restaurant is next to a self-serve launderette (open nightly until 21:30—clean your clothes while you dine).

$$ **Chez Janou,** a Provençal bistro, tumbles out of its corner building and fills its broad sidewalk with keen eaters. At first glance, you know this is a find. It's relaxed and charming, yet youthful and bustling with energy. The style is French Mediterranean, with an emphasis on vegetables (€14 *plats du jour*, €27 three-course *menu* that changes with the season, open daily, a block beyond place des Vosges at 2 rue Roger Verlomme, tel. 01 42 72 28 41).

$$ **Brasserie Bofinger**, an institution for over 100 years, is famous for fish and traditional cuisine with an Alsatian flair. You're surrounded by brisk, black-and-white attired waiters in plush rooms reminiscent of the Roaring Twenties. The non-smoking room is best—under the grand 1919 *coupole.* You'll see boys shucking and stacking seafood platters out front before you enter. Their €31 three-course (with wine) *menu* is a good value (daily and nightly, reservations smart, 5 rue de la Bastille, don't be confused by the lesser "Petite" Bofinger across the street, tel. 01 42 72 87 82).

$$ **L'Enoteca** is a high-energy, half-timbered Italian wine bar-restaurant serving reasonable Italian cuisine (no pizza) with a tempting antipasti bar. It's a relaxed, open setting with busy, blue-aproned waiters serving two floors of local eaters (allow €30 for meals with wine, daily, across from L'Excuse at rue St. Paul and rue Charles V, 25 rue Charles V, tel. 01 42 78 91 44).

$$ Lively ***rue de Lappe*** is what the Latin Quarter wants to be. This street, just beyond the more stately place de la Bastille, is one of the wildest night spots in Paris. You'll walk past a dizzying array of wacky eateries, bars, and dance halls. Then, sitting there like a van Gogh painting, is the popular, zinc-bar-classic **Bistrot les Sans Culottes**—a time-warp bistro serving traditional French cuisine with a proper respect for fine wine (€20 three-course *menu*, daily, 27 rue de Lappe, tel. 01 48 05 42 92). Stay out past your bedtime. Eat here. Then join the rue de Lappe party.

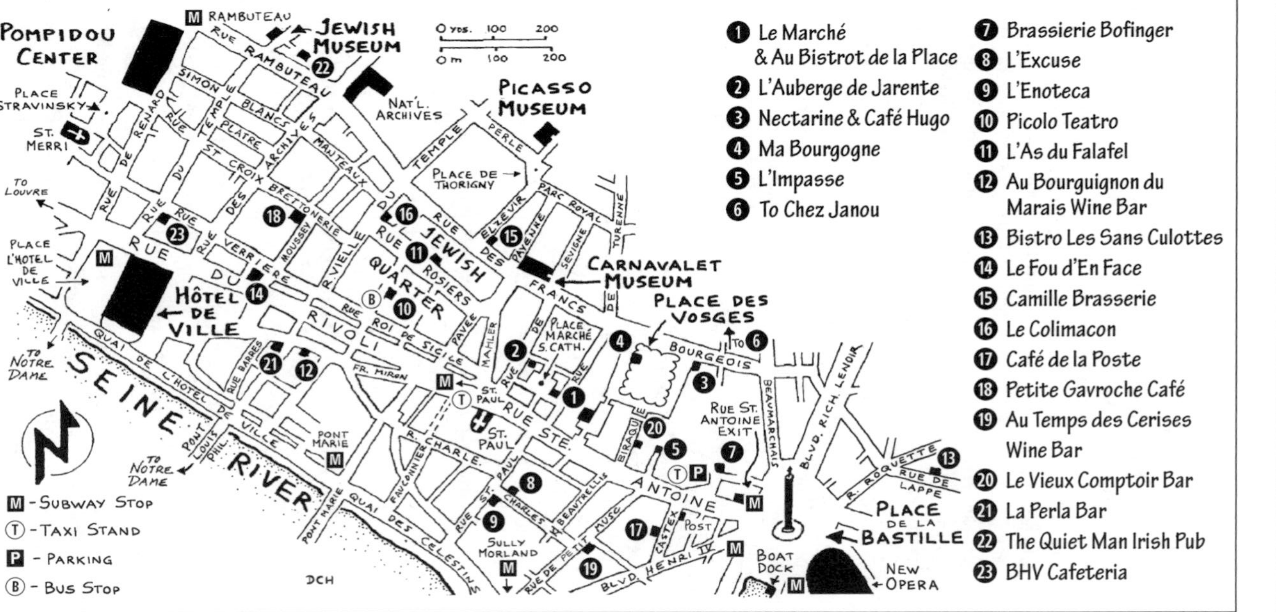
1 Le Marché & Au Bistrot de la Place
2 L'Auberge de Jarente
3 Nectarine & Café Hugo
4 Ma Bourgogne
5 L'Impasse
6 To Chez Janou
7 Brassierie Bofinger
8 L'Excuse
9 L'Enoteca
10 Picolo Teatro
11 L'As du Falafel
12 Au Bourguignon du Marais Wine Bar
13 Bistro Les Sans Culottes
14 Le Fou d'En Face
15 Camille Brasserie
16 Le Colimacon
17 Café de la Poste
18 Petite Gavroche Café
19 Au Temps des Cerises Wine Bar
20 Le Vieux Comptoir Bar
21 La Perla Bar
22 The Quiet Man Irish Pub
23 BHV Cafeteria
Pompidou Center
Place Stravinsky
St. Merri
Rambuteau
Jewish Museum
Nat'l. Archives
Picasso Museum
Place de Thorigny
Jewish Quarter
Carnavalet Museum
Place des Vosges
Hôtel de Ville
Place l'Hotel de Ville
Rue St. Antoine Exit
Place de la Bastille
New Opera
Boat Dock
Pont Marie
Sully Morland
St. Paul
Seine River
To Louvre
To Notre Dame
M - Subway Stop
T - Taxi Stand
P - Parking
B - Bus Stop
DCH

$$ **Camille,** a traditional corner brasserie, is a neighborhood favorite with great indoor and sidewalk seating. White-aproned waiters serve €9 salads and very French *plats du jour* for €15 to a down-to-earth but sophisticated clientele (daily, 24 rue des Francs Bourgeois at corner of rue Elzévir, tel. 01 42 72 29 50).

$ You can dine cheaply on the elegant place des Vosges at the mod and pastel **Nectarine**, a teahouse serving healthy salads, quiches, and inexpensive *plats du jour* both day and night. Its fun menu lets you mix and match omelets and crêpes (daily, 16 place des Vosges, tel. 01 42 77 23 78). **Café Hugo,** next door (open daily, named for the square's most famous resident), is a typical bistro serving good traditional favorites such as onion soup (€6) and crêpes (€5).

$ **Café de la Poste** is a tight little place serving good €11 *plats du jour* from a small but reliable menu (closed Sun, near place de la Bastille at 13 rue Castex, tel. 01 42 72 95 35).

$ **Au Temps des Cerises,** a *très local* wine bar, is relaxed and amiably run by the incredibly mustachioed Monsieur Vimard. This place is great for a colorful lunch or a very light dinner of cheese or cold meats with good wine (Mon–Fri until 20:00, closed Sat–Sun, at rue du Petit-Musc and rue de la Cerisaie).

$ **L'Auberge de Jarente,** is just off the charming place du Marché Ste. Catherine and offers a reliable, rainy-day, budget option, where a hard-working father-and-son team serve good Basque food (€18 three-course *menu* with wine, closed Sun–Mon, just off the square at 7 rue de Jarente, tel. 01 42 77 49 35).

$ **Piccolo Teatro** is where vegetarians should go for a fine meal (closed Mon, near rue des Rosiers, 6 rue des Ecouffes, tel. 01 42 72 17 79).

$ **L'As du Falafel** serves inexpensive Jewish cuisine with bustling ambience (closed Sat, tasty falafels for €5, 34 rue des Rosiers).

$ Several hard-working **Chinese fast food** places are along rue St. Antoine, great for a €6 meal.

Nearer the Pompidou Center and Hôtel de Ville

For eateries at and next to the Pompidou Center, see page 164.

$$$ **Au Bourguignon du Marais,** a small wine bar south of rue de Rivoli, is a place that wine-lovers shouldn't miss. Gentle English-speaking Jacques offers excellent Burgundy wines that blend well with his fine, though limited, selection of *plats du jour* (allow €45 with wine, closed Sat–Sun, call by 19:00 to reserve, 52 rue Francois Miron, tel. 01 48 87 15 40).

$$ **Le Fou d'En Face,** with dynamite ambience inside and out, is a wine-focused restaurant run by an amiable fellow who loves his lot in life. It's on a small square barely off rue de Rivoli near the recommended Hôtel de Nice. Try the *pot-au-feu* (beef stew-€16), and test the superb wine selection (closed Sun, 3 rue du Bourg-Tibourg, tel. 01 48 87 03 75).

$$ **Le Colimacon**, at #44, is a romantic little place twirled around

its spiral stairs *(colimacon)*, offering two-course (€18) or three-course (€23) *menus* of traditional cuisine including *magret de canard aux fruits de saison*—duck breast with a sauce of seasonal fruit (closed Tue, reservations required, tel. 01 48 87 12 01).

$ **BHV Department Store**'s fifth-floor cafeteria provides an escape from the busy streets below, nice views, and no-brainer, point-and-shoot cafeteria cuisine (Mon-Sat 11:30-18:00, closed Sun, at intersection of rue du Temple and rue de la Verrerie, one block from Hôtel de Ville).

$ **Petite Gavroche** is a charmingly basic place offering dirt-cheap French cooking (€8 *plats du jour*, 15 rue Ste. Croix de la Bretonnerie, tel. 01 48 87 74 26).

Picnicking

Picnic at peaceful place des Vosges (closes at dusk) or on the Ile St. Louis *quais* (see below). Stretch your euros at the basement supermarket of the **Monoprix** department store (closed Sun, near place des Vosges on rue St. Antoine). Two small grocery shops are open until 23:00 on rue St. Antoine (near intersection with rue Castex). For a cheap breakfast, try the tiny ***boulangerie-pâtisserie*** where the hotels buy their croissants (coffee machine-€0.70, baby quiche-€1.50, one block off place de la Bastille, corner of rue St. Antoine and rue de Lesdiguières).

Nightlife

The best scene is the bars and dance halls of rue de Lappe (beyond place de la Bastille, see above). Trendy cafés and bars also cluster on rue Vielle du Temple, rue des Archives, and rue Ste. Croix de la Bretonnerie (close about 2:00), and are popular with gay men. **Le Vieux Comptoir** is tiny, lively, and just hip enough (off place des Vosges at 8 rue de Birague). **La Perla** is full of Parisian yuppies in search of the perfect margarita (26 rue François Miron). **The Quiet Man** is a traditional Irish pub with happy hour from 16:00 to 20:00 (5 rue des Haudriettes).

Ile St. Louis

The Ile St. Louis is a romantic and peaceful place to window-shop for plenty of promising dinner possibilities. Cruise the island's main street for a variety of options, from cozy *crêperies* to Italian (intimate pizzeria and upscale) to typical brasseries (several with fine outdoor seating facing the bridge to Ile de la Cité). After dinner, sample Paris' best sorbet. Then stroll across to the Ile de la Cité to see an illuminated Notre-Dame. All listings below line the island's main drag, the rue St. Louis-en-l'Ile (see map on page 55). Consider skipping dessert to enjoy a stroll licking the best ice cream in Paris.

$$ **Le Tastevin** and **Auberge de la Reine Blanche** are two little family-run places that serve top-notch traditional French cuisine with white-tablecloth, candlelit elegance in small, 10-table rooms under

heavy wooden beams. Their *menus* start with three courses at about €29 and offer plenty of classic choices that change with the season for freshness. Le Tastevin at #46, run by Madame Puisieux, is a little more intimate (daily, tel. 01 43 54 17 31). Auberge de la Reine Blanche is a bit more touristy—but in the best sense—with friendly Françoise and her crew working hard to please in a characteristic little place with dollhouse furniture on the walls and a two-dove welcoming committee at the door (closed Wed, #30, tel. 01 46 33 07 87). Reservations are smart for each.

$$ **La Brasserie de l'Ile St. Louis** is situated at the prow of the island's ship as it faces Ile de la Cité, offering fine Alsatian cuisine (try the *choucroute garni* for €16), served in Franco-Germanic ambience with no-nonsense, brasserie service (closed Wed, no reservations, 55 quai de Bourbon, tel. 01 43 54 02 59).

$$ **Nos Ancêtres les Gaulois** and **La Taverne du Sergeant Recruteur,** next door to each other, are famous for their rowdy, medieval cellar atmosphere. They serve all-you-can-eat buffets with straw baskets of raw veggies (cut whatever you like with your dagger), massive plates of pâté, a meat course, and all the wine you can stomach for €36. The food is just food; burping is encouraged. If you want to eat a lot, drink a lot of wine, and holler at your friends while receiving smart-aleck buccaneer service, these food fests can be fun. Nos Ancêtres les Gaulois, or "Our Ancestors the Gauls," has bigger tables and seems made-to-order for local stag parties (daily from 19:00, at #39, tel. 01 46 33 66 07). If you'd rather be surrounded by drunk tourists than locals, pick La Taverne du Sergeant Recruteur. The "Sergeant Recruteur" used to get young Parisians drunk and stuffed here, then sign them into the army (daily from 19:00, #41, tel. 01 43 54 75 42).

$ **Café Med,** closest to Notre-Dame at #77, is best for inexpensive salads, crêpes, and lighter *menus* in a tight but cheery setting (daily, very limited wine list, tel. 01 43 29 73 17, charming Eva SE). There's a similar *crêperie* just across the street.

Riverside Picnic

On sunny lunchtimes and balmy evenings, the *quais* on the Left Bank side of Ile St. Louis is lined with locals who have more class than money, spreading out tablecloths and even lighting candles for elegant picnics. The grocery store on the main drag at 67 rue St. Louis-en-l'Ile is open daily until midnight if you'd like to join them. Otherwise, it's a great walk for people-watching.

Ice Cream Dessert

Half the people strolling Ile St. Louis are licking an ice cream cone, because this is the home of *les glaces Berthillon.* The original **Berthillon** shop, at 31 rue St. Louis-en-l'Ile, is marked by the line of salivating customers (closed Mon-Tue). It's so popular that the wealthy people who can afford to live on this fancy island complain about the congestion it causes. For a less famous but at least as tasty treat, the homemade Italian gelato a block away at **Amorino Gelati** is giving Berthillon competition (no line, bigger portions, easier to see what you want, and they offer little tastes—Berthillon doesn't need to, 47 rue St. Louis-en-l'Ile, tel. 01 44 07 48 08). Having some of each is a fine option.

The Luxembourg-Contrescarpe Neighborhood

There are a few diamonds for fine dining in this otherwise rough, but appealing restaurant area. Most come here for the lively and cheap eateries that line rue Mouffetard and rue du Pot-de-Fer. Study the many menus, compare crowds, then plunge in and have fun (see map on page 309).

$$ **Les Vignes du Panthéon,** near the Panthéon, is a homey, traditional place with a zinc bar and original flooring. It serves a mostly local clientele and will make you feel you're truly in Paris (allow €26 for à la carte, closed Sat–Sun, 4 rue des Fossés St. Jacques, tel. 01 43 54 80 81).

$$ Sprawling **Café Delmas,** on place de la Contrescarpe, is the place to see and be seen with a broad outdoor terrace, tasty salads (€12), and good *plats du jour* from €14 (open daily).

$$ **Le Jardin d'Artemis** is one of the better values on rue Mouffetard, at #34 (€17–26 *menus*, closed Tue).

$ **Le Bistro des Cigales,** between the Panthéon and place de la Contrescarpe, offers an escape to Provence, with deep yellow-and-blue decor and a purely Provençal *menu*, helpful staff, and air-conditioned rooms (€17–24 *menus*, daily, 12 rue Thouin, tel. 01 40 46 03 76).

$ **Gaudeamus,** with a low-profile café on one side and a pleasant bistro on the other, has friendly owners and cheap, €15 *menus* with good vegetarian options (daily, behind the Panthéon, 47 rue de la Montagne Ste. Geneviève, tel. 01 40 46 93 40).

$ **L'Ecurie** is for those who prefer ambience and setting over top cuisine. They serve inexpensive, acceptable meals on small, wood tables around a zinc bar in an unpretentious atmosphere with a few outdoor tables (*menus* from €16, daily, 58 rue de la Montagne Ste. Geneviève, tel. 01 46 33 68 49).

$ **Le Jardin des Pâtes** is popular with less strict vegetarians, serving pastas and salads at fair prices (daily, near Jardin des Plantes, 4 rue Lacépède, tel. 01 43 31 50 71).

$ **Café le Mouffetard** is in the thick of the street-market hustle and bustle (daily, at corner of rue Mouffetard and rue de l'Arbalète).

$ At **Cave de la Bourgogne**, the outdoor tables are picture-perfect (at the bottom of rue Mouffetard on rue de Bazeilles).

$ **Café de la Mosque** makes you feel like you've been beamed to Morocco. At this purely Arab café, order a mint tea, pour in the sugar, and enjoy the authentic interior and peaceful outdoor terrace (behind mosque, 2 rue Daubenton).

Montmartre

Montmartre is extremely touristy, with many mindless mobs following guides to cancan shows. But the ambience is undeniable, and an evening up here overlooking Paris is a quintessential experience in the City of Light. Along the touristy main drag and just off it, several fun piano bars serve reasonable crêpes with great people-watching. More eateries are mentioned in the Montmartre Walk chapter on page 94.

$$ **Restaurant Chez Plumeau,** just off the jam-packed place du Tertre, is a touristy yet cheery, reasonably priced place with great seating on a tiny characteristic square (€25 *menu*, daily, place du Calvaire, tel. 01 46 06 26 29).

$ **L'Eté en Pente Douce,** away from the crowds on a classic neighborhood corner, offers fine indoor and outdoor seating, €10 *plats du jour* and salads, veggie options, and good wines (daily, 23 rue Muller, hike from Sacré-Cœur basilica away from tourist zone and down the stairs, tel. 01 42 64 02 67).

Dinner Cruises

$$$ Several companies offer dinner cruises on the Seine. While touristy, they offer a unique chance to dine as illuminated Paris floats by. Prices vary from €38–125 depending on the "elegance" and drinks you require. Your hotel will have brochures and can reserve, though you might save by contacting them directly. At "Quai 55," the boat **Capitaine Fracasse** offers a basic €35 dinner cruise (daily in summer, closed Mon in winter, boats depart near Eiffel Tower, Mo: Bir-Hakeim, tel. 01 46 21 48 15, www.quai55.com). **Bateaux Parisiens Tour Eiffel** has €90 cruises, including a three-course meal with champagne, red and white wine, music and dancing (nightly, port de la Bourdonnais, Mo: Trocadéro, tel. 01 44 11 33 44, www.bateauxparisiens.com).

LES GRANDS CAFES DE PARIS

Please see "Café Culture" (above) for tips on Parisian cafés.

History of Cafés in Paris

The first café in the Western world was in Paris—established in 1686 at Le Procope (still a restaurant today, see below). The French had just discovered coffee, and their robust economy was growing a population of pleasure-seekers and thinkers looking for places to be seen, to exchange ideas, and to plot revolutions both political and philosophical. And with the advent of theaters like the Comédie Française, the necessary artsy, coffee-sipping crowds were birthed. By 1700, more than 300 cafés had opened their doors; at the time of the Revolution (1789), there were over 1,800 cafés in Paris. Revolutionaries from Jean-Paul Marat and Napoleon to Salvador Dalí enjoyed the spirit of free-thinking that the cafés engendered.

Café society took off in the early 1900s. Life was changing rapidly, with the Industrial Revolution and wars on a global scale. Many retreated to Parisian cafés to try to make sense of the confusion. Vladimir Lenin, Leon Trotsky, Igor Stravinsky, Ernest Hemingway, F. Scott Fitzgerald, James Joyce, Albert Einstein, Jean-Paul Sartre, Gene Openshaw, and Albert Camus were among the devoted café society. Some virtually lived at their favorite café, where they kept their business calendars, entertained friends, and ate every meal. Parisian apartments were small, walls were thin (still often the case), and heating (particularly during war times) was minimal, making the warmth of cafés all the harder to leave.

There are more than 12,000 cafés in Paris today, though their numbers are shrinking. They're still used for business meetings, encounter sessions, political discussions, and romantic interludes. Most Parisians are loyal to their favorites and know their waiter's children's names. And with the recently approved 35-hour workweek, most will have even more time to linger longer over their *café crème.*

Here's a short list of grand Parisian cafés, worth the detour only if you're not in a hurry and don't mind paying outrageous prices for a shot of espresso. Think of these cafés as museums. Try to understand why they matter just as much today as they did yesterday.

Grand Cafés by Neighborhood

St. Germain-des-Prés

Where the boulevard St. Germain meets rue Bonaparte (Mo: St. Germain-des-Prés), you'll find two famous cafés (both open daily). **Les Deux Magots** offers great outdoor seating and a warm interior. Once a favorite of Ernest Hemingway (in *The Sun Also Rises,* Jake met Brett here) and of Jean-Paul Sartre (he and Simone de Beauvoir met here), the café is today filled with international tourists. **Le Café de Flore,** right next door, feels much more local, hip, and literary—wear your black turtleneck. Pablo Picasso was a regular at the time he painted *Guernica.* The smoky interior is popular with Europeans.

For superb outdoor seating and the same delightful view for less, skip these places and set up for coffee or a light lunch at **Café Bonaparte** (big salads, from Les Deux Magots one block down rue Bonaparte toward river). You're farther from the large boulevards, but still in the thick of this pleasant café-sitting area.

Paris' first and most famous, **Café le Procope** lies an enchanting five-minute stroll away. From Café Bonaparte, walk down the rue de l'Abbaye (consider a 20-step detour to rue de Furstemberg en route), then continue onto rue de Bourbon-le-Château, veer left on the picturesque rue de Buci (more cafés), and turn right just after crossing rue de l'Ancienne Comédie. Go up the passageway at 59–61 to find Le

Procope. This place was a café célèbre, drawing notables such as Voltaire, Rousseau, Honoré de Balzac, Emile Zola, Maximilien de Robespierre, Victor Hugo, and two Americans, Benjamin Franklin and Thomas Jefferson (beautiful restaurant and café but average cuisine, Mon–Sat 10:00–24:00, closed Sun, 13 rue de l'Ancienne Comédie, tel. 01 40 46 79 00).

Boulevard du Montparnasse

An eclectic assortment of historic cafés gathers along the busy boulevard du Montparnasse near its intersection with boulevard Raspail (Mo: Vavin). Combine these historic cafés with a visit to the Luxembourg Garden that lies just a few blocks away down rue Vavin (next to Café le Select).

La Coupole, built in the 1920s, was decorated by aspiring artists (Fernand Léger, Constantin Brancusi, and Marc Chagall, among others) in return for free meals. This cavernous place feels like a classy train station, with grand chandeliers, velvet booths, brass decor, and waiters by the dozen. Today, an unappealing glass building towers above. Bring your friends and make noise. The food is fine, but not the reason you came. In fact, I prefer coffee and drinks rather than dinner here (allow €35 per person with wine, daily, 102 boulevard du Montparnasse, tel. 01 43 20 14 20).

Le Dome is right at the intersection of boulevard Raspail and boulevard du Montparnasse and forms a dramatic contrast to the party atmosphere of La Coupole. Smaller, more elegant, and refined in every way, this place makes me want to dress up and look better than I do. Have a drink at the tables just inside, facing the sidewalk. While La Coupole is not known for its cuisine, Le Dome is. Come here for a splurge dinner (figure €40/person with wine, daily, 108 bd. du Montparnasse, tel. 01 43 35 25 81).

Le Select was popular with the more rebellious types—Leon Trotsky, Jean Cocteau, and Pablo Picasso loved it. It feels more conformist today, with good salads €10–14, outdoor seating, and pleasant tables just inside the door (daily, 99 boulevard du Montparnasse, across from La Coupole tel. 01 45 48 38 24).

Avenue des Champs-Elysées

Ladurée is the classic 19th-century tea salon/restaurant/*pâtisserie* on Paris' grandest boulevard (open daily, a block below avenue George V at #75). Its interior is right out of the 1860s. Wander around...you can even peek into the cozy rooms upstairs. A coffee here with a selection of four little macaroons is *très élégant.* The bakery makes traditional macaroons, cute little cakes, and gift-wrapped finger sandwiches.

Fouquet's, a block uphill, opened in 1899 as a coachman's bistro. It gained fame as the hangout of France's WWI biplane fighter pilots—those who weren't shot down by Germany's infamous "Red Baron." I also served as James Joyce's dining room. Today, it's pretty stuffy—unless you're a film star. The golden plaques at the entry are from winners of France's film awards (like the Oscars), the Césars. While the intimidating interior is impressive, the outdoor setting is Champs-Elysées great with pay-for-view espresso (€4.50). Fouquet's was recently saved from foreign purchase and eventual destruction when the government declared it a historic monument (open daily, 99 avenue des Champs-Elysées, Mo: George V).

Near the Louvre

Within a short walk of the Louvre, you'll find melt-in-your-chair cafés (Mo: Palais Royal-Musée du Louvre). The staunchly Parisian **Café le Nemours,** serving pricey but good light lunches, is tucked into the corner of the Palais Royal adjacent to the Comédie Française (leaving the Louvre, cross rue de Rivoli and veer left). Elegant with brass and Art Deco, and with outdoor tables under an arcade two minutes from the pyramid, this place makes a great post-Louvre retreat (daily, 2 place Colette, tel. 01 42 61 34 14).

On Place de la Concorde

Hôtel Crillon's four-star elegance can be yours for an afternoon. Considered the most exclusive (and expensive) hotel in Paris (and the last of the great hotels to be French-owned), this is the place to experience château life. Wear the best clothes you packed, arrive after 15:00, let the bellhop spin the door, and settle into the royal blue chairs in the *salon du thé* (€9 for a pot of tea or double *café au lait,* €30 for high tea served daily 15:30–19:00 with a live harp serenade). You'll be surrounded by famous people you won't recognize (10 place de la Concorde).

At Gare de Lyon

Le Train Bleu is a vast restaurant with a small café-bar area built right into the train station for the Paris Exhibition of 1900 (which also saw the construction of the pont Alexandre III and Grand and Petit Palais). It's a simply grand-scale-everything experience with over-the-top, belle époque decor that speaks of another age—when going to dinner was an event, a chance to see and be seen, and intimate dining was out. Forty-one massive paintings of scenes along the old rail lines tempt diners to consider a short getaway. Reserve ahead for dinner, or drop in for a drink before your train leaves (€45 menu, open daily, up the stairs opposite track L, tel. 01 43 43 09 06, www.le-train-bleu.com).

PARIS WITH **CHILDREN**

Paris is surprisingly kid-friendly. After enjoying so many parks, squares, and sights, your children may want to return to Paris before you do. Consider these tips.

BEFORE YOU GO:

- Get your kids in the spirit: Rent or read Madeline stories by Ludwig Bemelmans, *The Hunchback of Notre-Dame* by Victor Hugo, or *The Man in the Iron Mask* by Alexandre Dumas.
- Hotel selection is critical. Stay in a kid-friendly area near a park. The rue Cler neighborhood is ideal. If you're staying a week or more, rent an apartment (see "For Longer Stays," page 311).
- Bring plenty of kids' books; they're hard to find and expensive in Paris.
- If traveling with infants, pack a light stroller and a child-backpack. Strollers are tough in the Métro and not allowed at many sights, but they're ideal for neighborhood walks.

IN PARIS:

- Don't overdo it. Tackle one key sight each day (Louvre, Orsay Museum, Versailles) and mix with a healthy dose of fun activities. The double-decker bus tours (see page 24) are a great way to start your visit.
- Follow this book's crowd-beating tips to a tee. Kids despise long lines more than you do.
- Eat dinner early (19:00–19:30 at restaurants, earlier at cafés). Skip romantic places. Try relaxed cafés (or fast-food restaurants) where kids can move around without bothering others. Picnics work well.
- The best, cheapest toy selection is in the large department stores, such as Bon Marché (see Shopping chapter, page 340).

- French marionette shows, called *guignols,* are fun for everyone. They take place in several locations in Paris, mostly in big parks. See *Pariscope* or *L'Officiel des Spectacles* (sold at newsstands), under "Marionettes," for times and places. Even in French, the plots are easy to follow. Arrive 20 minutes early for good seats.
- Involve your children in the trip. Let them help choose daily activities, lead you through the Métro, and so on.
- Some Paris parks host temporary amusement parks. The summer Ferris wheel and rides in the Tuileries Garden are the best—my daughter preferred it to Disneyland Paris (for Disneyland Paris details, see page 287).
- Keep in mind that Wednesdays can be busy days at children's sights, since school lets out early.

TOP TEN KIDS' SPOTS IN PARIS

1. Luxembourg Garden: This is my favorite place to mix kid business with pleasure. This perfectly Parisian park has it all, including an extensive big-toys play area with imaginative slides, swings, and jungle gyms (small fee, good for all day, open daily, many parents watch from chairs outside the play area). Kids also like the pedal go-carts, fun merry-go-round, and toy sailboats in the main pond (activities open daily in summer, otherwise Wed and Sat–Sun). Near the main building is a toddler wading pool and sandpit (free). Adults and kids enjoy the terrific puppet shows *(guignols)* held in the afternoons. And of course the park has big open areas perfect for kicking a ball (Mo: St. Sulpice, Odéon, or Notre-Dame-des-Champs, tel. 01 43 26 46 47).

2. Jardin des Plantes: These colorful gardens located across the river from the Marais area are short on grass but have a small zoo, a plant maze, and several kid-friendly natural-science museums (closed Tue). Kids love the dinosaur exhibit at the *Galerie d'Anatomie Comparée et de Paléontologie* (no English explanations but not really needed, kids-€3.10, adults-€5, Wed–Mon 10:00–17:00, closed Tue, includes *Musée de Minéralogie*). The *Grande Galerie de l'Evolution* at the non-river end of the park is a dazzling museum describing the evolution of animals, with huge models and fun exhibits (no English explanations, kids-€5, adults-€7, Wed–Mon 10:00–18:00, until 22:00 Thu, closed Tue). From the park entrance on place Valhubert, the museums line the left side of the park (Mo: Gare d'Austerlitz or Jussieu).

3. Eiffel Tower, Champ de Mars Park, and Trocadéro: You can easily fill an entire kid-fun day here. Come early and ride the elevator up the tower before crowds appear, or ride it above the lights at night (see page 33). The Champ de Mars park stretches out from the tower's base, with picnic-perfect benches, big toys, sand pits, and pony rides near the southwestern corner of the park. The center strip of grass is accessible only after the police leave (about dusk), though the corner grass pockets are fine anytime (Mo: Ecole Militaire or bus #69).

All ages enjoy the view from Trocadéro across the river to the Eiffel Tower, especially after dark (Mo: Trocadéro). In-line skaters and skateboarders make the area below the Trocadéro a gnarly teenage scene, particularly during afternoons and evenings. Two kid-friendly museums flank Trocadéro: the **Naval Museum** *(Musée de la Marine)* and the extensive **Museum of Man** *(Musée de l'Homme)*. Neither offers much information in English, but both are pretty self-explanatory. An impressive collection of ship models, submarines, torpedoes, and naval you-name-it—including a small boat made for Napoleon—are docked at the Naval Museum (kids-€4, adults-€7, covered by museum pass, Wed–Mon 10:00–18:00, closed Tue, on the left side of the Trocadéro Square with your back to the Eiffel Tower). On the other side of the square, the sprawling Museum of Man (*Musée de l'Homme*) is an anthropologist's dream, as cultures from Thailand to Lapland are creatively displayed on several floors with tools, costumes, and musical instruments (under 27-€2, adults-€3, not covered by museum pass, Wed–Mon 9:45–17:15, closed Tue).

4. Notre-Dame, Towers, and Crypt: Paris' famous Gothic cathedral doesn't have to be dry and dull. Replay Quasimodo's stunt and climb the tower (go early or late to avoid long lines). Kids love being on such a lofty perch with a face-to-face look at a gargoyle. The crypt on the square in front of Notre-Dame is quick and interesting. Kids can push buttons to highlight remains of Roman Paris and leave with a better understanding of how different civilizations build on top of each other. The small but beautiful park along the river and behind Notre-Dame has sandboxes, picnic benches, and space to run (Mo: Cité). ✪ See Historic Paris Walk, page 46.

5. Seine River Boat Rides: A variety of boats offer one-hour Seine cruises on huge glass-domed boats, with departures until 23:00. Or hop on a Batobus, a river bus connecting six stops along the river: Eiffel Tower, Orsay/place de la Concorde, Louvre, Notre-Dame, Hôtel de Ville, and St. Germain-des-Prés. Use the Batobus by day, and take a cruise on a Bateau-Mouche at twilight. See "Boat Tours," page 25.

6. Arc de Triomphe and Champs-Elysées: This area is popular with teenagers. Watch the crazy traffic rush around the Arc de Triomphe for endless entertainment, then stroll the avenue des Champs-Elysées, with its car dealerships (particularly Renault's concept-car exhibit), Virgin Megastore (music), Disney store, and the river of humanity that flows along its broad sidewalks. Take your teenager to see a movie on the Champs-Elysées ("*v.o.*" next to the show time means it's shown in the original language). ✪ See Champs-Elysées Walk, page 69.

7. Versailles: This massive complex of palaces, gardens, fountains, and forest can be a good family getaway if well-planned. Do the gardens first and the interior late, when crowds subside. Rent a bike for the gardens or a rowboat for the canal. The Hameau has barnyard animals. Be careful of weekend crowds when the fountains are flowing. ✪ See Versailles Tour, page 244.

8. Pompidou Center: The Pompidou Center appeals more to teens, with its crazy outdoor entertainers, throngs of young people, happening cafés, and fun fountains next door. Inside, the temporary exhibits on the main floor are visually impressive. The *Star Wars* escalator to the top is fun for all ages, but you need to have a museum pass or a ticket for the modern art museum to escalate (Mo: Rambuteau). ✪ See Pompidou Center Tour, page 163.

9. Jardin des Enfants Aux Halles: This is a terrific place to drop your child for an hour (ages 7-11 only, no adults allowed inside). It's outdoors, in front of Les Halles shopping center near St. Eustache church. Kids get one supervised hour (that's it) to negotiate a great play area filled with clever activities, including a small toboggan ride, a maze, a volcano, and much more (€0.40, Mon–Sat 9:00–12:00 & 14:00–18:00, no midday closing Wed or Sat, Sun 13:00–18:00, 105 rue Rambuteau, Mo: Les Halles, tel. 01 45 08 07 18).

10. Aquaboulevard: Paris' best pool/water slide/miniature golf complex is easy to reach and a great escape from the museum scene. Indoor and outdoor pools with high-flying slides, waves, geysers, and Jacuzzis draw kids of all ages. It's a pricey but fun opportunity to see soaked Parisians at play. Ride the Métro to the end of line 8 (Balard stop), walk two blocks under the elevated freeway, veer left across the traffic circle, and find Aquaboulevard in a complex of theaters and shops (kids under 12-€10/6 hrs, adults-€20/6 hrs, cheaper rates for more than one visit, English-speaking staff, keep a €1 coin for lockers, boys and men need Speedo-style swimsuits—€6–10 at the Decathlon sporting goods store right there, tel. 01 40 60 10 00).

SHOPPING

Shopping can provide a good break between Paris' heavyweight museums and monuments. And, if approached carefully, boutique browsing can be a culturally enlightening experience. In this chapter you'll find information on shopping for souvenirs, clothing, food, and bargains.

Most travelers are interested in finding a few souvenirs and maybe an article of clothing. Here's a simplified approach that works for most:

1) If you just need souvenirs, find a souvenir shop or consult your neighborhood's supermarket for that Parisian box of tea, jam, or cookies—perfect for tucking into your suitcase at the last minute.

2) For more elaborate purchasing plans, the city's large department stores offer relatively painless one-stop shopping in elegant surroundings.

3) Neighborhood boutiques offer the greatest reward at the highest risk. While clerks and prices can be intimidating, the selection is more original and the experience totally Parisian.

Tips

Before you enter a Parisian store, remember:

- In small stores, always say *"Bonjour, Madame/Mademoiselle/Monsieur"* when entering and *"Au revoir, Madame/Mademoiselle/Monsieur"* when leaving.
- The customer is not always right. In fact, figure the clerk is doing you a favor by waiting on you.
- Except in department stores, it's not normal for the customer to handle clothing. Ask first if you can look at an item.
- Forget returns (and don't count on exchanges).
- Saturdays are busiest.
- Observe French shoppers. Then imitate.
- Don't feel obliged to buy. The expression for window shopping in French is "*faire du lèche-vitrines*" (literally, window licking).

KEY PHRASES

Just looking.	*Je regards.* (zhuh ruh-gar)
How much is it?	*Combien?* (kohm-bee-ehn)
Too big/small/ expensive	*Trop grand/petit/cher.* (troh grahn/puh-tee/sher)
May I try it on?	*Je peut l'essayer?* (zhuh puh luh-say-yay)
Can I see more?	*Puis-je en voir d'autres?* (pweezh'en vwahr doh-truh)
I'll think about it.	*Je vais y penser.* (zhuh vayz-ee pahn-say)
I'd like this.	*Je voudrais ça.* (zhuh voo-dray sah)
On sale	*Solde* (sold-ay)
Discounted price	*Prix réduit* (pree ray-dwee)
Big discounts	*Prix choc* (pree shock)

Souvenir Shops

Avoid souvenir carts in front of famous monuments. Prices and selection are better in shops and in department stores. Look under the arcades of rue de Rivoli (across from Tuileries Garden), around the Pompidou Center, on the streets of Montmartre, and in department stores (see below). The riverfront stalls near Notre-Dame sell a variety of used books, magazines, and tourist paraphernalia in the most romantic setting.

Department Stores *(Les Grands Magasins)*

Like cafés, department stores were invented here (surprisingly, not in America). While the stores seem overwhelming at first, they generally work like ours, and those listed here are accustomed to wide-eyed foreign shoppers and generally have English-speaking staff. These stores are not only beautiful monuments to a more relaxed, elegant era, but also a great lesson in how others live. It's fun to see what's in style, check out Parisians' current taste in furniture, and compare the selection with Nordstrom's.

Parisian department stores begin with their spectacular perfume sections, almost always at ground zero and worth a visit to see how much space is devoted to scented water. Helpful information desks are usually near the perfume section (pick up the handy floor plan in English). Most stores have a good selection of souvenirs and toys at fair prices, plus reasonable restaurants; some have view terraces. Stores are generally open Monday through Saturday from 10:00 to 19:00.

Choose from these four great Parisian department stores:

Galeries Lafayette and Printemps

You'll find both Galeries Lafayette and Printemps (pran-tom) department stores in several Parisian neighborhoods. The most convenient and busiest are side by side behind the old Opéra (Mo: Chaussée d'Antin-La Fayette, Havre-Caumartin, or Opéra). Both stores sprawl over three buildings and consume entire city blocks. The selection is huge. Don't miss the belle époque dome at Galeries Lafayette or the rooftop view café at Printemps. Fashion shows open to the public are at Galeries Lafayette all year on Tuesdays at 11:00 (call 01 42 82 30 25 to reserve, they speak English). Continue your shopping by walking from this area to the place Vendôme (see "Boutiques," below).

Samaritaine

Samaritaine (sah-mah-ree-ten) is Paris' most central department store on the Seine at pont Neuf (Mo: Pont Neuf). Central and Old World elegant yet not high-priced, this is a handy place to take care of shopping business.

Bon Marché

Combine a visit to Paris' oldest department store with a great neighborhood shopping experience. Take the Métro to Sèvres-Babylone and find the Bon Marché behind a small park. The Bon Marché opened in 1852 when interest in iron and steel construction led to larger structures (like train stations, exhibition halls and Eiffel Towers). The Bon Marché was the first large-scale store to offer fixed-prices (no bargaining), and a huge selection of items under one glass roof. High-volume sales allowed low prices and created loyal customers.

Start your tour at the perfume section in the center, then escalate up a few floors for a better perspective. Consider a new couch (furniture on top floor) and review the toy selection in the basement. Graze the gourmet groceries in the store's second building (next door, ideal for food souvenirs like mustards, teas, and chocolates). I buy a small picnic here for the park in front.

To find my favorite boutique streets (see "Sèvres-Babylone to St. Sulpice," below), walk through the small park and down rue de Sèvres, passing the grand Hôtel Lutècia on your right.

Boutiques

I enjoy sifting through window displays, pausing at corner cafés, and feeling the rhythm of neighborhood life. It's like a vacation from my sightseeing-focused vacation. While shops are more intimate, sales clerks are more formal—mind your manners. Here are four very different areas to lick some windows:

Sèvres-Babylone to St. Sulpice

This shopping stroll allows you to sample smart clothing boutiques and

TIPS ON VAT REFUNDS AND CUSTOMS REGULATIONS

VAT Refunds: Wrapped into the purchase price of your Parisian souvenirs is a Value Added Tax (VAT) that's generally about 17 percent. If you make a purchase of more than €175 at a store that participates in the VAT refund scheme, you're entitled to get most of that tax back. Personally, I've never felt that VAT refunds are worth the hassle, but if you do, here's the scoop.

If you're lucky, the merchant will subtract the tax when you make your purchase; this is more likely if the store ships the goods to your home. If not, follow these steps:

Get the paperwork. Have the merchant completely fill out the necessary refund document, called a "cheque." You'll have to present your passport at the store.

Have your cheque(s) stamped at the border at your last stop in the European Union (usually the airport) by the customs agent who deals with VAT refunds. It's best to keep your purchases in your carry-on for viewing, but if they're too large or considered too dangerous to carry on, then track down the proper customs agent to inspect them before you check your bag. You're not supposed to use your purchased goods before you leave. If you show up at customs wearing your chic new French ensemble, officials might look the other way—or deny you a refund.

To collect your refund, you'll need to return your stamped documents to the retailer or its representative. Many merchants work with a service such as Global Refund or Cashback, which have offices at major airports, ports, or border crossings. These services, which extract a 4 percent fee, can refund your money immediately in your currency of choice or credit your card (within 2 billing cycles). If you have to deal directly with the retailer, mail the store your stamped documents, then wait. It could take months.

Customs Regulations: You can take home $800 in souvenirs per person duty-free. The next $1,000 is taxed at a flat 3 percent. After that, you pay the individual item's duty rate. You can also bring in duty-free a liter of alcohol (slightly more than a standard-sized bottle of wine), a carton of cigarettes, and up to 100 cigars. To check customs rules and duty rates, visit www.customs.gov.

clever window displays while enjoying one of Paris' more handsome neighborhoods. This leisurely, one-hour saunter starts at the Bon Marché department store (described above) and ends at the church of St. Sulpice (though it can easily be extended to the nearby Luxembourg Garden or boulevard St. Germain). After visiting the Bon Marché (Mo:

Sèvres-Babylone), walk by the small park and cross boulevard Raspail with Hôtel Lutècia to your right and start down the rue de Sèvres.

La Maison du Chocolat, next to Hôtel Lutècia (19 rue de Sèvres), sells handmade chocolates in exquisitely wrapped boxes and makes a good first stop. Then cross the street, walk down a block and find a seat at the atmospheric **Au Sauvignon Café** (10 rue de Sèvres), ideal for lunch or a drink and well-situated for watching the conveyor belt of shoppers glide by. Check out the zinc bar and picture-crazy interior. There's a **Mephisto** shoe store around the corner. A block farther down rue de Sèvres, a bizarre half-man, half-horse statue stands guard. From here, boutique-lined streets fan out like spokes on a wheel: rue du Dragon, rue du Cherche Midi, rue de Grenelle, and rue du Vieux Colombier. Each street merits a detour if you're a serious shopper. Rue du Cherche Midi (follow the horse's fanny) offers an ever-changing but always chic selection of shoe, purse, and clothing stores. Find Paris' best bread—beautiful round loaves with designer crust—at **Poilane** at #8.

Back to the horse, turn right and continue down rue du Vieux Colombier. At #57, watch ivory pieces being intricately carved or meticulously restored. At **Longchamps** (#21), you can hunt for a stylish bag in any color. Cross busy rue de Rennes, gasping at the dreadful Montparnasse Tower, and continue down Vieux Colombier. Many stores in this area offer just one or two items, but in a variety of colors and patterns. Check out **Vilebrequin** if the man or *petit-garçon* in your life needs a swimsuit. St. Sulpice awaits a block farther down. The **Café de la Mairie** has a privileged location on this lovely square. From here you can visit St. Sulpice (see page 36), then either cross the square and find Luxembourg Garden (page 37), or backtrack to rue Bonaparte, and turn right to reach the boulevard St. Germain (and our Grand Cafés of Paris stroll, page 332).

Place de la Madeleine, Rue Royale, Place Vendôme and Place de la Concorde

The ritzy streets connecting these high-priced squares are a miracle mile of gourmet food shops, jewelry stores, four-star hotels, perfumeries, and exclusive clothing boutiques. No area better shows the value Parisians place on outrageously priced products. If you include the place Vendôme detour (with brief stops to shop), this walk takes about two hours. For most, the one-hour walk sans detour ending on place de la Concorde offers a sufficient sample of conspicuous consumption.

Place de la Madeleine: Start at the place de la Madeleine (Mo Madeleine; see map on page 31) for a gourmet food fantasy. Work your way counterclockwise around the square, starting at the faded pink awnings of **Fauchon,** behind the basilica (26–30 place de la Madeleíne). This bastion of over-the-top food products has faded from its glory days and today caters to a largely tourist clientele—though it can still make your mouth water and your pocketbook ache. Four separate shops are necessary to meet demand: tea room *(salon de thé)*, meats *(charcuterie)*, pastries *(pâtisserie)*, and a grocery *(épicerie)*. The *charcuterie* and *pâtisserie* are each worth a quick glance (you'll see better elsewhere), but the *épicerie* is a must. Stroll downstairs for €7,000 bottles of Cognac (find *les Alcools de Prestige* in the small glass case at the rear—who buys this stuff?). There's also a room devoted to Champagne, and a wall of bottled waters, both bearing witness to French preoccupation with what they drink (bottled waters come in countless varieties and are evaluated with reverence). Ride the padded pink elevator up to the aromatic tea shop and exotic spice room.

Turn right out of Fauchon's and find **Hédiard** across the square (#21). This older, more appealing, and more accessible gourmet food shop was founded in 1854 and offers elegantly displayed produce and meats, a slick atrium wine shop, and a nifty café above (take the glass elevator up for a coffee or lunch). The small red containers make good souvenirs (with flavored mustards, jams, coffee, candies, and tea). Anyone can enter the glass doors of the wine cellar, but you need special permission to access *Les Vénérables* wines.

Next to Hédiard at #19 is **La Maison des Truffes,** the house of truffles. Check the window display of black mushrooms that sell for about €180/pound. Inside, you'll find seven cozy little tables (€53 tasting menu) and every food that can be made with truffles (even Armagnac brandy), as well as white truffles from Italy that sell for €2,500/pound.

At #17, **Caviar Kaspia,** you can add caviar from Iran, eel, and vodka to your truffle collection. The restaurant upstairs serves (at exorbitant prices) what you see downstairs.

Rue Royale: Passing the snazzy Baccarat crystal shop on your right and keeping straight, cross three crosswalks and trade expensive food for more expensive things. Next to the three-star restaurant **Lucas Carton** (allow €300 for dinner—per person) at 9 place de la Madeleine you'll find **Ecriture & Cie** selling pens that cost more than my car (find the €16,200 Namiki pens). Strut one block down the rue Royale with your new pen and detour into **Le Village Royale** for a cozy lineup of fine shops and a peaceful café break at **Le Coffee Shop.** Continue down rue Royale to rue St. Honoré. At the northeast corner of rue St. Honoré and Rue Royale, **Ladurée** offers an out-of-this-world pastry break in an 1800s setting (daily until 21:00).

Place Vendôme: A detour left on rue St. Honoré leads several blocks past clothing boutiques and a great toy store (**Au Nain Bleu** at #408) to place Vendôme (turn left on rue de Castiglione). The *très* elegant place Vendôme is home to the Ritz Hôtel on the left (Hemingway liberated the bar in World War II) and upper-crust jewelry stores—**Van Cleef & Arpels, Dior, Chanel, Cartier,** and others (if you have to ask how much...). Only jewelry stores are allowed on place Vendôme. The square was created by Louis XIV in the 17th century as a setting for a statue of himself. One hundred and fifty years later, Louis XIV was replaced by a statue of Napoleon. Leave place Vendôme by walking up rue de la Paix—strolling by still more jewelry, high-priced watches, and crystal—and enter place de l'Opéra (*Paris Story* film and the Opéra Garnier, page 39), or return to our walk on rue Royale.

Place de la Concorde: You can pass on the place Vendôme detour and continue two more blocks down rue Royale to its end at place de la Concorde. Browse the crystal shops (follow the lighted cobbles into the **Galerie Royale** at #11 for a royal selection of crystal), then cross rue Royale to pick up your new car at the **Audi Boutique**. At place de la Concorde, find **Hôtel Crillon** for the appropriate finish to this walk (see "Grands Cafés de Paris," page 332).

Marais

For more eclectic, avant-garde stores, peruse the artsy shops between the Pompidou Center and place des Vosges. Stick to the west-to-east axes formed by rue Ste. Croix de la Bretonnerie, rue des Rosiers, rue des Francs Bourgeois, and rue St. Antoine. (These streets are part of the Marais Walk; see map on page 80.) Rue des Francs Bourgeois bustles with trendy boutiques between place des Vosges and the Carnavalet Museum. On Sunday afternoons, when the rest of Paris naps, this area is jammed with shoppers and café crowds.

Bercy Village

For a contemporary, more casual, and less frenetic shopping experience, and to see Paris' latest urban renewal project, come to Bercy Village (daily 11:00–21:00 year-round). Once a thriving wine warehouse district, it traded barrels for boutiques and has been transformed into an outdoor shopping mall. The linear square, cour St. Emilion (named for one of Bordeaux's wine villages), is lined with cafés and appealing shops. Rail tracks are still embedded in the cobbles, and photos of its original purpose hang under the passages. **Club Med** greets you with its "*zone de plaisir*" complex of shops and restaurants that positively throb at night (quiz nights, concerts, and "Friday Night Fever" keep a young clientele well-entertained). Don't miss the **French National Museum store** and the **Animalis** pet shop.

Sleeping in Bercy Village: Hotel Ibis** is a chain hotel offering very cheap and small but clean, modern, and efficient rooms across from cour St. Emilion (Db-€70, 2 place de l'Europe, tel. 01 49 77 11 97, fax 01 49 77 81 91).

Getting to Bercy Village: Take Paris' newest Métro line (14) to the futuristic station at cour St. Emilion (just 2 stops east of Gare de Lyon), where signs lead you into the cour St. Emilion shopping area. The well-manicured parc de Bercy, with flowers and ponds, is next to the Métro stop.

Flea Markets

Paris plays host to three sprawling flea markets (*marché aux puces;* mar-shay oh-poos; literally translated, since *puce* is French for flea). These oversized garage sales were started in the Middle Ages, when middlemen would sell old, flea-infested clothes and discarded possessions of the wealthy at bargain prices to eager peasants. Buyers were allowed to rummage through piles of aristocratic garbage.

No event better brings together the melting-pot population of Paris than these carnival-like markets. Some find them claustrophobic and crowded, others find their French *diamants*-in-the-rough and return happy. All three of Paris' flea markets take place over weekends and two are open Mondays (the calmest day). Come early for the best deals and fewest crowds. You can bargain a bit, and you'll generally do better by paying with cash. Wear your moneybelt; pickpockets enjoy these wall-to-wall-shopper events.

The **Puces St. Ouen** (poos sahn-wahn, Sat 9:00–18:30, Sun–Mon 10:00–18:30, closed Tue–Fri) is the mother of all flea markets, with more than 2,000 vendors selling everything from flamingos to faucets, but mostly antiques (near as I can tell, the term "antique" covers anything from funky art objects to Louis XVI chairs). Thirteen different "antique markets" and endless stalls fill this strange area just outside Paris. Space was created in the 1800s when the city wall was demolished (now a freeway), which left large tracts of land open. The vacuum eventually was filled by street vendors, then antique dealers. The hodgepodge pattern of markets reflects their unplanned evolution. Strolling the markets can feel more like touring a souk in North Africa (narrow alleys packed with people and too much to see).

Even if antiques, African objects, and T-shirts aren't your thing, you'll still probably find this market worth the Métro ride. Come for lunch (many lively and reasonable cafés) and a reality check, away from the beautiful people and glorious monuments of Paris. You'll get a dose of life in "the burbs." Take Métro line 4 to Porte de Clingancourt (end of the line) then carefully follow *Sortie, Marché aux Puces* signs. Walk straight out of the Métro down avenue de la Porte de Clingancourt, passing by leather stores and through blocks of trinkets and cheap clothing stalls. Your destination is just beyond the elevated freeway (white bridge). Cross under the freeway (leaving Paris and entering the suburb of St. Ouen), veer left on the angled street, then turn left onto rue des Rosiers—the spine that links the many markets of St. Ouen. Most markets consist of a series of covered alleys, each specializing in a different angle on antiques, bric-a-brac, and junk. You'll see Marchés Vernaison, Dauphine, Biron, and Paul Bert by walking down rue des Rosiers, then turning left on rue Paul Bert, then left again on rue Jules Vallès and returning to the Métro.

Puces de Vanves is comparatively tiny and civilized (Sat–Sun

7:00–13:00, closed Mon–Fri, Mo: Porte de Vanves). The mega-**Puces de Montreuil** is the least organized and most traditional of them all, with chatty sellers and competitive buyers (Sat–Mon 8:00–18:00, closed Tue–Fri, Mo: Porte de Montreuil).

Street Markets

Several traffic-free street markets (like rue Cler) overflow with flowers, produce, fish vendors, and butchers, which illustrates how most Parisians shopped until the invention of supermarkets and department stores. Browse these markets for picnics, or find a corner café from which to appreciate the scene.

Here is a list of Paris' most appealing street markets (open daily except Sun afternoons and Mon; also closed for lunch 13:00–15:00):

Rue Cler is a refined street market serving an upscale neighborhood near the Eiffel Tower (Mo: Ecole Militaire, for details, see Rue Cler Walk, page 87).

Rue Montorgueil is a thriving and less touristed market street. Only blocks from the Louvre and Pompidou Center, rue Montorgueil is famous as the last vestige of the once-massive Les Halles market (just north of St. Eustache church, Mo: Etienne Marcel). Other traffic free streets cross rue Montorgueil—don't miss the nearby covered arcade, passage du Grand Cerf (down rue Marie Stuart at the Les Halles end of rue Montorgueil).

Rue Mouffetard is touristy but fun. Combine a visit to this market with the Luxembourg Garden (start at place de la Contrescarpe and work your way down, Mo: Cardinal Lemoine or Censier-Daubenton; for more, see Luxembourg Garden, page 37, and "Contrescarpe Orientation," page 307).

Rue Daguerre, near the Catacombs, is the least touristy of the four (off avenue du Général Leclerc, Mo: Denfert-Rochereau; for Catacombs description, see page 38).

Rue de Seine and rue de Buci combine to make a central and colorful market within easy reach of many sights (Mo: Odéon, see also Grand Cafés de Paris, page 332, and Left Bank Walk, page 105).

Weekly Markets: Offering cheaper prices and more selection, these markets take over selected boulevards and squares throughout Paris (8:00–12:30). Expect a lively combination of flea- and street-market atmosphere and items.

Marché de la Place d'Aligre, a few blocks behind the Opéra Bastille, runs daily and is a more intimate, locally popular open-air market (daily 9:00–12:00, place d'Aligre, Mo: Ledru-Rollin).

Marché de la Bastille is huge, with a vast selection of products (Thu and Sun, Mo: Bastille); consider combining either of these two markets with a stroll through Promenade Plantée park (see page 44) and the Marais Walk (page 79).

Marché Place Monge is comparatively minuscule, specializing in high-quality foods (Wed, Fri, and Sun, near rue Mouffetard, Mo: Monge).

Marché Boulevard de Grenelle, a few blocks southwest of the Champ de Mars park and the rue Cler area, is packed with produce, non-perishable goods, and Parisians in search of a good value (Wed and Sun, between Dupleix and La Motte Picquet-Grenelle Métro stops).

Marché Belleville is big and very untouristy (Tue and Fri, Mo: Belleville).

Arcaded Shopping Streets *(Passages)*

Over 200 of these covered shopping streets once crisscrossed Paris, providing much needed shelter from the rain. The first were built during the American Revolution, though the ones you'll see date from the 1800s. Today only a handful remain to remind us where department stores got their inspiration, although they now sell things you would be more likely to find in flea markets than at JCPenney. Here's a short list to weave into your sightseeing plan (they are located on the color map of Paris at the beginning of this book).

Galerie Colbert and **Galerie Vivienne**, behind the Palais Royal off rue du Petits-Champs and a few blocks from the Louvre (Mo: Pyramides or Palais Royal), are the classiest and most accessible of the passages for most, though they don't reflect the typical, more funky passages. Check out Le Grand Colbert, a surprisingly affordable yet elegant restaurant with decent cuisine.

Passage Choiseul and **Passage Ste. Anne,** four blocks west of galerie Colbert and galerie Vivienne (down rue des Petits-Champs toward avenue de l'Opéra, same Métro stops), are classic examples of most Parisian passages, selling used books, paper products, trinkets, and snacks.

Passage du Grand Cerf is a more elegant arcade, easily combined with a visit to the nearby rue Montorgueil street market, described above (Mo: Etienne Marcel).

Passage Panoramas and **Passage Jouffroy** are long galleries that connect with several other smaller passages to give you the best sense of the elaborate network of arcades that once existed (on both sides of boulevard Montmartre, between Métro stops Grand Boulevards/rue Montmarte and Richelieu Drouot).

NIGHTLIFE

Paris is brilliant after dark. Save energy from your day's sightseeing and experience the City of Light lit up. Whether it's a concert at the Sainte-Chapelle, a boat ride on the Seine, a walk in Montmartre, a hike up the Arc de Triomphe, or a late-night café, you'll see Paris come alive. Night walks in Paris are wonderful. Any of our walking tours are terrific after dark. *Pariscope* magazine (€0.40 at any newsstand, in French) offers a complete weekly listing of music, cinema, theater, opera, and other special events—I decipher this useful periodical for you below. The *Paris Voice* newspaper, in English, has a monthly review of Paris entertainment (available at any English-language bookstore, French-American establishments, or the American Church, www.parisvoice.com).

A Tour of *Pariscope*

The weekly *Pariscope* (€0.40) or *L'Officiel des Spectacles* (€0.35) is essential if you want to know what's going on in Paris. I prefer *Pariscope* and have explained its organization below. Pick one up at a newsstand and page through it.

There's a small English "*Time Out*" section at the end of the magazine listing the week's events and their top pick of movies, nightlife, music, and other odds and ends.

To decipher the French part: The magazine begins with culture news (*On en Parle*). The next section "Théâtre," lists what's playing at all key theater venues, including both opera houses (if performances are scheduled). "Musique" and Concerts Classiques" follow, listing each day's events (program, location, time, and price). Remember that some concerts are free *(entrée libre).*

"Enfants" section, covers the myriad of possible children's activities. "Spectacles" are shows (like magic shows); you'll also see many "Marionettes" shows and "Cirques" (circuses)—both are fun even for non-French speakers.

A third of the magazine is devoted to *Cinéma*—a Parisian forté. The "Films en Exclusivité" pages list all the films playing in town. While a code marks films as "Comédie," "Documentaire," "Karaté," "Erotisme," and so on, the key mark for tourists is "v.o.," which means *version originale* (original language version). "Dessin Animé" means cartoon. Films are listed alphabetically, by neighborhood ("Salles Paris") and by genre. To find a showing near your hotel, simply match the *arrondissement.* "Salles Périphérie" are out in the suburbs.

The next section, "Arts" lists current hours for temporary expositions, and all museums. (*tlj* = daily, *sf* = except, *Ent* = entry price, *TR* = reduced price, usually for students and children).

For cancan mischief, look under "Paris la Nuit."

Music

Jazz Clubs: With a lively mix of American, French, and international musicians, Paris has been an internationally acclaimed jazz capital since World War II. Unfortunately, many clubs are smoky, some wedge too many customers into too few tables, others are downright expensive, and some are guilty of all of the above. You'll pay €7–25 to enter a jazz club (one drink may be included; if not, expect to pay €5–10 per drink; beer is cheapest). See *Pariscope* magazine under "Musique" for listings, or better, the American Church's *Paris Voice* paper for a good monthly review, or drop by the clubs to check out their calendars posted on the front door. Music starts after 21:00 in most clubs. Some offer dinner concerts from about 20:30 on. Here are several good bets:

Caveau de la Huchette, a characteristic old jazz club, fills an ancient Latin Quarter cellar with live jazz and frenzied dancing every night (€9 weekday, €12 weekend admission, €5 drinks, Tue–Sun 21:30–2:30 or later, closed Mon, 5 rue de la Huchette, Mo: St. Michel, recorded info tel. 01 43 26 65 05).

For a hotbed of late-night activity and jazz, go to the two-block-long rue des Lombards, at boulevard Sébastopol, midway between the river and the Pompidou Center (Mo: Châtelet). **Au Duc des Lombards,** right at the corner, is one of the most popular and respected jazz clubs in Paris, with concerts generally at 21:00 (42 rue des Lombards, tel. 01 42 33 22 88). **Le Sunside** offers more traditional jazz—Dixieland and big band—and fewer crowds, with concerts generally at 21:00 (60 rue des Lombards, tel. 01 40 26 21 25).

At the more down-to-earth and mellow **Le Cave du Franc Pinot,** you can enjoy a glass of chardonnay at the main-floor wine bar, then drop downstairs for a cool jazz scene (good dinner-and-jazz values as well, located on Ile St. Louis where pont Marie meets the island, 1 quai de Bourbon, Mo: Pont Marie, tel. 01 46 33 60 64).

If it's a blues band you seek, join Parisian lovers of mostly American bands at **The Front Page** (58 rue St. Denis, Mo: Etienne Marcel).

Classical Concerts: For classical music on any night, consult *Pariscope* magazine; the "Musique" section under "Concerts Classiques" lists concerts (free and fee). Look for posters at the churches. Churches that regularly host concerts (usually March–Nov) include St. Sulpice, St. Germain-des-Prés, Ste. Madeleine, St. Eustache, St. Julien-le-Pauvre, and Sainte-Chapelle. It's worth the €15–23 entry for the pleasure of hearing Mozart while surrounded by the stained glass of the tiny Sainte-Chapelle (it's unheated—bring a sweater). Look also for daytime concerts in parks, such as the Luxembourg Garden. Even the Galeries Lafayette department store offers concerts. Many concerts are free *(entrée libre)*, such as the Sunday atelier concert sponsored by the American Church (17:00, Jan–June and Sept–Nov, 65 quai d'Orsay, Mo: Invalides, RER: Pont de l'Alma, tel. 01 40 62 05 00, www.acparis.org).

Opera: Paris is home to two well-respected opera venues. The Opéra Bastille is the massive modern opera house that dominates place de la Bastille. Come here for state-of-the-art special effects and modern interpretations of classic ballets and operas. In the spirit of this everyman's opera, unsold seats are available at a big discount to seniors and students 15 minutes before the show (Mo: Bastille, tel. 01 43 43 96 96). The Opéra Garnier, Paris' first opera house, hosts opera and ballet performances. Come here for less expensive tickets and grand belle époque decor (Mo: Opéra, tel. 01 44 73 13 99). For tickets, call 01 44 73 13 00, go to the opera ticket offices (open 11:00–18:00), or best, reserve on the Web at www.opera-de-paris.fr (for both opera houses).

Bus Tours

Several companies offer after-dark tours of Paris. I've described two here. These trips are sold through your hotel (brochures in lobby) or directly at the offices listed below. You save no money by buying direct.

Paris Illumination Tours, run by Paris Vision, connect all the great illuminated sights of Paris with a 100-minute bus tour in 12 languages. Double-decker buses have huge windows, but customers continuing to the overrated Moulin Rouge get the most desirable front seats.

You'll stampede on with a United Nations of tourists, get an audioguide, and listen to a tape-recorded spiel (interesting but occasionally hard to hear). Uninspired as it is, this provides an entertaining first-night overview of the city at its floodlit and scenic best (bring your city map to stay oriented as you go). Left-side seats are marginally better. Visibility is fine in the rain. You're always on the bus except for one five-minute cigarette break at the Eiffel Tower viewpoint (adults-€26, kids under 11 ride free, departures usually at 20:30 but earlier off-season, also at 21:30 April–Oct only, confirm departure time, departs from Paris Vision office at 214 rue de Rivoli, across the street from Mo: Tuileries, tel. 01 42 60 30 01, www.parisvision.com).

Touringscope offers the same kind of bus tour but with live guides (they try to keep the different languages to no more than three). This smaller, "we try harder" company offers better service and if their big buses don't fill up, they'll send you in a more personal minivan (buses depart from 11 boulevard Haussmann, Mo: Opéra or Chausée d'Antin-La Fayette, tel. 01 53 34 11 94, www.touringscope.com/home.html).

Minivan Tours

The same companies will take you on the same route for twice the price by minivan—maximum seven people (often fewer are in your van). Pick-up is at your hotel and the driver is a qualified (if not always charismatic) guide. You can get to places the big buses can't, though the ride is bumpier and you're not as high as in a bus. The guide is yours for 90 minutes, so have all your questions ready to make the most of this (adult-€48, ages 4–11-€25).

Seine River Cruises

Bateaux-Mouches offer one-hour cruises on huge glass-domed boats with departures along the Seine, including from the Eiffel Tower (every 20–30 min 10:00–22:30, see page 25).

Art in the Evening

Various **museums** are open late on different evenings, offering the opportunity for more relaxed, less-crowded visits: Louvre (Wed), Orsay (Thu), and Pompidou (Wed–Mon).

Art gallery openings are a fun way to check out new work by contemporary artists. Opening night receptions (*vernissage*) are both classy and free. Check upcoming events at www.associationdesgaleries.org.

Night Walks

Go for a walk to best appreciate the City of Light. Break for ice cream, pause at a café, and enjoy the sidewalk entertainers as you join the post-dinner Parisian parade. Use any of our self-guided walking tours as a blueprint, and remember to avoid poorly lit areas and to stick to main thoroughfares. Consider the following suggestions; most are partial versions of our longer walking tours.

Champs-Elysées and the Arc de Triomphe—✪ See Champs-Elysées Walk, page 69. The avenue des Champs-Elysées glows after dark. Start at the Arc de Triomphe, then stroll down Paris' lively grand promenade. A right turn on avenue George V leads to the Bateaux-Mouches river cruises. A movie on the Champs-Elysées is a fun experience (weekly listings in *Pariscope* under "Cinéma").

Trocadéro and Eiffel Tower—This is one of Paris' most spectacular views at night. Take the Métro to the Trocadéro stop and join the party on place de la Trocadéro for a magnificent view of the glowing Eiffel Tower. It's a festival of gawkers, drummers, street acrobats, and entertainers. Pass the fountains and cross the river to the base of the tower, worth the effort even if you don't go up. See "Eiffel Tower," page 33.

From the Eiffel Tower, you can stroll through parc du Champ de Mars past Frisbees, soccer balls, and romantic couples and take the Métro home (Ecole Militaire stop, across avenue de la Motte Picquet from far southeast corner of park). Or, there's a handy RER stop (Champ de Mars–Tour Eiffel) two blocks west of the Eiffel Tower.

Ile St. Louis and Notre-Dame—✪ See Historic Paris Walk, page 46. Take this beautiful stroll after dinner on Ile St. Louis (see page 329).

To get to Ile St. Louis, take the Métro (line 7) to the Pont Marie stop, then cross pont Marie to Ile St. Louis. Turn right up rue St. Louis-en-l'Ile, stopping for dinner—or at least a Berthillon ice cream at #31 or Amorino Gelati at #47. At the end of Ile St. Louis, cross pont St. Louis to Ile de la Cité with a great view of Notre-Dame. Cross to the left bank on quai de l'Archevêché and drop down to the river to the right for the best floodlit views. End your walk on place du Parvis Notre-Dame in front of Notre-Dame or continue across the river to the Latin Quarter.

Place de la Concorde, Place Vendôme and Place de l'Opéra—✪ See Shopping, page 340. These three squares tie together nicely for an elegant post-dinner walk. Take the Métro to place de la Concorde and consider an expensive drink at the most expensive hotel in Paris (Hôtel Crillon, see "Grands Cafés de Paris," page 332). Get out to the obelisk for a terrific view of the Champs-Elysées and the beautifully-lit Greek-looking National Assembly building (to your left looking up the Champs-Elysées). Now, walk up rue Royale toward the Madeleine church, turn right on rue St. Honoré, then left after several blocks on rue Castiglione. The sumptuous place Vendôme makes me wish I were rich. Exit place Vendôme at the opposite end and walk up the rue de la Paix to find the Opéra Garnier, stunning at night (see page 39, Mo: Opéra is right there to take you home).

Montmartre—✪ See Montmartre Walk, page 94. Take the funicular to the area near Sacré-Cœur and join the party. Follow our walking tour as far as you like, but keep to the top of the hill (avoid place Pigalle and boulevard de Rochechouart). Have a drink on place du Tertre and get your portrait sketched. Montmartre was a nighttime destination for Parisians in search of a lively evening even before the Impressionists arrived.

Rue de Lappe—Take a walk on Paris' wild side along the three-block stretch of rue de Lappe behind the Bastille from boulevard Richard Lenoir to rue de Charonne (Mo: Bastille). Nightclubs, bouncer-staffed bars, and youthful, boy-meets-girl energy power this late-night scene.

Place St. Germain-des-Prés—The square along the Left Bank's main east-west route hosts street theater and musicians that are better than ones you'll hear in the Métro. The church of St. Germain-des-Prés is often lit up and open at night, and Parisians sip drinks at two famous nearby cafés—see page 333 (Mo: St. Germain-des-Prés).

Odéon and Rue de Buci—In the heart of the Left Bank, Odéon is home to several movie theaters, and the surrounding area is colorful (Mo: Odéon).

TRANSPORTATION **CONNECTIONS**

This chapter covers Paris' two airports, six train stations, and main bus station, plus parking tips for drivers.

When leaving Paris, arrive at your departure point early to allow time for waiting in lines (three hours for an overseas flight, or one hour before a flight within Europe, a train trip—including Eurostar, or a bus ride). For the latest information on Paris airports, check www.adp.fr.

CHARLES DE GAULLE AIRPORT

Paris' primary airport has two main terminals: T-1 and T-2, and two lesser terminals, T-3 and T-9. United, US Airways, SAS, KLM, Northwest, and Lufthansa all normally use T-1. Air France dominates T-2, though you'll also find British Airways, Delta, Continental, American, and Air Canada. Smaller airlines use T-3 and charter flights leave from T-9. Airlines sometimes switch terminals, so verify your terminal before flying. Terminals are connected every few minutes by a free *navette* (shuttle bus, line #1). The RER (Paris subway) stops at T-2 and T-3 terminals, and the TGV (stands for *train à grande vitesse;* tay-zhay-vay) station is at T-2. There is no bag storage at the airport. Beware of pickpockets on *navettes* between terminals and (worse) on RER trains. Do not take an unauthorized taxi from the men greeting you on arrival (official taxi stands are well signed).

Those flying to or from the United States will almost certainly use T-1 or T-2. Below is information for each terminal. For flight information, call 01 48 62 22 80.

TERMINAL 1 (T-1): This circular terminal covers three floors—arrival (*arrivées*, top floor), departure (*départs*, one floor down) and shops/boutiques (basement level). For information on getting to Paris, see "Transportation between Charles de Gaulle Airport and Paris," below.

On the **arrival** level you'll find a variety of services at these gates.

Gate 36 (called *Meeting Point*): ADP, a quasi–tourist office, sells museum passes, offers free maps, and provides tourist/hotel information (daily 7:00–22:00). A nearby *Relay* store sells phone cards. To find the shuttle buses (*navettes*) for Terminal 2 and the RER trains to Paris, take the elevator down to level (*niveau*) 2, then walk outside (line #1 serves T-2 including the TGV station; line #2 goes directly to the RER station).

Gate 34: Outside are Air France buses to Paris and Orly Airport.

Gate 32: ATMs. Outside are Roissy Buses to Paris (buy tickets inside at gate 30 or from driver) and Disneyland Express buses.

Gate 22: SNCF train ticket office

Gate 20: Taxis outside

Gate 16: A bank with lousy rates for currency exchange.

Gates 10-24: Car-rental offices.

The **departure level** (*niveau* 3) is limited to flight check-in, though you will find ADP information desks here. Those departing from T-1 will find restaurants, a PTT (post office), a pharmacy, boutiques, and a handy grocery store one floor below the ticketing desks (level 2 on the elevator).

TERMINAL 2 (T-2): This long, horseshoe-shaped terminal is divided into several sub-terminals (or Halls), each identified by a letter. Halls are connected with each other, the RER, the TGV station, and T-1 every five minutes with free *navettes* (shuttle buses, line #1 runs to T-1). Here is where you should find these key carriers: in Hall A—Air France, Air Canada, and American Airlines; in Hall C—Delta, Continental, and more Air France; and in Hall D—British Airways. The RER and TGV stations are below the Sheraton Hotel (access by *navettes* or on foot). Stops for *navettes*, Air France buses, and Roissy Buses are all well-marked and near each Hall (see "Transportation between Charles de Gaulle Airport and Paris," below). ADP information desks are located near gate 5 in each Hall. Car-rental offices, post offices, pharmacies, and ATMs *(point d'argent)* are also well-signed.

Transportation between Charles de Gaulle Airport and Paris: Three efficient public-transportation routes, taxis, and airport shuttle vans link the airport's terminals with central Paris. All are well-marked and stops are centrally located at all terminals. (If you're carrying lots of baggage or just plain tired, airport shuttle vans or taxis are well worth the extra cost). The Roissy bus and Métro combination is the most convenient public transport route to rue Cler area hotels; the Air France bus to Gare de Lyon (then Métro line 1) is the easier route to hotels in the Marais (both described below).

RER trains, with stops near T-1 and at T-2 (€8), run every 15 minutes and stop at Gare du Nord, Châtelet-Les Halles, St. Michel, and Luxembourg in central Paris. When coming from Paris to the airport, T-1 is the first RER stop at Charles de Gaulle; T-2 is the second stop. Beware of pickpockets preying on jet-lagged tourists on these trains; wear your moneybelt. The other transportation options described below have far fewer theft problems.

Roissy Buses run every 15 minutes to Paris' Opéra Garnier (€8, 40-60 min). You'll arrive (and also depart) from a bus stop on rue Scribe at the American Express office on the left side of the Opéra. To reach rue Cler and Marais hotels, turn left out of the bus and find the Métro entrance in front of the Opéra. Take the Métro (direction Balard) to Ecole Militaire or La Tour Maubourg. For rue Cler hotels, take it in direction of Créteil Préfecture to Bastille stop for Marais hotels.

Air France bus routes serve central Paris about every 15 minutes (Arc de Triomphe and Porte Maillot-€10, 40 min; Montparnasse Tower/train station-€11.50, 60 min; or the Gare de Lyon station-€11.50, 40 min). To reach Marais hotels from Gare de Lyon, take Métro line 1 (direction La Défense) to the Bastille, St. Paul, or Hôtel de Ville stops.

Taxis with luggage will run €40–55 with bags. If taking a cab to the airport, ask your hotel to call for you (the night before if you must leave early) and specify that you want a real taxi *(un taxi normal)* and not a limo-service that costs €20 more.

Airport shuttles offer a less stressful trip between either of Paris' airports and downtown, ideal for single travelers or families of four or more (taxis are limited to three). Reserve from home and they'll meet you at the airport (€23 for one person, €27 for two, €41 for three, €55 for four, plan on a 30-min wait if you ask them to pick you up at the airport). Be clear on where and how you are to meet your driver. Choose between **Airport Connection** (tel. 01 44 18 36 02, fax 01 45 55 85 19, www.airport-connection.com) and **Paris Airports Service** (tel. 01 55 98 10 80, fax 01 55 98 10 89, www.parisairportservice.com).

Sleeping at or near Charles de Gaulle Airport: Hôtel Ibis**, outside the RER Roissy Rail station at T-3 (the first RER stop coming from Paris), offers standard and predictable accommodations (Db-€90, near *navette* stop, free shuttle bus to all terminals, tel. 01 49 19 19 19, fax 01 49 19 19 21, h1404sb@accor-hotels.com). **Novotel***** is next door and the next step up (Db-€155–170, tel. 01 49 19 27 27, fax 01 49 19 27 99, h1014@accor-hotels.com).

To avoid rush-hour traffic, drivers may consider sleeping north of Paris in either **Auvers-sur-Oise** (30 min west of airport, see accommodations on page TK) or in the pleasant medieval town of **Senlis** (15 min north of airport) at **Hostellerie de la Porte Bellon** (Db-€55-75, in the center at 51 rue Bellon, near rue de la République, tel. 03 44 53 03 05, fax 03 44 53 29 94).

ORLY AIRPORT

This airport feels small. Orly has two terminals: Sud and Ouest. International flights arrive at Sud. After exiting Sud's baggage claim (near gate H), you'll see signs directing you to city transportation, car rental, and so on. Turn left to enter the main terminal area, and you'll find exchange offices with bad rates, an ATM, the ADP (a quasi–tourist office that offers free city maps and basic sightseeing information, open until 23:00), and an SNCF French rail desk (closes at 18:00, sells train tickets and even Eurailpasses, next to ADP). Downstairs is a sandwich bar, WCs, a bank (same bad rates), a newsstand (buy a phone card), and a post office (great rates for cash or American Express traveler's checks). Car-rental offices are located in the parking lot in front of the terminal. For flight info on any airline serving Orly, call 01 49 75 15 15.

Transportation between Orly Airport and Paris: Several efficient public-transportation routes, taxis, and a couple of airport shuttle services link Orly with central Paris. The gate locations listed below apply to Orly Sud, but the same transportation services are available from both terminals.

The **Air France bus** (outside gate K) runs to Paris' Invalides Métro stop (€8, 4/hr, 30 min) and is handy for those staying in or near the rue Cler neighborhood (from Invalides bus stop, take the Métro two stops to Ecole Militaire to reach recommended hotels, see also RER Trains below).

Bus #285 (also called Jetbus, outside gate H, €5, 4/hr) is the quickest way to the Paris subway and the best way to the Marais and Luxembourg-Contrescarpe neighborhoods. Take Jetbus to Villejuif-Louis Aragon Métro stop, buy a *carnet* of 10 Métro tickets, then take the Métro to the Sully-Morland stop for the Marais area, or the Censier-Daubenton or Monge stops for the Contrescarpe area. If you're going to the airport, make sure your train serves Villejuif, as the route splits at the end of the line. The **Orlybus** (outside gate H, €6, 4/hr) takes you to the Denfert-Rochereau RER-B line and the Métro, offering subway access to central Paris.

These routes provide access to Paris via **RER trains**: an ADP shuttle bus takes you to RER line C, with connections to Gare d'Austerlitz, St. Michel, Musée d'Orsay, Invalides, and Pont de l'Alma stations (outside gate G, 4/hr, €5.50). The **Orlyval trains** are overpriced (€9) and require a transfer at the Antony stop to reach RER line B (serving Luxembourg, Châtelet-Les Halles, St. Michel, and Gare du Nord stations in central Paris).

Taxis are to the far right as you leave the terminal, at gate M. Allow €26–35 with bags for a taxi into central Paris.

Airport shuttle minivans are ideal for single travelers or families of four or more (see "Charles de Gaulle Airport," above, for the companies to contact; from Orly, figure about €18 for one person, €12/person for two, less for larger groups and kids).

Sleeping near Orly Airport: Hôtel Ibis** is reasonable, basic, and close by (Db-€60, tel. 01 56 70 50 60, fax 01 56 70 50 70, h1413@accor-hotels.com). **Hôtel Mercure***** provides more comfort for a price (Db-€120–135, tel. 01 49 75 15 50, fax 01 49 75 15 51, h1246@accor-hotels.com). Both have free shuttles to the terminal.

PARIS' TRAIN STATIONS

Paris is Europe's rail hub, with six major train stations, each serving different regions: Gare de l'Est (eastbound trains), Gare du Nord (northern France and Europe), Gare St. Lazare (northwestern France), Gare d'Austerlitz (southwestern France and Europe), Gare de Lyon (southeastern France and Italy), and Gare Montparnasse (northwestern France and TGV service to France's southwest). Any train station can give you schedule information, make reservations, and sell tickets for any destination. Buying tickets is handier from an SNCF neighborhood office (e.g., Louvre, Invalides, Orsay, Versailles, airports) or at your neighborhood travel agency—worth the small fee (SNCF signs in their window indicate they sell train tickets). For schedule information, call 08 36 35 35 35 (€0.50/min, English sometimes available).

All six train stations have Métro, bus, and taxi service. All have banks or change offices, ATMs, information desks, telephones, cafés, baggage storage *(consigne automatique*, none at Gare St. Lazare), newsstands, and clever pickpockets. Each station offers two types of rail service: long distance to other cities, called *Grandes Lignes* (major lines); and suburban service to outlying areas, called *banlieue* or RER. Both *banlieue* and RER trains serve outlying areas and the airports; the only difference is that *banlieue* lines are operated by SNCF (France's train system) and RER lines are operated by RATP (Paris' Métro and bus system). Paris train stations can be intimidating, but if you slow down, take a deep breath, and ask for help, you'll find them manageable and efficient. Bring a pad of paper for clear communication at ticket/info windows. All stations have helpful *accueil* (information) booths; the bigger stations have roving helpers, usually in red vests.

Station Overview

Here's an overview of Paris' major train stations. Métro, RER, buses, and taxis are well-signposted at every station. When arriving by Métro, follow signs for *Grandes Lignes*-SNCF to find the main tracks.

Gare du Nord: This vast station serves cities in northern France and international destinations north of Paris, including Copenhagen, Amsterdam (see "To Brussels and Amsterdam by Thalys Train," below), and the Eurostar to London (see "To London by Eurostar Train," below) as well as two of the day trips described in this book (Auvers-sur-Oise and Chantilly).

Arrive early to allow time to navigate this station. From the Métro,

France's Train Stations

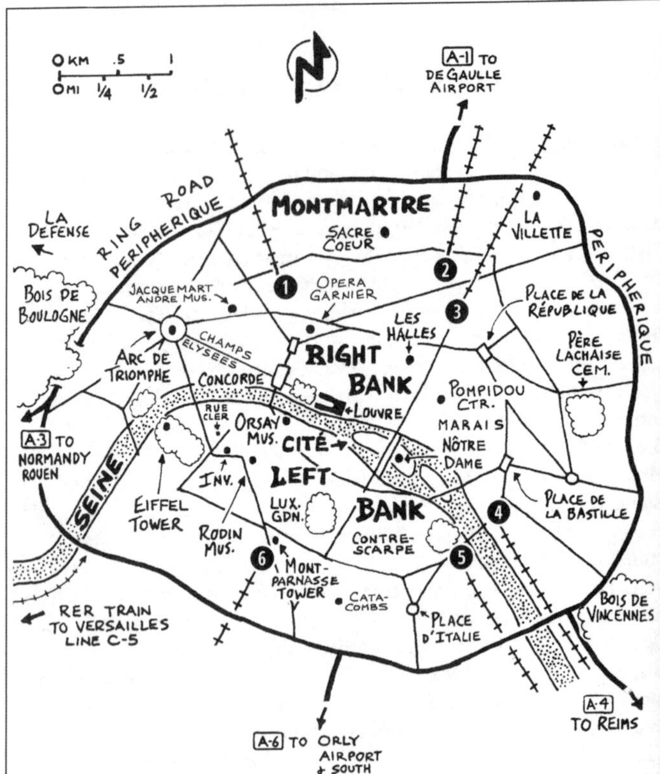

Paris train stations & destinations

1. Gare St. Lazare: To Normandy (including Giverny)
2. Gare Nord: To London & Brussels via Eurostar, to northern Europe (some trips via pricey Thalys trains)
3. Gare L'Est: To eastern France, southern Germany, Switzerland & Austria
4. Gare du Lyon: To southeast France & Italy, also Fontainebleau & Melun (for Vaux-le-Vicomte)
5. Gare d' Austerlitz: To southwest France, Loire & Spain
6. Gare Montparnasse: To Normandy, Brittany, Chartres, TGV trains to Loire & southwest France

follow *Grandes Lignes* signs (main lines) and keep going up until you reach the tracks at street level. *Grandes Lignes* depart from tracks 3–21, suburban (*banlieue*) lines from tracks 30–36, and RER trains depart from tracks 37–44 (tracks 41–44 are 1 floor below). Glass train information booths (*accueil*) are scattered throughout the station and information staff circulate to help (all rail staff are required to speak English).

The tourist information kiosk opposite track 16 is a hotel reservation service for Accor chain hotels (they also have free Paris maps). Information booths for the **Thalys** (high-speed trains to Brussels and Amsterdam) are opposite track 8. All non-Eurostar ticket sales are opposite tracks 3–8. Passengers departing on **Eurostar** (London via Chunnel) must buy tickets and check in on the second level, opposite track 6. (Note: Britain's time zone is one hour earlier; times listed on Eurostar tickets are local times.) Monet-esque views over the trains and peaceful, air-conditioned cafés hide on the upper level, past the Eurostar ticket windows. Lockers, baggage check, taxis, and rental cars are at the far end, opposite track 3 and down the steps.

Key destinations served by Gare du Nord *Grandes Lignes*: **Brussels** (12/day, 1.5 hrs, see "To Brussels and Amsterdam by Thalys Train," below), **Bruges** (18/day, 2 hrs, change in Brussels, one direct), **Amsterdam** (10/day, 4 hrs; see "To Brussels and Amsterdam by Thalys Train," below), **Copenhagen** (1/day, 16 hrs, two night trains), **Koblenz** (6/day, 5 hrs, change in Köln), **London** Eurostar via Chunnel (17/day, 3 hrs, tel. 08 36 35 35 39; see "To London by Eurostar Train," below).

By *banlieue*/RER lines: **Chantilly-Gouvieux** (hrly, fewer on weekends, 35 min), **Charles de Gaulle Airport** (2/hr, 30 min, runs 5:30–23:00, track 4), **Auvers-sur-Oise** (2/hr, 1 hr, transfer at Pontoise).

Gare Montparnasse: This big and modern station covers three floors, serves lower Normandy and Brittany, and offers TGV service to the Loire Valley and southwestern France, as well as suburban service to Chartres. At street level, you'll find a bank, *banlieue* trains (serving Chartres; you can also reach the *banlieue* trains from the second level), and ticket windows in the center, just past the escalators. Lockers *(consigne automatique)* are on the mezzanine level between levels 1 and 2. Most services are provided on the second level, where the *Grandes Lignes* arrive and depart (ticket windows to the far left with your back to glass exterior). *Banlieue* trains depart from tracks 10 through 19. The main rail information office is opposite track 15. Taxis are to the far left as you leave the tracks.

Key destinations served by Gare Montparnasse: Chartres (20/day, 1 hr, *banlieue* lines), **Pontorson-Mont St. Michel** (5/day, 4.5 hrs, via Rennes, then take bus; or take train to Pontorson via Caen, then bus from Pontorson), **Dinan** (7/day, 4 hrs, change in Rennes and Dol), **Bordeaux** (14/day, 3.5 hrs), **Sarlat** (5/day, 6 hrs, change in Bordeaux, Libourne, or Souillac), **Toulouse** (11/day, 5 hrs, most

France's Train Routes

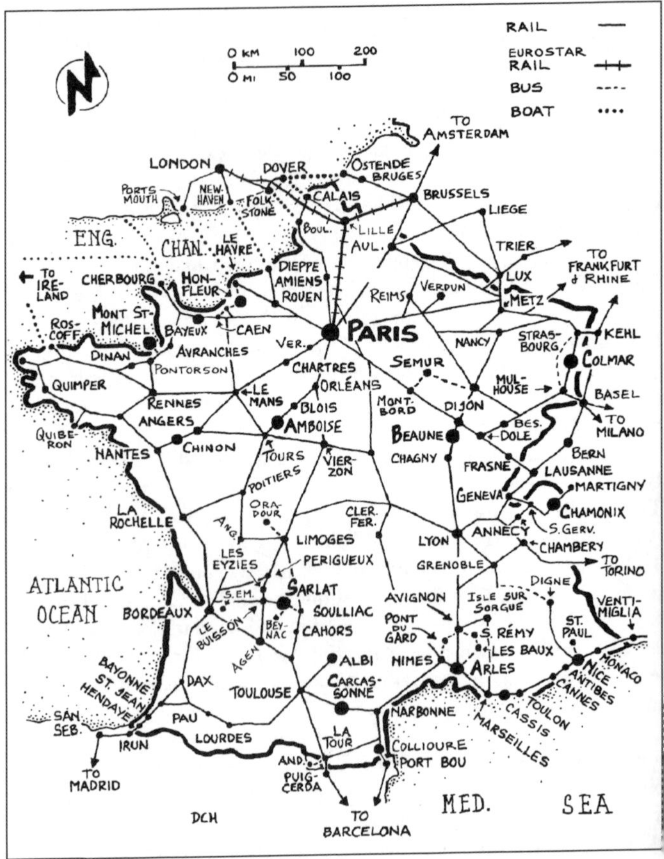

require change, usually in Bordeaux), **Albi** (7/day, 6–7.5 hrs, change in Toulouse, also night train), **Carcassonne** (8/day, 6.5 hrs, most require changes in Toulouse and Bordeaux, direct trains take 10 hrs), **Tours** (14/day, 1 hr).

Gare de Lyon: This huge and bewildering station offers TGV and regular service to southeastern France, Italy, and other international destinations (for more trains to Italy, see "Gare de Bercy," below). Frequent *banlieue* trains serve Melun (near Vaux-le-Vicomte) and Fontainebleau (some depart from the main *Grandes Lignes* level, more frequent departures are from one level down, follow RER-D signs, and ask at any *accueil* or ticket window where the next departure leaves from). Don'

KEY TRAIN PHRASES

accueil (ah-koy)	information/assistance
niveau (nee-voh)	level
billets (bee-yay)	tickets
départs (day-par)	departures
arrivées (ah-ree-vay)	arrivals
aller simple (ah-lay sam-pluh)	one-way
aller-retour (ah-lay ruh-toor)	round-trip
voyageurs munis de billets	travelers with tickets
Grandes Lignes (grahnd leen)	major domestic and international lines
RER (air-ay-air)	suburban lines
banlieue (bahn-lee-yuh)	suburb
quai (kay)	platform
voie (vwah)	track
retard (ruh-tar)	delay
salle d'attente (sahl dah-tahnt)	waiting room
consigne automatique (kohn-seen oh-to-mah-teek)	storage lockers
première classe (pruhm-yair klahs)	first class
deuxième classe (duhz-yehm klahs)	second class

leave this station without checking out Le Train Bleu Restaurant, up the stairs opposite track G (see "Grand Cafés of Paris," page 332).

Grande Ligne trains arrive and depart from one level but are divided into two areas (tracks A-N and 5-23). They are connected by the long platform along tracks A and 5, and by the hallway adjacent to track A and opposite track 9. This hallway has all the services, ticket windows, ticket information, banks, shops, and access to car rental. *Banlieue* ticket windows are just inside the hall adjacent to track A *(billets Ile de France)*. *Grandes Lignes* and *banlieue* lines share the same tracks. A helpful tourist office (Mon–Sat 8:00–20:00, closed Sun) and a train information office are both opposite track L. From the RER or Métro, follow signs for *Grandes Lignes Arrivées* and take the escalator up to reach the platforms. Train information booths *(accueil)* are opposite tracks G and 11. Baggage check is down the stairs opposite track 13. Taxi stands are well-marked in front of the station and one floor below.

Key destinations served by Gare de Lyon: Vaux-le-Vicomte (train to Melun, hrly, 30 min), **Fontainebleau** (nearly hrly, 45 min), **Beaune** (12/day, 2.5 hrs, most require change in Dijon), **Dijon** (15/day, 1.5 hrs), **Chamonix** (9/day, 9 hrs, change in Lyon and St. Gervais, direct night train), **Annecy** (8/day, 4–7 hrs), **Lyon** (16/day, 2.5 hrs), **Avignon** (9/day in

2.5 hrs, 6/day in 4 hrs with change), **Arles** (14/day, 5 hrs, most with change in Marseille, Avignon, or Nîmes), **Nice** (14/day, 5.5–7 hrs, many with change in Marseille), **Venice** (3/day, 3/night, 11–15 hrs, most require changes), **Rome** (2/day, 5/night, 15–18 hrs, most require changes), **Bern** (9/day, 5–11 hrs, most require changes, night train).

Gare de Bercy: This smaller station handles some night train service to Italy during renovation work at the Gare de Lyon (Mo: Bercy, one stop east of Gare de Lyon on line 14).

Gare de l'Est: This single floor station (with underground Métro) serves eastern France and European points east of Paris. Train information booths are at tracks 1, 18, and 26; ticket windows are in the big hall opposite track 8; luggage storage is through the hall opposite track 12.

Key destinations served by Gare de l'Est: Colmar (12/day, 5.5 hrs, change in Strasbourg, Dijon, or Mulhouse), **Strasbourg** (14/day, 4.5 hrs, many require changes), **Reims** (12/day, 1.5 hrs), **Verdun** (5/day, 3 hrs, change in Metz or Chalon), **Munich** (5/day, 9 hrs, some require changes, night train), **Vienna** (7/day, 13–18 hrs, most require changes, night train), **Zürich** (10/day, 7 hrs, most require changes, night train), **Prague** (2/day, 14 hrs, night train).

Gare St. Lazare: This relatively small station serves upper Normandy, including Rouen and Giverny. All trains arrive and depart one floor above street level. Follow signs to *Grandes Lignes* from the Métro to reach the tracks. Ticket windows are in the first hall on the second floor. *Grandes Lignes* (main lines) depart from tracks 17–27; *banlieue* (suburban) trains depart from 1–16. The train information office *(accueil)* is opposite track 15. There's a post office along track 27, and WCs are opposite track 19. There is no baggage check.

Key destinations served by Gare St. Lazare: Giverny (train to Vernon, 5/day, 45 min; then bus or taxi 10 min to Giverny), **Rouen** (15/day, 75 min), **Honfleur** (6/day, 3 hrs, via Lisieux, then bus), **Bayeux** (9/day, 2.5 hrs, some with change in Caen), **Caen** (12/day, 2 hrs).

Gare d'Austerlitz: This small station provides non-TGV service to the Loire Valley, southwestern France, and Spain. All tracks are at street level. The information booth is opposite track 17, and all ticket sales are in the hall opposite track 10. Baggage consignment (if open) and car rental are near *porte* 27 (along the side, opposite track 21).

Key destinations served by Gare d'Austerlitz: Amboise (8/day in 2 hrs, 12/day in 1.5 hrs with change in St. Pierre-des-Corps), **Cahors** (7/day, 5–7 hrs, most with changes), **Barcelona** (1/day, 9 hrs, change in Montpellier, night trains), **Madrid** (2 night trains only, 13–16 hrs), **Lisbon** (1/day, 24 hrs).

To Brussels and Amsterdam by Thalys Train

The pricey Thalys train has the monopoly on this route although the cheapest way to connect Paris with Brussels and Amsterdam is by bus (see "Buses," below). Without a railpass, you'll pay about €80–100 second-class for the Paris–Amsterdam train (compared to €35 by Eurolines bus) or about €60–80 second-class for the Paris–Brussels train (compared to €25 by Eurolines bus). Even with a railpass, you need to pay for train reservations (second class-€14, first class-€30). Book at least a day ahead as seats are limited. Or hop on the bus, Gus.

To London by Eurostar Train

The fastest and most convenient way to get to London is by rail. Eurostar is the speedy passenger train that zips you (and up to 800 others in 18 sleek cars) under the Channel from downtown Paris to downtown London (12-15/day, 2.5 hrs) faster and easier than flying. The train goes 190 mph in France but a doddering 80 mph in England. (Once the English segment gets up to speed, the journey time will shrink to 2 hours.) You might end up with a seat facing backward (feels strange). The actual tunnel crossing is a 20-minute, black, silent, 100-mile-per-hour non-event. Your ears won't even pop. Eurostar trains also run direct to London from Charles de Gaulle Airport (requires change in Lille) or Disneyland Paris (1/day direct, more frequent with transfer at Lille).

Eurostar Routes

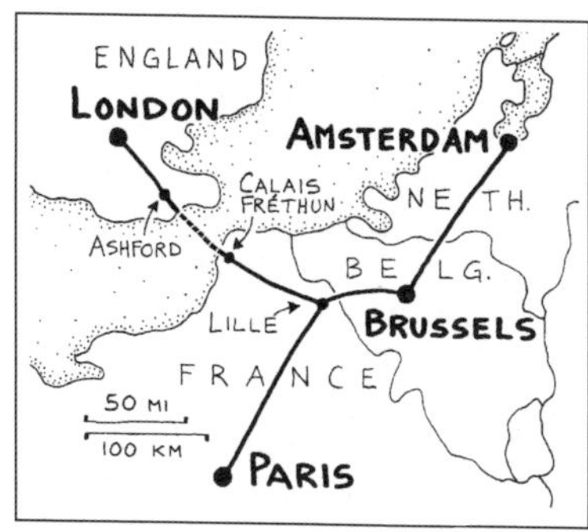

Eurostar Fares

Channel fares are reasonable but complicated. Prices vary depending on when you travel; whether you can live with restrictions; and whether you're eligible for any discounts (youth, seniors, and railpass holders all qualify). Rates are lower for round-trips and off-peak travel (mid-day, mid-week, low-season, and low-interest).

As with airfares, the most expensive and flexible option is a full-fare ticket with no restrictions on refundability (even refundable after the departure date; $223 one-way in second class, $312 in first). A first-class ticket comes with a meal (a dinner departure nets you more grub than breakfast)—but it's not worth the extra expense.

Also like the airlines, cheaper tickets come with more restrictions and are limited in number (so they sell out more quickly). Non-full-fare tickets have severe restrictions on refundability (best-case scenario: you'll get 25 percent back, but with many you'll get nothing). But several do allow you to exchange the ticket (only once) for another departure.

The two basic types of cheap tickets are the more easygoing Leisure Flexi ($195 one-way, one exchange allowed, 25 percent refund) and the highly-restricted Leisure ($90 one-way, no exchange or refund).

Several round-trip Leisure discounts are available: Leisure RT ($150 round-trip, no exchange or refund, 1-night stay required), Leisure RT Midweek ($90-120 round-trip, price based on availability; must travel on Mon, Tue, Wed, or Thu; no exchange or refund, 1-night stay required), and Leisure RT Same Day ($94, travel round-trip within 1 day, no exchange or refund). Even if you're only going one-way, a round-trip ticket can be cheaper; you can forget to return.

Those traveling with a railpass that includes Britain, France, or Belgium should look first at the passholder fare, an especially good value for one-way Eurostar trips ($75 one-way, one exchange, no refund).

There are a variety of other discounts: for seniors ($90 one-way, 60 years or older, one exchange, no refund), youth ($75 one-way during peak time, $45 off-peak, under 26 years old, one exchange allowed, no refund), and children ($38 one-way, ages 4-11, one exchange, no refund).

The ticket names, restrictions, and prices listed here are for tickets purchased in the United States. If you buy your ticket in Europe, your options are similar, though not necessarily identical. Sometimes it's a better deal to buy your ticket in France instead of the United States—or vice-versa. Compare. For updated U.S. fares, visit www.ricksteves.com/eurostar. For European fares, go to www.eurostar.com and input your travel date and time to see the available rates and restrictions.

Buying Eurostar Tickets

Refund and exchange restrictions are serious, so don't reserve until you're sure of your plans. If you're confident about the time and date of your crossing, order ahead from the U.S. Only the most expensive ticket (full fare) is fully refundable, so if you want to have more flexibility, hold off—keeping in mind that the longer you wait, the more likely the cheapest tickets will sell out.

You can check and book fares by phone or online in the United States (order online at www.ricksteves.com/eurostar, prices listed in dollars; order by phone at U.S. tel. 800/EUROSTAR) or in France (French tel. 08 92 35 35 39, www.eurostar.com, prices listed in euros). These are different companies, often with slightly different prices and discount deals on similar tickets; if you order from the United States, check out both. (If you buy from a U.S. company, you'll pay for ticket delivery in the United States; if you book with the European company, you'll pick up your ticket at the train station.) In Europe, you can buy your Eurostar ticket at any major train station in any country, at neigh-

Driving in Europe

orhood SNCF offices, or at any travel agency that handles train tick-
ts (expect a booking fee).

Note that France's time zone is one hour later than Britain's. Times isted on tickets are local times.

BUSES

The main bus station is the Gare Routière du Paris-Gallieni (28 venue du Général de Gaulle, in suburb of Bagnolet, Mo: Gallieni, tel. 1 49 72 51 51). Buses provide cheaper—if less comfortable and more ime-consuming—transportation to major European cities. Eurolines' uses depart from here (tel. 08 36 69 52 52, www.eurolines.com). urolines has a couple of neighborhood offices: in the Latin Quarter 55 rue St. Jacques, tel. 01 43 54 11 99) and in Versailles (4 avenue es Sceaux, tel. 01 39 02 03 73).

PARKING IN PARIS

Street parking is free after 19:00, on weekends, and in August. For a longer stay, consider parking for less at an airport (about €10/day) and taking public transport or a taxi into the city. You'll pay more to park in a downtown lot (€17–25/day) and it's a good idea to reserve ahead (the lot under Ecole Militaire works well for rue Cler–area hotels, €18/day, €40/3 days, and €10/day more after that; parking for less than three days is in their above-ground lot; www.vincipark.com). Otherwise, ask your hotelier for suggestions.

FRENCH **HISTORY**

Celts and Romans (52 B.C.–A.D. 500)

Julius Caesar conquered the Parisii, turning Paris from a tribal fishing village into a European city. The mix of Latin (southern) and Celtic (northern) cultures, with Paris right in the middle, defined the French character.

Paris Sights: Cluny Museum (Roman baths), Louvre (Roman antiquities), and Archaeological Crypt near Notre-Dame.

Dark Ages (500–1000)

Roman Paris fell to German pirates ("Franks" = France) and later to the Vikings ("Norsemen" = Normans). During this turbulent time, Paris was just another island state ("Ile de France") in the midst of many warring kingdoms. The lone bright spot was the reign of Charlemagne (A.D. 768–814), who briefly united the Franks, giving a glimpse of the modern nation-state of France.

Paris Sights: Cluny Museum artifacts and statue of Charlemagne near Notre-Dame.

Border Wars with England (1066–1500)

In 1066, the Norman duke William ("the Conqueror") invaded and conquered England. This united England, Normandy, and much of what is today Western France, sparked centuries of border wars, and produced many kings of England who spoke French. In 1328, King Charles IV died without an heir, and the Norman king of England tried to claim the throne of France, which lead to more than 100 years of Franco-Anglo battles (called the Hundred Years' War). Rallied by the teenage visionary Joan of Arc in 1429, the French finally united North and South, driving the English across the Channel in 1453. Modern France was born, with Paris as its capital.

Paris Sights: Notre-Dame, Sainte-Chapelle, Cluny Museu tapestries, Carnavalet Museum, the Sorbonne, and the Latin Quarter

Renaissance and Religious Wars (1500s)

A strong centralized France emerged, with French kings settin Europe's standard. François I made Paris a cultural capital, invitin Leonardo and *Mona Lisa* to visit. Catholics and Protestants fough openly, and 2,000 Parisians were slaughtered in the St. Bartholomew Day Massacre in 1572. The Wars of Religion subsided for a while whe the first Bourbon king, Henry IV, took the throne in 1589, after con verting to Catholicism (in 1598 he signed the Edict of Nantes, whic instituted freedom of worship).

Paris Sights: Louvre (palace and Renaissance art), pont Neuf, plac des Vosges, and Fontainebleau.

Louis XIV, the Absolute Monarch (1600s)

Louis XIV centralized the power, neutered the nobility, revoked th Edict of Nantes, and moved the capital to Versailles, which also becam the center of European culture. France's wealth sparked "enlightene ideas that became the seeds of democracy.

Paris Sights: Versailles, Vaux-le-Vicomte, Les Invalides, painting by Nicolas Poussin and Claude Lorrain.

Decadence and Revolution (1700s)

This was the age of Louis XV, Louis XVI, Marie-Antoinette, Voltair Jean-Jacques Rousseau, Maximilien de Robespierre, and Napoleon. financial crunch from wars and royal excess drove the French people t revolt. On July 14, 1789, they stormed the Bastille. A couple years late the First French Republic arrested and then beheaded the king an queen. Thousands lost their heads—guillotined if suspected of hinderin progress. A charismatic commoner rose amid the chaos, promising sta bility—Napoleon Bonaparte.

Paris Sights: Versailles, place de la Concorde, place de la Bastill Conciergerie, and paintings by Antoine Watteau, François Bouche Jean-Honoré Fragonard, and Jacques-Louis David.

Elected Emperors and Constitutional Kings (1800s)

Napoleon conquered Europe, crowned himself emperor, invaded Russi was defeated on the battlefields of Waterloo, and ended up exiled to a island in the Atlantic. The monarchy was restored, but rulers toed th democratic line—or were deposed in the popular uprisings of 1830 an 1848. The latter resulted in the Second French Republic, whose fir president was Napoleon's nephew. He rewrote the constitution wit himself as Emperor Napoleon III, and presided over a wealthy, middl ass nation with a colonial empire in slow decline. Although he trod arefully, the disastrous Franco-Prussian War in 1870 ended his reign, ading to the Third Republic. France's political clout was fading, even Paris remained the world's cultural center during the belle époque, or eautiful age.

Paris Sights: Arc de Triomphe, Baron Haussmann's wide boulevards, iffel Tower, Les Invalides and Napoleon's Tomb, pont Alexandre III, rand Palais, Petit Palais (closed through 2005), Montmartre, Opéra arnier, paintings by Jean-Auguste-Dominique Ingres and Eugène elacroix at the Louvre, and Impressionist and Post-Impressionist paintgs (Edouard Manet, Claude Monet, Pierre-Auguste Renoir, Edgar egas, Henri de Toulouse-Lautrec, Paul Cézanne, and so on) at the Orsay, Iarmottan, and L'Orangerie (scheduled to reopen in autumn 2004).

Var and Depression (1900–1950)

rance began the turn of the century as top dog, but the two World Vars with Germany (and the earlier Franco-Prussian War) wasted the ountry. France lost millions of men in World War I, sank into a epression, and was easily overrun by Hitler in World War II. Paris, ow dirt cheap, attracted foreign writers and artists.

This was the age of Pablo Picasso, Maurice Ravel, Claude Debussy, rik Satie, Igor Stravinsky, Vaslav Nijinsky, Ernest Hemingway, F. cott Fitzgerald, Gertrude Stein, Ezra Pound, Jean-Paul Sartre, Edith iaf, and Maurice Chevalier.

Paris Sights: Picasso Museum, Deportation Memorial, Pompidou enter (contains art from this period).

Postwar France (1950–Present)

fter the war, France reestablished a democracy with the Fourth epublic. But France's colonial empire dissolved after bitter wars in lgeria and Vietnam, which helped mire an already unsteady government. Vartime hero Charles de Gaulle was brought back to help in 1958, and e rewrote the constitution, beginning the Fifth (and current) Republic. nmigrants from former colonies flooded Paris. The turbulent '60s, proressive '70s, socialist-turned-conservative '80s, and the middle-of-theoad '90s bring us to the *début de siècle*, or the beginning of the century.

Paris Sights: Montparnasse Tower, La Défense, Louvre's pyramid, nd Pompidou Center (modern art).

Contemporary Politics in France

he key political issues in France today are high unemployment (about 9 ercent), a steadily increasing percentage of ethnic minorities, and the eed to compete in a global marketplace. The challenge is to address these sues while maintaining the social benefits the French expect from their overnment. As a result, national policies seem to conflict with each other

ANTI-AMERICANISM AND WEAPONS OF MASS UNFRIENDLINESS

In 2003 France refused to support President Bush's war against Iraq. Why? For reasons as numerous and varied as those for America's unilateral approach. Regardless of the reasons, the French government responded to the will of 80 percent of its people in attempting to deal with Iraq through the United Nations. This meant opposing the United States.

Incensed, many Americans burned their berets. They supported our troops by pouring French wine down the drain. Republicans renamed French fries "freedom fries" in the Congress cafeteria. And hard-hitting American patriots stopped buying French's Mustard (named for an American).

As newspapers reported that Yankees were being spat upon along the avenue des Champs-Elysées, North Americans heading to Paris wondered what kind of reception they'd receive.

Reading scores of e-mails and letters from Americans in France during this period, I learned that those who were outspoken in their support of President Bush reported being treated rudely, those who were opposed to America's unilateral action felt among friends, and those showing no interest in the situation found no anti-Americanism and enjoyed a fine time in France.

Before classifying the French as "surrender monkeys" when it comes to war, consider the scars recent wars have left on them. In 1918, after World War I, a full 50 percent of all French men between the age of 15 and 30 were casualties. Many, many times the French lost as many people in one day as America lost in the entire Vietnam War—out of a population only one-fourth as large as ours. And France had its own troubles in Vietnam, as well, encountering in the 1950s some of the same problems that America would endure a decade later.

Americans traveling in Europe should remember that, while a few governments supported the U.S.'s preemptive war in Iraq, most Europeans were quite strongly opposed. Still, most French people will judge you as an individual, not as a representative of your government. Having said all that, do I think anti-American sentiment in France will be a negative on your trip? No.

(e.g., France supports the lean economic policies of the European Union but recently reduced the French workweek to 35 hours).

The unification of Europe has been powered by France and Germany. The 15-member European Union, well on its way to becoming

"United States of Europe," is dissolving borders and freeing up trade. lost EU members share one currency—the euro.

French national politics are fascinating. While only two parties ominate American politics, France has five major parties. From left to ght, these include the reformed Communists (PCF—Parti Com-uniste Française), the moderate Socialists (PS—Parti Socialiste), the istocratically conservative UDF (Union pour la Démocratie Française), ne center-right RPR (Rassemblement pour la République), and the cist and isolationist Front National. In general, the UDF and RPR olit the conservative middle ground and the Socialists dominate the lib-al middle ground. But in France, unlike in the United States, informal oalitions are generally necessary for any party to "rule."

At the fringes, you'll read about the Front National party, led by an-Marie Le Pen. Le Pen's "France for the French" platform calls for ne expulsion of ethnic minorities and broader police powers. Although ne Front National has a staunch voter base of about 12 percent, the cent rise in unemployment and globalization worries have increased s following somewhat. In the 2002 presidential primary, 16 candidates new record) vied for office, and Le Pen's loyal following put him in econd place—ahead of the Socialist party candidate Lionel Jospin (who ad been prime minister), but behind conservative incumbent Jacques hirac (a former mayor of Paris). While Chirac won the regular election asily, Le Pen has been able to nudge the political agenda to the right. n the far left, the reformed Communists, still recovering from the fall f the Soviet Union, have had to work more flexibly with the less radical ocialists and the environmental (Green) parties, who see their fortunes se when the economy is strong and fall when it's weak.

While the French president is elected by popular vote every seven ears, he is more of a figurehead than his American counterpart. The ore powerful prime minister is elected by the parliament (Assemblée ationale) and confirmed by the new president. With five major par-es, a single majority is rare—it takes a coalition to elect a prime minis-r. Currently, the right is working together better than the left, as resident Jacques Chirac and Prime Minister Jean-Pierre Raffarin are oth conservatives.

APPENDIX

Let's Talk Telephones

Here are general instructions for making phone calls. (For information specific to France, see page 11). International access codes and country codes are listed below.

Making Calls within a European Country: About half of all European countries use area codes (like we do); the other half uses a direct-dial system without area codes.

To make calls within a country that uses a direct-dial system (France, Belgium, Czech Republic, Denmark, Italy, Portugal, Norway, Spain, and Switzerland), you dial the same number whether you're calling across the country or across the street.

In countries that use area codes (such as Austria, Britain, Finland, Germany, Ireland, Netherlands, and Sweden), you dial the local number when calling within a city, and you add the area code if calling long-distance within the country.

Making International Calls: You always start with the international access code (011 if you're calling from America or Canada, or 00 from anywhere in Europe), then dial the country code of the country you're calling (see chart below).

What you dial next depends on the phone system of the country you're calling. If the country uses area codes, drop the initial 0 of the area code, then dial the rest of the number.

Countries that use direct-dial systems (no area codes) vary in how they're accessed internationally by phone. For instance, if you're making an international call to the Czech Republic, Denmark, Italy, Norway, Portugal, or Spain, simply dial the international access code, country code, and phone number. But if you're calling France, Belgium, or Switzerland, drop the initial 0 of the phone number.

European Calling Chart

Just smile and dial, using this key:
AC = Area Code, LN = Local Number.

European Country	Calling long distance within...	Calling from the U.S.A./ Canada to...	Calling from a European country to...
Austria	AC + LN	011 + 43 + AC (without the initial zero) + LN	00 + 43 + AC (without the initial zero) + LN
Belgium	LN	011 + 32 + LN (without initial zero)	00 + 32 + LN (without initial zero)
Britain	AC + LN	011 + 44 + AC (without initial zero) + LN	00 + 44 + AC (without initial zero) + LN
Czech Republic	LN	011 + 420 + LN	00 + 420 + LN
Denmark	LN	011 + 45 + LN	00 + 45 + LN
Estonia	LN	011 + 372 + LN	00 + 372 + LN
Finland	AC + LN	011 + 358 + AC (without initial zero) + LN	00 + 358 + AC (without initial zero) + LN
France	LN	011 + 33 + LN (without initial zero)	00 + 33 + LN (without initial zero)
Germany	AC + LN	011 + 49 + AC (without initial zero) + LN	00 + 49 + AC (without initial zero) + LN
Gibraltar	LN	011 + 350 + LN	00 + 350 + LN From Spain: 9567 + LN
Greece	LN	011 + 30 + LN	00 + 30 + LN

European Country	Calling long distance within...	Calling from the U.S.A./ Canada to...	Calling from a European country to...
Ireland	AC + LN	011 + 353 + AC (without initial zero) + LN	00 + 353 + AC (without initial zero) + LN
Italy	LN	011 + 39 + LN	00 + 39 + LN
Morocco	LN	011 + 212 + LN (without initial zero)	00 + 212 + LN (without initial zero)
Netherlands	AC + LN	011 + 31 + AC (without initial zero) + LN	00 + 31 + AC (without initial zero) + LN
Norway	LN	011 + 47 + LN	00 + 47 + LN
Portugal	LN	011 + 351 + LN	00 + 351 + LN
Spain	LN	011 + 34 + LN	00 + 34 + LN
Sweden	AC + LN	011 + 46 + AC (without initial zero) + LN	00 + 46 + AC (without initial zero) + LN
Switzerland	LN	011 + 41 + LN (without initial zero)	00 + 41 + LN (without initial zero)
Turkey	AC (if no initial zero is included, add one) + LN	011 + 90 + AC (without initial zero) + LN	00 + 90 + AC (without initial zero) + LN

- The instructions above apply whether you're calling a fixed phone or mobile phone.
- The international access codes (the first numbers you dial when making an international call) are 011 if you're calling from the U.S.A./Canada, or 00 if you're calling from anywhere in Europe.
- To call the U.S.A. or Canada from Europe, dial 00, then 1 (the country code for the U.S.A. and Canada), then the area code and number. In short, 00 + 1 + AC + LN = Hi, Mom!

International Access Codes

When dialing direct, first dial the international access code. For the United States and Canada, it's 011. All European countries use 00 as their international access code.

Country Codes

After you've dialed the international access code, then dial the code of the country you're calling.

Austria—43
Belgium—32
Britain—44
Canada—1
Croatia—385
Czech Repub.—420
Denmark—45
Estonia—372
Finland—358
France—33
Germany—49
Gibraltar—350
Greece—30
Ireland—353
Italy—39
Morocco—212
Netherlands—31
Norway—47
Poland—48
Portugal—351
Slovenia—386
Spain—34
Sweden—46
Switzerland—41
Turkey—90
United States—1

Handy Phone Numbers

Directory Assistance for Paris and France (some English spoken): 12

Collect Calls to the U.S.: tel. 00 00 11

Lost Property (Bureau des Objets Trouvés, at the police station): Open Tue and Thu 8:30–20:00, 36 rue des Morillons, Mo: Convention, tel. 01 55 76 20 20

American Church: Open daily 9:00–22:00, 65 quai d'Orsay, Mo: Invalides, tel. 01 40 62 05 00

Office of American Services (lost passports, etc): See "U.S. Consulate," below

Sunday Banks: 115 and 154 avenue des Champs-Elysées

Emergency/Medical Needs

Police: 17

Emergency Medical Assistance: 15

American Hospital: 63 boulevard Victor Hugo, in Neuilly suburb, Mo: Porte Maillot, then bus #82, tel. 01 46 41 25 25

English-Speaking Pharmacy: tel. 01 45 62 02 41 (Pharmacie les Champs, 24 hrs, 84 avenue des Champs-Elysées, Mo: Georges V)

Chiropractic Centers: tel. 01 43 54 26 25 or 01 43 87 81 62

SOS Doctors: tel. 01 47 07 77 77 or 01 48 28 40 04

SOS Help (English-speaking hotline): Open daily 15:00–23:00, tel. 01 47 23 80 80

ape Crisis Hotline: 24-hr tel. 08 00 05 95 95
mbulance: tel. 01 45 67 50 50

onsulates/Embassies

.S. Consulate: Open Mon–Fri 9:00–12:30 & 13:00–15:00, 2 rue St. Florentin, Mo: Concorde, tel. 01 43 12 22 22
.S. Embassy: 2 avenue Gabriel (to the left as you face Hôtel Crillon), Mo: Concorde, tel. 01 43 12 22 22
'anadian Consulate and Embassy: 35 avenue Montaigne, Mo: Franklin D. Roosevelt, tel. 01 44 43 29 00

ourist and Transportation Information

aris Tourist Information: tel. 08 92 68 31 12 (recorded info with long menu)
e de France Tourist Information (covers Paris area, including Fontainebleau, Vaux-le-Vicomte, and Chantilly): tel. 01 42 60 28 62
'rain (SNCF) Information: tel. 08 36 35 35 35 (some English usually spoken)
us and Métro (RATP) Information: tel. 08 36 68 77 14 (French only)

ravel Companies

merican Express: 11 rue Scribe, Mo: Opéra, tel. 01 47 77 77 07

heap Flights

ccess Voyages: 6 rue Pierre Lescot, Mo: Châtelet, tel. 01 44 76 84 50
ny Way: 46 rue des Lombards, Mo: Châtelet or Hôtel de Ville, tel. 01 40 28 00 74
ash & Go: 34 avenue des Champs-Elysées, Mo: Franklin D. Roosevelt, tel. 01 53 93 63 63
SIT Voyages: 12 rue Vivienne, Mo: Bourse, tel. 01 42 44 14 00
ooking Service (for hotels, restaurants and other tourist activities): tel. 01 43 59 12 12, www.ely1212.com

ost or Stolen Credit Cards

isa: tel. 08 00 90 11 79
lasterCard: tel. 08 00 90 13 87
merican Express: tel. 01 47 77 72 00
iner's Club: call U.S. collect 00-1-702-797-5532

irports

harles de Gaulle: general info tel. 01 48 62 22 80, lost luggage tel. 01 48 62 10 46
rly: tel. 01 49 75 15 15

Airlines

Aer Lingus: tel. 01 55 38 38 55
Air Canada: tel. 08 25 88 08 81
Air France: tel. 08 20 82 08 20
Alitalia: tel. 08 02 31 53 15
American Airlines: tel. 08 10 87 28 72
British Airways: tel. 08 25 82 54 00
BMI British Midlands: tel. 01 41 91 87 04
Continental: tel. 01 42 99 09 09
Delta: tel. 08 00 35 40 80
Iberia: tel. 08 02 07 50 75
Icelandair: tel. 01 44 51 60 51
KLM: tel. 08 10 55 65 56
Lufthansa: tel. 08 20 02 00 30
Northwest: tel. 08 10 55 65 56
Olympic: tel. 01 44 94 58 58
Portugal Airlines: 08 03 08 38 18
SAS: tel. 08 10 25 25 25
Swiss: tel. 08 20 04 05 06
United: tel. 08 10 72 72 72
US Airways: tel. 08 10 63 22 22

Classes

French Language Classes

- American University of Paris (tel. 01 40 62 07 20, fax 01 47 05 34 32, www.aup.edu)
- Ecole France Langue (tel. 01 45 00 40 15, fax 01 45 00 53 41, www.france-langue.fr)

Cooking Schools

These have demonstration courses:

- Le Cordon Bleu (tel. 01 53 68 22 50, fax 01 48 56 03 96)
- Ritz Escoffier Ecole de Gastronomie Française (tel. 01 43 16 30 50)

Public Holidays and Festivals

Festivals in Paris

Paris is lively with festivals throughout the summer and fall. Kickin off the season in June is the month-long **Festival of St. Denis** in th Parisian suburb, featuring musicians from around the world at variou venues (tel. 01 48 13 06 07, www.festival-saint-denis.fr). Paris cel brates the solstice (June 21) at its **Music Festival** with concer throughout the city. In July, the prestigious **Tour de France** bicyc

2004

JANUARY

S	M	T	W	T	F	S
				1	2	3
4	5	6	7	8	9	10
11	12	13	14	15	16	17
18	19	20	21	22	23	24
25	26	27	28	29	30	31

FEBRUARY

S	M	T	W	T	F	S
1	2	3	4	5	6	7
8	9	10	11	12	13	14
15	16	17	18	19	20	21
22	23	24	25	26	27	28
29						

MARCH

S	M	T	W	T	F	S
	1	2	3	4	5	6
7	8	9	10	11	12	13
14	15	16	17	18	19	20
21	22	23	24	25	26	27
28	29	30	31			

APRIL

S	M	T	W	T	F	S
				1	2	3
4	5	6	7	8	9	10
11	12	13	14	15	16	17
18	19	20	21	22	23	24
25	26	27	28	29	30	

MAY

S	M	T	W	T	F	S
						1
2	3	4	5	6	7	8
9	10	11	12	13	14	15
16	17	18	19	20	21	22
23/30	24/31	25	26	27	28	29

JUNE

S	M	T	W	T	F	S
		1	2	3	4	5
6	7	8	9	10	11	12
13	14	15	16	17	18	19
20	21	22	23	24	25	26
27	28	29	30			

JULY

S	M	T	W	T	F	S
				1	2	3
4	5	6	7	8	9	10
11	12	13	14	15	16	17
18	19	20	21	22	23	24
25	26	27	28	29	30	31

AUGUST

S	M	T	W	T	F	S
1	2	3	4	5	6	7
8	9	10	11	12	13	14
15	16	17	18	19	20	21
22	23	24	25	26	27	28
29	30	31				

SEPTEMBER

S	M	T	W	T	F	S
			1	2	3	4
5	6	7	8	9	10	11
12	13	14	15	16	17	18
19	20	21	22	23	24	25
26	27	28	29	30		

OCTOBER

S	M	T	W	T	F	S
					1	2
3	4	5	6	7	8	9
10	11	12	13	14	15	16
17	18	19	20	21	22	23
24/31	25	26	27	28	29	30

NOVEMBER

S	M	T	W	T	F	S
	1	2	3	4	5	6
7	8	9	10	11	12	13
14	15	16	17	18	19	20
21	22	23	24	25	26	27
28	29	30				

DECEMBER

S	M	T	W	T	F	S
			1	2	3	4
5	6	7	8	9	10	11
12	13	14	15	16	17	18
19	20	21	22	23	24	25
26	27	28	29	30	31	

ace begins and ends in Paris (starts on Ile de France, www.letour.fr). **Bastille Day**, France's National Day (July 14), brings fireworks, dancing, and revelry countrywide. From mid-July to mid-August is the **Paris Neighborhoods Festival**, featuring theater, dance, and concerts round the city. **La Villette Jazz Festival** brings a week of outdoor jazz oncerts to this Parisian park in early- to mid-September. The first Saturday of October, Montmartre celebrates the **grape harvest** with a parade and festivities. The **Festival of Autumn** (www.festival-utomne.com) runs through autumn, with theater, dance, film, and opera performances. Also see www.franceguide.com, www.whatson-when.com, and www.festivals.com.

National Holidays

These national holidays (when many sights close) are observed throughout France. Note this isn't a complete list; holidays strike without warning.

Jan 1: New Year's Day
Jan 6: Epiphany
April 11: Easter Sunday
April 12: Easter Monday
May 1: Labor Day
May 8: VE Day
May 20: Ascension
May 30: Pentecost
July 14: Bastille Day
Aug 15: Assumption of Mary
Nov 1: All Saints' Day
Nov 11: Armistice Day
Dec 25: Christmas Day

Paris' Climate

First line, average daily low; second line, average daily high; third line, days of no rain.

J	F	M	A	M	J	J	A	S	O	N	D
34°	34°	39°	43°	49°	55°	58°	58°	53°	46°	40°	36°
43°	45°	54°	60°	68°	73°	76°	75°	70°	60°	50°	44°
14	14	19	17	19	18	19	18	17	18	15	15

Numbers and Stumblers

- Europeans write a few of their numbers differently than we do. 1 = 1, 4 = 4, 7 = 7. Learn the difference or miss your train.
- In Europe, dates appear as day/month/year, so Christmas is 25/12/04.
- Commas are decimal points and decimals commas. A dollar and a half is 1,50 and there are 5.280 feet in a mile.
- When pointing, use your whole hand, palm down.
- When counting with fingers, start with your thumb. If you hold up your first finger to request one item, you'll probably get two.
- What Americans call the second floor of a building is the first floor in Europe.
- Europeans keep the left "lane" open for passing on escalators and moving sidewalks. Keep to the right.

letric Conversion (approximate)

inch = 25 millimeters	32 degrees F = 0 degrees C
foot = 0.3 meter	82 degrees F = about 28 degrees C
yard = 0.9 meter	1 ounce = 28 grams
mile = 1.6 kilometers	1 kilogram = 2.2 pounds
centimeter = 0.4 inch	1 quart = 0.95 liter
meter = 39.4 inches	1 square yard = 0.8 square meter
kilometer = .62 mile	1 acre = 0.4 hectare

onverting Temperatures: Farenheit and Celsius

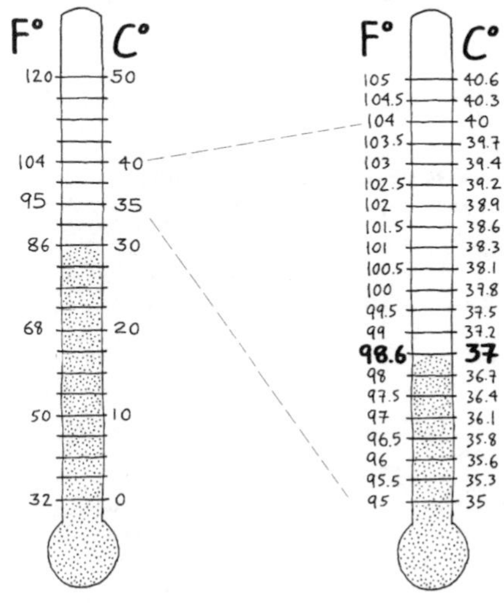

French Pronunciation Guide for Paris

Nasalize the underlined "n" if you can (let the sound come through your nose).

Arc de Triomphe ark duh tree-ohnf
arrondissement ah-rohn-dees-mohn
Art Nouveau art noo-voh
Auvers-sur-Oise oh-vehr-sur-wahz

Bateaux Mouches bah-toh moosh
Bon Marché bohn mar-chay
boulangerie boo-lahn-zheh-ree

Carnavalet kar-nah-val-eh
Champ de Mars shahn duh mar
Champs-Elysées shahn-zay-lee-zay
Chantilly shahn-tee-yee
charcuterie shar-koo-tuh-ree
Chartres shar-truh
château(x) shah-toh
Cité see-tay
Cité des Sciences see-tay day see-ahns
Conciergerie kon-see-ehr-zhuh-ree
Contrescarpe kohn-truh-scarp

droguerie droh-guh-ree

Ecole Militaire eh-kohl mee-lee-tehr
Egouts ay-goo

Fauchon foh-shohn
Fontainebleau fohn-tehn-bloh
fromagerie froh-mah-zhuh-ree

Galeries Lafayette
gah-luh-ree lah-fay-yet
gare gar
Gare d'Austerlitz gar doh-ster-leets
Gare de l'Est gar duh less
Gare de Lyon gar duh lee-ohn
Gare du Nord gar dew nor
Gare St. Lazare gar sahn lah-zar
Garnier gar-nee-ay
Giverny zhee-vehr-nee
Grand Palais grahn pah-lay
Grande Arche de la Défense
grahnd arsh duh lah day-fahns

histoire ees-twar
Hôtel d'Aignan oh-tehl day-nyahn
Hôtel de Sully oh-tehl deh soo-lee
Hôtel Salé oh-tehl sah-lay

Ile de la Cité eel duh lah see-tay
Ile St. Louis eel sahn loo-ee

Jacquemart-André
zhahk-mar-ahn-dray
jardin zhar-dan
Jardin des Plantes
zhar-dan day plahnt
Jeu de Paume juh duh pohm
La Madeleine lah mah-duh-lehn
La Marseillaise lah mar-seh-yehz
Le Hameau luh ah-moh
Les Halles lay ahl
Les Invalides lay-zan-vah-leed
Loire lwar
L'Orangerie loh-rahn-zhuh-ree
Louvre loov-ruh

Marais mah-ray
Marché aux puces mar-chay oh poos
Marmottan mar-moh-tahn
Métro may-troh
Monge mohnzh
Montmartre mohn-mart
Montparnasse mohn-par-nas
Moulin Rouge moo-lan roozh
musée mew-zay
Musée de l'Armée
mew-zay duh lar-may
Musée d'Orsay mew-zay dor-say

Notre-Dame noh-truh-dahm

orangerie oh-rahn-zhuh-ree
Orsay or-say

palais pah-lay
Palais de Justice
pah-lay duh zhew-stees
Palais Garnier pah-lay gar-nee-ay
Palais Royal pah-lay roh-yahl
Parc de la Villette park duh la vee-leht
Parc Monceau park mohn-soh
Père Lachaise pehr lah-shehz
Petit Palais puh-tee pah-lay
Pigalle pee-gahl
place plahs
Place Dauphine plahs doh-feen
Place de la Bastille
plahs duh lah bah-steel
Place de la Concorde
plahs duh lah kohn-kord
Place de la République
plahs duh lah ray-poo-bleek
Place des Vosges plahs day vohzh
Place du Tertre plahs dew tehr-truh
Place St. André-des-Arts
plahs sahn tahn-dray day zart
Place Vendôme plahs vahn-dohm

ompidou pohn-pee-doo
ont pohn
ont Alexandre III
pohn ah-leks-ahn-druh twah
ont Neuf pohn nuhf
romenade Plantée
proh-mohn-ahd plahn-tay
uai kay

ive Droite reeve dwaht
ive Gauche reeve gohsh
odin roh-dan
ue rew
ue Cler rew klehr
ue Daguerre rew dah-gehr
ue des Rosiers rew day roz-ee-ay
ue Montorgueil rew mohn-tor-goy
ue Mouffetard rew moof-tar
ue de Rivoli rew duh ree-voh-lee

acré-Cœr sah-kray-koor
ainte-Chapelle sahnt-shah-pehl

Samaritaine sah-mah-ree-tehn
Seine sehn
Sèvres-Babylone
seh-vruh-bah-bee-lohn
Sorbonne sor-buhn
St. Germain-des-Prés
sahn zhehr-man-day-pray
St. Julien-le-Pauvre
sahn zhew-lee-ahn-luh-poh-vruh
St. Séverin sahn say-vuh-ran
St. Sulpice sahn sool-pees

Tour Eiffel toor ee-fehl
Trianon tree-ahn-ohn
Trocadéro troh-kah-day-roh
Tuileries twee-lah-ree

Vaux-le-Vicomte voh-luh-vee-kohnt
Venus de Milo vuh-new duh mee-loh
Versailles vehr-sigh

Basic French Survival Phrases

Good day.	**Bonjour.**	bohn-zhoor
Mrs. / Mr.	**Madame / Monsieur**	mah-dahm / muhs-yur
Do you speak English?	**Parlez-vous anglais?**	par-lay-voo ahn-glay
Yes. / No.	**Oui. / Non.**	wee / nohn
I understand.	**Je comprends.**	zhuh kohn-prahn
I don't understand.	**Je ne comprends pas.**	zhuh nun kohn-prahn pah
Please.	**S'il vous plaît.**	see voo play
Thank you.	**Merci.**	mehr-see
I'm sorry.	**Désolé.**	day-zoh-lay
Excuse me.	**Pardon.**	par-dohn
(No) problem.	**(Pas de) problème.**	(pah duh) proh-blehm
It's good.	**C'est bon.**	say bohn
Goodbye.	**Au revoir.**	oh vwahr
one / two	**un / deux**	uhn / duh
three / four	**trois / quatre**	twah / kah-truh
five / six	**cinq / six**	sank / sees
seven / eight	**sept / huit**	seht / weet
nine / ten	**neuf / dix**	nuhf / dees
How much is it?	**Combien?**	kohn-bee-an
Write it?	**Ecrivez?**	ay-kree-vay
Is it free?	**C'est gratuit?**	say grah-twee
Included?	**Inclus?**	an-klew
Where can I buy / find...?	**Où puis-je acheter / trouver...?**	oo pwee-zhuh ah-shuh-tay / troo-vay
I'd like / We'd like...	**Je voudrais / Nous voudrions...**	zhuh voo-dray / noo voo-dree-ohn
...a room.	**...une chambre.**	ewn shahn-bruh
...the bill.	**...l'addition.**	lah-dee-see-ohn
...a ticket to ___.	**...un billet pour ___.**	uhn bee-yay poor
Is it possible?	**C'est possible?**	say poh-see-bluh
Where is...?	**Où est...?**	oo ay
...the train station	**...la gare**	lah gar
...the bus station	**...la gare routière**	lah gar root-yehr
...tourist information	**...l'office du tourisme**	loh-fees dew too-reez-muh
Where are the toilets?	**Où sont les toilettes?**	oo sohn lay twah-leht
men	**hommes**	ohm
women	**dames**	dahm
left / right	**à gauche / à droite**	ah gohsh / ah dwaht
straight	**tout droit**	too dwah
When does this open / close?	**Ça ouvre / ferme à quelle heure?**	sah oo-vruh / fehrm ah kehl ur
At what time?	**À quelle heure?**	ah kehl ur
Just a moment.	**Un moment.**	uhn moh-mahn
now / soon / later	**maintenant / bientôt / plus tard**	man-tuh-nahn / bee-an-toh / plew tar
today / tomorrow	**aujourd'hui / demain**	oh-zhoor-dwee / duh-man

When using the phonetics, try to nasalize the n sound.

For more user-friendly French phrases, check out *Rick Steves' French Phrase Book and Dictionary* or *Rick Steves' French, Italian & German Phrase Book and Dictionary*.

Road Scholar Feedback for PARIS 2004

*We're all in the same travelers' school of hard knocks. Your feedback helps us improve this guidebook for future travelers. Please fill this out (or use the online version at www.ricksteves.com/feedback), attach more info or any tips/favorite discoveries if you like, and send it to us. As thanks for your help, we'll send you our quarterly travel newsletter free for one year. Thanks! —**Rick***

Of the recommended accommodations/restaurants used, which was:

Best ______________________________

Why? ______________________________

Worst ______________________________

Why? ______________________________

Of the sights/experiences/destinations recommended by this book, which was:

Most overrated ______________________________

Why? ______________________________

Most underrated ______________________________

Why? ______________________________

Best ways to improve this book:

____

____

I'd like a free newsletter subscription:

____ Yes ____ No ____ Already on list

____
Name

____
Address

____
City, State, Zip

____
E-mail Address

Please send to: ETBD, Box 2009, Edmonds, WA 98020

Faxing Your Hotel Reservation

Use this handy form for your fax or find it online at www.ricksteves.com/reservation. Photocopy and fax away.

One-Page Fax

To: ______________________________ @ ______________________
hotel *fax*

From: ______________________________ @ ______________________
name *fax*

Today's date: ____ /_____ /____
day *month* *year*

Dear Hotel ____,

Please make this reservation for me:

Name: ____

Total # of people: _____ # of rooms: _____ # of nights: _____

Arriving: ____ /_____ /____ My time of arrival (24-hr clock): ______
day *month* *year* (I will telephone if I will be late)

Departing: ____ /_____ /____
day *month* *year*

Room(s): Single___ Double___ Twin___ Triple___ Quad___

With: Toilet___ Shower___ Bath___ Sink only___

Special needs: View___ Quiet___ Cheapest___ Ground Floor___

Credit card: Visa___ MasterCard___ American Express___

Card #: ____

Expiration date:____

Name on card: ____

You may charge me for the first night as a deposit. Please fax, e-mail, or mail me confirmation of my reservation, along with the type of room reserved, the price, and whether the price includes breakfast. Please also inform me of your cancellation policy. Thank you.

____
Signature

____
Name

____
Address

____
City ***State*** ***Zip Code*** ***Country***

____
E-mail Address

INDEX

ABOUT THE AUTHORS

RICK STEVES

RICK STEVES is on a mission: to help make European travel accessible and meaningful for Americans. Rick has spent 100 days every year since 1973 exploring Europe. He's researched and written 24 travel guidebooks. He writes and hosts the public television series *Rick Steves Europe*, now in its seventh season. With the help of his hardworking staff of 60 at Europe through the Back Door, Rick organizes and leads tours of Europe and offers an information-packed Web site (www.ricksteves.com). Rick, his wife (and favorite travel partner) Anne, and their two teenage children, Andy and Jackie, call Edmonds, just north of Seattle, home.

STEVE SMITH

STEVE SMITH has worked with Rick for 11 years managing tour logistics and for 15 years researching guidebooks. Fluent in French, he's lived in France on several occasions starting when he was seven, and has traveled there annually for the last 20 years. He recently restored a farmhouse in Burgundy where he hangs his beret in research season. Steve's wife, Karen Lewis, who's an expert on French cuisine and wine, provides invaluable contributions to his books.

GENE OPENSHAW

GENE OPENSHAW met Rick in the seventh grade, and they traveled through Europe together after high school. Gene, a Stanford graduate, has co-authored several books with Rick since they self-published their first book together, Europe 101, in 1984. Specializing in art and history, Gene writes the walking tours and museum tours for the city guidebooks. Also a composer, Gene wrote and produced an opera entitled *Matter*. He lives near Edmonds with his wife and daughter.

Rick Steves

COUNTRY GUIDES 2004

Best of Europe
Best of Eastern Europe
France
Germany, Austria & Switzerland
Great Britain
Ireland
Italy
Scandinavia
Spain & Portugal

CITY GUIDES 2004

Amsterdam, Bruges & Brussels
Florence & Tuscany
London
Paris
Provence & The French Riviera
Rome
Venice

MORE EUROPE FROM RICK STEVES

Europe 101
Europe Through the Back Door 2004
Mona Winks
Postcards from Europe

More Savvy. More Surprising. More Fun.

PHRASE BOOKS & DICTIONARIES

French, Italian & German
French
German
Italian
Portuguese
Spanish

VHS RICK STEVES' EUROPE

The Best of Ireland
Bulgaria, Eastern Turkey, Slovenia & Croatia
The Heart of Italy
London & Paris
Prague, Amsterdam & the Swiss Alps
Romantic Germany & Berlin
Rome, Caesar's Rome, Sicily
South England, Heart of England & Scotland
Southwest Germany & Portugal
Travel Skills Special
Venice & Veneto 2003

DVD RICK STEVES' EUROPE

Rick Steves' Europe All Thirty Shows 2000-2003
Britain & Ireland
Exotic Europe
Germany, the Swiss Alps & Travel Skills
Italy